The World Since 1945

SEVENTH EDITION

The World
Since 1945

A History of
International Relations

Wayne C. McWilliams
Harry Piotrowski

LYNNE
RIENNER
PUBLISHERS

BOULDER
LONDON

Published in the United States of America in 2009 by
Lynne Rienner Publishers, Inc.
1800 30th Street, Boulder, Colorado 80301
www.rienner.com

and in the United Kingdom by
Lynne Rienner Publishers, Inc.
3 Henrietta Street, Covent Garden, London WC2E 8LU

Library of Congress Cataloging-in-Publication Data
McWilliams, Wayne C.
  The world since 1945 : a history of international relations / Wayne C.
McWilliams Harry Piotrowski. — 7th ed.
      p. cm.
  Includes bibliographical references and index.
  ISBN 978-1-58826-662-0 (pbk. : alk. paper)
  1. World politics—1945–1989. 2. World politics—1989– 3. International
relations. 4. Military history, Modern—20th century. 5. Developing
countries—Economic conditions. I. Piotrowski, Harry. II. Title.
  D843.M34 2009
  327.09'045—dc22
                                                      2009002533

British Cataloguing in Publication Data
A Cataloguing in Publication record for this book
is available from the British Library.

Printed and bound in the United States of America

 The paper used in this publication meets the requirements
of the American National Standard for Permanence of
Paper for Printed Library Materials Z39.48-1992.

5   4

In Memoriam

Bill Sladek
1938–1993

friend and colleague

Contents

Illustrations

Maps

Photographs

Introduction

In this new edition of *The World Since 1945*, we take the story to early 2009—to the inauguration of US president Barack Obama—reflecting the changing political, ideological, and economic landscape as it emerged during the early years of the twenty-first century. Arguably the most significant development during these years was the increasing globalization of the economy, a process that produced an ever-tightening, interlocking economic relationship among nations. This brought prosperity to many nations, notably China (which by the end of 2008 had reached the rank of the world's third largest economy, behind only the United States and Japan) and India. The perils of globalization, however, came into sharp focus with the financial crises and the global recession that started in 2007.

We have also seen a new intensification of the Arab-Israeli conflict—part of a greater clash between militant Islam and the secular governments in the Islamic world—as well as the potentially deadly nuclear proliferation in western Asia. In Europe, Vladimir Putin (who still called the shots, although no longer president of Russia) made it plain with Russia's invasion of Georgia that the eastward expansion of the North Atlantic Treaty Organization could go only so far. And a number of nations—notably in Latin America, Africa, and Asia—struggled with the challenges of establishing democratic institutions and raising the standard of living of their people.

In his inaugural address, President Obama expressed the belief that the problems that his nation—and the world—face can be resolved. Whether his conviction was justified cannot yet be determined. But we can achieve an understanding of how we arrived at this particular point in history.

*   *   *

A survey of current world conditions and a reading of the recent past reveal that the world is neither a fair nor a friendly place. Insurrections and wars abound, and all too many of the world's inhabitants live in misery and hunger while others live in comfort and luxury. In this age of modern science and technology, of space exploration and heart transplants, how does one account for the absence of peace and the prevalence of poverty in a world of plenty? What are the roots of the perilous condition of human affairs? Today's students, young and old, must ask and seek to answer these questions. This book, a history of the world since 1945, was undertaken in order to assist them in that endeavor.

Tribal hostility and war between nations have been common throughout history, but in modern times, and especially in the twentieth century with the development of modern military technology, war has become increasingly deadly. World War II brought death and destruction on an unprecedented scale, and it ended with the use of a powerful new weapon of mass destruction, the atomic bomb. From the ruins of that war came a cry, expressed even by military leaders, that there must never be another such war. Yet, even as the ashes of World War II were still smoldering, friction developed among its victors, and they—the United States and Britain on one side and the Soviet Union on the other—became locked in a new power struggle that threatened the very peace they had sacrificed so much to attain. The postwar friction between them rapidly hardened into a political Cold War that soon turned into a military confrontation marked by mutual mistrust, suspicion, and hostility. After World War II the Cold War continued for more than forty-five years as the major determinant of international affairs. The two superpowers, the United States and the Soviet Union, aggressively sought to establish and maintain blocs of allies, thus dividing the world into two hostile camps. And since each claimed to be the champion of a superior system, one capitalist and the other Communist, the world became the arena of an ideological conflict that endured for nearly half a century.

Meanwhile, both superpowers engaged in a relentless arms race. Each claimed that security—both national and global—lay in military strength, but that the other's armaments threatened world peace. Thus they justified the building of massive arsenals containing thousands of nuclear weapons far more powerful than the ones used against Japan in 1945. Their arsenals have long since been large enough to destroy each other many times over and possibly extinguish human life on this planet, and yet year after year they continued piling up more expensive weapons. When they decided to scale back their nuclear arsenals, they found out that the genie was already out of the bottle, that even poor Third World nations had the capability to build and launch them.

The military standoff between the nuclear powers brought about a precarious truce between them, but the rest of the world was not free of war. On the contrary, there have been more than a hundred wars since World War II, and many of these lesser wars, though contained geographically and limited to conventional weapons, carried the potential of igniting a larger conflagration.

Indeed, the combatants were all too often clients of the major powers and were armed by them.

Equally dangerous to the safety and well-being of humanity was the growing gulf between the world's rich and poor, between the industrially advanced nations of the North and the underdeveloped nations of the South. In the South, often referred to as the Third World, one finds the world's lowest standards of living, lowest economic growth rates, lowest levels of education, lowest rates of life expectancy, and the highest population growth rates and infant mortality rates. Thus, millions of the inhabitants of the Third World are dreadfully impoverished, malnourished, disease-ridden, and unable to live productively and in dignity. Governments of Third World nations struggled, usually ineptly, to lift their countries from such impoverishment, and while some have made marginal progress, many others were merely marking time or slipping even farther behind. Many of these countries contracted enormous foreign debts they were unable to pay, and their indebtedness threatened the financial stability of the wealthier nations of the North. Economic failure made the Third World more volatile politically and more vulnerable to intervention and militarization by the superpowers. Nearly every war fought since World War II was fought in Third World countries, and all were fought with weapons supplied by industrialized nations.

This is the world into which the youth of today were born. Their chances of resolving the immense problems they have inherited, of reducing the nuclear threat, and of alleviating the misery of the majority of humankind, thus making this world a safer and more civilized place, depend to a great extent on what they know of the causes of these problems. The clear-eyed vision needed to come to terms with these difficult problems and to progress toward a resolution of them must be based on an understanding of the past. To remain unaware of that past is to compound the chances of either perpetuating the current problems or committing grievous and possibly irretrievable errors.

Our aim is to provide our readers with an evenhanded, yet critical, explanation of the political history of this troubled world and to expose them to more than one viewpoint. We seek to advance our readers' knowledge of the recent past and to develop a better understanding of the difficult issues and dangerous conditions in the world today. Above all, we hope to instill an appreciation of the need for greater objectivity and for careful, critical thinking about political issues. It is, therefore, our hope that this text will serve as a primer for responsible global citizenship.

It should be emphasized that we are primarily dealing with political history in this text, except in certain chapters where economic themes are particularly relevant. We do not address many of the social or cultural dimensions of recent world history, as interesting or important as they may be. We also wish to point out that a text with a scope as broad as the world cannot help but be selective. Not every political development around the globe can be discussed within these pages. We have attempted to provide a balanced coverage of global history, rather than a Western- or US-centered approach. Thus, a substantial portion of the text is devoted to Asia, Africa, and Latin America.

The study of the recent past is no substitute for studying the longer haul of human history. Obviously, World War II had antecedents, the knowledge of which deepens our understanding of that momentous event, its consequences, and the course of events in the postwar period. Nonetheless, because World War II represents a historic watershed, it is not inappropriate that it be taken as a starting point for the study of recent world history. And because the postwar period was distinctly a new era with many new features—the advent of nuclear warfare, the development of high-speed aviation, the emergence of two superpowers, and the end of European colonialism, to name just a few— it makes sense to treat it as a distinct historical period. To be sure, for certain topics treated in this text, such as the Arab-Israeli conflict or the revolution in China, it will be necessary to trace historical roots further back in time, but our focus remains on the postwar period.

Seven Major Consequences of World War II

The enormous consequences of World War II gave shape to the postwar world, and they are treated as major themes in this text. We have identified the following as the most important of those consequences:

1. *The end of the European age.* Europe ceased to be the center of international power. At war's end, Europe was in shambles; its nations were prostrate, its cities in ruins, its people exhausted, and its economies shattered. The total defeat and destruction of Germany created a power vacuum in central Europe, and since nature and politics both abhor a vacuum, the victors inevitably filled it.

2. *The rise of the United States to superpower status.* Having played a decisive role in the global war and emerging from it militarily and economically supreme among the nations of the world, the United States shed for good its earlier isolationism and assumed a leadership role in the international arena.

3. *The expansion of the Soviet Union and its rise to superpower status.* Despite its severe war damage and its dire economic condition, the Soviet Union was determined to extend its power, especially in Eastern Europe, and play a major role in world affairs.

4. *The emergence of the Cold War.* Contention, mistrust, and hostility between the two emerging superpowers, the United States and the Soviet Union, developed quickly and produced an ongoing, global, bipolar power struggle.

5. *The beginning of the nuclear age.* The use of the atomic bomb by the United States and the world's failure to achieve international control of atomic energy resulted inevitably in an ever-growing nuclear arms race.
6. *The rise of nationalism and independence movements in Asia and Africa.* Although the roots of nationalism may be traced back to prewar times, it was not until the postwar period that nationalist movements became strong enough to challenge successfully the colonial order in Asia and Africa. The struggle for independence, stimulated by Japan's victories over Western colonial powers during World War II, and the weakening of the European colonial powers resulted in an end to Western colonialism in a remarkably short span of time.
7. *A renewed effort to secure lasting peace through international organization.* The United Nations was created in the hope that it might help preserve the global peace and security that the old League of Nations had failed to maintain.

Most of these—interrelated—themes are discussed in Part 1, "The Origins of the Cold War," where we examine the global state of affairs at the end of World War II and the origins of the Cold War. In Part 2, "Nationalism and the End of Colonialism," we take up the sixth theme. There, we also trace the development of Arab and Israeli nationalism and the conflict arising from them. Part 3, "The Shifting Sands of Global Power," focusing mainly on the 1960s, examines the changing configuration of the Cold War, the strains within the Eastern and Western blocs, the Sino-Soviet split, and the resulting emergence of multipolarity, which replaced the bipolar confrontation of the earlier Cold War period. This section also includes coverage of the Vietnam War and its consequences.

Part 4, "The Third World," takes us back to Asia and Africa to trace their postindependence progress—or lack thereof—and to Latin America. In addition to investigating the political and economic patterns on the three Third World continents, we devote sections to such topics as the problem of the Third World's debt, the issue of apartheid in South Africa, and the economic progress of certain Asian nations.

Part 5, "The Emergence of a New Landscape," treats the major global developments since the 1980s. We have selected for special attention the rise of Japan and the European Community as new economic superpowers, in addition to later Cold War issues such as the rise of Solidarity in Poland, the Soviet invasion of Afghanistan, and the nuclear arms race. We also discuss the momentous changes in the Soviet Union and Eastern Europe since the end of the 1980s, changes that signaled the end of the postwar era. We conclude the book with a discussion of the rise of militant Islam, as manifested in the Iranian revolution and in the Arab world.

We urge our readers to join with us in a quest for a fuller, more objective understanding of the world of turmoil in which we live. And we would remind them that history, especially recent political history, is not merely the compilation of dead facts; it is alive with controversy and conflicting ideas. We challenge our readers to confront these controversies, to weigh the conflicting ideas and viewpoints, and to formulate their own opinions.

Part 1

The Origins of the Cold War

**In light of the enormous impact of the Cold War since World War
II**—the immeasurable human energies it exhausted, the gargantuan amounts of
wealth it consumed, the shifting of national priorities it demanded, the attention it diverted from other concerns, the civil liberties it impinged on and the
intellectual freedom it constrained, the anguish and fears it caused so many
people, the threat it posed to the earth's inhabitants, and the enormous loss of
life in the proxy wars (Korea, Vietnam, and Afghanistan)—it becomes necessary to inquire into its origins.

By its very nature, the Cold War was for many years so divisive a subject
that it was all but impossible to study it with detachment and objectivity. So
strong were the feelings and so total the commitment of each side to its cause,
and so contemptuous and mistrusting was each of the other side, that each had
its own self-serving version of the history of the Cold War.

The United States and the Soviet Union each perpetuated a series of Cold
War myths that sustained them over the years. The people of the United States
generally felt (1) that the Soviet Union broke its postwar promises regarding
Eastern Europe and was therefore responsible for starting the Cold War; (2)
that its aggressive action in Eastern Europe was a manifestation of the determination of the Soviet Union to capture the entire world for Communism; (3)
that so-called international Communism was a monolithic (i.e., singular)
movement centered in and controlled by the Soviet Union; (4) that Communism was enslavement and was never accepted by any people without coercion; and (5) that the great victory of the United States in World War II, as well
as its immense prosperity and strength, attested to the superiority of its values
and its system—that, in short, the United States represented humanity's best
hope.

The Soviets argued (1) that the United States and the Western allies pur-
posely let the Soviet Union bleed in World War II, and furthermore lacked
gratitude for the role that it played in the defeat of Hitler, as well as for the

losses it suffered in that cause; (2) that the United States was committed to the annihilation of Communism in general and to the overthrow of the Communist government of the Soviet Union in particular; (3) that the laws of history were on its side, meaning that capitalism was in decline and Communism was the wave of the future; (4) that the US political system was not really democratic but was controlled by Wall Street, or at any rate by a small clique of leading corporate interests; and (5) that capitalist nations were necessarily imperialistic and thus responsible for colonization across the globe, and that the leading capitalist nation, the United States, was the most imperialistic of them all.[1]

As unquestioned assumptions, these myths became a mental straitjacket. They provided only a narrow channel for foreign policy initiatives by either country. When notions such as these were embedded in the thinking of the two adversaries, it became all but impossible for the two countries to end the Cold War and equally impossible to analyze objectively the history of the conflict.

The myths came into play throughout the Cold War, and especially in its earliest phase even before the defeat of Nazi Germany—when the Allied leaders met at Yalta in February 1945. For this reason, in the opening chapter, we examine the wartime relationship between the United States and the Soviet Union, and their respective strengths at the end of the war. We also analyze the US decision to use the atomic bomb against Japan and the impact it had on US-Soviet relations. In Chapter 2, we turn to the Yalta Conference and examine its bearing on the beginning of the Cold War. We then trace the hardening of Cold War positions over critical issues in Europe in the four years following the end of World War II. By 1947, when the US policy of "containment" of Communism was in place, the Cold War myths were firmly entrenched on both sides.

In March 1964, William Fulbright, the chairman of the Senate Foreign Relations Committee, attempted to challenge some of these and other Cold War myths. He questioned whether Communist China's "implacable hostility" to the West was "permanent," whether Fidel Castro in Cuba posed "a grave danger to the United States," and whether there was something "morally sacred" about the US possession of the Panama Canal, which it had seized in 1903. Yet few listened; indeed, Fulbright spoke before a nearly empty Senate chamber.

The Cold War quickly became global, and in fact it was in Asia where it became most inflamed in the first decade after the war. In Chapter 3, we discuss the Cold War in Asia by treating the Allied Occupation of defeated Japan, the civil war in China, and the Korean War—all Cold War issues. The Allied Occupation of defeated Japan was thoroughly dominated by the United States over the feeble objections of the Soviets, and eventually the United States succeeded in converting Japan into an ally in the global Cold War. The Chinese revolution, which brought the Communists to power in 1949, was fought entirely by indigenous forces, but the stakes were great for the two superpowers. The United States responded to the Communist victory in China with still firmer resolve to stem the advance of Communism in Asia. Less than a year later, that resolve was tested in Korea, where Cold War tensions grew most intense and finally ignited in the Korean War. The armed conflict between East and West was contained within one Asian country, but it threatened to explode into the dreaded World War III.

After the standoff in Korea, Cold War tensions oscillated during the remainder of the 1950s. During this period, covered in Chapter 4, new leaders—Dwight Eisenhower in the United States and Nikita Khrushchev in the Soviet Union—exhibited a new flexibility, which made possible some reduction in tensions and the solution of a few of the Cold War issues. But the embrace of the Cold War myths remained undiminished during this period, as manifested by sporadic crises and the substantial growth in the nuclear arsenals of both countries. The two superpowers came to the brink of nuclear war in 1962 over the deployment of Soviet nuclear missiles in Cuba. The Cuban missile crisis was the most dangerous of the many confrontations between East and West.

Note

1. These myths are an adaptation of a similar set of Cold War myths in Ralph B. Levering, *The Cold War, 1945–1972* (Arlington Heights, Ill.: Harlan Davidson, 1982), pp. 8–9.

1 The End of World War II and the Dawn of the Nuclear Age

World War II was a cataclysmic event. It was by far the most deadly and destructive war in human history. The war raged on for almost six years in Europe, beginning with Nazi Germany's attack on Poland in September 1939, and ending with the surrender of Germany to the Allied Powers led by the United States, the Soviet Union, and Great Britain on May 9, 1945. The war lasted even longer in Asia, where it began with the Japanese invasion of China in July 1937, and ended with Japan's capitulation to the Allies on August 14, 1945. World War II represented a new dimension in warfare: total war. It was total in the sense that it involved or affected the entire population of nations, not just the men and women in uniform. Everyone was drawn into the war effort and everyone became a target. This was not merely a war between armies but between societies. Because a nation's military might rested ultimately on its industrial capacity, the civilian workforce contributed to the war effort and thus became targets and victims of new and more deadly modern weapons.

Another major dimension of World War II, one of immense importance in ending the war and shaping the postwar world, was the introduction of atomic weapons. There are many difficult questions to ponder concerning the US use of the atomic bomb against Japan, one of the most important and most controversial issues in modern history. But the fundamental question remains: Was it necessary or justifiable to use the bomb? It is also important to consider what bearing the emerging Cold War had on the US decision to drop the bomb on Japan, and what bearing its use had on subsequent US-Soviet relations.

After the war, the victorious nations—mainly the United States and the Soviet Union—took the lead in shaping the postwar world. In order to understand their respective postwar policies, one must consider the impact of World War II on these two nations, the new "superpowers."

The "Grand Alliance" fashioned by the United States, the Soviet Union, and Great Britain during the war hardly lasted beyond it. But before the alliance began to crumble and give way to Cold War hostility, leading politicians of these and other nations endeavored to create a new international structure for the maintenance of global peace through collective security—the United Nations (UN). Although the founding of the United Nations was attended by great hope, it was from the beginning severely limited in its capacity to attain its objective of world peace.

History's Most Destructive War

The carnage of World War II was so great as to be beyond comprehension. Much of Europe and East Asia was in ruins. Vast stretches of both continents were destroyed twice, first when they were conquered and again when they were liberated. Germany and Japan stood in ruins. It is impossible to know the complete toll in human lives lost in this war, but some estimates run higher than 70 million people. The nation that suffered the greatest loss of life was the Soviet Union. It lost an incredible 27 million people in the war, a figure that represents at least half of the total European war fatalities. Poland lost 5.8 million people, about 15 percent of its population. Germany lost 4.5 million people, and Yugoslavia, 1.5 million. Six other European nations—France, Italy, Romania, Hungary, Czechoslovakia, and Britain—each lost more than a half million people. In Asia, perhaps as many as 20 million Chinese and 2.3 million Japanese died in the war, and there were large numbers of casualties in various other Asian countries, from India in the south to Korea in the northeast. In some European countries and in Japan, there was hardly a family that had not lost at least one member in the war.[1]

Approximately two-thirds of those who died in World War II were civilians—many of them specifically targeted for destruction. In contrast, during World War I, fewer than half of the dead were civilians, who tended to be incidental victims of the consequences of the war, famine and disease. World War II, however, to an extent not witnessed in modern European history, became a war against civilians.

The German army's war of conquest in the East, under the direction of Adolf Hitler, led to the systematic murder of an estimated 12 million people—Jews, Slavs, gypsies. Other victims included the disabled, conscientious objectors, and political opponents (notably Communists). The Jewish Holocaust—replete with mass executions and gas chambers—reduced Europe's prewar Jewish population from 9.2 million to 3.8 million. In 1945 came the shocking revelations of forced labor and extermination camps in Eastern Europe—Theresienstadt, Auschwitz (where 1.5 million Jews died), Treblinka, Buchenwald. It raised the vexing question of how German society—heir to a humanist tradition that gave the world Beethoven, Goethe, Bach, and Schiller—descended (willingly or unwillingly, the debate continues) to such a level of depravity.

Another factor leading to the huge toll of civilian lives was the development of airpower—bigger and faster airplanes with longer range and greater carrying capacity. Indiscriminate bombing of the enemy's cities, populated by noncombatants, became common practice during the war.

Aerial bombardment actually began before World War II. Its deadliness was demonstrated in the late 1930s by the German bombing of Spanish cities in the Spanish civil war and the Japanese bombing of Shanghai and other Chinese cities. In World War II, Britain carried out bombing raids on Berlin before Germany began its bombardment of Britain, but the latter represents the first sustained, large-scale bombing attack on the cities of another country. It was not long before British and US bombers retaliated with a massive bombardment of Germany. At the end of the war, an Anglo-US bombing raid on the German city of Dresden in February 1945 (when Germany was all but defeated) killed some 135,000 people, mainly civilians. The Japanese, who also used airpower, suffered the destruction of virtually all of their cities by the saturation firebombing carried out by US bombers. And the war ended with the use by the United States of a dreadful new weapon of mass destruction, the atomic bomb, which wrought horrible devastation upon Hiroshima and Nagasaki in August 1945. In the end, the nations that fought in the name of democracy in order to put an end to militarism resorted to the barbaric methods of their enemies. If unrestrained warfare had come to mean sustained, indiscriminate bombing of noncombatants with weapons of mass destruction, what hope was there for humankind should total war ever again occur?

The suffering and sorrow, the anguish and desperation of the survivors of the war lingered long after the last bombs had fallen and the victory celebrations had ended. Never in history had so much of the human race been so uprooted. In Europe alone there were approximately 65 million refugees, a staggering figure. Among them were East Europeans—Poles, Ukrainians, Lithuanians, and others—fleeing the advancing Red Army; 13 million Germans expelled from Poland, Czechoslovakia, and other parts of Eastern Europe; as well as slave laborers—on farms, factories, and construction sites— employed in Nazi Germany.[2]

The ethnic cleansing that the Germans began in 1939 was completed by their victims in 1945. It was based on the eternal principle expressed in W. H. Auden's poem "September 1, 1939" that "those to whom evil is done, do evil in return." The Czechs showed the Germans little mercy as they expelled them from the Sudetenland; the Germans in East Prussia suddenly discovered that, after all, their armies had committed atrocities in the East and the Red Army would respond in kind. (Former German territories, which became parts of Poland, Czechoslovakia, and the Soviet Union, remained for decades among the unresolved issues of the Cold War.)

The figures cited above do not include the uncountable millions of refugees in China plus some 6 million Japanese—half of them military personnel—

scattered across Asia at war's end. After the war, the United States transported most of these Japanese back home and returned Koreans, Chinese, and others to their homelands. In Manchuria, however, which the Soviets occupied temporarily, several hundred thousand Japanese were never repatriated. They succumbed either to the severity of the Manchurian winter without adequate food, shelter, or clothing or to the brutality of Soviet labor camps in Siberia. In China, cities such as Beijing (Peking) and Shanghai were swollen with weary, desperate people for whom there was no livelihood and insufficient food and other staples. In these places people were plagued by disease, poverty, the black market, inflation, and corruption, all of which ran rampant in China during and well after the war.

The inferno of World War II left many cities gutted and vacant. Dresden, Hamburg, and Berlin in Germany and Tokyo, Yokohama, Hiroshima, and Nagasaki in Japan were virtually flattened, and many other cities in these and other countries were in large part turned to rubble. Some were entirely vacated and devoid of life for a while after the war, and most lost a substantial portion of their people. For example, the huge and once crowded city of Tokyo, which lay mostly in ruins, saw its population dwindle to only a third of its prewar size. In these once bustling cities, survivors scrounged in the debris in hopes of salvaging anything that might help them in their struggle for survival. At war's end homeless people moved into those few buildings that still stood—an office building, a railroad station, a school—and lived sometimes three or four families to a room, while others threw up shanties and shacks made of scraps of debris. Decades later one could still find here and there in many of these cities rubble left over from the war.

The physical destruction wrought by the war, estimated at over $2 trillion, continued to cause economic and social disruption in the lives of survivors long afterward. Not only were cities and towns destroyed but so too were industrial plants and transportation facilities. The destruction of factories, farmlands, and livestock and of railroads, bridges, and port facilities made it extremely difficult to feed and supply the needy populations in the war-torn nations. Acute shortages of food and scarcity of other life essentials continued well after the fighting was over. In these dire circumstances, many became desperate and demoralized, and some sought to ensure their survival or to profit from others' misfortune by resorting to hoarding goods and selling them on the black market. These were grim times in which greed, vengeance, and other base instincts of humanity found expression.

The widespread desolation and despair in Europe bred cynicism and disillusionment, which in turn gave rise to a political shift to the left, toward socialist solutions. Shaken and bewildered by the nightmarish devastation all about them, many Europeans lost confidence in the old political order and turned to other more radical political doctrines and movements. Many embraced Marxism as a natural alternative to the discredited fascism and as an ideology that offered hope for the future. The renewed popularity of the left was reflected primarily in postwar electoral victories of the moderate left, such as the Labour Party in Great Britain and the Socialist Party in Austria. But the Communists, too, were able to make strong showings in elections—if only for the time being—particularly in France and Italy. In Asia the political swing to the left could be seen in China, Indochina, and to a lesser extent in Japan. Alarmed by this trend, US leaders soon came to the view that massive aid was necessary to bring about a speedy economic recovery and thereby eliminate the poverty that was seen as the breeding ground for the spread of Communism.

During the war, in November 1943, the US Congress created the United Nations Relief and Rehabilitation Administration (UNRRA), the purpose of which was the rehabilitation of war-torn areas. Economic recovery, however, was a slow and painful process. By the fall of 1946, many of the transportation facilities and factories in Western Europe were rapidly repaired, and industrial production began to climb slowly. But the harsh winter of 1946–1947 brought new economic setbacks with a depletion of food supplies, raw materials, and financial reserves. Economic stagnation and attendant deprivation spread throughout nearly all of Europe—in defeated and devastated Germany as well as in victorious Britain. A similar situation prevailed in the war-ravaged nations of Asia, especially China and Japan.

When one considers the death, destruction, suffering, and social dislocation the war had brought, it becomes clear that World War II was much more than a series of heroic military campaigns and more than a set of war games to be played and replayed by nostalgic war buffs. It was human anguish and agony on an unprecedented scale. And nowhere were the scars any deeper than in the Japanese cities of Hiroshima and Nagasaki.

The Atomic Bombing of Japan

On August 6, 1945, the United States dropped an atomic bomb on Hiroshima and, three days later, another one on Nagasaki. In each instance a large city was obliterated and tens of thousands of its inhabitants were either instantly incinerated or left to succumb to radiation sickness weeks, months, and even years later. According to Japanese estimates, the atomic bomb strikes killed about 140,000 people in Hiroshima and about 70,000 in Nagasaki. US estimates of the death toll from the atomic bombings are 70,000 in Hiroshima and 40,000 in Nagasaki. The discrepancy in the fatality figures is partly the result of different methods of calculation and partly from differing intentions of those doing the counting. Thus, World War II ended and the nuclear age began with the use of a new weapon of unprecedented destructive power, one that a Japanese physicist later called "a magnificent product of pure physics."[3]

The people of the United States and their wartime president, Franklin Roosevelt, were determined to bring about the earliest possible defeat of Japan. Roosevelt, who had commissioned the building of the atomic bomb, was prepared to use it against Japan once it was ready, but he had died in April 1945. By the time Germany surrendered in May 1945, the bloody war in the Pacific had been raging for almost three and a half years. The decision to employ the revolutionary new weapon fell to the new president, Harry S. Truman, who had not even been informed of its existence until after he took office. In consultation with the secretary of war, Henry Stimson, Truman set up an advisory group known as the Interim Committee, which was to deliberate on the matter of introducing the weapon into warfare. Ultimately, the Interim Committee recommended that the atomic bomb be used against Japan as soon as possible, and without prior warning, on a dual target (meaning a military or war-plant site surrounded by workers' homes, i.e., a Japanese city).[4] The rationale for this strategy was to enhance the atomic bomb's shock value. The bomb was successfully tested in a remote New Mexico desert on July 16, just as Truman was meeting British prime minister Winston Churchill and Soviet leader Joseph Stalin at Potsdam, Germany. Nine days later, on July 25, Truman, elated by the news of the test, approved the military orders for its use.

Hiroshima, Japan, August 1945. Located near ground zero, this building with its "A-Bomb Dome" has been preserved as a peace monument. *(National Archives)*

The following day he issued the Potsdam Proclamation, which spelled out terms for Japan's surrender and warned of "prompt and utter destruction" for noncompliance, but it made no specific reference to the new weapon. The proclamation was rejected by the Japanese government, and thus the orders for the first atomic bomb strike were carried out as planned.

The Japanese government dismissed the proclamation, for it was silent on the most important question, a guarantee by the victors that Japan would be allowed to retain the most sacred of Japanese institutions, the emperor. The US intelligence community, which from the very beginning of the war had been able to decode Japanese diplomatic and military cables, was well aware that the Potsdam Proclamation had a "magnetic effect" on the emperor, Prime Minister Suzuki Kantaro, and the army. Some Japanese officials thought that Article 10 of the proclamation implied the retention of the emperor and thus could be used as the basis of a Japanese surrender; others wanted a clarification. The proclamation, far from triggering an expression of Japanese intransigence, had the earmarks of the terms of surrender of the armed forces of the empire of Japan. Only one question remained: Would the US government clarify Article 10 and accept a Japanese surrender before or after atomic weapons were used?[5]

Many people have since questioned the use of the atomic bomb, and opinions differ sharply. The orthodox view, presented by US officials and generally shared by the US public, is that, by cutting short the war and sparing the casualties that would have occurred in the planned invasion of Japan, the atomic bomb actually saved many lives, Japanese as well as US. This explanation concludes that, although use of the bomb was regrettable, it was nonetheless necessary. Japan's diehard military leaders were determined to fight to the bitter end, as they had in the Pacific islands, and they were prepared to fight even more fanatically on their own soil to prevent defeat (as exemplified in the late spring of 1945 by the bloodiest battle in the Pacific, at Okinawa, where more than 12,000 US soldiers and Marines lost their lives in less than three months of fighting). To bring about the earliest possible surrender of Japan and an end to the long and costly war, US officials felt compelled to use the revolutionary, powerful new weapon at their disposal.

One commonly finds in US literature the figure of 1 million as the estimate of Allied (mainly US) soldiers who would have been killed in the invasion of Japan had the atomic bomb not been used. But the figure is grossly exaggerated since it is more than three times the total number of US military deaths resulting from World War II—both in Europe and in the Pacific—in four years of warfare. The 1 million figure was used by Secretary of War Stimson after the war in an article intended to justify the use of the atomic bombs. At a meeting of military officials to discuss the planned invasion of Japan, on June 18, 1945, General George C. Marshall, the army chief of staff, expressed the view that it was impossible to give an estimate of the casualties in such an invasion, but he said that in the first month they would probably not exceed those suffered in the invasion of Luzon—31,000.[6]

This interpretation, basically a justification of the atomic bombing of Japan, neglects many important historical facts. First, Japan was all but defeated. Its home islands were defenseless against the sustained US naval and air bombardments, its navy and merchant marine were sunk, its armies were weakened and undersupplied, and it was already being strangled by a US naval blockade. US leaders, who had underestimated the Japanese at the beginning of the war, were now overestimating Japan's remaining strength. Although the diehard determination of its military leaders kept Japan from surrendering, the nation's capacity to wage war had been virtually eliminated.

Second, before the United States had tested the atomic bomb in mid-July, the Japanese were already attempting to initiate negotiations with Washington in order to end the war. They sought to do this through Soviet mediation, since direct communication between Tokyo and Washington had been broken off during the war; Japan, however, was not at war with the Soviet Union. The US government was fully aware of these efforts and of the sense of urgency voiced by the Japanese in their communications to Moscow. US decisionmakers chose to ignore these diplomatic overtures, which they dismissed as unreliable and possibly a trick. The major obstacle to Japan's effort to achieve a diplomatic settlement to the war was the US insistence upon unconditional surrender, which called for Japan's acceptance of complete submission to the will of the United States, as opposed to a negotiated settlement to end the war. This was unacceptable to the Japanese, who wanted at least a guarantee of the safety of their sacred imperial institution—which is to say, they insisted on the retention of their emperor, Hirohito, in whose name the imperial forces fought the war. The US government steadfastly refused to offer any such exception to the unconditional surrender policy. The Potsdam Proclamation, the Allies' ultimatum issued on July 26, 1945, did not offer Japan any guarantees regarding the emperor, and thus the Japanese did not accept it as a basis for surrender. This condition was the only one the Japanese insisted upon, and eventually it was granted by the United States, but only after the nuclear destruction of Hiroshima and Nagasaki, on August 6 and 9, respectively. On August 11, the Japanese government still insisted on a surrender that "does not comprise any demand which prejudices the prerogatives of His Majesty as a sovereign ruler."[7] The Truman administration accepted this condition in its reply when it demanded the unconditional surrender of the Japanese forces "on behalf of the Emperor of Japan." If this condition had been granted beforehand, the Japanese may well have surrendered and the atomic bombs would then have been unnecessary.

Third, the Japanese might have been spared the horrendous fate of Hiroshima and Nagasaki had the US government provided them with an explicit warning about the nature of the new weapon and possibly an actual demonstration of an atomic blast as well. If Tokyo had still refused to accept the surrender

General Douglas MacArthur on the deck of the USS *Missouri* signing the Japanese surrender documents. *(National Archives)*

The formal Japanese surrender ceremony, September 2, 1945, onboard the USS *Missouri. (National Archives)*

terms after such a warning or demonstration, the use of the atomic weapons might have been morally justifiable. The Japanese were given no warning of the atomic bombing outside of the vague threat in the Potsdam Proclamation of "prompt and utter destruction." The Interim Committee ruled out the idea of providing Japan with either a warning or a demonstration of the bomb in favor of its direct use on a Japanese city in order to shock the Japanese into surrender. It was argued that a demonstration would be risky because of the possibility of the bomb's failing to work, thus causing the United States to lose credibility and the Japanese military leaders to gain confidence.

Fourth, an unquestioned assumption of most of those who defend the use of the two atomic bombs is that it produced the desired results: Japan quickly surrendered. Still, questions arise. Did the atomic bombings actually cause the Japanese to surrender? And was the second bomb necessary to bring it about? (The plan was for a "one-two punch" using both bombs in rapid succession and then, if necessary, a third, which was to be ready within ten days, so as to maximize the new weapon's shock value and force Japan to capitulate as rapidly as possible.)

Those who specifically protest the bombing of Nagasaki as unnecessary, and therefore immoral, assume that the bombing of Hiroshima was sufficient to cause Japan's surrender, or that Japan should have been given more time to assess what had hit Hiroshima. One may indeed question whether the interval of three days was long enough for the Japanese military leaders to assess the significance of the new force that had destroyed one of their cities. But a more fundamental question is whether the atomic bombings indeed caused Japan's surrender. Japanese newspapers, the testimony of Japanese leaders, and US intercepts of Japanese diplomatic cables provide reason to believe that the Soviet entry into the war against Japan on August 8 was as much a cause for Japan's surrender as the two atomic bombs. The Soviet Union was the only major nation in the world not at war with Japan, and the Japanese leaders were still desperately hoping for continued Soviet neutrality or possible Soviet mediation to bail them out of the war. They took heart in the fact that the Soviet Union had neither signed the Potsdam Proclamation nor signified support for it, even though Stalin was meeting with Truman and Churchill when it was issued. But with the Soviet attack the last shred of hope was gone, and Japan could no longer avoid admitting defeat. As for the effect of the atomic bombings on Japanese leaders, Japan's inner cabinet was divided three-to-three for and against accepting the Potsdam Proclamation before the bombing of Hiroshima, and it remained so afterward. It remained equally divided after the Soviet entry into the war and the bombing of Nagasaki, until finally the emperor himself broke the deadlock in favor of ending the war.

At the Yalta Conference in February 1945, Roosevelt and his military advisors strongly desired the early entry of the Soviet Union into the war against Japan, and he was willing to concede much to Stalin to attain this. But five

Nagasaki before. *(National Archives)*

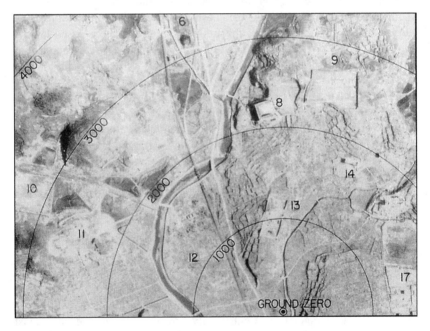

Nagasaki after. *(National Archives)*

months later, after the Battle of Okinawa (during which an estimated 200,000 Japanese—soldiers and civilians—died) and after the atomic bomb was successfully tested, leading figures in the Truman administration were not so sure they wanted the Soviet Union to enter the war against Japan. Nor did they want the Soviets to know anything about the atomic bomb. In fact, both Roosevelt and Truman pointedly refused to inform Moscow about the development and planned use of the new weapon (about which Stalin's spies had already informed him).

This last point raises intriguing and important questions about the connection between the US use of the bomb and its policies toward the Soviet Union at the end of the war. One historical interpretation asserts that the United States used the atomic bomb on defeated Japan not so much as the last attack of World War II, but as the first expression of US power in the Cold War. In other words, the bomb was used in order to coerce the Soviet Union into behaving itself in Europe, Asia, and elsewhere. This interpretation would explain the hurried use of the bomb before the Soviet Union had entered the war and nearly three months prior to the planned US invasion of Japan. It would explain Truman's refusal to inform Stalin officially about the new weapon before (or even after) its use against Japan. In this way, it is argued, the United States sought to maintain its nuclear monopoly (shared with Britain) and to engage in what became known as "nuclear diplomacy" as a means to curb Soviet expansion.

This interpretation by revisionist historians, based on substantial evidence and logic, remains speculative; those who hold the orthodox view, of course, reject it and offer counterarguments. They emphasize the fanaticism and intransigence of the Japanese military leaders, who even resorted to suicidal kamikaze airplane attacks on US ships. And they argue that the atomic bomb was needed to subdue an irrational enemy who seemed determined to fight suicidally to the bitter end. Therefore, in this view, it was solely for military purposes that Truman decided to use the atomic bomb. They also argue that Truman, as commander in chief, had the responsibility to use the military power at his command to produce the earliest possible defeat of Japan, and that, if he had not used the atomic bomb and more US military personnel had died in the continuing war, he would surely have been condemned as being politically and morally liable for their deaths.

Those who hold this view also argue that Truman could hardly have decided against use of the atomic bomb. As a new occupant of the White House following the popular Roosevelt, Truman inherited Roosevelt's cabinet, his policies, and specifically his resolve to treat the atomic bombs as a legitimate weapon of war. General Leslie Groves, head of the Manhattan Project (the code name of the secret program to build the atomic bomb), certainly assumed and fully expected that the bomb would be used as soon as it became operational. The military planning for its use was well under way. There was, among many of the scientists and military personnel involved in the project, a rising anticipation of the successful deployment of the weapon they had brought into being after four years of expensive and herculean effort. Truman, who had learned about the new weapon only after he became president in April, could hardly have stemmed the momentum. General Groves was especially determined to deploy the new weapon in order to know its destructive force. Military planners decided upon a set of Japanese cities as targets and ordered that these cities be spared from conventional bombing so that they would remain unspoiled targets for the nuclear experiment.

The Political Fallout

Historians are also in disagreement over the impact of the atomic bomb on the Cold War. Did the Truman administration actually attempt to employ nuclear diplomacy after the war? If it did, it is safe to say that it did not work. The nuclear threat, implicit in the exclusive Anglo-US possession of the atomic bomb, did not seem to produce any significant change in Soviet behavior and policies anywhere. But it did, no doubt, affect attitudes on both sides that contributed to Cold War mistrust. US possession of the bomb caused its leaders to be more demanding and less flexible in dealing with Moscow, and the US possession and use of the bomb surely caused Stalin, in turn, to increase his suspicions of the West.

It is fairly certain that the secretive manner of the United States in building and then using the atomic bomb made a postwar nuclear arms race likely, if not inevitable. Truman's secretary of state, James Byrnes, who also served on the Interim Committee, contended that it would take the Soviet Union at least ten years to develop an atomic bomb and that in the interim the United States could take advantage of its "master card" in dealing with the Soviet Union. However, leading US nuclear scientists, including lead scientist Robert Oppenheimer, predicted that the Soviet Union could build the bomb within four years.[8] Several of the Manhattan Project scientists attempted to warn the Truman administration that the atomic monopoly could not be maintained for long and that a nuclear arms race would surely follow and threaten the peace of the world if the US government did not inform the Soviet Union about this revolutionary new weapon of mass destruction and did not attempt to bring it under international control. This advice, given both before and after the Hiroshima and Nagasaki bombings, went unheeded, and the result was exactly what the scientists had predicted. Indeed, Oppenheimer's prediction that the Soviets would have their own atomic weapon in four years was right on target.

The US government did, however, after months of careful study of the complicated issues involved, offer a proposal for international control of atomic power. This proposal, the Baruch Plan, presented to a United Nations committee in June 1946, was unacceptable to the Soviet Union because, among other reasons, it permitted the United States to retain its nuclear arsenal indefinitely while restricting Soviet efforts to develop one. The Soviets countered by proposing the immediate destruction of all existing nuclear weapons and the signing of a treaty outlawing any future production or use of them. The United States, understandably unwilling to scuttle its atomic monopoly, flatly rejected this proposal. Talks continued for the next three years at the United Nations, but they proved fruitless. In the meantime, the Soviet Union's frantic effort to build an atomic bomb did bear fruit as early as the US atomic scientists had predicted—July 1949. The nuclear arms race was thus joined.

The United States and the Soviet Union at War's End

The two nations that emerged from the war as the most powerful shapers of the postwar world, the two new superpowers, the United States and the Soviet Union, had very different wartime experiences. No nation has ever suffered as many wartime casualties as the Soviet Union, and no major nation in the war suffered as few as the United States.

In June 1941, the German army of more than 2 million soldiers invaded the Soviet Union. Immense areas of the Soviet Union were devastated by the ensuing conflict, leaving some 1,700 cities and 70,000 villages in ruins and some 70 percent of its industries and 60 percent of its transportation facilities destroyed. During the war, the Germans took several million Soviet prisoners, many of whom did not survive their ordeal, and several million others were forcibly conscripted to labor in German factories and on farms until the end. The horrors of the German invasion and the siege of Soviet cities (notably Leningrad, Moscow, and Stalingrad) aroused the patriotism of Russians as well as non-Russian peoples of the Soviet Union, who fought heroically to defend the nation in what became known as the second Great Patriotic War (the first one being against the Napoleonic invasion of 1812), celebrated ad infinitum in songs, memorials, and paintings.

Ultimately, the Soviet people endured, and the Soviet Red Army chased the German army back to Berlin. But the cost in lives was enormous: an estimated 7.5 million military deaths and twice—possibly three times—as many civilian lives. There were perhaps twice as many Soviet battle deaths in the Battle of Stalingrad alone (and that does not include the civilians) as the United States suffered in the entire war (330,000); another estimate was that 1 million (largely civilians) died in the siege of Leningrad. Any discussion of postwar policies of the Soviet Union and its relations with the United States must begin with a recognition of the incredible losses it suffered in its war against Nazi Germany and the insistence that there be no repetition of this history.

In contrast, the United States emerged from the war, comparatively speaking, largely unscathed. Except for the Japanese attack on Pearl Harbor at the outset of the war and the brief Japanese occupation of Attu and Kiska at the far end of the Aleutian Islands, it was not invaded or bombed. In comparison with the huge Soviet death toll, the number of US soldiers killed in the war—approximately 330,000—was small. For every US death resulting from the war there were more than 80 Soviet deaths.

In comparison to the immense physical destruction sustained by the Soviet Union, the US infrastructure suffered no damage. On the contrary, the US economy experienced a great wartime boom, which brought it out of the Great Depression. While the Soviet Union's industrial output fell by 40 percent during the war years, that of the United States more than doubled. And while the Soviet Union sorely needed economic rehabilitation to recover from the ravages of war, the United States possessed unparalleled economic power. Indeed, no nation had ever achieved such economic supremacy as that achieved by the United States at the end of World War II. In a war-ravaged world where every other industrial nation had suffered extensive damage and declining production, the US economy, with its wartime growth, towered over all others like a colossus. What is more, the United States had the capacity to greatly extend its huge lead. It possessed in great abundance every resource necessary for sustained industrial growth in the postwar era: large, undamaged industrial plants; skilled labor; technology; raw materials; a sophisticated transport system; and, last but not least, a huge supply of capital for investment.

The United States came through the war with another important although intangible asset: a greatly inflated national ego. The nation was brimming with renewed confidence and optimism, and the pessimism spawned by the Great Depression became a thing of the past. The US people saw their victory in war as proof of the superiority of their way of life. With their nation standing tall at the pinnacle of power in the war-torn world, the people exhibited what has been called an "illusion of American omnipotence."[9] Here we have, indeed, what Henry Luce, the publisher of *Time* and *Life* magazines, had predicted five years earlier, the dawn of the "American Century." Bolstered by this new confidence and sense of supremacy, the United States now displayed a new determination to play the role of a great power and to exercise its leadership in shaping the postwar world. Under these conditions, it was astonishing to see that self-confidence so rapidly shaken once the Cold War got under way.

The Quest for Collective Security

The task of establishing a new world order after the defeat of Germany and Japan fell, of course, to the victors, especially the most powerful among them, the United States, the Soviet Union, and to a lesser degree Great Britain. During the war, the leaders of the "Big Three" countries—Franklin Roosevelt, Joseph Stalin, and Winston Churchill—met not only to coordinate war plans but also to lay plans for a postwar settlement. Roosevelt, in particular, was confident that the harmony and—relative—trust developed during the war would endure and that through personal diplomacy they could settle the enormous problems of the postwar world, such as the futures of Germany, Eastern Europe, Japan, and the rest of Asia. However, before the war ended, two of the three were no longer in power: Roosevelt died in April 1945, and Churchill was defeated in the election of July of that year. But it was already apparent before Roosevelt's death that the wartime alliance would not outlast the war. In retrospect, it became clear that the Big Three had little more in common than a common enemy, and once Nazi Germany was defeated, their conflicting interests came to the fore.

Wartime solidarity could not be counted on to guide the postwar world to safety and security and would not, in any case, endure beyond the war. The Big Three did, however, endeavor, albeit cautiously, to erect a new international structure designed to settle international problems. Even though sharp differences arose among the Big Three over a number of issues as the war was ending, they were in general agreement on the concept of maintaining peace through collective security. Roosevelt was most ardent in advocating the creation of a new international peacekeeping organization to replace the defunct League of Nations. Early during the war, Roosevelt began sounding out Churchill on this idea and then found occasion to discuss it with Stalin as well.

The Big Three. Soviet marshal Joseph Stalin, US president Franklin D. Roosevelt, and British prime minister Winston Churchill at the Tehran conference in November 1943. *(National Archives)*

All three were concerned about maintaining a postwar working relationship among the "united nations," as the Allied powers were sometimes called. Roosevelt wished to avoid a return of his country to isolationism, and Stalin had a similar concern. He did not want the Soviet Union to be isolated as it had been prior to World War II.

There was much discussion about what shape the new collective security organization should take—its structure, functions, and authority. The most difficult issue was the conflict between a commitment to internationalism, on one hand, and nationalist concerns, on the other. Specifically, the question was how much of any member nation's sovereignty was to be surrendered to the new supranational body in the interest of maintaining world peace. Would the new international organization have enough authority to enforce its decisions on member nations and yet permit each the right to protect its national interests? Another key question was the relationship of the major powers to the many smaller nations within the international body. From the outset the Big Three were in agreement that they would not sacrifice their power to majority rule. They insisted that their own nations, which had played the major role in World War II, should be entrusted with the responsibility to maintain the postwar peace, and that the new international organization should invest authority in them to exercise leadership unobstructed by the collective will of the smaller, but more numerous, member states.

These issues were resolved among the Big Three at a series of wartime conferences. At a meeting in Moscow in October 1943, the Allied foreign ministers agreed in principle to the creation of the organization that would come to be known as the United Nations. In August 1944, as victory in the war approached, representatives of the Big Three, now joined by Nationalist China, met at Dumbarton Oaks (in Washington, D.C.) to hammer out the shape of the new international body. At the Yalta Conference in February 1945 (see Chapter 2), the Big Three came to terms on the matter of securing for each of the major powers the right to veto decisions of the new international body. This cleared the way for convening a conference at San Francisco in April 1945, where the United Nations Charter, which spelled out the principles and the powers of the new organization as well as its organizational structure, was signed by representatives of the fifty-one founding nations. In September 1945, the United Nations officially opened its headquarters in New York City.

The principal organs of the United Nations were the Security Council, the General Assembly, the Economic and Social Council, the International Court of Justice, and the Secretariat. The most powerful and important of these was the Security Council, which was given the responsibility to keep the peace. It was empowered to determine whether an action such as armed aggression by a member nation constituted a breach of the United Nations Charter and to recommend corrective measures or sanctions, including the use of force under the principle of collective security. The Council was composed of five permanent members (the five great powers: the United States, the Soviet Union, Great Britain, China, and France) and six other nations elected for two-year terms. The permanent members were given absolute veto power, which is to say the Council could not enact a binding resolution unless there was unanimity among the big five. It was in this manner that they intended to protect themselves from actions by the world body against their own interests. It must be noted that both the United States and the Soviet Union insisted on this veto power, and without it they would not have joined the United Nations. And it should also be noted that it was this same provision that soon rendered the United Nations Security Council ineffective, because in the ensuing Cold War, unanimity among the major powers was all but impossible to attain. In the early years of the United Nations, the Soviet Union, which often stood alone against the other four major powers, resorted again and again to the veto.

The UN General Assembly was composed of all of the member nations, each of which had an equal voice and a single vote. It acted as an open forum in which international problems and proposed solutions were discussed. The Assembly passed resolutions by majority vote, but these were treated merely as recommendations and were not binding on the member nations. This body was important mainly for giving the smaller nations a voice—albeit generally ignored—in world affairs.

The UN Secretariat was the permanent administrative office concerned primarily with the internal operations of the organization. It was headed by a secretary-general, who was the highest and most visible officer of the United Nations. He was appointed by the General Assembly on the recommendation of the Security Council. In effect, it meant finding a compromise candidate from a neutral country acceptable to the two sides in the Cold War. As such, the secretary-general's authority tended to be limited since he took his marching orders from the Security Council.[10]

The other bodies of the United Nations, especially the specialized agencies (e.g., the World Health Organization) under the Economic and Social Council, functioned more effectively than the Security Council precisely because they were more operational than political in nature, and the problems they addressed could be separated from Cold War polemics. This also was essentially true for such UN bodies as the International Court of Justice, its highly effective World Health Organization, UNESCO (United Nations Educational, Scientific, and Cultural Organization), and UNHCR (the UN High Commissioner for Refugees, an agency that, in 1951, took over the functions of UNRRA).

The founding of the United Nations was an expression of hope by the survivors of a catastrophic world war, and it was greeted by them as the fulfillment of dreams for an organization that would ensure international peace and order. The political leaders who took part in its creation also had high hopes for it. It was not long, however, before the United Nations proved unable to fulfill those dreams and even became an object of derision for many. The United Nations did on several occasions intervene to settle or moderate international disputes in such places as Iran, India, Malaya, and the Middle East, when and where the interests of both the United States and the Soviet Union were either minimal or not in conflict. However, the veto power that both superpowers had insisted on and the Cold War contention between them rendered the Security Council all but powerless to keep the peace in the postwar era.

Recommended Readings

World War II

Calvocoressi, Peter, and Guy Wint. *Total War: Causes and Courses of the Second World War.* New York: Pantheon, 1972.
    A comprehensive account of the war both in Europe and Asia.
Dower, John W. *War Without Mercy: Race and Power in the Pacific War.* New York: Pantheon, 1986.
    A frank analysis of the racial nature of the war.
Hart, B. H. Liddell. *History of the Second World War.* New York: Putnam, 1971.
    One of the most highly regarded single-volume studies of World War II.
Saburo, Ienaga. *The Pacific War: World War Two and the Japanese, 1931–1945.* New York: Pantheon, 1978.
    A strong indictment of Japanese militarism.
Werth, Alexander. *Russia at War, 1941–1945.* New York: Dutton, 1964.
    Excellent look at the Soviet Union's wartime experience, by a British war correspondent, a native of St. Petersburg.
Wright, Gordon. *The Ordeal of Total War.* New York: Harper and Row, 1968.

The Atomic Bomb

Alperovitz, Gar. *Atomic Diplomacy: Hiroshima and Potsdam.* New York: Simon and Schuster, 1965.
    The foremost revisionist interpretation of the atomic bomb decision.
———. *The Decision to Use the Atomic Bomb.* New York: Knopf, 1995.
Bernstein, Barton J., ed. *The Atomic Bomb: The Critical Issues.* Boston: Little, Brown, 1976.
    An excellent anthology, which provides excerpts from the writings of some of those involved in the atomic bomb project and by various other writers.
Committee for the Compilation of Materials on Damage Caused by the Atomic Bombs in Hiroshima and Nagasaki. *Hiroshima and Nagasaki: The Physical, Medical, and Social Effects of the Atomic Bombs.* New York: Basic Books, 1981.
    The definitive study on the subject from the Japanese perspective.
Feis, Herbert. *The Atomic Bomb and the End of World War II.* Princeton: Princeton University Press, 1966; originally published in 1961 as *Japan Subdued.*
    A standard work that focuses on both the military and diplomatic aspects of the atomic bomb decision.
Herken, Gregg F. *The Winning Weapon: The Atomic Bomb in the Cold War, 1945–1950.* New York: Knopf, 1981.
    A discussion of the role of the atomic bomb in immediate postwar diplomacy.

Hersey, John. *Hiroshima*. New York: Bantam, 1959.
A classic on the death and destruction caused by the first atomic bomb attack.
Nobile, Philip, ed. *Judgment at the Smithsonian: The Bombing of Hiroshima and Nagasaki*. New York: Marlowe, 1995.
The Smithsonian's catalog for its controversial 1995 exhibit, before veterans' organizations and Congress banned it since it challenged the orthodox interpretation.
Rhodes, Richard. *The Making of the Atomic Bomb*. New York: Simon and Schuster, 1986.
Sherwin, Martin J. *A World Destroyed: The Atomic Bomb and the Grand Alliance*. New York: Knopf, 1975.
Among the best studies of the politics and diplomacy involved in the decision to drop the atomic bomb on Japan.

Notes

1. The magnitude of the slaughter was such that no exact figures are possible. For a breakdown of the figures, particularly in Asia, see John W. Dower, *War Without Mercy: Race and Power in the Pacific War* (New York: Pantheon, 1986), pp. 295–301.
2. United Nations High Commissioner for Refugees (UNHCR), *The State of the World's Refugees, 2000: Fifty Years of Humanitarian Action* (New York: Oxford University Press, 2000), chapter 1, "The Early Years."
3. Dr. Yoshio Nishina, "The Atomic Bomb," Report for the United States Strategic Bombing Survey (Washington, D.C.: National Archives), p. 1, Record Group 243, Box 56.
4. "Notes of the Interim Committee," Record Group 77, Manhattan Engineering District Papers, Modern Military Branch, National Archives (Washington, D.C.: National Archives, May 31, 1945), pp. 9–10.
5. Pacific Strategic Intelligence Section, intelligence summary of August 7, 1945, "Russo Japanese Relations (28 July–6 August 1945)," National Archives, Record Group 457, SRH-088, pp. 3, 7–8, 16. For the Japanese attempts to surrender, beginning on July 13, 1945, see "Magic Diplomatic Extracts, July 1945," MIS, War Department, prepared for the attention of General George C. Marshall, National Archives, Record Group 457, SRH-040, pp. 1–78.
6. Herbert Feis, *The Atomic Bomb and the End of World War II* (Princeton: Princeton University Press, 1966), pp. 8–9.
7. Harry S. Truman, *Memoirs, I, 1945: Year of Decisions* (New York: Signet, [orig. 1955] 1965), p. 471.
8. "Notes of the Interim Committee," May 31, 1945, pp. 10–12; Gregg Herken, *The Winning Weapon: The Atomic Bomb in the Cold War, 1945–1950* (New York: Random House, 1981), pp. 109–113. Byrnes was apparently less influenced by the views of the scientists than he was by General Groves, who speculated that it would take the Soviet Union from ten to twenty years to produce an atomic bomb.
9. Sir Denis Brogan, cited in Louis Halle, *The Cold War as History* (New York: Harper and Row, 1967), p. 25.
10. The first secretary-general was Trygve Lie of Norway (1946–1952), who was followed by Dag Hammarskjöld of Sweden (1953–1961), U Thant of Burma (1961–1971), Kurt Waldheim of Austria (1972–1981), Javier Pérez de Cuéllar of Peru (1982–1991), Boutros Boutros-Ghali of Egypt (1992–1996), Kofi Annan of Ghana (1997–2006), and Ban Ki Moon of South Korea (2007).

2 The Cold War Institutionalized

At the end of 1944, it became clear that it was only a matter of time until the Allies would defeat Nazi Germany. It also became evident that the reason for the wartime alliance—always a marriage of convenience—was coming to an end. Postwar considerations were beginning to play an ever-increasing role in the relations between the Allies. Throughout the war, the Allies repeatedly had made clear that they fought for specific aims and not merely for the high-sounding principles of liberty and democracy. In 1945, the moment thus came to consider the postwar world. For these reasons the Allied heads of state—Franklin Roosevelt of the United States, Joseph Stalin of the Soviet Union, and Winston Churchill of Great Britain—met in February 1945 in the Soviet resort of Yalta on the Crimean peninsula on the Black Sea. It was here that the Big Three attempted to sort out four central issues.

The Yalta Conference

The main topic at Yalta was the status of postwar Eastern Europe, mainly that of Poland, which had been—and still was at the time of the conference—an ally in the war against Germany. It was on behalf of the government of Poland that Great Britain and France had declared war on Germany in 1939. This action by the Western powers had transformed the German-Polish war into a European conflict, which then spilled over into the Atlantic, the Mediterranean, and North Africa, and with the Japanese attack on Pearl Harbor in December 1941, into Asia and the Pacific. In short, the governments of France and Great Britain had taken the momentous decision to go to war—and thus risk the lives and fortunes of their own people—to prevent the German conquest of a nation in Eastern Europe.

As the war drew to a conclusion and the Germans were expelled from Poland, the fate of that nation became the overriding political concern of the Allies. To complicate matters for the West, the prewar government of Poland, virulently anti-Russian and anti-Communist, had fled Warsaw in the wake of the German invasion and had taken up residence in London, waiting to return to power at the end of the war. The Polish leaders in London now insisted that the West had an obligation to return them to Warsaw as the legitimate government of Poland. The Western leaders, Churchill and Roosevelt, wanted to oblige, but it was the Red Army of the Soviet Union that was in the process of occupying Poland. It became increasingly clear that Stalin, not Roosevelt or Churchill, would determine the nature of the government in postwar Poland.

The second issue at Yalta was one of prime importance for the US armed forces, which at that time were still engaged in a bitter war with Japan that promised to continue perhaps into 1946. The sustained bombing of Japanese cities was under way, but Japanese resistance was as fierce as ever and the Battle of Okinawa (where the United States first set foot on Japanese soil) had not yet taken place. For the US Joint Chiefs of Staff, therefore, Yalta was primarily a war conference with the aim of bringing the seasoned Red Army into the war against Japan in the Pacific.

The third question was the formation of the United Nations to replace the old League of Nations, a casualty of World War II. Roosevelt sought an organizational structure that was acceptable to Churchill and Stalin, as well as to constituents back home. Roosevelt firmly believed that there could be no effective international organization without US and Soviet participation.

Finally, there was the question of what to do with the German state, whose defeat was imminent. The Allies would soon be in control of the devastated land of the once powerful Germany, whose uncertain future was in their hands.

The Polish Question

The first question, the status of Poland, proved to be the thorniest. It came up in seven of the eight plenary (full, formal) sessions. Roosevelt and Churchill argued that Poland, an ally, must be free to choose its own government. Specifically, they sought the return of the prewar—pro-West and anti-Communist and anti-Russian—government of Poland, in exile in London.

This "London government" consisted of Poles who did not hide their strong anti-Moscow sentiments, the result of age-old struggles between Russians and Poles. Their animosity toward the Communist government in Moscow was so great that on the eve of the war with Germany they had refused even to consider an alliance with the Soviet Union. Stalin then made his famous deal in 1939 with Hitler whereby the two agreed to a Non-Aggression Pact,[1] by which Stalin hoped to sit out the war. As part of the bargain, Hitler offered Stalin the eastern region of Poland, a large piece of territory that the victorious Poles had seized from a devastated Soviet state in 1921. The Polish conquest (1921) of what the Soviets considered part of their empire and the subsequent Soviet reconquest (1939) of these lands (with Hitler's complicity) were but two events in the long and bloody relationship between these two peoples. In 1941, Hitler used Poland as a springboard to invade the Soviet Union and at the end of the war the Soviets returned to Poland with a powerful army once more.

Stalin understood only too well the nationalistic and bitterly anti-Russian attitudes of the Poles, particularly that of the prewar government, which had sworn eternal hostility to his government. As the Soviet soldiers moved into Poland they became targets of the Polish resistance, which took time out from fighting the Germans to deal with the invader from the east. Stalin had no difficulty understanding the nationalistic and religious divisions in Eastern Europe. As an ethnic Georgian, Stalin was, after all, a product of the volatile ethnic mix of the old tsarist empire. He understood, as he told his Western allies at Yalta, that the Poles would be "quarrelsome."[2]

Hitler's invasion of the Soviet Union cost the Soviet Union an estimated 27 million lives. At Yalta, Stalin was determined to prevent the reestablishment of a hostile Poland along his western border. Stalin had no intentions, therefore, to permit the London Poles to take power in Warsaw. This was a major concern Stalin repeatedly conveyed to his allies, Roosevelt and Churchill, who grudgingly accepted in principle the reality that Eastern Europe in general, and Poland in particular, already had become part and parcel of the Soviet Union's sphere of influence. To this end, even before Yalta, Stalin had created his own Polish government, with its seat in the eastern Polish city of Lublin, which consisted of Communists and socialists.

Roosevelt and Churchill faced a dilemma. World War II had been fought for the noble ideals of democracy and self-determination. But in postwar Poland there would be neither. Britain, moreover, still had a treaty obligation with the London Poles. The treaty with the Polish government in London, however, consisted of an obligation on the part of Britain to defend its ally only against Germany, not the Soviet Union, a point the British government stressed in April 1945, when it released a secret protocol of the 1939 treaty. With this release, Britain's legal obligation to the Polish government came to an end. But there was still the moral duty to defend a former ally against the aspirations of a totalitarian ally of convenience. Yet that moral obligation was trumped by the Red Army's control of Poland.

The long disputation on the Polish question pitted the demands of Roosevelt and Churchill for self-determination against Stalin's insistence on a government answerable to Moscow. Specifically, it came down to an argument over the composition of a provisional (interim) government, with Stalin arguing for recognition of the Lublin regime as the provisional government and Roosevelt and Churchill insisting that Poland's provisional government include "democratic" (that is, pro-Western) politicians. Finally, the two sides arrived at an ambiguous agreement that papered over their broad differences.

The Polish government was to be "reorganized on a broader democratic basis with the inclusion of democratic leaders from Poland itself and Poles abroad."[3] This reorganized government was to be provisional until the "free election" of a permanent government. The ambiguity of the agreement allowed both sides to interpret it as they saw fit.

After the conference, Roosevelt and Churchill chose to accentuate Stalin's concession to allow "free elections" so as to claim that they had won at Yalta a victory for the London Poles and for democracy. Stalin, however, had no intention of allowing "democratic" politicians—that is, the Western-oriented and anti-Soviet London Poles—into the provisional government or of permitting them to run for office later. In any case, his definition of free elections was so narrow that the supposed promise of free elections became meaningless. When elections were finally held, the slate of candidates was restricted to "safe" political figures who posed no threat to the Soviet domination of Poland.

Stalin apparently was under the impression that the Western powers had essentially yielded at Yalta to the Soviet Union's presence in Poland and that their complaints were largely cosmetic and for domestic consumption. He thus considered the question resolved. But in Britain, and in particular the United States, the Soviet Union's control of Poland never sat easily. Events showed that Stalin subsequently violated his promise of free elections, that his control of Poland was in direct conflict with the Western war aims, such as freedom and democracy, and that the Red Army in Poland pushed Stalin's political and military influence toward the center of Europe.

From these events came the following arguments, which Roosevelt's Republican critics often made: (1) Roosevelt had yielded Poland (as well as the rest of Eastern Europe) to Stalin; and (2) Stalin had broken his promise at Yalta to hold free elections, and this act of infidelity precipitated the Cold War. The Democrats, stung by these charges, replied that Roosevelt had not ceded Eastern Europe to the Soviets. Geography and the fortunes of war, they contended, had been responsible for putting the Red Army into Eastern Europe, not appeasement on the part of Roosevelt or of his successor, Harry Truman, who became president upon Roosevelt's death on April 12, 1945.

The Ghost of Munich

At this juncture the two major allies in World War II became locked into positions that were the result of their peculiar readings of the lessons of history—particularly, the "lessons of Munich." This refers to the event that many politicians and historians have considered the single most important step leading to World War II.

In the autumn of 1938, Adolf Hitler insisted that a part of western Czechoslovakia—the Sudetenland with a population of 3 million ethnic Germans—must be transferred to Germany on the basis of the principle of national self-determination, a principle ostensibly dear to the victors of World War I, who had created the sovereign state of Czechoslovakia. Germans must live in Germany, Hitler threatened, otherwise there will be war. France had a treaty of alliance with Czechoslovakia that committed France to war in case Germany attacked that country. But the French government was psychologically and militarily incapable of honoring its treaty and sought a compromise solution. At this point England's prime minister, Neville Chamberlain, stepped in. The result was the Munich Conference, by which the Western powers avoided war, if only for the time being, and Hitler obtained the Sudetenland. Hitler promised that this was his last demand in Eastern Europe. Chamberlain returned to London proclaiming famously that he had "brought peace in our time."

Events quickly showed that Hitler had lied. In March 1939, he annexed the rest of Czechoslovakia and then pressured the Poles to yield on territorial concessions. When the Poles refused to budge, the British, and later the French, determined that the time had come to take a stand and offered the Poles a treaty of alliance. Hitler then invaded Poland, and a European war was in the making.

The lessons of Munich for the West were clear. A dictator can never be satisfied. Appeasement only whets his appetite. In the words of the US secretary of the navy, James Forrestal, there were "no returns on appeasement."[4] When Stalin demanded his own sphere of influence in Eastern Europe after the war, the West quickly brought up the lessons of Munich and concluded that Western acceptance of the Soviet Union's position would inevitably bring further Soviet expansion and war. Western leaders, therefore, proved to be psychologically incapable of accepting the Soviet Union's presence in Eastern Europe: There could be no business-as-usual division of the spoils of victory.

The Soviets had their own reading of these same events. To them, Munich meant the first decisive move by Hitler (in collusion with the capitalist West) against the Soviet Union. The men in the Kremlin long believed that they, and not the West or Poland, were Hitler's main target. Throughout the latter half of the 1930s, the Soviet Union had repeatedly called for an alliance with the West against Germany, but the pleas had always fallen on unreceptive and suspicious Western ears. From Moscow's perspective, the West's deal with Hitler at Munich deflected Hitler toward the East. In rapid order Hitler then swallowed up Czechoslovakia and a host of other East European nations, confirming the Soviet leaders' deep suspicions. By June of 1941, when Hitler launched his invasion of the Soviet Union, he was in control of all of Eastern Europe—not to mention most of the rest of Europe as well—and proceeded to turn it against the Soviet Union.

For the Soviets the lessons of Munich were obvious. Eastern Europe must not fall into the hands of hostile forces. Stalin would tolerate neither the return to power of the hostile Poles in London nor that of the old regimes in Hungary, Romania, and Bulgaria, which had cooperated with the Nazis. No foreign power would have the opportunity to do again what Hitler had done and turn

PRE–WORLD WAR II BOUNDARIES

POST–WORLD WAR II BOUNDARIES

TERRITORIAL CHANGES RESULTING FROM WORLD WAR II

FINLAND

PORRKALLA, LEASED TO U.S.S.R. 1946 - 1956

Leningrad

NORWAY

SWEDEN

North Sea

Baltic Sea

ESTONIAN S.S.R.

LATVIAN S.S.R.

DENMARK

OCCUPATION ZONES IN GERMANY

ADMINISTRATION U.S.S.R.

LITHUANIAN S.S.R.

U.S.

U.S.S.R.

EAST PRUSSIA

SOVIET UNION

NETH.

BR.

Berlin

ADMINISTRATION POLAND

BELG.

GERMANY

POLAND

EASTERN PRE-WAR POLAND

LUX.

FR.

FRANCE

FR.

U.S.

CZECHO-SLOVAKIA

U.S.S.R.

OCCUPATION ZONES IN AUSTRIA

SWITZ.

FR.

U.S.

AUSTRIA

BR.

HUNGARY

Trieste

ROMANIA

YUGOSLAVIA

ITALY

Adriatic Sea

ALBANIA

BULGARIA

GREECE

TURKEY

Dodecanese Is. (Gr.)

0   300
miles

Central and Eastern Europe:
Territorial Changes After World War II

Eastern Europe against the Soviet Union. The old order of hostile states aligned with the Soviet Union's enemies must give way to a new reality that served Moscow's interests.

From the same events the two antagonists in the Cold War thus drew diametrically opposed conclusions. The West focused on the military containment of the Soviet Union accompanied by an unwillingness to legitimize the Kremlin's dominant position in Eastern Europe. A lack of resolve, it was argued in the West, would surely bring war. The Soviets in their turn were just as adamant in insisting that the buffer they had created in Eastern Europe kept the capitalist West at bay and preserved the security of their nation. These opposing visions of the lessons of history were at the core of the conflict between the West and the Soviet Union.

Polish Borders

At Yalta, Stalin also insisted on moving Poland's borders. He demanded a return to the Soviet Union of what it had lost to the Poles in the Treaty of Riga in 1921 (after the Poles had defeated the Red Army). At that time Lord Curzon, the British foreign secretary, had urged the stubborn Poles to accept an eastern border 125 miles to the west since that line separated more equitably the Poles from the Belorussian and Ukrainian populations of the Soviet Union. But in 1921, the victorious Poles rejected the Curzon Line and, instead, imposed their own line upon the defeated Soviets. In 1945, it became Stalin's turn to redraw the border.

To compensate the Poles for land lost on the east to the Soviet Union, Stalin moved Poland's western border about 75 miles farther west into what had been Germany, to the Oder and Western Neisse Rivers. At Yalta, Stalin sought his allies' stamp of approval for the Oder-Neisse Line but without success.

A third readjustment of Poland's border called for the division between the Soviets and the Poles of East Prussia, Germany's easternmost province. Stalin insisted that East Prussia become part of the spoils of war. His reasoning was simple. The Soviet Union and Poland had suffered injury at the hands of the Germans and their peoples deserved compensation. The West reluctantly acceded to Stalin's demands, which, in any event, had already been accomplished.

Since 1945, the Soviets and Poles have considered the border changes at the expense of Germany a fait accompli. A fair number of Germans, however, were reluctant to accept these consequences of the war. When, after World War II, the Western powers and the Soviet Union failed to reach an agreement on the political fate of a unified Germany, the result was the division of that nation into the US-sponsored Federal Republic of Germany (commonly known as West Germany) and the Soviet creation, the Democratic Republic of Germany (or East Germany). The East German government had little choice but to accept the new German-Polish border. The West German government, however, always insisted that it was the sole legitimate German government and that it spoke for all Germans, East and West. The first West German government of Chancellor Konrad Adenauer—a determined champion of German territorial integrity—bitterly opposed Soviet expansion westward and refused to accept the new, Soviet-imposed boundaries.

In the late 1960s, the West German government, under the leadership of Willy Brandt, began to acknowledge that new borders existed in fact; but for the first 42 years of its existence, no West German government (not even that of Brandt) formally accepted the legality of the transfer of German territory. Until the reunification of Germany in 1990, it remained one of the unresolved consequences of the war.

The Japanese Issue

The second issue at Yalta was more straightforward. The US Joint Chiefs of Staff wanted the Soviet Red Army to enter the war against Japan. The Soviets, as it turned out, needed little prodding. Stalin promised to enter the Japanese war ninety days after the end of the war in Europe. The Japanese had handed Russia a humiliating defeat in the Russo-Japanese War of 1904–1905 and took the island of Sakhalin, which previously had been under Russian control. In the wake of the Bolshevik Revolution of 1917 and the civil war that followed, the Japanese had invaded eastern Siberia and remained there until 1922.[5] In the 1930s, it seemed for a while as if the Soviet Union might become Japan's next target after the Japanese annexation of the northeastern Chinese region of Manchuria. In fact, in late summer 1939, the Red Army and the Japanese army were engaged in a bloody battle along the Mongolian-Chinese border at Khalkin Gol. Japan's thrust southward—which ultimately brought it into conflict with the United States—and the Soviet Union's preoccupation with Nazi Germany kept the two from resuming their old rivalry. When the Soviets attacked the Japanese army in Manchuria at the very end of World War II, it marked the fourth Russo-Japanese conflict of the twentieth century. From the Soviet point of view, here was a golden opportunity to settle past scores and to regain lost territories.

The UN Question

The third major topic at Yalta dealt with the organization of the United Nations. Roosevelt proposed, and Churchill and Stalin quickly accepted, the power of an absolute veto for the world's great powers over any United Nations action they opposed. In 1919, when President Woodrow Wilson unsuccessfully proposed the US entry into the League of Nations, his opponents argued that in doing so, the foreign policy of the United States would be dictated by the League. A US veto would prevent such an eventuality in the new United

Nations. The United States, however, could not expect to be the only nation with a veto. Roosevelt proposed that each of the "Big Five"—the United States, the Soviet Union, Great Britain, France, and China—be given the power to veto a UN action. It also meant that the United Nations could not be used against the interests of any of the major powers. The United Nations thus could act only when the Big Five were in concert—and that proved to be a rare occasion. The weakness of the United Nations was thus built into its charter.

An example of what this sort of arrangement meant in practice may be seen in this exchange between Stalin and Churchill at Yalta (concerning the issue of Hong Kong, a colony Great Britain had taken from China in the nineteenth century):

> Stalin: Suppose China . . . demands Hong Kong to be returned to her?
> Churchill: I could say "no." I would have a right to say that the power of [the United Nations] could not be used against us.[6]

The German Question

The fourth question, the immediate fate of Germany, was resolved when the Big Three decided that, as a temporary expedient, the territory of the Third Reich—including Austria, which Hitler had annexed in 1938—was to be divided into zones of occupation among the three participants at the Yalta Conference. Shortly, the French insisted that as an ally and a major power they, too, were entitled to an occupation zone. Stalin did not object to the inclusion of another Western, capitalist power, but insisted that if France were to obtain a zone, it must come from the holdings of the United States and Great Britain. The result was the Four-Power occupation of Germany and Austria, as well as of their respective capitals, Berlin and Vienna.

As the Big Three returned home from Yalta, they were fairly satisfied that they had gotten what they had sought. As events would show, however, Yalta immediately became the focal point of the Cold War. Poland and its postwar borders, the United Nations, the Red Army's entrance into the war against Japan, and the German and Austrian questions all became bones of contention between East and West in the months and years ahead.

The Potsdam Conference

By mid-summer 1945, with Berlin in ruins and the defeat of Japan all but a certainty, the Grand Alliance of World War II fell apart with remarkable speed. The first signs of tension already had appeared upon the conclusion of the war in Europe, when the West and the Soviet Union sought to carve out spheres of influence in Eastern Europe. Whatever cooperation had existed during the war had turned into mutual suspicion. Still, the two sides were consulting with each other and they were slated to meet again in July 1945, this time for a conference in Germany at Berlin, the capital of Hitler's Third Reich. The near-total destruction of Berlin led to a change in venue to the nearby city of Potsdam.

The Big Three at Potsdam were Joseph Stalin, Harry Truman (who had succeeded Roosevelt in April 1945), and Winston Churchill (who later in the conference would be replaced by Britain's new premier, Clement Attlee). This meeting accomplished little. The Polish question came up at once, particularly the new border drawn at the expense of Germany, which the Western leaders reluctantly accepted. The Western leaders also grudgingly recognized the new socialist government in Poland, but they repeatedly voiced their objections to other client governments Stalin had propped up in Eastern Europe, particularly those of Romania and Bulgaria. The Soviets considered the transformation of the political picture in Eastern Europe a closed issue, comparing it to the creation of the new government in Italy under Western supervision that had replaced the previous fascist government, an ally of Nazi Germany. The sharp exchanges at Potsdam only heightened suspicions and resolved nothing.

Another source of disagreement was the issue of reparations from Germany. The Soviets insisted on $20 billion from a nation that was utterly destroyed and could not possibly pay such a huge amount. This demand meant the transfer of whatever industrial equipment Germany still possessed to the Soviet Union. It would leave Germany impoverished, weak, and dependent on outside help. This scenario presented several disadvantages to the West: A helpless Germany was no physical deterrent against potential Soviet expansion westward; it might succumb to Communism; and it would be neither an importer of US goods nor an exporter of the goods. Moreover, the United States was already contemplating economic aid to Germany, and thus the Soviet demand meant that US money and equipment would simply pass through Germany to the Soviet Union as reparations.

The Soviets insisted that at the Yalta Conference in February 1945 their allies had promised them the large sum of $20 billion. US representatives replied that this figure was intended to be the basis of discussion, depending upon conditions in Germany after the war. The devastation of Germany at the very end of the war, therefore, meant that the Soviets would have to settle for far less.

To Truman the solution was simple. He would exclude the Soviets from the Western zones of occupation, leaving the Soviets to find whatever reparations they could come up with in their Eastern zone. They did so by plundering the eastern part of Germany. The reparations question marked the first instance of the inability of the wartime allies to come to an agreement on how to govern Germany. It established the principle that in each zone of occupation the military commander would have free rein. As such, the occupation powers never came up with a unified policy for Germany. The main consequence of this was the long-enduring division of Germany. Within three years there was no point in pretending that a single German state existed.

The only thing on which Truman and Stalin agreed at Potsdam was their position on Japan. Neither, it seems, was willing to let the Japanese off the hook. Surrender could only be unconditional. While at Potsdam, Truman received word that the first atomic bomb had been successfully tested at Alamogordo, New Mexico. Truman knew of Japanese efforts to end the war through negotiations, but with the atomic bomb he could now end the conflict on his own terms and keep the Soviet Union out of postwar Japan. Stalin, for his part, did not want a quick Japanese surrender. At Yalta he had pledged to enter into the war ninety days after hostilities against Germany had ended, and he had every intention of doing so. It would give him the chance to redress old grievances against Japan and to extend his influence in the Far East. Truman did not tell Stalin about the atomic bomb—of which Stalin already was well aware—and his plans to use it against Japan. Stalin was led to believe that Truman still wanted the Soviet Union to attack Japan. With the United States secretly planning to drop atomic bombs on Japan, and Stalin secretly planning to attack its forces in Manchuria, Japan was doomed.

The defeat of Japan, however, brought no improvement in East-West relations. Both sides constantly voiced their grievances and suspicions of each other. Indeed, the bombing of Hiroshima and Nagasaki gave the Soviets still more reason to distrust and suspect the intentions of the United States. Each point of disagreement was magnified; each misunderstanding became a weapon; each hostile act was positive proof of the other side's evil intentions.

But one could not yet speak of a full-blown, irreversible Cold War. This came in 1947, when the conflict reached a new plateau. In fact, many historians, in the Soviet Union as well as in the West, see that year as the true beginning of the Cold War. It was then that the United States declared its commitment to contain—by economic as well as military means—all manifestations of Communist expansion wherever it occurred. In the same year, a Soviet delegation walked out of an economic conference that concerned itself with the rebuilding of Europe. With this act all East-West cooperation came to an end and the battle lines were more clearly drawn.

The Truman Doctrine

"The turning point in American foreign policy," in the words of President Truman, came early in 1947 when the United States was faced with the prospect of a Communist victory in a civil war in Greece.[7] The end of World War II had not brought peace to Greece. Instead, it saw the continuation of a bitter conflict between the right and the left, one that in early 1947 promised a Commu-

President Harry S. Truman and General Dwight Eisenhower, January 1951. Two years later, the general would succeed Truman as president. *(National Archives)*

nist victory. The British, who for a long time had played a significant role in Greek affairs, had supported the right (the army and the Greek monarchy), but they were determined to end their involvement in Greece. Exhausted by the war, Britain could not go on. Unceremoniously, London dumped the problem into Washington's lap: If the United States wanted a non-Communist government in Greece, it would have to see to it and it would have to go it alone. Truman, a man seldom plagued by self-doubt, quickly jumped into the breach. But he also understood that the US public would be slow to back such an undertaking. At the end of World War II, the US public had expected that within two years the US military presence in Europe would end. Truman's involvement in Greece, however, would extend it and postpone the US disengagement from Europe indefinitely. In fact, it meant an increased, continued US presence in Europe. To achieve his aim, Truman knew he would have to "scare the hell out of the American people."[8] And he succeeded admirably.

In March 1947, Truman addressed a joint session of Congress to present his case. In his oration, one of the most stirring Cold War speeches by a US political leader, Truman expounded his views: The war in Greece was not a matter between Greeks; rather, it was caused by outside aggression. International Communism was on the march and the orders came from its center,

Moscow. It was the duty of the United States "to support free peoples who are resisting attempted subjugation by armed minorities or by outside pressures." The United States must play the role of the champion of democracy and "orderly political processes." There was more at stake than the upholding of political and moral principles. A Communist victory in Greece threatened to set off similar events in other countries, like a long chain of dominoes. "If Greece should fall under the control of an armed minority, the effect upon its neighbor, Turkey, would be immediate and serious. Confusion and disorder might well spread throughout the entire Middle East."[9] This speech, which became known as the Truman Doctrine, firmly set US foreign policy on a path committed to suppressing radicalism and revolution throughout the world. All US interventions since that day invoked what became known as the "domino theory": If country X falls, then Y and Z will surely follow.

But there was no clear evidence that the guiding hand of Stalin was behind the Greek revolution. Stalin, it seems, kept his part of the bargain he made with Churchill in October 1944, by which the two agreed that after the war Greece would fall into Britain's sphere of influence. Churchill later wrote that Stalin adhered to this understanding.[10] If anything, Stalin wanted the Greek revolt to "fold up . . . as quickly as possible" because he feared precisely what ultimately happened.[11] He told the Yugoslav vice president, Milovan Djilas: "What do you think? That . . . the United States, the most powerful state in the world will permit you to break their line of communications in the Mediterranean Sea? Nonsense, and we have no navy."[12] But to Truman and most of the US public it was a simple matter: All revolutions in the name of Karl Marx must necessarily come out of Moscow.[13] The Republican Party, not to be left behind in the holy struggle against "godless Communism," quickly backed Truman. Thus, a national consensus was forged, one that remained intact until the divisive years of the Vietnam War.

The first application of the Truman Doctrine worked remarkably well. US military and economic aid rapidly turned the tide in Greece; the Communists were defeated and the monarchy was spared. All this was achieved without sending US troops into combat. There appeared to be no limits to US power. This truly appeared to be, as Henry Luce, the influential publisher of *Time* and *Life* magazines, had said earlier, the "American Century."[14] Yet, at about the same time, events in China showed that there were in fact limits on the ability of the United States to affect the course of history, when the US-supported government and its army there began to unravel.

The Marshall Plan

Three months after the pronouncement of the Truman Doctrine, the United States took another step to protect its interests in Europe when the Truman administration unveiled the Marshall Plan, named after General George Marshall, Truman's secretary of state, who first publicly proposed the program. The program was intended to provide funds for the rebuilding of the heavily damaged economies of Europe. The Marshall Plan was in large part a humanitarian gesture for which many Europeans expressed their gratitude and remained grateful for decades to come. The Marshall Plan was also intended as a means to preserve the prosperity the war had brought to US society. At the very end of the war, the United States took the lead in establishing an international system of "free trade"—or at least relatively unrestricted trade. But international commerce—in this case access to European markets—demanded a strong and prosperous Europe that in turn was capable of purchasing US goods. The United States proved to be extremely successful in shoring up the financial system of the Western, capitalist world. In this sense, the Marshall Plan well complemented the Truman Doctrine as a potent political weapon in the containment of Soviet influence. The Marshall Plan, Truman explained, was but "the other half of the same walnut."[15]

The Marshall Plan helped to stymie the floundering Communist parties in Western Europe. The Soviet Union's influence there was dependent on the strength of these parties. After initial strong showings, particularly in France and Italy, the Communist parties' fortunes declined rapidly under the impact of the Marshall Plan.

At the end of World War II, the US wartime Lend-Lease program—war materiél valued at $11 billion—with the Soviet Union had come to an end. Moscow applied for continued economic assistance from the United States, but nothing came of it since any subsequent aid was dependent upon proper Soviet behavior in Eastern Europe. Officially, Washington was willing to extend Marshall Plan aid to Eastern Europe, including the Soviet Union, but not without preconditions. The money would have to be administered, as in Western Europe, by the United States, not by its recipients. Several East European states were receptive to the plan, particularly Poland and Czechoslovakia, both of which were governed by coalitions of Communist and non-Communist parties. The Soviet Union, too, at first appeared to be ready to participate in the rebuilding of Europe under the auspices of the Marshall Plan. Its foreign minister, Viacheslav Molotov, came to Paris with a large entourage of economic experts to discuss the implementation of the plan. But shortly afterward, he left the conference declaring that the US conditions were unacceptable since their implementation would entail the presence of US officials on East European and Soviet soil and would, therefore, infringe upon his country's national sovereignty. Molotov did not say publicly that the presence of US representatives in Eastern Europe would reveal the glaring weaknesses of the Soviet Union and its satellites. The Marshall Plan was a gamble Stalin apparently felt he could not afford. Stalin then pressured the governments of Poland and Czechoslovakia to reject the Marshall Plan.

George Marshall as chief of staff. *(National Archives)*

Stalin went beyond merely applying pressure on Czechoslovakia. In February 1948, a Communist coup in that country ended the coalition government and brought Czechoslovakia firmly into the Soviet orbit. This act regenerated in the West the image of an aggressive, brutal, and calculating leadership in Moscow. The Communist coup in Czechoslovakia, only ten years after Hitler had taken the first steps to bring that nation under his heel, did much to underscore in the West the lessons of Munich. During the coup, Czechoslovakia's foreign minister, Jan Masaryk, was probably murdered under mysterious circumstances, an act generally attributed in the West to Stalin. The coup had a deep impact on public opinion in the West and it became prima facie evidence that one could not do business with the Soviets.

Stalin's rejection of Marshall Plan aid also meant that the East European countries would have to rebuild their war-torn economies with their own limited resources, under Moscow's umbrella and without US aid and Western technology. Moscow's power now extended to the center of Europe. In response to this, Churchill, in a speech in Fulton, Missouri, in 1946, reminded his audience that an "Iron Curtain" had descended across Europe—from Stettin on the Baltic Sea to Trieste on the Adriatic Sea.

Limits of Soviet Power

Yet, immediately after Stalin appeared to have consolidated his position in Eastern Europe, the first crack appeared in what had been a monolithic facade. The Yugoslav Communist leadership, under the direction of Joseph Tito, broke with the Kremlin over the fundamental question of national sovereignty. Moscow insisted that the interests of a foreign Communist party must be subordinate to those of the Soviet Union, officially the center of an international movement. The Yugoslavs insisted, however, on running their own affairs as they saw fit. In the summer of 1948, the bitter quarrel became public. Tito refused to subordinate the interests of his state to those of Stalin, and consequently Yugoslavia became the first Communist nation in Eastern Europe to assert its independence from the Soviet Union.

In the West, the prevailing view was that "Titoism"—a nationalist deviation from the international Communist community—was a unique, singular incident. Stalin knew better. He understood that Titoism was no isolated phenomenon. Other East European nations could readily fall to the same temptation. In order to forestall such an eventuality, Stalin launched a bloody purge of East European "national Communists." The purge was so thorough that, until Stalin's death in March 1953, Eastern Europe remained quiet.

In 1948, it also became evident that the division of Germany and Berlin would become permanent. All talks on German reunification had broken down, and the West began to take steps to create a separate West German state, with West Berlin, a city 110 miles inside the Soviet sector, becoming a part of West Germany. When, during World War II, Stalin had agreed on the division of Berlin among the allies, he had not bargained on such an eventuality. The last thing he wanted was a Western outpost inside his zone. Berlin had little military value for the West since it was trapped and outgunned by the Soviet

West Berlin children on rubble mounds cheer the arrival of a US aircraft filled with food during the airlift, 1948. *(German Information Center)*

army, which occupied East Germany. But it served as a valuable political, capitalist spearhead pointing into Eastern Europe. Moreover, West Berlin was invaluable as a center of espionage operations. In June 1948, Stalin took a dangerous, calculated risk to eliminate the Western presence in that city. He closed the land routes into West Berlin in the hope of convincing the West to abandon Berlin. The West had few options. It neither wanted World War III nor could afford to abandon West Berlin and its 2 million people to the Communists. The result was the "Berlin Airlift," by which the West resupplied West Berlin by transport planes flying over East Germany. During the next ten months, over 270,000 flights were made, carrying an average of 4,000 tons of supplies a day to the beleaguered city. Stalin dared not attack the planes for he, too, would not risk World War III. Finally, in May 1949, Stalin yielded by reopening the highways, linking the city once again with West Germany. Stalin had lost his gamble and there was no point in perpetuating the showdown. This crisis, which had brought both sides to the edge of war, was over, if only for the time being.

Throughout the late 1940s, the US assumption was that the Soviet Union was preparing for an attack on Western Europe, an assumption based largely on fear rather than on fact. The image of an expansionist, aggressive Soviet Union was the result of three conditions. First, the Soviet army was ensconced in the center of Europe. Second, this act was seen not so much as the logical consequence of the war but as the fulfillment of Soviet propaganda stressing the triumph of socialism throughout the world. Third, the differences of opinion between the Soviet Union and the West quickly took on the character of a military confrontation, and people began to fear the worst.

Once the specter of an inevitably expansionist Soviet state gripped the Western imagination, it became almost impossible to shake this image. This view of Soviet intentions buttressed the US arguments that the Soviet Union must be contained at all costs. The subsequent "containment theory," first spelled out in 1947 in a lengthy essay by George Kennan, a State Department expert on the Soviet Union, seemed to be working reasonably well with the application of the Truman Doctrine and the Marshall Plan. But Kennan never made clear the nature of the containment of the Soviet Union he had in mind. Later, he insisted that he had meant the political, and not the military, containment of the Soviet Union. Yet, the central feature of Truman's containment policy was its military nature. In 1949, the United States created NATO, the North Atlantic Treaty Organization, an alliance that boxed in the Soviet Union along its western flank. One person's containment theory is another person's capitalist encirclement. Stalin responded by digging in.

Recommended Readings

Andrzejewski, Jerzy. *Ashes and Diamonds.* London: Weidenfeld and Nicholson [orig. 1948], 1965.
   The classic novel on life in Poland at the very end of World War II.
Clemens, Diane Shaver. *Yalta.* New York: Oxford University Press, 1970.
   Discusses Yalta not as an ideological confrontation but as an exercise in horse-trading.
de Zayas, Alfred M. *Nemesis at Potsdam: The Anglo-Americans and the Expulsion of the Germans: Background, Execution, Consequences.* 2nd rev. ed. London: Routledge and Kegan Paul, 1979.
   Focuses on the refugee problem after the war, a topic generally ignored in Cold War histories.
Fleming, D. F. *The Cold War and Its Origins, 1917–1960.* 2 vols. Garden City, N.Y.: Doubleday, 1961.
   By one of the first practitioners of the revisionist school of history of the Cold War.
Halle, Louis J. *The Cold War as History.* New York: Harper and Row, 1967.
   One of the few earlier books on the Cold War that put it into historical perspective.
Ulam, Adam B. *The Rivals: America and Russia Since World War II.* New York: Viking, 1971.
   Discusses the first phase of the East-West confrontation.
———. *Expansion and Coexistence: Soviet Foreign Policy, 1917–1973.* 2nd ed. New York: Praeger, 1974.
Volkogonov, Dmitri. *Stalin: Triumph and Tragedy.* Rocklin, Calif.: Prima Publishing, 1991.
   A product of Gorbachev's "new thinking" and glasnost, a critical reassessment of the reign of Stalin.

Notes

1. Often called the Molotov-Ribbentrop Pact, after the foreign minister of Nazi Germany, Joachim Ribbentrop, and the Soviet Union's commissar for foreign affairs, Viacheslav Molotov, who worked out the details of the arrangement.

2. Winston S. Churchill, *The Second World War, VI, Triumph and Tragedy* (New York: Bantam, [orig. 1953] 1962), p. 329.

3. Quoted from "The Yalta Declaration on Poland," as found in US Department of State, *Foreign Relations of the United States: The Conferences at Malta and Yalta, 1945* (Washington, D.C.: US Government Printing Office, 1955), p. 938.

4. Quoted from a cabinet meeting of September 21, 1945, in Walter Millis, ed., *The Forrestal Diaries* (New York: Viking, 1951), p. 96.

5. The US president, Woodrow Wilson, also sent troops into eastern Siberia at that time, ostensibly to keep an eye on the Japanese. Earlier, at the end of World War I, Wilson had sent troops into European Russia, ostensibly to protect supplies that had been sent to the Russian ally—led at the time by Tsar Nicholas II—to keep them from falling into German hands. The Soviets have always rejected this explanation and have argued that US intentions were to overthrow the fledgling Communist government.

6. James F. Byrnes, *Frankly Speaking* (New York: Harper and Brothers, 1947), p. 37.

7. Harry S. Truman, *Memoirs, II, Years of Trial and Hope* (Garden City, N.Y.: Doubleday, 1956), p. 106.

8. The words are Senator Arthur Vandenberg's, cited in William A. Williams, *The Tragedy of American Diplomacy*, rev. ed. (New York: Delta, 1962), pp. 269–270.

9. "Text of President Truman's Speech on New Foreign Policy," *New York Times*, March 13, 1947, p. 2.

10. Churchill's report to the House of Commons, February 27, 1945, in which he stated that he "was encouraged by Stalin's behavior about Greece." *The Second World War, VI*, p. 334. In his "Iron Curtain" telegram to Truman, May 12, 1945, Churchill expressed concern about Soviet influence throughout Eastern Europe, "except Greece"; Lord Moran, *Churchill: Taken from the Diaries of Lord Moran, The Struggle for Survival, 1940–1965* (Boston: Houghton Mifflin, 1966), p. 847. Churchill to the House of Commons, January 23, 1948, on Greece: "Agreements were kept [by Stalin] when they were made." Robert Rhodes James, *Winston S. Churchill: His Complete Speeches, 1897–1963, VII, 1943–1949* (New York: Chelsea House, 1974), p. 7583.

11. Milovan Djilas, *Conversations with Stalin* (New York: Harcourt, Brace and World, 1962), pp. 181–182.

12. Ibid., p. 182.

13. After World War II, the most militant Communist head of state was Joseph Tito of Yugoslavia. It was Tito, rather than Stalin, who openly supported the Greek Communist insurgency by providing them weapons and refuge in Yugoslavia. Tito's actions were seen in the West as evidence of Stalin's involvement via a proxy; yet even Tito, once he broke with Stalin in 1948, shut his border to the Greek Communists and abandoned them.

14. Henry Luce, "American Century," in W. A. Swanberg, *Luce and His Empire* (New York: Dell, 1972), pp. 257–261.

15. Quoted in Walter LaFeber, *America, Russia, and the Cold War, 1945–1984*, 5th ed. (New York: Knopf, 1985), pp. 62–63.

3 The Cold War in Asia: A Change of Venue

The Cold War, which had its origins in Europe, where tensions mounted between East and West over the status of Germany, Poland, and other East European countries, became even more inflamed in Asia. In 1945, US policy in East Asia was focused primarily on the elimination of the menace of Japanese militarism and on support of the Nationalist government of China under Jiang Jieshi (Chiang Kai-shek)[1] as the main pillar of stability in Asia. But within five short years the United States was confronted with a set of affairs very different from what Washington had envisioned just after the war.

The Nationalist regime in China was defeated by the Chinese Communists who, under the leadership of Chairman Mao Zedong (Mao Tse-tung), proclaimed the founding of the People's Republic of China (PRC) on October 1, 1949. The largest nation on earth, in terms of population, was now under Communist rule. Only nine months later the Communist forces of North Korea attacked the US-supported, anti-Communist regime in South Korea. For the first time, the rivals of the Cold War, by way of proxies, clashed on the field of battle. These two events had a profound effect on the US-led military occupation of defeated Japan, an East Asian military outpost directed against the Soviet Union and Communist China.

The Allied Occupation of Japan

The Allied Occupation of Japan, which lasted almost seven years (from September 1945 to May 1952), was unique in the annals of history, for, as the historian Edwin Reischauer wrote, "never before had one advanced nation attempted to reform the supposed faults of another advanced nation from within. And never did the military occupation of one world power by another prove so satisfactory to the victors and tolerable to the vanquished."[2] From the outset, the US policy in Japan was benevolent and constructive, although it had

49

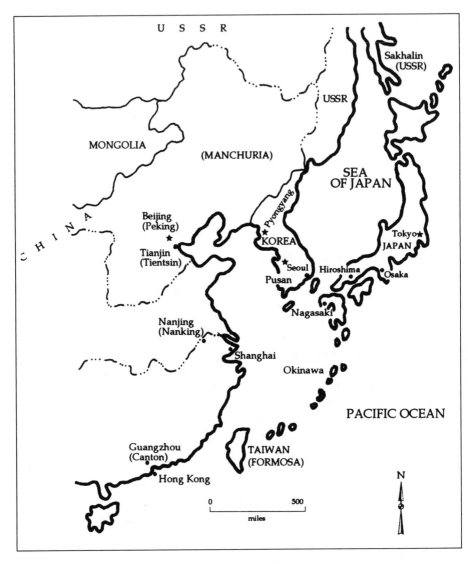

East Asia (1945)

its punitive aspects as well. The Japanese, who had never in their long history been defeated and garrisoned by foreign troops, expected the worst. Not only did their fears of US brutality prove unfounded, but so also did US fears of continued hostility by Japanese diehards. The two nations, which had fought each other so bitterly for almost four years, made amends, and in a remarkably short time they established enduring bonds of friendship and cooperation. This

Mao Zedong (Mao Tse-tung), chairman of the Chinese Communist Party, October 1, 1950, the first anniversary of the founding of the People's Republic of China. *(National Archives)*

was partly the result of the generous treatment by the US occupation forces, and partly the result of the receptivity and goodwill of the Japanese themselves. They welcomed the opportunity to rid themselves of the scourge of militarism that had led their nation into the blind alley of defeat and destruction. And they appreciated the sight of US GIs brandishing not rifles, but chocolate bars and chewing gum. Even more important for securing the active support of the Japanese was the decision by US authorities to retain the emperor on the throne rather than try him as a war criminal, as many in the United States had demanded. Indeed, one important reason why the Japanese were so docile and cooperative with the US occupation forces was that their emperor, whom they were in the habit of dutifully obeying, had implored them to be cooperative.

Prior to the defeat of Japan, officials in Washington were already planning a reform program under a military occupation. The Allied Occupation of Japan was, as the name implies, supposedly an Allied affair, but it was in fact dominated by the United States, despite the desire of the Soviet Union and other nations to play a larger role in it. General Douglas MacArthur was appointed Supreme Commander of Allied Powers (SCAP), and under his authority a broad-ranging reform program was imposed on Japan. The government of Japan was not abolished and replaced by a military administration as was the case in defeated Germany; rather, the Japanese cabinet was maintained as the instrument by which the reform directives of SCAP were administered. Also, unlike the case of Germany, Japan was not divided into separate occupation zones, largely because of the insistence of the United States on denying the Soviet Union its own occupation zone in Japan.

The principal objectives of the US-controlled occupation program were demilitarization and democratization. Demilitarization was attended to first and was attained promptly. Japan's army and navy were abolished, its military personnel brought home from overseas and dismissed, its war plants dismantled, and its weapons destroyed. Some 3 million Japanese soldiers were repatriated to Japan from all over Asia and the Pacific mainly by US ships, as were almost as many Japanese civilians. Also, as a measure to rid Japan of militarism, Japanese wartime leaders were put on trial at an international military tribunal in Tokyo. In court proceedings similar to the Nuremberg trials of Nazi war criminals, twenty-eight leading figures were accused of "planning a war of aggression" and "crimes against humanity," found guilty, and given severe sentences. Seven of them were hanged and seventeen others were sentenced to prison for life. Additionally, several thousand other Japanese military officers were tried and found guilty of a variety of wartime atrocities.

The occupation reformers also sought to rid Japan of its ultranationalist ideology, steeped in Shintoism and emperor worship. On January 1, 1946, the emperor was called upon to make a radio speech to the nation renouncing imperial divinity. Steps were also taken to abolish "State Shinto," the aspect of the religion native to Japan that promoted the belief in the divine descent of Japan's imperial ruler. Textbooks were censored to rid them of such ideas and other content considered militaristic.

Democratization of Japan was a more complex matter and would take longer to achieve, but the first major step in that direction was taken with the writing of a new constitution for Japan in 1947. Drafted by MacArthur's staff, it provided for a fundamental political reform. It provided Japan with a parliamentary system similar to that of Britain, an institution consistent with Japan's prewar political experience. The people of Japan were made sovereign (meaning, in effect, that government power ultimately rested on the consent of the governed, the people). The emperor, who had been sovereign in the old constitution, became no more than a symbol of the state, which is to say, he would no longer have any political authority. All laws were to be passed by a majority in the popularly elected House of Representatives in the Diet (Japan's parliament). The 1947 constitution also included extensive provisions spelling out the civil rights of Japanese citizens in great detail. The most striking feature of the new constitution—one in keeping with the demilitarization objective—was Article Nine, which outlawed war and forbade Japan to maintain land, sea, or air forces. MacArthur himself ordered that this provision be put into the constitution, but the idea was enthusiastically endorsed by the political leaders and a war-weary nation.

As the occupation continued under the watchful eye of MacArthur, a host of other reforms were imposed upon the Japanese. The economic reforms included the dismantling of the old *zaibatsu* (the huge financial cartels that dominated Japan's prewar economy), a land reform that redistributed farmland for the benefit of poor farmers and at the expense of wealthy landowners, and a labor reform creating Japan's first genuine trade union movement. There were also far-reaching social and educational reforms, all of which were intended to make Japan a more democratic society. Generally, these various reform programs were remarkably successful, largely because they addressed real needs in Japan and because the Japanese themselves desired the reforms.

One of the anomalies of the occupation is that democracy was being implanted in Japan by a military command, that is, by General MacArthur and his staff. SCAP's mode of operation was military: It censored the Japanese press, disallowed free speech, ruled by fiat, and issued directives to the Japanese government, not arrived at by a democratic process. Also anomalous was the character of General MacArthur as a reformer. In Japan he was aloof, arrogant, and almighty. The defeated Japanese seemed to need an august authority figure, and the imperious MacArthur seemed destined to play just such a role. Although he claimed to like the Japanese people, his manner toward them was condescending, and he often expressed contempt for their culture. In his view, the Japanese were but twelve-year-old children who must be shown the way from "feudalism" to democracy.[3] But despite MacArthur's arrogance and the military cast of the occupation, he and his staff possessed a genuine reformist zeal, and their sense of mission contributed greatly to the successful rooting of democratic ideas and institutions in Japan.

The menace of Japanese militarism was thus eliminated and supplanted by democracy, but US minds soon perceived a larger menace looming on the Eastern horizon: the spread of Communism in Asia. The Communist victory in the civil war in China in 1949, and Communist aggression in Korea in the following year, caused the US government to recast its policy in Japan reflecting Cold War exigencies. Safely under US control, Japan was to be prepared to play a key role in the US policy of containment of Communism.

It is difficult to arrive at a final assessment of the occupation of Japan, for opinions differ greatly according to one's ideology and nationality. That the occupation program, with its various reforms, was in every instance a grand success is certainly debatable. Many Japanese historians as well as revisionist historians in the United States have argued that the US exercise of power in postwar Japan was excessive, that the "reverse course" policies (see below) negated many of the democratic reforms, and that Japan was victimized by zealous US anti-Communist policies. But there is little question that Japan emerged from the experience with a working democratic system of government and a more democratic society, a passionate pacifism, the beginnings of an economic recovery, and a large measure of military security. And the United States emerged with a new, potentially strong ally strategically located in a part of the world confronted with the spread of Communist revolution.

The Civil War in China

The victory of the Chinese Communists over the Nationalist government of China in 1949 was the culmination of a long struggle between two revolutionary parties—the Communists and the Nationalists—that began back in the 1920s. After winning the first round of that struggle and coming to power in 1928, the Nationalist Party, under its domineering leader Jiang Jieshi, sought to exterminate the rural-based Communist Party led by Mao Zedong. In 1935, the Communists barely escaped annihilation by embarking on the epic "Long March," a trek of over 6,000 miles, after which they secured themselves in a remote area in northwestern China. When the war with Japan began in mid-1937, Mao persuaded Jiang to set aside their differences and form a united front for the purpose of defending China from the Japanese invaders. During the war against Japan (1937–1945), the Chinese Communist Party (CCP) and its army grew enormously while the Nationalist regime deteriorated badly. The Communists' success was the product of inspired leadership, effective mobilization of the peasantry for the war effort, and skillful use of guerrilla warfare tactics against the Japanese. By the end of the war the Communists controlled nineteen "liberated areas," rural regions mainly in northern China, with a combined population of about 100 million, and the size of their army had increased tenfold from about 50,000 to over half a million. In contrast, the Nationalist government and army had retreated deep into the interior to Chongqing (Chungking) during the war and failed to launch a successful counteroffensive against the Japanese. Meanwhile, wartime inflation became rampant, as did corruption within Jiang's Nationalist government and army. Growing political oppression was met by growing public discontent and declining morale. The Nationalist Army, supplied and trained by the United States, was hardly used against the Japanese, but rather was deployed to guard against the spread of Communist forces or languished in garrison duty. Thus, military morale sank as well.

When World War II ended with the US defeat of Japan, civil war within China was all but a certainty as the two rivals, Nationalists and Communists, rushed to fill the vacuum created by the defeated Japanese. Both sought to expand their areas of control and particularly went after the major cities in northern China. Jiang issued orders, sanctioned by the United States, that Japanese commanders were to surrender only to Nationalist military officers rather than turn over areas under their control to the Communists. Moreover, the United States landed some 53,000 Marines to take and hold several key cities in northern China until the Nationalist forces arrived.

While the United States continued to support Jiang's government as it had during the war, it wished to avert the impending civil war and thus urged Jiang Jieshi to find a peaceful solution to his conflict with the Communists. Even before the war had ended, Washington had sent a special envoy, Patrick Hurley, to China to serve as a mediator between the two sides. He was successful only in bringing the rivals Mao and Jiang to the negotiating table in August 1945, but not in finding a solution to their feud. After these efforts ended in failure, President Harry Truman sent General George C. Marshall to China in December 1945 to mediate the dispute. Despite Marshall's initial success in getting the two sides to agree—on paper at least—to an immediate cease-fire and to a formula for mutual military demobilization and political cooperation, he too ultimately failed as the conflict escalated into a full-fledged civil war in the spring of 1946. The US efforts to mediate between the CCP and Jiang's regime were destined to failure largely because Jiang refused to share power with the Communists. Essentially, Mao demanded the formation of a coalition government, followed by the mutual reduction and integration of Communist and Nationalist military forces, whereas Jiang insisted on the reduction of Communist forces and their integration into the Nationalist Army as the precondition for sharing power with the Communists. The US position as mediator was weakened by its lack of neutrality, for continued US military and economic aid to the Nationalists served to alienate the Communists. However, the civil war that the United States had tried so hard to prevent was not initiated by Mao, but rather by Jiang, who was convinced that the only solution to the problem was a military one and that it was obtainable.

At the outset of the Chinese civil war, the Nationalists had good reason to be confident of victory. Despite Communist gains, the Nationalist Army still had a numerical superiority of three to one over the Communist forces. The Nationalist Army was much better equipped, having received huge amounts of US military aid, including artillery pieces, tanks, and trucks, as well as light arms and ammunition. Moreover, the Nationalists benefited by having the use of US airplanes and troop ships for the movement of their forces. In contrast, the Communist army, reorganized as the People's Liberation Army (PLA), was relatively poorly equipped and had practically no outside support. Given the Nationalist edge, it is not surprising that Jiang's armies were victorious in the early months of the war, defeating the PLA in almost every battle in northern China. But within a year of fighting the tide began to shift.

The battle for China took place mainly in Manchuria, the northeastern area of China, which had been under Japanese control since the early 1930s. It was prized by both sides for its rich resources and as the most industrialized area of China (thanks to the Japanese and to the earlier imperialist presence of Russia). Immediately after World War II, Manchuria was temporarily under the control of the Soviet Union, whose Red Army had attacked the Japanese forces there in the closing days of the war and "liberated" the area. On August 14, 1945, the Soviet Union concluded with the Nationalist government of China a treaty of friendship, which included provisions for the withdrawal of Soviet forces from Manchuria to be completed within three months after the surrender of Japan. Before the Nationalists could occupy the area with their forces, the Soviet Red Army hastily stripped Manchuria of all the Japanese military and industrial equipment it could find and shipped it—together with Japanese prisoners of war—into the Soviet Union in order to support its own economic rehabilitation. Meanwhile, Chinese Communist forces had begun entering Manchuria immediately after the surrender of Japan. A poorly equipped PLA force of about 100,000 troops was rapidly deployed in rural areas surrounding the major cities of Manchuria. Jiang was determined to maintain Nationalist military control of Manchuria, and he decided—against the advice of his US military advisors—to position his best armies in that remote area, where they could be supported or reinforced only with great difficulty. Thus, when the battle for Manchuria began, Jiang's Nationalist forces held the major cities, railways, and other strategic points, while the PLA held the surrounding countryside. The Chinese Communists were not assisted by the Soviet Red Army in Manchuria (or elsewhere), but before the Soviets left Manchuria they did provide the PLA with a much needed cache of captured Japanese weapons (mainly light arms—rifles, machine guns, light artillery, and ammunition).

In the major battles in Manchuria in late 1947 and 1948, the Chinese Communists were big winners. Not only did the Nationalist Army suffer great combat casualties, running into the hundreds of thousands, but it lost almost as many soldiers to the other side either as captives or defectors. Moreover, the PLA captured large amounts of US weapons from the retreating Nationalist Army. The Communist forces, which were better disciplined and had stronger morale, used their mobility to advantage, since they were not merely trying to hold territory as were the Nationalists. In the end, it was they, not the Nationalists, who took the offensive. With their greater maneuverability they were able to control the time and place of battle and to inflict great losses on their less mobile enemy. The Nationalists had spread their forces too thin to maintain defensive positions and were unable to hold open the transportation lines needed to bring up reinforcements and supplies.

After the last battle in Manchuria, the momentum in the civil war shifted to the Communists. The last major engagement of the war was fought in the fall of 1948 at Xuzhou (Hsuchow), about 100 miles north of the Nationalist capital of Nanjing (Nanking). In this decisive battle Jiang deployed 400,000 of his best troops, equipped with tanks and heavy artillery. But after two months of fighting, in which the Nationalists lost 200,000 men, the larger and more mobile Communist army won a decisive victory.

From that point it was only a matter of time before the Nationalist collapse. During the spring and summer of 1949, Jiang's forces were rapidly retreating southward in disarray, and in October Jiang fled with the remainder of his army to the Chinese island of Taiwan. There the embattled Nationalist leader continued to claim that his Nationalist regime (formally titled the Republic of China) was the only legitimate government of China, and he promised to return to the mainland with his forces to drive off the "Communist bandits." In the meantime, on October 1, 1949, Mao Zedong and his victorious Communist Party proclaimed the founding of the PRC with Beijing (Peking) as its capital.

The Chinese civil war, however, was not entirely over, but instead became a part of the global Cold War. The new Communist government in Beijing insisted it would never rest until its rival on Taiwan was completely defeated; conversely, the Nationalist government was determined never to submit to the Communists. The continued existence of "two Chinas," each intent on destroying the other and each allied to one of the superpowers, would remain a major Cold War issue and source of tension in East Asia for decades.

The outcome of the Chinese civil war was the product of many factors, but direct outside intervention was not one of them. Neither of the superpowers, nor any other nation, became engaged militarily in the conflict once it began in 1946. By that time the United States had pulled its troops out of China. Indeed, after Jiang launched a full-scale civil war in mid-1946, General Marshall made clear to him that the United States would not underwrite his war. Thereafter, Washington turned down Jiang's urgent requests for additional military aid and provided only a reduced amount of economic aid after the end of 1946. Nor was indirect foreign assistance a major factor in determining the outcome of the conflict. If military aid had been a factor, the Nationalists surely should have won, for the United States provided them far more assistance, military and otherwise, during and after World War II than the Soviet Union provided the Chinese Communists. The United States had provided Nationalist China with a massive amount of military and economic aid since 1941, amounting to more than $2 billion.

The postwar policy of the Soviet Union toward Nationalist China was ambivalent, as was its attitude toward the Chinese Communists. It is noteworthy that at the end of World War II, Stalin signed a treaty with the Nationalist government of China and publicly recognized Jiang's rule of China. The Soviet Red Army did little to deter the takeover of Manchuria by Jiang's Nationalist Army, and it withdrew from Manchuria not long after the date to which the two sides had agreed.

The Soviet Union's looting of Manchuria for "war booty" was of benefit to neither of the combatants in China and was objectionable to both. Moreover, Stalin made no real effort to support or encourage the Chinese Communists in their bid for power in China, except for turning over the cache of Japanese arms in Manchuria. On the contrary, Stalin is known to have stated in 1948, when the victory of the Chinese Communists was all but certain, that from the outset he had counseled the Chinese Communist leaders not to fight the Nationalists because their prospect for victory seemed remote. Indeed, when we take all this into account and take note of how guarded Moscow was in its dealings with the Chinese Communists after their victory, we can speculate that Stalin might have been happier with a weak Nationalist government in China than with a new and vigorous Communist government. Jiang's regime could more readily be exploited than could a strong fraternal Communist regime.

More important as a determinant of the civil war's outcome than outside support (or the lack of it) were domestic factors: the popular support of the peasantry for the Communists, the high morale and effective military strategy of the Communist forces, the corruption of the Nationalist regime, the low morale and ineffective strategy of its army, and the inept political and military leadership of General Jiang Jieshi. Still another factor was the deteriorating situation on the Nationalist home front, where runaway inflation, corruption, and coercive government measures combined to demoralize the Chinese population. The Communists, by contrast, enjoyed much greater popular support, especially from the peasantry (which made up about 85 percent of the population), because of their successful land redistribution programs. The Nationalists had alienated the peasantry for lack of a meaningful agrarian reform, having provided neither a program of land redistribution nor protection for tenant farmers against greedy and overbearing landowners.

The turn of events in China had immediate political repercussions in the United States. Shortly before the civil war ended, the US Senate Foreign Relations Committee heard the testimony of US teachers, businesspeople, journalists, and missionaries who had lived in China for years. They were unanimous in their criticism of Jiang's regime and warned that any additional aid would only fall into the hands of the Communists. The Truman administration understood this, but it nevertheless continued to provide aid. It knew that to cut off aid to its client promised to invite the inevitable political charge that Truman had abandoned a worthy ally, albeit a hopelessly corrupt one, in the struggle against international Communism. The Republicans, of course, who had been sharpening their knives for several years, did precisely what Truman had feared. No sooner had the civil war ended in China than they were blaming the Democratic administration of Truman for "losing China." Republican senator Joseph McCarthy went so far as to blame the "loss of China" on Communists and Communist sympathizers within the State Department. Although McCarthy's charges proved unfounded, the Democrats were nonetheless saddled with the reputation of having lost China to Communism.

The "loss of China," as perceived by the US public, and the intensified Cold War mentality it engendered within the United States, served to drive the Truman administration farther to the right in its foreign policy. Truman became ever more vigilant to check the spread of Communism to other parts of Asia, and when, soon afterward, he was faced with a Vietnamese Communist revolution against French colonialism in Indochina, Communist aggression in Korea, and the prospect of "losing" Korea, it was little wonder that he responded immediately and forcefully.

The Korean War

On June 25, 1950, only nine months after the Communist victory in China, the armed forces of Communist North Korea launched a full-scale attack on South Korea. The United States and its major allies responded swiftly and decisively to halt what they perceived to be the forceful expansion of international Communism and a blatant violation of the United Nations Charter. Korea thus became the first real battleground of the Cold War and the first major threat of an all-out war between the East and West. Even though it remained a limited war and resulted in an inconclusive stalemate, it proved to be a bitter and bloody conflict that lasted over three years, produced over 2 million fatalities, and left Korea devastated and hopelessly divided. The Korean War, a product of the Cold War, had profound effects on its continuation.

The roots of the Korean conflict go back to the last days of World War II, when the United States and the Soviet Union divided the Korean peninsula at the thirty-eighth parallel. The division, which was agreed to by US and Soviet diplomats at Potsdam in July 1945, was meant to be a temporary arrangement for receiving the surrender of Japanese military forces in Korea after the war. Soviet occupation of northern Korea and the US occupation of the southern half were to last only until a unified Korean government could be established—an objective agreed to by both parties. However, before any steps were taken to achieve that objective, Korean Communists, who during the war had been in exile in either the Soviet Union or northern China, established in the north a Soviet-styled government and speedily carried out an extensive land reform program. Meanwhile, in the south, US occupation authorities attempted to bring order to a chaotic situation. Korean nationalists opposed continued military occupation of their country and agitated for immediate independence. Rival nationalist parties, some of which were virulently anti-Communist, contended with each other in a political free-for-all.

In 1948, South Korea's first president, Syngman Rhee, who had spent the war years in exile in the United States, joined the "free world" under US auspices. It would take another forty years, however, before democracy became established. In the meantime, force prevailed. The "April 3 Cheju Incident" is a case in point. In March and April 1948, on the island of Cheju, off the southern coast of Korea, socialist "people's committees" organized demonstrations against the US presence in Korea and against the upcoming elections in the south designed to legitimize a separate national government and, in effect, divide the country. US forces and local police fired on demonstrators, killing several. US authorities then branded Cheju as "the second Moscow" and its people as Communists. A general insurrection that began on April 3 was put down, with a loss of life estimated at 14,000 (official South Korean count), 30,000 (US estimates), and 80,000 according to the islanders. Another 40,000 fled to

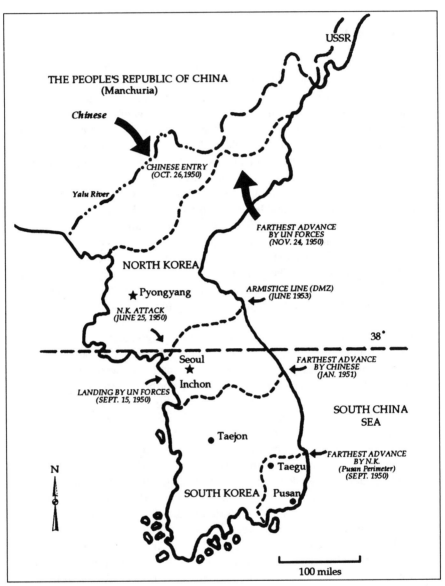

The Korean War (1950–1953)

Japan. Under penalty of the National Security Law of December 1948, it became forbidden to mention the Cheju massacre for the next 45 years. Not until after a democratic government had come to power 45 years later could it be discussed publicly. In 1998, at the fiftieth anniversary of the massacre, President Roh Moo-hyun profusely apologized to the residents of the island.[4]

Political disorder in the south was further exacerbated by economic problems—namely, runaway inflation and the demand for land redistribution. Under these circumstances, unification of Korea proved impossible. US and Soviet diplomats had agreed in late 1945 to set up a provisional Korean government, which for five years would operate under a joint US-Soviet trusteeship. However, the first session of this commission in March 1946 produced a typical Cold War scene, with US and Soviet officials hurling accusations at one another. The Soviets accused the US military command in South Korea of fostering an undemocratic anti-Communist regime in the south, and the US side similarly accused the Soviets of creating an undemocratic Communist regime in the north. The Soviets insisted that no "antidemocratic" (meaning anti-Communist) Korean political party be allowed to participate in the political process, while US representatives insisted on the right of all parties to participate. The Soviets also proposed the immediate withdrawal of both Soviet and US occupation forces from Korea, but the United States, concerned about the Soviet advantage of having a better-organized client state in the north, insisted on a supervised free election to be carried out in both the north and the south prior to troop withdrawal.

Failing to solve the impasse, the United States took the issue of a divided Korea to the United Nations in September 1947. The UN General Assembly passed a nonbinding resolution calling for free elections throughout Korea and a UN commission to oversee these elections. In May 1948, the National Assembly elections were held under UN supervision, but in the south only, since the Communist regime in North Korea refused to permit the UN commission into the north. On the basis of his party's victory in the UN-sanctioned election, Syngman Rhee proclaimed the founding of the Republic of Korea, which purported to be the only legitimate government of all of Korea. Less than a month later, in September 1948, the Communist regime in the north, led by Kim Il Sung, formally proclaimed the founding of the Democratic People's Republic of Korea, and it too claimed to be the rightful government of all of Korea. With the peninsula now divided between two rival regimes, the hope of peaceful unification was dashed. Despite this and despite the steadily mounting tensions between the two opposing regimes, both the Soviet Union and the United States began withdrawing their forces from the peninsula, and by mid-1949 the withdrawal was completed. (There remained in North Korea a 3,500-troop Soviet military mission and in South Korea a 500-troop US military advisory group.)

Tensions were mounting not only in Korea but elsewhere in the global Cold War struggle. By the end of the 1940s, the US policy of containment of the Soviet Union began to show signs of cracks, especially when, in August 1949, the US public was hit with twin shocks. First, the Soviet Union successfully tested an atomic bomb, thus breaking the US monopoly in four short years. Second, only two months later, the civil war in China came to an end with a Communist victory, and with it, the world's most populous nation had fallen to what the West perceived to be militant, expansionist Communism. Predictably, the people of the United States believed that the Communist triumph in China somehow had been engineered by Moscow.

As noted previously, the loss of China to Communism had immediate political repercussions in the United States. The Republican charge, that Truman had lost China to the Communists just as Roosevelt had lost Eastern Europe to the Soviets, served to create a perception of dominoes falling one after another. The relentless Republican criticism of the Democrats for being "soft on Communism" caused the Truman administration (and especially Secretary of State Dean Acheson, a favorite target of McCarthy) to strengthen even more its resolve to stand up to the Communists.

* * *

In April 1950, Truman received and accepted a set of recommendations from his National Security Council (NSC), the president's own advisory committee. These recommendations, known as NSC-68, were based on the premise that there could be no meaningful negotiations with the Kremlin until it "changed its policies drastically." According to NSC-68, Stalin understood only force. It recommended, therefore, that the United States develop the hydrogen bomb to offset the Soviet Union's atomic bomb, and that it rapidly increase US conventional forces. The cost of such a program would have to be borne by a large increase in taxes. The US people would have to be mobilized; the emphasis must be on "consensus," "sacrifice," and "unity." NSC-68 also expressed the hope of making "the Russian people our allies in this enterprise" of ridding the world of "Communist tyranny." This hope, however, was based on the questionable assumptions that people never willingly accept Communism, that it is always forced on them, and that they will always welcome US forces as liberators. This set of assumptions later produced fatal consequences for US foreign policy in Cuba and in Vietnam, where the local populations refused to rally to the US cause.

The National Security Council, created in 1947, duplicates much of the work of the State Department. During the Kennedy administration (1961–1963) a tendency emerged where presidents began to consult the NSC rather than the professionals in the State Department. The discussion in 1950 on the nature of the Soviet threat proved to be one of the first instances where the professionals in the State Department played second fiddle to the NSC. The State Department's experts on the Soviet Union, Charles Bohlen and George Kennan, both of whom later served as ambassadors to Moscow, challenged the argument that Stalin had a master plan of conquest. They saw the Soviet threat largely as a potential political problem in Western Europe. But they were overruled by Dean Acheson, who sided with the hard-liners on the National Security Council who argued that the United States must maintain order throughout the world.

*   *   *

The first test of the mobilization of the US people came two months after the president approved NSC-68, when the Korean War broke out. At this point, the remilitarization of the United States began in earnest. It should be noted, however, that earlier in the year top US military leaders (including the Joint Chiefs of Staff and Generals Dwight Eisenhower and Douglas MacArthur) had concluded that Korea was not of sufficient importance to US national interests to be included within its defensive perimeter. This assessment was based mainly on the higher priority given to defending Europe and Japan and on the insufficiency of US ground forces at the time. Secretary of State Acheson stated publicly in January 1950 (as MacArthur had done earlier) that the US defense perimeter stretched from Alaska through Japan to the Philippines, and that Korea was outside that perimeter. In making this statement Acheson can hardly be faulted for inviting the North Korean attack on the south, as his critics would later charge, because he was merely stating what was already quite clearly US policy. North Korea and the Soviet Union were well aware of US strategic priorities and troop limitations. US military doctrine at the time emphasized preparation for "total war" (and not so-called brushfire wars) and focused primarily on resisting the Soviet threat in Europe, not in Asia.

When the invasion came on June 25, 1950, Washington acted as if it had been caught off guard and denounced it as an unwarranted surprise attack. In fact, both MacArthur's military intelligence and that of Syngman Rhee had monitored North Korean troop movements and preparations and had abundant evidence of the impending attack. It appears that both Rhee and MacArthur withheld this information to maximize the psychological impact of what they called a "surprise attack."[5]

It is not altogether clear what roles the Soviet Union and Communist China played in the decision of North Korea to attack the south, but neither Soviet nor Chinese troops were involved initially. Nor were they deployed near Korea prior to the war. North Korea, however, was a Communist state that received substantial Soviet political, economic, and military support and was considered in the West to be under Soviet control. The United States and its allies concluded, therefore, that this was another case of Soviet aggression, and they were quick to lay the blame at Joseph Stalin's feet. Testimony by men who were close to Stalin, which came to light only after the collapse of the Soviet Union, makes clear that Kim Il Sung did visit with Stalin in Moscow in March 1949 and again in March 1950 and in the latter meeting sought Stalin's support for an invasion of South Korea aimed at unifying Korea by force. But the Soviet dictator's response is less clear. By some accounts Stalin acknowledged Kim's plans for war and wished him success but did not offer specific instructions, much less orders for carrying out such plans. Stalin neither blocked Kim's proposed war nor gave it enthusiastic support. Stalin did advise Kim to consult first with Mao Zedong, which Kim did in Beijing in May 1950. It seems that he was there merely to inform the Chinese leader of his plans and that Mao, although skeptical, raised no objections and speculated that the United States was not likely to intervene in such a distant and small country.[6] Thus, on the evidence available, it is reasonable to conclude that the decision for war—specifically the strategy and timing of the attack—was made by Kim himself in Pyongyang, the North Korean capital, after he had secured at least general acquiescence from both Stalin and Mao. Soviet sources show that, throughout 1949, Stalin opposed a North Korean attack on the south, repeatedly telling Kim that "the 38th parallel must remain peaceful." Stalin feared that a war would give the United States a pretext for getting involved in Korean affairs. Kim, however, continued to lobby for a green light from Stalin. It was not until April 1950 that Stalin accepted Kim's view that the war could be contained in the Korean peninsula and would not draw foreign intervention.[7] Kim, whose nationalist convictions were as strong as his Communist ones, was convinced that his army was strong enough to gain a swift victory by waging a full-scale offensive. He also assumed that the United States lacked either the will or the means to come to the rescue of South Korea, but this would prove to be a serious miscalculation.

Far from ignoring or standing by idly while its former client was being overrun by a superior Communist force, the US government rapidly swung into action. First, Truman immediately ordered US naval and air support from bases in nearby Japan to bolster the retreating South Korean army, and, second, he immediately took the issue of North Korean aggression to an emergency session of the UN Security Council. In the absence of the Soviet delegate, who was boycotting the United Nations in protest against its refusal to seat the People's Republic of China in the world body, the Security Council passed a resolution on June 25 condemning the invasion by North Korea and calling for the withdrawal of its forces from South Korea. Two days later the Security Council passed a second resolution calling for UN member nations to contribute forces, for what later became known as a UN "police action," to repel the aggression. It seems unlikely that the Soviet delegate to the United Nations would not have been at his seat in the Security Council—or even in New York—if Moscow had known in advance of, much less planned, the North Korean attack on the south.

By virtue of the second resolution, US military involvement in Korea was authorized by the United Nations. Actually, Truman had already, the previous day, ordered US ground troops (in addition to air and naval support) into action in Korea. The Soviet Union made use of this point to argue that US military action in Korea was an act of aggression. Moreover, Moscow contended that the war was started by South Korea and that the deployment of UN forces

United Nations Security Council session, New York, June 27, 1950, at which the resolution condemning North Korean aggression was approved in the absence of the
Soviet representative, who was then boycotting the UN. *(National Archives)*

in Korea was in violation of the UN Charter because neither the Soviet Union
nor the People's Republic of China had been present at the Security Council
session to cast a vote. The Soviets protested that the UN operation in Korea
was actually a mask for US aggression.

The authors of NSC-68 welcomed the outbreak of war as an opportunity
for the United States to roll back Communism on the Korean peninsula.[8] Although some sixteen nations ultimately contributed to the UN forces in Korea,
the bulk of UN troops, weapons, and matériel were from the United States; UN
operations in Korea were largely financed by the US government; the UN
forces were placed under the command of US Army general Douglas
MacArthur; and the military and diplomatic planning for the war was done
mainly in Washington.

The swift and resolute US response to halt Communist aggression in
Korea belied the Acheson statement of January 1950 that Korea was outside
the US defensive perimeter. It reflected, instead, the thinking of NSC-68. The
Truman administration, which had been ready to write off Korea earlier in the
year, decided that it must meet the Communist challenge to its containment
policy. On second look, Washington determined that South Korea's defense

During the Korean War, a GI reads the *Stars and Stripes* of August 9, 1950. In the headline, MacArthur claims the war to have been won, less than three months before the Chinese came in. *(National Archives)*

was vital to the defense of US interests in Asia, especially since the prospect of a Soviet-controlled Korea would threaten the security of Japan, which had suddenly become the major US ally in Asia. Moreover, Truman saw the defense of Korea as important to the maintenance of US credibility and defense commitments elsewhere in the world, and thus to the maintenance of the NATO alliance. Indeed, he likened the situation in Korea in June 1950 to the

Nazi aggression in the late 1930s and invoked the lesson of Munich: Appeasement of an aggressor does not bring peace but only more serious aggression. Korea represented a test of US will; the United States must not fail to stand up to that test.

The South Korean army, which lacked tanks, artillery, and aircraft, was no match for the heavily armed North Korean forces, and it therefore took a beating in the early weeks of the war. The first units of US ground troops coming to its rescue were also undermanned and ill-equipped, but still they succeeded in holding the Pusan perimeter in the southeastern corner of Korea. Then, in September 1950, MacArthur engineered a dramatic reversal of the war with his successful landing of a large US/UN force at Inchon several hundred miles behind the Communist lines. Taken by surprise by this daring move, the North Korean forces then beat a hasty retreat back up the peninsula. By early October the North Koreans were driven across the thirty-eighth parallel; the US/UN forces had gained their objective in spectacular fashion.

At this juncture the US government had a critical decision to make: whether or not to pursue the retreating enemy across the thirty-eighth parallel. General MacArthur, riding the wings of victory, was raring to go, and so, of course, was Syngman Rhee, who hoped to eliminate the Communist regime in the north and bring the whole of Korea under his government. But the use of military force to achieve the unification of Korea had not been part of the UN resolution, which had called only for repelling the North Korean invasion. Moreover, a push into North Korea ran the risk of intervention by Communist China and possibly the Soviet Union as well in an expanded conflict. At the United Nations, Truman's ambassador rejected proposals by the Soviet Union and India aimed at achieving an overall peace in Asia, which would include an armistice in Korea and the seating of the People's Republic of China in the United Nations. Instead, Truman succeeded in getting a nonbinding resolution passed in the UN General Assembly that called for nationwide elections in Korea after "all appropriate steps [are] taken to ensure conditions of stability throughout Korea."

In the meantime, Truman authorized the entry of the South Korean army into the north and then granted the same authority to MacArthur's UN forces—on the condition that they would halt their advance northward if either Chinese or Soviet forces entered the war. Nonetheless, by entering North Korea the US war objective was now significantly altered; the goal was no longer limited to repelling an attack but was extended to eliminating the Communist regime in the north and militarily unifying the whole of Korea. Despite the caution manifested in Washington, General MacArthur, sensing the imminent collapse of the North Korean army, pressed on, rapidly advancing his forces toward the Yalu River, the boundary between Korea and China. In doing so he ignored the repeated warnings from skeptics in Washington and those from Beijing, which threatened intervention by Chinese forces if its territory were threatened. To the Beijing leadership, with its memory of Western imperialism in China over the past century, the prospect of a hostile "imperialist" military presence across the border of Manchuria, its most industrialized region, was intolerable.

MacArthur's aggressive pursuit of the enemy raised more than a few eyebrows among Truman's advisors. In mid-October, Truman and his field commander met on Wake Island in the Pacific, where the president urged caution against provoking Chinese or Soviet entry into the war. MacArthur, however, confidently predicted an imminent victory and assured Truman that if the Chinese dared to intervene, they could get no more than 50,000 troops across the Yalu and the result would be "the greatest slaughter."[9] Back in Korea, MacArthur launched a major offensive, which, he predicted, would have the US soldiers back home in time for Christmas.

With US forces rapidly advancing toward the Chinese border, the Chinese did exactly as they had warned they would: They sent their armed forces into battle in Korea. Beijing insisted that these troops were "volunteers," thereby disclaiming official involvement in the war in order to ward off a possible retaliatory attack by UN forces on China itself. After an initial surprise attack on October 25, the Chinese made a strategic retreat for about a month, only to come back in much greater numbers. MacArthur's intelligence reports badly underestimated the number of Chinese troops involved and China's capacity to increase the size of its forces. Suddenly, on November 26, a vast Chinese army of 300,000-plus soldiers opened a massive counteroffensive. Overwhelmed by this superior force, MacArthur's UN forces swiftly retreated over 250 miles to a line 50 miles south of the thirty-eighth parallel.

The Chinese intervention with a force much larger than MacArthur thought possible made it, in his words, "an entirely new war," and it also provoked a sharp dispute with Truman over political and military policy. MacArthur, frustrated by having an imminent victory denied him and by the limitations placed on him by his superiors in Washington, favored widening the war, including using Chinese Nationalist forces from Taiwan, bombing Chinese Communist bases in Manchuria, and blockading the coast of China. The president, his military advisors, and his European allies feared that such steps might touch off World War III—possibly a nuclear war with the Soviet Union—or that the overcommitment of US forces in an expanded Korean War would leave Europe defenseless against a possible Soviet attack. MacArthur publicly criticized the policy of limited warfare that he was ordered to follow.

In March 1951, MacArthur clearly exceeded his authority by issuing a public statement threatening China with nuclear destruction if it refused to heed his demand for an immediate disengagement from Korea. It was this unauthorized ultimatum that caused Truman to dismiss the general from his command. Truman, who later stated that this was the most difficult decision he had ever made, felt it necessary to reassert presidential authority over the military and make it clear to both enemies and allies that the United States spoke with a single voice. Moreover, there was good reason to fear that continued insubordination by MacArthur, in his quest for total victory, might indeed instigate an all-out war between East and West. For his part, MacArthur minimized such prospects and argued that the West was missing an opportunity to eliminate Communism not only from Korea but from China as well.

It has been frequently alleged that it was General MacArthur's advocacy of use of the atomic bomb against the Chinese that resulted in his dismissal. Although there may be some truth to the allegation, it must be pointed out that on at least three separate occasions US presidents considered the use of the bomb in the Korean War. Truman threatened use of the bomb in a press conference in November 1950, just after Chinese soldiers entered the war in large numbers, and he suggested that the decision rested with the field commander in Korea. The latter point caused so much consternation among US allies and Truman's own advisors that he quickly modified his statement, saying that the final decision on the use of the bomb rested, after all, with the president. Several months later, when a new UN offensive was stymied by Chinese forces near the thirty-eighth parallel, Truman conferred with his advisors on the possibility of using the bomb. And near the end of the war, in June 1953, when armistice talks were deadlocked, the new US president, Dwight Eisenhower, seriously considered using the atomic bomb to break the stalemate.

The dismissal of MacArthur on April 11, 1951, brought no significant change in the war. His replacement, General Matthew Ridgway, held against a new Chinese offensive in late April, and several weeks later he was able to force the Chinese to retreat to near the thirty-eighth parallel. Soon thereafter, the war stalemated, with the battle line remaining in that general vicinity. The war dragged on for two more years without a major new offensive by either side. Still, the toll of casualties mounted as patrol actions on the ground continued. All the while, the United States conducted devastating bombing attacks on North Korea, destroying virtually every city as well as hydroelectric plants and irrigation dams. The toll on the civilian population of Korea of these bombing attacks was immeasurably large.

The military deadlock in the spring of 1951 brought about the beginning of peace talks. In June of that year, Moscow and Washington agreed to begin negotiations for a cease-fire, and both Beijing and Pyongyang concurred. Talks began in July and continued on-again, off-again for the next two years at Panmunjom, a town situated along the battle line. Two main questions divided the negotiators: the location of the cease-fire line and the exchange of prisoners. The Communist side insisted on returning to the thirty-eighth parallel but finally agreed to the existing battle line, which gave South Korea a slight territorial advantage. On the second issue, the Communists insisted on a complete exchange of all prisoners, but the US negotiators called for allowing the prisoners to decide for themselves whether they wished to be returned to

General MacArthur, September 15, 1950, observing the shelling of Inchon, from the USS *Mt. McKinley. (National Archives)*

North Korean prisoners, September 11, 1950, in the town of Yongsan. *(National Archives)*

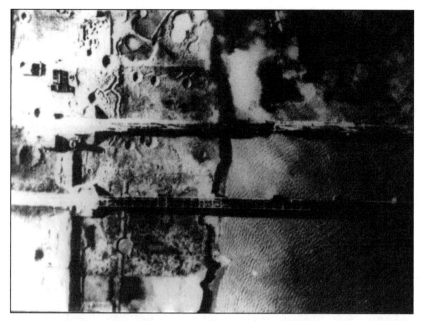

US bombing of bridges at Sinuiyu, across the Yalu River into Manchuria, November 15, 1950. *(National Archives)*

US Army trucks at the thirty-eighth parallel, crossing into North Korea, October 1950, heading toward a showdown with the People's Liberation Army of Communist China. *(National Archives)*

their homelands. The truce talks remained deadlocked on this issue, which carried great propaganda value for the United States. Indeed, many North Korean captives—perhaps as many as 40,000—did not wish to be repatriated, and the United States wanted to exploit this matter as much as the Communists wanted to prevent this mass defection and thereby deny the United States a major propaganda victory.

After the emergence in 1953 of new leadership in Moscow with the death of Stalin and in Washington with the inauguration of Eisenhower, the two sides finally exhibited the flexibility necessary to break the impasse and to end the costly stalemated war. On June 8, 1953, the negotiators at Panmunjom signed an agreement that made repatriation of prisoners voluntary, but allowed each side the opportunity (under the supervision of a UN commission) to attempt to persuade their defectors to return home. However, the truce settlement was delayed because of a drastic attempt by South Korean president Syngman Rhee to sabotage it. Rhee, who desired to continue the fight to unify the country under his regime, released some 25,000 North Korean prisoners, who allegedly rejected repatriation to the north. The Chinese responded with a new offensive against South Korean units. Finally, after US negotiators offered assurances to pacify and restrain Rhee, the two sides signed a truce on July 23, 1953. The fighting ended with the final battle line as the truce line, which was widened to become a two-and-a-half-mile-wide demilitarized zone (DMZ). The truce, however, did not mean an official end of the war; it merely meant a halt in the fighting by the exhausted adversaries. Officially, a state of war continued and the truce line between North and South Korea remained the most militarized border anywhere in the world. For over fifty years it remained a potential flash point in the Cold War.

Even though the Korean War ended roughly along the same line where it began, its costs and its consequences were enormous. The United States lost over 35,000 men in combat (and more than 55,000 in all); South Korea, an estimated 300,000; North Korea, 52,000; and China, 900,000 (Washington estimates). The historian Bruce Cumings estimated that the total number of fatalities was as high as 2 million.[10] While the outcome represented something short of victory for either side, both could claim important achievements. The United States succeeded, with the help of its allies, in standing firm against Communist aggression. This brought greater security to Japan and it contributed to the strengthening of NATO as well. The Chinese emerged from the Korean conflict with greatly enhanced prestige, especially insofar as its now battle-hardened army had stood up to technically superior Western armies in a manner that no Chinese army ever had.

For the Koreans in both the north and the south, the war was disastrous. The war had been fought with great ferocity by Korean partisans, who did not hesitate to inflict vicious punishment on their enemies—not only enemy soldiers but civilians thought to be informers or collaborators. Consequently, many atrocities were committed by both sides, and caustic bitterness would persist for years to come. In addition to the great death and destruction suffered by the Koreans, the division of their country was made permanent, and there would be no reduction of tensions and animosity between the Communist regime in the north and the anti-Communist regime in the south. The war produced millions of refugees, and when the fighting ended, several hundred thousand Korean families remained separated. The Cold War thus remained deeply entrenched in Korea.

The United States and the Cold War in Asia

The Communist victory in China represented a major setback for US foreign policy. The threat to US power in East Asia was made all the greater when the new Communist government of China promptly cemented its relations with the Soviet Union with a thirty-year military alliance aimed at the United States, and vehemently denounced US "imperialism." The United States was then confronted by what seemed to be a global Communist movement that had suddenly doubled in size and now included the world's most populous nation. The turn of events in China meant that the US immediate postwar Asian policy, which had envisioned the emergence of a strong, united, democratic China to serve as the main pillar of stability in Asia, was completely shattered. Now the US government fashioned a new Asian policy that called for the containment of Communism and featured Japan, former enemy of the United States, in the role of its strategic partner and base of operations.

In 1948, when it became apparent that the Chinese Communists would defeat the Nationalists in the civil war raging in China, the US occupation policy in Japan took a strong turn to the right. The new policy, known as the "reverse course," called for rebuilding the former enemy, Japan, so that it would play the role of Washington's major ally in Asia, acting as a bulwark against the spread of Communism. Beginning in 1948, Washington, which heretofore had made no effort to assist Japan economically, now began pumping economic aid into Japan and assisting its economic recovery in other ways. The reverse course was evidenced by a relaxation of the restrictions against the *zaibatsu*, a new ban on general labor strikes, and the purge of leftist leaders. With the outbreak of war in Korea in 1950, the security of Japan became an urgent concern to the United States. In order to maintain domestic security within Japan, MacArthur authorized the formation of a 75,000-person Japanese National Police Reserve, thus reversing his earlier policy for an unarmed Japan. This was the beginning of the rearmament of Japan, and it was bitterly disappointing to many Japanese who were sincere in their conversion to pacifism.

In the midst of the intensified Cold War, the United States not only groomed Japan to become its ally, but also took the lead in framing a peace treaty with Japan in 1951 that would secure the new relationship. The treaty, which formally ended the Allied Occupation and restored full sovereignty to Japan, was crafted by the US diplomat John Foster Dulles in consultation with major US allies. The Communist bloc nations, which were not consulted, objected to the final terms of the treaty and they chose not to sign it. Tied to the treaty, which went into effect in May 1952, was a US-Japan Mutual Security Pact, which provided that the United States would guarantee Japan's security. It also allowed US military bases to remain in Japan to provide not only for Japan's security but also for the defense of US interests in Asia or, more specifically, for the containment of Communism. Moreover, the United States retained control of the Japanese island of Okinawa, on which it had built huge military installations. The reborn nation of Japan thus became a child of the Cold War, tied militarily and politically as well as economically to the apron strings of the United States.

Within Japan the Cold War was mirrored by political polarization between the right and the left. The right (the conservative political parties, which governed Japan for the next four decades) accepted the Mutual Security Pact and favored the maintenance of strong political and military ties with the United States. It recognized the threat that the war in nearby Korea represented and the advantages provided by the security arrangement with the United States. Moreover, it was fully aware of Japan's economic dependence on the United States and did not wish to jeopardize these vital ties. The left (labor unions and many—probably most—of Japan's intellectuals and university students) was bitterly opposed to the Mutual Security Pact, to US military forces remaining on Japanese soil, and to the rearmament of Japan. It favored instead unarmed neutrality rather than Japan becoming a party to the Cold War. But since the conservative party remained in power, Japan continued to be a close partner of the United States in the international arena, and more than 40,000 US forces remained on US military bases in Japan.

The Korean War had a great and lasting impact on the global Cold War. Beyond the fact that the two sides fought to a standstill in Korea, the war occasioned a large general military buildup by both East and West, and this meant the militarization of the Cold War. "Defense" budgets of both the United States and the Soviet Union skyrocketed during the Korean War to record peacetime levels, and they continued to grow thereafter. The military budget of the People's Republic of China also grew commensurately, and that nation remained on a war footing in the years that followed.

A less tangible, but no less important, consequence of the Korean War was the great intensification of hostility between the United States and the People's Republic of China. The possibility for accommodation between them, which still existed before they crossed swords in Korea, vanished. Both continued to accuse each other of aggression, and both increased their vigil against each other. For the PRC, the increased US military presence in Asia meant a rising threat of US "imperialism," and for decades to come this perceived threat remained the central point of Chinese diplomacy and security policy. For the United States, the continuing threat of "Chinese Communist aggression" required a greatly strengthened commitment to the containment of Communist China, and this became the central feature of US Asia policy for the next twenty-five years. This was reflected in the policy of making Japan the major US ally and base of operations in Asia, a decision to guarantee the security of South Korea and maintain US forces there, a commitment to defend the Nationalist Chinese government on the island of Taiwan against an attack from the mainland, and a growing US involvement in Vietnam in support of the French in their efforts to defeat a Communist-led revolutionary movement. The United States thus locked itself into a Cold War position in Asia in its endeavor to stem the spread of Communism. In their turn, the Communists in Asia—China, North Korea, Vietnam, and others—strengthened their own resolve to resist US intervention and "imperialism." The Cold War battle lines in Asia were drawn by the early 1950s, and for the next two decades, the two sides maintained their respective positions in mutual hostility.

Recommended Readings

Japan

Dower, John W. *Empire and Aftermath: Yoshida Shigeru and the Japanese Experience, 1878–1954.* Cambridge, Mass.: Harvard University Press, 1979.
An in-depth analysis of the politics of the US occupation authorities and the government of occupied Japan.
Kawai, Kazuo. *Japan's American Interlude.* Chicago: University of Chicago Press, 1960.
A firsthand account of the occupation by a Japanese American scholar who edited an English-language newspaper in Japan during the period.
Minear, Richard. *Victor's Justice: The Tokyo War Crimes Trials.* Princeton: Princeton University Press, 1971.
Argues that the war crimes trials were unjust.
Perry, John C. *Beneath the Eagle's Wings: Americans in Occupied Japan.* New York: Dodd, Mead, 1980.
Reischauer, Edwin O. *Japan: The Story of a Nation.* 4th ed. New York: Knopf, 1988.

China

Bianco, Lucien. *The Origins of the Chinese Revolution, 1915–1949.* Stanford: Stanford University Press, 1971.
Analysis of the Communist revolution stressing the strengths of the Communists and the failures of the Nationalists.
Fairbank, John K. *The United States and China.* 4th ed. Cambridge, Mass.: Harvard University Press, 1979.

Pepper, Suzanne. *Civil War in China: The Political Struggle, 1945–1949.* Berkeley: University of California Press, 1979.

Purifoy, Lewis M. *Harry Truman's China Policy: McCarthyism and the Diplomacy of Hysteria, 1947–1951.* New York: New Viewpoints, 1976.
Strongly critical of the US policy of supporting Jiang Jieshi.

Tsou, Tang. *America's Failure in China, 1941–1950.* Chicago: University of Chicago Press, 1963.
Argues that the United States had neither the means nor the will to achieve its goals in China.

Tuchman, Barbara. *Stilwell and the American Experience in China, 1911–1945.* New York: Macmillan, 1970.
A criticism of Jiang Jieshi and of US support for him.

Korea

Cumings, Bruce. *The Origins of the Korean War: Liberation and the Emergence of Separate Regimes, 1945–1947.* Princeton: Princeton University Press, 1981.

———, ed. *Child of Conflict: The Korean American Relationship, 1943–1953.* Seattle: University of Washington Press, 1983.
Essays by revisionist historians that refute orthodox Western interpretations of the origins of the war.

———. *The Origins of the Korean War: II, The Roaring of the Cataract, 1947–1950.* Princeton: Princeton University Press, 1990.
The best scholarly analysis of the background and the early stages of the war.

Rees, David. *Korea: The Limited War.* Baltimore: Penguin, 1964.
Its focus is on the uniqueness of this conflict as the first US limited war.

Spanier, John W. *The Truman-MacArthur Controversy and the Korean War.* New York: Norton, 1965.

Stone, I. F. *The Hidden History of the Korean War.* New York: Monthly Review Press, 1952.
A provocative early revisionist version of the Korean War.

Whiting, Alan S. *China Crosses the Yalu: The Decision to Enter the Korean War.* New York: Macmillan, 1960.

Notes

1. One finds in English-language materials on China two different spellings of Chinese names depending on when they were published. In the People's Republic of China, the Wade-Giles system of romanization of Chinese names and words was replaced by the pinyin system and subsequently adopted, in 1979, by US publishers. After 1979, Chiang Kai-shek's name was rendered as Jiang Jieshi, and that of Mao Tse-tung as Mao Zedong; Peking become Beijing, and so on. This text uses the pinyin system, but in most instances the old spelling of Chinese names will also be provided in parentheses. Also note that personal names for Chinese, Japanese, Vietnamese, and Koreans are given in the manner native to their countries, that is, the surname or family name precedes the given name.

2. Edwin O. Reischauer, *Japan: The Story of a Nation,* 3rd ed. (New York: Knopf, 1981), p. 221.

3. MacArthur's testimony to the joint committee of the US Senate on the military situation in the Far East in April 1951; cited in Rinjiro Sodei, "Eulogy to My Dear General," in L. H. Redford, ed., *The Occupation of Japan: Impact of Legal Reform* (Norfolk, Va.: The MacArthur Memorial, 1977), p. 82.

4. Chalmers Johnson, *Blowback: The Costs and Consequences of Empire* (New York: Henry Holt, 2000), pp. 98–100. US authorities, too, participated in the cover-up.

5. The first to make this case was I. F. Stone, *The Hidden History of the Korean War* (New York: Monthly Review Press, 1952), pp. 1–14. Also see Bruce Cumings, "Introduction: The Course of Korean-American Relations, 1943–1953," in Bruce Cumings, ed., *Child of Conflict: The Korean American Relationship, 1943–1953* (Seattle: University of Washington Press, 1983), pp. 41–42.

6. See Sergei N. Goncharov, John W. Lewis, and Xue Litai, *Uncertain Partners: Stalin, Mao, and the Korean War* (Stanford: Stanford University Press, 1993), pp. 136–146.

7. See Natal'ia Bazhanova, "Samaia zagadochnaia voina XX stoletniia," *Novoe vremia* no. 6 (February 1996), pp. 29–31.

8. Cumings, "Introduction: The Course of Korean-American Relations, 1943–1953," pp. 29–38.

9. Quoted in Richard Rovere and Arthur Schlesinger Jr., *The General and the President* (New York: Farrar, Straus, 1951), pp. 253–262.

10. Bruce Cumings, *The Origins of the Korean War, II, The Roaring of the Cataract, 1947–1950* (Princeton: Princeton University Press, 1990).

4 Confrontation and Coexistence

For centuries the nations of Europe had waged war against each other. France and Britain had been enemies in past centuries, and in modern times the strife between France and Germany has been even bloodier. Within the span of seventy-five years, they fought in three wars. Twice in the first half of the twentieth century, European nations divided into warring camps and fought each other with ever more destructive consequences. During and immediately after World War II, leading political representatives of war-ravaged Europe spoke fervently of the necessity of burying the violent past and embarking on a search for peace and unity among Europeans.

The onset of the Cold War and the closing of the Iron Curtain by Stalin over Eastern Europe meant that Western designs for European unity would be limited to Western Europe. Indeed, the East-West division of Europe and the perceived threat posed by the Soviet Union to the security of West European nations served to reinforce the need for greater unity among them. To counter the Soviet Union's hegemony in Eastern Europe, the United States and its allies began to take steps in the late 1940s to secure the integration of Western Europe. In its turn, Moscow set out to create its own unified empire in Eastern Europe. The result was the rigid political division of the continent.

West European Economic Integration

After 1945, the focal point in the East-West power struggle was Germany, a nation divided into four occupation zones. Disagreements over reparations to be extracted from Germany and other issues led to a closing off of the Russian zone in East Germany from the US, British, and French zones in West Germany. By early 1947, less than two years after the conclusion of the war, it became clear that the chances for a settlement of the German question had vanished in the Cold War climate of acrimony, suspicion, and fear. The United

States began to consolidate its position in Western Europe, a position centered on a North Atlantic community of nations with common economic and political systems and security interests. In essence, it meant the integration of parliamentary, capitalist nations of Western Europe, such as Great Britain, France, Italy, Belgium, the Netherlands, Luxembourg, Denmark, and Norway (but excluding the dictatorial states of Spain and Portugal), into a defensive alliance. Within a decade, West Germany, by virtue of its location, size, and economic potential, also joined this community and it was destined to play a major role in it. Thus, in the late 1940s, West Germany, like Japan in East Asia, became the first line of defense for the United States against Soviet expansion.

The creation of a separate West German state and its economic recovery became matters of high priority for US government officials. The United States, with the concurrence of Britain and France, took the lead in creating a parliamentary government in West Germany, officially known as the Federal Republic of Germany. From the very moment of its formation in May 1949, the West German government insisted that it spoke for all of Germany, including what at the time was still the Soviet zone of occupation. West Germany's choice of a capital, the small provincial city of Bonn, signified its provisional and temporary status. The traditional German capital, Berlin (which was divided into East and West German sectors), was within East German territory.

In rapid order, the United States integrated West Germany into a system of international trade, supplied it with generous amounts of economic aid (through the Marshall Plan), introduced a new currency, and eventually brought West Germany into the US-led military alliance, NATO. Under such circumstances, West German democracy flourished, as did its economy. Indeed, West Germany was the first of the world's war-torn industrial nations to attain an economic recovery, and by the late 1950s its postwar growth was considered an economic miracle, or *Wirtschaftswunder.*

When the government in Bonn introduced the new German mark into West Berlin, it underscored the fact that the new West German state had an outpost 110 miles inside the Soviet zone. When, during the war, the Soviets had agreed to the Allied occupation of Berlin, they did not expect a permanent Western outpost within their zone. In June 1948, Stalin attempted to force the West to abandon Berlin by closing the overland routes into West Berlin. Unable to reopen the roads by military means and unwilling to abandon West Berlin, the Allies responded with the Berlin Airlift, an operation involving daily flights of US, British, and French transport planes over East Germany delivering food and other necessities to West Berlin. For political, psychological, and practical reasons, the West was in no mood to yield. West Berlin's value to the West was that it was a most important center of intelligence operations as well as a symbol of the steadily improving West European standard of living. It stood out in sharp economic contrast to that of East Germany, by which it was surrounded. When Stalin finally relented by lifting the overland blockade in May 1949, it was a tacit recognition that West Berlin would remain part of West Germany.

Once West Germany came into existence in 1949, its chancellor, Konrad Adenauer, doggedly pursued a policy of integrating it into the community of West European nations. He insisted that the postwar West German state develop democratic, liberal institutions under the aegis of the West. In fact, there is ample evidence to suggest that Adenauer, who came from the westernmost part of Germany—the Rhineland—and whose credentials as an opponent of the Nazi regime were impeccable, did not trust the German people. He feared that, left alone, they would succumb once more to the lure of political, economic, and, in particular, military power. Germans, he felt, needed to be under the lengthy tutelage of the Western democracies. Such an arrangement suited him and many of his compatriots just fine. In fact, in March 1952, when Stalin sought talks with the West about the possibility of establishing a neutral, unified Germany, it was Adenauer who lobbied strenuously—and successfully—with his Western allies to reject Stalin's diplomatic note without even bothering to discuss it.[1] For Adenauer, the inclusion in the company of Western nations was more important than German unification. The unification of Germany had to wait, and it had to be accomplished on Western, not Stalin's, terms.

What endeared the Roman Catholic Adenauer to the West was his conservatism and staunch opposition to Communism. The West German voters, not inclined to another round of social experimentation, gave their votes to Adenauer's conservative Christian Democratic Union. *Der Alte* ("the old man") Adenauer, already seventy-three years old at the time of his first election as chancellor, held that post until 1963 and put West Germany firmly onto its postwar path.

During Adenauer's tenure, West Germany experienced rapid economic recovery, established viable democratic institutions, and tried to come to grips with its recent past. It acknowledged Germany's responsibility for World War II and the Jewish Holocaust and paid large sums in reparations to Jewish victims. It took steps to purge the nation of its Nazi past; the Nazi Party and its symbols were outlawed, and students were taught the causes and consequences of the rise of Nazism.

When dealing with the West, Adenauer always said the right things, but he and many Germans had a more difficult time acknowledging the crimes the German armies committed in the East. Not only did Adenauer insist that Poland and the Soviet Union return German lands they had seized at the end of the war, but his government refused to pay reparations to the millions of Poles, Russians, and others in Eastern Europe who had been forced to work in Nazi slave labor camps or had family members murdered. Under Adenauer, there was no diplomatic or economic contact with Eastern Europe, except with the Soviet Union. Stalin had created the Iron Curtain, but politicians such as

Adenauer also played a role in maintaining the partition of Europe. (For details, see Chapter 18.)

West European economic integration had its beginnings in the Marshall Plan, the US economic aid program announced in June 1947, which was intended to rescue Europe from the economic devastation of the war. However, insofar as the Marshall Plan was rejected by Moscow, which spoke for most of Eastern Europe, the aid and the integrative impact of the program were limited to Western Europe.

In short order, the countries of Western Europe took bold steps toward greater economic integration. In April 1951, six nations—France, West Germany, Italy, and the Benelux countries (Belgium, the Netherlands, and Luxembourg)—signed a treaty establishing the European Coal and Steel Community. This program, designed primarily by the French economist Jean Monnet and French foreign minister Robert Schuman (both of whom have been called the "father of Europe"), called for the pooling of the coal and steel resources of the member nations. It created a High Authority that, on the basis of majority vote, was empowered to make decisions regulating the production of coal and steel in the member countries. In effect, it internationalized the highly industrialized Saar and Ruhr regions of West Germany. Not only did this program eliminate a source of national contention and greatly raise production, but it was considered at the time as the platform on which to build the economic and political integration of Europe.

So well did the integrated coal and steel program work that in a few years, the same six nations formed the European Economic Community (EC), also known as the Common Market or European Community, to further integrate their economies. The Treaty of Rome of March 1957 brought a more comprehensive organization formally into existence. A central feature was the formation of a customs union for the purpose of lowering tariffs among the member states and of establishing one common tariff rate on imports from outside countries. This easing of trade restrictions greatly increased the flow of goods within the EC, which in turn stimulated production, provided jobs and capital accumulation, and increased personal income and consumption. Western Europe began to reemerge as one of the thriving economic regions of the world. In fact, the economic growth rate of the Common Market countries surpassed that of the United States by the end of the 1950s and remained significantly higher for many years thereafter.

Great Britain did not share in the benefits of the Common Market because it initially chose not to join. Britain already enjoyed the benefits of a preferential tariff system within its own community of nations—the British Commonwealth—and it could not reconcile its Commonwealth trade interests with those of its European neighbors in the Common Market. Other reasons for Britain's rejection of the Common Market included its conservative inclination to retain the old order rather than join in the creation of a new one, its reliance on its strong ties with the United States and Commonwealth friends, and its reluctance to give up a measure of its national sovereignty to a supranational body whose decisions were binding on member nations. However, after both its economy and its international status faltered in the 1950s, Britain saw fit in 1961 to apply for membership in the Common Market, only to find that admission now was not for the mere asking. The issue of Britain's entry was hotly debated both within Britain, where the Labour Party opposed it, and within France, where President Charles de Gaulle had his own terms for British admission. After over a year of deliberation, de Gaulle, who was critical of Britain's close political and economic ties with the United States and with the Commonwealth nations in other parts of the globe, suddenly announced in January 1963 his firm opposition to British membership in the EC. Since decisions within the Common Market required unanimity—a point de Gaulle had insisted upon—the French president's veto unilaterally kept Britain out. When Britain renewed its application to join the Common Market in 1966, de Gaulle still objected, and it was only after his resignation as president of France in 1969 that Britain gained entry. After lengthy negotiations, Britain finally joined the EC in January 1973 (together with Denmark and Ireland).

From its inception, the EC was divided between the "supranationalists," who desired comprehensive integration, and the "federalists," who wished to retain for each nation essential decisionmaking powers. The tug-of-war between these two camps remained unresolved. Moreover, since decisions on key issues were binding for all member states, certain members (most notably France and later Britain) successfully insisted on unanimity rather than majority vote on issues such as expansion of the membership, a common currency, social legislation, and so on.

NATO: The Military Integration of Western Europe

In April 1949, a number of nations heeded a call on the part of the United States to create an alliance against a potential Soviet threat. The result was the creation of NATO, the North Atlantic Treaty Organization, a collective security system for Western Europe and North America. It was the military counterpart to the Marshall Plan, designed to extend US protection to Western Europe. The ten European members (Britain, France, Iceland, Norway, Denmark, Belgium, the Netherlands, Luxembourg, Portugal, and Italy), together with the United States and Canada, signed a treaty of mutual assistance: An attack on one was an attack on the others. (NATO remained intact even after the demise of the Soviet Union, against which it was directed. It was invoked for the first time after al Qaeda's September 11, 2001, assault on the World Trade Center in New York and the Pentagon in Washington.) NATO brought US airpower and nuclear weapons to bear as the primary means to prevent the Soviet Union from using its large land forces against West Germany or any of the member states. Each of the NATO nations was to contribute ground forces to a collective army under a unified command.

Once again, the main obstacle was the force of nationalism, especially as personified by France's Charles de Gaulle. The first serious question facing NATO was whether to include West Germany. Its territory was covered by the initial NATO security guarantee, but it was not a treaty member; in fact, it was still under Allied military occupation until 1952 and had no armed forces of its own. As early as 1950, after the outbreak of the Korean War, US officials began to encourage the rearmament of Germany and integration of its forces into NATO. But the French and other Europeans, fearing the return of German militarism, were reluctant to allow the rearmament of Germany.

The fear of a reappearance of German militarism was, however, overshadowed by the fear of potential Soviet aggression. Moreover, German troops were badly needed to beef up the understrength NATO ground forces. At the urging of the United States, Britain, and West Germany itself, the NATO members agreed by the end of 1954 on West Germany's entry into NATO—on the conditions that it supply twelve divisions of ground forces and that it be prohibited from the development of nuclear, bacteriological, and chemical weapons as well as warships and long-range missiles and bombers.

The Soviet Union, too, opposed the rearmament of West Germany and made an eleventh-hour attempt to block its entry into NATO. In March 1952, Stalin proposed the immediate and total evacuation of all occupation forces from Germany—East and West—the reunification of Germany, and the creation of a security pact to defend it as a neutral nation. It is idle to speculate whether such a generous proposal would have received a better reception in Western capitals had it been made earlier, but Western leaders—particularly Adenauer—rejected it out of hand as a Soviet propaganda ploy aimed at disrupting the Western military alliance.

In NATO's first decade, the weak link in the collective security system was France, which lacked political stability until the emergence of General Charles de Gaulle as president of the newly established Fifth French Republic in 1958. France had been unable to supply its share of ground troops to NATO because they were needed first in Indochina and later in Algeria, where it was desperately trying to hold on to its colonial empire. De Gaulle, however, eventually decided on cutting France's losses abroad and regaining for France a dominant position in Europe. De Gaulle, France's great World War II hero and always the supreme nationalist, wished to remake Europe in his own way. His vision of a powerful Europe was not one of economic integration as suggested by the Common Market, but rather an association of strong nations. He was staunchly opposed to the notion of supranationalism, for his real objective was to elevate the role of France in a reinvigorated Europe. His determined pursuit of French domination of the new Europe was the cardinal point of what came to be called Gaullism.

French president Charles de Gaulle and visiting US president John F. Kennedy, Paris, June 2, 1961. *(National Archives)*

De Gaulle's boldly assertive nationalism was also reflected in his view of the security needs of France (and Europe). Because he sought the strengthening of the posture of France within Europe and the reassertion of European power in global affairs, de Gaulle wished to put the United States at a greater distance from Europe. He felt that Europe, especially NATO, was dominated by the United States and, secondarily, by its closest ally, Great Britain. De Gaulle also questioned the commitment of the United States to the defense of Europe. He thought that while the United States might wage a nuclear war in defense of its West European allies in case of a nuclear attack by the Soviet Union, it could not be counted on to risk its own nuclear destruction to defend Western Europe from an invasion by conventional Soviet ground forces.

De Gaulle rejected a US offer to place nuclear weapons in France; instead, he went ahead with the development of France's own nuclear arsenal, its *force de frappe,* or "strike force." It promised to enhance France's international prestige by joining the exclusive club of nuclear powers. De Gaulle also felt that, even if France's nuclear force were far smaller than that of the superpowers, it still would serve as a deterrent. In the 1960s, de Gaulle turned a deaf ear to foreign critics when he refused to join other nations in signing a series of nuclear arms control agreements and to halt France's atomic bomb testing program in the Pacific Ocean.

In 1966, de Gaulle decided to withdraw all French troops from NATO (although he did not formally withdraw France from the alliance) and he called for the withdrawal of all US forces from French soil. French security, the general insisted, must remain in French hands.

Occasionally, de Gaulle also conducted a foreign policy at odds with that of the United States. In 1964, for instance, he extended diplomatic recognition to the People's Republic of China. He disliked the confrontational approach taken by the United States in the Cold War, especially during the 1962 Cuban missile crisis (to be discussed later), and he did not want to be left out of diplomatic meetings between the superpowers where decisions might be made affecting the security and interests of France. He countered US Cold War diplomacy and its domination of the Western allies by conducting his own diplomacy with the Soviet Union and Communist China, and by strengthening France's ties with the most powerful continental West European state, West Germany.

The *entente* (understanding) between France and West Germany was achieved by the political skills of de Gaulle and West Germany's aged chancellor, Konrad Adenauer. After Adenauer accepted an invitation to meet with de Gaulle in Paris in July 1962, de Gaulle undertook a triumphant tour of West Germany two months later. The Franco-German summit meetings were followed by the signing of a Franco-German treaty aimed at strengthening their relations and thereby making it the cornerstone of West European solidarity. The treaty, meant to check the Anglo-US domination of the Western alliance, did not result in putting greater distance between West Germany and the United States, as de Gaulle had wished. It did, however, symbolize the marked improvement in the postwar era of the relations between these two powerful European nations with a long history of mutual hostility.

East European Integration

In Eastern Europe, Moscow had its own program of political and economic integration. What had begun in 1944–1945 as a military occupation by the Red Army shortly became a social, political, and economic experiment with Stalin's Soviet Union serving as the model. In 1949, in response to the Marshall Plan, Stalin's foreign minister, Viacheslav Molotov, introduced the Council of Mutual Economic Aid, commonly known as COMECON. Its purpose was to integrate the economies of the East European nations of Poland, Hungary, Romania, Czechoslovakia, and Bulgaria (and later Albania) with that of the Soviet Union. It was designed to aid in the postwar reconstruction of the Soviet Union and in the industrial development of Eastern Europe, which was still largely an agricultural region. It also supplemented the Kremlin's political control of Eastern Europe by giving it an economic lever.

The transformation of the East European economies took place along Soviet lines. The emphasis was on heavy and war industries, with consumer goods taking a backseat. Expropriation decrees, issued as early as September 1944 in Poland, led to the confiscation of the estates of nobles and the churches. These measures eliminated the "landlord" classes and paved the way for collectivization of agriculture.

The economic transformation of Eastern Europe was accompanied by sweeping political changes. In Bulgaria, Albania, Yugoslavia, and Romania, the monarchies were officially abolished. Moscow's East European satellites followed the Soviet example by adopting constitutions similar to Stalin's constitution of 1936. Everywhere, parties in opposition to the new political order were declared illegal.

The dominant force in Eastern Europe since the end of World War II was the Soviet army, augmented by the forces of the new socialist regimes. In 1955, the Soviet Union, in response to the inclusion of West Germany in NATO, created its own military alliance, the Warsaw Treaty Organization, commonly known as the Warsaw Pact. Its membership included Albania, Bulgaria, Czechoslovakia, East Germany, Hungary, Poland, Romania, and the Soviet Union. Unlike NATO, its members did not have the right to withdraw from the organization, an act the Kremlin considered the supreme political sin its satellites could commit. Albania, by virtue of its geographic position and relative lack of importance, did manage to leave the Warsaw Pact in 1968, but Hungary's flirtation with neutrality in 1956 met with an attack by the Soviet army. When Czechoslovakia in 1968 and Poland in the early 1980s moved dangerously close to a position similar to that of Hungary in 1956, the Soviet leadership made it clear that it would not tolerate the disintegration of its military alliance.

The most interesting manifestation of the force of nationalism in Eastern Europe was that of Romania, which since the mid-1960s sought to carve out a measure of independence from Moscow. Under the leadership of Nicolae Ceauşescu, the Romanian Communist Party successfully maneuvered to secure a limited economic and political independence, particularly in its dealings with Western Europe. Over the years, Romania retained diplomatic ties with Israel after all other East European nations had broken relations after the 1967 Six Day War, refused to participate in Warsaw Pact maneuvers, maintained diplomatic relations with the People's Republic of China at a time of ever-increasing hostility between Moscow and Beijing, gave warm receptions to visiting US presidents, and sent its athletes to the 1984 Olympic Games in Los Angeles in defiance of the Soviet boycott of the Games. Throughout, the Kremlin cast a wary eye on the Romanian maverick but refrained from taking drastic action. There was no pressing need to discipline Ceauşescu since he remained a loyal member of the Soviet Union's military alliance and, perhaps even more important, he showed absolutely no tendency toward any sort of political reform. Moscow always considered political reform in Prague and Warsaw a greater threat to its hegemony in Eastern Europe than Ceauşescu's actions, which, although an irritant, did not pose a major problem.

Despite the Kremlin's insistence on maintaining its hegemony over Eastern Europe, the forces of nationalism repeatedly made clear that Eastern Europe contained restless populations with whom the Kremlin's control did not sit easily. In the face of repeated Soviet pronouncements that considered Eastern Europe a closed issue (notably General Secretary Leonid Brezhnev's statement in 1968 that the Soviet Union's defensive borders were at the Elbe River separating East and West Germany), the region remained a potentially volatile problem.

Europe (1990)

The First Attempts at Détente

The Korean War, one of the most dangerous moments in the Cold War, brought about the remilitarization of both the United States and the Soviet Union. After World War II, the two nations had reduced their armed forces despite the shrill accusations in Washington and Moscow focusing on the evil intentions of the other. US intelligence records show that a Soviet attack was not in the cards—unless an uncontrolled chain of events led to miscalculations on the part of the leaders in the Kremlin. By early 1947, US forces had dwindled from a wartime strength of 12 million to fewer than 1 million soldiers under arms. Because of this reduction, Western Europe was exposed to a possible assault by the Soviet army. If that occurred, US troops in Western Europe were under orders not to fight but to find the quickest way across the English Channel.

The Soviets showed no inclination to initiate World War III on the heels of the just-concluded World War II. Stalin reduced the Soviet army to its prewar level of about 3.5 million soldiers, much of the Soviet Union was in ruins and in need of rehabilitation, and there was always the US trump card, the atomic bomb. Washington did not consider it likely that Stalin's army would cross the Iron Curtain; similarly, Moscow did not contemplate a US attack. For the next five years the protagonists maintained their forces at a level just sufficient to repel a potential attack. In 1950, the outbreak of the Korean War proved to be the catalyst for the rapid remilitarization of both sides.

In April 1950, nine weeks before the outbreak of the Korean War, a National Security Council directive (NSC-68) recommended to President Harry Truman a drastic increase in the military budget. The prospects of attaining this were slim, however, for popular sentiment was against it. The opportunity to implement NSC-68 came in June 1950 when, as Secretary of State Dean Acheson put it, "Korea came along and saved us."[2]

In the Soviet Union a similar process took place. In the late 1940s, Stalin renewed his insistence on unity and sacrifice, that the socialist, Soviet fatherland be defended at any cost. A renewed emphasis on ideological rigidity and conformity became the order of the day, and with it purges of individuals suspected of ideological nonconformity. When the war in Korea broke out, Stalin rapidly increased the size of the Red Army from 3.5 million to about 5–6 million troops, the approximate level the Soviet armed forces retained until the late 1980s. The five-year period after World War II during which both sides had reduced their armed forces and had curtailed their military expenditures was at an end.

Truman retired from political life in January 1953 and Stalin suddenly died six weeks later. The departure of the two chief combatants during the initial stages of the Cold War made it possible for the new leaders to try a different tack, for they were not locked into the old positions to the same degree their predecessors had been.

President Dwight Eisenhower and Nikita Khrushchev, who had emerged as the Soviet Union's new leader by September 1953, began a dialogue that resulted in the lessening of tensions. It was in this context that the word *détente* (from the French, the easing of tensions or the relaxation of strained international relations) first entered the vocabulary of the Cold War. Eisenhower, the hero of World War II, had no need to establish his anti-Communist credentials. He had greater latitude in dealing with the Soviets than did Harry Truman or his secretary of state, Dean Acheson, whom Republicans (notably Senator Joseph McCarthy and Richard Nixon) had berated time and again for being "soft on Communism." There was little the Democrats could do to shake off the Republican charges, and in fact, McCarthy went far beyond charging Truman with a lack of vigilance when he alleged that Truman's State Department was filled with Communist subversives.

Khrushchev and his colleagues began to move away from the Stalinist pattern of conduct at home and abroad. Khrushchev was determined to avoid a military showdown with the West and declared, by dusting off an old Leninist phrase, that "peaceful coexistence" (the Soviet euphemism for détente) with the West was possible. With it he rejected the thesis of the inevitability of war between the socialist and capitalist camps.

In short order, the great powers convened at Geneva in 1954 to deal with the central problems of the day. The more relaxed climate made possible the "Spirit of Geneva" and in turn paved the way for the disengagement of the occupying powers from Austria, which had been under four-power occupation since the end of the war. It proved to be the first political settlement of any significance by the belligerents in the Cold War.[3] In May 1955, Austria gained its independence as a neutral state, a nonaligned buffer in the heart of Europe, separating the armies of the superpowers. The stubborn fact that it took the two sides ten years and new leaders to agree on the Austrian solution—and on little else—was testimony to the intensity of the Cold War.

With the Austrian settlement, the Iron Curtain shifted eastward to the borders of Czechoslovakia and Hungary. Western and Soviet troops thus disengaged along a line of about 200 miles. In return, Austria pledged its neutrality in the Cold War, a condition that suited the Austrian temperament perfectly. In particular, Austria was not to join in any alliance—particularly military or economic—with West Germany. Austria quickly became a meeting ground between East and West. Its capital, Vienna, became a neutral site for meetings of world powers as well as a city with one of the largest concentrations of foreign spies in the world.

A solution similar to the Austrian settlement had earlier been envisioned for Germany. But in contrast to Austria, by 1955 two Germanies already existed. Austria's good fate was that at the end of the war it was treated not as a conquered nation but as a liberated nation. Also, it had a relatively small population of just over 7 million and was insignificant as an economic and military power. Yet this may also be said of Korea and Vietnam, where no political solutions were forthcoming. The main reason a solution for Austria ultimately proved to be feasible was Stalin's unilateral action in April 1945. He appointed the moderate socialist Karl Renner as the new head of Austria, and in this fashion Austria, unlike Germany, Korea, and Vietnam, was from the very beginning under one government, which all of the occupying powers eventually recognized. Churchill and Truman were initially unhappy with Stalin's action, not because they objected to Renner, but because he had acted without consulting them. Renner then proceeded to guide his nation carefully on a middle course between the superpowers. When the time came to disengage in 1955, Austria already had a neutral government ten years in existence. The German experience had been quite different. At the end of the war the Allies had spoken of creating a German government that all sides could accept, but instead wound up creating two German states.

The partial rapprochement between the United States and the Soviet Union made possible Nikita Khrushchev's visit to the United States in 1959. His itinerary took him to New York City, a farm in Iowa, Los Angeles, and the Camp David presidential retreat in the hills of western Maryland, where he and Eisenhower conferred in private. The "Spirit of Camp David" produced recommendations for disarmament and a decision for the two men to meet again at a summit meeting in Paris in May 1960, to be followed by an Eisenhower visit to the Soviet Union.

The Austrian settlement and talks between the heads of state did not mean that the Cold War was over. Nor did it mean that a comprehensive process of disengagement had begun. Détente was always tempered by a heavy residue of mistrust and a continued reliance on military might. At the high point of détente in the 1950s, the Cassandras were always in the wings warning of dire consequences.

The Soviets spoke of peaceful coexistence, but the ideological struggle and the preservation of the empire continued. Nikita Khrushchev always had his critics at home, particularly the old Stalinist, Viacheslav Molotov, who remained foreign minister until Khrushchev replaced him in 1956.[4] Détente did not mean, therefore, the abandonment of one's spheres of influence. The Soviets were unwilling to cede territory they considered vital to their security. When they were challenged in Eastern Europe, they did not hesitate to act. They accepted the defections of Yugoslavia and Albania, at the fringes of their sphere of influence, but after that they drew the line. When rebellions broke out in East Germany in 1953 and in Hungary in 1956, they quickly suppressed them.

A conflict between détente and Cold War aspirations was also evident in the United States. While the Republican president, Eisenhower, pursued the high road of compromise and negotiations, his secretary of state, John Foster Dulles, was an uncompromising anti-Communist. Containment of the Soviet

Union, a policy initiated by his Democratic predecessors Dean Acheson and George Marshall, was not enough for Dulles, for it suggested tolerance of an evil, godless system. To Dulles, the Cold War was not merely a struggle between two contending economic and political orders; it was also a clash between religion and atheism. Dulles, therefore, proposed the "rollback" of the Soviet Union's forward position and the "liberation" of lands under Communist rule. Officially, US foreign policy abandoned what had been the defensive position of containment and took on a "new look," an offensive character. But as events showed, particularly in Hungary in 1956, it is the president who ultimately determines foreign policy, and Eisenhower had no desire to start World War III by challenging the Soviets in their sphere. Despite Dulles's rhetoric, US foreign policy had to settle for containment.

Dulles acted vigorously to preserve and protect the US presence throughout the world. When in 1954 the Communist Vietminh of Vietnam triumphed over the French, he moved to preserve the southern half of that country for the Western camp. When the United States felt its interests threatened in Iran in 1953 and in Guatemala in 1954, the US Central Intelligence Agency (CIA), under the guidance of Allen Dulles, John Foster's brother, quickly moved into covert action and accomplished some of its most successful coups. In Iran, the CIA returned the shah to power when it engineered the overthrow of Premier Mohammed Mossadegh, who had sought to nationalize the nation's oil industry in order to take it out of the hands of British and US companies. In Guatemala, the CIA ousted the socialist Jacobo Arbenz, who had proposed the nationalization of lands held by US corporations, replacing him with a military junta.

Moscow's Response to Containment

In the mid-1950s, the Kremlin's foreign policy underwent a significant transformation when Khrushchev took the first steps to negate the US-led system of regional alliances designed to contain the Soviet Union. Until that time the country and its satellites had resembled a beleaguered fortress, defying the West. In 1954, the United States had created the Southeast Asia Treaty Organization and, in 1955, the Baghdad Pact. The latter treaty was intended to be a Middle Eastern alliance of Arab states, yet the only Arab state to join was Iraq; its other members were the United States, Britain, Turkey, Pakistan, and Iran. Washington, with NATO and its military ties in the Far East (South Korea, Japan, and Taiwan), was about to close a ring around the Soviet Union.

The change in Soviet foreign policy did not come without intense debate in the high echelons of the Soviet Union's ruling circle. From the end of World War II until Stalin's death, the Soviet Union had conducted a relatively conservative foreign policy. Stalin had refused to yield to the West on a number of central issues, notably Eastern Europe, but he had not challenged the West outside the confines of his own sphere. The successful Communist insurgencies in Vietnam and China, for instance, had not been of his making. Shortly after Stalin's death, the CIA, in a special report to Eisenhower and the National Security Council, described Stalin as a man "ruthless and determined to spread Soviet power," who nevertheless "did not allow his ambitions to lead him to reckless courses of action in his foreign policy." The CIA warned, however, that Stalin's successors might not be as cautious.[5]

Events quickly bore out the CIA's prediction. In 1954, a bitter debate took place in the Kremlin over the nation's foreign policy. One faction, led by Prime Minister Georgi Malenkov and Foreign Minister Viacheslav Molotov, urged caution, favoring a continuation of the Stalinist pattern of defiance and rearmament. The majority in the Presidium of the Central Committee of the party,[6] led by Nikita Khrushchev, who was the first secretary of the party and thus its leader, argued for a more active foreign policy, calling for a breakout from what they called capitalist encirclement. This argument stressed that those who accept the status quo and merely stand still will suffer defeat at the hands of the enemy. (Interestingly, this position echoed that of John Foster Dulles, who could not tolerate the mere containment of the foe. The conflict, both sides argued, must be taken to the enemy.)

Molotov and his allies warned that involvement in the Middle East was bound to fail. After all, British and US navies controlled the Mediterranean Sea and were bound to stop all shipments, as the United States had intercepted a Czechoslovak arms shipment to Guatemala earlier in 1954. But Khrushchev and his faction prevailed, and the Soviet Union began early in 1955 to arm in secret Gamal Abdel Nasser, Egypt's military dictator, a fait accompli revealed to the world later that year.

In return for its support of Nasser, the Soviet Union obtained a client in the Middle East, and it was thus able partially to offset the effects of the Baghdad Pact, an alliance that, at any rate, did not last long, nor did it accomplish much. Khrushchev's support of Nasser had primarily a symbolic value: The Soviet Union had become a global player.

For the first time the Soviet Union had a foothold in a region beyond the Communist world. The person largely responsible for this significant departure in Soviet foreign policy and who reaped handsome political dividends at home was Khrushchev. He had challenged the West in what had formerly been a Western preserve. It marked the beginning of a contest for the hearts and minds of the nonaligned world. With this in mind, Khrushchev undertook in 1955 a much publicized journey to South Asia. He visited India and on his way home stopped in Kabul, the capital city of Afghanistan, to forestall apparent US designs on that country. "It was . . . clear that America was courting Afghanistan," Khrushchev charged in his memoirs. The US penetration of that country had "the obvious purpose of setting up a military base."[7] In 1960,

Khrushchev paid a second visit to Asia. Eisenhower, concerned with the growing Soviet influence in southern Asia, followed in 1960 in Khrushchev's footsteps when he visited India and other nonaligned nations.

The Soviet Union's foray into the Third World had little to do with ideology, but everything to do with balance-of-power politics. Nasser, contrary to Western charges, was hardly a Communist. In fact, Nasser had outlawed the Egyptian Communist Party. The Soviet Union turned a blind eye to Nasser's jailing of Communists in order not to jeopardize its new relationship with the Arab world. Similarly, when the Soviets began to sell arms to the Sukarno government of Indonesia, the powerful Indonesian Communist Party complained bitterly. The party's fears were well founded; in October 1965, the Indonesian army launched a bloodbath, killing up to half a million actual and suspected Communists. The Soviet Union, however, first and foremost, wanted clients outside its sphere of influence to challenge the West. What those clients did to their Communist parties was of secondary concern.

The United States sought to bring Nasser to heel by withdrawing funding for the Aswan High Dam on the upper Nile River. Nasser then turned to the Soviet Union to help him complete the project. By that time he had already concluded an arms agreement with the Soviet Union (its first with a non-Communist state). When, in the summer of 1956, Nasser nationalized the Suez Canal, which had been in British hands since 1887,[8] the stage was set for a retaliatory strike. In October 1956, France and Britain joined Israel in an attack on Egypt. The Cold War once again spilled over into the Third World.

In May 1960, relations between the Soviet Union and the United States took a sudden turn for the worse when a US spy plane, a U-2, was shot down deep inside the Soviet Union. The Soviet Rocket Force Command had finally been able to bring down one of the high-flying planes, which had periodically violated Soviet airspace since 1956. This event wrecked the summit between Khrushchev and Eisenhower later that month, and it canceled Eisenhower's scheduled goodwill visit to the Soviet Union. Khrushchev's vehement denunciation of Eisenhower overstepped the boundaries of both common sense and good manners. Western historians have often speculated that Khrushchev had to placate the hard-liners at home, who had never been happy with his rapprochement with the West. U-2 flights had proved to be an embarrassment for Khrushchev; after all, the Soviet military and scientific establishment had launched the first earth satellite and the first intercontinental missile, yet it had been unable to bring down a US plane at 75,000 feet until engine trouble apparently forced it to a lower altitude.

The U-2 incident also embarrassed Eisenhower, who had first lied about it and then had to acknowledge that he had approved the spying mission. In the United States, 1960 was a presidential election year. During the campaign, the "outs," in this case John Kennedy and his Democratic Party, accused the "ins," Richard Nixon (Eisenhower's vice president) and the Republicans, of having fallen asleep on the job. They charged that the Soviets had opened a "missile gap" that endangered the security of the United States. The Cold War was back in full bloom.

From the days of the Korean War, the Cold War belligerents engaged in an open-ended arms race—both conventional and nuclear—in preparation for a military showdown that neither wanted. In conventional land forces, the Soviet bloc always held the lead, while the West relied primarily upon the US nuclear umbrella. The US nuclear monopoly, however, was short-lived. In 1949, the Soviet Union tested its first atomic weapon; in the early 1950s, it exploded its first thermonuclear bomb; and starting in 1955, it had the capability of delivering these weapons by means of intercontinental bombers. By the end of the 1950s, both Washington and Moscow had successfully tested intercontinental missiles. Essentially, the nuclear arms race was deadlocked. A nuclear exchange was bound to lead to Mutually Assured Destruction (MAD) for both belligerents. But this did not keep them from adding to their arsenals. The focus of the nuclear showdown shifted in October 1962 to a most unlikely place, Cuba. The confrontation—the most dangerous episode in the Cold War—grew out of the Cuban revolution of the 1950s that brought Fidel Castro to power.

The Cuban Missile Crisis

Cuba's successful war for independence against Spain, completed in 1898 with US assistance, had come with a high price, the overbearing presence of the "colossus of the north." Cuba's national hero, José Martí, had warned that US support of the Cuban independence movement would come precisely with that price. Indeed, after 1898, one Cuban dictator after another made his peace with Washington at the expense of Cuban sovereignty.

March 1952 saw the return to power, by virtue of a military coup, of the dictator Fulgencio Batista (who in 1933 had been a participant in the "revolt of the sergeants" and then ruled Cuba until 1944). In the 1950s, with the return of prosperity on the island nation, US economic influence grew considerably and Batista did much to facilitate it. US businesses—both legitimate (farming, mining, tourism) and illegitimate (the mafia with its reach into hotels, nightclubs, prostitution, narcotics)—dominated the Cuban economy. Indeed, the mafia— accustomed to demanding protection money from others—paid the obliging Batista to protect its investments. It was a symbiotic relationship that served both very well. Batista made sure it worked smoothly by brandishing both the carrot (such as bribes and the granting of licenses) and the stick (terror). The brutality and venality of the Batista regime—which had sold Cuba to foreign and criminal interests accompanied by the unequal distribution of wealth—bred resentment among Cubans of all walks of life.

Resentment, however, failed to produce an organized resistance, and dissenting voices remained amorphous and thus ineffective. And even when meaningful resistance began to take shape under the direction of Fidel Castro, he managed to organize no more than 300 comrades under arms at any one time, although increasingly the population became more sympathetic to it. When Castro came to power in January 1959, it was not so much that he had gained power by force of arms but that Batista had lost his hold on it. Castro himself admitted that had Batista enjoyed a measure of popular support, his revolution would easily have been crushed. At the end, however, there was no one—including the military—to defend Batista.

Castro launched his revolution on July 26, 1952, in a supreme act of recklessness, an attack on the Moncada military barracks in Santiago, in the southeastern corner of Cuba. Everything went wrong from the outset: the planning, the dearth of arms, the fact that Castro's 120 men were outnumbered by a factor of ten to one. Castro's forces were decimated; he was captured, tried, and sentenced to a 15-year prison term. Popular revulsion against Batista (on the part of the Roman Catholic Church, mothers openly protesting, students, the middle class) led to an amnesty of political prisoners. In May 1956, a defiant Castro walked out of prison and went into exile in Mexico to plot his next step. It was there he and his brother, Raúl, met Ernesto "Ché" Guevara of Argentina. Guevara, who had been in Guatemala City at the time of the 1954 CIA-backed military coup that overthrew Jacobo Arbenz, had been appalled by Arbenz's lack of resolve. Events showed that he and Castro were made of sterner stuff.

Castro's moderate success in raising money from the Cuban community-in-exile in south Florida forced him to settle for returning to Cuba on a used thirty-eight-foot cabin cruiser, named *Granma* after its US owner's grandmother. In November 1956, *Granma*, with 81 rebels aboard, in a re-creation of José Martí's fateful return to Cuba in 1895, set sail for Cuba's Oriente Province. There, they immediately ran into an ambush that devastated their ranks. Havana newspapers declared Castro dead, his revolution crushed. Castro was down to sixteen men, but among the survivors were Ché Guevara and Raúl Castro, who set out to rebuild their organization and recruit new fighters.

This time Castro refrained from frontal assaults against a stronger enemy. Operating out of the rugged Sierra Maestra Mountains of southeastern Cuba, his guerrillas attacked lightly defended military outposts, gathering weapons, supplies, and experience in the process. In May 1957, eighty Castro guerrillas scored a significant psychological victory over the undermanned garrison at Uvero. It signified (in Guevara's words) that the revolution had "reached full maturity." As the confidence of the rebels waxed, that of Batista's military waned. The rebels' radio messages had their intended effect. When, in May 1958, Batista dispatched 10,000 troops into the Sierra Maestras, Castro's 300 guerrillas halted their advance and captured large amounts of weapons. When the last battle took place, at the end of December 1958, for control of Cuba's fourth largest city, Santa Clara, on the road to Havana, which should have been strenuously defended, the military simply gave up. Abandoned by his military (some of whom were plotting against him) and encouraged by the US ambassador to leave the country, Batista fled in the middle of the night. It was New Year's Day, 1959.

Castro's rebels immediately began the "purification" of Cuba. "The dead shout out for justice," Castro declared. Justice included the execution of Batista's top officials for "treason, rebellion, sedition, desertion, malfeasance, robbery and fraud." It meant the closing of crooked numbers games, casinos, and news offices in the pay of Batista, and the mass dismissal of officials. It also meant the denial of constitutional rights.[9]

Castro's revolution sought to establish Cuba's sovereignty—political and economic—at the expense of the overbearing US presence. To that end, he insisted on the nationalization—with compensation, initially—of US investments estimated at just under $1 billion. With the Cuban treasury virtually empty and much of the nation's assets deposited in accounts abroad (Batista alone plundered Cuba of an estimated $300 million), the nationalization process would have to be underwritten by international banking institutions (an unlikely prospect). Just in case there was compensation, US businesses now claimed assets of $2 billion. Castro reminded them that for the purpose of taxation, they had previously grossly undervalued their investments. At stake, however, was something much more important than money. US businesses were less interested in compensation than in maintaining their profitable businesses. The mafia, which had long labored to establish a foothold in Cuba and to that end had cultivated politicians such as Batista, had no intention of abandoning their golden goose in Havana.

Castro's revolution soon began to feel the full brunt of the US business community, the mafia, the CIA, the State Department, and the Pentagon. Initially, the CIA did not believe Castro to be a Communist (unlike his brother, Raúl), but merely one of the many Cuban rebels, inspired by José Martí, who had railed against the United States only to come around (as Batista had done) and, in the end, continue business as usual. As pressure mounted, Castro found an unlikely patron in the Kremlin.

Shortly, the Eisenhower administration began to charge that Castro was a Communist. (It is difficult to pinpoint when his conversion to Communism took place, but apparently it was after the revolution.) Either way, Castro had to be overthrown. There were solid reasons to believe that the CIA could duplicate its successes in Iran and Guatemala.

*   *   *

The crisis in Iran was the consequence of a decision in April 1951 by Iran's parliament, the *majlis*, to nationalize the property of the Anglo-Iranian Oil Company (AIOC), Britain's most profitable business in the world. Not only had the AIOC taken Iran's wealth out of the country, but its workers in Abadan suffered the indignities of surviving on wages of fifty cents a day, living in a shantytown (called "paper city"), and battling pollution, rats, and disease. In May, the *majlis*, under the leadership of the nationalist Mohammed Mossadegh, forced the shah, Mohammed Reza Pahlavi, to establish the National Iranian Oil Company, the first step toward the nationalization of the oil industry. Britain's prime minister, the old imperialist Winston Churchill, appealed to the CIA to help him get rid of Mossadegh. The Truman administration, however, was unwilling to become involved in the dispute. Churchill had to wait until the Eisenhower administration, with its "new look," came to power. The new secretary of state, John Foster Dulles, and his brother, Allen, the head of the CIA, were more than willing to launch a covert operation to overthrow Mossadegh, a man already demonized in the US press.

Eisenhower gave the Dulles brothers the green light to initiate the operation. The CIA spent money to foment demonstrations in the streets, paid off religious leaders, and bribed army officers. In August 1953, after the nationalists had driven the shah into exile, the CIA managed to create a volatile situation that led to the army's arrest of Mossadegh and the shah's return from Rome. Three hundred Iranians died in the violence, but on balance, CIA intervention had worked as planned. When the leading CIA operative in Iran, Kermit Roosevelt (Theodore Roosevelt's grandson), briefed John Foster Dulles on the agency's success, Dulles "purred like a giant cat."

But that was not the end of the story. As a critic of the operation later explained, "nations . . . cannot be manipulated without a sense on the part of the aggrieved that old scores must eventually be settled." The day came in 1979, when demonstrations forced the shah into exile once more and when Iranian students took possession of the US embassy in Tehran. While Dulles purred, many in the CIA understood that the United States might pay a price someday.[10] In the month after the overthrow of Mossadegh, a CIA report spoke for the first time of "blowback."[11]

In the following year, in Guatemala, the CIA moved into action once more. A revolution in 1944 had overthrown Guatemala's military dictatorship and had brought to power civilians who sought to address the country's social and economic problems. In 1950, 2.2 percent of landowners owned 70 percent of the land (of which they cultivated but one-quarter) and the annual income of agricultural workers was $87. Most of the economy was in foreign—mostly US—hands and, consequently, large profits went abroad. The greatest employer was the United Fruit Company, *El Coloso*, with its vast landholdings, 85 percent of which consisted of excess, uncultivated land.

The nationalist Jacobo Arbenz, upon winning a democratic election, became president of Guatemala in March 1951. Arbenz and his congress—which had but a handful of Communist deputies with little influence—then proceeded to take steps to limit the power of foreign corporations, notably United

Fruit. They nationalized unused land and supported strikes against foreign businesses. In March 1954, Arbenz told his congress that this was a matter of protecting the "integrity of our national independence." John Foster Dulles raised the specter of Communism. The nationalization of land did not sit well with the Dulles brothers. They decided to act for reasons of national security, ideology, and the fact that both owned stock in United Fruit and had previously provided legal services to the company. The CIA organized and armed disaffected elements of the Guatemalan army, led by Colonel Carlos Castillo Armas, who once before, in November 1950, had sought (unsuccessfully) to overthrow the civilian government and then fled into exile. A successful coup took place in July 1954, when Arbenz's own army would not support him.

For Washington, the crisis was over. For Guatemala, it was the first step of a descent into hell. Castillo Armas, who was assassinated in July 1957, never managed to bring order or prosperity to Guatemala. Instead, a revolutionary movement began to gain strength. In the early 1960s, a succession of military regimes—some of them extraordinarily brutal—launched a campaign in an attempt to return the country to the "quiet days" before 1944.[12]

For more than three decades, the military killed an estimated 200,000 Guatemalans, most of them indigenous Mayans. Of particular viciousness was the reign of General Efrain Rios Montt, a born-again Christian who became the darling of the US religious right in the early 1980s. During his seventeen-month reign, his army killed an estimated 70,000 people, mostly Mayan peasants, and razed thousands of villages. Rios Montt's scorched-earth policy, directed primarily against an ethnic group, came close to the definition of genocide. Rios Montt was arguably the worst human rights abuser in Latin American history since the arrival of the Spanish *conquistadores*. Guatemala's civil war produced more fatalities than the "dirty wars" of El Salvador, Nicaragua, Argentina, and Chile combined.

*   *   *

There was little reason to believe that the United States could not repeat in Cuba the Iranian and Guatemalan scenarios. The first weapon Washington employed was economic; if needed, other weapons would be used later. It closed the US market to Cuba's main source of income, the export of sugarcane. The US market previously had taken half of Cuba's exports and had provided nearly three-quarters of its imports. As anticipated, the US trade embargo had severe repercussions for the Cuban economy.

At this point events began to move rapidly. Castro refused to yield to US pressure and, instead, turned to the Soviet Union for economic, political, and military support. Also, he saw his revolution as a model for other countries in Latin America, and as such he posed a direct challenge to US hegemony there. His reform program at home acquired increasingly a socialist flavor and resulted in the exodus of thousands of Cubans. They settled mainly in Florida, waiting to return to their native land.

In March 1960, a frustrated Eisenhower administration turned the Cuban problem over to the CIA and subsequently to the new president, John Kennedy. Cuba became Kennedy's first foreign policy challenge. In the spring of 1961, Allen Dulles assured Kennedy that Castro could be removed with little difficulty. After all, the CIA had dealt successfully with similar problems before. Dulles worked out a plan that called for Cuban exiles, trained and supplied by the CIA, to land on the beaches of Cuba and appeal to the Cuban population to rise against Castro. It was based on the assumption that Castro's regime had scant popular support; all that was needed was a push and the corrupt house of cards would come down.

Kennedy, although skeptical of the plan, decided to put it into operation in April 1961, since by that late date it could not be called off without recrimination by the Cubans in Florida. Kennedy had good reason to be skeptical, for the CIA operation stood little chance of success. The population did not rise against Castro, and his armed forces—in the course of seventy-two hours— destroyed the contingent of 1,500 Cuban exiles on the beaches at the Bay of Pigs. A vague understanding between the CIA and the Cuban exiles had led the exiles to believe that the United States would not abandon them in case they ran into difficulties. When Kennedy did not respond militarily to the fiasco at the Bay of Pigs, many Cubans in the United States felt betrayed. But Kennedy never had contemplated the need for such a contingency. Moreover, direct US involvement would have been in violation of international law and surely promised international and domestic repercussions.

Kennedy, stung by this defeat, blamed Allen Dulles for the fiasco. Castro's Cuba then became an obsession with Kennedy that made it difficult for him to accept the new government of Cuba. Three days after the Bay of Pigs, he offered Castro a warning: "Let the record show that our restraint is not inexhaustible."[13]

The Soviet Union could do little to aid Castro. It could not readily challenge the United States in the Caribbean and protect Cuba. The United States enjoyed a vast naval superiority in that region, not to mention a large advantage in delivery systems of nuclear weapons. When John Kennedy entered the White House, the United States possessed over 100 intercontinental and intermediate-range ballistic missiles, 80 submarine-launched missiles, 1,700 intercontinental bombers, 300 nuclear-armed airplanes on aircraft carriers, and 1,000 land-based fighters with nuclear weapons. In contrast, the Soviets possessed 50 intercontinental ballistic missiles, 150 intercontinental bombers, and an additional 400 intermediate-range missiles capable of reaching US overseas bases.[14] The overwhelming ratio (17:1) stood in favor of the United States.

Soviet leader Nikita Khrushchev and Cuban president Fidel Castro at the United Nations, New York, November 1960. *(National Archives)*

In the presidential election of 1960, Kennedy had charged that the Eisenhower administration had been responsible for a "missile gap" to the detriment of the United States. But that political myth was laid to rest shortly after Kennedy became president. In October 1961, his deputy secretary of defense, Roswell Gilpatric, announced that there was no missile gap favoring the Soviet Union; on the contrary, there was a large gap favoring the United States. "We have a second-strike capability," Gilpatric stated, "which is at least as extensive as what the Soviets can deliver by striking first."[15]

Nikita Khrushchev understood all too well that his boasts of Soviet military might had only masked the unyielding reality that the Soviet Union was trailing badly in the nuclear arms race. But one day in 1962, a solution came to him in a flash. He reasoned that if he could establish a Soviet nuclear presence in Cuba, he could solve several problems in one bold stroke. He was, after all, a man of action, not of reflection. In 1955, Khrushchev had argued for a secret arms shipment to Nasser's Egypt, and it had proven to be a bold and successful initiative. In Cuba, he could perhaps do the same. Success promised impressive dividends. First, Khrushchev would be able to present himself as the defender of a small and vulnerable state. Second, and more important, medium-range missiles in Cuba would essentially give the Soviet Union nuclear parity—if only symbolically—with the United States. The missile gap, which favored the United States, would be no more. Third, nuclear parity with the United States would greatly enhance the international prestige of the Soviet Union.

Khrushchev's memoirs suggest that neither he nor his advisors spent much time considering the consequences of this rash step. In the past, Khrushchev had several times taken decisive yet potentially dangerous steps that nevertheless had brought him political rewards. Now the stakes were higher than ever. Success promised to bring great gains, but failure promised dire consequences. Indeed, two years after the Cuban missile crisis, when his party turned him out, it accused Khrushchev of unspecified "hare-brained" and "wild schemes, half-baked conclusions and hasty decisions," none too subtle reminders of what had gone wrong in the Caribbean.[16]

When the CIA became aware of the construction of Soviet missile sites in Cuba, Kennedy had to act. Military and domestic political considerations demanded it. The Joint Chiefs of Staff understood that the presence of perhaps ninety Soviet intermediate-range missiles in Cuba, while posing a formidable threat to much of the eastern United States, did not change the balance of terror. Both sides were already capable of annihilating the other. Kennedy and his advisors knew they had first of all a domestic political problem. At the height of the crisis, Secretary of Defense Robert McNamara told National Security Advisor McGeorge Bundy: "I'll be quite frank, I don't think there is a military problem here. . . . This is a domestic, political problem. . . . We said we'd act. Well, how will we act?"[17]

One option was to launch preemptive air strikes against the missile sites, which would bring about the deaths of Soviet troops, humiliate a great power, and conceivably touch off a nuclear war. Two of Kennedy's advisors, the Air Force chief of staff, General Curtis LeMay, and the commander of the Strategic Air Command, Thomas Power—both of whom for over a decade had advocated a preemptive nuclear war against the Kremlin—now took the opportunity to urge a nuclear resolution of the crisis. In the unlikely event of a Soviet nuclear retaliation, they argued, the Kremlin would be able to inflict only minimal damage on the United States. LeMay said that "the Russian bear has always been eager to stick his paw in Latin American waters. Now we've got him in a trap, let's take his leg off right up to his testicles. On second thought, let's take off his testicles too." Somehow, LeMay thought the bear would accept his castration without trying to reclaim his manhood. After the crisis was over, a disappointed LeMay publicly berated Kennedy for having "lost" the showdown.[18]

The Joint Chiefs of Staff and the CIA had a more sanguine assessment. They told Kennedy that in an all-out war the Soviet nuclear arsenal was capable of destroying the United States without the Cuban missiles. This bleak assessment had a sobering impact on Kennedy and his advisors, who met around the clock in an effort to find a political solution to the confrontation.

A second alternative was the invasion of Cuba, but that option was as dangerous as the first. The destruction of Soviet forces in Cuba would leave Khrushchev with few options. He could accept a defeat, contemplate a nuclear

This low-level reconnaissance photograph, taken by the United States on October 23, 1962, provided evidence that the Soviet Union was setting up missile bases in Cuba. *(US Department of Defense)*

exchange, or attack the West's isolated and vulnerable outpost in Berlin, where the Soviet army had a marked advantage.

Kennedy decided on a third option, a blockade of Cuba (which he called a "quarantine" since a blockade is an act of war) that would give both sides additional time to resolve the issue. The blockade was a limited one since its purpose was only to intercept ships carrying missile components. Khrushchev, in the face of US action, was prepared to back down. But he, like Kennedy, had his own political problems at home. Since he could not afford to come away from the confrontation empty-handed, he demanded concessions. First, he insisted on the Soviet Union's right to place defensive missiles in Cuba. After all, the United States had done the same when it had placed missiles in Turkey, along the Soviet Union's southern border. At the least, therefore, the US missiles should be removed from Turkey. But Kennedy refused publicly to discuss this demand. He, too, could not afford to appear to back down, despite the fact that the US missiles in Turkey were obsolete and already had been scheduled for removal. Second, Khrushchev wanted a pledge from the United States not to invade Cuba and to respect the sovereignty of that nation.

The standoff was resolved with the help of two unlikely intermediaries. Soviet journalist Alexander Feklisov (who was also a KGB agent) and US journalist John Scali (who had contacts in the White House) met in a restaurant in Washington on October 26 to discuss the crisis. Feklisov pointed out that "mutual fear" drove the two superpowers: Moscow feared a US invasion, and Washington feared the rockets in Cuba. A US pledge not to invade Cuba would resolve the matter. Feklisov got in contact with his embassy, Scali with the White House. They met again for dinner that same day, and Scali informed

Feklisov that "the highest power"—namely, John Kennedy—had accepted the deal to trade the Soviet rockets for a public pledge that the United States would not invade Cuba.[19]

Kennedy ignored Khrushchev's belligerent statements and instead replied to a conciliatory letter from the Soviet prime minister in which Khrushchev had expressed his desire to resolve the dilemma:

> We and you ought not to pull on the ends of the rope in which you have tied the knot of war, because the more the two of us pull, the tighter that knot will be tied. And a moment may come when that knot will be tied too tight that even he who tied it will not have the strength to untie it. . . . Let us not only relax the forces pulling on the ends of the rope; let us take measures to untie that knot.[20]

Robert Kennedy, the president's brother and closest advisor, met with Soviet ambassador Anatoly Dobrynin to tell him that the United States was prepared to pledge not to invade Cuba in the future and that after a sufficient interval it would remove the missiles from Turkey. But there would be no official US acknowledgment of this second concession. On the next day, Dobrynin told Robert Kennedy that the Soviet missiles would be withdrawn. The crisis was over.

After the first Soviet ships were turned back by the US blockade, Secretary of State Dean Rusk famously remarked that "we looked into the mouth of the cannon; the Russians flinched."[21] That statement became the basis of the widely held view in the United States that Kennedy had stared down Khrushchev. It suggested that US warships and Soviet freighters carrying missile components had met in the waters off Cuba. But the reality was that the Soviet freighters had turned around more than 500 nautical miles (575 miles) from the nearest US warships.[22]

Yet it was not merely the Soviets who had flinched. Both sides realized that the constant state of confrontation had been in part responsible for the nuclear showdown. The time had come for a sobering, constructive dialogue. And, in fact, relations between the United States and the Soviet Union improved markedly shortly thereafter. The most notable, immediate achievement was the partial Nuclear Test Ban Treaty of 1963, which forbade nuclear testing in the atmosphere. It set the stage for further East-West discussions and the beginning of the détente of the late 1960s.

In the aftermath of the crisis, historians, politicians, and military brass sought to determine the lessons of the confrontation. A view commonly held in the United States emphasized that the crisis showed that the Soviets yielded only in the face of determination. Force was the only thing they understood. Khrushchev, indeed, had surrendered to Kennedy's demands by removing the Soviet missiles from Cuba. But this explanation has several serious flaws. On balance, the victory did go to Kennedy. But it came at a price. Until the very end, Khrushchev always insisted on a quid pro quo—something in return—

and he continued to hold out for concessions until he received them. In the meantime, his government granted Kennedy nothing. As long as the deadlock persisted, the Soviets continued to work on the missile sites and they challenged the US U-2 spy planes that continued their surveillance flights. A Soviet tactical ground-to-air missile—fired by Cubans at the express order of Fidel Castro—shot one down and killed its pilot, Major Rudolph Anderson. And when, during the crisis, a US intelligence plane entered Soviet airspace, the Soviet air force chased it back.

The Cuban missile crisis was first and foremost a political test of wills. Nothing that either side did or contemplated doing would have changed the military balance of power. The crisis was political in nature, one that called for a political solution, a quid pro quo. And that is how it was resolved, not by one side dictating a settlement to the other. It ended only after Kennedy gave assurances on the missiles in Turkey and a pledge of noninterference in Cuban affairs. As Khrushchev emphasized in his memoirs, the crisis was resolved by political compromise, and he spared no words in thanking Kennedy for taking that road rather than going to war.[23]

What the crisis revealed was the Soviet Union's relative weakness in the face of US military might. This imbalance in favor of the United States had been in part the result of a modest build-down on the part of the Soviets, which had begun under Khrushchev in the late 1950s. When Kennedy and his secretary of defense, Robert McNamara, continued to push for an increase in their already bloated US nuclear arsenal, the Soviet leadership committed itself to the quest for genuine—and not just symbolic—nuclear parity with the United States, something they had failed to achieve by the time of the Cuban missile crisis. Afterward, they vowed that the United States would never again humiliate them. The result was a renewed—this time successful—Soviet effort to establish nuclear parity with the United States.

The United States honored Kennedy's verbal pledge not to invade Cuba. Castro, however, remained an obsession to the Kennedy brothers, who turned to organized crime to do what the CIA had failed to accomplish. The mafia, of course, had the best of reasons for trying to eliminate Castro. Their profits had been of such magnitude that when Castro's revolution ruined everything, they had been paying Batista a monthly bribe of $1.28 million.[24] It was not surprising they sought to assassinate Castro.

Recommended Readings

Western Europe

Calmann, John. *The Common Market: The Treaty of Rome Explained.* London: Blond, 1967.

Hiscocks, Richard. *The Adenauer Era*. Philadelphia: Lippincott, 1966.
Judt, Tony. *Postwar: A History of Europe Since 1945*. New York: Penguin, 2005.
The magisterial, detailed treatment of the first sixty years.
Williams, Philip, and Martin Harrison. *Politics and Society in de Gaulle's Republic*.
New York: Doubleday, 1971.
A focus on the politician most responsible for the political orientation of postwar
France.

The Cold War, 1953–1962

Beschloss, Michael. *Mayday: Eisenhower, Khrushchev, and the U-2 Affair*. New York:
Harper and Row, 1986.
An analysis of the U-2 incident and its impact on US-Soviet relations.
———. *The Crisis Years: Kennedy and Khrushchev, 1960–1963*. New York: Harper-
Collins, 1991.
Detailed account of the Cold War confrontations of the early 1960s.
Bundy, McGeorge. *Danger and Survival: Choices of the Bomb in the First Fifty Years*.
New York: Random House, 1988.
By the assistant to Secretary of War Henry Stimson and national security advisor
to Lyndon Johnson.
Dallin, David. *Soviet Foreign Policy After Stalin*. Philadelphia: Lippincott, 1961.
Lebow, Richard Ned, and Janice Gross Stein. *We All Lost the Cold War*. Princeton:
Princeton University Press, 1994.
A discussion of the resolutions of three East-West confrontations: the Cuban missile
crisis, the Yom Kippur War of 1973, and the management of the nuclear deterrent.
Ra'anan, Uri. *The USSR Arms the Third World: Case Studies in Soviet Foreign Policy*.
Cambridge, Mass.: MIT Press, 1969.
On the debates in the Kremlin over foreign policy after Stalin's death.

Cuba

Abel, Elie. *The Missile Crisis*. Philadelphia: Lippincott, 1966.
A journalist's account of the nuclear confrontation.
Dobbs, Michael. *One Minute to Midnight: Kennedy, Khrushchev, and Castro on the
Brink of War*. New York: Knopf, 2008.
The definitive account of the crisis.
English, T. J. *Havana Nocturne: How the Mob Owned Cuba—and Then Lost It to the
Revolution*. New York: Morrow, 2008.
Kennedy, Robert F. *Thirteen Days: A Memoir of the Cuban Missile Crisis*. New York:
Norton, 1969.
By the president's brother and close advisor, who presents what may be called the
official US view.
Kinzer, Stephen. *All the Shah's Men: An American Coup and the Roots of Middle East
Terror*. Hoboken, N.J.: John Wiley and Sons, 2003.
How the CIA overthrew Mossadegh's elected government in Iran.
Schlesinger, Stephen, and Stephen Kinzer. *Bitter Fruit: The Untold Story of the Amer-
ican Coup in Guatemala*. New York: Anchor Books, 1990.
The definitive account of the CIA's coup of 1954.
Szulc, Tad. *Fidel: A Critical Portrait*. New York: Morrow, 1986.

A detailed biography that offers the thesis that Castro was already a Communist before seizing political power.

Walton, Richard J. *Cold War and Counterrevolution: The Foreign Policy of John F. Kennedy*. New York: Viking, 1972.
Contains two chapters highly critical of Kennedy's handling of the Bay of Pigs and the missile crisis.

Wyden, Peter. *Bay of Pigs: The Untold Story*. New York: Simon and Schuster, 1979.
On the CIA's ill-fated attempt to overthrow Fidel Castro.

Notes

1. For details, see Rolf Steininger, *Eine Chance zur Wiedervereinigung? Die Stalin-Note vom 10. März 1952: Darstellung und Dokumentation auf der Grundlage unveröffentlichter britischer und amerikanischer Akten* (Bonn: Neue Gesellschaft, 1985).

2. Cited in Walter LaFeber, *America, Russia, and the Cold War: 1945–1990*, 6th ed. (New York: McGraw-Hill, 1991), p. 98.

3. Other agreements on trade, arms limitations, travel, and the like must not be lightly dismissed. Yet none of them settled a major political problem.

4. In 1957, Andrei Gromyko became foreign minister; he retained his post until July 1985, when Mikhail Gorbachev kicked him upstairs to take the ceremonial post of president of the Soviet Union.

5. CIA special estimate, advance copy for National Security Council, March 10, 1953, "Probable Consequences of the Death of Stalin and the Elevation of Malenkov to Leadership in the USSR," p. 4, in Paul Kesaris, ed., *CIA Research Reports: The Soviet Union, 1946–1976* (Frederick, Md.: University Publications of America, 1982), reel II, frames 637–648.

6. The Presidium (known as the Politburo during 1966–1991) of the Central Committee of the Communist Party was the decisionmaking body, which consisted of approximately a dozen individuals. The number was not fixed; it varied frequently.

7. N. S. Khrushchev, *Khrushchev Remembers: The Last Testament* (Boston: Little, Brown, 1974), pp. 299–300.

8. The Suez Canal was owned by a joint-stock company in which British and (to a lesser extent) French money had been invested.

9. "Purification," *Time*, February 9, 1959.

10. Stephen Kinzer, *All the Shah's Men: An American Coup and the Roots of Middle East Terror* (Hoboken, N.J.: John Wiley and Sons, 2003), pp. 2, 5–6, 67, 161–163, 209. The citation is by William Roger Louis, p. 215.

11. Chalmers Johnson, "Abolish the CIA!" *London Review of Books*, October 21, 2004, p. 25.

12. Stephen Schlesinger and Stephen Kinzer, *Bitter Fruit: The Untold Story of the American Coup in Guatemala* (New York: Anchor Books, 1990), pp. 49–63, 76, 108, 253–254.

13. Cited in Richard J. Walton, *Cold War and Counter-Revolution: The Foreign Policy of John F. Kennedy* (Baltimore: Viking, 1972), p. 50.

14. David Horowitz, *The Free World Colossus: A Critique of American Foreign Policy in the Cold War*, rev. ed. (New York: Hill and Wang, 1971), pp. 342–345. Also, Edgar M. Bottome, *The Balance of Terror: A Guide to the Arms Race* (Boston: Beacon Press, 1971), pp. 120–121, 158–160.

15. "Gilpatric Warns US Can Destroy Atom Aggressor," *New York Times*, October 22, 1961, pp. 1, 6.

16. "Nezyblemaia leninskaia general'naia linia KPSS," *Pravda*, October 17, 1964, p. 1.

17. Kai Bird and Max Holland, "Dispatches," *The Nation*, April 28, 1984, p. 504.

18. See Richard Rhodes, *Dark Sun: The Making of the Hydrogen Bomb* (New York: Simon and Schuster, 1995), pp. 571, 574–575.

19. See A. S. Feklisov, "Neizvestnoe o razviazke karibskogo krizisa," in M. V. Filimoshin, ed., *KGB otkryvaet tainy* (Moscow: Patriot, 1992), pp. 118–132.

20. Robert F. Kennedy, *Thirteen Days: A Memoir of the Cuban Missile Crisis* (New York: Norton, 1969), pp. 89–90.

21. Ibid., p. 18.

22. Michael Dobbs, *One Minute to Midnight: Kennedy, Khrushchev, and Castro on the Brink of War* (New York: Knopf, 2008).

23. Khrushchev, *Khrushchev Remembers*, pp. 513–514.

24. For Batista and the mafia, see T. J. English, *Havana Nocturne: How the Mob Owned Cuba—and Then Lost It to the Revolution* (New York: William Morrow, 2008), pp. 16, 58–59, 132–133, 266–267, 318, passim.

Part 2

Nationalism and the End of Colonialism

After World War II, a wave of nationalism swept across Asia and Africa, and in its wake a host of new nations proclaimed independence from their European colonial masters. Within two decades about one-third of the world's population was freed from colonial rule. The scope and the speed of the dismantling of the colonial empires were unforeseen. By 1960, it had become clear to even the more conservative rulers of the colonial powers that they could no longer stem the tide. None stated it better than British prime minister Harold Macmillan in his famous "Wind of Change" speech delivered at the end of a tour of Africa in January 1960:

> We have seen the awakening of national consciousness in peoples who have for centuries lived in dependence upon some other power. Fifteen years ago this movement spread through Asia. . . . Today the same thing is happening in Africa and the most striking of all the impressions . . . is the strength of this African national consciousness. The wind of change is blowing through the continent, and whether we like it or not this growth of national consciousness is a political fact.[1]

Several historical developments merged to bring about this phenomenon. First, the war itself had weakened the European imperial powers. Some of them had lost their colonies during the war and found it difficult to restore control of them afterward, and others were so exhausted by the war that they came to view the maintenance of a colonial empire as a burden greater than it was worth. Another factor was the emergence of a Western-educated elite among the natives of the colonies, who took seriously the lessons they had learned in the Western universities and now demanded popular representation leading to national sovereignty. In many cases the colonial peoples took part as allies in the war and, having contributed to the victory of the "four freedoms" (Franklin Roosevelt's not too subtle swipe against colonialism), they now demanded a measure of that freedom for themselves.

Still another factor, with relevance to Asia, was the role of Japan in bringing an early end to European colonialism. Japan had promoted and provoked nationalist movements in various Asian countries. Britain responded to the strength of the independence movement with greater alacrity than France and the Netherlands and took the lead in decolonization. Once it granted independence to India, long its most important colony, the grounds for maintaining its rule over lesser colonies vanished. France, however, refused to grant independence to its colonies, for it saw in the restoration of the French empire a means of compensating for its humiliating defeats in World War II. In the end, France was unable to stem the tide of anticolonialism when it lost to a determined Vietnamese nationalist-Communist movement led by Ho Chi Minh.

In Africa, decolonization came later than in Asia largely because national consciousness and strong nationalist movements were slower to develop. The persistence of ethnic divisions in Africa was a major obstacle to the development of nationalism. In general, Britain did more to prepare its African colonies for self-rule and independence than France, Belgium, or Portugal. In fact, the abrupt departure of France and Belgium from Africa left their former colonies particularly ill prepared for either political or economic independence. Moreover, France refused to abandon Algeria, which many French citizens called home and which their government considered a province of France and not a colony, despite its large Muslim majority. The result was that France had on its hands another long and bitter revolutionary struggle it was unable to win.

Nationalism was a key ingredient in the postwar struggles in the Middle East as well. Here, two peoples, Jews and Arabs, clashed over claims to the same land. The Jews, fortified by their particular brand of nationalism—Zionism—returned to settle a land they had parted from centuries before, while the Palestinians, who had occupied this same land for centuries, were determined to establish their own state. The state of Israel came into being in 1948, at the expense of the Palestinians, and ever since it has been embattled by its Arab neighbors.

The continuing struggle for national self-determination in Vietnam is treated in Chapter 9, and the postindependence drive of the new nations of Asia and Africa for political and economic modernization is taken up in Part 4, "The Third World."

Note

1. James J. McBath, ed., *British Public Addresses, 1828–1960* (Boston: Houghton Mifflin, 1971), pp. 75–83.

5 Decolonization in Asia

Independence movements in Asian nations had been brewing since about the beginning of the twentieth century and by the end of World War II could no longer be contained. In some cases, independence was achieved peacefully, because the imperial nation became resigned to the termination of its colonial rule, as was the case of the United States in the Philippines and Great Britain in India and Burma. In other cases, imperial powers were determined to resist the national independence movements in their colonies, granting independence only after engaging in a long and bloody struggle, as was the case of the French in Indochina and the Dutch in the East Indies.

The primary ingredient in all independence movements was nationalism. Gradually, the colonized peoples awakened to their precolonial traditions and developed a sense of national consciousness mixed with strong anti-imperialist sentiment. They were outraged by colonialist domination, by being treated as inferior citizens in their own native lands. They could point out to the Europeans the blatant contradiction between their own professed ideals of democracy and self-government—of *liberté, égalité, fraternité*, in the case of the French—and their denial of the same to their Asian colonies. After witnessing the destruction European nations had wrought upon one another in World War I, the Asian colonial peoples began to doubt the superiority of their colonial masters. During World War II, that sentiment only grew.

The Impact of World War II

World War II, and especially the role played by Japan in the war, greatly stimulated Asian independence movements. During the war, several of the imperial powers of Europe were either overrun by Nazi Germany, as were France and the Netherlands, or were fighting desperately for survival, as was Great Britain. These nations were unable to defend their colonies once Japan set out

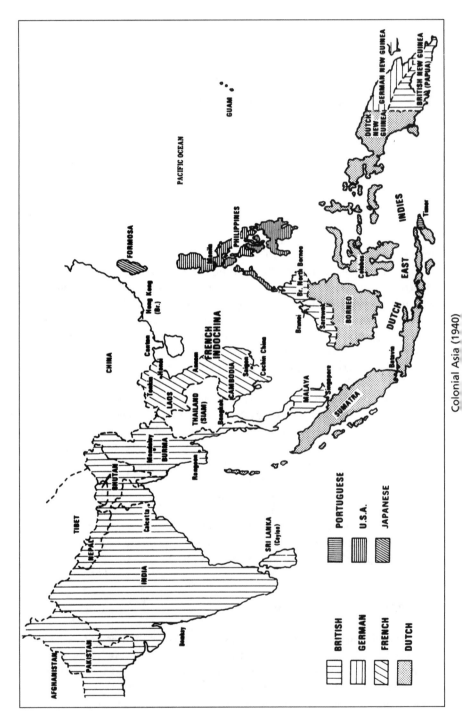

Colonial Asia (1940)

to bring Southeast Asia into its own colonial orbit. The Japanese claimed that they came as liberators, fighting to free Asians from the chains of Western imperialism and to make Asia safe for Asians. While it is true that under Japanese rule Asian colonies merely replaced one master for another, Japan did much to strengthen nationalist movements in Southeast Asia. The swiftness and apparent ease with which the Japanese defeated the European forces in Asia signaled to Vietnamese, Indonesians, Burmese, Indians, and others that their former European masters were not as powerful as they had thought.

In Indonesia the Japanese released native political prisoners from the jails and threw the Dutch colonial officials into the same cells. They banned the use of the Dutch language and promoted the use of native languages. In Indochina, under French rule for sixty years, they granted Vietnam its independence, albeit under Japanese tutelage. They granted nominal independence to the Philippines and to Burma in 1943, and promised it to others. In some cases, such as in India and Burma, Japan helped arm and train national armies to fight the British. By the end of the war, when Japan was forced out, the nationalist organizations Japan had assisted stood ready to oppose the efforts by the European powers to reimpose their colonial rule. This was especially the case in Indonesia, where nationalist leaders immediately issued a declaration of independence at the time of Japan's surrender.

The United States, too, played a role in hastening the end of colonialism in East Asia. During the war, President Franklin Roosevelt had been outspoken in his opposition to the continuation of European colonialism; indeed, after the war, the United States became the first Western nation to relinquish its colonial power in Asia. It had long before promised independence to the Philippines, a colony since 1898, and no sooner was the war over than plans for the transfer of power were made. In 1946, with great fanfare, the Republic of the Philippines was proclaimed on an appropriate date, July 4.

Independence and the Partition of India

The decolonization of British India has deep historical roots. Resistance to British rule began in the nineteenth century with the founding of the Indian National Congress (a political party usually known as Congress). When World War II broke out, the British Raj (rule) faced a well-organized independence movement led by Jawaharlal Nehru and Mohandas Gandhi.

While Nehru was the leading purely political figure, Gandhi represented a moral argument against British colonialism, which found expression in passive resistance to British colonial laws. Gandhi had become a unique force to be reckoned with because of his long-suffering and selfless pursuit of national independence using such nonviolent methods as refusing to pay British-imposed taxes, organizing work stoppages, and fasting until near death.[1] Britain's viceroy (the crown's representative in India) described him as a "terribly difficult little person,"[2] while Prime Minister Winston Churchill called him a "half naked" fakir, something Gandhi took as a compliment. They had good reasons to fear Gandhi, someone who had inexorably undermined British pretentions of moral and legal authority to control India.

It did not help that when World War II broke out in Europe in September 1939, the British viceroy—without consulting with Indian leaders—declared war on Germany on behalf of India. Churchill had no intention of even discussing Indian independence, but he found that the exigencies of war demanded a more flexible position. In March 1942, his government dispatched a special envoy, Sir Stafford Cripps, on a mission aimed at placating the Indian nationalists. In August 1942, at a time when the Japanese armies appeared to be moving inexorably toward India (Britain's major military base in Southeast Asia, with Singapore having fallen in February), Cripps offered India dominion status (self-government but continuing membership in the British Commonwealth) and an election for a native constituent assembly to draft an Indian constitution—*after* the war. Congress responded with the Quit India Resolution demanding, as Gandhi put it, that Britain leave India "to God, or to anarchy."

The British response to the Quit India Resolution was to arrest tens of thousands, including Gandhi and Nehru. Congress followers rebelled but were suppressed in several weeks. One expatriate Indian nationalist leader, Subhas Chandra Bose, went so far as to put an army in the field (with Japanese assistance) to fight the British. Toward the end of the war, the British viceroy repeatedly advised London that the demand for independence in India was so strong that it could be postponed no longer. Churchill, the guardian of Britain's empire, disliked Indians, had little tolerance for their nationalist movement, and had no intention of granting independence. In his public reaction to the Quit India Resolution he famously declared:

> We intend to remain the effective rulers of India for a long and indefinite period. . . . I have not become the King's First Minister in order to preside over the liquidation of the British Empire. . . . Here we are, and here we stand, a veritable rock of salvation in this drifting world.[3]

Churchill reduced the issue to two clear-cut alternatives: The British could either stand and rule or they could cut and run, and he never seriously considered the latter. He did, however, consider adopting a policy aimed at undermining Congress by enlisting the support of the impoverished rural masses with a land reform program that would benefit them at the expense of wealthy landowners, who were identified with Congress.

In the end, Churchill was unable to prevent the inevitable. In June 1945, in anticipation of the end of the war, British authorities in India convened a conference of Indian leaders (several of whom were released from prison so that they could take part) aimed at creating an interim coalition government pending the granting of independence after the war. These talks, however, were complicated by the presence of a third party, the Muslim League. Muslims made up the largest religious minority in India, and they feared political domination on the part of the far more powerful Hindu majority. They feared becoming a helpless minority in an Indian nation in which the Hindu-Muslim population ratio was about five to one. Centuries of Hindu-Muslim antagonism could not easily be resolved, and the Muslim League, led by Mohammed Ali Jinnah, insisted on nothing less than a separate state for the Muslims. Gandhi and Nehru were staunchly opposed to such a division, and they tried—without success—to reassure Jinnah and the British that Muslim autonomy and safety would be guaranteed within the new Union of India. The British, too, wished to preserve the unity of India, but Jinnah remained adamant in his demands for a separate Muslim state.

In London, the new prime minister, Clement Attlee, whose Labour Party had unseated Churchill's government in July 1945, agreed to the transfer of power to the Indian people as soon as possible, and at the same time to preserve the unity of India. In an effort to resolve the Muslim-Hindu dispute, Attlee dispatched, in March 1946, a cabinet mission to India, where tensions were rapidly mounting. Indian nationalism was made manifest in a mutiny by Indian sailors against their British naval officers, and by the outpouring of the inspired nationalist rhetoric of Gandhi and Nehru. The Muslim leader, Jinnah, was equally articulate and passionate in his demand for the creation of a separate nation for the Muslims. The British mission released its report, rejecting partition as impractical but favoring instead a formula for ensuring the autonomy of Muslim provinces within a greater Indian unity. But efforts to implement this compromise were forestalled by mutual mistrust and quarreling. With the outbreak of communal violence between Hindus and Muslims (and among other minorities), there was too little time to work out a peaceful solution.

The tense situation in India caused the British to advance the timetable for independence. The British government appointed a new viceroy of India, Lord Louis Mountbatten, the popular wartime hero, who arrived in India in March 1947. Mountbatten announced July 1948 as the new deadline for the transfer of power from the British to the Indians. Instead of pacifying the Indians—both Hindus and Muslims—as he had intended, his announcement had the opposite effect. Fearful and mistrustful of each other, Hindus and Muslims initiated a new cycle of violence.

Although Mountbatten at first reaffirmed the British desire to preserve the unity of India, he could not satisfy the Muslim League with anything less than partition, and he therefore decided to settle the matter speedily by establishing two successor states to British rule. The result was a hasty agreement on the independence and partition of India to go into effect on a new, earlier date, August 15, 1947.

Thus, not one but two nations came into being: India and Pakistan, the new Muslim state. The problem was compounded by the new maps—drawn up in haste by a London judge, Cyril Radcliffe, who was granted only forty days to draw up the Radcliffe Line—which suddenly put people in regions where they were now a religious minority. He well understood the nature of his task, writing at the time that "there will be roughly 80 million people with a grievance looking for me. I do not want them to find me." The partition of India led to a flood of some 15 million refugees, one of history's largest. Radcliffe departed for home, never to return to India, explaining that "I suspect they'd shoot me out of hand—both sides."[4]

The transfer of the refugees was accompanied by unbridled violence, particularly in the provinces of Punjab and Bengal, which had been cut in half. Trains carrying nothing but corpses were but one symptom of it. Hysterical mobs of Hindus, Muslims, Sikhs, and others savagely attacked one another in acts of reprisal, bitterness, and desperation. In many cities, terrorism raged out of control for days when arson, looting, beatings, murder, and rape became common. Villages became battlegrounds of warring groups, and massacres were frequent along the highways clogged with poor and usually unprotected migrants. Before all was over, an estimated 1 million people lost their lives.

Indian prime minister Jawaharlal Nehru, addressing an audience in the United States, October 11, 1947, two months after independence was granted to India. *(National Archives)*

Mohammed Ali Jinnah, president of the Muslim League and later the first president of Pakistan, August 9, 1945. *(National Archives)*

The result was a legacy of bitterness that plagued Indian-Pakistani relations for decades to come.

Violence ultimately claimed even the life of Mohandas Gandhi, the supreme symbol of nonviolent resistance. In January 1948, a Hindu extremist, believing that Gandhi had been too conciliatory to the Muslims, shot him to death. Between 1937 and 1948, Gandhi had been nominated five times for the Nobel Peace Prize, only to be denied the honor because "he was neither a real politician nor a humanitarian relief worker." Perhaps, but nonviolent dissident movements across the globe continue to carry the imprint of Gandhi's legacy.

The agreement on the partition of India did not specify the future status of the Sikhs, another religious minority, and the 565 small, independent princely states scattered throughout India. It was presumed, however, that they would look to one or the other of the two new governments for protection and thus become integrated into either India or Pakistan.

The new nation of Pakistan—made up almost exclusively of Muslims (whereas India retained a sizable Muslim minority, who a half century later became hostages to Hindu extremists)—came into being in a strange configuration. It consisted of two parts—West Pakistan and East Pakistan—situated on Indian's western and eastern flanks, separated by 1,000 miles.

The British and Dutch in Southeast Asia

The process of decolonization in Southeast Asia—the region stretching from Burma to the Philippines and includes such countries as Thailand, Vietnam, Indonesia, and Malaysia—varied from country to country. In general, it was more orderly in the US and British colonies (excepting, of course, the violence involved in the partition of India) than it was in the French and Dutch colonies. The British granted independence to Ceylon (now known as Sri Lanka) in 1947 and to Burma (now called Myanmar) in 1948. They were prepared to transfer power to a Malayan union in 1948, but this was delayed for a decade by internal strife between the Malays, who represented the Muslim majority, and the Chinese, who were in the minority except in the city of Singapore. An unsuccessful ten-year Communist insurgency further complicated matters. Finally, in August 1957, after the Communist movement was suppressed and a greater degree of ethnic harmony between the Malays and the Chinese was attained, the British granted full independence to the Federation of Malaya.

Brunei, another British protectorate, in northern Borneo, was scheduled to join its neighbors, Sarawak and North Borneo, in becoming members of the new union of Malaysia, but, prompted by Indonesia, it refused to do so at the last minute. It remained a source of contention among Britain, Malaysia, and Indonesia until it attained self-government under British tutelage in 1971. Singapore separated from Malaysia in 1965 and became a sovereign state.

In contrast to Britain, the Netherlands had no intention of granting independence to the Dutch East Indies, a colony comprising 8,000 ethnically diverse islands, which the Dutch had exploited for three centuries. But Dutch intransigence was met by equally strong resistance on the part of the Indonesian nationalists. During World War II, the Japanese military rulers, who had seized the Dutch colony, gave their active support to an anti-Dutch nationalist organization known as Putera. By the end of the war, this organization, under the leadership of Achem Sukarno, had developed a 120,000-troop army. When news of Japan's surrender reached the capital of Jakarta, Sukarno, who had been under intensive pressure from the more radical student element in Putera, quickly drafted a declaration of Indonesian independence and read it on August 17, 1945, to a huge crowd that had gathered to celebrate the event. At about the same time, the British landed an occupying force to receive the Japanese surrender and to maintain order until Dutch forces could arrive.

The Dutch intended to restore colonial rule, only to be confronted by a strong nationalist movement with a large, well-equipped army and by an even more hostile Communist movement. Negotiations produced a compromise in late 1946 whereby the Dutch would recognize Indonesian independence only on the islands of Java and Sumatra, on the condition that this new Indonesian republic remain within the Dutch colonial empire in a "Union of Netherlands and Indonesia." Indonesian leaders, however, rejected this plan, and when the Dutch resorted to police action to quell demonstrations in July 1947, they were met by armed resistance. Despite UN efforts to arrange a cease-fire, and diplomatic pressures by the United States and Britain on the Dutch, the Indonesian war of independence continued for another two years, with thousands of casualties on both sides. Finally, in 1949, the Dutch conceded, and a fully independent Federation of Indonesia came into being with Sukarno as its president.

The French in Indochina

After World War II, a succession of French governments were resolutely opposed to granting independence to their Asian colonies. The retention of their colonies was a matter of *honneur* and a commitment to their *mission civilisatrice*.

France's colonial presence in Vietnam dates back to 1858, when its troops first arrived. It took a quarter of a century, but in 1883, the native ruling dynasty submitted to French rule. The Vietnamese nationalist resistance began literally the very day the emperor surrendered his country's sovereignty to France. It took the French another dozen years to establish a sense of stability, but they never did extinguish Vietnamese resistance, something the Vietnamese had honed for 2,000 years against any and all enemies, primarily the Chinese to the north. For the next half-century, French rule appeared to be secure. Military might, imprisonment, and the public use of the guillotine had their intended impact.

The central figure in the Vietnamese independence movement was Ho Chi Minh, who, starting as a young man, questioned the moral and legal authority of France to be in Vietnam. In 1919, he happened to be living in Paris, where the victors of World War I were meeting to decide the fate of the losers. US president Woodrow Wilson had come to the conference as the champion of national self-determination, someone who spoke for the rights of all subjugated peoples. Ho Chi Minh humbly submitted a petition to the US delegation asking for Vietnamese self-rule, amnesty for all political prisoners, equal justice, freedom of the press, and "the sacred right of all peoples to decide their own destiny."[5] The French rejected Ho's petition and the US delegation ignored it. The delegates at the conference had more pressing issues to consider, and the French, whose overriding concern was the punishment of Germany, were in no mood to abandon their prized colony (which by then had become a money-making enterprise through the ruthless exploitation of Vietnam's people and resources).

In the following year, Ho became one of the founders of the French Communist Party, because he saw Communism as the only political movement in France that concerned itself "a great deal with the colonial question." For Ho,

Ho Chi Minh at Dien Bien Phu, May 1954. *(National Archives)*

Communism thus became a vehicle for national liberation of his native land from French colonialists who professed the sacred principles of liberalism and democracy. Ho's identity as a Marxist and anticolonialist took him to Moscow in 1923, just as the Kremlin began to focus on domestic problems and all but abandoned its commitment to international revolution. By the late 1920s, he made his way to China, where revolutionary ferment promised to spread to the rest of Asia. For nearly thirty years, he was a man without a country, living in exile and waiting for a chance to return to Vietnam to challenge the French.

The opportunity came in 1941, during the early years of World War II. The French army, one of the world's best on paper, had collapsed in the face of the German attack in the spring of 1940. In the following year, when the Japanese swept over Southeast Asia, the French again offered no resistance. Japan had humbled one of Europe's great powers, but this proved to be little solace for the Vietnamese, since they had merely exchanged one exploitative master for another. The Japanese conquest of Southeast Asia, however, put into sharp focus the vulnerability of the European colonial presence in Asia, a lesson that was not lost on the Vietnamese.

In the meantime, Ho had returned to Vietnam in 1941 to create a native resistance movement, the Vietminh (the League for the Independence of Vietnam). When he turned against the Japanese, who now controlled Vietnam, by a strange twist of fate, Ho and the United States became allies during World War II. The US military recognized the usefulness of the Vietminh, and in fact officers of the US Office of Strategic Services (the forerunner of the CIA), generally anti-French and quite sympathetic to the Vietnamese revolution, provided Ho's troops with training, weapons, and supplies—even medical assistance when they nursed the chronically ill Ho back to health.

When the war ended in 1945, it was Ho and his men who controlled most of Vietnam. France's colonial ambitions in Southeast Asia seemed to be at an end. During the war, US president Franklin Roosevelt had urged the French to follow the US example in the Philippines and grant Vietnam its independence. But the French, humiliated in World War II, insisted on returning to Vietnam as one of the world's great powers and refused to accept the loss of a prized colony. They sought refuge in a maxim out of the nineteenth century, which equated colonialism with national pride and prestige. They insisted on reasserting France's authority as they had in the past and could not imagine that they would not be able to do it.

In the meantime, the Vietminh forced the abdication of the last emperor of Vietnam, and on September 2, 1945, before a massive throng of Vietnamese in Hanoi's main square, Ho declared the independence of Vietnam. He drew on hallowed French and US political documents—the 1789 French Declaration of the Rights of Man and Citizen and the US Declaration of Independence—to justify a Vietnam free from colonial rule. The governments in Paris and Washington, however, turned a deaf ear to Ho's pleas. Subsequent talks between Ho and the French achieved little. At a minimum, Ho insisted on a genuine measure of autonomy within the context of the French empire. Ho did agree, however, upon the return of the French army to the north of Vietnam (the region of Tonkin) to deal with the rapacious Chinese Nationalist army that had arrived there in September 1945 to disarm the Japanese army. Ho had his work cut out to convince his followers that the Chinese were the primary threat to Vietnamese independence (indeed, the Chinese head of state, Jiang Jieshi, claimed Tonkin as part of China) and that they could be forced out only with French help.

As tensions between the Vietnamese and the French rose, the French navy replied with a classic example of gunboat diplomacy. In November 1946, it bombarded the Vietnamese sector of the port of Haiphong, killing, according to French estimates, 6,000 civilians. In December 1946, the Vietminh, fearful that the French would replicate the Haiphong scenario in Hanoi, launched an attack on the French garrison in that city. The first Indochina war was under way.

The First Indochina War

Initially, the Vietminh proved to be no match for the French army, which possessed superior weapons as well as more troops. The French were able to put into battle airplanes, tanks, trucks, and heavy artillery. In a conventional head-to-head clash the French were destined to win. The Vietminh had no choice except to pursue the tactics of the weak against the strong: guerrilla warfare.

Guerrillas (from the Spanish meaning "little war") have little chance of defeating their more powerful enemy in a decisive battle, because they do not have the means to do so. They rely instead on a series of small campaigns designed to tie down enemy soldiers without engaging them directly. Once the enemy brings superior power into play, the guerrillas break off the fight and withdraw, leaving the battlefield to the conventional forces, who then plant their banners and proclaim victory. Armies fighting guerrillas generally can point to an uninterrupted string of "victories," in the traditional sense of the word. The guerrillas are almost always "defeated."

Such a scenario is misleading. Ché Guevara, one of the better-known practitioners of guerrilla warfare and who had fought alongside Fidel Castro in Cuba in the 1950s, compared a guerrilla campaign to the minuet, the eighteenth-century dance. In the minuet, the dancers take several steps forward and then back.[6] The "steps back" are of central importance. Retreat is central to guerrilla warfare since the guerrillas cannot afford to try to hold their ground lest they be decimated. Instead, the guerrillas gather their dead, their wounded, and their supplies and reorganize to fight another day. Little wonder that the conventional forces are always able to claim that they are winning and that it will only be a matter of time until the guerrillas suffer their "final" defeat.

The guerrillas' ultimate victory comes after a prolonged struggle that wears down the enemy physically and psychologically. Of utmost importance for the guerrillas is the sophisticated conduct of political action necessary to gain recruits for their cause. For conventional forces, the conflict is frequently of a purely military nature; in contrast, successful guerrilla movements always focus on the psychological and political nature of the conflict. The French colonel Gabriel Bonnet reduced this to a quasimathematical formula: "RW = G + P (revolutionary warfare is guerrilla action plus psychological-political operations)."[7]

The French, certain of victory, were constantly able to discern "light at the end of the tunnel" (an unfortunate phrase the US military later borrowed). The Vietminh, however, always managed to reappear and fight again. Thus, what was intended as a short punitive action by the French turned into a long and costly war of attrition. And because all wars have political and economic repercussions, successive French governments were beginning to feel the heat. At the outset of the Indochina war, the French public had supported the suppression of the anticolonial rebellion, but, as the years went by, the financial burden became increasingly heavy and public dissatisfaction grew.

In the late spring of 1950, the United States became involved—indirectly—in the Indochina war and—directly—in the Korean War. Washington considered both wars as manifestations of a general Communist offensive in East Asia. President Harry Truman became concerned with the increasingly precarious French position in Vietnam, and he thus became the first US president to involve the United States in that region when he offered the French US military and financial aid. At the end of the war, in 1954, it was the US taxpayer who underwrote most of the French expenditures in Vietnam. Truman and his staunchly anti-Communist secretary of state, Dean Acheson, never hesitated to support French colonialism. In the process, for the next twenty-five years Southeast Asia became a focal point of the Cold War.

Cold War orthodoxy in Washington insisted that Communist revolutions were fomented from the outside. The Soviet Union, however, offered the Vietminh no aid. Indeed, Ho's revolution—the formation of the Vietminh, the seizure of power in Hanoi, and the attack on the French garrison in that city—was carried out without Moscow's advice, support, or even knowledge. When the Chinese Communists came to power in 1949, Ho Chi Minh emphatically rejected the idea of using Chinese troops against the French, although he did accept Chinese supplies, particularly artillery. Chinese-Vietnamese enmity is age-old, and Ho feared the Chinese, their Communism notwithstanding, even more than he did the French. He believed, correctly, that the days of the white colonizers in Asia were numbered, but if the Chinese came they would stay for 1,000 years (as they had done in the past).

After years of fighting, the French were bogged down with little chance of winning the war. To suppress a guerrilla insurrection, conventional armies need vast troop superiority, somewhere between four and ten conventional soldiers for every guerrilla soldier. But in some of the important contested regions in the north, notably in the Red River delta, the Vietminh were able to match the French one to one. It is a truism of guerrilla warfare that as long as the guerrillas are not defeated, they are winning. In retrospect, by 1953 the French had already lost the war in Indochina.

French public support of the war began to wane. Predictions of victory by French generals and politicians had proven to be hollow promises. In desperation, the French military command, hoping to find a solution to the elusiveness of the Vietminh guerrillas, sought to entice the Vietnamese to stand up and wage a final, conventional battle at the remote outpost of Dien Bien Phu, near the border of Laos. If the Vietminh took the bait, it would result in a conventional showdown, one that the French—in possession of superior firepower as well as control of the air and the roads—felt certain they were destined to win.

General Vo Nguyen Giap, the military genius of the Vietminh, decided to oblige the French, but only after making adequate preparations for the battle. With great difficulty he brought into combat heavy artillery (courtesy of the Chinese Communists), which the Vietminh had not used previously to any great extent. To the surprise of the French, Giap placed his artillery on the hilltops overlooking the valley of Dien Bien Phu. The French soon realized their position was doomed and they appealed for US intervention.

The new US president, Dwight Eisenhower, weighed in on the side of colonialism, as Truman had done before him. Some of Eisenhower's advisors urged a nuclear strike, but he rejected this option. It made no sense to incinerate Dien Bien Phu—French and Vietnamese alike—to "save" it. Eisenhower refused to become directly involved in Vietnam, particularly after the Senate majority leader, Lyndon Baines Johnson, told him that the US people would not support another war in Asia, particularly in light of the fact that the ceasefire in Korea had been signed only the previous year.[8] Eisenhower did, however, offer the French clandestine assistance at Dien Bien Phu. The CIA flew 682 airdrop missions, and two of its pilots were killed,[9] the first US citizens to die in Vietnam in hostile action.

The battle of Dien Bien Phu ("hell in a very small place," in the words of the French historian Bernard Fall) took place in the spring of 1954. The French forces fought heroically against tremendous odds against nearly 50,000 Vietminh who pounded their fortifications and gradually, yet inexorably, inched ever closer in the tunnels and trenches they dug. The French commander, Henri Navarre, safely ensconced in Hanoi, demanded that there be no surrender. Despite his orders, white flags appeared over the French fort in early May. Two thousand of France's finest soldiers lay dead; 10,000 were taken prisoner (along with 4,000 indigenous troops), and only seventy-three managed to escape (nearly all of them indigenous troops).[10] The Vietminh lost up to 10,000 of their best soldiers. The French defeat was total and the French role in Indochina was over. A new French government and the public both welcomed the end.

By coincidence, the world's leading powers—both Communist and capitalist—were engaged at that time in discussing several issues in Geneva and had agreed to take up the question of Indochina. The French and Vietnamese agreed, even before the battle of Dien Bien Phu began, to take their dispute to this forum. It was incumbent for Ho and Giap to attain a victory before the talks on Indochina began and, indeed, they were able to do so on the day before the conference opened. At the conference, however, the Vietnamese Communists received no support from the other Communist powers, the Soviet Union and China, both of whom were more interested in normalizing relations with the West. As a consequence, the talks produced a strange agreement—which none of the parties signed. The Geneva Agreement called for a Vietnam temporarily divided along the 17th parallel with a Communist government in the north and a non-Communist government in the south. This division was to last until a nationwide election, scheduled for July 1956, meant to give the country a single government and president and thus finally bring about the "unity and territorial integrity" of Vietnam. In the meantime, the agreement demanded the neutrality of both parts of Vietnam, north and south.

The US delegates at Geneva were hypnotized by the specter of a global monolithic Communism. But they need not have worried. Both the Communist Chinese and the Soviets were more interested in cutting a deal with the French than in coming to the aid of their Vietnamese comrades. It appears that it was the Chinese foreign minister, Zhou Enlai (Chou En-lai), much to the surprise of the French, who first proposed a division of Vietnam. The Vietminh finally yielded, but they insisted on a dividing line along the 13th parallel, which would leave them with two-thirds of the country. The Vietnamese, under Chinese and Soviet pressure, backed down and accepted the 17th parallel, which cut the country in half. At the farewell banquet, Zhou hinted to the South Vietnamese delegation that he favored a permanent partition of Vietnam. Zhou's comment reflected China's centuries-old animosity toward Vietnam rather than solidarity among Communist nations.

The Vietminh also yielded on the question of the timetable for the scheduled election. They wanted an election as soon as possible to cash in on their stunning defeat of the French. It was the Soviet foreign minister, Viacheslav Molotov, who asked rhetorically: "Shall we say two years?"[11] The French and the US delegates quickly endorsed Molotov's proposal. It was the best deal the US delegation could hope to obtain. Secretary of State John Foster Dulles knew that any southern, anti-Communist candidate stood little chance against the popular Ho Chi Minh. Earlier in the conference, Dulles had cabled his ambassador in Paris:

> Thus since undoubtedly true that elections might eventually mean unification Vietnam under Ho Chi Minh this makes it all more important that they should be held only as long after cease-fire agreement as possible. . . . We believe important that no date should be set now.[12]

As it was, losing even half of the nation to Communism did not sit well with Dulles. US representatives refused to sign the Geneva Agreement, but in a separate statement the chief US negotiator, General W. Bedell Smith, acting on behalf of Eisenhower, pledged US adherence to the agreement.

In the end, Washington made clear it wanted no part of the elections. Thus, in a development reminiscent of Korea and Germany, two separate governments came into being: a pro-Western dictatorship in the South (with its capital city of Saigon) and a Communist dictatorship in the North (with the capital in Hanoi). The United States began to prop up the anti-Communist government in the South, which it dubbed as "democratic" and which refused to abide by the Geneva Agreement calling for free elections. Instead, Washington became increasingly tied to the unpopular and repressive regime of Ngo Dinh Diem in South Vietnam. From the very beginning, the United States provided military assistance, as well as economic aid, thus sowing the seeds for direct US intervention once the very existence of the Diem regime was threatened.

With US assistance, South Vietnam became the "guardian" of the "free world." Once that metaphor took root in popular thought, the anti-Communist regime in South Vietnam became identified with the very survival of the United States. For psychological, geopolitical, and domestic political reasons, therefore, US–South Vietnamese relations became a Gordian knot that a succession of US presidents did not dare to cut. When the repressive Diem regime was challenged by an insurgency in the late 1950s, the Second Indochina War began.

Recommended Readings

India and Pakistan

Brown, W. Norman. *The United States and India, Pakistan, Bangladesh.* 3rd ed. Cambridge, Mass.: Harvard University Press, 1972.

Hutchins, Francis G. *India's Revolution: Gandhi and the Quit India Movement.* Cambridge, Mass.: Harvard University Press, 1973.

Merriam, Allen H. *Gandhi vs. Jinnah: The Debate over the Partition of India.* Calcutta: Minerva, 1980.

Scott, Paul. *The Raj Quartet.* Published in various editions between 1966 and 1975. A novel that examines the dark side of the British Raj—its legal and moral pretensions; the questions of race, ethnicity, religion; sexual mores guiding the rulers and their subjects; and the independence movement—at the time of its demise, 1942–1947.

Thorne, Christopher. *Allies of a Kind: The United States, Britain, and the War with Japan.* Oxford, UK: Oxford University Press, 1978.

Vietnam

Duiker, William J. *Ho Chi Minh.* New York: Hyperion, 2000. Definitive biography that emphasizes Ho's nationalism, not Communism, as the wellspring of Ho's ideology.

Fall, Bernard B. *Hell in a Very Small Place: The Siege of Dien Bien Phu.* Philadelphia: Lippincott, 1966. By one of the leading Western authorities on Indochina until his death in Vietnam in 1967.

———, ed. *Ho Chi Minh on Revolution: Selected Writings, 1920–66.* New York: Praeger, 1967. A collection of primary sources.

Joint Chiefs of Staff. *The Joint Chiefs of Staff and the War in Vietnam: History of the Indochina Incident, 1940–1954.* Washington, D.C.: Joint Chiefs of Staff, 1955; declassified 1981. The Pentagon's assessment of why the French lost.

Patti, Archimedes. *Why Vietnam? Prelude to America's Albatross.* Berkeley: University of California Press, 1980. By a US OSS officer who established a working relationship with Ho Chi Minh in 1945.

Vo Nguyen Giap. *People's War, People's Army.* New York: Praeger, 1962. Vo Nguyen Giap's discussion of the nature of wars for national liberation and the reasons for his victory at Dien Bien Phu.

Notes

1. Gandhi's career of passive resistance to the laws of Britain that he considered immoral drew upon the writings of the nineteenth-century US writer Henry David Thoreau, and in turn he influenced the US civil rights leader Martin Luther King Jr.

2. For this and other citations below, see Pankaj Mishra, "Exit Wounds: The Legacy of Indian Partition," *The New Yorker*, August 13, 2007, pp. 80–84.

3. Cited in Francis G. Hutchins, *India's Revolution: Gandhi and the Quit India Movement* (Cambridge, MA: Harvard University Press, 1973), p. 143.

4. Basharat Peer, "The View from Jantar Mantar," *The Nation*, November 19, 2007, p. 42; Mishra, "Exit Wounds," p. 84.

5. Jean Lacouture, *Ho Chi Minh: A Political Biography* (New York: Random House, 1968), pp. 24–25; Chalmer M. Roberts, "Archives Show Ho's Letter," *Washington Post*, September 14, 1969, p. A-25.

6. Ché Guevara, *Guerrilla Warfare* (New York: Vintage Books, 1969), p. 13.

7. Bernard B. Fall, *The Two Vietnams: A Political and Military Analysis*, 2nd rev. ed. (New York: Frederick A. Praeger, 1967), pp. 349–350; Bernard B. Fall, *Last Reflections on a War* (Garden City, NY: Doubleday, 1967), pp. 209–223.

8. David Halberstam, *The Best and the Brightest* (New York: Random House, 1969), p. 141; also Stanley Karnow, *Vietnam: A History* (New York: Viking, 1983), p. 197.

9. James Bamford, *Body of Secrets: Anatomy of the Ultra-Secret National Security Agency* (New York: Doubleday, 2001), p. 286. The names of the pilots, however, are not inscribed in the Vietnam War Memorial in Washington.

10. Bernard B. Fall, "Dienbienphu: A Battle to Remember," in Marvin E. Gettleman, ed., *Vietnam: History, Documents, and Opinions* (Greenwich, CN: Fawcett, 1965), p. 107.

11. Karnow, *Vietnam*, pp. 198–204.

12. Neil Sheehan et al., eds., *The Pentagon Papers* (New York: Bantam, 1971), p. 46. Dulles also sent a copy of the cable to the US delegate at Geneva, Bedell Smith. Eisenhower wrote in his memoirs that Ho Chi Minh would have defeated the last emperor, Bao Dai, with 80 percent of the vote.

6 Decolonization in Africa

Africa was the last frontier of European colonialism. At the close of World War II, the European powers—Britain, France, Belgium, Portugal, and Spain—still held firmly to their colonies, virtually the entire continent. But this was soon to change with the awakening of African nationalism. In 1945, there were only three independent nations on the African continent (Ethiopia, Liberia, and South Africa), but by 1980 there were more than fifty independent African nations.

By the mid-1950s, the British government, already having lost India and Palestine, recognized the inevitability of decolonization and began preparing for it. By the end of that decade the French, too, had resigned themselves—even in Algeria—to the new reality. The 1960s in Africa were full of excitement and expectation as power changed hands from the white colonial masters to new black African rulers who were flush with nationalistic pride and eager to face the new challenges of nationhood. The transition was relatively smooth in many colonies and was achieved faster and with less bloodshed than an earlier generation—black or white—had dreamed possible. Yet it was also a process that many European colonialists—notably in Algeria and Kenya—bitterly resisted.

The Rise of Nationalism

The idea that Africans belonged to a nation was difficult to instill among the population who, as a rule, identified with their tribe or ethnic group, not a centralized state. The colonies had boundaries that had been artificially created by the Europeans in the previous century. The inhabitants of any given colony were not all of the same ethnic group, and in some cases one ethnic group was spread over more than one colony. In sub-Saharan Africa, no colony came close to containing a majority ethnic group. The growth of nationalism thus required

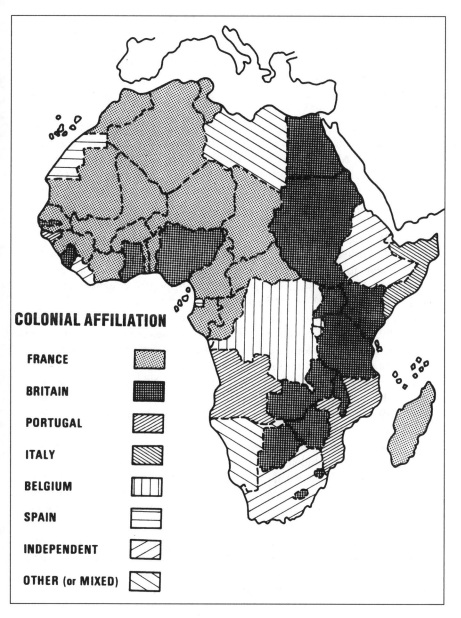

COLONIAL AFFILIATION

FRANCE

BRITAIN

PORTUGAL

ITALY

BELGIUM

SPAIN

INDEPENDENT

OTHER (or MIXED)

Colonial Africa (1945)

that loyalty to tribe be shifted to loyalty to nation. The timing of decolonization in the various colonies therefore depended, to a great extent, on the growth of a national consciousness and the development of a sense of political unity. This was a slow and difficult process to achieve and was still far from complete in the 1950s. After independence, the persistence of tribal loyalties continued to plague the new nations.

Prior to World War II, European colonial rule was hardly challenged by the subject peoples of Africa. The colonial administrations seemed so secure that they needed little military force to protect them. In some cases, especially in British colonies, this was achieved by use of the protectorate system, whereby local African rulers were allowed to retain considerable autonomy and were protected by the colonial "overlords," a classic case of divide-and-conquer. Local rulers were made more secure by the military, political, and financial support supplied by their colonial masters. In this fashion, the Europeans blocked the development of African unity, or even tribal unity, that might threaten their colonial rule. In general, the Africans, the majority of whom were illiterate, viewed the Europeans with mixed awe and fear, and they were hesitant to attempt armed insurrection. And since political consciousness remained relatively low, there seemed little prospect of effective, organized anticolonialist action by the African blacks.

Gradually this situation changed as more Africans received an education— ironically, at the hands of the Europeans—and gained more experience in and exposure to the world of the Europeans. The very presence of Europeans in Africa fundamentally altered African society, particularly in the cities. On the one hand, the Europeans created a labor class among the blacks, whose cheap labor was exploited; and on the other hand, the Europeans created new educational and economic opportunities as well as new models for the Africans. Colonialism carried within it the seeds of its own destruction, especially when the Europeans espoused democracy and civil liberties, ideas antithetical to colonialism—an institution based on force, racial superiority (and a professed desire to civilize the natives), economic exploitation, and the rule of the few. After generations under colonial rule, a native elite emerged, marked by its Western education and values. Many of the early leaders tended to be lawyers or officers in the colonial armies. It was this class that first developed a sense of grievance and frustration, and then a political and historical consciousness marked by a strong desire to liberate black Africa. The bond among these new nationalist leaders developed into a pan-Africanist movement in which they sought unity in the cause of liberating the whole of Africa from colonial rule.

Although signs of African restiveness appeared in the prewar period, especially as Africans felt the effects of the Great Depression of the 1930s, it was not until World War II that nationalism and the demand for independence gained strength. Some African leaders pointed out that their people, who had been called upon to participate in that war to help defeat tyranny and defend liberty, deserved their just reward, a greater measure of that liberty. They were also stimulated by the example of colonies in Asia winning their independence from the same Europeans who ruled them. The French defeat at Dien Bien Phu, for instance, had an electrifying impact on African independence movements. And in India, Jawaharlal Nehru vigorously championed the cause of decolonization in the United Nations and other forums. The founding of the United Nations also gave heart to the African nationalists, who looked forward to the day when their new nations would join its ranks as full-fledged member nations. The two superpowers, the United States and the Soviet Union, as the professed champions of oppressed peoples everywhere, also urged early decolonization.

As important as the growth of nationalism in Africa was in preparing the way for independence, that objective would not have been achieved so swiftly had Britain, France, and the other colonial nations not come to the realization— albeit grudgingly—that it was not in their interest to perpetuate their colonial empires on that continent. The British were the first to come to that realization, but eventually the French and Belgians also came to the same view.

The British Departure

In a gradual, step-by-step manner, the British permitted greater participation by the native peoples in the governing of their colonies. They established executive and legislative councils to advise the royal governors of the colonies, and began to appoint a few well-educated black Africans to these councils. Next, black political leaders were permitted to seek election to the legislative council. Once this was granted, the nationalist leaders began convening national congresses and organizing political parties, which became organs of nationalistic, anti-imperialist propaganda. They also began agitating for expanding the right to vote in the legislative council elections. The granting of universal suffrage—the right to vote—was the turning point, for it paved the way for the nationalist, pro-independence parties to gain power. According to the parliamentary system that operated in British colonies, the party that won the election and gained the majority seats in the legislature earned the right to appoint the prime minister.

The first native Africans to achieve this position were usually charismatic figures who had long been recognized as leaders of the national independence movement. Typically, the one chosen was an able and articulate leader who had a Western education, had spent many years as a political organizer and agitator, and had spent not a few years in the jails of the British colonial administration.

This procedure took place first in the Gold Coast, the first of Britain's African sub-Saharan colonies to gain independence. In this West African colony, the able nationalist leader Kwame Nkrumah organized an effective political movement, taking advantage not only of the legal political process, but also of various forms of illegal political pressure, including "positive action"— namely, strikes and boycotts. In 1951, in the first election under universal suffrage, Nkrumah managed his party's campaign while sitting in a British prison. After Nkrumah's party won a large majority, the British governor had little choice but to release him, now a national hero, and granted him a seat on the executive council. Three years later, in March 1957, the colony gained its independence, with Nkrumah becoming its first prime minister. Henceforth, the Gold Coast became known as Ghana, after the ancient empire of Ghana that controlled much of West Africa.

Ghana became the model for other African independence movements, and Nkrumah became the continent's most outspoken champion of liberation. In 1958, Nkrumah invited leading African politicians, representing African peoples from the entire continent, to two conferences at Accra, the capital of Ghana. These conferences greatly promoted and advanced the cause of pan-African unity. It was there that the Organization of African Unity was created. The delegates unanimously endorsed Nkrumah's call for the complete liberation of Africa.

The demand for independence spread rapidly across Africa. In Nigeria, the most heavily populated British colony, whose nationalist leaders were

Kwame Nkrumah, first prime minister of Ghana, on a visit to the United States, addresses a New York audience. *(National Archives)*

Kenyan prime minister Jomo Kenyatta, November 1964, ruler of Kenya from independence in 1963 until his death in 1980. *(National Archives)*

among the earliest and most vocal in demanding liberation, the process was delayed until 1960 by serious ethnic conflicts. And in East Africa, Kenya's independence was forestalled by other, very different problems.

Kenya was one of several settler colonies in Africa—among them Algeria, South Africa, and Southern Rhodesia—that contained an entrenched permanent class of European settlers, many of whom had been born in Africa and, indeed, called themselves Africans. Their status was at the expense of the once independent African farmers, who now were reduced to serving the Europeans. In Kenya, the white settlers, numbering about 40,000, lived in the Kenyan highlands, possessed the best lands, and controlled the economic and political levers of power. Their opposition to any independence movement based on majority rule ran deep.

The largest tribe in Kenya, the Kikuyu, reacted against the domination and exploitation by the white settlers. In World War II, 75,000 Kenyans had served in the British army and now they expected fairer treatment. In 1952, the hitherto peaceful Kikuyus launched a movement known as the "burning spear," or Mau Mau. The primary aim of the Mau Mau was to return the land to the black population. Not only had blacks been dispossessed, but they were also forbidden to compete with the white farmers. Cash crops for export—such as coffee, tea, and sisal—were to be grown only by the Europeans.

The uprising, between 1952 and 1960, terrorized the white settlers but eventually directed most of its violence toward other blacks who represented the hierarchy the British had created. The Mau Mau insurrection thus also became a civil war between the Mau Mau and those loyal to Britain (such as local chiefs and Christians). The Mau Mau killed approximately 2,000 black Africans, thirty-two European settlers, and fewer than 200 British soldiers and police.

The British response was all out of proportion to the uprising they faced. After the loss of India and Palestine, the British saw Kenya as their most important colony, and to hold on to it they used any and all means—arbitrary arrests, hard labor, the bribing of judges to obtain convictions, torture of every conceivable sort (including dogs that mauled prisoners, castration, men forced to sodomize each other), collective punishment of entire villages (some of which were set on fire), the resettlement of nearly the entire Kikuyu population of 1.5 million in 800 "new villages" (detention camps surrounded by barbed wire), and the strafing of villages from airplanes, in the end killing, at a minimum, 100,000 Kikuyus. Between 1953 and 1958, the British hanged 1,090 Kikuyus. Nowhere in the annals of British imperialism had the authorities executed so many. Kenya became a police state in the proper sense of the word.

At first, British authorities dismissed accounts of the stark brutality the British employed as rumormongering or the acts of a few individuals who had strayed from the norms of civilization. After eleven Kikuyus died at the Hola prison in March 1959, however, the British position in Kenya became untenable.

Investigations revealed that the prisoners had been clubbed to death. The murders at Hola marked the end of Britain's "civilizing mission" in Kenya.[1]

The Kikuyu and other tribes eventually formed a national party under the leadership of Jomo Kenyatta. Kenyatta, a London-educated member of the Kikuyu tribe, had languished in a British jail for over seven years as a political prisoner. One of the many mistakes the British committed was to conclude that the moderate Kenyatta headed the Mau Mau uprising. In May 1960, while still in prison, he led his party, the Kenyan African National Union, to political victory. When Kenya gained its independence in December 1963, he became its first prime minister. Kenyatta's party and the outgoing British colonial authorities worked out a political formula, embodied in a new constitution, designed to provide for majority rule and yet protect the white minority.

Included was a tacit agreement not to dwell on the atrocities the British had committed. A small number of Europeans left, but those who remained were victimized neither by Kenya's black majority nor by the new government. Indeed, Kenyatta made sure that the losers in the new Kenya were the Mau Mau. There was no land reform and the Europeans and black loyalists kept their government jobs. Kenyatta went so far as to bury this sordid episode in British colonial history, declaring the Mau Mau "a disease which has been eradicated, and must never be remembered again." To this day, there is no official memorial to the Mau Mau—the architects of Kenyan independence—in Nairobi.

In south-central Africa there remained three British settler colonies: Nyasaland, Northern Rhodesia, and Southern Rhodesia. They were joined to form a federation in 1953, partly for economic reasons and partly as a means of retaining rule by the white minorities. However, in response to increasing pressure by the majority black populations, the British dissolved the federation and imposed on Nyasaland and Northern Rhodesia constitutions guaranteeing majority rule, thus ending white minority rule. In 1961, Nyasaland under black rule became independent Malawi, and in 1963, Northern Rhodesia became the African-ruled state of Zambia.

In Southern Rhodesia, however, a white minority regime, led by Ian Smith, defied the British government and its own black majority by rejecting its British-made, majority-rule constitution and by unilaterally declaring its independence in 1965 and withdrawal from the British Commonwealth. Only after prolonged guerrilla attacks by African nationalist parties from bases in neighboring countries and sustained international pressure did Smith finally relent, accepting a plan in 1976 to allow majority rule two years afterward. Continued fighting among rival nationalist parties delayed until 1980 the creation of a black majority government in the country, now known as Zimbabwe. The hero of the resistance, Robert Mugabe, became the nation's first prime minister elected by popular vote.

The French Departure

The French colonial system was different from the British, and this meant that the decolonization process was also different, even though the timetable was similar. The aim of French colonial policy had been the assimilation of its African colonies into the French empire and the transformation of the African natives into French citizens. The blacks were enjoined to abandon their culture in favor of the "superior" French civilization. They were taught the French language and culture, and the elites among them received their higher educations at French universities. No attempt was ever made to prepare the native Africans for independence; however, because the colonies were part of the French empire, they were permitted to send elected representatives to Paris, where they held seats in the French National Assembly.

There always was a problem with the French program of assimilation in that it assumed that the population of the French African colonies wanted to become and in fact were somehow capable of becoming "French." In the case of Algeria, the assimilation of Muslim Arabs proved to be impossible, as the French settlers and the Arabs both rejected it. The Arabs and black Africans always understood that they were, first and foremost, conquered subjects. There was no point for black schoolchildren to recite the lessons written for French children in Paris: "Our ancestors the Gauls had blue eyes and blond hair." At its worst, assimilation as Paris envisioned it was racist; at its best, it was unabashedly ethnocentric. A greater French union of France and the former colonies could have succeeded only on the basis of equality and on the recognition of cultural and racial diversity.

Until the mid-1950s, none of the short-lived cabinets in postwar France—desperately trying to suppress an anticolonial rebellion in Indochina—responded to the African demands for self-rule. However, at this juncture, immediately after abandoning Indochina, France was faced with a revolutionary movement in Algeria and a growing demand for independence in its other African colonies. With the exception of Algeria, where the French refused to budge, the African colonies of France were surprised to find a new French receptiveness to change. The French no longer insisted upon assimilation; instead, they began to search for a workable alternative.

African nationalists who desired the liberation of their people still found it necessary to work within the French system. The most politically successful of the black African leaders from the French colonies was Félix Houphouët-Boigny, a medical doctor from the Ivory Coast. Shortly after World War II, he had taken the lead in forming a political party that championed the cause of the blacks. As a member of the French National Assembly, Houphouët-Boigny played a leading role in drawing up a new colonial policy that set in motion the movement for colonial self-government. The effect of this bill, which was passed by the assembly in June 1956, was to permit greater autonomy for the separate French colonies, which heretofore were under one centralized colonial administration, the Ministry of Overseas France. Each colony was now to have a French prime minister and African vice-ministers, as well as elections for legislative assemblies under universal suffrage. Meanwhile, in the various French colonies, Houphouët-Boigny's party established branches, which began organizing for elections under the banner of nationalism.

Still, it remained the intent of France to maintain some form of indirect control over its African colonies. A plan for continued association was endorsed by President Charles de Gaulle, after he came to power in Paris in May 1958. Later that year, he offered the twelve sub-Saharan colonies the option of membership in the French Union or immediate and full independence. The former meant autonomy but continued association with France; more important, it meant continued French economic and military aid. This was the preference of all of the colonies except Guinea, which opted instead for independence. In response to Guinea's decision, France immediately pulled out all of its personnel and equipment and terminated all economic aid in hopes of forcing the maverick back into the fold. Guinea, however, stuck with its decision.

The example of Guinea, and nearby Ghana as well, inspired the nationalist leaders in the neighboring French colonies in West Africa. In 1960, after two years of agitation and negotiations, President de Gaulle, with his hands full in Algeria, abruptly granted independence to all of the remaining French colonies in sub-Saharan Africa. These new nations were relatively unprepared either politically or economically for independence, and consequently they tended to remain politically unstable and economically dependent on France for years to come.

The French in Algeria

France's determination to retain control over Algeria must be viewed in the historical context of its war in Vietnam, a conflict that had drained the French people emotionally, physically, and economically. When defeat came in 1954, the French accepted the loss of Vietnam without bitter recrimination. Vietnam was finally seen as a burden to be lifted from their shoulders. There were few dissenting voices in the spring of 1954 when Prime Minister Pierre Mendès-France promised to end the war by granting the Vietnamese their independence. With the Geneva Conference of July 1954, the French colonial presence on the Asian mainland came to an inglorious end.

Yet, within five months of the Geneva settlement, the French faced once more the prospect of losing another important colony. This time it was Algeria. The French, having lost one colony, were in no mood to accept another humiliation at the hands of a colonized people of a different color and religion. At stake were France's honor and its role as a great power.

The French insisted that Algeria was not a colony but an integral part of France, a province across the Mediterranean, in the same manner that Brittany, Alsace, and Lorraine were provinces. (US president Dwight Eisenhower compared it to Texas.) More important, Algeria was the home of 1 million Europeans, individuals who considered themselves to be living in France. Mendès-France, the prime minister who had taken France out of Vietnam, now insisted that Algeria was "part of the republic," that it had "been French for a long time. Between it and the mainland, no secession is conceivable. . . . Never will France . . . yield on this fundamental principle." His minister of the interior, François Mitterrand, added: "Algeria is France."[2]

France's presence in Algeria dated back to 1830 when its troops first landed there. It took the French seventeen years to complete the conquest of a people who spoke Arabic and professed the faith of Islam, a religion remarkably impervious to Christian missionaries. (For a summary of Islam, see Chapter 20.) In 1848, the first French Roman Catholic settlers arrived. The French quest for empire here became a bitter struggle between two cultures and two religions. In 1870–1871, in the wake of France's defeat in its war with Prussia, the Arab population rose in rebellion. The uprising was put down in blood and was followed by the widespread confiscation of Muslim lands. Algeria became a land divided between the immigrant French, who had seized the best lands along the coast and who enjoyed the rights and protection of French citizenship, and the native Algerians, for whom the law offered little protection. The French always justified their conquest as part of their *mission civilisatrice*, yet the blessings of French democracy were meant only for Europeans in Algeria, not for the indigenous Arab and Muslim population.

In the years between the two world wars (1918–1939), the French government grappled repeatedly with the question of the status of native Algerians. Liberals, both French and Algerian, urged the integration of the Muslim Algerians into French society by granting them citizenship without first having to convert to Catholicism. In 1936, France's premier, Leon Blum, proposed a bill granting a number of select Arabs—soldiers with distinguished records in World War I, teachers, graduates from French institutes—the privilege of French citizenship even though they continued to profess the faith of their ancestors. Unrelenting opposition killed the bill—and with it the opportunity of integrating Algeria with France.

A synthesis of Algerian and French societies was a pipe dream pursued by a liberal minority. The French settlers in Algeria refused to consider it; the same may be said of most Muslims. They, too, could not envision themselves as French. As one Muslim scholar put it: "The Algerian people are not French, do not wish to be and could not be even if they did wish." Children in Muslim schools were taught to recite: "Islam is my religion. Arabic is my language. Algeria is my country."[3]

World War II had been fought for the noblest of reasons: against fascism, racism, and colonialism, and for democracy and human rights. It was little wonder that at the end of the war the colonial peoples in Asia and Africa demanded the implementation of these ideals for which, moreover, many of their compatriots had died fighting in the armies of the colonial powers. Inevitably, after the war the Algerians presented the bill for their services to the French.

The first manifestation of the new Algerian attitude became apparent even before the guns fell silent in Europe. On May 1, 1945, during the May Day celebrations in Algiers, Algerian demonstrators staged an unauthorized march carrying banners denouncing French rule and demanding Algerian independence. The French attempt to halt the demonstration led to the deaths of ten Algerians and one European. The French then boasted that they had ended all disorder. But several days later, on May 8, 1945, the V-E (Victory-in-Europe) Day parade in the Algerian city of Setif turned into a riot. The French had hoisted their victorious tricolor flag. Algerian participants, however, had their own agenda. Again they came with banners calling for the independence of Algeria—and one young man defiantly carried Algeria's forbidden green-and-white flag with the red crescent. A police officer shot him to death.

This act touched off a spontaneous anticolonial rebellion—and one of the bloodiest repressions by a European power. The heavy-handed French response included aerial and naval bombardments of Algerian villages. The British, as they did later that year in Vietnam when they secured Saigon for the French upon the defeat of the Japanese, came to the assistance of their French colonial counterparts when they provided airplanes to carry French troops from France, Morocco, and Tunisia. When the fighting was over, the French conducted wholesale arrests—the traditional European policy after colonial outbreaks. The French killed between 1,165 (according to their official count) and 45,000 Arabs (according to Algerian estimates).[4] The Office of Strategic Services, the US wartime intelligence-gathering organization, put the number of casualties at between 16,000 and 20,000, including 6,000 dead,[5] a figure that is still generally accepted. The rebellion claimed the lives of 103 Europeans. On May 13, the French staged a military parade in Constantine to impress upon the Algerians the decisive nature of their victory. The Algerians quickly found out that World War II had been a war for the liberation of the French from German occupation, not for the liberation of the French colonies from French domination.

French society was nearly unanimous in its response to Algerian defiance. Politicians of all stripes, including the Communist Party—whose official position was one of anticolonialism—strongly supported the suppression of the uprising. The French colonial authorities blamed the violence in part on food shortages, refusing to acknowledge that the rebellion had been fueled primarily by a deep-seated opposition to French racism and colonialism.

For nine years relative stability prevailed in Algeria. When the next rebellion broke out, it was not a spontaneous uprising as had been the case in 1945. This time the revolution was organized by the FLN (Front de Libération Nationale), which turned to the traditional weapon of the weak—terror and guerrilla warfare.[6] Terrorists and guerrillas have little hope to defeat an adversary whose military strength is formidable. They seek, instead, to intimidate and to keep the struggle alive in the hope of breaking the other side's will.

The conflict became one of extraordinary brutality. The FLN resorted to bombing attacks against European targets; the Europeans then, predictably, bombed Muslim establishments. The French army responded with its own terror, torturing and executing prisoners in order to uncover the FLN's organizational structure. In 1956, France's Parliament—with the express support of the Communist Party—granted General Jacques Massu of the Tenth Parachute Division absolute authority to do whatever was necessary. The subsequent "Battle of Algiers" ended with the destruction of the FLN's leadership. Brute force had triumphed over brute force, and within a year the uprising appeared to be over.

But the rebellion continued as new leaders emerged. Algerians such as Ferhat Abbas, who had devoted their lives to cooperation with the French, joined the rebellion. The million French settlers in Algeria demanded an increase in military protection. French military strength, initially at 50,000, rose to 400,000, and that figure does not include the number of Algerians who fought on the French side and who alone outnumbered the estimated 25,000 armed rebels. In the end, 2–3 million Arabs (out of a population of 9 million) were driven from their villages to become refugees, and perhaps as many as a million had died.

Gradually, many in France began to comprehend the unpalatable truth that Algeria would never be French. By the late 1950s, the French, who had been unified on the Algerian question in 1954, began an intense debate of the subject. The war now divided French society to the point that it threatened to touch off a civil war. One of the telling arguments against the continued French presence in Algeria was that it corrupted the soldiers who were serving in an army guilty of repeated atrocities. Many French (not unlike many of their US counterparts during the war in Vietnam) became more concerned about the effect that the killing, the brutality, and the torture had on their own society than their impact on the Arab victims. The costs of the continuing struggle were outweighing the benefits. The time had come to quit Algeria.

It took an exceptional political leader, General Charles de Gaulle, who had emerged from World War II as the supreme symbol of French resistance to Nazi Germany and of French honor, to take a deeply divided France out of

Algeria. The colonials in Algeria continued to insist that as French citizens they had the right of military protection; the army, too, was determined to stay. By 1957, the gravest issue before France was no longer the Algerian uprising, but a sequence of "white rebellions," led by the military officers who sought numerous times to assassinate de Gaulle. This threatened to topple the constitutional government of France itself and plunge the nation into a civil war.

A decade earlier, in 1947, de Gaulle had tied the fate of Algeria to France's status as a great power: "We must never allow the fact that Algeria is our domain to be called into question in any way whatever from within or from without." Since then conditions had changed, however, and so had de Gaulle's position. After he became president in June 1958, he sought at first to resolve the conflict by offering the Algerians what all previous French governments had refused. He announced the rectification of inequalities between Algerians and Europeans, which included the Algerians' right to vote. In this way, Algeria was to remain a part of France. Arab nationalists, however, rejected this solution, which might have worked before hostilities had commenced in 1954. Now nothing short of independence would do. De Gaulle's choices were now narrowed down to either crushing the rebellion or withdrawal. He chose the latter. In the summer of 1960, he began talking publicly of an *"Algérie algeriénne,"* which, he declared, would have "its own government, its institutions and its laws."[7] When he took an inspection trip to Algeria in December 1960, the European residents organized a general strike to protest his policies, demanding an *"Algérie française!"*

In July 1962, de Gaulle quit Algeria in the face of intense opposition within his own army and from the settlers in Algeria, nearly all of whom left for France and never forgave de Gaulle for his betrayal. Only 170,000 French citizens remained when Algeria formally declared its independence in July 1962. The withdrawal marked the end of France as a colonial power.

The rebellion was led by men who had been educated by the French, many of whom had fought with distinction in the French army during World War II. Although Muslim leaders threw in their lot with the FLN, the French-educated, socialist leadership had no regard for Islam. (The Algerian women who joined the rebellion did so in opposition to both French colonialism and the Islamic veil.) They had no intention of establishing an Islamic republic. Indeed, at the time of the FLN's creation in Cairo in March 1954, Ahmed Ben Bella, one of the legendary nine founders of the FLN, profusely apologized to an Egyptian audience for his inability to address them in Arabic.[8] Nor did these men seek a social revolution, although they described themselves as socialists—in line with the prevailing trend in Western Europe and in the colonial world. Nearly all independence leaders after World War II—from Mao to Nehru, Ho Chi Minh, Castro, and so on—professed one form of socialism or another.

The new leaders of Algeria were interested, first and foremost, in the exercise of power. Ben Bella, who became independent Algeria's first president, was soon overthrown by his defense minister and then imprisoned. The revolution was over. The military then sought—successfully—to preserve one-party rule. When, in 1991–1992, under the influence of the Islamic revolution in Iran and the rise of Islamic fervor throughout the Arab world, the Islamic Salvation Front party was about to win the elections, the military cancelled the elections. The result was an extraordinarily bloody civil war during which an estimated 100,000 people perished, the army and the Islamic militants both committing untold atrocities. Journalists were prevented—by means of press censorship and assassination—from investigating independently the army's complicity in massacres it attributed to the insurgents. The army continued to control the political candidates, settling in 1999 on Abdelaziz Bouteflika, the new front man for the continuing military dictatorship. In late 2001, US president George W. Bush welcomed Algeria as an ally in his global war on terror.

The Belgian and Portuguese Departures

The Belgian government paid even less attention than France to preparing the Belgian Congo for independence. The Congo, once the private domain of King Leopold II, was one of the largest and richest of the African colonies. Between 1885 and 1908, Leopold controlled what he called euphemistically the Congo Free State, where he exercised complete control, referring to himself as its "proprietor." He never visited his possession, preferring to live off his fortune (estimated at more than $1 billion in current dollars) on yachts and luxury villas on the French Riviera. His legacy was the rule of terror and exploitation leading to the deaths of perhaps up to 10 million Africans—nearly half of the population—during the next forty years, either killed outright, ravaged by disease, or worked to death mining ore and harvesting rubber.[9]

In the twentieth century, the Belgian colonial policy changed little. In response to the outbreak of insurrection in the city of Leopoldville in early January 1959, however, the Belgian government hastily issued plans for the creation of what it described as a new democratic order for the Congo. The new government in Leopoldville was to be based on universal suffrage and was to guarantee the liberties of all of its people and eliminate any further racial discrimination. In January 1960, the Belgian government made the stunning announcement that in only six months it would formally transfer power to the new sovereign state of the Republic of the Congo.

The turbulent events that followed independence gave proof that the Congo was ill prepared for self-rule and that it had been too hastily abandoned by Belgium. The Belgians left behind but a handful of university-trained Congolese. Among the 5,000 senior administrators, only three were native Congolese. Kwame Nkrumah charged that the Belgians' motto was "no elite, no trouble."[10] The sudden Belgian departure contributed to an explosion of ethnic rivalry (the Congo had over 200 different ethnic groups) and separatist wars. The violence was also the consequence of the lack of development of a nationalism sufficient to pull the new country's ethnic groups into a national union. Even before the Belgians exited, a rift had developed between the two most noted nationalist leaders: Patrice Lumumba and Joseph Kasavubu. Lumumba traveled throughout the Congo exhorting people to see themselves as citizens of a unitary state with a strong central government. Subsequently, he became the country's only democratically elected prime minister. Kasavubu, in contrast, insisted upon a loose federation of autonomous regions based on tribal affiliation. No sooner had the two established rival regimes than Moise Tshombe, the separatist leader of the rich copper-mining province of Katanga, announced the secession of that province from the new republic. The result was not only a complicated, three-sided political struggle, but also a tragic war that soon involved outside forces, including Belgian and UN troops, the CIA, Soviet advisors, and Ché Guevara, fresh from the Cuban revolution. Foreign intervention could only contribute to what became an extraordinarily violent war that lasted over two years and left tens of thousands dead.

The Congolese army, weakened by the mutiny of black soldiers against their white officers and divided in loyalty between the contending leaders, Lumumba and Kasavubu, was unable to maintain order. Nor could either leader match the Katangan forces of Tshombe, whose army remained under the command of Belgian officers. Tshombe, who had the support of the Union Minière, the huge corporation that controlled the copper mines, and of the white settlers, invited Belgian reinforcements into Katanga to defend its independence. Desperate to maintain Congolese national unity, Lumumba requested military assistance from the United Nations. The UN Security Council called upon Belgium to withdraw its forces from the Congo and dispatched a peacekeeping force with instructions to prevent a civil war. The United Nations, however, proved to be impotent as its member states were in disagreement about its role in the Congo.[11] Frustrated by the UN failure to act decisively against Katanga, and still unable to defeat Katanga's Belgian-led forces, Lumumba then turned to the Soviet Union for support. This complicated the situation all the more as the Western powers moved to check the Soviet influence. Kasavubu, with the help of Colonel Joseph Mobutu and the CIA, overthrew Lumumba, who was then delivered to his Katangan enemies, who murdered him. The democratic experiment was over.

The Republic of the Congo managed to survive with the province of Katanga included, but only after Kasavubu brought Tshombe and his followers into the government on their own terms. About a year later, in November 1965, both Kasavubu and Tshombe were overthrown in a military coup by their erstwhile ally Mobutu, by now a general, who then established a lasting, brutal, and dreadfully corrupt regime. Under Mobutu, the Congo (which

Mobutu renamed Zaire in 1971, as part of an Africanization campaign) reverted to the status under King Leopold when Mobutu, too, treated it as his private preserve. In the process, Mobutu—like Leopold before him—became one of the richest men on earth, even acquiring villas on the Riviera, while his country descended into poverty and degradation.

The Katangan secessionist war and its aftermath severely damaged the credibility of African nationalists who had insisted on the readiness of Africans for self-government. It also had the effect of exposing the weakness of the United Nations as a neutral peacekeeping body. There was little, however, that the United Nations could do as its two most influential members were competing for influence. The conflict in the Congo was part and parcel of the recurrent East-West power struggles in the Third World.

* * *

By the end of the 1960s, in the south of Africa, Portugal still stubbornly held on to its colonies, Angola and Mozambique. Portugal, a small country under the dictatorship of António Salazar from 1929 to 1968, regarded its African possessions—which together amounted to twenty times the size of Portugal itself—as "overseas provinces," that is, as integral parts of the nation and not colonies at all. Portugal savagely suppressed a nationalist insurrection in Angola in 1961, killing about 50,000 people, and quashed a similar uprising in Mozambique in 1964. The Salazar regime ignored UN condemnation and continued its use of force to subdue guerrilla resistance. Not until the overthrow of Salazar's dictatorship in April 1974 (Salazar himself having died in 1970) did Portugal take steps to grant independence to its African colonies. The transfer of power to an independent Angola in 1975 was accompanied by the eruption of warfare among rival nationalist parties, each of which had international supporters, and the country remained a scene of domestic violence and East-West contention for many years. The Portuguese, exhausted by the conflict in Angola, decided in June 1975 to grant independence to Mozambique as well.

African solidarity, as expressed in Nkrumah's African Union, remained an impossible dream thwarted by ethnic and national differences, ambitious rulers who had their own national and personal agendas, and the question of what, specifically, it was meant to accomplish. In the early twenty-first century, when the African Union sought to deal with genocide in the Darfur region of Sudan, it had only modest success in mitigating the violence there.

The African nationalists who had led the struggle for independence also championed the cause of democracy, but it soon became clear that the attainment of the former did not guarantee the success of the latter. Even where genuine efforts were made to establish democratic institutions, officials who had gained power by the democratic electoral process were, all too often, loath to risk their positions in another election. The principle of a loyal opposition (i.e., tolerance of opposing political parties) remained an abstraction. Eventually, most elected African governments gave way to dictatorships, the notable exceptions being Senegal, Ivory Coast, Tanzania, and Botswana.

The rulers of the newly independent African nations, especially the former French colonies, also found it extremely difficult to maintain a sound economy and raise their people's standard of living—as they had earlier promised. They were soon to find that independence itself brought no magic solution to the struggle against poverty and that they would remain far more dependent economically on their former colonial rulers than they had hoped. One unanticipated financial burden on the new governments of Africa was the ever increasing cost of maintaining armed forces that they deemed were necessary to safeguard internal security. Eventually, such armies became the major threat to the security of African rulers and their governments.

Despite the numerous problems that lay ahead (see Chapter 12), the liberation of Africa stands as a momentous historical event. In retrospect, however, the tasks of nation-building, sustaining economic growth, and maintaining democratic institutions proved to be more difficult than anyone had anticipated.

Recommended Readings

Black Africa

Anderson, David. *Histories of the Hanged: The Dirty War in Kenya and the End of Empire.* New York: Norton, 2005.
> Based largely on the official record in London.

Brendon, Piers. *The Decline and Fall of the British Empire, 1781–1997.* New York: Knopf, 2008.
> A reminder that the history of empires, in the words of Edward Gibbon, "is the history of human misery," rebellion, and decline.

Cameron, James. *The African Revolution.* New York: Random House, 1961.
> A stirring contemporary account of the independence movement in Africa by a British journalist.

Cartey, Wilfred, and Martin Kilson, eds. *The African Reader: Independent Africa.* New York: Random House, 1970.
> A useful anthology of writings by participants in the African independence movement.

Elkins, Caroline. *Imperial Reckoning: The Untold Story of Britain's Gulag in Kenya.* New York: Henry Holt, 2005.
> An oral history telling the stories of the survivors.

Hochschild, Adam. *King Leopold's Ghost: A Story of Greed, Terror, and Heroism in Colonial Africa.* Boston: Houghton Mifflin, 1999.
> The story of unchecked colonialist exploitation, slavery, and the murder of millions.

Mazrui, Ali A. *The Africans: A Triple Heritage.* Boston: Little, Brown, 1986.
> An introduction to the culture and politics of Africa by a native of Kenya whose emphasis is on the European colonial heritage; a companion volume of the BBC/WETA television series.

Mazrui, Ali A., and Michael Tidy. *Nationalism and New States in Africa.* London: Heinemann Educational Books, 1984.
A survey of the decolonization process in Africa, focusing on Ghana.
Oliver, Roland, and Anthony Atmore. *Africa Since 1800.* 3rd ed. New York: Cambridge University Press, 1981.

Algeria

Fanon, Frantz. *A Dying Colonialism.* New York: Monthly Review Press, orig. 1959; English edition, 1965.
By a native of the West Indies, a psychiatrist, whose focus is on the psychological oppression and disorientation French colonialism created in Algeria.
———. *The Wretched of the Earth.* New York: Grove Press, 1963.
Fanon's most influential book on the psychological and economic impacts of colonialism.
Horne, Alistair. *A Savage War of Peace: Algeria, 1954–1962.* New York: Viking, 1977.
Reissued in paperback nearly thirty years later, in 2006, still the authoritative history of the war.
Talbott, John. *The War Without a Name: France in Algeria, 1954–1962.* New York: Random House, 1980.

Notes

1. David Anderson, *Histories of the Hanged: The Dirty War in Kenya and the End of Empire* (New York: W. W. Norton, 2005); also Caroline Elkins, *Imperial Reckoning: The Untold Story of Britain's Gulag in Kenya* (New York: Henry Holt, 2005).

2. Pierre Mendès-France and François Mitterrand, cited in John Talbott, *The War Without a Name: France in Algeria, 1954–1962* (New York: Random House, 1980), p. 39.

3. Abdelhamid Ben Badis, one of the founders in 1931 of the Society of Reformist Ulema, in Tanya Matthews, *War in Algeria: Background for Crisis* (New York: Fordham University Press, 1961), p. 20.

4. Frantz Fanon, *A Dying Colonialism* (New York: Monthly Review Press, 1965), p. 74.

5. "Moslem Uprisings in Algeria, May 1945," Record Group 226, OSS Research and Analysis Report 3135, May 30, 1945, pp. 1–6, National Archives, Washington, D.C.

6. The distinction between terrorism and guerrilla tactics has always been blurred. Guerrilla action is a type of warfare (which frequently uses terror); terror is a form of political propaganda. The FLN in Algeria was primarily a terrorist organization. The guerrillas of the NLF in Vietnam, no stranger to the uses of terror, went into combat. All guerrillas have been labeled by their opponents as terrorists, bandits, and the like. None of the studies on contemporary terror have yet come up with a generally accepted definition of the term. Richard E. Rubenstein, *Alchemists of Revolution: Terrorism in the Modern World* (New York: Basic Books, 1987), defines it as "politically motivated violence engaged in by small groups claiming to represent the masses." That would include the FLN and the French government. To complicate matters further, no one ever admits to being a terrorist.

7. Samuel B. Blumenfeld's epilogue in Michael Clark, *Algeria in Turmoil: The Rebellion, Its Causes, Its Effects, Its Future* (New York: Grosset and Dunlap, 1960), pp. 443–454.

8. Gamal Nkrumah, "Ahmed Ben Bella: Plus ça change," *Al-Ahram Weekly Online*, May 10–16, 2001.

9. Revelations of Leopold's greed and brutality prepared the way for the first great human rights crusade—augmented by the writings of Mark Twain and Joseph Conrad—of the twentieth century. See Adam Hochschild, *King Leopold's Ghost: A Story of Greed, Terror, and Heroism in Colonial Africa* (Boston: Houghton Mifflin, 1999).

10. Kwame Nkrumah, *Class Struggle in Africa* (New York: International Publishers, 1970), p. 38.

11. Secretary-General of the United Nations Dag Hammarskjöld made great efforts to resolve conflicts among the disputants in the Congo and among member states of the United Nations disputing the Congo issue. In this effort, he made frequent trips between the UN headquarters in New York and the Congo, and on a trip to Katanga in September 1960 he died in an airplane crash.

7

The Middle East:
The Arab-Israeli Conflict

The Middle East did not escape the anticolonial revolts of the twen-
tieth century. There, however, the resistance to foreign domination was first directed not against a European power but against the Ottoman Turkish Empire,
which had been in control of the region for centuries. But with the defeat of
Turkey in World War I, the Middle East fell under the dominion of other outside forces, Britain and France. Thus, the Arab states merely exchanged one
master for another and, predictably, the anticolonial movement continued. The
result was the gradual weakening of the hand of the European colonial overlords, who slowly began to understand that ultimately they would have to
leave. The Arab world had long been impervious to European cultural penetration, a lesson hammered home to the French during their bloody attempt to
suppress the Algerian revolution. Arab nationalism and culture steeped in Islamic tradition undermined, gradually yet irrevocably, the French and British
positions in the Middle East.

Yet, by a twist of fate, at the same time Arab cultural and political nationalism began to assert itself, the Middle East saw the introduction in the 1880s
of another cultural and political element: the first attempts to re-create a home
for Jews, to reestablish the biblical Zion in Jerusalem, in a region populated
largely by Arabs. The Zionists, primarily of European background, thus
launched their experiment at a time when the European presence in the world
beyond Europe was under direct challenge and retreat.

The Rebirth of Zionism

Contemporary Zionism has its origins in the rebirth of European nationalism,
which soon became transformed—in Germany and elsewhere—into virulent
manifestations of racism. The nineteenth century witnessed the revival of ro-
mantic national consciousness among Europeans who sought to define their

histories, origins, and contributions to civilization. The result was an increased fragmentation of what is commonly called "European civilization." The Germans, Italians, Russians, and Irish, to mention just a few, discovered their uniqueness in their ancient histories and traditions and professed cultural superiority over their neighbors. They all had this in common: They sought to find their proper places in the context of European civilization.

The Jews of Europe were another case in point. Their religion set them apart from the rest of Christian Europe and generally made it impossible for them to achieve cultural and political assimilation. Moreover, the nineteenth century was an extraordinarily race-conscious age. The relative toleration of Jews during the previous century, the Age of Reason, was no more. The legal status of Jews was beginning to deteriorate, particularly in Eastern Europe. As a consequence, a number of European Jews began to contemplate the re-creation of the ancient Jewish state in the biblical land of Zion. The result was the rebirth of Jewish nationalism,[1] an escape from the destructive fury of a rejuvenated anti-Semitism during the last decades of the nineteenth century.

Appropriately, the father of modern Zionism was Leon Pinsker, a Jew from Russia, a nation where anti-Semitism had become state policy. The assassination of Tsar Alexander II in 1881 was blamed on the Jews and touched off anti-Semitic pogroms (massacres). Jews made up a large percentage of the revolutionary movement, and even though it was ethnic Russians who carried out the murder of the tsar, the assassination let loose anti-Semitic passions of unprecedented scope and intensity. It became evident to Pinsker and others that self-preservation demanded the creation of a Jewish state. In 1882, Pinsker published his pamphlet, *Auto Emancipation: An Appeal to His People by a Russian Jew*. The book was instrumental in the creation of a Zionist organization (the "Lovers of Zion") that launched the first wave of emigrants to Palestine. As a result, by the end of the 1880s, the Jewish population of Palestine was 30,000–40,000, about 5 percent of the total population.

In 1897, an Austrian Jew, Theodor Herzl, became the best-known publicist of the Zionist cause when he organized the First World Zionist Congress and published his pamphlet, *The Jewish State*. The creation of such a state, however, faced numerous obstacles. Palestine, as well as nearly the entire Middle East, was in the hands of the Ottoman Empire, a power that sought to suppress manifestations of Jewish as well as Arab nationalism. It was little wonder that Herzl called the first Zionists "beggars . . . with dreams."[2]

The nationalist movements of modern times (i.e., since the end of the Middle Ages) have grown up in the main as reactions to foreign imperialism. The Napoleonic Wars gave birth to German nationalism; the Mongol invasion of Russia gave rise to Russian nationalism; American nationalism came with the wars against the British. Modern Jewish nationalism was the product of an assault on the culture and, ultimately, on the very existence of the Jews. Similarly, the resurgence of Arab nationalism meant resistance against the Turkish

Ottoman Empire. Jewish and Arab nationalism reappeared in Palestine at about the same time. Arabs sought to reclaim their lands; desperate Jews, seeking a safe haven from the gathering fury of anti-Semitism, were claiming the same land.

The early Zionists were slow to grasp that their struggle would ultimately be against the Arabs. Eventually, it became clear to them that the defeat of Turkey would be but the first step of a long journey. David Ben-Gurion, one of the early Zionist settlers and later Israel's first prime minister, overlooked the Arabs until 1916. It was a friend, a Palestinian Arab, who awakened him to the prospect of an Arab-Jewish conflict. The Arab expressed his concern over Ben-Gurion's incarceration when he visited him in a Turkish military prison. "As your friend, I am deeply sorry," he told Ben-Gurion, "but as an Arab I am pleased." "It came down on me like a blow," Ben-Gurion later wrote, "so there is an Arab national movement *here*."[3]

The possibility of a Jewish state surfaced during World War I when Britain launched a drive against Turkey, an ally of imperial Germany. In December 1916, the British advanced from Egypt, and in the following month they entered Jerusalem. By this time, Britain and France had already agreed to carve up the Middle East after Turkey's defeat. By the secret Sykes-Picot Agreement of May 1916, Britain was to extend its influence into Palestine, Iraq, and what shortly became Trans-Jordan, while France claimed Lebanon and Syria.

The British did not foresee the troubles ahead. While fighting the Turks, they had enlisted Arab support and had promised the Arabs nationhood after the war. These pledges had contributed to anti-Turkish rebellions in Jerusalem, Damascus, and other cities long controlled by the Turks. At the same time, however, the British government also enlisted Jewish aid and in return "viewed with favour" the creation of a "national home for the Jewish people" in Palestine. This pledge came in November 1917 in the Balfour Declaration (named after the British foreign secretary) in a one-page letter to Baron Lionel Rothschild, a representative of the Jewish community in England. The declaration also insisted, however, that "nothing shall be done which may prejudice the civil and religious rights of the existing non-Jewish communities in Palestine."[4] The declaration and its later endorsement by the League of Nations gave international sanction to what since 1881 had been a haphazard experiment to create a homeland for Jews.

The Arabs rejected the Balfour Declaration. The promises made by the British, they argued, were at best limited and conditional. A Jewish "national home" in Palestine, they insisted, did not constitute a Jewish state. Moreover, Great Britain had no right to give away Palestine over the heads of its inhabitants. If anything, Britain earlier had promised Palestine to the Arabs in the Hussein-McMahon Letters of 1915–1916. This exchange of letters had led to the Hussein-McMahon Agreement of 1916 (between Sherif Hussein, the emir of

Mecca, and Henry McMahon, Britain's high commissioner in Egypt), whereby the Arabs, in exchange for Britain's recognition of a united Arab state between the Mediterranean and Red Seas, joined Britain in the war against Turkey.

The best that can be said about the British policy is that the authorities in London did their best to satisfy all claimants to the lands of the Middle East that became a part of the British postwar mandate. First, to satisfy the Arabs, they granted Abdullah, the second son of Sherif Hussein, a stretch of territory east of the Jordan River. The British here transferred the easternmost portion of Palestine to what became the Emirate of Trans-Jordan, today's Kingdom of Jordan. The creation of this artificial realm constituted the first partition of Palestine. The remainder of Palestine west of the Jordan River, with its restless Arab and Jewish populations, remained under British rule.

The British soon found out, however, that one cannot serve two clients with conflicting claims without arousing their animosity. Arabs and Jews both suspected that the British were backing away from the commitments they had made. Arabs feared the British sought to establish a Zionist state; Jews feared the British favored the numerically superior Arabs and thus had no intention of honoring the Balfour Declaration. The British, however, had no clear policy except to try to keep the antagonists apart. The consequence of this fence-straddling was that the British eventually came under fire from both Jews and Arabs.

After World War I, Jews and Arabs were determined to create their own national states in Palestine. The clash between Zionists and Palestinians became a conflict fueled by passion, anger, and hatred between two movements insisting on their historic and religious rights to the same land. The Balfour Declaration had asserted the rights of two peoples whose claims and aspirations clashed. The result was that Jews and Arabs acted out a tragedy of classic proportions in which the protagonists became victims of inexorable forces over which they had but little control.

From the very outset, Jews and Arabs were engaged in mortal strife. Each side engaged in acts of violence that led to additional violence. Particularly bloody were the riots of 1929, the first instance of large-scale bloodshed between Jews and Arabs. In Jerusalem, in a dispute over the Wailing Wall and the Dome of the Rock, 133 Jews and 116 Arabs lost their lives. In Hebron, the Jewish inhabitants, a people with an ancient linear connection to biblical times in that city, were driven out of it in a riot that claimed 87 Jewish lives. The British authorities sought to keep the peace but with limited success. Both sides felt the British had betrayed them for not fulfilling the promises made during the war. In 1939, Britain, to placate the Arabs who had risen in bloody rebellion (1936–1939), issued its controversial "white paper," or position paper. With it the British authorities sought to limit the Jewish population of Palestine to one-third and to curtail severely the transfer of land to Jews. (The Jewish population at that time was already at 30 percent of the total population, up from 10 percent in 1918.)

The Dome of the Rock, Jerusalem. *(Harry Piotrowski)*

The Western Wall—or Wailing Wall—in Jerusalem. *(Harry Piotrowski)*

The new British directive came at a time when life in Nazi Germany had become perilous for Jews. Yet no country would take them in, and Hitler later initiated his program of extermination of Jews. Militant Zionists began to suspect the worst, namely, collusion between the British and the Nazis. The British decision closed the door to Palestine for Jews who sought a safe haven trying to escape the Nazi jackboot. It created a lingering legacy of bitterness among many Zionists. After the war, it led to violence between the British army and militant Jewish organizations, such as the Irgun (Irgun Zvai Leumi, or National Military Organization, headed by Menachem Begin), which captured and executed British soldiers and blew up the King David Hotel in Jerusalem in July 1946, killing ninety-one, including twenty-eight British citizens, the group's main target.

The murder of 6 million European Jews at the hands of Nazi Germany during World War II, all too frequently with the collusion of peoples—Poles, Ukrainians, French, and others—who themselves had been conquered by the Germans, seared the consciousness of Jews. It underscored the necessity of a Jewish state as a matter of self-preservation, as the only place where Jews could be assured a sanctuary against the fury of anti-Semitism. Israel was created by survivors of the Holocaust, whose actions were constantly marked by the remembrance of that cataclysmic event. Years later, when Egyptian president Gamal Abdel Nasser spoke of the destruction of Israel, its citizens could not help but invoke the memory of Hitler's attempt to annihilate the Jews.

After World War II, the British decided to wash their hands of Palestine. At this point, the United Nations agreed to take its turn in trying to solve this problem. It was clear by then, however, that a single Palestinian state consisting of Arabs and Jews, as the Balfour Declaration had suggested, was an impossibility. Few Zionists or Arabs were interested in such a solution. Too much blood had already been shed between them; besides, both saw themselves as the legitimate heirs to the land of Palestine. In November 1947, the United Nations, therefore, called for the creation of separate Israeli and Arab states. Jerusalem, a holy city for Jews and Muslims (as well as Christians), was to have international status with free access for all worshippers. The UN decision marked the second partition of Palestine, at least of the territory that remained after the British had initially granted the eastern bank of the Jordan River to the emir of Trans-Jordan.

Nearly all Arabs rejected the UN resolution. They were in no mood for such a compromise with the Zionists, whom they considered a foreign presence in their land. The Arabs also harbored the suspicion that Zionism in control of only half of Zion—and the fact that the very heart of Zion itself, Jerusalem, was slated to remain a separate entity, apart from the state of Israel—would ultimately satisfy few Israelis and inevitably lead to additional Zionist expansion. Most Jews were generally willing to accept the borders the United Nations had drawn, despite the fact that they fell far short of what the Zionist

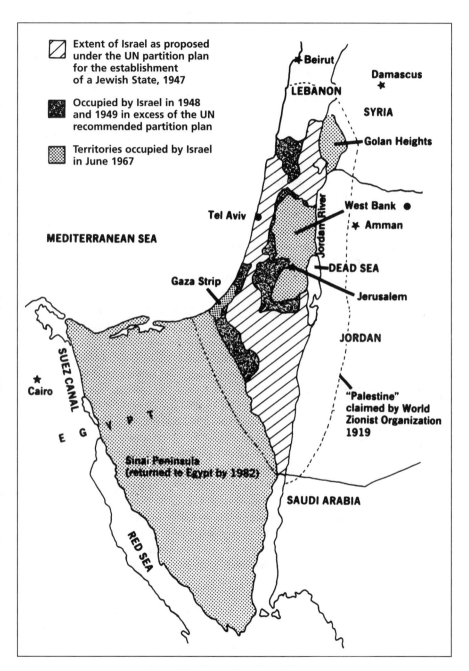

Extent of Israel as proposed under the UN partition plan for the establishment of a Jewish State, 1947

Occupied by Israel in 1948 and 1949 in excess of the UN recommended partition plan

Territories occupied by Israel in June 1967

Beirut

Damascus

LEBANON

SYRIA

Golan Heights

MEDITERRANEAN SEA

Tel Aviv

West Bank

Amman

Jordan River

DEAD SEA

Gaza Strip

Jerusalem

JORDAN

SUEZ CANAL

Cairo

E G Y P T

"Palestine" claimed by World Zionist Organization 1919

Sinai Peninsula (returned to Egypt by 1982)

SAUDI ARABIA

RED SEA

The Expansion of Israel

movement had originally envisioned. David Ben-Gurion, who once had argued that Israel's eastern border must reach the Jordan River, rejected pressures for expansion in the hope of gaining Arab recognition of what in his youth had been but a dream—the state of Israel. The more militant Zionists, people such as Begin, whose Irgun military organization had as its logo a map of Israel with borders beyond the Jordan River, had a much larger Israel in mind than the one the UN plan defined.

The Arabs remained adamant in their refusal to recognize Israel's existence. At best, some were willing to accept the presence of a Jewish minority in an Arab state. More significant, many Arabs were convinced that they could prevent the establishment of the Israeli state by military means and could drive the Zionists into the sea.

In 1947, the Zionist dream had finally borne fruit. The state of Israel (no longer merely a homeland for Jews) had obtained international sanction. The first country to extend diplomatic recognition to Israel was the United States; the Soviet Union and several Western nations quickly followed suit. No Arab state, however, recognized Israel. Indeed, after King Abdullah of Jordan met in secret talks with Zionists in 1949, it cost him his life at the hand of a Palestinian assassin. Arab intransigence—coupled with the threat of another event like the Holocaust a scant three years after Hitler's defeat—made it clear that Israel's right to exist would have to be defended by the sword.

The Arab-Israeli Wars

The British were slated to withdraw from Palestine in May 1948, and both sides prepared for that day. Violence between Arabs and Jews, already endemic, escalated. On April 9, 1948, Begin's Irgun killed between 116 and 254 Palestinians (depending upon whose account one credits) in the village of Deir Yassin, and three days later an Arab reprisal caused the deaths of 77 Jews. These and other acts of violence became etched into the collective memory of both peoples. Each massacre had its apologists who defended the bloodletting as a just action in a just war. In this fashion the first Arab-Israeli war began.

The 1948 war was essentially over in four weeks. A number of Arab states—Jordan, Syria, Egypt, Lebanon, and Iraq—invaded Israel, but their actions were uncoordinated and ineffectual. The Israeli victory resulted in the third partition of Palestine. The Israelis wound up with one-third more land than under the UN partition plan when they seized West Jerusalem, the Negev Desert, and parts of Galilee. King Abdullah of Jordan made the best of his defeat at the hands of the Israelis by annexing the West Bank and East Jerusalem. The Palestinians, defeated by Israel and betrayed by the Kingdom of Jordan, saw the dream of a state of their own vanish.

The war also led to a refugee problem that continued to plague the Middle East. By the end of April 1948, even before the outbreak of the war, Israeli forces expelled 290,000 Palestinian Arabs. During the war, the victorious Israelis expelled another 300,000 Palestinians. By 1973, the number of refugees topped 1.5 million; in 2004, their number plus those of their descendants stood at 4 million, many of them wards of the UN relief organizations. Most of the refugees fled across the Jordan River into Jordan. As a result, 70 percent of the population of the Kingdom of Jordan consisted of Palestinians, from which came the argument in some quarters in Israel that a Palestinian state already existed.

The flight of the Palestinians determined the nature of the new state of Israel. It guaranteed that Israel would be a Zionist state dominated by a Jewish majority at the expense of what was now an Arab minority left behind. Whatever property the Arabs had abandoned, if only to seek shelter elsewhere during the war, was confiscated by Israel.[5] The displaced Palestinians settled in refugee camps in Jordan, Lebanon, and Gaza. They considered their status as temporary and looked—in vain—to the day of return to lands and homes that had once belonged to them.

When the war ended, the Israelis considered the armistice lines, which gave them the additional lands, to be permanent and refused—in violation of international law—to permit the return of the refugees. For Arabs, the new borders and the refugees were a humiliating reminder of their defeat, and they remained incapable of accepting the consequences of the war. These factors, coupled with Arab intransigence on the question of Israel's right to exist, remained at the core of the continuing deadlock in Arab-Israeli relations.

The partitions of Palestine were the result of actions taken by Great Britain, the United Nations, Israel, and Jordan with the complicity of the nations of Europe, both capitalist and Communist. From the beginning, the United States and other major Western powers offered the Israelis diplomatic support, whereas the Soviet bloc had provided most of the weapons for the Jewish victory in the first Arab-Israeli war.

It was only a matter of time until the second war broke out. The 1948 war had been a bitter blow to the pride and national consciousness of the Arabs. The war had exposed their weaknesses and their inability to unite. Throughout that war, Israeli forces had outnumbered those of the Arabs by a ratio of roughly two to one. Arabs spoke fervently of Arab unity and of fighting another war against Israel to drive the Israelis into the sea, but their rhetoric only masked their impotence and frustration.

A palace revolution in Egypt in 1952 swept aside the ineffectual King Farouk and in 1954 brought to power one of the conspirators, Gamal Abdel Nasser, who promised the regeneration of the Arab world. He envisioned a pan-Arab movement uniting all Arabs, and for a short time Egypt and Syria were in fact merged into one nation, the United Arab Republic. Nasser's rejuvenation of Arab pride was coupled with a call for the ouster of the Western presence—notably that of the British, French, and Israelis—which in the past had been responsible for the humiliation of the Muslim world. Another war between Israel and the Arabs seemed inevitable. Nasser, instead of coming to grips with the reality of Israel, was busy putting another Arab-Israeli war on the agenda.

As tensions in the Middle East increased, so did the arms race. Nasser turned to the Soviet Union and in September 1955 announced a historic weapons deal by which he became the recipient of Soviet MiG-15 fighter planes, bombers, and tanks. The Soviet Union, in turn, gained for the first time a client outside its Communist sphere of influence. Israel immediately renegotiated an arms agreement with France. The Middle East was now on a hairtrigger alert waiting for a crisis to unfold. The wait was not long. In July 1956, Nasser boldly seized the Suez Canal, thus eliminating British and French control and operation of that important waterway.

The British and French prepared a counterattack to retake the Suez Canal. They were joined by the Israelis, who, for a number of years, had listened to Nasser's bloodcurdling rhetoric promising the destruction of their state. They now saw their chance to deal with Nasser and to halt the border raids by the Arab *fedayeen* (literally "those who sacrifice themselves"). These raids had produced an unbroken circle of violence, a series of "little wars" consisting of incursions and reprisals, which in turn led to other raids and reprisals.

Britain, France, and Israel, in preparation for a second Arab-Israeli war, signed the secret Treaty of Sèvres in October 1956. Israel attacked in Egypt's Sinai Desert and swept all the way to the Suez Canal and the southern tip of the Sinai at Sharm el-Sheikh. British and French naval, air, and land forces joined the battle against the outgunned Egyptians. The war lasted only a few days, from October 29 until November 2, 1956. Egypt's defeat on the battlefield—not to mention its humiliation—was complete.

When the Anglo-French forces launched an assault aimed at retaking the Suez Canal, President Dwight Eisenhower's stated opposition to more war, Soviet threats of intervention, and UN condemnations persuaded Britain, France, and Israel to halt the attack. Israel eventually agreed to withdraw from the Sinai, whereas Egypt pledged not to interfere with Israeli shipping through the Strait of Tiran, which gave Israel an outlet to the Red Sea. The United Nations negotiated the evacuation of the British and French from the canal zone, leaving Nasser in control of the Suez, which remained bottled up with war-damaged ships for several years. The United Nations also agreed to patrol the border between Egypt and Israel and in this fashion helped to preserve an uneasy truce for more than ten years.

The 1956 war resolved none of the grievances held by the Israelis and Arabs. Officially, the state of war between the Arab nations and Israel continued. Israel was still unable to obtain recognition from any Arab government, and the Arabs continued to call for the destruction of the Israeli state. Both sides had no illusions that another war was in the offing, and they took steps to prepare for it.

In the spring of 1967, Nasser, in an attempt to negate the consequences of the 1956 war, closed the Strait of Tiran to Israeli shipping in the face of Israeli warnings that such an action constituted a *casus belli*, a cause for war. Inevitably, tensions rose rapidly. Nasser then demanded that the UN forces leave Egyptian territory along the Israeli border and concluded a military pact with King Hussein of Jordan. When Iraq joined the pact, the Israelis struck, initiating the Six Day War of June 1967.

In less than a week Israeli forces decimated those of Egypt, Syria, and Jordan and in the process rearranged the map of the Middle East. The political repercussions still haunt the region. Once again—as it had done in the 1956 war—Israel conquered the Sinai all the way to the Suez Canal. It also seized from Egypt the Gaza Strip, a small stretch of land inhabited by Palestinian refugees. It then turned against Syria and stormed the Golan Heights, a seemingly impregnable 20-mile-wide strategic plateau rising 600 feet above Galilee from which the Syrian army had fired repeatedly on Israeli settlements below. But most significant, Israel also took what had been under Jordan's administration, the lands west of the Jordan River and the Dead Sea—a region generally known as the West Bank (i.e., west of the Jordan River). With it, Israel also came into possession of the entire city of Jerusalem. All the conquered territories—the Sinai Peninsula, the Golan Heights, the West Bank, Gaza, and East Jerusalem—became Israeli-occupied lands, and as such they became the source of still further contention between Arabs and Israelis.

In November 1967, the great powers once again sought to use the United Nations to resolve the conflict. The United States and the Soviet Union were fearful of being increasingly drawn into the Arab-Israeli wars, each backing one of the belligerents. In a rare display of US-Soviet cooperation, the UN Security Council sought to resolve the crisis by passing Resolution 242, which called for an Israeli withdrawal from territories conquered in the Six Day War, accompanied by a political settlement that would include Arab recognition of Israel and a fair deal for the Palestinian refugees. After some hesitation, Egypt and Jordan accepted Resolution 242, but Syria and the militant Palestinians rejected it. The Israelis were not inclined to give up all the spoils of victory, and they, too, rejected it. In the decades to come, leaders of various political and national persuasions repeatedly reached for Resolution 242 as a potential answer to this deadly dispute. But the overwhelming strength of Israel's military in effect negated the resolution. The Israeli government had no pressing need to return to its pre-1967 borders; moreover, it never contemplated the return of East Jerusalem to the Arabs. And the Arabs always insisted that in Resolution 242, "the territories occupied [by Israel] in the hostilities" meant "all territories."[6]

General Moshe Dayan, one of the architects of Israel's victory in the Six Day War, expressed the extremist conviction when he said, "I would rather have land than peace," to which King Hussein of Jordan prophetically replied, "Israel can have land or peace, but not both."[7] The resultant deadlock became but another manifestation of how in the Middle East the militants nearly always carried the day.

With the acquisition of the West Bank, Israel now came into possession of land containing 750,000 hostile Arabs. Three days after the end of the war, on June 13, 1967, the first Jewish settlers arrived at the village of Gush Etzion, from which Jews had been expelled in 1948. Other Jews began to reclaim property in East Jerusalem.[8] In 1977, after an election in Israel had brought to power Menachem Begin, who had always insisted that the West Bank was not merely conquered Arab territory or a bargaining card to be played eventually in exchange for Arab recognition of Israel's right to exist, the widespread Israeli settlement of the West Bank began. That territory, Begin insisted, consisted of the biblical lands of Judea and Samaria, an integral part of Israel's religious heritage, the historic part of Zion. Despite objections from Arab states as well as the United Nations, United States, and other nations, Begin considered the annexation of the West Bank a closed matter. His government also officially annexed the Golan Heights and considered that matter closed as well.

The problem of the West Bank was complicated by the fact that its largest city, Hebron, contains the tomb of Abraham, who is revered by both Jews and Muslims. Both groups consider Abraham as God's messenger and their spiritual and biological patriarch. Jews consider themselves the direct descendants of one of Abraham's sons, Isaac; Arabs claim descent from his other son, Ishmael.

The 1967 Arab defeat had another unexpected result. It strengthened the hand of Palestinian liberation/terrorist organizations, which now operated under the aegis of a recently established umbrella organization, the Palestine Liberation Organization (PLO), led by Yassir Arafat. Henceforth, it was the PLO's guerrilla fighters, rather than the armies of the Arab nations generally, that challenged Israel's right to exist. During the 1972 Summer Olympics in Munich, for instance, Palestinian terrorists dramatized their cause before a worldwide audience by taking hostage Israeli athletes and coaches, eventually killing eleven of them. This act propelled the Palestinian question into the consciousness of the Western world. But this example of "propaganda by the deed" (to use a phrase from the Russian revolutionary movement of the nineteenth century) strengthened the hands of the extremists on both sides and continued to impede any and all efforts to resolve the conflict. It should not have been surprising, therefore, that the consequence of the inability to resolve Arab-Israeli differences was yet another war.

The Yom Kippur War took place in October 1973, when Egyptian president Anwar Sadat, who had succeeded Nasser in 1970, initiated an offensive against the seemingly impregnable Israeli positions across the Suez Canal.

Owing to its surprise attack, Egypt enjoyed initial successes, but Israeli forces counterattacked and threatened to destroy the Egyptian army. The United Nations, United States, and Soviet Union hastily intervened to stop the war. Neither Israel nor Egypt was to be permitted to destroy the other. Egypt was permitted to retain a foothold on the eastern side of the Suez Canal, and the United Nations then created a buffer zone to keep the two sides apart.

The Egyptian offensive proved to be the first time an Arab state had been able to wrest any territory—however small—from the Israelis. After suffering one humiliation after another for a quarter of a century, an Arab army had finally proven its battleworthiness. Sadat felt he could now negotiate with Israel as an equal. With encouragement from Washington, Sadat began to take steps to recognize the existence of the state of Israel and eventually became the first Arab head of state to do so. In an act of supreme courage, Sadat responded to an invitation from the Israeli government and flew to Jerusalem in 1977 to address the Knesset, Israel's parliament. Israeli prime minister Begin reciprocated with his own visit to Cairo.

These remarkable diplomatic actions set the stage for a September 1978 summit meeting between Sadat and Begin at the US presidential retreat at Camp David, Maryland, mediated by US president Jimmy Carter. The Camp David Accords led directly to an Egyptian-Israeli peace treaty in 1979 that

Egyptian president Anwar Sadat, US president Jimmy Carter, and Israeli prime minister Menachem Begin after signing the Middle East peace treaty at Camp David, Maryland, March 27, 1979. *(AP/Wide World Photos)*

ended a state of war of thirty years' duration between Egypt and Israel and brought about Egypt's diplomatic recognition of Israel. In turn, Israel agreed to return the Sinai to Egypt and did so by April 1982. This marked the first instance in which an Arab state managed to regain territory lost to Israel. Sadat had achieved through negotiation what no Arab nations had achieved by war. For their efforts, the three leaders were nominated for the Nobel Peace Prize. In the end, Begin and Sadat—former terrorists turned diplomats—shared the prize; inexplicably, Jimmy Carter was excluded.

But the Camp David Accords did not adequately address the thorny questions of Jerusalem, the West Bank, and the Palestinian refugees. Sadat showed little interest in the Palestinians. Begin spoke vaguely of Palestinian "autonomy" within the state of Israel, but he was more interested in peace with Egypt and diplomatic recognition than in discussing the fate of the inhabitants of what he considered to be an integral part of Israel and thus an internal matter. Nor did the Camp David Accords settle the issue of Jerusalem, the Israeli capital. Virtually all Israelis insisted that Jerusalem remain one and indivisible. But the Palestinians, too, envisioned Jerusalem as the capital of their future state.

The PLO was neither consulted nor interested in these negotiations. Sitting down with Begin would have meant the de facto recognition of Israel. Inevitably, many Arabs saw Sadat as a man who had betrayed the Palestinian and Arab causes. His new relationship with Israel contributed to his domestic problems. As critics became more vocal, his regime became increasingly dictatorial and his opponents, in turn, became increasingly embittered. Radical Muslims, members of the Egyptian Islamic Jihad, assassinated Sadat in October 1981.[9]

The festering Palestinian problem continued to vex the region. In 1970, King Hussein of Jordan drove the PLO leadership from his country after it had become clear that its presence posed a threat to his regime. Searching for a home, the PLO found a new base of operation in Lebanon, a nation already divided between a politically dominant Christian minority and the majority Muslim population, who at that time were already on the edge of civil war. Lebanon's political factions operated their own private armies, and it was into this volatile environment that the Palestinians introduced their own armed insurgents who periodically launched raids into Israel.

The Israelis responded in kind. Raids and reprisals became the order of the day along the Lebanese-Israeli border. In July 1981, however, the PLO and Israel agreed on a "cessation of all armed attacks." The cease-fire over the next ten months was in part the work of the special US envoy to the Middle East, Philip Habib. Both sides abided by the terms of the agreement until June 1982, when the government of Menachem Begin attempted to eliminate the Palestinian threat in Lebanon once and for all by launching an invasion into southern Lebanon.

The Israeli government's official explanation for the resumption of war against the Palestinians was to secure "Peace for Galilee" and to root out the Palestinians across the border. This rationale for the invasion had a hollow ring to it since there had been no Palestinian attacks across that border for nearly a year. The scope of the operation, the Begin government announced, would be limited. The Israeli army would go no farther than 40 kilometers (25 miles) into Lebanon. Events proved, however, that Begin and his defense minister, Ariel Sharon, had more ambitious plans.

In December 1981, Sharon outlined his scenario to Philip Habib, one that called for a strike into Lebanon in the hope of quickly resolving several problems at once. Sharon would dislodge the Syrians, who had been invited several years earlier by the Lebanese government to restore order at a time when the country was beginning to disintegrate into civil war. Once invited, however, the Syrians had stayed. Sharon considered the Syrians, with whom the Israelis had been on a war footing since 1948, to be the real masters of Lebanon. Next, Sharon intended to destroy the PLO, a "time bomb" in Sharon's words, in southern Lebanon and with it subdue the restless Palestinian population in Israel, numbering about half a million.[10] When Habib asked of the fate of the 100,000 Palestinians directly across the border in Lebanon, Sharon told him that "we shall hand them over to the Lebanese. . . . Fifty-thousand armed terrorists won't remain there, and the rest will be taken care of by the Lebanese." Habib protested the impending violation of the cease-fire that he had worked out. Shortly afterward, US president Ronald Reagan warned Prime Minister Begin against any moves into Lebanon, but to no avail.

The invasion of Lebanon did bring about the military (although not the political) defeat of the PLO as well as the Israeli bombardment and destruction of the parts of Beirut containing Palestinian populations. The invasion also led to the massacre of an estimated 700–2,000 Palestinian civilians at the refugee camps of Sabra and Shatila. The slaughter—first with knives, then with firearms—was the handiwork of Lebanese Maronite Christian Phalangist (fascist) militia forces, with the approval and assistance of the Israeli armed forces who witnessed the massacres.[11] Israeli forces also crippled Syrian forces in Lebanon and destroyed much of the military hardware the Soviets had provided them, but the Syrians quickly recovered their losses and remained as deeply entrenched in Lebanon as ever. Israel did not withdraw completely but left some of its forces in a self-imposed buffer region in southern Lebanon.

The cost of the invasion was considerable. The greatest losers were the Palestinians, who suffered at the hands of first the Israelis, then the Christian Phalangists, and finally the Shiite Muslims in Lebanon. The war also pitted the Israelis against the Shiites; the Shiites against the Maronite Christians and their army, the Phalangists; and a faction of the PLO (the rebels supported by the Syrians) against Arafat's faction. It produced the evacuation of the PLO guerrillas (who found a heaven far from Palestine, in Tunis), the deaths of over 600 Israeli soldiers, the de facto partition of Lebanon between Syria and Israel, and a deep emotional split within the population in Israel. The volatile political debates in Israel centered on whether the invasion had been necessary, for this was the first war initiated by Israel in which its survival had not been an immediate issue.

There were additional costly consequences. Under UN auspices, a peacekeeping force made up of US, French, and Italian troops oversaw the evacuation of PLO fighters from Lebanon. Soon afterward, the US and French peacekeeping forces ran head-on into an opposition of fury and anger few in the West were able to understand. Two Shiite Hezbollah (Army of God) suicide bombers blew up trucks filled with explosives, killing 242 US troops (mostly Marines) and 59 French paratroopers. Nearly two decades later, the violence continued as Israeli forces in southern Lebanon remained engaged in sporadic combat with Lebanese Shiites.

The Israeli-Palestinian Impasse

In the mid-1980s, the PLO was no closer than before to achieving its goal—the creation of a Palestinian state and the destruction of Israel. After its 1982 expulsion from Lebanon, it was in disarray. For the next several years, its nominal leader, Yassir Arafat, now based in Tunis, struggled to maintain the unity of the organization.

Little changed until December 1987, when the Palestinian population took matters into its own hands. The so-called *intifada* (literally, "shaking off" the Zionist yoke), began in Gaza after an Israeli truck collided with two cars, killing four Palestinian refugees. The protests escalated and spread to the West Bank. Israel put itself into the uncomfortable position of using armed soldiers against stone-throwing Palestinians. By early 1990, Israeli soldiers had killed more than 600 Palestinians. Israeli hard-liners tried to deflect criticism by blaming the violence on the PLO.

The intifada spurred debate within Israel over the future of Gaza and the West Bank as well as a debate within the PLO over strategy and tactics. In November 1988, the PLO met in Algiers, where it passed a resolution proclaiming its willingness to recognize Israel on the condition that it officially endorse UN Resolutions 242 and 338, which called for Israeli withdrawal—both its military and settlers now numbered 70,000—from the Occupied Territories and for the right of all parties in the Middle East to live in peace and security. For the PLO, this was a remarkably conciliatory position. Arafat also declared that "we [the PLO] totally and absolutely renounce all forms of terrorism."[12] Israeli prime minister Yitzhak Shamir and his party, the right-wing Likud, did not believe the peaceful protestations of these mortal enemies. There would be no talks with the PLO and no Palestinian state. Shamir could not forget that the PLO had vowed in the past to destroy the state of Israel and that, in fact, several of its factions still held this position.[13]

The end of the Cold War in 1990 led to significantly improved relations between Israel and the Soviet Union. The two nations reestablished diplomatic relations (which the Soviet Union had broken off after the Six Day War of 1967), and when Moscow opened its doors for the emigration of Jews, Israel welcomed them. The mass immigration of Jews into Israel (200,000 in 1990 alone) had consequences beyond the domestic issues of providing housing and jobs. Many Soviet Jews were settled in the West Bank and East Jerusalem, areas the Palestinians claimed. Although intifada violence subsided, the influx of the Soviet Jews into the occupied lands again inflamed Arab passions. Shamir, however, reiterated his pledge that he would keep intact for future generations the "Greater Israel," by which he meant all areas currently under Israeli control.

The Search for a Political Solution

The Arab-Israeli dispute became more acute during the crisis in the Persian Gulf occasioned by Iraq's invasion of Kuwait in August 1990 (see Chapter 20). Israel's most urgent concern was for its own security; earlier in the year Iraqi ruler Saddam Hussein had threatened to "scorch half of Israel" in reprisal of any Israeli action against Iraq. Hussein, in his efforts to secure Arab support, proclaimed his willingness to withdraw from Kuwait if Israel were to withdraw from all the Occupied Territories.

The defeat of Iraq by the US-led coalition in the Gulf War in early 1991 improved conditions for achieving a breakthrough in the Middle East. After the war, it was clearer than ever that Israel was a permanent fact of life in the Middle East. The PLO already had publicly contemplated recognition of Israel in exchange for the land taken in 1967. Syrian president Afez Assad, deprived of Soviet backing, ceased pretending that he had the military capability of regaining the Golan Heights. Many Israelis, too, sought an end to the costly confrontation. The time had come to sit down and talk.

In June 1992, in a tight race for prime minister, Labor Party leader Yitzhak Rabin defeated Shamir. Rabin had promised greater flexibility in the search for peace and suggested he was willing to trade some land for peace. Rabin was a military man who in January 1964 had become the chief of staff of the Israeli army (IDF). His hawkish position had contributed to rising tensions in the years leading up to the Six Day War of 1967; during that war, he was as responsible as anyone for the Israeli conquest of Arab lands. Yet it was this man who now had to deal with the consequences of that war. Rabin declared that the most urgent task was to negotiate self-rule for Palestinians in the West

Bank and Gaza, and toward that end he announced a curb on building new settlements in the Occupied Territories, but he was not willing to return to the 1967 borders.

The Oslo Accords

At the end of summer 1993, secret talks in Oslo, Norway, between PLO functionaries and members of Israel's Peace Now movement (acting at first independently of the Rabin government) offered hope for a solution to the Arab-Israeli conflict. The negotiations produced a remarkable breakthrough when Arafat and Rabin accepted the broad outlines of an agreement. The signing ceremony took place on the White House lawn in Washington, on September 13, 1993, where a reluctant Rabin shook Arafat's hand. Oslo called for an Israeli military withdrawal from Gaza (except for the Jewish settlements there) and from the West Bank city of Jericho, with further withdrawals sometime in the future. Political control of these regions would fall to a Palestinian Authority under Arafat.

Yet a final settlement proved to be as elusive as ever. The key defect of Oslo was that it failed to define the shape of a permanent peace. It said nothing about the fate of Jewish settlements in Gaza and the West Bank, the status of East Jerusalem, where the population was still almost exclusively Palestinian, or the refugees and a Palestinian state. Most important, it had virtually no effect on the ongoing expansion of Jewish settlements in the West Bank. Without a halt of the expansion, there could be no peace.

Moreover, the two sides had different visions of what Oslo meant, something that was apparent at the signing ceremony. Rabin spoke vaguely of the two sides "destined to live together on the same soil, in the same land." Arafat, in contrast, spoke of the Palestinians' "right to self-determination" and "coexistence" with Israel on the basis of "equal rights," calling for the implementation of UN Resolutions 242 and 338, which demanded an Israeli withdrawal from lands conquered in 1967.[14]

Oslo prompted Jordan's King Hussein to act. Secret talks between his representatives and Israel soon produced a peace treaty, signed in Washington in July 1994, officially ending a forty-six-year state of war.

Not surprisingly, there was strong opposition to the agreement from radical elements in both Israel and among the Palestinians. Rabin's foreign minister, Shimon Peres, explained that "a peace negotiation is with your own people as well as with the other one."[15] Jewish militants, particularly those who had set up residence in Hebron, deep inside the West Bank, wanted no part of Oslo.

Palestinian and Israeli leaders who contemplated dealing with the enemy knew that many of their compatriots saw them as traitors negotiating away their patrimony. To complicate matters for Israel, it now faced another Palestinian social, political, and military force, namely, Hamas ("zeal" in Arabic), a militant Islamic organization based in Gaza, which had gained considerable support with its uncompromising call for the destruction of Israel. Hamas, the Palestinian branch of the Muslim Brotherhood (see Chapter 21), was founded in Gaza in 1987 by its spiritual leader, Sheik Ahmed Yassin. Hamas emerged, slowly yet surely, as a voice for the Palestinian community, an alternative to the increasingly corrupt and ineffective PLO leadership. It wanted nothing to do with Oslo, charging that Arafat had obtained too little and that he had betrayed the Palestinian cause.

In February 1994, a US-born Zionist, Baruch Goldstein, shot and killed twenty-nine Muslim worshippers at the Cave of the Patriarchs (the resting place of Abraham and other Old Testament figures) in Hebron. Goldstein was a member of an extremist organization whose attitudes were capsulized by a statement a rabbi made in a eulogy to the killer: "One million Arabs are not worth a Jewish fingernail."[16]

But as long as the Oslo Accords remained in force, the possibility continued that even the most intractable issues could be resolved. It was for this reason that the Nobel Peace Prize committee, as it had done several times in the past, presented its award for 1994 to former enemies—Rabin, Arafat, and Peres—who had attempted to resolve their differences at the conference table rather than on the battlefield.

Arafat now had to shoulder the work of governing the Palestinians and improving their livelihood. Poverty was especially severe in Gaza, where the unemployment rate was around 50 percent. By the end of 1994, the World Bank and several nations contributed the small sum of $180 million in developmental aid to the Palestinian Authority, but the amount was far lower than was needed. In addition to having to fend off complaints about the economy, Arafat faced critics of his autocratic and corrupt rule. Most serious was the challenge posed by Hamas. In October 1994, a Hamas suicide bomber blew up a crowded bus in Tel Aviv, killing twenty-one people. A rally in Gaza drew more than 20,000 Hamas supporters who praised the bomber as a martyr and denounced the PLO's agreement with Israel.

In September 1995, Arafat and Rabin affixed their signatures to a detailed plan that established a timetable for the withdrawal of Israeli forces from about 30 percent of the West Bank (including its major cities and about 400 towns) and put the Palestinian Authority immediately in charge of public services for most of the residents of the West Bank. Yet no progress was made on the more crucial questions of halting Jewish settlements or the formation of a Palestinian state.

The militants in Israel stepped up their criticism of Rabin. Benjamin Netanyahu, the new leader of the opposition Likud Party, went so far as to accuse Rabin of treason. One of Netanyahu's campaign posters showed Rabin wearing the *kaffiyeh*, Arafat's trademark Arab headdress. In November 1995, a twenty-one-year-old Israeli extremist, Yigal Amir, assassinated Rabin. He justified his act on religious grounds: A Jew who harmed Jewish society must be killed. Rabin's successor was his foreign minister, Shimon Peres, one of the architects of the Oslo peace process who was committed to moving it forward, but first he had to face Netanyahu in an election.

Return to Impasse

The first direct election of an Israeli prime minister took place in May 1996 under the shadow of escalating violence. The election became a referendum on the nearly three-year-long peace process. By a razor-thin margin, the victory went to Netanyahu, a hard-liner who had opposed the Oslo process every step of the way. Netanyahu rejected Rabin's "land for peace" formula; he promised, instead, "peace with security."

Once elected, Netanyahu was reluctant to meet with Arafat, whom he considered a terrorist and not a worthy negotiating partner. When Netanyahu and Arafat did meet, in January 1997, to sign an agreement on an Israeli military pullback from Hebron, it was telling that they did so in the middle of the night, at 2:45 A.M., away from the glare of publicity. Netanyahu continued to demolish Palestinian homes and authorize the building of additional Jewish settlements and Jewish-only access roads in the West Bank. In the seven years after the signing of the Oslo Accords, settlement construction had increased by more than 50 percent and the settler population by 72 percent, their numbers reaching 380,000 amid more than 3 million Palestinians.[17] Moreover, economic conditions for the Palestinians steadily declined. In February 2000, Egyptian president Hosni Mubarak warned that Palestine had become a time bomb.

In the May 1999 election, Ehud Barak, the centrist candidate of the Labor Party and a former career military man who had risen to the post of IDF chief of staff as a protégé of Rabin, defeated Netanyahu after promising to revive the stalled Oslo Accords. But Barak was unable to come to a final agreement with Arafat. Instead, he focused on the withdrawal of Israeli troops from southern Lebanon, where they had been since 1982. Once that had been achieved in July 2000, Barak then turned his attention to Syria in the hopes of coming to an understanding over the Golan Heights. The new leader of Syria, Bashar Assad, showed little interest in negotiations and insisted, instead, on a maximalist position, the unconditional withdrawal of Israel's 18,000 settlers and its military from the Golan Heights.

Barak then returned to the Palestinian question. He convinced US president Bill Clinton to convene a meeting at Camp David in July 2000, during which he offered Arafat concessions that went beyond the Israeli consensus. He promised Arafat most—but not all—of the West Bank, the potential return of an unspecified number of the 3.5 million Palestinian refugees, and the withdrawal of an unspecified number of Israeli settlers from the West Bank and Gaza.

A sticking point again was the status of Jerusalem. Arafat continued to insist on Palestinian sovereignty over its eastern half. When Barak refused to discuss the issue, Arafat returned home to a hero's welcome. Before he left Camp David, he told Clinton: "If I make concessions on Jerusalem, I will be killed, and you will have to talk to Sheikh [Ahmed] Yassin," the spiritual head of Hamas.[18]

Barak and Clinton blamed Arafat for the breakdown. The head of Israel's military intelligence, however, concluded that Arafat had sought a diplomatic solution but could not accept the loss of 9 percent of West Bank territory and of East Jerusalem. Nor could he ignore the Palestinian refugee problem[19] or the fact that Jewish settlers in the West Bank, Gaza, and East Jerusalem now numbered more than 400,000.

In September 2000, Ariel Sharon—the man primarily responsible for the 1982 Israeli invasion of Lebanon that had resulted in the slaughter of Palestinians there, who had participated in a massacre of Palestinians in 1953, who once had referred to Palestinians as "cockroaches," and who as cabinet minister had overseen the building of Israeli settlements in the Occupied Territories—paid a visit to a most sensitive site, the Temple Mount in the Old City of Jerusalem. It was there that the temple of Solomon once stood; its Wailing Wall at the foot of the Mount is the holiest place in the Jewish faith. At the end of the seventh century C.E., however, Muslims had built on the top of the Mount, which they call the Haram al-Sharif (Noble Sanctuary), two mosques—the Dome of the Rock and the al-Aqsa Mosque. According to Muslim tradition, it was from there that the Prophet Mohammed took his "Night Journey" to heaven where he received Allah's command of five daily prayers. After the Six Day War, General Moshe Dayan, one of the architects of Israel's victory, had granted the Muslims sovereignty over the Temple Mount but at the same time had granted Israelis the right to visit it.

The Temple Mount/Haram al-Sharif has long been a focal point of Arab-Israeli tension. The bloody riots of 1929 were the result of the Palestinians' belief that Zionists were about to seize control of it. In 1990, an Israeli group, the Temple Mount Faithful, sought to lay a cornerstone for a future temple. In the aftermath, Israeli forces killed seventeen Palestinians, whose memory is honored in the museum of the Haram al-Sharif. Over the years, Israeli zealots called for the establishment of a new temple, even threatening to blow up the mosques.

Under heavy guard from 1,000 Israeli soldiers and police, Sharon ascended the Temple Mount to underscore that it belonged to the Jews. Predictably, this incident touched off the time bomb Mubarak had predicted. Thus began the second intifada, which pitted mostly young Palestinians against Israeli soldiers and citizens. It featured the lynching of two Israeli soldiers and the death of a thirteen-year-old Palestinian boy caught in the cross-fire, both acts caught on videotape and replayed endlessly on television.

Oslo was dead and Sharon, the candidate promising the restoration of order, became the next Israeli prime minister. Order, however, eluded Sharon. During the next four years, Palestinians carried out more than 170 suicide attacks, most of them by Hamas; one-third of them, however, were carried out by the al-Aqsa Martyrs' Brigade, an offshoot of Arafat's Fatah organization. The Martyrs' Brigade may have been out of Arafat's control, but he showed little interest in reining it in.

Israel responded with helicopters, tanks, and bulldozers, demolishing even more Palestinian homes in the West Bank and in Gaza. In March 2004, Sharon carried out the assassinations of Sheikh Ahmed Yassin and his immediate successor, and threatened the same fate for Arafat. All the while, the number of Jewish settlers in Gaza and the West Bank continued to increase. Between the beginning of 1997 and the end of June 2004, their numbers rose from 156,100 to 243,749. Another 150,000 had taken root in East Jerusalem. The uninterrupted building of new settlements turned any and all talks about peace into a receding mirage. Instead, during the first four years of the second intifada (September 2000–September 2004), 1,002 Israelis and 2,780 Palestinians lost their lives as a result.

Sharon and Arafat, two old men, were engaged in their last battle. Arafat, seventy-five years old and suffering from Parkinson's disease, was trapped in his bombed-out compound in Ramallah and was threatened with expulsion by the seventy-six-year-old Sharon. Meanwhile, Hamas challenged Arafat for the hearts and minds of the Palestinians.

In order to prevent suicide bombers from entering Israel from Gaza and the West Bank, Sharon began to build a security wall. Arafat replied that he had no problem with such a wall provided it was built on Israeli territory. But the wall, scheduled to run 410 miles, cut deep into the West Bank, transferring nearly 17 percent of its territory to Israel. It had a direct impact on the lives of 38 percent of the West Bank population[20]—cut off from other Palestinian communities, schools, hospitals, and farmlands. The Arabs charged that what was left of Palestine consisted of a collection of *bantustans* reminiscent of what white settlers had done to blacks in South Africa, that is, ghettos roped off by an "apartheid wall."

The administration of President George W. Bush in Washington, busy with the war on terror and the invasion of Iraq, made a few pronouncements calling for a "roadmap" for peace, but then lost interest. It labored under the illusion that a political transformation in Iraq would force the Palestinians to accept whatever Israel had in store for them. The "roadmap" called for the dismantling of Israeli settlements as a step toward Palestinian nationhood. The only thing Sharon was willing to do, however, was to eliminate Jewish settlements in Gaza, where 8,100 settlers required the costly protection of 6,000 demoralized soldiers. That still left 450,000 settlers in the West Bank and Jerusalem. Bush soon saw things from Sharon's perspective. In the autumn of

2004, Sharon's chief negotiator in the "roadmap" talks declared they were already "dead" and went on to say that he had come to an understanding with the Bush administration that there would be no talks with the Palestinians until they "turn into [peaceful] Finns." The issue of a Palestinian state "has been removed indefinitely from our agenda . . . all with a [US] presidential blessing and the ratification of both houses of Congress."[21]

In November 2004, Yassir Arafat, a man without a country, died in a Paris hospital. After the Egyptian government honored him with a state funeral, he was interred in his compound in Ramallah in the West Bank to which he had been forcibly confined during the last three years of his life.

Bush spoke of the power of democratic institutions to transform the Middle East. To that end, he put pressure on the Egyptian dictator Hosni Mubarak, the recipient of an annual US subsidy of $2 billion, who had governed his country with an iron hand since 1981, to permit contested, multiparty elections for president. When Mubarak agreed, First Lady Laura Bush, during a visit to Egypt, praised him for his "wise and bold" decision. But things turned out differently than Bush had envisioned. When the Muslim Brotherhood showed remarkable strength in preliminary elections, Mubarak arrested 1,300 Brotherhood activists and, in December 2005, the presidential candidate Ayman Nour was sentenced to prison for five years at hard labor. In April 2006, Mubarak extended the twenty-five-year-old emergency law for another two years.

Fair and free Palestinian elections in January 2006 produced a seismic political shift when Hamas gained political control of Gaza and won an absolute majority of the seats (74 out of 132) in the Palestinian Authority parliament. Hamas's victory came at the expense of the PLO's Fatah party—corrupt, spineless, and without a sense of purpose—now led by Arafat's successor, Mahmoud Abbas, to whom Ariel Sharon once referred—contemptuously yet accurately—as a "plucked chicken." Over the years, Fatah's leadership had failed to achieve anything of substance. Israel continued to build settlements in the West Bank and showed no signs of accepting an independent Palestinian state. Yet it was precisely for these reasons that Bush and the Israeli leadership were willing to deal with Abbas. Talks with Hamas, however, remained out of the question. Instead, the government of Ehud Olmert, who had succeeded Sharon, responded to the election results by arresting Hamas parliamentary deputies in Ramallah.

Olmert then turned his attention to Lebanon, where Shiite Hezbollah, under the charismatic leader Hassan Nasrallah, held sway. Hezbollah, well funded by Iranian petrodollars, represented the largest religious faction in Lebanon, deeply entrenched as a political (twelve members in the legislature as well as a cabinet minister), social (running schools, hospitals, and orphanages and providing radio and television services), and military force (having successfully insisted on maintaining its well-armed private army after Israel's withdrawal in 2000). After Hezbollah kidnapped two Israeli reservist soldiers in July 2006, Olmert sent the Israeli military into Lebanon.

Hezbollah was stunned by the strong Israeli response, but held its ground. In 1982, the Israeli forces had reached Beirut within a week; this time, despite massive aerial bombardments, the going was much tougher. After thirty-three days, Israel called off the attack without having gained its main objectives, neither the destruction of Hezbollah's military capability nor the release of its two soldiers (who, in any case, unbeknownst to the Israelis, were already dead). Instead, the invasion of Lebanon only increased the prestige of Hezbollah, which had stood up to the Israeli assault, effectively using antitank rockets and shorter-range missiles against northern Israel. An estimated 1,200 Lebanese died, more than 4,000 were injured, more than 100,000 were rendered homeless, and three-quarters of Lebanon's roads and bridges were severed. Israeli losses amounted to 116 soldiers and more than forty civilians killed.

The Bush administration, expecting an easy victory, had given its blessing to the Israeli attack on Hezbollah even before the soldiers' kidnapping. When the war was over, Bush described it as an Israeli victory; his secretary of state, Condoleezza Rice, went so far as to declare that the Middle East had just experienced the "birth pangs" of a "new" democratic age. But that was wishful thinking. Instead, the war strengthened those who opposed a Pax Americana in the Middle East.

Israelis understood that they needed to find a solution with the Palestinians. Israel's 5.4 million Jewish citizens had to contend with 1.3 million Arab citizens and another 3.4 million Arabs in the West Bank and East Jerusalem. The Arab population's birthrate, being three times that of Jews, produced the possibility that by 2020, Jews would be in danger of making up but 47 percent of the population in the region between the Jordan River and the Mediterranean Sea. Then there were the moral, economic, political, and military implications of controlling a sullen, resentful Arab population. Yet Israelis were divided on how to resolve the issue. The prime minister's own family was a microcosm of Israel's political deadlock. Olmert's wife was sympathetic to Peace Now (which advocated a withdrawal to the 1967 borders), and their four children opposed the father's incursion into Lebanon (one son, a reservist, even refusing to serve in the Occupied Territories, the other avoiding the military draft altogether). At the dinner table, Olmert acknowledged, "I am a minority of one." In September 2008, Olmert, among the first to urge Jewish control over all of Jerusalem, now urged a return to the 1967 borders, including joint Israeli-Palestinian control of Jerusalem.[22]

In the meantime, however, there was still the problem of Hamas and its control of Gaza, the result of its 2006 election victory. Yet a host of nations refused to accept the legitimacy of the election, including Egypt (long at war with the Muslim Brotherhood that had given birth to Hamas), Israel, the Palestinian Authority in the West Bank, the United States, European Union, Saudi

Arabia, and Jordan. Diplomatically and economically isolated, Gaza, the most densely populated piece of real estate on earth, barely survived, subjected to arguably history's tightest blockade—an act of war according to international law. Palestinians gained direct access to the outside world only after constructing a series of tunnels along the southern Gaza border with Egypt, through which they smuggled needed supplies, including weapons.

In April 2008, Hamas announced a six-month truce with Israel, one that held until November 4 (at a time when the world's attention was riveted on the US presidential election), when Israel bombed Gaza, killing six Palestinians. Hamas responded immediately by launching missiles against southern Israel. Israel countered with a massive bombardment of Gaza. During the previous seven years, Hamas rockets had killed no more than three Israelis, and between July 2008 and the resumption of violence in November one Israeli had died at the hands of Hamas.[23] A cease-fire that had held up reasonably well now gave way to all-out war.

The goal was to destroy Gaza's infrastructure in the vain hope of turning the population against Hamas. The sustained bombing campaign began at the end of December. Nothing was off-limits: rocket launchers, residences of Hamas leaders, government buildings, police stations, roads and bridges, schools and universities, mosques, water, and sanitation and power facilities. A week later Israel followed up with a ground invasion—the seventh Arab-Israeli war and the fourth Israeli conquest of Gaza, testimony to an intractable conflict. Israel was certain that the Bush administration would not object and, moreover, gave notice to the incoming Barack Obama administration not to expect too much from a resumption of the peace process.

The invasion, however, had more to do with domestic matters, namely, the election of a new prime minister, which was scheduled for February 10, 2009. The seeming beneficiary was the Labor Party candidate, the defense minister Ehud Barak. He was the architect of the invasion, which he had carefully planned over several months,[24] and trailed badly in the polls against Tzipi Livni (Kadima) and the hawkish Benjamin Netanyahu (Likud). In Israel, where public opinion overwhelmingly supported the invasion, it became known as the "election war." It was Livni's party that won a slight plurality of the seats in the Knesset, but none of the three major parties were able to gain a majority of the seats in the Knesset. After lengthy negotiations, Netanyahu was able to form a coalition government with Labor and the ultranationalist Yisrael Beiteinu party. Ehud Barak thus retained his post as defense minister while the head of Yisrael Beiteinu, Avigdor Lieberman, became foreign minister. Lieberman, a resident of the West Bank, was an advocate of a two-state solution. He had no intention, however, of abandoning the Israeli settlements on the West Bank. A Palestinian state would have to be a severely truncated entity.

Israel's aims in Gaza remained murky. Olmert and Barak spoke of eliminating Hamas once and for all, a tall order indeed; Hamas was more than a fighting force—it had become a religious and social organization with deep roots among the Palestinians. In the end, they settled on weakening the military capability of Hamas. They achieved that goal by destroying Gaza's infrastructure—at the cost of 1,300 Palestinians killed, as compared to thirteen Israelis—and with it they destroyed the chance of an equitable settlement with the Palestinians anytime soon.

Recommended Readings

Avineri, Shlomo. *The Making of Modern Zionism: The Intellectual Origins of the Jewish State.* New York: Basic Books, 1981.
An explanation of the intellectual climate of the nineteenth century that produced the Zionist movement.
Elon, Amos. *The Israelis: Founders and Sons.* New York: Holt, Rinehart and Winston, 1971.
On the roots of Zionism and the first two decades of the existence of Israel.
Fisk, Robert. *The Great War for Civilization: The Conquest of the Middle East.* New York: Knopf, 2007.
By arguably the best informed Western reporter on the Middle East, writing for Britain's *Independent.*
Kimmerling, Baruch, and Joel S. Migdal. *Palestinians: The Making of a People.* New York: Free Press, 1993.
How a clan-centered Arab population acquired a national collective character.
Lilienthal, Alfred M. *The Zionist Connection: What Price Peace?* Rev. ed. New Brunswick, N.J.: North American, 1982.
A critical account of Zionism.
Oz, Amos. *In the Land of Israel.* New York: Random House, 1983.
By an Israeli novelist who dwells on Israel's dilemma.
Peters, Joan. *From Time Immemorial: The Origins of the Arab-Jewish Conflict over Palestine.* New York: Harper and Row, 1984.
An ambitious, controversial attempt to prove that the Jews did not displace the Arabs in Palestine but instead that Arabs had displaced Jews.
Rabinovich, Abraham. *The Yom Kippur War: The Epic Encounter That Transformed the Middle East.* New York: Schocken, 2004.
An Israeli journalist's definitive account of the war told from the Israeli side. The Arab view of the "Ramadan" War is covered only sketchily.
Ross, Dennis. *The Missing Peace: The Inside Story of the Fight for Middle East Peace.* New York: Farrar, Straus and Giroux, 2004.
By the US envoy to the Middle East who had served US presidents George H. W. Bush and Bill Clinton.
Said, Edward W. *The Question of Palestine.* New York: Random House, 1980.
By a US scholar of Palestinian descent, this is the classic study championing the Palestinian cause.
———. *The End of the Peace Process: Oslo and After.* New York: Pantheon, 2000.
Collection of essays by a leading spokesman of the Palestinian cause, highly critical of both the Palestinian and Israeli leaderships.
Segev, Tom. *1949: The First Israelis.* New York: Free Press, 1985.
A controversial best-seller in Israel, a reinterpretation, particularly of the origin of the refugee problem.
———. *One Palestine, Complete: Jews and Arabs.* New York: Henry Holt, 2000.

A revisionist, also known as "post-Zionist," treatment of the British mandate period from the Zionist and Palestinian perspective by an Israeli journalist and historian.
Shehadeh, Raja. *Samed: Journal of a West Bank Palestinian.* New York: Adama Publishers, 1984.
Life on the West Bank from a Palestinian's perspective.

Notes

1. Jewish nationalism has existed ever since the diaspora, the dispersion of the Jews, that began in the sixth century B.C. with the destruction of Solomon's temple and culminated with the destruction of the second temple in Jerusalem in A.D. 70 and the defeat of Bar Kochba in A.D. 135. British philosopher Bertrand Russell, in reminding his readers that modern nationalism is a relatively new concept, pointed out that at the end of the Middle Ages "there was hardly any nationalism except that of the Jews."
2. Quoted in Amos Elon, *The Israelis: Founders and Sons* (New York: Holt, Rinehart and Winston, 1971), p. 106.
3. Palestinian Arab and Ben-Gurion cited in ibid., p. 155 (emphasis in the original).
4. "Balfour Declaration," in *Times* (London), November 9, 1917, p. 7.
5. Charles Glass, "'It Was Necessary to Uproot Them,'" *London Review of Books*, June 24, 2004, pp. 21–23.
6. "UN Resolution 242," *Yearbook of the United Nations: 1967* (New York: United Nations, 1969), pp. 257–258.
7. Moshe Dayan and King Hussein quoted in Dana Adams Schmidt, *Armageddon in the Middle East* (New York: John Day, 1974), p. 249. For a discussion of the views of Dayan and Hussein, see Bernard Avishai, *The Tragedy of Zionism: Revolution and Democracy in the Land of Israel* (New York: Farrar, Straus and Giroux, 1985), pp. 275–278.
8. Tom Segev, "A Bitter Prize," *Foreign Affairs* (May/June 2006), p. 145.
9. Hosni Mubarak, Sadat's successor, jailed a number of suspects, among them Sheik Omar Abdel Rahman and Ayman al-Zawahiri, both of whom eventually were released. Once freed, they joined Osama bin Laden's al Qaeda. In 1993, Rahman led an attempt to blow up one of the towers of the World Trade Center in New York City; al-Zawahiri became one of the leading figures in al Qaeda.
10. "What can be done," Sharon told Habib, "and this is not actually a plan, but it is practicable, is a swift and vigorous strike of 24 to 48 hours, which will force the Syrians to retreat and inflict such heavy losses on the PLO that they will leave Lebanon." Sharon also expected the Lebanese government to regain control of the Beirut-Damascus highway, thus driving the Syrians farther north. From a report of a US diplomatic summary of the conversation between Sharon and Habib, published by the Israeli Labor Party newspaper, *Davar.* The US ambassador to Israel, Samuel W. Lewis, and the State Department confirmed the basic outlines of the conversation. Thomas L. Friedman, "Paper Says Israeli Outlined Invasion," *New York Times*, May 26, 1985, p. 15.
11. John Fisk, *Pity the Nation: The Abduction of Lebanon*, 4th ed. (New York: Thunder's Mouth Press/Nation Books, 2002), chapter 11, "Terrorists," pp. 359–400. In 1983, an Israeli commission declared that Sharon was not fit as defense minister, that he bore personal responsibility for the massacres. That did not prevent him from becoming the minister of housing and construction who oversaw the expansion of settlements in the West Bank. In 2001 he became prime minister.

12. Text of Arafat statement, *Baltimore Sun*, December 15, 1988.

13. Yitzhak Shamir, "Israel at 40: Looking Back, Looking Ahead," *Foreign Affairs* 66, no. 3 (1988), pp. 585–586.

14. The speeches of Rabin and Arafat, in Walter Laqueur and Barry Rubin, eds., *The Israel-Arab Reader: A Documentary History of the Middle East Conflict*, 5th rev. ed. (New York: Penguin, 1995), pp. 613–614.

15. Peres, cited in Connie Bruck, "The Wounds of Peace," *The New Yorker*, October 14, 1996, p. 64.

16. Cited in William Pfaff, "Victory to Extremists," *Baltimore Sun*, March 7, 1994, p. 14A.

17. According to the estimates of Arie Arnon of Peace Now; Graham Usher, "Middle East Divide," *The Nation*, December 25, 2000, p. 6.

18. Cited by Ben Macintyre, "Arafat: If I Sign, I'll Be Killed," *Times* (London), July 27, 2000, p. 17.

19. Amos Malka, cited in Robert Malley, "Israel and the Arafat Question," *New York Review of Books*, October 7, 2004, p. 23.

20. From the website of B'Tselem, the Israeli human rights organization, www.btselem.org. See also John Ward Anderson and Molly Moore, "Israel Blunts Uprising's Impact," *Washington Post*, October 5, 2004, p. A22, and "A Bloody Vacuum," *Economist*, October 2, 2004, pp. 23–25.

21. Dov Weisglass, one of Sharon's closest advisors, cited in John Ward Anderson, "Sharon Aide Says Goal of Gaza Plan Is to Halt Road Map," *Washington Post*, October 7, 2004.

22. Olmert interview in *Yedioth Ahronoth*, reprinted in *New York Review of Books*, December 4, 2008, pp. 6–8.

23. The precise numbers are murky, but nearly all of the thirty-one Israeli terrorist victims in 2008 (according to Israeli government figures) died at the hands of non-Hamas terrorists. "Where Will It End?" *Economist*, January 10, 2009, p. 24; Human Rights Watch, "Letter to Hamas to Stop Rocket Attacks," November 20, 2008, www.theisraelproject.org.

24. Barak Ravid, "Disinformation, Secrecy, and Lies: How the Gaza Offensive Came About," *Haaretz*, December 31, 2008.

Part 3

The Shifting Sands
of Global Power

The Cold War created a bipolar world in which the two contending superpowers pulled other nations toward one pole or the other. But gradually the bipolar East-West confrontation underwent a transformation marked by divisions within each camp and the emergence of other centers of power. The first ten years of the Cold War were marked by a straightforward adversarial relationship featuring the hard-nosed diplomatic combat of Joseph Stalin and Harry Truman. It also featured the US containment policy, the division of Europe, the creation of two military alliances (NATO and the Warsaw Pact), a war in Korea, persistent ideological attacks and counterattacks, and the massive rearmament of both sides. Despite the conciliatory gestures by the successors of Stalin and Truman and talk of peaceful coexistence, the bipolar struggle carried over into the 1960s, even to the point of the superpowers coming close to a nuclear exchange during the Cuban missile crisis.

By that time, however, it was clear to the superpowers that they could not make military use of their huge nuclear arsenals and that the day of direct confrontation was over. Indeed, the Cuban settlement was testimony to that reality. Additionally, by the early 1960s, the superpowers could no longer take for granted the solidarity of their respective alliances. The bipolar world began to give way to multipolarity.

To understand this process, Joseph Stalin's political legacy is our point of departure in Chapter 8. Here we trace the efforts of his successor, Nikita Khrushchev, to put to an end the excesses of Stalinism, the terror, and the arbitrary and abusive use of state power, and to institute reforms aimed at restoring orderly and legal procedures to Soviet rule and revitalizing the economy. The consequences of this reform effort and the pattern of Soviet politics under Khrushchev's successors are also discussed. We also examine the stresses and strains within the Communist bloc and particularly the impact of Khrushchev's reforms in Eastern Europe. The impact of Khrushchev's de-Stalinization was a controlled process in the Soviet Union, but that was not the case in the satellite countries, especially in Poland and Hungary, where it rekindled nationalist sentiments and unleashed pent-up desires for political liberalization and liberation from Moscow's control.

The revolts in Poland and Hungary and later in Czechoslovakia were snuffed out by the Soviet Union. A recalcitrant Communist China, however, could not so easily be dealt with. In Chapter 8, we analyze the causes and the course of the Sino-Soviet split, which divided the Communist world. Their bitter and long-lasting feud signified that ideological bonds were not stronger than national interests and that international Communism was not the monolithic movement it was generally thought to be.

Meanwhile, in the 1960s, the US government, still convinced that Communism was monolithic, went off to war in distant Asia to stop its spread. In Chapter 9, we explain how and why the United States took up the fight in Vietnam. The staunch anti-Communist logic prevalent in Washington caused a misreading of the revolution in that country, its causes and strengths, coming up with the erroneous conclusion that its source was Beijing-based Communist aggression rather than Vietnamese nationalism. We discuss the prolongation and expansion of the war in Vietnam and the difficulty the United States had in extracting itself from that war. We also examine the war's tragic consequences and impact on the remainder of Indochina, especially Cambodia, and the plight of the refugees, the "boatpeople."

In the late 1960s, despite the fact that the United States was still mired in Vietnam, progress was made in lowering East-West tensions elsewhere. New leadership in West Germany, specifically that of Chancellor Willy Brandt, took bold steps seeking to break up the twenty-year-old Cold War logjam in Central Europe. In Chapter 10, we examine Brandt's conciliatory policy toward the Communist nations of Eastern Europe and the role it played in bringing détente—the relaxation of tension—to East-West relations. By the early 1970s, détente became the basis also of Soviet-US diplomacy. The new relations between Washington and Moscow left Beijing isolated as an enemy of both. In fact, the US-Soviet détente at first brought jeers from China, which suspected an anti-Chinese conspiracy. But as we show in Chapter 10, Chinese leaders came to realize the dangers of China's continued isolation and judged that it had more to gain in terms of economic development and national security by normalizing its relations with the United States. In a dramatic diplomatic turnabout, the United States and Communist China, two nations that had been the most intransigent of ideological foes for over two decades, suddenly in 1972 buried the hatchet.

With US-Soviet détente and the normalization of US-Chinese relations, a new era of delicate tripolar power relations had arrived. Moreover, with the resurgence of Western Europe and the emergence of an economically powerful Japan, the international arena was now multipolar. The simpler world of East versus West, of the struggle between the "free world" and the "Communist world," gave way to a more complex world of power-balancing diplomacy, one calling for greater political flexibility.

8 The Communist World After Stalin

When Stalin died in March 1953, he had ruled the Soviet Union for nearly thirty years and in the process left his imprint on the Communist Party and the nation. In the late 1920s, Stalin and his party had set out to initiate a program of rapid industrialization with a series of Five-Year Plans. In order to feed the growing proletariat (the industrial workforce), he introduced a program of rapid collectivization whereby the small and inefficient individual farms were consolidated into larger collectives. In effect, it made the Soviet peasant an employee of the state. The state set the price that collective farms received for their agricultural commodities, a price kept low so that the countryside wound up subsidizing the cities, where an industrial revolution was taking place. In this fashion, agriculture became one of the "stepchildren" of the Communist revolution.

At the time of the revolution in 1917, the peasants briefly realized an age-old dream, the private and unrestricted ownership of their land. Predictably, they resisted the Stalinist drive toward collectivization. Stalin, faced with intense opposition, had two choices: curtail the program of collectivization and industrialization or pursue it with force. He chose the latter. Collectivization became a bloody civil war during the late 1920s and early 1930s, in which several million peasants perished, accompanied by the widespread destruction of equipment and livestock. In such a wasteful and brutal manner, the countryside was forced to subsidize the industrial revolution and the growth of the city.

Stalin subordinated Soviet society to one overriding quest: to create an industrial state for the purpose of bringing to an end Russia's traditional economic backwardness, the root cause of its military weakness. In 1931, he spoke to a conference of factory managers on the question of whether the mad dash toward industrialization could be slowed. He offered his audience a capsule history of Russia:

> To slacken the tempo would mean falling behind. And all those who fall be-
> hind get beaten. . . . One feature of the history of old Russia was the continual
> beatings she suffered because of her backwardness. She was beaten by the
> Mongol khans . . . the Turkish beys . . . the Swedish feudal lords . . . the Pol-
> ish and Lithuanian gentry . . . the British and French capitalists . . . the Japa-
> nese barons. All beat her—because of her backwardness, military backward-
> ness, cultural backwardness, political backwardness, industrial backwardness.
> . . . Such is the law of the exploiters, to beat the backward and the weak. . . .
> Either we do it [catch up with the capitalist West], or we shall be crushed. . . .
> In ten years we must make good the distance which separates us from the ad-
> vanced capitalist countries. . . . And that depends on us. Only on us![1]

Stalin's Five-Year Plans gave the Soviet Union a heavily centralized
economy capable of withstanding the supreme test of fire, the German attack
on the Soviet Union in 1941. In fact, during World War II the Soviet war economy, despite massive destruction at the hands of the Germans, outproduced
that of Germany. Studies conducted after the war for the US Joint Chiefs of
Staff repeatedly paid tribute to Stalin's industrial revolution, which had transformed the Soviet Union from a weak, backward country into a formidable opponent that in short order broke the US nuclear monopoly (1949) and later was
the first to venture into the frontiers of space (1957).

All of this did not come without a heavy price. The Soviet Union's "dictatorship of the proletariat"[2] became a dictatorship of the party over the proletariat and the peasantry, and eventually a dictatorship of the secret police over
the proletariat, the peasantry, and the party itself. In 1937, Stalin initiated the
bloodiest of a series of purges of the party by which he eliminated all opposition within the Communist Party. The Bolshevik Revolution of 1917, which
had begun as an uprising by the proletariat, rank-and-file soldiers, and peasants, had become a monument to the triumph of the secret police.

Khrushchev and Stalin's Ghost

When Stalin died in 1953, the party immediately took steps to reassert the position of preeminence it had enjoyed in the days of Vladimir Lenin, the architect of the Bolshevik Revolution, who had led the Soviet Union until his death
in 1924. Within a week after Stalin's death, the party forced Stalin's designated
successor, Georgi Malenkov, to give up one of the two posts he held. The party
told him to choose between the post of first secretary of the party (i.e., the head
of the party) and that of prime minister. Malenkov, inexplicably, decided to
hold on to the position of prime minister. As a result, a lesser member of the
ruling circle, the Politburo, Nikita Khrushchev, became the new first secretary
of the party in charge of its daily operations. The party then took another step
to prevent the consolidation of power in the hands of one person. It officially

Soviet leader Nikita Khrushchev, flanked by Foreign Minister Andrei Gromyko and Marshal Rodion Malinovski, at a press conference in Paris, May 16, 1960. *(National Archives)*

established a collective leadership, a *troika* (Russian for a sled pulled by three horses) consisting of Malenkov as prime minister, Viacheslav Molotov as foreign minister, and Lavrentii Beria as the head of the secret police. Beria, who had been an agent of Stalin's terror, remained a threat to the party. In the summer of 1953, the party, with the help of generals in the Soviet army (which also had suffered greatly during the secret police's unchecked reign of terror), arrested Beria. It charged him with the abuse of power and then shot him.

The party continued in its attempts to come to terms with the Stalinist legacy. The reformers, however, repeatedly clashed with those who sought to prevent meaningful changes. Gradually, in the mid-1950s, the reformers gained the upper hand and some of the shackles of the Stalinist past were cast off. A general amnesty freed political prisoners. Writers, many of whom had been "writing for the desk drawer," succeeded in seeing their works in print. Détente with the West now became a possibility. Western visitors began to arrive in Moscow.

The most dramatic assault on the status of Stalin came in February 1956, at the Communist Party's Twentieth Congress, when Nikita Khrushchev delivered a scathing attack on Stalin's crimes. It became known as the "Secret Speech," but it did not remain secret for long—since any address before an assembly of hundreds of delegates, many of whom had much to gain by making it public, would certainly reach the light of day. The speech was the result of a commission the party had set up to report on Beria's and Stalin's crimes committed against the party. Khrushchev told the assembled delegates that Stalin's terror, including the destruction of the party's role in the affairs of the state, had been an act of lawlessness, one that the party now sought to prevent in the future. "Socialist legality" was to take the place of one-person rule.

The speech was essentially an attempt by the party at self-preservation. And it was limited to just that. It did not address the larger question of Stalin's terror directed against the peasants, religious organizations, writers, and composers— in short, the public at large. One of Khrushchev's Western biographers wrote that the Secret Speech was a smokescreen as well as an exposure.[3] It did not tackle the question of one-party rule by the "vanguard of the proletariat," the Communist Party. Neither did it challenge the Stalinist system of agriculture, which the party admitted at the time was in ruins, or the system of industrial organization, which still worked reasonably well. Instead, Khrushchev's speech focused on the dictatorship of the police over the party.

The Secret Speech signaled the end of the arbitrary terror of Stalin's time. The secret police was brought under the party's control and its wings were clipped, particularly in dealing with party members. Arbitrary arrests were largely ended. Censorship restrictions were partially lifted, breathing new life into the Soviet Union's intellectual community. Throughout his tenure Khrushchev repeatedly waged war against the memory of Stalin, particularly in 1956 and then in 1961, when he went so far as to remove Stalin's body from the mausoleum it shared with Lenin's remains and to rename cities and institutions that had been named in Stalin's honor. The city of Stalingrad, for example, the supreme symbol of the Soviet Union's resistance to Hitler, where an entire German army found defeat, became merely Volgograd, the "city on the Volga."

After Khrushchev's ouster in October 1964, the party made no concerted effort to rehabilitate Stalin's image, although overt criticism of Stalin was brought to an end. It was clear, however, that one day Soviet society again would have to come to grips with Stalin's legacy. The transformation of Stalin's image from a hero and generalissimo, to a murderous tyrant in violation of "Leninist legality," and finally to a shadowy figure who appeared scarcely to have existed, simply would not do. In 1961, the party published the long-awaited second edition of its *History of the Communist Party of the Soviet Union*. The first edition, published in 1938 under Stalin's direct editorship, had heaped voluminous praise on Stalin. The second edition, in contrast, was an example of revisionist history with a vengeance. It never mentioned Stalin's name. It was only after a quarter-century, under the impetus of Mikhail Gorbachev's reforms, that Soviet society once more was brought face-to-face with Stalin's legacy.

To many observers in the West, these changes were of little consequence. The Communist Party still retained its control and the economy remained unchanged. But in the context of Russian and Soviet history, the changes were significant. This was something on which both Khrushchev and his opponents agreed. Khrushchev needed to tread carefully without stirring up major repercussions, for, as Alexis de Tocqueville (the French political writer of the nineteenth century) noted, harking back to the French Revolution, the most difficult time in the life of a bad government comes when it tries to reform itself. Khrushchev soon found that out.

Philosophically, Khrushchev expressed the view that art must not be censored. But the flood of writings portraying Soviet reality as it in fact existed, warts and all, soon overwhelmed the party, and Khrushchev himself became a censor. In 1962, Khrushchev permitted the publication of Alexander Solzhenitsyn's exposé of Stalin's labor camps, *One Day in the Life of Ivan Denisovich,* the literary sensation of the post-Stalin age; yet, several years earlier, Khrushchev had supported "administrative measures" to prevent the publication of Boris Pasternak's *Doctor Zhivago,* admittedly without having read it. Late in life, a repentant Khrushchev wrote that "readers should be given a chance to make their own judgments" and that "police measures shouldn't be used."[4] As the first secretary of the party, however, Khrushchev never did manage to come to grips with his contradictions. The result was that he was unable to bring the restless writers under control. This task fell to his successor, Leonid Brezhnev, a man lacking all subtlety.

By the early 1960s, Khrushchev had worn out his welcome. The majority of the party increasingly viewed his erratic moves and innovations as harebrained schemes. The classic case in point was the attempt to place nuclear missiles in Cuba in 1962, a rash, impulsive act. Poorly thought out and hasty reforms in the areas of agriculture and industry also came back to haunt Khrushchev.

In 1958, Khrushchev demanded a drastic rise in meat production to surpass the United States. The ambitious first secretary of the party in Riazan, A. N. Larionov, publicly pledged a doubling of meat production in 1959. Khrushchev then ordered that other regions follow the Riazan example. In February 1959, before Larionov could even get started, Khrushchev went to Riazan to bestow on him personally the prestigious Order of Lenin. A desperate Larionov fulfilled his pledge by slaughtering whatever livestock was available. Eventually, he went outside the region to purchase milk cows and breeding stock. In December 1959, Larionov declared a hollow "victory" for which, nevertheless, he was once again decorated. In 1960, meat production declined by 200,000 tons, a decline that took years to reverse. At the end of 1960, Larionov, a Hero of Socialist Labor, shot himself in his office.[5]

In October 1964, Khrushchev initiated a shakeup in the party. It proved to be the last straw, for it threatened the exalted positions of many. By then Khrushchev had lost the support of the majority in the Central Committee, officially the major decisionmaking body of the Communist Party. The party, in a vote of no confidence, sent him out to pasture with the stipulation that he stay out of politics. Leonid Brezhnev succeeded him as the head of the party.

Khrushchev's demise proved to be his finest hour. He had dealt with his opponents within the bounds of "socialist legality," that is, by using the rules and procedures written into the party's statutes and by using the support many in the party at one time gave him enthusiastically. But when his behavior became increasingly irrational, embarrassing, and reckless, the party then turned against him. Once he faced the cold, hard fact that he had lost the support of the majority, he stepped down. There was never a question of using the military or the secret police.

Khrushchev's successors gave the Soviet Union twenty years of stability, a significant increase in the standard of living, and rough military parity with the West. At the same time, this was an era when the status quo was maintained. A freewheeling discussion of Stalin's role in Soviet history had no place in the scheme of the Brezhnev vision of Soviet society. The intellectuals were eventually brought under control by intimidation, jailing, and, in several cases, notably that of Solzhenitsyn, expulsion from the country. Brezhnev's prime minister, Alexei Kosygin, contemplated economic reforms but they were soon shelved when it became apparent that all too many factory managers had their fill of reforms under Khrushchev and fought for the retention of the status quo.

By the time Brezhnev died in 1982, the party was beginning to accept the need for another round of reform. Yuri Andropov and Konstantin Chernenko initiated the first modest steps, but both were hampered by what turned out to be incurable illnesses. In 1985, Mikhail Gorbachev, the new first secretary of the party, took on the nation's problems. In a direct challenge to Brezhnev's political, economic, and intellectual inertia, Gorbachev committed his nation to a wide-ranging discussion of its shortcomings and to the restructuring of the economy (see Chapter 18).

Eastern Europe: The Satellites

As the Communist Party in the Soviet Union wrestled with Stalin's ghost, a similar drama began to unfold in Moscow's East European satellites. There, the conflict was fought with much more intensity and conviction. The reformers were willing to go much farther than their counterparts behind the Kremlin walls. Although much of Eastern Europe subsequently moved farther from the Stalinist model than did the Soviet Union, Moscow always made clear that the reforms must remain within certain parameters, which, although not rigidly defined and constantly shifting, must not be transgressed. In its dealings with the restless East Europeans, Moscow did not hesitate to brandish its big stick, the Soviet army, just in case someone stepped out of line.

The West considered Soviet postwar expansion a threat to its security and saw it as a source of Soviet strength. Stalin, however, saw it in a different light. He knew that the East European buffer offered his state a measure of security but that it was also a potential source of headaches. At the Yalta Conference he had described the Poles as "quarrelsome." He well understood the volatile mix of nationalism, religion, and anti-Russian sentiments in Eastern Europe. Soviet occupation of Eastern Europe had strengthened his forward position in a future confrontation with the capitalist West, but it also promised to bring problems.

By 1948, Stalin appeared to have consolidated his position in Eastern Europe. The Communist parties there were for the most part the creation of the Soviet Union, and on the surface loyal members of the Communist camp lined up in solidarity against the capitalist threat. But the Communists of Eastern Europe were soon showing nationalist tendencies; it became clear they were more interested in championing the causes of their own nations instead of serving the Kremlin's interests.

Yugoslavia

The classic example of such "nationalist deviation" was the case of Joseph Tito, the Communist ruler of Yugoslavia. In the late 1930s, Tito had spent time in Moscow under Stalin's tutelage, and during World War II he had fought with the Red Army (as well as the Western Allies) against Nazi Germany. His loyalty to Stalin and the cause of international Marxist solidarity appeared beyond reproach. Soon after the war, however, at the very moment the West and the Soviet Union were taking steps to consolidate their respective positions, the Yugoslav and Soviet Communists had a falling-out over the question of who was to play the dominant role in running Yugoslavia. The upshot of this quarrel was that Tito established his independence from Moscow. He did not, however, move into the capitalist camp. He accepted aid from the West, but always maintained a position of neutrality between East and West.[6] The Tito-Stalin split pointed to a central problem the Soviets faced in Eastern Europe, the volatile force of nationalism.

The immediate consequence of Tito's defection was Stalin's reorganization of the Communist governments of Eastern Europe. He executed and jailed Communists (such as Poland's Wladyslaw Gomulka, of whom more later) whom he suspected of nationalist (or Titoist) tendencies. The loyalty of foreign Communists, Stalin had always insisted, must be to the Soviet Union, not to their native lands. Stalin's definition of a loyal Communist was one who faithfully served the interests of the Kremlin. An international "*revolutionary*," he wrote in 1927, is one "who is ready to protect, to defend the U.S.S.R. without reservation, without qualification."[7] In short, the interests of the Soviet Union outweighed the considerations of all other socialist governments. Stalin never budged on this definition of an international revolutionary. Only one Marxist was permitted to be a nationalist, namely, Stalin himself.

The damage Stalin did to Communist movements abroad was seldom adequately appreciated or understood in the West. Not only did he subordinate the Communist parties to the interests of his state, but in doing so he tainted them with a brush wielded by a foreign power. As such, these movements found themselves struggling for support, their association with Moscow a millstone dragging them down, and their thunder stolen by reformist socialists in the West. After World War II, the shifts to the left were the result of wars, poverty, and disillusion with the old order, not the creation of Stalin; the left's demise, however, was in part Stalin's responsibility.

Stalin's brutal cleansing ("purging") of the East European Communist parties did have its desired effect. Until Stalin's death in March 1953, these parties were outwardly loyal to the Soviet Union, and Eastern Europe remained calm.

Poland

Soon after Stalin's death, however, the East European Communist parties began to work toward partial independence from Moscow. It did not mean that they sought to leave the socialist camp or to legalize capitalist political parties, but they did insist on dealing with their own internal problems without direct intervention by Moscow. An element of self-preservation played a large part in the restructuring of the relationship between the East European Communist parties and Moscow. The East Europeans sought to do away with Moscow's repeated and arbitrary purges of their ranks and interference in their internal affairs. The Polish party took the lead when it quietly released from house arrest (December 1954) and later readmitted (August 1956) into the party the nationalist Wladyslaw Gomulka.

Stalin had good reason to mistrust Gomulka. As early as 1945, Stalin's agents in Poland had warned him that the "deviationist" Gomulka had repeatedly and publicly advocated a "Polish road" to socialism, a "Polish Marxism." Gomulka's variation of Communism, unlike the Soviet version, sought a peaceful rather than a bloody transformation of society. It rejected the collectivization of agriculture, spoke of a "parliamentary democracy" for Poland, and even suggested that the Polish Communist Party had seized political power in 1945 in its own right—as it was "lying in the street" ready to be picked up—thus failing to show proper gratitude for the role of the Red Army. What we are dealing with here, Stalin's agents pointed out, is more a case of "Polish nationalism" than of Communism based on the Soviet model.[8]

The return to power of East European Communists who had been driven from power by Stalin was greatly speeded up by Nikita Khrushchev's denunciation of Stalin's "mistakes" and "excesses," namely, his crimes against members of the Communist Party in the Soviet Union itself. Khrushchev had sought to discredit his Stalinist political opponents at home, but his action had unforeseen and important repercussions in Eastern Europe.

After Khrushchev attacked Stalin in his Secret Speech at the Twentieth Congress of the Communist Party of the Soviet Union in February 1956, the Polish Communist Party, which had sent delegates to the congress, leaked a copy of the speech to the West. Khrushchev later wrote in his memoirs: "I was told that it was being sold for very little. So Khrushchev's speech . . . wasn't appraised as being worth much! Intelligence agents from every country in the world could buy it cheap on the open market."[9] If Khrushchev could denounce Stalinism at home, the Poles reasoned, then they ought to be able to do the same. The Poles then used the speech to justify their attempt to travel their own road toward socialism without, however, leaving the Soviet camp.

At home the reformist wing of the Polish Communist Party had its work cut out. The summer of 1956 saw rioting by workers, particularly in Poznan, where seventy-five were shot dead in confrontations with police. To deal with the crisis, the party convened in October 1956 to initiate a program of reform and to elect Gomulka as its first secretary. Upon his election, Gomulka delivered a speech in which he affirmed Poland's right to follow a socialist model other than the Soviet example. He also insisted on his country's "full independence and sovereignty," as part of every nation's right to self-government. Polish-Soviet relations, he said, must be based on equality and independence.

What particularly had galled the Poles was that their defense minister, Konstantin Rokossovsky, was a Soviet citizen. Rokossovsky, a native of Poland, had left his country for the Soviet Union and had risen to the highest military rank, that of marshal of the Red Army. As Poland's minister of defense he thus served a foreign master. Understandably, Rokossovsky became one of the first casualties of Poland's peaceful "October Revolution" when he was dismissed as defense minister.

The behavior by the Polish Communists alarmed their Soviet comrades. In October, a high-level Soviet delegation, led by Khrushchev, arrived uninvited in Warsaw. The Poles refused to back down. They made clear they would continue to travel down the socialist road, yet at the same time, they insisted on the right to take care of their own internal problems. To mollify their Soviet counterparts, they pledged loyalty to the Warsaw Pact, the Soviet-led military alliance.

The Soviet Union, here, gave tacit assent to the principle that there existed several different roads to socialism, that the Soviet model was not the only one and thus not necessarily the correct one. In effect, the Kremlin yielded and accepted the legitimacy of what once was a heresy, the right to nationalist deviation. If the Soviets had the right to find their own path to socialism, so did the other socialist countries. In fact, Khrushchev had already buried the hatchet in the ideological dispute with Tito. In May 1955, he had gone to Belgrade on a state visit and when he and Tito embraced, it signaled an end to the intra-Marxist feud. The Soviet Union's monopoly on interpreting the writings of Marx and Engels was no more. The Italian Communist Palmiro Togliatti coined a word to describe the new reality, "polycentrism." The world now had several centers of Marxist orthodoxy.

The Poles, although still in the shadow of the Soviet Union, embarked on their own road to socialism. The Communist Party set out to placate the restless population. The gradual process of collectivizing farmland was halted and then reversed. (Unlike the Soviet Union, where the state owned all the land, most farmland in Communist Poland was in the hands of private farmers.) Political parties other than the Communist Party were permitted to exist and they received subordinate representation in the government. Small businesses were tolerated. Gomulka released from jail the prelate of the Roman Catholic Church in Poland, Stefan Cardinal Wyszynski, and the church regained the traditional right to administer its own affairs. In turn, Gomulka received the church's endorsement.

Hungary

Across the border, the Hungarians watched the events in Poland with increasing intensity. If the Poles could eliminate some of the baleful effects of Stalinism, why could not they? Heated discussions took place in intellectual circles and within the Hungarian Communist Party. The upshot was that the Stalinists were forced to resign and Imre Nagy, Hungary's "Gomulka," took over.

Initially, events in Hungary paralleled those in Poland. But Nagy could not control the rebellious mood that was building up in his country. Reformers argued that a reformed Communist Party, freed of the Stalinists, was not enough; nothing short of independence from Moscow would do. Deep-seated Hungarian animosity toward the Russians had its historic roots in the intervention by the Russian army during the revolution of 1848, when Hungarians had sought to free themselves of Austrian domination. Also, the Stalinist secret police had bred deep resentment. These factors, as well as economic grievances, led to massive street demonstrations and the lynching of secret police agents. Budapest had become unmanageable, and on November 1, 1956, Nagy suddenly announced that Hungary was now an independent nation. With this declaration came the pledge to hold free elections—elections that would no doubt bring an end to Communist Party rule in Hungary.

The events in Hungary left Nikita Khrushchev few choices, particularly when Radio Free Europe, a station operating out of Munich under the aegis of the CIA, encouraged the Hungarians by offering vague promises of US aid. At this highly charged moment in the Cold War, a neutral Hungary was out of the question. John Foster Dulles, the US secretary of state, had said earlier that neutrality in this holy, ideologically charged crusade against the forces of ab-

Hungarian secret police executed in the street by "freedom fighters," October 1956. *(National Archives)*

solute evil was the height of immorality.[10] The leaders in the Kremlin held a similar view. Hungary's destiny remained to be but a pawn in an ideological and military tug-of-war. The question in the fall of 1956 was whether it would serve the interests of Washington or Moscow. With the Soviet position in Eastern Europe beginning to disintegrate, Khrushchev acted.

For several days, the Soviets hesitated. At first, they saw the disturbances in Budapest as anti-Soviet (as had been the case in Poland) but not anti-Communist. They expected to work with Nagy and even discussed the possibility of withdrawing their troops from Hungary. But then came the news that Communists were being lynched in the streets of Budapest. Any withdrawal, Khrushchev now argued, would "cheer up the imperialists." "We had to act," he wrote in his memoirs, "and we had to act swiftly."[11]

The Soviet army attacked Budapest three days after Nagy's proclamation. After a week of savage fighting, the Soviets reestablished their control over Hungary. The Kremlin installed János Kádár as the Hungarian party's new first secretary, who came to power with blood on his hands. He became known as the "butcher of Budapest" for having come to power by dint of the Soviet Union's violent suppression of the revolution and because of his execution of Nagy and others in 1958.

In time, however, Kádár proved to be a cautious reformer. Over the next three decades, he introduced the most sweeping economic reforms anywhere in the Soviet bloc, culminating in the legalization of private enterprises in the early 1980s. This combination of the carrot (tolerance of reforms) and the stick (the Soviet army) lifted many restrictions, raised the standard of living, and kept Hungary quiet.

The United States could do little but watch with indignation the Soviet suppression of the Hungarian uprising and offer political asylum to many of the nearly 200,000 Hungarians who fled their country. John Foster Dulles, who in the past had repeatedly stated that the aim of the United States was the liberation of Eastern Europe and the rollback of the Soviet presence there, could do no more than watch in frustration. The events in Hungary offered him the opportunity to put his policy into operation, but President Dwight Eisenhower's cautious response revealed that Dulles's rhetoric was just that. The Hungarian rebellion also made clear that the United States would not challenge the Soviet Union in Eastern Europe; it would not start World War III over Poland or Hungary. The lesson was not lost on the Soviets when they had to deal with Czechoslovakia in 1968.

Czechoslovakia

Events in Poland and Hungary did not affect Czechoslovakia during the 1950s. The country continued to be ruled by Antonin Novotny, whom Stalin had placed in power in 1952. In the late 1960s, Czechoslovakia, therefore, appeared to be the least likely candidate for social and political reform. Yet many in Czechoslovakia bitterly resented the unreconstructed Stalinist Novotny, particularly the writers but also members of his own party. When a writers' rebellion began late in 1967, Novotny found himself unable to deal with it because his own party did not support him. It asked him to resign, and he did so in January 1968. After the party dutifully checked with the Kremlin, Leonid Brezhnev responded that "this is your matter." The party then elected Alexander Dubček as its first secretary.

The writers, however, many of whom were Communists, had raised a number of basic questions—those of civil rights, censorship, and the monopoly of the Communist Party in the political, economic, and social affairs of the nation. After Novotny's ouster, the party continued the discussions. Under Dubček's stewardship, it introduced numerous reforms at breakneck speed. It attempted to create "socialism with a human face," one that sought to combine Eastern-style socialism with Western-style democracy. One restriction after another was lifted. The results were freedom of the press, freedom to travel, freedom from fear of the police. An intense and open debate of the nature of the reforms took place in the uncensored pages of the press. The "Prague Spring" was under way. In the spring and summer of 1968, euphoria swept a nation that became oblivious to the inherent dangers of such radical reforms. Soon there was the inevitable talk of the possibility of leaving the Soviet bloc and of neutrality.

The Soviet leadership watched these developments intensely. Several high-ranking delegations arrived from Moscow and other East European capitals. The Communist parties of Eastern Europe urged Dubček and his party to bring the movement under control before it completely got out of hand. Several of the East European governments (particularly those of Yugoslavia and Hungary) did not want to give the Soviet Union an excuse for intervention. But it was to no avail. Dubček neither wanted to nor was able to put an end to the discussions and experiments. The hopeful Prague Spring continued unabated. The border between Czechoslovakia and Austria became but a line on a map that Czechs—and visitors from the West—crossed without restriction. The Iron Curtain ceased to exist in this part of Europe.

Until August 1968, the Soviet leadership was divided on what course to take. The hard-liners in Moscow became convinced that Dubček and his party were no longer in control. To them, what was happening in Czechoslovakia was not a local matter but a counterrevolution in the making, one Dubček was unable and unwilling to bring to an end. Dubček was well aware of the inherent danger of this situation, that the Soviets had a contingency plan to use force. In a telephone conversation with Brezhnev on August 13, a week before the invasion, Dubček said, "If you consider us traitors, then take the measures which your Politburo considers necessary."[12]

Events in Czechoslovakia also threatened to create repercussions in the Soviet Union. The non-Russian population of the Soviet empire—approximately half of the population—watched the events in Czechoslovakia with growing interest. The party chiefs in the non-Russian republics, particularly those of Ukraine and Lithuania, took the lead in urging strong action. Brezhnev convened a plenary session of the party's Central Committee to inform the party that the Warsaw Pact was about to put an end to the Prague Spring. On August 20, 1968, Brezhnev ordered the Soviet army into action. When the Soviet tanks rolled into Prague, the Czechs, as expected, did not resist to any appreciable degree. The Soviets then replaced Dubček with Gustav Husak.

The Soviets justified their invasion by claiming that they had to protect Czechoslovakia against a counterrevolution. Moreover, Brezhnev declared that the Soviet Union possessed the inherent right to intervene in all socialist countries similarly threatened. This unilateral Soviet right of intervention in Eastern Europe became known in the West as the Brezhnev Doctrine. In 1979, Brezhnev used it anew to justify intervention in Afghanistan, when he sent the Soviet army to bail out a bankrupt socialist government. And in 1980, Brezhnev resurrected it to warn Poland's Solidarity movement against going too far.

Ironically, the Soviet Union had been able to count on a certain measure of goodwill among the population of Czechoslovakia until the invasion of 1968. It had been the Red Army in 1945 that had liberated Prague from the Germans, and only the Soviets had appeared to be willing to come to the aid of Czechoslovakia when Hitler carved it up in 1938. But whatever goodwill had existed before 1968 became a thing of the past.

East Germany

East Germany was unique among the Communist states in Eastern Europe. For one, it was the last of the Communist states Stalin established. It is not clear what Stalin had in mind for Germany after World War II, but after the West had formally created West Germany in May 1949, Stalin had little choice but to create his own state in October of that year. As late as March 1952, Stalin still proposed to the West a unified—but demilitarized and neutral—Germany. A West German historian concluded that East Germany was "Stalin's unloved child,"[13] a burden he wanted to be rid of. Stalin's proposal to unload East Germany came too late, however, as the Cold War by 1952 was in full bloom and attitudes had hardened. By then, West Germany was well on its way to rearmament as a member of NATO.

Second, East Germany was the Communist state with the least popular support. Its leaders understood only too well that without Soviet backing their state had no chance of existing. The politicians in Bonn considered it part of West Germany and bided their time until reunification. As a result, East German leaders, such as Walter Ulbricht and Erich Honecker, were the most hawkish of all the East European Communist rulers. They wanted the Soviets to dig in as deeply as possible in defiance against the West. Shortly after Stalin died in March 1953, politicians in Moscow once again contemplated the abandonment of East Germany. But when widespread uprisings took place on June 17, 1953,[14] Moscow, after initial hesitation, came to the "fraternal" assistance of a Communist client in deep political trouble. It was Soviet army tanks that put an end to the disturbances in East Berlin and other cities.

Third, the Western challenge East Germany faced was not only political but also economic. As East Germany gradually rebuilt its economy under Soviet auspices, West Germany experienced a sustained economic boom. By the late 1950s, West Germany had reached its prewar standard of living, and it continued to improve. As a booming West German economy suffered from a shortage of skilled workers, many East Germans left their country to participate in the political and economic benefits in the West. East Berliners were able to travel by public transport to West Berlin, where they automatically received West German citizenship. Berlin became the biggest hole in the Iron Curtain. By the early 1960s, the hemorrhage was so serious for East Germany that Khrushchev repeatedly threatened war to drive the West out of Berlin.

The Berlin Blockade (1948–1949) and Khrushchev's saber-rattling proved to be ineffective in dislodging the Western powers. Another way had to be found to stop the bleeding. Khrushchev's solution was the erection of a ten-foot barrier around West Berlin. The Berlin Wall, built in August 1961, solved East Ger-

View of the Berlin Wall, part of the "German-German" border, where eighty East Germans lost their lives trying to leave for the West. Another 720 died along the rest of the 850-mile-long border. *(German Information Center)*

many's most pressing problem when it sealed off the last remaining gap in the Iron Curtain. The East Germans left behind were shut off from the rest of the German-speaking world. The Berlin Wall became the supreme symbol of the division of Europe, the most visible manifestation of the Iron Curtain.

The Sino-Soviet Split

After Stalin's death, the Soviet leaders faced another crisis within the Communist world. By the mid-1950s, the Communist rulers of the People's Republic of China (PRC) began to strike out on their own. Before long, it became apparent that the two Communist giants were at loggerheads. The rift between them became more serious with each passing year, and by the early 1960s, relations were openly hostile. The feud between the Communist giants had a great impact on international relations. The Cold War, initially a bipolar struggle between East and West, gave way to a triangular pattern of relations among the Soviet Union, China, and the United States.

From the time of its formation in October 1949, the PRC sought to establish and maintain close relations with the Soviet Union. At the time, Moscow and Washington were engaged in a potentially dangerous rivalry that already had turned into a nuclear standoff. Chairman Mao Zedong's mission to Moscow in early 1950 seemed to confirm the suspicion that Mao and Stalin were comrades united in the cause of international Communism and mutually dedicated to the defeat of the capitalist world. In February 1950, they signed a thirty-year military alliance aimed at the United States, and the Soviet Union took up the cause of seating the PRC in the United Nations to replace the Republic of China (Nationalist China, i.e., Taiwan). The Soviet Union also provided much needed economic assistance to China in the form of loans, technicians, and advisors. In November 1950, Beijing sent its troops against the US-led forces of the United Nations in Korea. Moscow and Beijing rallied in support of Communist North Korea during the Korean War. And of course they spoke the same Marxist language as they denounced US imperialism. Moscow and Beijing thus faced a common foe and professed a common ideology. There was little reason to believe that their alliance would be short-lived. Yet, a scant six years after the PRC had come into existence, the two began to pull apart.

It was little wonder that the United States was skeptical about the early reports of difficulties between the two Communist states. The US assumption, fostered by the Cold War, was that Communism was a monolith, a single unitary movement directed by Moscow. This assumption was much slower to die than the reality of Communist unity.

In retrospect, we can recognize signs of friction between Beijing and Moscow from the very outset. The Chinese could hardly be pleased by the rather cavalier manner in which Stalin treated them. The terms of the Moscow agreement (1950) were not at all generous. Stalin offered Mao a development loan of no more than $300 million to be spread over five years and to be repaid by China in agricultural produce and with interest. As a price for that loan, China agreed to continued Soviet use and control of the principal railroads and ports in Manchuria and to the creation of joint Sino-Soviet stock companies to conduct mineral surveys in Xinjiang (Sinkiang), the innermost province of China. The paucity of Soviet aid and the concessions Stalin demanded from China suggest that Stalin's purpose was to accentuate Soviet supremacy and Chinese dependency. Indeed, it would seem that Stalin was wary of this new Communist friend and that he would have preferred dealing with a weaker, more vulnerable Nationalist China than with a vigorous new Communist regime in China. If the Chinese harbored ill feelings toward Stalin or resented the continued Soviet presence in Manchuria and Xinjiang, they prudently remained silent, publicly accepting Stalin's leadership and extolling their fraternal relationship with the Soviet Union. The backwardness of China's economy was such that Chinese leaders considered Soviet economic assistance and diplomatic support too important to be sacrificed on the altar of national pride.

The unspoken Chinese misgivings during the early 1950s did not lead directly to the Sino-Soviet split later that decade. Nor is that feud to be explained as a direct consequence of earlier Sino-Russian troubles. One can surely trace the historical roots of animosity between the two countries back in time, to tsarist imperialism in the nineteenth century, or even to the Mongol invasions of Russia in the thirteenth century. But it would be too simple to argue that the conflict in the late 1950s was, therefore, the inevitable result of that history. The two sides dredged up the conflicts of the past, such as territorial claims, only after the dispute began to develop over other contemporary issues in the mid-1950s.

The first strains of conflict between Moscow and Beijing came in consequence of Soviet leader Nikita Khrushchev's famous Secret Speech in February 1956. The Chinese leaders were caught by surprise by this sudden, scathing attack on Stalin and by Khrushchev's call for peaceful coexistence with the capitalist world. Chinese Communists had no particular reason to defend the departed Stalin, but they feared that the attack on Stalin's "cult of personality" might, by implication, undermine Mao's dictatorship in China. Moreover, they questioned the wisdom of peaceful coexistence and they disputed the right of Moscow to unilaterally make such a major ideological shift with significant global implications. The Chinese chafed at Khrushchev's bold reinterpretation of Marxist-Leninist doctrine, without so much as consulting with Mao in advance. Mao, who had led the Chinese Communist Party since 1935, was the world's senior ranking Communist leader, and he had reason to object to being ignored by the brash new leader of the Soviet Union. The Chinese were, in effect, questioning Khrushchev's authority to dictate policy to the Communist world.

The new Soviet line of peaceful coexistence soon became the major bone of contention between Moscow and Beijing. The Soviet leadership had become alarmed about the nuclear arms race and came to the conviction that the Soviet Union must avert a devastating nuclear war with the United States, whose burgeoning nuclear arsenal posed a serious threat to the survival of their country. Khrushchev, therefore, concluded that it would be necessary to coexist peacefully with the capitalist superpower. However, at the same time that they were offering the olive branch to the other side, the Soviets worked feverishly to close the gap in the arms race, and in 1957, they made two remarkable technological breakthroughs. They launched their first intercontinental ballistic missile (ICBM) in August, and in October they stunned the world with *Sputnik*, the first artificial satellite sent into orbit around the earth. The enormous strategic significance of this Soviet advance in military technology was not lost on the Chinese. Mao, attending a meeting of world Communist leaders in Moscow in November 1957, contended that the international situation had reached a new turning point and that the Communist world had stolen the march on the capitalist world in the contest for global power. Mao asserted that "at present, it is not the west wind which is prevailing over the east wind, but the east wind prevailing over the west wind."[15] He argued that the Communist camp should put its newfound military superiority to work to attain the final victory over capitalism. Khrushchev strongly rejected these ideas and concluded the meeting with a reaffirmation of peaceful coexistence.

This was the origin of the dispute over global strategy that ultimately split the two Communist giants. The Chinese argued that, by making peace with the capitalists, the Soviet Union was departing from essential Marxist-Leninist doctrine. Peaceful coexistence might suit the Soviet Union, already an industrialized nation with secure borders and nuclear weapons, but it did not serve China, which had none of these. Mao well remembered that his army had fought a bloody war with the United States in the not too distant past in Korea, a war the imperialists in Washington were sure to resume. Mao argued that Communist nations should continue the international struggle by assisting Communist forces engaged in wars of national liberation. Moreover, the PRC sought assurances of Soviet support in its own unfinished war of national liberation: the civil war against Jiang Jieshi's Nationalist regime, which controlled the island of Taiwan. In 1958, Beijing intensified its pressure on Taiwan by launching a sustained artillery barrage against two offshore islands occupied by Nationalist forces, Quemoy and Matsu. It seems that Mao's purpose was to test the resolve of the United States to defend Nationalist China and to test Soviet willingness to provide active military support to the PRC. The United States did make clear its commitment to the defense of Taiwan, but the Soviets, instead of pledging support, denounced China's actions as reckless. The Soviet Union would not allow itself to be drawn into a nuclear war with the United States over Taiwan.

The two Communist powers also disagreed on the means to attaining Communism. The Chinese had adopted the Soviet model for economic development when, in 1953, they put into operation a Soviet-style Five-Year Plan. But by 1957, the leaders in Beijing were beginning to question the appropriateness of the Soviet model for China. In early 1958, Mao called for scrapping the Second Five-Year Plan and replaced it with his own program, the Great Leap Forward. Boldly, Mao proclaimed that China had overtaken the Soviet Union in the quest to build a Communist society. But Mao was too quick to trumpet success, for within a year the Great Leap Forward, with its hastily created communes, produced an economic disaster (see Chapter 14). The Kremlin was concerned about the implications of any departure from Soviet orthodoxy since its East European satellites, like China, had similar ideas of departing from the Soviet model. From the very beginning, Khrushchev criticized the new experiment in China. When it failed, he heaped all the more scorn on Mao's heralded Great Leap Forward.

In September 1959, Khrushchev gave Mao reason to suspect that the Soviet Union was plotting against China. At the invitation of President Eisenhower, Khrushchev made a two-week visit to the United States. Mao, who remained adamantly opposed to peaceful coexistence, took a dim view of this diplomatic venture. His suspicious mind was left to speculate on what had transpired at Camp David during the private talks between Khrushchev and Eisenhower. He suspected that Khrushchev was making concessions at China's expense, specifically, striking a bargain that would trade Western concessions on the Berlin question for a Soviet commitment to oppose the PRC's use of force to settle the Taiwan question.

In 1960, the polemical feud between Moscow and Beijing became an open confrontation as each side, for the first time, made public their attacks on the other. The Chinese Communist Party struck first, in April 1960, with an article titled "Long Live Leninism" in *Red Flag*, an official organ of the Chinese Communist Party. It argued that peaceful coexistence was contrary to the precepts of Leninism.

> We believe in the absolute correctness of Lenin's thinking: War is an inevitable outcome of systems of exploitation and the source of modern wars is the imperialist system. Until the imperialist system and the exploiting classes come to an end, wars of one kind or another will always occur.[16]

Khrushchev responded quickly. In July 1960, he abruptly pulled out of China its 1,300 Soviet economic advisors, engineers, and technicians, who took their blueprints with them and left behind many unfinished projects. This was a serious blow to China's industrialization efforts. At the same time, Moscow rescinded an earlier agreement to provide China nuclear technology to build the atomic bomb.

Khrushchev's purpose was not to terminate the alliance but to force Beijing back into line and to coerce its acceptance of Moscow's policies and position of leadership. In the year that followed, Beijing seemed to acquiesce while a more conciliatory Moscow seemed to be backing away from détente with the United States. But this proved to be only a brief respite, for in October 1961, at the Twenty-Second Party Congress of the Communist Party of the Soviet Union, Khrushchev again lashed out at the Chinese. He attacked China's economic policies and ideology and argued that modern industrial development must precede experiments with creating communes. Communism was to be achieved by following the Soviet lead. In response, Chinese foreign minister Zhou Enlai led the entire Chinese delegation out of the congress and back to Beijing.

In 1962, new diplomatic issues divided Moscow and Beijing and exacerbated their conflict. China and India engaged in a brief war in October over a border dispute, and Moscow, instead of supporting China (with which it had a military alliance), offered diplomatic support to India while joining the United States in condemning China for its reckless aggression. And shortly afterward, in the wake of the Cuban missile crisis, in which the United States and the Soviet Union came perilously close to a nuclear war, the Chinese scorned

Khrushchev as weak-kneed for caving in to the US demand to pull his missiles from Cuba.

The Chinese once thought that the Kremlin would support them in their military quest to "liberate" Taiwan. Having failed in this, Beijing then sought to strengthen its position by cultivating its relations with other Communist and national liberation movements in Asia, Africa, and Latin America—that is, the Third World. China had already moved in this direction by identifying with the nonaligned nations of these parts of the world by its participation in the Bandung Conference in Indonesia in 1955.[17] Increasingly in the 1960s, the PRC sought to befriend leaders of revolutionary movements and of newly independent nations in the Third World, even to the point of providing economic aid that China, with its own economic problems, could ill afford.

In the early 1960s, when the breach with China became wide open, Khrushchev seemed to have become as obsessed with the recalcitrant China as Mao had become obsessed with what he regarded as Soviet treachery. After publishing an open letter demanding Beijing's submission to Soviet leadership, Khrushchev began formulating plans for a meeting of world Communist leaders at which he would either force China back into the fold or force it out. Several Communist parties, however, declined the invitations because they opposed Khrushchev's confrontational approach. Before this meeting could be arranged, Khrushchev himself was suddenly ousted from power in Moscow. And on the very day that this was reported in the world press, October 16, 1964, the PRC announced it had successfully tested an atomic bomb. Proudly, the Chinese proclaimed that the PRC too was now a superpower. They had successfully defied Khrushchev's efforts to dictate policy and his efforts to deny them nuclear weapons.

No significant change occurred in Sino-Soviet relations in consequence of the fall of Khrushchev and his replacement by Leonid Brezhnev. Nor did the escalation of the US involvement in the Vietnam War in 1965 bring the two Communist powers together; instead, they rivaled one another for influence over the Communist regime in North Vietnam. In April 1965, Moscow proposed to Beijing that the two nations cooperate in support of North Vietnam. It asked the Chinese to allow Soviet aircraft use of Chinese airports and airspace. After lengthy debate within ruling circles in Beijing, Mao rejected the proposal. Mao feared not only a Soviet military presence in China but also the possibility of a full-scale war with the Soviet Union.

Mao Zedong's tirade against the Soviet Union reached new heights in the summer of 1966, when he launched the Great Proletarian Cultural Revolution, a campaign designed to revitalize the Chinese revolution by mass mobilization (see Chapter 14). This political program contained a strong anti-Soviet aspect, for Mao called upon the Chinese people to purge the party of leaders whom he condemned for trying to establish a Soviet-type Communism in China. He pronounced them guilty of the same crimes that he pinned on Soviet leaders:

bureaucratic elitism, revisionism, sabotage of the Communist movement, and taking China down the capitalist road. The political and economic chaos caused by his Cultural Revolution gave the Soviet Union still more reason to ridicule Mao and Maoism. Nevertheless, despite the upheaval it caused, Mao proclaimed that he had set the revolution back on the track to true Communism, and he called upon all Communists throughout the world to abandon the revisionist Soviets and turn instead to China for their model.

Tensions between the two Communist giants escalated even higher on yet another front: the Sino-Soviet border. From time to time during their feud, Mao had called into question the Soviet claim to territory north of the Amur River boundary between the two countries in East Asia. In two separate treaties in 1858 and 1860, China had relinquished to tsarist Russia territory north of the Amur River and east of the Ussuri River (the latter territory known as the Maritime Province). But Mao now contended that these were ill-gotten gains and that, since the treaties were foisted upon China by an imperialist government, they should not be honored or considered binding.

During the 1960s, as the feud heated up, the two sides fortified their common border with ever larger forces. On the Ussuri River were several disputed islands, and in February and March 1969, skirmishes between Chinese and Soviet armed forces suddenly broke out on the island of Damanskii. After the Chinese launched an assault, the Soviets retaliated with artillery, tanks, and aircraft and drove back the Chinese. The warfare left about 800 Chinese troops dead as compared with about sixty Soviet soldiers killed.

Although a cease-fire was arranged, a war of nerves continued throughout the year. A full-scale war between China and the Soviet Union seemed imminent. It was in this context that leaders in Beijing began to consider ending their diplomatic isolation by improving relations with the United States. Tension along the border continued into the late 1980s as both sides reinforced their border security. Ultimately, the Soviet Union deployed an estimated 2 million troops along its 2,700-mile-long China border and armed them with the most modern of weapons, including tactical and intermediate-range nuclear missiles. China's border forces were thought to be as large as the Soviets' but not as well equipped.

One of the major consequences of the Sino-Soviet split, specifically the military confrontation, was the normalization of relations between the PRC and the United States in the early 1970s. This had a profound effect on global power relations, supplanting the bipolar Cold War with what may be called a strategic triangle. Throughout the 1970s and 1980s, the PRC moved closer to the United States and still farther away from the Soviet Union. It charged the latter with "socialist imperialism" and "hegemonism." In fact, "antihegemonism" became the main pillar of China's foreign policy in the 1970s, when it endeavored to attain the active support of the United States, Japan, and other nations in its standoff with the Soviet Union.

The Thirty-Year Feud Is Ended

The estrangement between the two Communist giants continued into the late 1980s. Although Moscow showed signs of desiring a thaw, Deng Xiaoping, the new Chinese Communist ruler who came to power after Mao's death in 1976, hunkered down with an inflexible policy. He insisted on three changes in Soviet foreign policy before relations could be normalized. He demanded a withdrawal (or at least a substantial reduction) of Soviet forces from the Chinese border, an end to the Soviet invasion of Afghanistan, and an end to Soviet support for the Vietnamese army in Cambodia. Although bilateral trade and diplomatic exchanges were gradually restored, further progress was blocked by Chinese and Soviet intransigence on the "three obstacles."

As both Beijing and Moscow focused their attention on economic reform in the 1980s, the prospects for Sino-Soviet rapprochement improved. Mikhail Gorbachev, who came to power in the Kremlin in 1985, brought a dynamic new pragmatism to Soviet diplomacy. Determined to regenerate the faltering economy, Gorbachev saw it necessary to reduce the size of the Soviet Union's military establishment, including the large deployment of forces in East Asia. With this in mind, Gorbachev in July 1986 went to Vladivostok, the largest Soviet city in East Asia, to deliver a speech that boldly proclaimed a new Soviet initiative to establish peaceful relations with China and other Asian nations. In his conciliatory speech, Gorbachev addressed Beijing's three burning issues, declaring Soviet readiness to seek accommodation on all three. He indicated that steps were already being taken toward the evacuation of Soviet forces from Afghanistan, that Soviet troops would be withdrawn from Mongolia on the Sino-Mongolian border, and that Moscow was prepared to discuss the issue of mutual reduction of military forces on the Sino-Soviet border and a resolution of the Vietnamese occupation of Cambodia.

Deng Xiaoping responded positively. In April 1987, Chinese and Soviet negotiators began addressing "regional issues," particularly border disputes, and the Cambodian question. Negotiations continued on various levels through the following year as both parties reciprocated with confidence-building gestures and agreements. By 1989, substantial improvement had been made toward the restoration of peaceful relations. The Soviet Union withdrew from Afghanistan, reduced its troops along the Chinese border, and pressured Vietnam to begin evacuation of its troops from Cambodia.

In December 1988, Gorbachev pledged at the United Nations to cut Soviet military forces by half a million, 200,000 of which would be from military units in Asia. He also announced plans to withdraw three-quarters of the Soviet troops in Mongolia and indicated that the first contingent of 12,000 soldiers was already being taken out. Placated by these conciliatory measures, Deng accepted Gorbachev's proposal for a summit meeting and extended an invitation to him to visit Beijing in May 1989.

Gorbachev's visit to China signaled the end of the thirty-year-long rift. He arrived in Beijing, however, in the midst of the mammoth student demonstrations in the Chinese capital, and his historic visit was upstaged by this tumultuous event (see Chapter 14). The summit meeting was, nonetheless, a success. Gorbachev, who acknowledged that the Soviet Union was partly to blame for the deep split between the two countries, proclaimed the summit a "watershed event." The two sides pledged to continue talks aimed at mutually reducing military troop strength along their long shared border "to a minimum level commensurate with normal, good-neighborly relations," to seek expanded trade and cultural relations, and to restore relations between the Communist parties of the two countries.[18] On Cambodia, they acknowledged a lack of agreement but pledged to continue efforts to avert a full-fledged civil war in that country and to help it become independent and nonaligned. On the whole, the summit advanced the new rapprochement between China and the Soviet Union and reflected their mutual objectives of lessening tensions and improving economic relations.

In 1992, the Russian parliament ratified Gorbachev's agreement with China. It recognized that Damanskii Island on the Ussuri River, where the fighting had broken out in 1969, was indeed Chinese territory. Russian historians estimated that Soviet troop deployment along the Amur and Ussuri Rivers from the onset of hostilities in 1969 to Gorbachev's visit to Beijing cost the state the massive sum of 200–300 billion rubles (in 1960s rubles), roughly the equivalent of $200–300 billion.[19]

Recommended Readings

Bethell, Nicholas. *Gomulka: His Poland, His Communism*. New York: Holt, Rinehart and Winston, 1969.
An explanation of the Polish road to socialism.
Chen Jian. *Mao's China and the Cold War*. Chapel Hill: University of North Carolina Press, 2001.
Clubb, O. Edmund. *China and Russia: The "Great Game."* New York: Columbia University Press, 1971.
A comprehensive, detailed, and evenhanded analysis of the Sino-Soviet split by a US diplomat-turned-scholar.
Crankshaw, Edward. *Khrushchev: A Career.* New York: Viking, 1966.
Deutscher, Isaac. *Stalin: A Political Biography.* Rev. ed. New York: Oxford University Press, 1966.
The classic biography by a Trotskyite.
Hinton, Harold C. *China's Turbulent Quest.* 2nd ed. New York: Macmillan, 1973.
An analysis of the Sino-Soviet rift.
Kecskemeti, Paul. *The Unexpected Revolution: Social Forces in the Hungarian Uprising.* Stanford: Stanford University Press, 1961.
London, Kurt, ed. *Eastern Europe in Transition.* Baltimore: Johns Hopkins University Press, 1966.
A study of the forces of nationalism in Eastern Europe.

Medvedev, Roy A. *Let History Judge: The Origins and Consequences of Stalinism.* New York: Knopf, 1971.
An indictment of Stalin by a Soviet "Leninist" historian.

Medvedev, Roy A., and Zhores A. Medvedev. *Khrushchev: The Years in Power.* New York: Norton, 1978.

Shipler, David K. *Russia: Broken Idols, Solemn Dreams.* New York: Times Books, 1983.
A discussion of Soviet society at the end of the Brezhnev era, by a correspondent of the *New York Times.*

Solzhenitsyn, Alexander. *One Day in the Life of Ivan Denisovich.* New York: Praeger, 1962.
An exposé of Stalin's forced-labor camps, the novel that brought Solzhenitsyn international acclaim.

Tatu, Michel. *Power in the Kremlin: From Khrushchev to Kosygin.* London: William Collins Sons, 1968.
A well-received study of Soviet politics by a French expert.

Taubman, William. *Khrushchev: The Man and His Era.* New York: Norton, 2003.
The definitive biography.

Ulam, Adam. *Stalin: The Man and His Era.* New York: Viking, 1973.
A highly readable, detailed biography written from a Western perspective.

Valenta, Jiri. *Soviet Intervention in Czechoslovakia in 1968.* Baltimore: Johns Hopkins University Press, 1979.
An analysis of the Kremlin's reasons for ending the Czechoslovak experiment in liberalization.

Notes

1. J. V. Stalin, "The Tasks of Business Executives," February 4, 1931; J. V. Stalin, *Works* (Moscow: Foreign Languages Publishing House, 1955), vol. 13, pp. 40–41.

2. A proletarian—a member of the proletariat—is a wage-earner or, more commonly, a factory worker. In Marxist jargon, the words "proletarian" and "worker" are used interchangeably.

3. Edward Crankshaw, *Khrushchev: A Career* (New York: Viking, 1966), p. 228.

4. N. S. Khrushchev, *Khrushchev Remembers: The Last Testament* (Boston: Little, Brown, 1974), p. 77.

5. Roy A. Medvedev and Zhores A. Medvedev, *Khrushchev: The Years in Power* (New York: Norton, 1978), pp. 94–101.

6. Tito's independence of both the Soviet Union and the West led him to take a "third" road. Tito, Nehru of India, and Nasser of Egypt became the early leaders of the Third World, that is, nations that refused to align themselves with either the Western or socialist blocs. The term later lost its original meaning, for it came to designate the world's underdeveloped nations.

7. J. V. Stalin, "The International Situation and the Defense of the U.S.S.R.," speech delivered on August 1, 1927, to the Joint Plenum of the Central Committee and Central Control Commission of the C.P.S.U. (b); J. V. Stalin, *Works*, vol. 10, pp. 53–54.

8. G. M. Adibekov, *Kominform i poslevoinnaia Evropa* (Moscow: Rossia molodaia, 1994), pp. 90–95.

9. Khrushchev, *Khrushchev Remembers*, p. 351; for the full text of the "Secret Speech" see pp. 559–618.

10. For a summary of Dulles's views on Communism, see his testimony before Congress, January 15, 1953; Walter LaFeber, ed., *The Dynamics of World Power: A Documentary History of United States Foreign Policy, 1945–1973*, vol. 2, *Eastern Europe and the Soviet Union* (New York: Chelsea House, 1973), pp. 465–468.

11. Khrushchev, *Khrushchev Remembers*, pp. 416–420. See also the documents made public at a conference in Budapest commemorating the fortieth anniversary of the uprising: Timothy Garton Ash, "Hungary's Revolution: Forty Years On," *New York Review of Books*, November 16, 1996, pp. 18–22; Reuters, "Soviets Almost Recognized Hungary Revolt, Data Show," *Baltimore Sun*, September 28, 1996, p. 7A; Jane Perlez, "Thawing Out Cold War History," *New York Times*, October 6, 1996, p. 4E.

12. R. G. Pikhoia, "Chekhoslovakiia, 1968 god. Vzgliad iz Moskvy: Po dokumentam TsK KPSS," *Novaia i noveishaia istoriia* 1 (January–February 1995), p. 42.

13. Wilfried Loth, *Stalins ungeliebtes Kind: Warum Moskau die DDR nicht wollte* (Berlin: Rohwolt-Berlin, 1994).

14. That day became an official holiday in West Germany, the Day of Unity, commemorating the victims of the uprising and underscoring the commitment to unification. After Germany was unified in 1990, October 3 became the new official Day of Unity.

15. Mao cited in "At Present It Is Not the West Wind," *Survey of the China Mainland Press*, US Consulate General, Hong Kong, no. 1662, December 2, 1957, p. 2.

16. Mao on Lenin, *Current Background*, US Consulate General, Hong Kong, no. 617, April 26, 1960.

17. At this conference of twenty-nine African and Asian nations, China's representative, Zhou Enlai, shared the spotlight with India's neutralist prime minister, Nehru. China joined with these Third World nations in pledging peace and mutual noninterference.

18. Scott Shane, "Gorbachev Returns Home from 'Watershed' Summit," *Baltimore Sun*, May 19, 1989.

19. Viktor Usov, "'Goriachaia vesna' na Damanskom," *Novoe vremia* 9 (1994), pp. 36–39.

9 The War in Indochina

When the fighting stopped in Korea, in 1953, it became an article of faith in the Pentagon that the United States must "never again" become bogged down in a war on the Asian mainland. Yet a scant dozen years later, the United States became tied down in a lengthy war in Southeast Asia.

After the Vietminh had defeated the French at Dien Bien Phu, the Geneva Agreement of July 1954 called for France's withdrawal from Indochina and the formation of the independent states of Laos, Cambodia, and Vietnam. Vietnam, however, was to remain temporarily divided along the 17th parallel. In the interim, in the South, a new pro-Western and anti-Communist nation, the Republic of Vietnam, came into existence. The northern half became the Communist-led Democratic Republic of Vietnam, headed by Ho Chi Minh, the hero of the Vietnamese revolution.

The Geneva Agreement also called for an internationally supervised nationwide election of a president for a unified Vietnam. The election was to be held by July 1956 at the latest. In the meantime, Geneva also permitted the voluntary transfer of peoples across the 17th parallel. The result was an exodus from the North (organized by the US Navy) of 860,000 people, the majority of them Catholics fearful of the future under Communism. "God and the Virgin have gone south," priests told their parishioners, and "only the devil remains in the north." In the South, approximately 140,000 Vietminh went to the North, hoping to return once unification had been achieved.

The Eisenhower administration immediately became involved in the affairs of South Vietnam. It provided economic and military assistance to its government. The US military and CIA officers gradually replaced the French presence in Saigon, South Vietnam's capital, and began to carry out sabotage and intelligence missions against the North.

The chief of state of South Vietnam was the former playboy emperor, Bao Dai, known as the "Emperor of Cannes." He prudently remained in exile in

France, leaving matters to his newly appointed prime minister, Ngo Dinh Diem, the scion of a famous and influential Roman Catholic family. Diem, however, was a man with only limited following in Saigon. He had not been in Vietnam during its long and difficult struggle for independence against the French but instead had resided abroad, including in the United States, where he had sought to cultivate contacts with influential Catholic clergy and politicians.

Diem lobbied long and hard, and ultimately successfully, with Bao Dai for his appointment as prime minister. Relations between the two had never been good, however. Diem, a staunch Vietnamese nationalist, thought that Bao Dai had been too ready to compromise as emperor, too ready to serve the French, the Japanese, the Vietminh—whoever was in control of Vietnam. The pliant Bao Dai well understood that Washington was poised to take over from France and thus gave the Eisenhower administration a prime minister to its liking. Years later, Bao Dai wrote that he had selected Diem because he was "well known to the Americans, who appreciated his [anti-Communist] intransigence," his "fanaticism and messianic tendencies."[1]

Diem had not terribly impressed anyone during his lengthy stays in the United States. The fervidly anti-Communist secretary of state, John Foster Dulles, was not sure that Diem was up to the job. The chief of the CIA mission in Saigon, Edward Lansdale, however, took an immediate liking to Diem. Lansdale, a former advertising executive, had just arrived from the Philippines, where he had played a role in consolidating the power of the nation's new president, the effective and popular anti-Communist Ramon Magsaysay. Upon arriving in Saigon, Lansdale was certain he had in Diem a similar product that he could readily sell to his bosses in Washington. This time, however, Lansdale was peddling merchandise highly defective from the very start.

Rigid and righteous, Diem was at heart a mandarin (a high-ranking educated official who ruled at the behest of the emperor) who believed that it was his people's duty to obey him. He did not entertain the idea that it was his obligation to gain the goodwill of his people; instead, it was up to the people to gain his goodwill. A century earlier, Diem might have been an effective ruler, but his return to Saigon came at a time when a social revolution already had swept away much of the old order (including the monarchy and the mandarinate).

Diem's other problem was his Catholicism. Catholics supported him in large numbers, but they made up only 10 percent of the population in Vietnam. Diem had to decide whether to reconcile with his (mostly Buddhist) fellow citizens and govern by consensus and social contract or by decree. Psychologically incapable of reconciliation, he chose to govern by decree.

Upon arriving in Saigon in June 1954, Diem faced a number of serious problems. His first task was to secure control of Saigon, a city dominated by a powerful crime syndicate, Binh Xuyen, which controlled the narcotics market, prostitution, and gambling. More significant, Bao Dai (in order to pay off

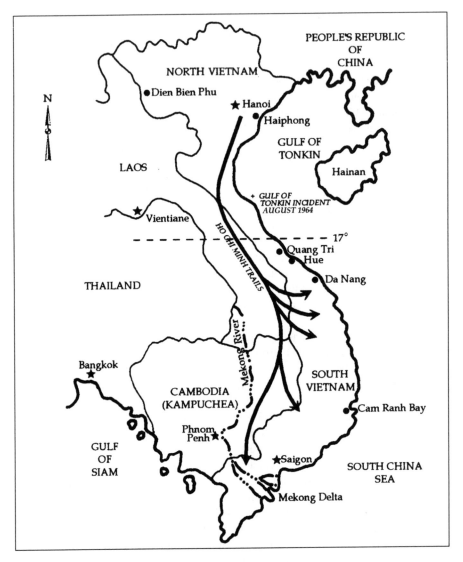

Indochina: The Vietnam War

his gambling debts) had also consigned the police to Binh Xuyen's control. Diem, unwilling to share power with anyone, let alone with organized crime, declared war on Binh Xuyen and in short order routed the organization. He also neutralized several high-ranking French-trained generals who had plotted against him, exiling them to Paris. Finally, he turned against religious sects— Cao Dai and Hoa Hao—under the control of warlords with their own private armies. He drove any resistance underground—until they reemerged later as part of the insurrection coalescing around the Vietcong guerrillas.

After ten months in power, Diem had exceeded Washington's expectations. Doubts about him gave way to the certitude that he was the man to rule South Vietnam. Diem decided to concentrate all power in his own hands. In a popular referendum in October 1955, Diem asked voters to choose between him and Bao Dai. The result was a smashing—albeit fraudulent—electoral victory for Diem by which he became president of South Vietnam. He obtained an incredible 98.2 percent of the votes cast nationwide, and in Saigon he received 605,025 votes from the 450,000 registered voters, a mathematically implausible 134 percent.[2] During its short existence, South Vietnam never held a free election. Diem's sister-in-law, for example, the widely reviled Madame Nhu, won her seat in the National Assembly with a vote of 99.4 percent in Long An Province in the Mekong Delta, which was under Vietcong control.[3]

Diem's next target was the remaining Vietminh, who were tracked down, imprisoned, and often executed. Washington liked what Diem was doing. He was well on his way to being hailed as the "Churchill of Southeast Asia," as *Life* magazine dubbed him, the guardian at the gates of the "free world," the savior of South Vietnam. In May 1957, during a highly publicized state visit to Washington, he was given the honor of addressing both houses of Congress—where he explained that democracy "is neither material happiness nor the supremacy of numbers." By this time Diem had already rejected the Geneva Agreement's call for an internationally supervised nationwide (i.e., all of Vietnam) election. He and his patrons in Washington were well aware that in a national election "the supremacy of numbers" favored Ho Chi Minh, the man who had defeated the French (and who, ironically, by defeating the French had made possible Diem's return as prime minister to an independent South Vietnam). Better to keep Vietnam divided than take a chance on an election in which the numbers were sure to go against Diem.

Diem turned on any and all opponents, real or imagined: former Vietminh, Communists, liberals, Buddhists, peasants. His rejection of the elections in 1956 stirred protests, especially by former Vietminh who had remained in the South in the expectation of reunification. Diem's reign of terror (which included the use of the guillotine) dealt the Vietminh in the South a near-mortal blow. Diem's war against the Vietminh included the negation of land redistributions that the Vietminh had already carried out. The lands were now returned to their former landlords. Other beneficiaries of Diem's land program were newly arrived Catholics from the North who became the largest landowning bloc in South Vietnam.[4]

Diem persecuted the very same individuals who had fought and bled in the struggle against the French. He added insult to injury when he desecrated the graves of Vietminh war dead. In doing so, he violated the sacred Vietnamese tradition of ancestor worship. Diem's desecration was more than a crime; it was a serious mistake, one of the many that eventually brought him down.

*   *   *

In the mid-1950s, the Vietminh's desperate appeal for help from Hanoi, North Vietnam's capital, received only a tepid response. North Vietnam was exhausted from the Indochina war against the French; its economy was in shambles, the railroad system was in need of reconstruction, foreign technicians and engineers had left, and rice grown in the South was no longer available. In Hanoi an intense political debate took place over whether to assist the southern Vietminh and thus resume the war, this time against the US "puppet regime" of Diem. For the time being, the faction that stressed rebuilding the northern economic infrastructure carried the day. The party's sacred quest for unification would have to wait.

Economic reconstruction in the North was accompanied by a drastic—and disastrous—"land reform" program that meant dispossessing the landlord class. It was carried out despite Ho Chi Minh's warnings against undertaking such a measure. He had promised, more than once, that the "patriotic elements" had nothing to fear from the new order. This included the holders of large estates. Ho lost the debate in the Politburo, however, and it is not certain that he ever regained his once dominant position.

Within a year, by the end of 1956, the Communist Party could no longer ignore the consequences of the land reform—between 3,000 and 15,000 dead (the exact number has never been established) as well as widespread physical damage. An uprising in Nghe An Province—once the staunchest of Vietminh bastions—had to be put down by the army. The party now eased off on land reform—without, however, ever truly abandoning it. The landlords never regained their once lofty status. It was Ho Chi Minh who wound up apologizing profusely to the victims.

Once land reform was put aside, the party saw its way clear to return to events in the South, where the rebellion was gaining strength. At this point, the South-first faction became ascendant, and it was this faction—led by Le Duan and Le Duc Tho—that eventually oversaw the unification of Vietnam in 1975. It would take many years, however, before the North played a meaningful role in the South. In the meantime, what transpired in the South was all-out civil war, which only gradually drew the North into the conflict in the South.

*   *   *

In the late 1950s, the desperate southern Vietminh had virtually no weapons. They did, however, have revolutionary propaganda on their side—a vision of a better future in a unified Vietnam—and they had organizational skills, a carryover from the war against France. Moreover, despite Diem's attempt to extend his control over all of South Vietnam, the Vietminh still controlled wide stretches of land where they had established themselves during the war against France. That was particularly true in the Mekong River delta, along the Cambodian border, and even in Saigon. Their control also extended to include Route 1, the main road north from Saigon, which the French had dubbed the "street without joy"—into Quang Ngai Province, all the way to Danang and beyond. It was there that US combat troops would first meet the enemy.

Government terror now clashed with guerrilla terror, with levels of violence steadily increasing. Starting in the late 1950s, as the resistance grew, rebels managed to capture ever more weapons from the Army of the Republic of (South) Vietnam (ARVN), which was well equipped with US armaments but poorly led. The resistance acquired, in early 1960, its first significant cache of arms from an ARVN post in Phu My Hung, just nine miles from Saigon.[5]

In December 1960, various opposition groups and parties, led by former Vietminh and Communists, formed the National Liberation Front (NLF). Diem, encouraged by his US advisors, labeled all resistance as Communist in nature. Thus, the NLF became known as the Vietcong (or Vietnamese Communists). At first, the NLF considered the label an insult, but eventually it became a

Ngo Dinh Diem, president of the Republic of Vietnam from 1955 to November 1963, arrives in Washington on May 8, 1957, to meet with President Eisenhower and Secretary of State John Foster Dulles during a state visit. *(National Archives)*

badge of honor. US soldiers referred to this determined enemy as "VC," "Charlie," and eventually "Mr. Charles," a term of respect.

Until 1961, the resistance appeared little more than a nuisance. Indeed, when President-elect John Kennedy met with Dwight Eisenhower to discuss the state of the world, the outgoing president did not deem it important enough to dwell on Vietnam. At that time, the Vietcong were still on their own, receiving no material support from Hanoi, merely advice by the occasional party functionary who had made the difficult, time-consuming, and dangerous trek to the South.

Imperceptibly, the Vietcong grew in size and strength. When Diem replaced locally elected village headmen with his own bureaucrats in an attempt to control the countryside, these interlopers became targets for Vietcong assassinations. To secure the villages of South Vietnam, Diem resorted in 1962 to the drastic and expensive measure of resettling villagers in compounds called "strategic hamlets." It proved to be counterproductive. The peasants, uprooted from their native villages—the soil of their ancestors—became ever more resentful. Diem's heavy-handedness merely pushed the villagers into the welcoming embrace of the resistance.

Diem's government was a little more popular in the cities. His cult of personality did not sit well. It was based on a vague theory called "personalism," a doctrine steeped in a mixture of Catholic and Confucian traditions. Diem demanded obedience; individual freedom must take second place to the collective betterment of society, which is achieved by dutiful loyalty to the morally superior ruler. In practice, it meant absolute obedience to an imperious autocrat. Meanwhile, Diem surrounded himself with a clique of loyal supporters, several of whom were his brothers. The most notorious among them was Ngo Dinh Nhu, the head of the secret police—Diem's "Siamese twin," as the US ambassador called him—without whom Diem was incapable of governing.

Diem never trusted his own armed forces—and for good reason. There were units loyal to him, usually under the command of Catholic generals, but he was unwilling to risk them against the Vietcong, since he needed them to protect the presidential palace against generals he did not trust. In February 1962, two disgruntled air force officers—in an attempt to assassinate Diem or, at the least, spark a popular uprising against him—bombed the palace. Diem and his relations escaped with their lives. Diem characterized the attack as an "isolated act" and his survival as a manifestation of "divine protection."

Diem's Downfall

In July 1959, the Vietcong infiltrated the huge military base at Bien Hoa, just north of Saigon, where they assassinated two US officers, officially the first US soldiers to die in Vietnam. As the Vietcong became better equipped, through their seizure of weapons and supplies from the ARVN, they began to refer to Diem as their "supply sergeant."

At first, in classic guerrilla style, Vietcong attacks consisted of ambushes followed by retreats in the face of the ARVN's superior firepower. In January 1963, however, near the village of Ap Bac in the Mekong Delta, forty miles southwest of Saigon, a well-prepared Vietcong unit engaged the ARVN in a head-to-head battle for the first time. The Vietcong, who knew of the ARVN's battle plans beforehand, suffered eighteen fatalities, but they killed eighty ARVN soldiers and three US advisors and destroyed five helicopters and three armored personnel carriers. The Diem government proclaimed it a victory for the ARVN. US reporters, who rushed to the battle scene, were able to see with their own eyes, however, the carnage the Vietcong had inflicted on the well-equipped ARVN troops under the leadership of US advisors. It was a jolting foreshadow of events to come.

It was one thing for Diem to favor the Catholic minority; it was another to engage in an unnecessary confrontation with the Buddhist majority, particularly since its leaders were politically passive and, moreover, looked with a jaundiced eye upon the Vietcong and Communists in general. Indeed, Diem and the Buddhists should have been allies against the Vietcong. Instead, Diem went to war against the Buddhists.

In the city of Hue, in May 1963, during celebrations of Buddha's birthday, Diem banned the flying of multicolored Buddhist flags; only the yellow-and-red South Vietnamese national flag was permitted to be flown, even though earlier that month Diem had made an exception for Catholics. After the police, without warning, shot and killed nine Buddhist demonstrators, Diem placed the blame on the Vietcong, something no one believed. The protests escalated. An old Buddhist monk resorted to the dramatic act of self-immolation. Seated in a meditative posture in a public square in Saigon, he was doused with a homemade version of napalm, which was then set aflame. In the weeks to come, other monks followed his example. Graphic depictions of these acts of self-sacrifice, indictments of the Diem regime, were carried around the world in newsprint and on television. Madame Nhu, Diem's sister-in-law and the nation's first lady, did not help when she derided the self-immolations as "barbecues." "Let them burn," she said, "and we shall clap our hands."[5]

US officials, including Ambassador Henry Cabot Lodge, were appalled by events in Saigon and concluded that Diem had to be replaced. The CIA thus gave the green light to a group of ARVN officers to replace Diem, which they did in early November 1963. Instead of sending Diem and Nhu into exile, however, they murdered both, much to the shock of the principals in Washington. Edward Lansdale, who supported Diem until the end, saw his project turn to ashes. In South Vietnam, virtually no one lamented Diem's passing; instead, people celebrated in the streets.

The new junta (a military ruling group) now in power was immediately recognized by the Kennedy administration, but it proved to be no more effective than the previous one in dealing with the nation's problems. If anything, the Vietcong grew in strength during the next year and a half.

Johnson's War

During the Kennedy administration, the US presence had grown already from approximately 800 advisors in the days of Eisenhower to 16,000 "special forces." Lyndon Johnson, who succeeded the slain Kennedy as president on November 22, 1963, soon expanded the US presence to 20,000, even though he knew this was not enough to counter the growing strength of the Vietcong, who were poised for victory.

The great irony was that Johnson doubted the very wisdom of US involvement in Vietnam. In May 1964, in a telephone conversation with his former mentor in the Senate, Richard Russell, a frustrated Johnson thought that Vietnam "is the damndest worst mess that I ever saw . . . and it's going to get worse." "How important is that [Vietnam] to us?" Russell wanted to know. Neither Vietnam nor Laos, Johnson replied, was worth "a damn." But he could not withdraw because the Republican Party would denounce him for it. "It's the only issue they've got," Johnson said.[6] That, and the fact that Johnson, the proud son of Texas, refused to become the first president to lose a war, meant that he had little choice but to try to win the war by sending in combat troops.

To sell his escalation of the war in Vietnam, Johnson argued that the revolution in the South was the consequence of Beijing-directed Communist aggression. If South Vietnam fell, other states would fall like a long row of dominoes. It was a scenario first publicly raised by Eisenhower in 1954. The war was portrayed as an international conflict, not a civil war in South Vietnam. For that reason, there could be no retreat from the defense of a "democratic" South Vietnam against "Communist aggression from outside."

During the presidential election of 1964, Johnson faced the Republican "hawk" Barry Goldwater, whose answer to Vietnam was to send in the Marines, finish the job, and return home to a victory parade. Johnson played the role of the "dove," assuring the electorate that "we are not going to send American boys nine or ten thousand miles away from home to do what Asian boys ought to be doing for themselves." Still, he spoke of his commitment to "defend freedom" in South Vietnam and stop the "Communist aggression." The dove thus had to show he had the talons of a hawk. That opportunity came in early August, during the Gulf of Tonkin incident.

In August 1964, during the runup to the November election, the Pentagon reported that one of its naval ships, the destroyer *Maddox*, had been attacked by North Vietnamese torpedo boats in the Gulf of Tonkin off the coast of North

Vietnam. Johnson claimed that the attack had taken place on the high seas (i.e., in international waters) and that it was unprovoked. It turned out that the destroyer (at the disposal of the National Security Agency, an intelligence arm of the US government) had been within the twelve-mile territorial limit of North Vietnam gathering electronic intelligence and providing support for covert military operations (including bombing raids) against North Vietnam by South Vietnamese commandos (which had been ongoing since January 1964). Put simply, *Maddox* had engaged in an act of war against North Vietnam.

Nevertheless, on the basis of a reported second "attack" two days later, this one in international waters, Johnson went to Congress for authorization to deploy direct military force against North Vietnam. With almost no deliberation, and with virtual unanimity (unanimous in the House of Representatives, and by an 88–2 vote in the Senate), Congress passed the Gulf of Tonkin Resolution, which authorized him to take "all necessary measures to repel any armed attacks against the forces of the United States and to prevent further aggression." Johnson's supporters called it a "functional equivalent of a declaration of war." The Democratic Johnson and his successor, the Republican Richard Nixon, used it as the legal basis for massive military operations in Vietnam and in neighboring countries. There is still no evidence today that the second attack had even taken place. North Vietnam always denied it, and it was never confirmed by any investigation, not even by the NSA. Secretary of Defense Robert McNamara wrote in his memoirs, more than thirty years later, that it appeared that no second attack had occurred.[7]

After Johnson defeated Goldwater in a landslide victory in November 1964, Vietnam became "Johnson's war." The president's critics—and they were still rather few at this stage—disputed the claim that South Vietnam was the victim of foreign aggression, that the NLF was a puppet of Hanoi. Hanoi and the NLF had similar objectives and had the same enemies, and the NLF no doubt looked for and received guidance and—eventually—supplies from Hanoi. But the NLF fought its own battles, at least until the massive intervention by US troops in 1965, which in turn brought about direct North Vietnamese intervention. In June 1966, Democratic senator Mike Mansfield of Montana revealed that when US escalation began in March 1965, only 400 of the 140,000 enemy forces in South Vietnam were North Vietnamese soldiers, figures confirmed by the Pentagon.[8] A lengthy study commissioned by Secretary of Defense McNamara (which became known as the *Pentagon Papers*) points to similarly low estimates of North Vietnamese forces during the years 1963 and 1964. Washington's panicky reaction to events in Vietnam was not in response to what the North was doing, but rather to the weakness of South Vietnamese forces and the fear of a Vietcong victory.[9]

In February 1965, the State Department, headed by the hawkish Dean Rusk, sought to prove that the war in South Vietnam was the result of Communist aggression from the North. It issued, with great fanfare, its famous but poorly

Secretary of Defense Robert S. McNamara, on a visit to South Vietnam, with the commander of US forces (1964–1968), General William C. Westmoreland, meeting with South Vietnamese officers, August 1965. *(National Archives)*

US troops on a "search-and-destroy" mission, May 1966, in Cu Chi district, about 20 miles northwest of Saigon, the most heavily bombed territory in history. *(National Archives)*

reasoned White Paper. Its centerpiece claim was that, among the weapons captured from the NLF, several were of Communist origin. But the number—179 weapons out of a total of 15,100, a little more than 1 percent—only proved that the NLF depended overwhelmingly on weapons it had captured from the inept and demoralized ARVN rather than from outside Communist sources.[10]

Shortly after his inauguration in January 1965, Johnson ordered Operation Rolling Thunder, the sustained aerial bombing of North Vietnam. In March 1965, US Marines landed on the beaches of Danang, ostensibly to protect its military airfield in that city, a vital component of Rolling Thunder. It was not long, however, before the Marines began "search-and-destroy" missions extending the scope of their operations in ever widening circles. Danang and its environs, long a Vietminh-Vietcong stronghold, were not easily pacified. With US forces unable to engage the furtive enemy directly, large stretches of the region were declared "free-fire zones" where anything that moved was fair game. Winning over the "hearts and minds" of the population quickly became an afterthought. And it was here where the Marines first engaged in hand-to-hand combat with the North's People's Army of Vietnam (PAVN) in the bloody battle of Ia Drang Valley in November 1965.

The enemy "body count" rose ever higher; yet the US commander, General William Westmoreland, asked for additional troops. By the end of 1965, the US contingent numbered 200,000; by the end of 1967, it stood at nearly 550,000, augmented by 1 million ARVN troops. Facing them, ultimately, were 200,000–300,000 Vietcong and 140,000 PAVN troops. The troop ratio favoring the US-Saigon side (approximately 3:1) was not enough considering that it takes nearly a ten-to-one advantage to defeat an insurgency, especially one that was organized, dedicated, and well supplied (particularly as Moscow and Beijing stepped up their arms shipments to North Vietnam).

In the meantime, there was no political stability in Saigon as military coups became the order of the day. In June 1965, yet another coup brought to power Air Marshal Nguyen Cao Ky and army general Nguyen Van Thieu. In September 1967, by virtue of a controlled election, Thieu became president and Ky vice president. Ky explained that, in case a civilian won the election, he would respond "militarily" because in a "democratic country you have the right to disagree with the views of others."[11] As if such a perverted definition of democracy was not enough, Ky declared that he had but one hero and that was Adolf Hitler. The election served further to dispel the fiction that Washington was fighting in defense of South Vietnamese democracy.

The Tet Offensive of 1968

Johnson expected that the bombing of North Vietnam's supply routes into the South (nicknamed the Ho Chi Minh Trail) and the heavy commitment of US

Vietnamese president Nguyen Van Thieu and vice-president Nguyen Cao Ky meet with US president Lyndon Johnson, Honolulu, Hawaii, February 7, 1966. *(National Archives)*

Vietcong prisoners under US military guard. *(National Archives)*

forces would bring victory, at the latest, at the outset of the 1968 presidential campaign. The task, however, was much more difficult than expected. At the beginning of 1965, the number of US dead stood at 401; by the end of 1967, it was over 16,400. And by the end of 1967 the war had become an escalated military stalemate. Hanoi did what Pentagon planners had thought impossible: matching US escalation with its own increased commitment. US bombing was unable to shut down Hanoi's pipeline bringing ever more PAVN soldiers and supplies into the South. The PAVN and Vietcong took heavy losses, but they managed to replenish them with men and women willing to fight and die in a war against yet another foreign invader. None of that had an impact on the drumbeat of pronouncements coming out of Washington that the war was being won. In November 1967, General Westmoreland declared that a lull in the fighting meant "we have reached an important point, when the end begins to come into view."

The shocking realization that there just might be no victory came in the wake of the Tet Offensive of 1968, at the time of the Vietnamese lunar new year. It began at the end of January, when the Vietcong and PAVN launched a surprise offensive across the breadth of South Vietnam. They were able to take thirty-six of the forty-four provincial capitals, and most surprising of all, they staged a major attack on Saigon, where suicide commandos even penetrated the grounds of the US embassy. The psychological and political impact of the Tet Offensive, as Hanoi had calculated, shattered the popular illusion in the United States that victory, the proverbial "light at the end of the tunnel," was within reach.

US forces launched a furious counterattack making full use of their massive firepower. Enemy losses were staggering as they were driven out of Saigon and the other cities and towns. After a month of heavy fighting, Westmoreland claimed that the Tet Offensive had been a military disaster for the enemy, who had surfaced and been hunted down. This was not an empty claim, for the US counterattack greatly weakened the Vietcong and the regular PAVN.

During the Tet Offensive, particularly harsh were the fates of the beautiful old imperial city of Hue, the provincial Mekong Delta town of Ben Tre, and the village of My Lai. After the North Vietnamese seized Hue, they immediately rounded up and executed an estimated 3,000 city residents suspected of collaborating with the Saigon government. By the end of February, US troops reconquered Hue, a city largely in ruins.

Ben Tre suffered an even worse fate. US artillery destroyed it completely. When asked why the city had been leveled, a US major offered what became his country's epitaph in Vietnam: "It became necessary to destroy the town to save it."[12] It was the only answer he could give. The US military's involvement in Vietnam no longer made sense.

It took another year and a half for the My Lai story to break—the massacre of more than 500 Vietnamese villagers, including women, children, and

Top: Antiwar demonstrators confront military police, Pentagon, Washington, D.C., October 21, 1967. *(National Archives)*
Bottom: Antiwar sentiment among troops: Sky trooper from 1st Cavalry Division (Airmobile) tracks time left in Vietnam, 1968. *(National Archives)*

US Marines during Operation Hastings in a search-and-destroy mission to clear Quang Tri province, south of the seventeenth parallel, of North Vietnamese troops, July 1966. (*National Archives*)

Marines on ribs of rice paddies. *(National Archives)*

Boatpeople onboard the USS *Wabash,* August 7, 1979. *(National Archives)*

old men, at the hands of US Army troops—graphically retold in color photographs in *Life*. Initially, the Pentagon (as well as Congress) ignored all reports of the massacre, then pinned it on a single lieutenant, whom President Nixon absolved of all wrongdoing and then pardoned. Further investigations revealed that My Lai had not been an isolated incident.

The Tet Offensive was a military setback for the enemy, but it was a psychological and political victory for them. Hanoi gave notice during the 1968 presidential election year that the war was far from over. Johnson, faced with mounting opposition to his Vietnam policy, was forced to reassess the war and his political future. Even his own secretary of defense, Robert McNamara, once a true believer in the war, had begun to doubt the wisdom of continuing it. In early March 1968, Johnson replaced him with Clark Clifford, who also concluded within a few weeks that the United States had reached a dead end in Vietnam and that the time had come to find a way out.

In March 1968, Johnson received from Westmoreland a request for 206,000 additional soldiers, despite Westmoreland's consistent claims that his troops were winning the war. In a presidential election year, Johnson was in no position to take the US troop level to 750,000. His advisors prevailed upon him to find a political solution to the war. At the end of the month, in a televised address to the nation, Johnson announced a halt to the bombing of North Vietnam and stated that he was willing to sit down with Hanoi to negotiate a settlement. The real surprise came at the end of his address, when he announced that he would not seek reelection as president of the United States.

Hanoi had long been willing to sit down with Johnson, but on its own terms. Its four-point proposal of April 1965 called for an end to US bombing of the North, withdrawal of all foreign forces from Vietnam, adherence to the Geneva Agreement, and the right of the Vietnamese alone to settle their problems. It also insisted, as a precondition for negotiations, that the NLF be recognized and be allowed to take part in the negotiations. The Johnson administration and the generals in Saigon, however, had steadfastly refused to have any dealings with the NLF. In the end, Johnson yielded on that issue, and in October 1968, Hanoi and Washington began to talk in Paris, with the NLF and a reluctant Saigon represented as well.

Nixon and the Vietnamization of War

In the presidential election of 1968, the Republican candidate, Richard Nixon, defeated by the smallest of margins Johnson's vice-president, Hubert Humphrey, a man tied to the war and despised by the growing antiwar movement. Nixon's appeal to voters consisted primarily of his "secret plan" to end a war in which he had played no direct role. He appeared to be the candidate best suited to extricate the United States from a bloody conflict that already had claimed the lives of 32,000 US troops.

Nixon's great fear on the eve of the election was a negotiated settlement of the war. In Saigon, the South Vietnamese president, Nguyen Van Thieu, too, wanted no part of an agreement that, he feared, would come at his expense. Nixon secretly contacted Thieu and offered him a deal: If Thieu sabotaged the talks with Hanoi by refusing to participate in any settlement, Nixon, should he be elected president, would continue to support Thieu. Thieu did his part in undermining the talks, and Nixon delivered on his promise and sustained the

Thieu regime for another four years—at the expense of more than 20,000 US war dead.

Years later, Nixon admitted that he had no plan at all on how to end the war. He knew, however, that he had to end direct US involvement by the time the next presidential election rolled around. In the meantime, he and his national security advisor, Henry Kissinger, pursued an elusive victory. The plan Nixon and Kissinger finally worked out consisted of yet another escalation of the war, followed by what became known as "Vietnamization." Once more, a US president announced, the fighting and the dying would be by Asian boys. As the fighting abilities of the ARVN increased, Washington would decrease its forces. For the time being, Nixon honored Johnson's bombing halt of the North, but he did not spare the South, which took the full brunt of the firepower Nixon had at his disposal. Vietnamization gradually reduced the number of US troops and thus casualties, but not those of the Vietnamese.

Negotiations

A third element of Nixon's blueprint for an exit from Vietnam was to put pressure on Hanoi's patrons, the Soviet Union and Communist China. Neither Moscow nor Beijing, however, was interested in helping him out. They welcomed détente with Washington, but they were unwilling to help Nixon achieve victory in South Vietnam. Nixon, during his visit to China in February 1972, brought up Vietnam, but foreign minister Zhou Enlai and party chief Mao Zedong refused to discuss it.

Nixon's election and his pursuit of victory put on hold further talks with Hanoi. It was not until February 1970 that Nixon's negotiator, Henry Kissinger, and the North Vietnamese representative, Le Duc Tho, met in Paris to resume negotiations.

Even though US troop levels were reduced from 542,000 in February 1969 to 139,000 in December 1971, violence in Indochina did not diminish. In fact, an ever more frustrated Nixon expanded the war into Laos and Cambodia in order to destroy Vietcong and PAVN sanctuaries there. Over a period of fourteen months (March 1969 to May 1970), Nixon ordered secret B-52 bombing raids of Cambodia, which were illegal under US law. A CIA-engineered overthrow of the ruler of Cambodia, the neutralist Prince Norodom Sihanouk, in March 1970 brought to power a pro-US general, Lon Nol. Sihanouk had managed to keep his country out of the Vietnam War but had been unable to prevent the Vietcong and Vietminh from establishing bases in eastern Cambodia; indeed, he had permitted China to supply them through the port of Sihanoukville. He had also been unable prevent Nixon's retaliatory air strikes against them. In April 1970, Nixon ordered a joint US-ARVN "incursion" (as Nixon put it) into Cambodia. For more than two months, more than 50,000 US and ARVN troops searched the jungles of eastern Cambodia in a futile effort to find the headquarters of the enemy's southern operations.

The geographical widening of the war inflamed protest demonstrations by antiwar activists in the United States. By this time, US society was already deeply split over a host of issues, including civil rights, poverty, women's rights, and cultural issues—what the political right called "amnesty, acid and abortion"—and the war itself. Nixon exacerbated the split by appealing, in a televised address in November 1969, to the "great silent majority," his political base among the resentful, patriotic, God-fearing, socially conservative (mostly southern) white electorate who yearned for simpler times among the tumult. After the Cambodian invasion, antiwar students ("bums," Nixon called them) at Columbia University and other campuses sought to shut down their schools in protest. They were intent on "bringing the war home," and in a sense that is what happened on the campus of Kent State University, where four students were shot to death (and another nine wounded) by the Ohio National Guard during an antiwar rally on May 4, 1970.

An incursion into southern Laos in March 1971 demonstrated the failure of Vietnamization. ARVN forces, in an attempt to gain control of the Ho Chi Minh Trail, entered Laos with US air support but were badly routed by the PAVN. Television crews sent back images of panic-stricken ARVN troops hanging on to the skids of evacuation helicopters in a desperate effort to escape the North Vietnamese counterattack.

As the 1972 election approached, Nixon had to find a way to bring home the remaining US troops. To complicate matters for him, beginning in late March, Hanoi launched its Easter Offensive across the 17th parallel. To stop the offensive, Nixon ordered the most devastating bombing campaign yet against North Vietnam—Operation Linebacker. Bombing targets included North Vietnam's infrastructure—factories, bridges, harbors, and power stations—as far north as Hanoi.

As the fighting raged, Henry Kissinger and Le Duc Tho resumed their on-again, off-again talks in Paris. This time, they hammered out the broad outlines of a final settlement. In the end, Nixon gave Hanoi what it had always demanded: withdrawal of all US troops and the right to retain PAVN troops in South Vietnam. In return, Hanoi promised to release its US prisoners, mostly navy and air force personnel shot down over North Vietnam. What Nixon was unwilling to grant, however, was another of Hanoi's demands, the abandonment of Thieu's government in Saigon. He saw it as a matter of international prestige: A great power does not turn its back on its allies. When Hanoi eventually yielded on this point, meaning that Washington would continue to provide assistance to Saigon, the stage was set for the signing of a "peace agreement."

On the eve of the 1972 presidential election, Kissinger announced that "peace is at hand." The terms of the preliminary agreement that Kissinger and Le Duc Tho had agreed on stipulated that within sixty days after a cease-fire the United States would complete the withdrawal of its remaining troops from Vietnam, Hanoi would release all US prisoners, and the political settlement in South Vietnam would be left for the Vietnamese to work out. But one problem remained, essentially the same one that had existed in 1968: Thieu refused to accept these terms. To win over Thieu, Kissinger traveled to Saigon, carrying with him threats and Nixon's vague pledge of continued US protection for his government, including $1 billion in additional armaments.

To demonstrate his continuing commitment to defend Thieu's government, Nixon delivered one final savage punishment of North Vietnam— Operation Linebacker II—another round of bombings against Hanoi and Haiphong. The around-the-clock raids (dubbed by his critics the "Christmas bombings"), which began on December 18 and continued until the end of the month, turned large parts of these two cities into rubble. The bombings did not bring any significant change in the terms of the peace agreement finally signed in January 1973. Its terms were essentially those agreed to by Kissinger and Le Duc Tho the previous October. But Nixon, who had a pathological fear of being perceived as weak, was able to claim that he had bombed the enemy back to the conference table.

Hanoi's Victory

The so-called peace treaty did not bring an end to the war. The fighting continued. ARVN forces, despite their US-made arsenal, proved to be no match against the PAVN. Public opinion in the United States made impossible a return of troops or even bombing raids. And Congress, reflecting the will of the nation, cut off further aid to South Vietnam.

Moreover, Nixon was now mired in the Watergate scandal, a direct outgrowth of the war. In June 1971, Daniel Ellsberg, who had once served as a zealous administrator of official US policy in Vietnam and who had since become an equally zealous opponent of it, leaked the *Pentagon Papers* to the media (including the *New York Times* and *Washington Post*); this history of the war in Vietnam, commissioned by the former secretary of defense Robert McNamara, was explosive. Nixon, furious at this and other leaks of classified information, created a group inside the White House, the "plumbers," whose task it was to plug intelligence leaks and to investigate Ellsberg and other "subversives" undermining his presidency. For reasons still unclear decades later, in June 1972 the "plumbers" broke into the headquarters of the Democratic National Committee at the Watergate, a hotel-office-apartment complex in Washington. They were caught and arrested, and as evidence of wrongdoing began to implicate Nixon himself, he ordered his subordinates to commit perjury, that is, lie under oath. Unfortunately for Nixon, he had tape-recorded his own crimes, and for reasons also still not clear, he had not destroyed the

Refugees on Route 1 near Quang Tri, South Vietnam, 1972. *(National Archives)*

Exhausted troops of the 1st Marine Division, after five hours of "humping" to Hill 190, six miles northwest of Danang, late December 1969 or early January 1970. *(National Archives)*

evidence. The upshot was probable impeachment by Congress. When it became obvious to Nixon that his removal from office was all but a certainty, he resigned and was replaced by his vice-president, Gerald Ford.

Finally, in early 1975, a North Vietnamese attack in the northern highlands produced a panic throughout the ARVN. The expected battle for Saigon never took place. In April 1975, North Vietnamese forces entered the city unopposed. The US embassy in Saigon became the scene of a frantic airlift of remaining US personnel and as many of their Vietnamese cohorts as they could crowd into the last departing helicopters.

The final cost of the war for the United States included more than 58,000 troops killed and more than 300,000 wounded. The price tag, an estimated $165 billion, contributed to the inflation, national debt, and balance-of-payments problems that plagued the United States during the 1970s. It produced a new activism among the country's young people and a new political consciousness. But it also produced an even more powerful conservative political backlash that was still evident a generation later.

In 1995, Robert McNamara, who had been the US secretary of defense and one of the principal architects of US involvement in Vietnam, published memoirs in which he confessed that the United States "could and should have withdrawn from South Vietnam" in late 1963. At that point, only seventy-eight US troops had died there. Looking back, McNamara saw things much more clearly. He listed eleven major errors on the part of the United States, including misjudging the strength and resolve of North Vietnam, underrating nationalism as a force in Vietnam, failing to understand the history and culture of Vietnam, and failing to recognize the limitations of modern technological warfare.

The costs of the war for the peoples of Indochina were extraordinary. The US estimate of ARVN deaths was over 200,000, and for enemy forces—both NLF and PAVN—almost 500,000. We will never know how many civilians died or how many became refugees. In an interview in 2002, McNamara put the number of dead in Indochina at 3.4 million.[13] The physical mutilation of the country was also staggering. The United States dropped three times more bombs on Indochina than it had dropped on its enemies in the entirety of World War II. In addition, it defoliated over 5 million acres with chemicals such as Agent Orange, a powerful, cancer-causing herbicide.

The Continuing Tragedy of Indochina

In the wake of the North's victory, the South Vietnamese braced themselves for the terrible, vengeful "bloodbath" that Nixon had predicted, but it did not come. Still, those identified as high-ranking former government or military officers of the overthrown Saigon regime were singled out for severe punishment, usually involving confiscation of property, arrest, and long sentences to hard labor in remote rural "reeducation" camps. Saigon, renamed Ho Chi Minh City, saw its bars, brothels, and dance halls closed.

Within a year, severe economic problems gripped Vietnam. The government's plan to quickly restore the agricultural productivity of the South to complement the industrial development of the North proved too optimistic. Vast areas of the countryside were no longer under cultivation due to the flight of peasants and the defoliated and bomb-cratered land. Hundreds of thousands of unemployed city-dwellers were lured to rural "New Economic Zones" with promises of houses, land, and food. Many of them soon fled from the harsh, primitive rural conditions. To compound matters, southern regions experienced three successive years of droughts and devastating floods.

Nor was there international deliverance. Vietnam was unable to attract foreign investment, without which its hopes of economic recovery were dim. The economic assistance that Nixon had once promised never came. Instead, Washington pressured international lending agencies to reject Vietnam's requests for loans. Increasingly, Hanoi was forced to turn to the Soviet Union (which had its own severe economic problems) for assistance. Vietnam's reliance on the Soviet Union contributed to a worsening of its relations with China, which until 1978 had provided a modicum of aid to Hanoi.

The Plight of Cambodia

Yet a bloodbath did occur, not in Vietnam but in neighboring Cambodia. When the United States disengaged from Vietnam in early 1973, it also terminated its military support for the Lon Nol government in Cambodia, which was embattled by the Khmer Rouge, a native Communist force. In April 1975, just before Saigon fell to the North Vietnamese, the Khmer Rouge swept into Phnom Penh, the Cambodian capital.

Cambodia braced itself for a new order under a Communist government led by Pol Pot, who immediately began a reign of revolutionary terror. In theory, Communist revolutions, upon inheriting the existing capitalist industrial base, transfer ownership from the capitalists to the workers. The Khmer Rouge, however, set out to eradicate the old order completely, root and branch, to reorganize society to a degree no revolutionary regime had ever attempted. Pol Pot's ideal society, in direct contrast to the tenets of Marxism, demanded a return to the land. The entire urban population was evacuated to the countryside. Those who resisted—members of the old regime, the Western-educated elite, city-dwellers, and all real or suspected "enemies of the revolution"— were exterminated. In the space of three years, the Khmer Rouge murdered an estimated 1.5 million Cambodians—almost one-fifth of the population.

Pol Pot also rejected the old borders of Cambodia that the French had drawn up. He initiated attacks against neighboring Thailand and Communist

Vietnam (with which, by necessity, he had cooperated over the years). Vehemently anti-Vietnamese, as were many Cambodians, he looked with misgivings upon the substantial Vietnamese population in eastern Cambodia. In 1978, he unleashed a furious attack against them, committing every conceivable atrocity.

For a while, Hanoi sought—unsuccessfully—to negotiate with Pol Pot. In January 1979, it sent its battle-tested army into Cambodia, scattered the Khmer Rouge, and then took control of Phnom Penh, where it installed a former Khmer Rouge officer, Heng Samrin, as head of a new pro-Vietnamese government. The Vietnamese conquest of Phnom Penh, however, did not bring peace to Cambodia. A Vietnamese army of about 170,000 continued to battle remnants of Pol Pot's forces, who had retreated into the mountainous jungles of western Cambodia.

Even though Vietnam had ended the genocidal fury of the Khmer Rouge, the international community was slow in showing its gratitude. As long as Vietnam remained a client of the Soviet Union, then Washington and Beijing continued to support the Khmer Rouge—the Chinese providing military assistance, the Carter and Reagan administrations diplomatic and economic aid. Beijing even sent its army into Vietnam in February 1979 to "teach it a lesson." That Communist China would be at war with Communist Vietnam, so soon after the war, proved how utterly wrong was Washington's conviction that a Communist victory in Vietnam would be a victory for Beijing.

By the end of the 1980s, with the Cold War winding down, opportunities arose to resolve the stalemate in Cambodia. The new Soviet leader, Mikhail Gorbachev, disengaged from the Third World and thus ended economic and military assistance to Vietnam. In 1989, Hanoi withdrew from Cambodia, leaving behind a pro-Vietnamese regime in Phnom Penh.

By the summer of 1991, the Soviet Union unraveled and, with the Soviet threat gone, Washington and Beijing lost interest in Cambodia. The United Nations was thus able to work out a political solution. Sihanouk returned from exile in Beijing, and in 1993 the UN oversaw a nationwide election won by the royalist party. Pol Pot, old and in ill health, was still holed up in the jungle near the Thai border. In April 1998, just as one of his own Khmer Rouge factions was about to hand him over to the government to stand trial for his crimes, Pol Pot cheated the hangman when he died of an apparent heart attack.

Another consequence of the Indochina wars was the desperate flight of refugees from Vietnam, which saw an estimated 1.5 million of its citizens escape by boarding vessels and taking to the sea. Many of these "boatpeople" died on the South China Sea from exposure, drowning, and attacks by pirates.

The first wave of boatpeople came in 1975 after the fall of Saigon, when about 100,000 people fled the country. In 1978 and 1979, during the war between Cambodia and Vietnam, a second and much larger wave of refugees fled Vietnam. They arrived in neighboring countries—Malaysia, Thailand, Singapore, the Philippines—which, however, did not want them. In July 1979, the UN secured an agreement with Vietnam to limit the refugee outflow. It also provided relief to nations of "first asylum" (such as Malaysia) and secured promises from other nations to open their doors to refugees.

The majority of those who left Vietnam were ethnic Chinese who had long dominated private business in Vietnam and fell victim to government policies in early 1979 that abolished "bourgeois trade" and introduced a currency reform that rendered their accumulated savings nearly worthless. Curiously, many were assisted in their flight by Communist authorities, who collected exit fees of up to $2,000 in gold from each departing refugee. In northern Vietnam, where the brief Chinese invasion had taken place, the exodus meant the expulsion of 250,000 of the region's approximately 300,000 ethnic Chinese.

Recommended Readings

Appy, Christian G. *Patriots: The Vietnam War Remembered from All Sides.* New York: Penguin, 2003.
An oral history consisting of approximately 140 interviews of participants, US as well as Vietnamese.

Arnett, Peter. *Live from the Battlefield: From Vietnam to Baghdad, 35 Years in the World's War Zones.* New York: Touchstone, 1994.
By an AP reporter from New Zealand.

Fall, Bernard B. *Vietnam Witness, 1953–1966.* New York: Praeger, 1966.
One of several books by a French historian, widely considered the West's leading authority on Vietnam.

FitzGerald, Frances. *Fire in the Lake: The Vietnamese and the Americans in Vietnam.* New York: Random House, 1972.
Places the US intervention in a context of Vietnamese history.

Halberstam, David. *The Best and the Brightest.* New York: Random House, 1972.
By a former *New York Times* reporter, still the best account of how Washington was drawn into the war.

———. *The Making of a Quagmire: America and Vietnam During the Kennedy Era.* Rev. ed. New York: Knopf, [1964] 1988.
Reportage at its best.

Hersh, Seymour. *My Lai Four: A Report on the Massacre and Its Aftermath.* New York: Random House, 1970.

Isaacs, Arnold R. *Without Honor: Defeat in Vietnam and Cambodia.* Baltimore: Johns Hopkins University Press, 1983.

Just, Ward, ed. *Reporting Vietnam: American Journalism, 1959–1975.* New York: Library of America, 1998.
Excellent selection of articles.

Langguth, A. J. *Our Vietnam: The War, 1954–1975.* New York: Simon and Schuster, 2000.
A definitive, detailed treatment of the war.

Mangold, Tom, and John Penycate. *The Tunnels of Cu Chi.* New York: Berkley Books, 1986.

An account of the Vietcong's 200-mile-long tunnel complex stretching from the "Iron Triangle" to the outskirts of Saigon.

McNamara, Robert S. *In Retrospect: The Tragedy and Lessons of Vietnam.* New York: Times Books/Random House, 1995.
The mea culpa of the secretary of defense for Presidents Kennedy and Johnson.

Shawcross, William. *Sideshow: Kissinger, Nixon, and the Destruction of Cambodia.* New York: Simon and Schuster, 1979.
A discussion of the widening of Nixon's war into Cambodia.

Sheehan, Neil. *A Bright Shining Lie: John Paul Vann and America in Vietnam.* New York: Random House, 1988.
A critical account of the US conduct of the war in Vietnam.

———, et al., eds. *The Pentagon Papers.* New York: Bantam, 1971.
A useful, abridged version of the official Pentagon collection of documents and interpretation.

Notes

1. Cited in Edward Miller, "Vision, Power, and Agency: The Ascent of Ngo Dinh Diem, 1945–1954," *Journal of Southeast Asian Studies* (October 1954), pp. 455–456.

2. Bernard B. Fall, *Last Reflections on a War* (Garden City, N.Y.: Doubleday, 1967), p. 167.

3. David Halberstam, *The Making of a Quagmire: America and Vietnam During the Kennedy Era*, rev. ed. (New York: Knopf, [1964] 1988), pp. 27, 29.

4. Stanley Karnow, *Vietnam: A History* (New York: Viking, 1983), p. 281.

5. Wilfred G. Burchett, *Vietnam: Inside Story of the Guerrilla War*, 3rd ed. (New York: International Publishers, 1968), p. 111.

6. Johnson's telephone conversation with Russell, May 27, 1964, Lyndon B. Johnson Library, Tape WH6405.10, Side A.

7. Robert S. McNamara, *In Retrospect: The Tragedy and Lessons of Vietnam* (New York: Times Books/Random House, 1995), pp. 128–142.

8. Theodore Draper, "The American Crisis: Vietnam, Cuba, and the Dominican Republic," *Commentary* (January 1967), p. 36.

9. Neil Sheehan et al., *The Pentagon Papers* (New York: Bantam, 1971), documents 61–64, pp. 271–285.

10. For the White Paper "Aggression from the North" and I. F. Stone's reply, see Marcus G. Raskin and Bernard B. Fall, eds., *The Vietnam Reader: Articles and Documents on American Foreign Policy and the Viet-Nam Crisis*, rev. ed. (New York: Vintage, 1967), pp. 143–162.

11. Associated Press, *New York Times*, May 14, 1967, p. 3.

12. Peter Arnett, *Live from the Battle Field: From Vietnam to Baghdad—35 Years in the World's War Zones* (New York: Touchstone Books, 1994), p. 256.

13. Errol Morris (director), documentary, *The Fog of War: Eleven Lessons from the Life of Robert S. McNamara* (2003).

10 Détente and the End of Bipolarity

Ironically, the years of US military involvement in Vietnam, 1965–1973, which represented a crusade against international Communism, saw a gradual improvement in relations between Washington and the two great Communist states. Toward the end of that period, the Cold War took several unexpected turns. First, détente eased the tensions between Moscow and Washington. Second, the early 1970s saw the normalization of relations between the United States and the People's Republic of China. In the end, President Richard Nixon, the quintessential anti-Communist who had always urged strong measures against the Vietnamese, Soviet, and Chinese Communists—all part of a great conspiracy—visited Moscow and Beijing. The bipolar world, with Moscow and Washington at center stage, was at an end.

The United States and China: The Normalization of Relations

The split between the Soviet Union and the People's Republic of China gave the United States a golden opportunity. Monolithic Communism, or "international socialist solidarity" as its proponents frequently called it, proved to be an ideological quest that ran aground on the shoals of nationalist interests. A succession of governments in Washington, tied to the principle of thwarting an international Communist conspiracy, had been slow in taking advantage of the falling-out between the two most important Communist states. But by the early 1970s, the time had come to cash in on what clearly had become a windfall for Washington.

Rapprochement between the United States and the vast Chinese empire could only give the Soviets a headache. At first, it was Moscow that played the "China card." With it, the Soviet Union's first line of defense in the East had been on the shores of the Yellow Sea. Washington's ability to play the same card promised to pay immeasurable dividends. The Chinese in their turn, however, a proud and ancient people, had no intentions of playing the pawn and instead sought to carve out their own niche as a major player in the superpower game. When Beijing and Washington took the first steps toward the normalization of relations in the early 1970s, the result was an end to great-power bipolarity and increased complexity in international relations.

For more than twenty years the United States and the PRC had no official relations; instead, they were hostile adversaries. Successive US presidents denounced "Red China" as a menace to the peace-loving peoples of Asia, as a reckless, irresponsible, aggressive regime unworthy of diplomatic recognition or UN membership. The United States maintained relations instead with the Nationalist regime on Taiwan, adhering to the fiction that it was the only legitimate government of China and pledging to defend it against "Communist aggression." The United States did not immediately commit itself to the defense of the government on Taiwan, but it did so in 1954, after having engaged Chinese Communist forces in battle for three years in Korea. Beijing denounced the US military alliance with Jiang's Nationalist government and the US military presence on Taiwan as "imperialist aggression" and as interference in the internal affairs of China. Meanwhile, the United States effectively blocked the PRC from gaining admission into the United Nations, contained it within an arc of military bases—running from South Korea to Japan, Taiwan, the Philippines, and South Vietnam—maintained a rigid embargo on all trade with China, and denied its citizens the right to travel there.

Nor was this merely a bilateral feud, since both antagonists called upon their respective Cold War allies for support. Supporting China, at least in the first decade of the Beijing-Washington clash, was the Soviet Union, its satellite states in Eastern Europe, and Communist parties in other parts of the world. The Soviet Union had supported from the outset the PRC's bid to replace the Republic of China (Jiang's government) in the United Nations. The United States, which perceived itself as leading and speaking for the "free world," applied diplomatic pressure on its friends and allies for support of its uncompromising China policy. Washington also pressured them to stand united against diplomatic recognition of the PRC and against its entry into the United Nations. It reacted negatively, for example, when in 1964 the independent-minded French government broke ranks and extended formal recognition to the PRC.

While Washington tirelessly denounced "Red China" and condemned Mao and the Chinese Communists for their brutal enslavement of the Chinese people, Beijing regarded the United States, the most powerful capitalist nation in the world, as its "Number One Enemy" and argued persistently that US imperialism was the major threat to world peace. The United States pointed to the Chinese intervention in the Korean War and China's border war with India in 1962 as examples of Chinese aggression. But Beijing (and some observers in the West) countered that in both cases China acted legitimately to protect its borders. The Chinese pointed to the ring of US military positions on their periphery as proof of the aggressive imperialism of the United States. So intense was this ideological conflict between the two countries that any reduction of tensions seemed impossible.

The Sino-Soviet split in the late 1950s did not bring about an improvement in Sino-US relations. Instead, relations worsened since it was China, not the Soviet Union, that argued for a stronger anti–United States line. When the United States and the Soviet Union began to move toward détente in the late 1960s, Beijing's anti-imperialist, anti–United States rhetoric became even more shrill as it sought to make its point: The Soviet Union had grown soft on capitalism, while China had not. China complained bitterly of Soviet "socialist imperialism," arguing that it was linked with US "capitalist imperialism" to encircle China. Mao spoke fervently of China's support for revolutionary movements throughout the world and support for wars of national liberation, such as that waged by Communist forces in Vietnam. He even taunted the United States to make war on China, saying that the atomic bomb was merely a "paper tiger" and that China would prevail in the end. Mao's inflammatory rhetoric made it easy for both superpowers to condemn China as a reckless warmonger, the greatest threat to world peace.

The seemingly interminable hostility between China and the United States ended quite suddenly in the early 1970s, in one of the most dramatic turnabouts in modern diplomatic history. On July 15, 1971, Republican president and diehard anti-Communist Richard Nixon made an unanticipated announcement that stunned the world. He would travel to China within six months, at the invitation of the Chinese government, for the purpose of developing normal relations with that government. He revealed that his secretary of state, Henry Kissinger, had just returned from a secret trip to Beijing, where he and Chinese premier Zhou Enlai had made arrangements for the diplomatic breakthrough.

The Nixon administration had begun making subtle overtures to the PRC in the previous year. In Warsaw, Poland, where the US and Chinese ambassadors had periodically engaged in secret talks, the US side intimated its desire for improved relations. In his televised "State of the World" address to the nation in February 1971, Nixon referred to the Beijing government as the People's Republic of China, instead of the usual "Red China" or "Communist China," and Chinese leaders took note of the fact that for the first time the US government had publicly used the proper name of their government. This opened the door to what became known as "ping-pong diplomacy." A US table-tennis team was invited to play an exhibition tournament in Beijing, and Premier Zhou gave them a warm reception and noted that their visit "opened a new page in the relations between the Chinese and US peoples."[1] Nixon responded by announcing a relaxation of the US trade embargo with China, and

US president Richard Nixon and Chinese premier Zhou Enlai at a reception banquet in Beijing, February 21, 1972. *(National Archives)*

this was followed by Kissinger's secret trip to Beijing in early July 1971 that prepared the ground for Nixon's dramatic announcement.

The following February, Nixon made his heralded two-week visit to China. He was welcomed with great fanfare by Chinese leaders. At the Beijing airport he extended a hand to Premier Zhou, the same Chinese leader whom John Foster Dulles had pointedly snubbed eighteen years earlier at Geneva by refusing to shake hands. In addition to his own large staff, Nixon was accompanied by a large retinue of journalists and television camera crews who recorded the historic event and gave the US people their first glimpse of life inside Communist China. For two weeks they were treated to pictures of China and its friendly, smiling people. And they were treated to the extraordinary spectacle of Nixon, a man known for his trenchant anti–Chinese Communist pronouncements, saluting the aged and ailing Chairman Mao Zedong and toasting the new bond of friendship with China's most able diplomat, Premier Zhou Enlai. For the United States and China alike, it was a mind-boggling, 180-degree turnabout.

At first blush, it appeared ironic that Nixon, a conservative, Communist-hating Republican, would be the one to go to China and establish friendly relations with its Communist government. But the task required just such a politician. A Democratic president would have found it impossible to do so, because the Democratic Party still carried the scars of allegedly having "lost China" to Communism in the first place. A Republican president whose anti-Communist credentials were beyond question would encounter much less opposition for reversing US policy toward Communist China.

In any case, the normalization of US-PRC relations was an event whose time had come and, indeed, was long overdue. Both sides understood that they had much more to gain by ending their mutual hostility than by continuing it. The Chinese needed to end their isolation in the face of a growing Soviet threat after the Ussuri River border clash in March 1969. The Soviets had greatly increased their ground forces along the Chinese border and equipped them with tactical nuclear weapons. Menaced by a superior Soviet force on their border, the Chinese leaders came to view closer ties with the United States as a means to decrease the possibility of a preemptive Soviet nuclear attack. By ending its isolation and reducing tensions with the United States, the PRC stood to gain greater security against becoming engaged in a war with either of the two superpowers, much less with both of them in a two-front war. The PRC also saw it as a means to gain entry into the United Nations and to solve the Taiwan question. China's international prestige would be greatly enhanced by its new relationship with the United States, while that of its rival, the Nationalist government on Taiwan, would be diminished. In addition, China had much to gain economically from trade opportunities that would come with normalization of relations with the United States and its allies.

The United States stood to benefit from normalization as well. One of the prime reasons for Nixon going to China was to obtain Beijing's assistance to negotiate an end to the Vietnam War on US terms. Nixon calculated—incorrectly it turned out—that Beijing could bring influence to bear on Hanoi to withdraw from South Vietnam. The Chinese, however, showed no interest whenever Nixon brought up Vietnam.

Nixon and his ambitious secretary of state, Henry Kissinger, developed a grand design for achieving a new global balance of power. They postulated that the bipolar world dominated by the two opposing superpowers was giving way to a world with five major power centers: the United States, the Soviet Union, Western Europe, Japan, and China. To achieve an international balance of power it was necessary to end the isolation of China. Détente with the Soviet Union was already well under way, but now the United States sought to "play the China card" when dealing with Moscow. By cautiously drawing closer to China, the United States sought to gain greater leverage in its diplomacy with Moscow. The Nixon administration saw that détente with the Soviet Union and normalization of relations with China were possible at the same time and that together these policies would perhaps constitute a giant step toward ending the Cold War. At the least, it would provide greater national security for the United States at a reduced cost. The opportunity for trade with China was also a motivating factor, but not as important as the diplomatic factors.

The major obstacle to improving relations between the two countries was—as had always been the case—Taiwan. The United States was still standing by the Nationalist regime on Taiwan, recognizing it as the sole legitimate government of China, and had a commitment to defend it. The United States envisioned a compromise solution to the Taiwan question, the so-called two-China formula. It called for formal diplomatic recognition of two separate Chinese governments, one on the mainland, the other on Taiwan. But this proved to be impossible since both Chinese governments firmly refused to accept that formula. Neither would give up its claim as the sole legitimate government of the whole of China.

When Nixon first communicated his desire for talks aimed at improving relations with the PRC, Zhou Enlai replied that he was ready to join in that effort on the condition that the United States be prepared for serious negotiations on the Taiwan issue. Beijing was not willing to compromise on that question. It was Washington that yielded when it ended its objection to the PRC's entry into the United Nations. In the past, the United States had voted against the PRC replacing the Republic of China in the United Nations but now made it known that it would not block this move as it had for over two decades. In October 1971, the PRC was admitted to the United Nations on its terms, namely, as the single legitimate government of China and as the rightful claimant of the seat that had been occupied by the Republic of China.

It was a test of the diplomatic skills of Henry Kissinger and Zhou Enlai to arrive at an agreement on Taiwan that would recognize the PRC's claim to Taiwan and yet would be less than a complete sellout of the Nationalist government on Taiwan by its US ally. They reached a tentative agreement on Taiwan in the carefully worded Shanghai Communiqué at the end of Nixon's visit to China in February 1972. In it, the United States acknowledged that all Chinese maintain "there is but one China and that Taiwan is part of China" and that the United States would not challenge that position. In the communiqué, the US side reaffirmed "its interest in a peaceful settlement of the Taiwan question by the Chinese themselves." The United States also agreed to reduce its military forces on Taiwan "as tension in the area diminishes." (This was in reference to the war in Indochina from which US forces were gradually withdrawing.) The PRC obtained important concessions on the Taiwan issue—namely, the US acknowledgment that the island was part of China proper and a US promise to withdraw its military force from that island. The United States conceded more than it gained but came away with an understanding that the PRC would not attempt to take over Taiwan by military means and with the satisfaction that its new relationship with China would serve to enhance stability in Asia.

This was not the end but the beginning of the normalization process. Full normalization of relations, involving the formal recognition of the PRC by the United States and the breaking off of US diplomatic ties with Nationalist China, was yet to be achieved. However, in accordance with the Shanghai

Communiqué, the two countries established liaison offices in each other's capital; began a series of exchanges in the fields of science, technology, culture, journalism, and sports; and initiated mutually beneficial trade relations that grew steadily in subsequent years.

It was not until January 1979 that full diplomatic relations between the two countries were achieved. There were two main reasons for the seven-year delay: political leadership problems in both countries in the mid-1970s, and the still unresolved Taiwan issue. In the United States, Nixon was hamstrung by the Watergate scandal and finally resigned in disgrace in August 1974. And in China, both Chairman Mao and Premier Zhou died in 1976, leaving behind a succession problem that was not resolved until Deng Xiaoping consolidated his leadership in 1978. It was left to new political leaders, Deng and President Jimmy Carter, to settle the Taiwan question. Deng came to the view that establishing diplomatic ties with the United States was of greater importance than liberating Taiwan and that a formula could be found to achieve the former by postponing the latter. Secret negotiations produced an agreement in December 1978, the terms of which included restoration of full diplomatic relations between the United States and the PRC and the termination of official US relations and the US defense pact with the Republic of China. It did allow, however, for continued US commercial and cultural ties with Taiwan and continued US arms sales to Taiwan. On the latter point, the Chinese government agreed to disagree, which is to say that it did not formally agree to such arms sales but would set aside that issue so that the normalization agreement could be made without further delay. To further strengthen the new diplomatic relations, Deng Xiaoping accepted an invitation to visit the United States, and he was given a warm reception during his nine-day visit that began less than a month after the mutual diplomatic recognition had gone into effect.

The agreement was a severe blow to Taiwan, which remained in the hands of the anti-Communist Nationalist government now headed by Jiang Jingguo (Chiang Ching-kuo), son of Jiang Jieshi, who had died in 1975. The US government attempted to soften the blow by passing the Taiwan Relations Act, which affirmed the resolve of the United States to maintain relations with the people (not the government) of Taiwan and to consider any effort to resolve the Taiwan issue by force as a "grave concern to the United States."

The consequences of the normalization of Chinese-US relations were immense. The United States ended the anomaly of recognizing a government that ruled only 17 million Chinese in favor of one that governed over 900 million. Normalization led to a significant reduction of tensions and provided greater stability in Asia. Both countries attained greater security, and at the same time they gained greater maneuverability in dealing with other powerful nations, notably the Soviet Union. Normalization opened the way to a vast increase in trade, which provided China with much-needed capital and technology. In the United States it was hoped that China's large market might serve to offset the mounting US trade deficit in other world markets. That hope soon vanished. Indeed, as early as 1996, China ran up the largest trade surplus of any nation trading with the United States (overtaking Japan).

One of the most important consequences of the normalization of Sino-US relations was the ending of China's diplomatic isolation. Not only did the PRC gain a permanent seat on the UN Security Council, but many nations of the world that had withheld formal ties with the PRC now followed the US lead by breaking off official ties with Taiwan and recognizing the PRC instead. In 1969, sixty-five countries had recognized Taiwan as the legal government of China, but by 1981 only twenty countries did so.

The breakthrough in Sino-US relations brought in its wake an equally abrupt turnaround in Sino-Japanese relations, which was of great significance to both countries as well as for peace and stability in Asia. Initially, the Japanese were stunned by Nixon's surprise announcement in July 1971, not because they opposed the move but because they were caught off guard by it and felt that they should have been consulted beforehand. The Japanese prime minister, Sato Eisaku, had for years stressed the mutual trust between his government and Washington, and, in order not to jeopardize the strong ties with the United States, he had consistently resisted popular pressure for normalization of relations with China. For the United States to suddenly reverse its China policy without consulting its major Asian ally was considered by the Japanese a diplomatic slap in the face.

Once the Japanese got over the "Nixon shock," as they referred to it, they hastened to work out their own rapprochement with China. Prime Minister Tanaka Kakuei responded to mounting public pressure for normalization of relations with China. He was able to obtain from the Chinese government an invitation to visit Beijing. His trip, in September 1972, was of great historical importance, being the first visit to China by any Japanese head of state and coming after almost a century of hostile Sino-Japanese relations. In Beijing, the Japanese prime minister contritely expressed his regret over the "unfortunate experiences" between the two nations in the past and stated that "the Japanese side is keenly aware of Japan's responsibility for causing enormous damage in the past to the Chinese people through war and deeply reproaches itself."[2]

The result of Tanaka's talks with Zhou Enlai was an agreement on the restoration of full diplomatic relations between the two countries on the following terms: Japan affirmed its recognition of the PRC as the sole legal government of China and agreed to the claim that Taiwan was an inalienable part of the territory of the PRC. China waived its claim to reparations of several billion dollars and agreed to discontinue its protest against the US-Japan Mutual Security Pact and to drop its insistence that Japan end its trade relations with Taiwan. The two countries also agreed to negotiate a new treaty of peace and friendship in the near future. China and Japan reaped enormous benefits from their improved relations, particularly from the huge volume of trade that developed between them in the following years. The two countries were natural trading partners; China had raw materials to offer resource-poor Japan in exchange for Japan's technology, machinery, and finished goods. The diplomatic rewards of the Sino-Japanese détente were probably even greater, for relations between these two major Asian nations had never been better than this since the nineteenth century, and the new relationship between these once hostile neighbors brought an era of stability and security to East Asia.

The government most disaffected by the PRC's new diplomatic achievements was, of course, the Republic of China on Taiwan. It bitterly denounced its former allies—the United States, Japan, and others—for abandoning a friend and argued that leaders in Washington and Tokyo had been duped by the Communist government in Beijing, toward which Taiwan leaders directed their strongest attacks. Although it was becoming isolated diplomatically, Taiwan carefully sought to retain ties with the United States, Japan, and other Western nations with whom it still maintained a lucrative commercial relationship. The diplomatic setback had no impact on Taiwan's continued high rate of economic growth, which produced a far higher standard of living for its people than the Chinese on the mainland. Stubbornly, its government, still dominated by the Nationalist Party, rebuffed every overture by the PRC for a peaceful reunification. Meanwhile, the PRC, careful not to risk damaging its good relations with the United States, patiently refrained from forceful gestures toward Taiwan and waited for a softening of Taiwan's position. But, insofar as the *raison d'être* of the Nationalist government on the island was to overthrow the Communist rulers of the mainland, it neither wavered in its resolute anti-Communist policy nor moderated its strident anti-Beijing propaganda. Not until the late 1980s, when the global Cold War ended, did the Taiwan government retreat from its rigid stance.

Détente Between East and West

The rapprochement between Washington and Beijing took place in an era of thawing of frozen relations across a wide front. It pointed to significant changes in the Cold War mentality in both camps. Originally, both sides had taken the position that there could be no improvement of relations until such issues as Taiwan, Germany, and the like had been resolved. In the mid-1960s, however, the belligerents backtracked when they concluded that a normalization of relations—such as in the areas of trade, international travel and contact, and arms limitations—could contribute ultimately to resolving the greater issues—the unification of divided nations, the nuclear arms race—and perhaps even put an end to the Cold War. The result was détente, the lessening of tensions in international relations.

*   *   *

The Cold War that began in the late 1940s had created two German nations—a West German state aligned with the West and ultimately with the North Atlantic Treaty Organization, and an East German state whose government had been installed by the Red Army and which then joined the Soviet Union's military organization, the Warsaw Pact. The conservative anti-Communist West German governments of the 1950s and the early 1960s, particularly that of Chancellor Konrad Adenauer, considered the Soviet creation of East Germany as illegitimate and refused to recognize or deal with it. The West German leaders treated Germany as a whole, claimed to speak for all Germans, and automatically granted citizenship to East Germans who made it across the border into West Germany. They considered the West German capital, Bonn, as a provisional seat of a provisional state; the true political heart of Germany was Berlin.

Adenauer stated his position forcefully when his government issued the Hallstein Doctrine (named after the state secretary of the West German Foreign Office) in 1955. It emphasized that West Germany would not recognize any state (with the exception of the Soviet Union) that had diplomatic relations with East Germany. In practical terms it meant that West Germany would have no dealings with the Soviet client states of Eastern Europe. It would make no attempt to raise the Iron Curtain.

But in 1966, Willy Brandt, West Germany's new foreign minister, reversed Adenauer's stand when he took the first steps to establish contact with the socialist nations of Eastern Europe. He was willing to recognize the political realities in place for more than two decades, ever since the Red Army had rolled into the center of Europe. The president of the United States, Lyndon Johnson, anticipated Brandt's new position when he stated that the reunification of Germany could only come about as a result of détente. In other words, Brandt and Johnson took the position that détente was a precondition for a unified Germany, whereas Adenauer and Hallstein had earlier argued that there must first be a unified Germany before there could be talk of improved relations with the Soviet bloc. Brandt and Adenauer sought the same end; they only differed over the means.

Brandt's departure from Adenauer's stance also meant that he was willing to grant de facto recognition to the existence of East Germany, as well as to the borders of the two Germanies, the consequence of Germany's defeat in World War II. To achieve the normalization of relations between East and West, the Brandt government was willing to recognize the Oder-Neisse Line as the border between East Germany and Poland. The new border had been in existence since the end of the war, when the Soviet Union moved Poland's western border about seventy-five miles (into the region of Silesia, which before the war had been German territory) to the Oder and Western Neisse Rivers. Of the 6 million former German inhabitants of the area lost to Poland, many had been killed during the war, others had fled before the advancing Red Army, and nearly all of the remaining 2 million were expelled. The Germans

West German chancellor Willy Brandt after placing a wreath at the Tomb of the Unknown Soldier in the Polish capital of Warsaw, December 1970. *(German Information Center)*

Soviet leader Leonid Brezhnev and US president Richard Nixon at the White House, Washington, D.C., June 19, 1973. *(AP/Wide World Photos)*

also had lost East Prussia, the easternmost province of the German Reich, to the Soviets, who took the northern half, and to the Poles, who took the southern half. And in Czechoslovakia, the Germans had lost the Sudetenland, which the British and the French had granted Hitler in 1938. The Czechs, of course, wasted little time after the war in expelling what was left of the 3 million Sudeten Germans.[3]

The Adenauer government had been most adamant in its refusal to accept the loss of German territory to Poland. Willy Brandt, however, acknowledged that the Oder-Neisse Line had existed as the new German boundary for over twenty years and had few Germans living east of it. Brandt also stopped believing that his government could ever hope to reclaim East Prussia. Any attempt to do so would lead to another war in Europe and only drive Poland and the Soviet Union into each other's arms. (In 1945, the Poles and the Soviets had been able to agree on only one thing, that Germany must pay for the war with the loss of territory.) Brandt also abandoned all claims to the Sudetenland. This was the least controversial of the steps Brandt was willing to take, for the region had been Czechoslovakia's before the war and its transfer to Hitler's Reich was one of the most significant events leading to World War II. That the Sudetenland would be returned to Czechoslovakia after the war had been a foregone conclusion. (What had not been a foregone conclusion was the expulsion of Germans whose ancestors had lived there for centuries.)

The Soviet Union and East Germany, however, wanted more than a mere West German recognition of the borders. They also wanted West German recognition of the East German government, which of course would legitimize it. Such recognition, however, would also undermine the West German government's claim that it spoke for all Germans. This was not something Brandt—or any other West German leader—was willing to do.

Still, the two German governments did begin to talk to each other. On March 19, 1971, a historic meeting took place in Erfurt, East Germany, between Willy Brandt, who by then was West Germany's chancellor, and his counterpart Willi Stoph, the East German prime minister. (The power behind the throne in East Germany, however, was the Communist Party's chief, Walter Ulbricht.) This event led to the Basic Treaty of 1972 between the two German states. East Germany did not obtain full diplomatic recognition from West Germany, but the treaty did call for "good neighborly" relations, and it led to increased contacts of a cultural, personal, and economic nature. The Iron Curtain was partially raised.

Brandt's attempts to establish contacts with Eastern Europe became known as *Ostpolitik* (an opening toward the East, literally "eastern politics"). It included a partial thaw in relations with the Soviet Union and other East European countries. In 1968, West Germany established diplomatic relations with Yugoslavia. In 1970, West Germany and the Soviet Union signed in Moscow a nonaggression treaty. Later that year, Brandt went to Warsaw to sign a similar treaty with the Polish government, and his government accepted the Oder-Neisse Line.

Brandt's de facto recognition of the line meant that he would not permit it to stand in the way of better relations with the East. But not everyone was willing to accept the new borders. The critics pointed out that a central feature of the West German position—one spelled out during the early 1950s—had not changed. There could be no final, de jure acceptance of the borders until Germany signed peace treaties with Poland and the Soviet Union. Until the treaties were ratified there could be no de jure recognition of the postwar borders. With the deterioration of East-West relations during the late 1970s, West German conservatives, including Chancellor Helmut Kohl, dusted off this argument in the mid-1980s, thus keeping the question of Germany's borders an open issue.[4]

Détente and Brandt's *Ostpolitik* made possible a series of US-Soviet arms limitation talks, including SALT I and SALT II (see Chapter 19), which led directly to the European Security Conference of August 1975 in Helsinki, Finland. The Soviets had proposed such a conference as early as 1954 and again in the late 1960s to ratify the consequences of World War II. The Soviet proposals were to no avail. Since no formal treaty or conference had recognized the redrawn map and the new governments of Eastern Europe, the Soviet leaders continued to press for such a conference. At Helsinki in 1975, thirty years after the fact, they hoped to obtain such recognition.

The participants at Helsinki included all European states (except Albania) as well as the United States and Canada. The agreement signed at Helsinki recognized the postwar borders of Europe, but it left open the prospect that the borders could be changed, although only by peaceful means. West Germany renounced its long-standing claim as the sole legitimate German state. East and West agreed to observe each other's military exercises to avoid the misreading of the other's intentions. Last, all signatories of the Helsinki Agreement promised greater East-West contacts and to guarantee the human rights of their citizens. In Eastern Europe, however, the rights of citizens were defined differently than in the West, and this point later became a central issue when détente was shelved by the United States during the late 1970s.

Détente between East and West also produced the first steps on the road to limit the unchecked nuclear arms race. Until 1972, there were no limits on the nuclear arsenals of the United States and the Soviet Union. Both had more than enough firepower to destroy each other several times over, and there was little point in adding to stockpiles already of grotesque proportions. By 1970, the Soviet Union had concluded its concerted effort to catch up with the United States and had achieved a rough sort of parity. The US strategic nuclear arsenal consisted at that time of 3,854 warheads; the Soviet total was 2,155.

The year 1975, the year of the Helsinki Agreement, saw the high point of détente. After that, relations between the United States and the Soviet Union began to deteriorate, and by 1980, détente was a thing of the past. A number of factors contributed to the new climate.

Détente never sat well with a number of influential US policymakers. To them, détente was always a snare and a delusion. One cannot do business, they warned, with an ideological system that professes world revolution. They seized every opportunity to sabotage détente. Eventually, a number of liberals joined their chorus. These liberals—together with the old hard-liners—became known as the neoconservatives, or simply "neocons," who heavily influenced the foreign policy of presidents from Ronald Reagan to George W. Bush.

With the intensification of the Cold War came a reassessment of Soviet military strength and intentions. In 1976, the head of the CIA, George H. W. Bush, brought in a group of Cold War warriors (known as the "B Team") who overruled a CIA estimate of Soviet military spending. According to the B Team, the Soviets were spending nearly twice as much on their military as the CIA had reckoned. These ominous interpretations placed Soviet intentions and capabilities in a new light. Reporters, editorial writers, politicians, and academicians quickly accepted these new figures, which then became part and parcel of the new orthodoxy during this latest phase of the Cold War. This was not the last time the neocons would challenge CIA findings. Their greatest success came when they beat the drums for war against Iraq in 2003.

In 1983, the professionals in the CIA, in a report to Congress, cast off the shackles of George H. W. Bush and the B Team when they restated the validity of their original estimates of Soviet military spending. They cut the B Team's estimates by more than half. But while the B Team's findings had received much publicity, the CIA's declaration of independence from meddling outsiders received scant attention. Nor did a NATO study of January 1984, which concluded that Soviet military spending since 1976 had, in fact, declined to less than 2.5 percent of gross national product (GNP), as compared to 4–5 percent during the early 1970s.

These reassessments of Soviet military spending notwithstanding, the B Team's estimates of Soviet military spending became the new orthodoxy. Between 1976 and 1980, Republican presidential hopeful Ronald Reagan got considerable mileage out of an argument that the Soviets had opened up a lead on the United States in the nuclear arms race. He promised to restore US military might, a pledge that, probably more than anything else, gained him the presidency in 1980, particularly after the incumbent Jimmy Carter proved impotent in gaining the release of the US hostages in Iran (see Chapter 20). The B Team's findings, the seizure of the hostages in Iran, and the burning of US flags in full view of television cameras had a profound effect. A new militancy set in.

The Soviets, too, contributed to the scuttling of détente. Their definition of détente had always been different from that of the West. They insisted on the right to conduct their foreign and domestic affairs as they had in the past.

What they did in Africa, they insisted, had nothing to do with Soviet-US relations. But many in the United States perceived the Soviet activities in Africa differently. In 1975, the Brezhnev government signed the Helsinki Agreement and in the same breath began sending arms to clients in Angola, Somalia, Ethiopia, and Mozambique, while Cuban soldiers arrived in Soviet planes in Angola and Ethiopia to train African soldiers.

The result was stepped-up competition between Moscow and Washington, not just in Africa but also elsewhere. Close Soviet ties with the Marxist leader of Somalia, Siad Barre, dated to the early 1970s. Then, in late 1976, the Soviet Union began to send arms shipments to the Marxist head of Ethiopia, Mengistu Haile Miriam. In 1978, the Communist governments of Somalia and Ethiopia went to war over a stretch of desert in the Somalian border province of Ogaden. The Soviets had to choose, and they decided to stay with Ethiopia. The United States then became the supplier of weapons to Siad Barre.

Elsewhere, Moscow had a client in Vietnam who, in 1979, marched into Phnom Penh, the capital of Cambodia. And in December 1979, the Soviet army moved into Afghanistan to prop up a bankrupt and brutal Communist government. Then, in 1981, the head of the Polish state invoked martial law in an attempt to destroy the only independent labor union in the Soviet bloc. To many in the West, Moscow and its surrogates appeared to be on the march. Under such circumstances, détente could not survive.

Soviet domestic actions also undermined the spirit of détente when Jewish emigration was drastically curtailed. During the 1970s, Jews who wished to leave the Soviet Union had been bargaining chips in East-West relations. During that decade, about 270,000 Jews emigrated. Afterward, emigration slowed to a trickle. Dissidents, the most famous of whom was the nuclear physicist Andrei Sakharov, were either jailed or exiled, in violation of the Helsinki Agreement. Détente became a memory of the not too distant past.

Recommended Readings

Bueler, William M. *US China Policy and the Problem of Taiwan*. Boulder: Colorado Associated University Press, 1971.
   An analysis of the Taiwan issue on the eve of Nixon's visit.
Fairbank, John K. *The United States and China*. 4th ed. Cambridge, Mass.: Harvard University Press, 1983.
   A standard work that provides a historical account of Sino-US relations as well as a survey of Chinese history.
Garthoff, Raymond. *Détente and Confrontation: American-Soviet Relations from Nixon to Reagan*. Washington, D.C.: Brookings Institution, 1985.
   A most detailed analysis of a complex relationship.
Griffith, William E. *Peking, Moscow, and Beyond: The Sino-Soviet Triangle*. Washington, D.C.: Center for Strategic International Studies, 1973.
   Discusses the implications of Nixon's visit to Beijing.

Hersh, Seymour M. *The Price of Power: Kissinger in the Nixon White House.* New York: Summit Books, 1983.
A devastating analysis of Kissinger's foreign policy.
Schaller, Michael. *The United States and China in the Twentieth Century.* New York: Oxford University Press, 1979.
A useful study that takes the story well beyond the Nixon visit to China.
Ulam, Adam B. *Dangerous Relations: The Soviet Union in World Politics, 1970–1982.* New York: Oxford University Press, 1983.
Discusses the rise and fall of détente.

Notes

1. Immanuel C. Y. Hsu, *The Rise of Modern China*, 3rd rev. ed. (New York: Oxford University Press, 1983), p. 373.

2. Cited in ibid., p. 751.

3. For a map of the transfer of land after World War II, see Chapter 2, "The Cold War Institutionalized."

4. Bernt Conrad, "How Definite Is the Oder-Neisse Line?" *Die Welt*, December 24, 1984; reprinted in *The German Tribune: Political Affairs Review* (a publication of the West German government), April 21, 1985, pp. 15–16. See also *The Week in Germany*, a weekly newsletter of the West German Information Center, Washington, D.C., June 21, 1985, p. 1.

Part 4

The Third World

The East-West confrontation was surely the dominant theme in international relations in the postwar period, but since the 1970s, another cleavage, the North-South divide, became increasingly important. "North" refers to the modern industrialized nations, most of which happen to be located in the temperate zones of the Northern Hemisphere, and "South" signifies the poorer nations, most located in the equatorial region or in the Southern Hemisphere. The nations of the South are scattered throughout Asia, Africa, and Latin America. They are sometimes euphemistically called "developing countries," even though some were hardly developing at all, or "underdeveloped countries." More commonly, they were referred to collectively as the "Third World."

By the end of the twentieth century, the Third World as a nonaligned, non-Western entity had largely ceased to exist. The term, however, continued to be used—as we use it here—to describe nations lacking sustained economic development, notably in the area of industrialization. Indeed, the principal identifying characteristic of Third World nations was and remains poverty.

The economic dilemma of the Third World is the theme of Chapter 11. First we examine the gap between North and South and the reasons for the retarded economic development of the latter. We particularly focus on the population factor and problems in agricultural and industrial development. In the remainder of the chapter, we examine a global economic dilemma that strongly affected many Third World nations and became especially acute in the 1990s: the crisis of debt. Many of the nations of the Third World—even those with an industrial base such as Brazil, Mexico, and Argentina—amassed foreign debts so large they were unable to pay either the principal or the interest on their loans.

Economic and political development are interrelated, one being a function of the other, and this was surely the case in Africa, which is the focus of Chapter 12. It is necessary, therefore, to seek political reasons for the economic problems in the Third World and economic reasons for its political problems.

We examine the political patterns of postindependence sub-Saharan Africa, where the demise of fledgling democratic governments and the rise of militarism were common. We also take note of a new push for democracy in the early 1990s that ultimately bore little fruit. We also examine in this chapter South Africa, which stood apart from its northern neighbors, not so much because it was more prosperous but because it alone among African nations continued to be ruled until 1994 by a white minority. After explaining the policy of apartheid in South Africa, we relate the story of the abolition of apartheid and the role of Nelson Mandela in the creation of a nonracial democratic South Africa.

The militarization of politics, new to Africa after independence, has a long history in Latin America. There, in countries large and small, postwar economic development was disappointing, and the disaffected classes—mainly laborers and landless farmers—continued to be victimized by an elitist system that has endured for centuries. In Chapter 13, we examine the patterns of politics—the swings between democratic rule and militarism in Latin America, particularly in Argentina, Brazil, Chile, and Peru. Next we turn to the struggle for economic and political modernization in Mexico. Economic problems and political struggle were even more acute in Central America, where several Central American nations—notably Nicaragua and El Salvador—became hotbeds of revolution. Finally, we take up the issue of Latin American narcotics trade, centering on Colombia, and its connection to the US intervention in Panama.

In Chapter 14, we turn to Asia to study the twists and turns of the Communist rule in the People's Republic of China as it attempted to put that huge Third World nation on the track of economic development. China, the world's largest nation—with over 1 billion people in 1990—faced the problems of feeding a burgeoning population and maintaining political order. China is unique not only because of its great size but because for almost three decades, while under the rule of Mao Zedong, the political goal of creating a Communist society was given higher priority than the economic goal of industrial development. From the late 1970s, however, China's new leader, Deng Xiaoping, gave priority to economic growth. We relate the remarkable success of Deng's policies as well as the lack of corresponding political liberalization, as seen in the crushing of the prodemocracy demonstration in Tiananmen Square in Beijing in 1989. Next we turn to the other China—Taiwan—and its economic and political development and its ongoing rivalry with Communist China.

The focus shifts in Chapter 15 to South Asia and Southeast Asia, where the trials and tribulations of India—the world's second-largest nation—Pakistan, and Bangladesh are given primary attention. We also examine briefly the politics and the economic surge of the Southeast Asian countries of Indonesia, Thailand, and Malaysia, and the problems of the Philippines, where a corrupt dictatorship was overthrown in 1986.

11 Problems of Economic Development in the Third World

In addition to the East-West ideological division, the world was divided between the rich nations and the poor nations. About three-quarters of the world's wealth was produced and consumed by a relatively small proportion of its people, those of the North. Conversely, the large majority of the earth's people, those in the South, alternatively known as the Third World, produced and consumed but a small proportion of the world's wealth.

The concept of a North-South division of the world was popularized by the West German foreign minister (and later chancellor) Willy Brandt, who argued that the East-West division (between the Western and Soviet blocs) can readily be overcome; the division between the haves and the have-nots, however, was a much more difficult matter to resolve.

The disparity in wealth between the North and the South during the early 1990s may be seen in the figures in Table 11.1 on per capita GNP (gross national product).

During the 1950s, French journalists coined the phrase "Third World" to describe nations that were neither part of the Western world nor of the Communist bloc. In 1955, the leaders of these nations met for the first time at an Afro-Asian conference in the Indonesian city of Bandung. The spiritual father of the nonaligned Third World movement was the prime minister of India, Jawaharlal Nehru. As early as 1947, at a time when India had just gained its independence from Great Britain and the Cold War was already in full bloom, Nehru had declared that "we will not attach ourselves to any particular group," neither the Communist nor the Western camp.[1] At Bandung, seven years later, he called for an "unaligned area" as a buffer between the two camps, if only to lessen the danger of war between them.[2] The Bandung Conference criticized "colonialism in all of its manifestations," a direct swipe at the remaining Western colonial presence in the Third World as well as the Soviet Union's presence in Eastern Europe.

Table 11.1   Per Capita Gross National Product, 1990

North	
United States	$21,790
Switzerland	$32,680
Japan	$25,430
West Germany (before unification)	$22,320
South	
Sub-Saharan Africa	$340
East Asia and the Pacific (without Japan)	$600
South Asia	$330
Middle East and North Africa	$1,790
Latin America and the Caribbean	$2,180
World	$4,200

Source: World Bank, *World Development Report 1992,* pp. 196, 218–219.

Among the other leaders in attendance were Gamal Abdel Nasser (Egypt), Kwame Nkrumah (Ghana), Achem Sukarno (Indonesia), and Zhou Enlai (China). Eventually they were joined by Joseph Tito of Yugoslavia, the head of a European Communist nation that had taken a neutral stance in the Cold War. Collectively, the representatives of twenty-nine African and Asian nations spoke for more than one-half of the world's population. They had much in common; they had participated in the postwar struggle for independence from colonial control and now sought to resolve the host of problems of their newly independent nations. They tended to reject capitalism, the economic model of the former colonial powers, and instead opted for some variant of socialism. Officially, they were nonaligned in the Cold War, although some leaned toward the Soviet bloc and some toward the West. The tilt to one or the other bloc often depended on the assistance they received from either Washington or Moscow. Genuine neutrality was difficult to maintain, particularly because the superpowers constantly bid for the nonaligned nations' loyalty.

The alarming increase in the gap between the impoverished South and the more prosperous North was the focus of an international conference in Cancún, Mexico, in September 1981. Figures presented at the conference indicated that the 140 countries that classified themselves as "developing nations" comprised 75 percent of the world's population but had only 20 percent of the world's income. These nations were developing, yet the gap between them and the North continued to grow larger in the 1980s (see Table 11.2).

The statistical average of $700 annual per capita GNP for the Third World in 1985 masked the great disparity in wealth among Third World nations. In fact, per capita GNP for most sub-Saharan African countries was far below $700. According to World Bank figures, in 1984, Ethiopia had a per capita GNP of only $110—the lowest among African nations—followed by Mali ($140), Zaire ($140), and Burkina Faso ($160).[3] Moreover, most of the nations of Africa had low economic growth rates. Indeed, at least fourteen African nations

Table 11.2 North Versus South, 1985

	North	South
Population	1.18 billion	3.76 billion
Annual per capita GNP	$9,510	$700
Life expectancy	73 years	58 years
Annual rate of population growth	0.6%	2.0%

Source: Population Reference Bureau, *1986 World Population Data Sheet.*

registered "negative growth," that is, a decline of the per capita GNP. Zaire, for example, had a negative growth rate of –1.2 percent and Uganda one of –3 percent for the decade between 1972 and 1982. The poor were getting poorer.

Within each impoverished nation of the South, a great disparity existed between the wealthy and the poor. The maldistribution of wealth in the underdeveloped nations of the Third World was greater than that in industrialized nations of the North.[4] The majority of people in Third World nations, mainly peasants but many city-dwellers as well, had far less than the national average per capita income. Taking this into account, as well as considering the increasing population and low per capita income figures to begin with, we can begin to fathom the dimensions of poverty and hunger in the Third World. In the mid-1980s, at least one-fifth of the earth's inhabitants lived in dire poverty and suffered from chronic hunger and malnutrition.

The Population Factor

Population growth was a major factor in the persistence of poverty. In the twentieth century, the population of the world grew at an increasing rate and at an especially alarming rate in the Third World. It had taken about 5 million years for the world's population to reach 1 billion, around 1800. The second billion mark was reached in about 130 years, by 1930; the third billion in 30 years, by 1960; the fourth billion in 15 years, by 1975; and the fifth billion in only 11 years, by 1986. The rate of population growth, however, decreased since the mid-1960s, as witnessed by the fact that the sixth billion was reached after 14 years (see Figure 11.1). The rate of growth of world population peaked at 2.4 percent annually in 1964; by the mid-1990s it fell to about 1.5 percent.

The pressure of overpopulation was much greater in the Third World, where population growth rates remained high compared with the developed nations of the North. Indeed, after World War II, the Third World witnessed a veritable population explosion, an increase at a historically unprecedented rate. During the late 1980s in Africa, for example, many nations had growth rates of more than 3 percent, and some even reached more than 4 percent. In contrast, the industrialized nations had a much lower rate of growth, and—notably East

Figure 11.1   Past and Projected World Population, C.E. 1–2150

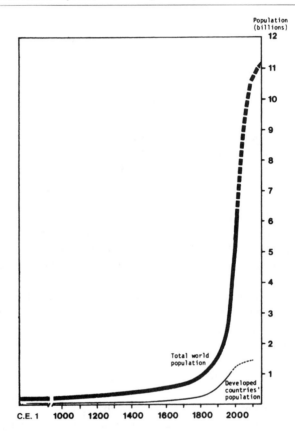

Germany, West Germany, and Austria—attained a stable population (no growth at all) or even a negative growth rate. (See Figure 11.2.)

Because of unchecked population growth rates, many Third World nations were on a treadmill. The increase in economic output, never large to begin with, was all too often swallowed up by relentless population growth. During the 1970s and 1980s, Africa's population growth rate of roughly 3 percent was about nine times that of Europe and about three times that of the United States and Canada. These ominous statistics meant that unless the trend was reversed, the continent's population of 450 million would double in only twenty-three years—as, indeed, it did. The growth rate in Kenya throughout the 1970s stood at 3.5 percent, and by the mid-1980s it had risen to 4.2 percent. Kenya's fertility rate (the average number of children born to a woman) was 8.0. These figures were among the highest in recorded history. But Kenya was not alone,

Figure 11.2 Population Growth Rates, 1950–1985

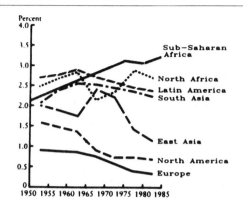

Source: World Bank, 1986.

for all of these African countries had population growth rates approaching 4 percent: Rwanda, Burundi, Zimbabwe, Tanzania, Uganda, Ghana, and Libya.

How is the population explosion in the Third World to be explained? In briefest terms, the death rate fell while the birthrate either rose or remained constant. The introduction of modern medicines, the eradication of communicable diseases (such as smallpox), and improved public health and education all contributed to a reduced rate of infant mortality and an increased life expectancy. But there was no corresponding decrease in fertility. In most developing countries, most families had at least four children and in rural areas often more than five. In these countries—similar to the developing European countries in the nineteenth century—the larger the number of children in a family, the greater the number of hands in the fields or in the factories, where they were able to earn money to supplement their parents' meager income. Having large families was a means to escape poverty and was, therefore, considered economically rational. The responsibility for overpopulation in the Third World is often attributable to men, who tended to disdain all artificial birth control methods and for whom having many children was a sign of virility and moral rectitude. Yet, it was the women who bore the children and wound up caring for the large families. But it was also true that in most of the Third World, women also typically shared the men's desire for many children.

Programs of governments and international agencies to control population growth in the Third World initially met with mixed success. The most dramatic reduction of the birthrate occurred in China, where the Communist government instituted a stringent birth control program that included paramedical services, free abortions (even at near full term), public education, social pressure, and economic sanctions. Government-supported family-planning programs were moderately successful in other Third World countries, notably South Korea, Colombia, Mauritius, Sri Lanka, Argentina, Uruguay, and Egypt. In many other countries, governments were less active in, or were slow to begin, birth control efforts. In India, birth control programs had mixed results but were generally more effective in regions where public education was more widespread. Until the 1960s, such programs had little impact on many countries in Latin America (especially Central America) and in sub-Saharan Africa.

The problems of overpopulation in the Third World were compounded by an ongoing exodus of people from the surrounding countryside migrating into already overcrowded cities in quest of a better life. In 1940, 185 million people lived in Third World cities; by 1975 the number rose more than fourfold, to 770 million. In the early 1970s, 12 million people a year—33,000 a day— were arriving in the cities of the Third World.[5] Third World cities became the largest in the world—Mexico City, São Paulo, Buenos Aires, Seoul, Calcutta, and Cairo. In Africa in 1950, only three cities had a population of 500,000; thirty-five years later there were twenty-nine cities of at least that size. The urban population of Kenya doubled in a decade. The population of Lagos, Nigeria, grew incredibly from 300,000 in 1970 to over 3 million in 1983.

Although the cities typically offered more and better employment opportunities, medical services, and education than the villages, they could not readily accommodate the massive influx of newcomers. They did not provide adequate employment, housing, sanitation, and other services for the numerous new inhabitants—many of whom remained unemployed and impoverished. Mexico City was the most extreme case. Its population doubled in a decade to over 18 million. More than one-third of the new arrivals lived in squatter settlements in the world's largest slum. This scene was duplicated in most other Third World cities, such as Cairo, where many thousands lived in the city's cemeteries and refuse dumps, and Calcutta, where nearly 1 million of the city's 10 million inhabitants lived in the streets. The concentration of such huge numbers of disaffected peoples, living in the shadows of the edifices of the more opulent class and often within marching distance of the centers of political power (many of the largest Third World cities are capital cities), heightened the potential for political unrest.

One of the most critical problems associated with overpopulation was how to feed the people. In the 1960s, television began to bring home to people in the North the tragedy of mass starvation in Ethiopia and Somalia, but most viewers remained unaware that hundreds of thousands of people in other African countries—Sudan, Kenya, Mozambique, Chad, Mali, Niger, and others—also suffered from starvation. Estimates of the extent of world hunger varied greatly, depending in part on how hunger was defined, but there was little doubt that an enormous number of Third World people—perhaps 1 billion—were chronically malnourished.

In the late 1980s, a number of international agencies began to single out overpopulation as a leading factor threatening the quality of life. The UN Population Fund, in its Amsterdam Declaration of November 1989, urged a recognition of responsibility to future generations. It stressed that men must recognize that "women are in the center of the development process" and that their freedom to make choices "will be crucial in determining future population growth rates." Without rights for women—legal, social, educational, and reproductive—there would be little hope of solving the problem of rapid population growth.[6]

Similarly, the Organization for Economic Cooperation and Development in 1989 argued that "women must be fully involved as decision makers in the planning and implementation of population programs."[7] The committee concluded that one of the priorities for international assistance should be the slowing of population growth. The World Bank's fifteenth annual *World Development Report* (1992) emphasized for the first time the link between unchecked population growth and environmental degradation, slow economic growth, declining health care, and declining living standards.

The international organizations understood that the implementation of effective family-planning programs would not be easy because they frequently clashed with deeply entrenched cultural and religious values held particularly (but not exclusively) by adherents of Islam, Hinduism, and Roman Catholicism. Pope John Paul II, for instance, in his encyclical "On the Hundredth Anniversary of Rerum Novarum" (May 1991), denounced, as he had done before, all measures "suppressing or destroying the sources of life." "Anti-childbearing campaigns," he argued, rested "on the basis of a distorted view of the demographic problem." Birth control, the pope declared, was responsible for "poisoning the lives of millions of defenceless human beings, as if in a form of 'chemical warfare.'"[8]

If the world experienced a population explosion immediately after World War II, from the mid-1960s on, it witnessed another demographic trend, a considerable *decline* in the population growth rate, from 2.4 percent to 1.5 percent by the end of the century. The world was slowly moving toward the zero-growth fertility rate of 2.1 infants per female.

Conventional wisdom declared that a falling birthrate was necessarily tied to prosperity, but the increasingly wider availability of birth control in many poorer countries upset this theory. One example was Bangladesh, which not only ranked among the poorest of nations but was also overwhelmingly Muslim. The tenets of Islam prohibit family planning, yet 40 percent of that country's women used some sort of birth control. This trend produced a shift from the view that "development is the best contraceptive" to "contraceptives are the best contraceptives."[9] In addition, Third World feminists stressed that birth control frequently was tied to levels of education. At a UN conference on population control in April 1994, they produced statistics pointing to the correlation be-tween higher female education and a lower fertility rate.[10]

By the summer of 2008, the world's population stood at 6.7 billion. China, at 1.33 billion people still the most populous nation, was followed closely by India with 1.15 billion and destined to overtake China in the not too distant future. Africa remained the fastest growing continent, which col-lectively broke the 1 billion mark—160 million people living in the northern Arab-speaking belt and another 860 million in sub-Saharan Africa. Of the twenty-one countries with the highest birthrates, nineteen were in Africa; of the seventeen countries with the highest fertility rate, fifteen were in sub-Saharan Africa.[11]

The Agrarian Dilemma

Food production in the South increased at about 3.1 percent annually from the late 1960s to the late 1980s, but population growth ate up this increase almost entirely. Although most Asian nations made considerable progress in agricul-tural production, fifty-five Third World nations—again most of them in Africa—registered a decline in food production per capita after 1970. In the early 1970s, the nations of the South collectively were net exporters of food, but by the early 1980s they were net importers.

There were several major causal factors why many nations of the Third World, all of them primarily agrarian, were unable to increase their food pro-duction to a level of self-sufficiency.

1. *Natural causes.* Most Third World nations are in the tropics, where the climate is often very hot and where both extended droughts and torren-tial rainstorms occur. Desertification is a major problem in Africa, where the Sahara Desert has pushed its frontier southward into West Africa and eastward into Sudan. Indeed, much of that continent suffers from prolonged drought. The Third World also suffers from other nat-ural catastrophes, such as flooding, cyclones, and even earthquakes.
2. *Abuse of the land.* Great amounts of topsoil are lost to wind and water erosion every year, in part because of climate conditions, in part be-cause of human activity, such as deforestation, overgrazing, and over-cultivation, all of which exhaust the land's nutrients.
3. *Primitive farming methods.* Most Third World peasants work with sim-ple tools, many with nothing more than a hoe, and most plowing is still done with draft animals. Peasants are usually too poor to afford modern equipment. In some instances, intensive farming with traditional meth-ods and tools is efficient, especially in the case of paddy farming (rice growing) in Asia, but in many other areas—especially in Africa—

Ethiopian famine victims, 1984.
(AP/Wide World Photos)

Cambodian children receiving relief food at a refugee camp in Trat, Thailand, June 4, 1979. *(AP/Wide World Photos)*

toiling in parched fields with hand tools is an inefficient mode of production. In some parts of Africa, most of this toil was done by women. Traditionally, African men were hunters and herdsmen, and women worked in the fields. The tradition has changed with the depletion of wild game; few men continued to hunt. Too proud to toil in the fields, men either supervised women or sought other employment. A 1985 UN report, *State of the World's Women*, estimated that between 60 and 80 percent of farmwork in Africa was still done by women.[12]

4. *Inequality of landholdings.* Throughout the Third World, agricultural production often suffered because the majority of the peasants had too little land and many were tenants burdened with huge rent payments. In 1984, an international study concluded that in Latin America 80 percent of the farmland was owned by 8 percent of landowners, and the poorest peasants—66 percent of all owners—were squeezed onto only 4 percent of the land.[13]

5. *Lack of capital for agricultural development.* Third World food-producing farmers all too often lacked irrigation works, better equipment, chemical fertilizers, storage facilities, and improved transport. Yet all too often, their governments were unwilling or unable to supply the capital needed to provide these essentials.

6. *One-crop economies.* In many Third World nations, the best land with the best irrigation belonged to wealthy landowners (and sometimes to multinational corporations) who grew cash crops—peanuts, cocoa, coffee, and so on—for export rather than food for domestic consumption. Generally, Third World leaders accepted the dogma that economic progress depended on what they produced for sale to the developed countries. Dependence on a single cash crop for export, however, placed the developing nations at the mercy of the world market, where competition was fierce and where prices fluctuated greatly. This situation proved disastrous when prices of agricultural exports dropped sharply while prices of necessary imports (especially petroleum, fertilizers, and finished goods) rose. Meanwhile, Third World leaders neglected the needs of the majority of the food-producing farmers in favor of support for the cash-crop farmers. In many cases, governments—out of political considerations—kept food prices artificially low to the benefit of the growing number of city-dwellers and to the detriment of the farmers who grew the food.

Many of these problems were caused by the political leaders rather than the farmers. The solution to these problems consisted of land redistribution, diversification of agriculture, and the building of irrigation systems, roads, storage facilities, fertilizer plants, and agricultural schools. But these efforts required a large amount of capital, political stability, and strong and able political leadership—all of which were frequently lacking.

A number of Third World nations obtained relief in the form of large shipments of food to feed starving people. Although such aid was beneficial and humane, it did not go to the root of the problem, and, in fact, it often did not reach those who needed it most.

Prerequisites for Industrialization

Upon gaining independence from Europe, Third World nations blamed their economic backwardness on their former colonial masters. They looked forward to rapid progress as independent nations, hoping to close the gap that separated them from the wealthier nations. They saw industrial development as the primary road to economic modernization. By giving priority to industrial growth, however, they tended to neglect agriculture and its role in economic development. They expected rapid progress but found, to their dismay, that industrial development is a difficult process. The following prerequisites—the minimal necessary conditions for industrial development—were often lacking in Third World countries.

1. *Capital accumulation.* Money for investments to build plants and buy equipment has to come from somewhere: the World Bank, foreign powers (which usually seek to gain political or military leverage), heavy taxation (often falling upon people who can least afford it), or the export of raw materials or cash crops. This last method of capital accumulation often led to an anomaly: With the focus on cash crops and the attendant neglect of growing food, agrarian nations of the Third World found themselves importing food, often from the developed nations, in ever increasing amounts and at ever increasing cost. Thus money tended to flow out of their economies rather than in.

   Third World nations received substantial sums of capital from abroad for many years, but too often the money was mismanaged, squandered on unproductive projects, or simply siphoned off by corrupt leaders. Moreover, overreliance on outside financial aid came with strings attached. It led to foreign intrusions into national sovereignty. The loans produced excessive indebtedness (see discussion below and Chapter 17). Having gained national independence, Third World nations became economic dependencies and debtors beholden to their former colonial masters.

2. *Technology.* To compete with highly sophisticated industries abroad, developing nations must rapidly incorporate new technology. But

technology transfer is a complicated matter, and its acceptance and implementation in tradition-bound societies can be a slow process. Meanwhile, technological change in developed nations was rapid, and developing countries too often fell farther behind.

3. *Education.* An industrialized society requires an educated, literate workforce—assembly-line workers, engineers, and managers. The attainment of mass education in the Third World is a long-term and costly undertaking all too often neglected.

4. *Favorable trading conditions.* In general, the system of free trade erected by the industrial West after World War II was designed primarily to serve it—rather than the developing world. Third World nations sought new trade agreements that would, in some manner, underwrite their exports with guaranteed minimum purchases at prices not to fall below a fixed level. At the same time, they wanted to maintain higher tariffs on imports to protect their native industries.

5. *Political stability.* Capital accumulation and the conduct of business require safety and stability. Domestic strife and wars are disruptive and costly, draining off the meager resources for economic development. (Nearly all of the wars since 1945 were fought in Third World countries. The list seems endless: China, Korea, Vietnam, Iran, Iraq, Afghanistan, Ethiopia, Angola, Chad, Nigeria, Lebanon, India, Pakistan, El Salvador, Nicaragua, and so on.) Even developing nations not engaged in wars spent an extraordinary amount on sophisticated weapons, which they were scarcely able to afford, including expensive purchases from the industrialized powers—primarily the United States and Soviet Union.

6. *Capital investment.* The economies of the Third World tend to be exploitative of their own people. Available capital was spent time and again on expensive imports for those in power—luxury items of every sort, weapons, showcase airports, hotels, and the like—and not on the economic substructure for industrial and agricultural growth—an activity that would benefit the population as a whole. Thus, we see in Third World cities great contrasts of wealth coexisting with grinding poverty—elegant mansions in one part of town and tin-roof hovels in another.

Third World Debt: Africa and Latin America

The 1970s saw the emergence of a phenomenon with potentially serious international repercussions: the increasing indebtedness of the Third World to the industrial First World. Traditionally, nations seeking to develop their economies rely upon capital from abroad. This was true, for example, of the industrial revolutions in England, the Netherlands, the United States, and Russia. Foreign capital—in the form of profits from sales abroad, loans, or capital investments—has long been a catalyst for speeding up the expensive process of industrialization.

Prerevolutionary tsarist Russia drew heavily upon foreign capital and foreign engineers to begin the industrialization process. Stalin's industrial revolution of the 1930s, in contrast, was accomplished largely without foreign assistance. In the early 1960s it became one of the models considered by a number of newly independent nations of the Third World. Their economic planners found out, however, that their economic base was so primitive, in contrast to what Stalin had inherited from the tsars, that they had little choice but to turn to capital available from the industrialized First World.

The emerging, developing economies of the Third World increasingly sought this shortcut. Until the oil crises of the 1970s, the reliance on foreign money had been kept in bounds. The money borrowed was doled out in reasoned, and at times sparse, amounts—until the surfeit of "petrodollars" (i.e., money invested in Western banks by the oil-rich nations) created a binge of lending by these same banks and an orgy of borrowing by the nations of the Third World. There appeared to be no limit to the banks' willingness to extend credit and the recipients' willingness to take it. Foreign capital promised the road out of the wilderness. It would generate rapid economic development and, with it, the ability to repay the loans. By the mid-1980s, the consequence was a staggering debt among Latin American and African nations in excess of $500 billion, a sum far beyond the capacity of the debtor nations to repay. Many were staring bankruptcy in the face, and if they defaulted, they threatened to take the lending institutions and the international banking system itself down the road to ruin.

Africa

The African debt had its roots in the political instability that followed independence, which resulted in frequent government turnovers, secessionist movements, and civil wars. Among the first casualties were the budding democratic institutions. Political and military considerations quickly began to take precedence over economic development, for the first priority of dictatorships is the retention of power. As such, precious resources were diverted to the military, whose main task was not so much the defense of the nation against a foreign foe, but the suppression of domestic opposition.

Political instability led to the flight of Europeans, who took with them their skills and capital. This was the case particularly in the new states where independence was won by force and where a legacy of bitterness and mistrust remained after the violence had subsided. Algeria, Mozambique, Angola, Zimbabwe (formerly Southern Rhodesia), and Kenya readily come to mind. South

Africa, too, saw the flight of whites as racial tensions mounted during the early 1980s. The exodus left many African nations with a badly depleted industrial base and a continued reliance on the agricultural sector. Yet, Africa's agriculture remained the world's most primitive.

Until the late 1970s, the African economies limped along, but then the roof began to cave in when a number of conditions came together. The result was that much of the continent was bankrupted. First came the oil crisis with its accompanying rise in the cost of crude oil. The crisis had a greater impact on the poorer nations than on the industrial West, which had the means of meeting the higher payments. (Although several oil-producing nations of sub-Saharan Africa, such as Nigeria and Cameroon, benefited from the new, higher price tag on oil, most suffered greatly. And when oil prices began to fall in the early 1980s, Nigeria was among the hardest hit, having become saddled with mounting debts and attendant political instability.) In the West, the oil crisis contributed to a global recession, which in turn lessened the demand for raw materials. The prices for copper, bauxite (aluminum ore), and diamonds fell. Prices for agricultural exports fell similarly, as a result of a worldwide glut in agricultural commodities that played havoc with the African economies. Cacao, coffee, cotton, peanuts, and such no longer brought the prices African exporters had been accustomed to. After 1979–1980, prices for African commodity exports declined by as much as 30 percent. All the while, prices for crude oil and for goods manufactured in the West—such as machinery, tools, electronics, and weapons—continued to rise.

Appreciation of foreign currencies, particularly the US dollar, added to the dilemma. Since the debts of nations were calculated in US dollars, the increasing purchasing power of the dollar in the early 1980s played havoc with the pay rate of debtor nations. Debts now had to be repaid in dollars with greater purchasing power; this meant that Third World nations had to export more. Indeed, this condition—as well as high interest payments—forced African nations to repay more than they had borrowed.

As Africa's indebtedness to the industrial world increased during the first half of the 1980s, the poorest continent became a net exporter of capital. In 1985 alone, African nations were required to pay $7 billion to banks and governments of the developed world. On average, African nations used 25 percent of their foreign currency earnings to repay their foreign debts. They were reaching the point where they were dismantling their social and economic development plans in order to meet their debt obligations. They were, in effect, cannibalizing their economies and social programs (notably health and education) to meet their interest payments. After more than three decades, that dilemma remained. Between 1970 and 2003, African countries borrowed $540 billion and repaid $580 billion in debt service (principal and interest), yet remained saddled with a crippling debt of $300 billion—$108 billion owed by the Arabic-speaking states in the north and $194 billion by sub-Saharan Africa.[14]

Africa reached a point where it could neither repay its debt nor borrow any appreciable sums of money. (Not surprisingly, Nigeria, a major oil-exporting nation, ran up the largest debt on the basis of its projected ability to repay its obligations.) Moreover, significant foreign investment in Africa declined after 1980. The continent was on a treadmill, pledged to come up with interest payments over an indefinite period to the industrialized West and its banks. Under such circumstances, the indebtedness to the West became a permanent fixture, since there was no question of making a dent in the principal (i.e., the debt itself). The African nations listed in Table 11.3 increased their foreign debts between 1987 and 1990.

Predictably, African leaders pointed an accusing finger at the international banking system. In July 1985, the African heads of government met under the aegis of the Organization of African Unity (OAU) in Addis Ababa, Ethiopia's capital, to address this bleak situation. They placed part of the blame on an "unjust and inequitable [international] economic system," but they also acknowledged that natural calamities such as droughts, as well as "some domestic policy shortcomings," had contributed to Africa's problems. The chair of the OAU, Tanzanian president Julius Nyerere, hinted at the creation of a defaulter's club, which sought the cancellation of government-to-government loans and the restructuring of interest rates in order to avoid default and, with it, national bankruptcy. African politicians considered their national obligations as illegitimate, "odious debts" (a principle in international law). The Western lenders, in their turn, saw the debts as legal, binding national obligations. The task was to find a compromise with which both could live.

It took the Western nations another decade to come around to a discussion of debt relief, even cancellation—but only for the most desperately poor nations. In 1996, the Club of Paris, an informal group of creditors that in the mid-1950s began its work to find solutions for national debt obligations, looked for another solution to the developing nations' insurmountable debts, which ran to $2 trillion. Its 1996 Heavily Indebted Poor Countries (HIPC) initiative was

Table 11.3   African Nations with Foreign Debt Increases, 1987–1990

Nation	Debt in 1987 (US$, billions)	Debt in 1990 (US$, billions)	Percentage of Increase, 1987–1990
Nigeria	$28.7	$36.1	26
Ivory Coast	13.5	17.9	33
Sudan	11.1	15.4	39
Zaire	8.6	10.1	17
Zambia	6.4	7.2	13
Kenya	5.9	6.8	15
Tanzania	4.3	5.9	37

Sources: World Bank, *World Development Report, 1989,* p. 205; *World Development Report, 1992,* p. 258.

embraced by the World Bank and the International Monetary Fund (IMF), which then began to provide relief to 41 of the poorest nations (more than three-quarters of them in Africa). By July 2006, 21 nations received 100 percent IMF–World Bank debt cancellation; others had their debts brought down to more sustainable levels. By 2005, about one-third of the debt was cancelled, which, however, still left the HIPC nations with about $90 billion in debt.[15]

Latin America

During the late 1970s, Latin America witnessed sharp economic downturns similar to the ones in Africa, and for similar reasons. The rapid increase in oil prices in the 1970s and the drop in agricultural commodity prices produced a decline in the standard of living.

Latin America has long been a region of economic promise. This was especially the case with Brazil, a land of seemingly unlimited potential, resources, and workers. On the basis of future earnings, the Brazilian government was able to borrow huge sums of money during the 1970s. Within a decade, the borrowing binge came back to haunt it. By 1987, Brazil's foreign debt was well over $120 billion, and in 2003 it was more than $220 billion, sums beyond the country's capacity to repay. The best that Brazil could do was merely make interest payments and in this fashion avoid a declaration of bankruptcy. The country's potential bankruptcy threatened the international banking system, and for this reason, despite its staggering debt, Brazil was able to demand additional loans until the time—sometime in the distant, nebulous future—when it would be able to begin to repay the principal. In the meantime, Brazil remained beholden to the Western banks and governments.

Argentina was another Latin American nation that accumulated a large foreign debt. It had traditionally been a nation with a strong and vigorous economy, which made it relatively easy for its governments to borrow money from abroad. But a succession of military regimes (1976–1983) contributed to the ruination of the nation's economy. The regimes' brutality (see Chapter 13) and a losing war with Great Britain over the Falkland Islands in 1983 brought about the return to civilian rule that year. At that time, Argentina's foreign debt was thought to be about $24 billion—a large sum by anyone's yardstick. The new civilian government discovered, however, that the military had in fact run up twice that amount of debt, some $48 billion, the third-largest foreign debt (after Brazil and Mexico) among the developing countries.

In contrast to most Third World nations, the oil shortages of the late 1970s did not initially harm Mexico's economy. Instead, the shortages appeared to work to its benefit, for Mexico's oil reserves were potentially among the world's largest. It was oil that promised to solve Mexico's economic problems, caused in part by its large and rapidly growing population, weak industrial base, and inefficient agricultural system. Mexico was able to borrow large sums of money in the expectation that oil shortages and high oil prices would make it possible to repay the loans. In short, Mexico borrowed against future income. At the end of 1981, Mexico's foreign debt was at about $55 billion. Four years later, that figure had risen to well above $100 billion. By 1990, Latin America's leading debtors, unlike those of Africa, had a measure of success in reducing their debts—through a combination of increasing exports, selling off equity, and debt cancellation by lenders.

Still, the external debt continued to grow. In the mid-1980s, Latin America's obligation to international lending institutions stood at $360 billion; by 2007, it had ballooned to more than $820 billion. The leaders, as in the past, were Brazil (holding steady at $224 billion), Mexico (up to $180 billion), and Argentina (up to $136 billion). Chile, Venezuela, Colombia, South Africa, and Peru owed, in descending order, somewhere between $50 billion and $31 billion.[16]

The Third World's Continuing Poverty

In the 1960s, when many Third World nations gained independence, there already existed a huge gap between their levels of economic development and wealth and those of the industrialized world. For much of the Third World, however, the gap was even wider at the end of the century. The 1990s were a time of vastly increasing wealth in the industrialized world, but many of the poorest nations became even more deeply in debt to the rich. Saddled with enormous debt payments that squeezed national budgets, Third World nations had a most difficult time digging themselves out of the hole. While per capita GNP figures for most industrialized countries rose ever higher over the previous forty years, the figures for most Third World countries (particularly in Africa and Latin America) rose only slightly, if at all. Per capita GNP for the industrialized nations remained as much as 100 times higher than that for the poorest of Third World countries.

It should be pointed out that GNP figures do not give a complete picture of the standard of living in a developing nation since much of the economy is informal. GNP statistics tend to understate real income in Third World nations because many of the people meet their needs by barter or may be paid for by in-kind labor—such as a sharecropping arrangement—and informal arrangements are not measured and thus do not enter into GNP figures. To go beyond economic statistics and assess the quality of life, the UN conducted a "human development" survey, assessing and ranking 174 nations on such things as health care, life expectancy, education levels, and access to clean water, as well as income. But even in this assessment, published in the annual UN *Human Development Report* released in June 2000, Third World nations were generally in the bottom half of the ranking. At the very bottom of the list were twenty-four African countries.[17]

Not all Third World countries, however, remained mired in poverty at the end of the twentieth century. Some had made moderate economic progress, and a few others, particularly in Asia, had made significant progress and were able to climb from Third World status to become newly industrializing countries.

Recommended Readings

Barnet, Richard J. *The Lean Years: Politics in the Age of Scarcity.* New York: Simon and Schuster, 1980.
A study of the political factors involved in sharing limited global resources.

Brown, Lester R., et al. *State of the World, 1986.* New York: Norton, 1987.
An annually updated reference on food and environmental issues around the globe.

Ehrlich, Paul E., and Anne H. Ehrlich. *The Population Explosion.* New York: Simon and Schuster, 1990.
This sequel to Paul Ehrlich's *The Population Bomb* (1968) warns of the dangers of rampant population growth.

Emerson, Steven. *The American House of Saud: The Secret Petrodollar Connection.* Danbury, Conn.: Franklin Watts, 1985.

George, Susan. *Ill Fares the Land: Essays on Food, Hunger, and Power.* Rev. and expanded ed. London: Penguin, 1990.
A sociological inquiry into what went wrong with agricultural planning in the Third World.

Harrison, Paul. *Inside the Third World.* 2nd ed. New York: Penguin, 1984.
An excellent comprehensive description and analysis of the dilemmas of the Third World.

Kapuscinski, Ryszard. *The Soccer War.* New York: Knopf, 1991.
A Polish journalist's explanation of the political problems of the Third World.

Lacey, Robert. *The Kingdom: Arabia and the House of Sa'ud.* New York: Avon, 1983.

Sampson, Anthony. *The Sovereign State of ITT.* 2nd ed. New York: Fawcett, 1974.
By an English muckraking reporter who has written several popular books on the world of international finance. This book discusses ITT's foreign operations, particularly in Latin America.

―――. *The Seven Sisters.* New York: Viking, 1975.
A chronicle of the activities of the major international oil companies.

―――. *The Money Lenders: The People and Politics of International Banking.* New York: Penguin, 1982.

World Bank. *World Development Report: Development and Environment.* New York: Oxford University Press, 1992.
Fifteenth in an annual series, this report discusses the link among economic development, population pressures, and the environment.

Notes

1. Nehru's foreign policy address to India's Constituent Assembly, December 4, 1947, in Dorothy Norman, ed., *Nehru: The First Sixty Years*, vol. 2 (New York: John Day, 1965), pp. 353–356.

2. See Nehru's address to the Bandung Conference, in G. M. Kahin, *The Asian-African Conference* (Ithaca: Cornell University Press, 1956), pp. 54–72.

3. GNP, or gross national product, is the wealth—the total goods and services—a nation produces per year. The per capita GNP is calculated by dividing the figure for wealth generated (calculated in US dollars) by the nation's population.

4. See Paul Harrison, *Inside the Third World*, 2nd ed. (New York: Penguin, 1984), pp. 414–415.

5. Ibid., p. 145.

6. For the text of the Amsterdam Declaration, see *Population and Development Review,* March 1990, pp. 186–192.

7. For the text of the OECD's statement, see "Population and Development—DAC Conclusions," *Population and Development Review,* September 1990, pp. 595–601.

8. "Pope John Paul II on Contemporary Development," *Population and Development Review,* September 1991, p. 559. The citations are from chapter 4 of the encyclical.

9. The statement is by Bryant Robey of the Johns Hopkins School of Hygiene and Public Health and the editor of *American Demographics,* cited in William K. Stevens, "Poor Lands' Success in Cutting Birth Rate Upsets Old Theories," *New York Times,* January 2, 1994, p. 8.

10. Susan Chira, "Women Campaign for New Plan to Curb the World's Population," *New York Times,* April 13, 1994, pp. A1, A12.

11. CIA, *The World Factbook,* 2008, www.cia.gov/library/publications/the-world-factbook.

12. Barber Conable, president of the World Bank, at a joint World Bank–International Monetary Fund meeting, stated that women did two-thirds of the world's work, earned 10 percent of the world's income, and owned less than 1 percent of the world's property. As such, women remained "the poorest of the world's poor." Clyde Farnsworth, "World Bank Chief Outlines Strategy," *New York Times,* October 1, 1986, p. D23.

13. Harrison, *Inside the Third World,* p. 455.

14. Africa Action, "Africa Action Statement on 100% Debt Cancellation for Africa," September 23, 2005; CIA, *The World Factbook,* 2008.

15. Jubilee USA Network, "The Unfinished Agenda on International Debt," *Spotlight,* July 2006; "At Last, $350 Billion Debt Write-off in Sight for Africa," *The East African,* April 18, 2005.

16. CIA, *The World Factbook,* 2008.

17. Cited in United Nations, "Rankings of World's Nations in Human Development," June 29, 2000. Among Third World nations Cuba ranked highest (56th), followed by Belize, Panama, Venezuela, Colombia, and Brazil.

12 Africa

In the early 1960s, when most African nations gained their independence, proud African leaders heralded the dawn of a new age. Freed from the shackles of European colonialism, they looked confidently to a new political and economic order that promised an end to the continent's economic backwardness and its dependence on the West. But the euphoria of the early 1960s soon gave way to a more somber reality, for as years went by, African leaders' shared goals of economic growth, of national self-reliance and dignity, and of African unity remained elusive. Indeed, forty years later those dreams were in shambles, as most African countries had become increasingly impoverished and more dependent on foreign aid than ever before. Across the continent one found declining economies, grinding poverty, civil strife, corruption, crop failures, hungry and starving people, spreading disease, overcrowded and deteriorating cities, massive unemployment, and growing numbers of refugees.

The plight was exacerbated by the political turmoil that became common throughout Africa. In one African country after another, democratic rule gave way to military rule, and several countries experienced a series of military coups. Many countries were torn apart by civil wars, which were often internecine struggles among ethnic groups. Often the flames were fanned by the rival superpowers who armed the combatants. Political stability necessary for economic growth was sorely lacking.

Africa had the world's lowest economic growth rates, highest infant mortality rates, and highest population growth rates. In the 1970s, the population of Africa grew at about twice the rate of the increase in food production. Chronic malnutrition and starvation became more common in subsequent years. Perhaps as many as 200,000 people succumbed to starvation in the Ethiopian famine in the early 1970s, and another famine a decade later—more publicized than the earlier one—took an equally large toll.

Media attention focused on Ethiopia diverted attention from the hundreds of thousands of people malnourished and on the verge of starvation in Sudan,

Chad, Niger, and Mali, nations most affected by the relentless expansion of the Sahara Desert. Farther south, countries such as Kenya, Uganda, Gabon, and Mozambique were also drought-stricken. The Economic Commission for Africa, a UN agency, reported that from 1960 to 1975 there was no significant improvement in most African nations' economies. In 1960, Africa had been 95 percent self-sufficient in food, but twenty-five years later every African country except South Africa was a net importer of food.

The nations of sub-Saharan Africa were not equally impoverished. By far the most prosperous nation on the continent was South Africa, which stood as an exception to the economic decline characteristic of the remainder of sub-Saharan Africa. In the 1980s, South Africa's per capita income was more than $12,500, far higher than that of any other African country. Blacks, however, who outnumbered whites (who had one of the highest standards of living in the world) by five to one, earned only about one-sixth of what white workers were paid. Nigeria, burdened with Africa's largest population and yet blessed with large deposits of oil, prospered greatly following independence, only to find its economy in collapse as a result of political corruption and plummeting world oil prices in the 1970s. An examination of per capita GNP growth rates in the decade after 1973 reveals that black African nations were either struggling to maintain marginal economic progress, marking time, or actually declining. According to World Bank figures, only Benin, Botswana, Cameroon, the People's Republic of Congo, Ivory Coast, and Rwanda had marginal growth. Fourteen countries had a decline in per capita GNP.[1] Most tragic were those states that had displayed the potential for economic growth and had made progress in the first decade of independence only to slide backward, especially Ghana, Nigeria, Kenya, Uganda, Zimbabwe, and Zaire.

Political Instability in Sub-Saharan Africa

Africa's problems were economic as well as political. Political chaos often followed economic disaster; conversely, political problems often contributed to economic woes.

Following the independence of many nations from their colonial masters, Africa witnessed the steady erosion of democratic institutions and the steady militarization of politics. After initial trial runs in parliamentary democracy, elected governments often retained power by eliminating the electoral process altogether. Subsequently, military coups—not popular elections—were the primary vehicle for the transfer of power. Dictatorships became common throughout Africa, where about three-quarters of the governments were controlled either by one-party regimes or by military men. Only about a half-dozen states in sub-Saharan Africa permitted opposition parties to engage in the political process, and until 1991 no African head of state was ever voted

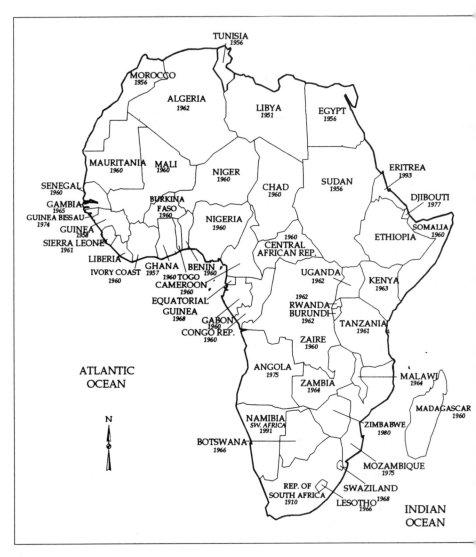

Africa After Independence

out of office. Political repression became the order of the day, especially in countries such as Uganda, Zimbabwe, Zaire, and Guinea, where political opponents were routinely massacred. And more often than not, African leaders were as corrupt as they were repressive.

The Colonial Legacy

Many African leaders were quick to blame a century of European colonialism for their nations' problems. After a century of dependency on Europeans, Africans were ill prepared for the task of nation-building. The Europeans, time and again, left too abruptly, leaving behind political institutions that few Africans, beyond a small circle of Western-educated elites, appreciated or well understood. Also, the Europeans did little to develop national economies in their colonies; instead, they had mainly built up enterprises focused on export commodities such as coffee, cacao, copper, and bauxite. The economic system inherited by the newly independent African nations had been designed for export rather than for producing goods and services for domestic consumption. These export-oriented economies were directly linked with the former colonial power instead of with African neighbors.

Perhaps the most baleful legacy of European colonialism was the artificiality of the national boundaries it had created. In the nineteenth century, the European imperialists often hastily drew new boundaries with little or no recognition of the ethnic makeup of Africa. One British commissioner later joked: "In those days we just took a blue pencil and a rule, and we put it down at Old Calabar, and drew that blue line up to Yola. . . . I recollect thinking when I was sitting having an audience with the [local] Emir . . . it was a very good thing that he did not know that I . . . had drawn a line through his territory."[2] Nonetheless, the new African nations kept and guarded these boundaries as they fended off ethnic conflicts and secessionist wars. As a result of the political boundaries created by the Europeans, most African states were much larger than the precolonial political units and contained within them many more ethnic groups—and thus were more difficult to manage than smaller states. Only two countries in sub-Saharan Africa—Lesotho and Swaziland—retained ethnic uniformity. All others had mixed populations made up of many different ethnic entities. The most extreme cases, such as Nigeria and the former Belgian Congo, included within their borders more than 200 diverse ethnic groups with their own distinct languages, histories, and traditions. The new nations tended to be artificial constructs, and their rulers had the task of superimposing a new national identity over the existing ethnic configurations. In most instances, however, ethnic identity prevailed over nationalism—a relatively new and foreign concept—to the detriment of the process of nation-building. The results were conflicts ranging from bloody civil wars, to secessionist wars, and even to genocides. Ethnic strife claimed a frightful toll on life in Nigeria during the Biafran War in the 1960s; in Rwanda and Burundi in the 1960s, 1970s, and again in the 1990s; and in Darfur (a region of western Sudan) starting in the late 1970s.

Tribalism is a legacy not of colonialism but rather of African history. It persisted during the colonial era—in some places strengthened by colonial policy, in others diluted—and remained strong after independence. Typically, an African's strongest loyalties were to family and ethnic group (tribe). Given the relative lack of geographic mobility in Africa, people of one ethnic group maintained local roots and mixed little with others. Governments often represented one dominant ethnic group to the exclusion of others, and the discontent of the excluded ethnic groups was often the source of instability and repression.

Tribalism relates to another aspect of African heritage that plagued African politics: corruption. In kinship-based societies such as those in Africa, communal elders were entrusted with authority not only to make decisions binding for the group but also to divide the wealth among its members. At the national level in postcolonial Africa, self-aggrandizement and corruption on an immense scale were often the result, with politics often degenerating into ethnic contests for the spoils of power.

The combination of unbridled corruption and the cult of personality in Africa produced some of the world's most outrageous displays of extravagance. Not a few African rulers lived in regal splendor in fabulous palaces, owned fleets of luxury cars, and stashed vast amounts of money in Western banks. For bizarre extravagance none exceeded Colonel Jean-Bedel Bokassa, emperor of the Central African Republic, who spent about $20 million—one-quarter of his nation's revenue—on his coronation ceremony in 1977. He wore a robe bedecked with 2 million pearls that cost $175,000 and donned a $2 million crown topped with a 138-carat diamond. This in a country that had no more than 170 miles of paved roads. Two years later, Bokassa was deposed.

Most of the newly independent nations of Africa began with inherited parliamentary systems in which executive power was in the hands of a prime minister who was elected by and responsible to a popularly elected legislative body. Typically, the African prime ministers revised the constitutions to allow themselves to become presidents with broadened executive powers and longer terms of office. (A prime minister is elected by and responsible to the parliament and may be called to resign at any time by a vote of no confidence in the parliament. But a president is elected by the people for a fixed, usually longer term and is not so easily expelled from office.) Without an effective check on their new powers, the presidents began exercising them in a dictatorial manner and no longer tolerated political opposition. They argued that opposition parties were divisive, a threat to political stability, even unpatriotic, and thus needed to be abolished. This notion undermined the concept of a "loyal opposition," an out-of-power political party opposed to the party currently in power but loyal to the nation and qualified to govern if elected.

African dictators used all the levers of power available to stay in office. They replaced local officials with ruling party members and cronies loyal to them, made use of state wealth and especially foreign loans to buy off or secure the loyalties of others, made sure to control all outlets of information (the press, radio, television), and subjected their people to a heavy dose of propaganda through which they constructed a cult of personality. When all else failed, they relied on military force to consolidate their power, to suppress dissent, and to terrorize the population.

The Militarization of African Politics

African leaders could not always be certain of the loyalty of the military, and this proved to be the Achilles' heel for many of them. In many nations, military revolts supplanted presidential dictators with military dictators. Many of Africa's first line of rulers were, in fact, overthrown by their own armies.[3] The overthrow of Ghana's Kwame Nkrumah in 1966 gave rise to a wave of military coups across Africa, and by 1980, no fewer than sixty coups had taken place. In Benin, between 1963 and 1972, there were five military coups and another ten attempted coups. Military officers with their own esprit de corps and political ambitions had little difficulty in finding cause to overthrow unpopular corrupt rulers. Some promised to restore rule to civilian politicians, but few actually did so. Others, like Zaire's Joseph Mobutu, retired their military uniforms and became presidents; still others became victims of subsequent military coups. Most of the earlier coups were carried out by high-ranking officers, but as time went on, lower-ranking officers and even noncommissioned officers thrust themselves into power behind the barrel of a gun. In Sierra Leone, army generals took power in 1967 but were overthrown several months later by other army officers, who in turn were soon ousted by a sergeants' revolt.

New military regimes were often welcomed by a disillusioned people, but because the new rulers were usually less prepared than the ousted politicians to cope with the problems of poverty, economic stagnation, and political unrest, they seldom succeeded. As they became more tyrannical and as corrupt as the civilian rulers they had overthrown, they quickly lost popular support and became ripe for overthrow by still other ambitious military officers.

Take the case of Ghana, a nation once looked upon as the pacesetter in Africa's drive for independence and modernization. The charismatic Kwame Nkrumah, who had led the fight for independence, provided vigorous leadership as prime minister for a nation that, in the early 1960s, had the second-highest per capita income in Africa. A most outspoken champion of pan-Africanism, Nkrumah became the spokesman for the liberation of other African colonies. He adopted a socialist program for Ghana that entailed nationalization of industries and state planning, but he did not attempt a social revolution involving land redistribution. By the 1960s, Ghana became the victim of a drastic decline in the world price for cocoa, its principal cash crop. In the decade following independence, the price fell to one-third of its previous level. Nkrumah's own corruption and extravagance became targets of criticism, something he did not tolerate well. With the pressures of a bankrupt economy and popular unrest mounting, the volatile Nkrumah, now a dictator, jailed the opposition and silenced dissent. Finally, in February 1966, when he was away on a visit to China, the army toppled his regime.

In the years that followed, as coup followed coup, Ghana became the epitome of political instability. The officers who grasped power in 1966 made good on their promise to restore civilian rule, but in 1969 a group of junior officers staged another coup, eliminating by firing squads former government leaders. After still another coup in 1972, Ghana remained under military rule through the 1970s. In 1979, a youthful air force flight lieutenant, Jerry Rawlings, shot his way into power and carried out another wave of executions. In 1980, however, he made good on his promise to give democracy another chance in Ghana. This, too, proved short-lived when, at the end of 1981, Rawlings once again seized power by force. Despite a host of problems, however, Rawlings remained popular; in 1992 and again in 1996, he won multiparty elections. In 2000, he decided to leave office—in compliance with the constitutional limit of two terms—provided the election was "fair, genuine and sincere."[4] All the while, however, Ghana's economic and social woes continued to worsen.

Few of Africa's military men exceeded the brutality of Idi Amin of Uganda. In 1971, Amin—an army officer—staged a coup, overthrowing the dictatorship of Milton Obote. Soon Amin found scapegoats for the economic and social ills of Uganda in several minority tribes and in the community of Asian (mainly Indian) residents of the country. In 1972, Amin forcefully expelled some 50,000 Asians, an act most detrimental to the economy since many of them were merchants and professionals. As conditions worsened, Amin resorted to torture, public execution, and assassination. After surviving a number of plots against his life, he was finally overthrown in 1979 by a force from Tanzania, which then installed a civilian government. Before his removal from power, however, Amin had massacred an estimated 250,000 of his own people, caused about as many to flee the country, and left Uganda in shambles. In 1980, Milton Obote returned to power as dictator. His regime continued military "cleanup operations" but never succeeded in restoring order. In the end, he eventually killed almost as many people as Amin had and caused another wave of refugees to flee the stricken country.

The Biafran War

Nigeria provides another case of militarization as well as an object lesson on the consequences of ethnic warfare. During the early years of independence, no country made greater efforts to overcome ethnic disunity, yet none spilled more blood in ethnic strife in the aftermath of independence. At the time of independence, Nigeria, Africa's most populous nation and one of its wealthiest, was a federal republic of three self-governing regions, each dominated by a major ethnic group—the Hausa-Fulani (mostly Muslim) in the northern region (approximately 15 million strong), the Yoruba in the western region (15 million), and the Ibo in the southeastern region (10 million). After independence, tensions remained high among the three factions as each feared domination by the other. The first census in independent Nigeria only added to the suspicion that the northerners were about to abolish the federal system of power-sharing. The census, manipulated by northerners, declared that the northern region contained an absolute majority of the population and thus could create a government dominated by Hausas and Fulanis. The census upset the balance of power, charged the political atmosphere, and set the stage for the political crisis that followed.[5]

In January 1966, military officers—mainly Ibos—staged a coup and established a military regime under General J. T. Ironsi. The northerners, who were mainly Muslims, feared and resented the largely Christian and better-educated Ibos, who had enjoyed commercial and political privileges under British rule. The northerners saw the coup as an attempt to destroy the power of the Hausa-Fulani oligarchy.

At the end of May 1966, the northern general, Yakubu Gowon, staged his own coup and kidnapped (and later murdered) Ironsi and members of his government. It was at this point that the first wave of assaults against Ibos took place, first in the north, where tens of thousands were massacred; 2 million were driven to flight. In July 1966, Ibo soldiers in the Nigerian army were massacred. Additional attacks on Ibos followed. An Ibo brotherhood called upon Ibos throughout the country "to come home." On May 30, 1967, at the regional capital of Enugu, an Oxford-educated lieutenant colonel, C. O. Ojukwu, issued the declaration of independence of the Republic of Biafra. The declaration denounced the "evils and injustices"—not the least of which were the "premeditated and planned" pogroms—carried out by the military government.[6] Now came the difficult task of defending the independence of Biafra.

The Biafran rebels quickly found out that they stood alone. Only four of Africa's fifty-odd nations and one European state, France, recognized Biafra. France did so because Biafra was located in the oil-rich southeastern corner of Nigeria and contained the nation's largest oil field and its only refinery. The African nations, even though they had denounced repeatedly the arbitrary borders that the European colonialists had carved out, did not want to see a dangerous secessionist precedent take place.

General Gowon treated the rebellion as a Nigerian matter that was not the business of others. The United Nations and the rest of the world accommodated him. When the great powers did become involved, notably Britain and the Soviet Union, they did so in support of a united Nigeria. Britain sought to maintain its political and economic influence in Nigeria. Moreover, within a week after the Biafran declaration of independence, the Six Day War in the Middle East closed the Suez Canal, and Nigeria's oil suddenly became more important for Britain. The Soviets, in turn, sought to increase their influence in Africa and provided Gowon's army—the likely winner—with modern weapons. This was the first time in modern history an African nation fought a war using weapons provided by outside powers, but it would not be the last. Civil wars and secessionist movements armed by outside powers were later responsible for the destruction of much of Angola, Mozambique, Ethiopia, and Somalia.

Biafra's resistance ended after thirty months. Defeats on the battlefield, bombing raids, and widespread starvation took their toll. In January 1970, the Ibo surrendered. Gowon insisted that no retribution be taken and that Ibos be reintegrated into Nigerian society. A Nigerian colonel described the aftermath to a US reporter: "It was like a referee blowing a whistle in a football game. People just put down their guns and went back to the business of living."[7]

Foreign Intervention

At the outset of independence, African leaders sought to eliminate dependence on foreign powers and insisted on "African solutions to African problems." Political and economic instability, however, made Africa ripe for intervention by outside powers. The Organization of African Unity, formed in 1963, never achieved a meaningful concert of Africa, as the nations tended to pull apart and most maintained closer ties with their former colonial masters in Europe than with neighbors. They continued to rely on Europeans for economic aid and military assistance, and the Europeans continued to intervene in Africa in order to protect investments. France, in particular, maintained a military presence of more than 15,000, its highly mobile *force d'intervention*. As the gap between African economic development and that of the industrialized nations widened, especially after the oil crises in the 1970s, Africans were forced all the more to depend on foreign aid and became even more vulnerable to meddling by outside powers. These powers were not limited to the former colonial powers of Europe but came to include the United States and the Soviet Union, which, in their global struggle, were eager to make themselves indispensable to new African friends and to check the spreading influence of the other.

China, too, competed for influence in Africa. Its boldest undertaking in Africa was the construction of the 1,200-mile Tanzam "Great Freedom" railroad in the mid-1970s, linking landlocked Zambia with the Tanzanian port city of Dar es Salaam. The $500 million project—which employed some 20,000 Chinese and 50,000 African workers—was undertaken after Britain, Canada, and the United States declined the project. The United States had earlier missed an opportunity to expand its influence in northern Africa when, in 1956, it rejected Egypt's request for financial backing to build the Aswan Dam on the Nile River. The Soviet Union moved in within a year to build the dam and temporarily gained Egypt as a client state.

The United States offered security arrangements, weapons, and economic aid to its African clients; the Soviet Union similarly supplied weapons and economic assistance, especially to those nations whose leaders paid lip service to Marxism. Although the United States provided much more developmental aid to African nations than did the Soviet Union, it did not win more friends. Nowhere was this more evident than in the United Nations, where African nations and the Soviet Union—sharing an anticolonialist viewpoint—often voted the same way, whereas the United States was seldom able to count on the votes of these nations.

Advocacy of Marxism by an African leader, however, did not necessarily signify successful Soviet intervention. Marxism-Leninism was in vogue in the early postindependence years, as new African leaders were attracted to the ideology for its explanation of past colonial exploitation and neocolonialism. The leading theoretician of neocolonialism, Ghana's Kwame Nkrumah, defined it a colonialism by economic means.[8] Nkrumah and others turned to Marxism-Leninism as a model for political organization and state planning. But governments that adopted Marxism and established close ties with Moscow, such as Guinea and Angola, found developmental aid from the Soviet Union to be disappointingly meager. Some African leaders—Nkrumah and Tanzania's Nyerere, for instance—conjured up their own brands of "African socialism," a blend of Marxist ideas and indigenous African notions, which were usually vague and had little resemblance to either Marxism or the Soviet system. In any case, it was difficult to distinguish between those African states that were nominally socialist and those that claimed to be capitalist, for in all of them state planning and control of the economy were common. "The distinction between socialist and capitalist states in Africa," two noted African specialists explained, "has often proved to be more one of rhetoric than reality. . . . In the last resort, the socialist or capitalist jargon employed in any individual state is often a reflection of where external aid was coming from at a particular time."[9]

It was not until the mid-1970s, with the end of Portuguese colonial rule in southern Africa, that a direct confrontation between the superpowers occurred in Africa. The departure of Portugal created a volatile situation across southern Africa, not only because power was up for grabs in Portugal's former colonies but also because the buffer between black African nations and the white supremacist regime of South Africa had been removed. South Africa now found itself threatened by the accession of a Marxist regime in Mozambique in 1975, the transfer of power to a black government in Zimbabwe (formerly Southern Rhodesia) in 1980, and the increasing resolve of Botswana,

Zambia, and other black African nations to oppose its racist policies. As a consequence, South Africa resorted increasingly to military force, intervening in Angola, Mozambique, and Lesotho.

In defiance of the United Nations, South Africa continued to occupy nearby Namibia, thereby thwarting its demand for independence. In 1975, South Africa installed a puppet black government in Namibia and promised to grant it independence. The left-leaning South-West Africa People's Organization (SWAPO), the largest Namibian party, was left out of the government and, supported by black African nations, continued guerrilla resistance in its fight for Namibian independence.

The focal point of international struggle in sub-Saharan Africa between 1975 and 1990 was Angola, where the largest buildup of foreign military forces in Africa in postcolonial times took place. The outside forces were from nations such as the United States, the Soviet Union, the People's Republic of China, Cuba, Zaire, and South Africa. When Portugal withdrew in April 1975, three separate, professedly Marxist Angolan revolutionary groups rivaled each other for power. The Popular Movement for the Liberation of Angola (MPLA), a group founded in 1956, was in control of the capital city of Luanda. The National Front for the Liberation of Angola (FNLA), established in 1962, held the mountainous region in the north. And the National Union for the Total Independence of Angola (UNITA), founded in 1966, representing the Ovimbundu—the largest ethnic group in Angola—ruled in the central and southern regions. The transitional government established by the Portuguese collapsed in June 1975, and foreign powers intervened in support of rival revolutionary groups.

The United States and the Soviet Union accused each other of meddling in Angola, all the while claiming that their own involvement was justified by the actions of the other. MPLA received Soviet financial and military support, assisted by several thousand Cuban advisors and a Zairean military unit. FNLA and UNITA each received financial support and covert military assistance from the CIA and South Africa. By the end of the year, MPLA, on the threshold of victory, formed a new Angolan government.

In Washington, the administration of Gerald Ford and the US secretary of state, Henry Kissinger, refused to accept what they considered a Soviet victory. Continued US military aid to UNITA rebels and South African military involvement in the years that followed served to perpetuate the Angolan civil war. Indeed, this issue was one of several that, by the end of the 1970s, brought an end to détente between the United States and Soviet Union.

The Worsening Economic Plight of Sub-Saharan Africa

The 1980s saw an increase in living standards throughout much of the globe, except for nations at war, such as Afghanistan, Nicaragua, El Salvador, Cambodia, Iran, and Iraq. The most important exception, however, was sub-Saharan Africa, the region that covers all of Africa with the exception of the Arabic-speaking belt along the shores of the Mediterranean Sea in the north.

From 1965—that is, shortly after independence—through the 1980s, per capita income in sub-Saharan Africa grew a mere 0.6 percent.[10] Overall, economic growth averaged 3.4 percent per year, barely above the increase in population. Between 1970 and 1987, the rate of growth of agricultural production declined; it grew at a pace of less than half the rate of population growth, 1.4 percent versus 3.3 percent. Droughts and the increasing drying-up of the Sahel, the belt directly south of the Sahara, were in part to blame for the decline in agricultural production. Whatever economic gains sub-Saharan Africa had enjoyed during the preceding thirty years were eaten up by the phenomenal rise in population. A World Bank report concluded that "never in human history has population grown so fast." In the half-century since the first African nation obtained its independence, the population doubled to nearly 1 billion. Often the result of such growth was hunger. Nearly one-quarter of the population faced "chronic food insecurity." Family planning was needed to reduce the threat of hunger and to improve health care. Sub-Saharan Africa had the highest rates of maternal and infant mortality in the world. In the poorest countries (Burkina Faso, Ethiopia, and Mali), one-quarter of the children died before they reached the age of five.

During the 1980s, per capita income and food production continued to decrease; the share of sub-Saharan Africa's exports in world markets declined from 2.4 percent in 1970 to 1.3 percent in 1987; and the region witnessed, in the terse language of a World Bank report, "accelerated ecological degradation." Several countries—among them Ghana, Liberia, and Zambia—slipped from the middle-income group to the low-income group. In 1987, the region's population of 450 million produced only as much wealth as Belgium's 10 million. The world's per capita GNP in 1987 stood at $3,010; for sub-Saharan Africa, the figure was $330.[11]

Another problem, one that went back to the 1960s, was the high level of public expenditures for standing armies. The World Bank stressed that a direct link existed between low military spending and good economic performance, pointing to Botswana and Mauritius. It also touched for the first time the question of official corruption, although only briefly and gingerly. "Bad habits," it noted, "are hard to undo," such as the siphoning of millions of foreign aid dollars into private overseas accounts. An unfettered and vigilant press, playing the role of watchdog, was all too rare. The nations with the best economic performance—Botswana and Mauritius—had parliamentary democracies and a free press.

Meanwhile, the nations of sub-Saharan Africa were increasingly unable to pay off their mounting debts. The region was overburdened by an external debt that totaled nearly $106 billion in 1987, up from $5.3 billion in 1970 and $41.2 billion in 1980 (see Chapter 17).

Africa in the Early 1990s: The Call for Democracy

By the early 1990s, the Cold War came to an end. It was no longer necessary for Moscow and Washington to prop up African dictators. It became possible, therefore, for political factions to try to resolve their problems without outside interference. The world's leading international lending institutions, notably the International Monetary Fund and World Bank, increasingly stressed that the continent's economic plight could not be resolved unless governments became accountable for their actions. Britain's foreign secretary, Douglas Hurd, declared in 1990 that "governments which persisted with repressive policies, corrupt management and wasteful, discredited economic systems should not expect us to support their folly with scarce aid resources."[12] French president François Mitterand delivered the same message at a Franco-African summit, saying that there could be "no development without democracy and no democracy without development."[13]

The year 1990 saw the rise of protest from below as political discontents—students and scholars, labor unions (often including government employees), and the poor—railed against oppressive government, corruption, and deprivation. Strikes, protest marches, and riots suddenly had an effect on dictators who for many years had been impervious to criticism. Opposition leaders demanded the convening of "national conferences" to deliberate the political future of the nation. One of the common demands was for multiparty elections.

In Benin, President Mathieu Kérékou—military dictator for seventeen years—bowed to political pressure and convened a national conference, which proceeded to strip him of his powers, appoint an interim president, call for a presidential election, and draft a new constitution. Kérékou accepted the decisions of the national conference and, after losing the election to his opponent by a two-to-one margin in the March 1991 election, became the first African ruler to be voted out of office. Benin's national conference became a model for political change in Africa, particularly in the former French colonies.

Most of Africa's strongmen, however, were unwilling to go quietly into retirement. A case in point was Joseph Mobutu, the heavy-handed dictator of Zaire since 1965. In April 1990, he announced an end to one-party government and promised to accept the verdict of a free, multiparty election. When elections were finally held, Mobutu received over 99 percent of the votes, hardly the hallmark of a free election. In the Central African Republic, strongman president André Kolingba authorized opposition parties and scheduled an election for October 1992 but then abruptly arrested the opposition. Another holdout was President Daniel arap Moi of Kenya, who denounced the movement for multiparty elections as "garbage" and an invitation for chaos. In July 1990, Kenyan police opened fire on several hundred dissidents during a peaceful demonstration demanding the legalization of opposition parties, killing at least twenty-six and jailing more than 1,000. After a year and a half of continued political agitation and after Western governments terminated economic aid to Kenya, arap Moi finally consented to legalize opposition parties in December 1991 and to call an election a year later. He then manipulated the election, however, to make certain he remained in power. In October 1990, demonstrations forced the president of the Ivory Coast, Félix Houphouët-Boigny, one of Africa's more benevolent dictators, in power since the early 1960s, to legalize opposition parties. It did not prevent him, however, from making sure he won the subsequent election decisively.

By the end of the twentieth century, freedom of the press existed in only three of Africa's fifty-five states: South Africa, Senegal, and Mali.[14] Not until 1986 did the OAU come up with an African Charter of Human Rights and the Rights of Peoples. The charter's interpretation of human rights, however, differed from the Western definition, which stresses the protection of the individual against the powers of the state. In Africa the traditional group—whether family or state—is more important and the rights of individuals are limited. The right of assembly, for example, is subject to "necessary limitations," and individual liberties have to be reconciled with the rights of others (i.e., collective security, customs, and social interests). The OAU hesitated to condemn member states, even in the case of systematic human rights violations, as with Emperor Bokassa of the Central African Republic, who in 1972 led his soldiers into a prison to quell a disturbance and ended up maiming and murdering prisoners and then displaying the dismembered bodies to the crowds outside.[15]

Flash Points in Africa in the 1990s

Throughout the 1990s, Africa experienced widespread ethnic violence, civil wars, and larger conflicts in a number of countries.

Namibia, Angola, and Mozambique

The impact of the end of the Cold War was felt quickly in three war-torn countries in southern Africa: Namibia, Angola, and Mozambique. Soviet ruler Mikhail Gorbachev withdrew financial support for the leftist government in Angola and the Cuban troops deployed there and in Namibia. US-sponsored and Soviet-supported negotiations produced an agreement in December 1988 that led to the evacuation of Cuban troops from Angola in exchange for a South African troop withdrawal from Namibia. UN negotiators brought together opposing revolutionary groups who (again with US and Soviet support) drafted one of Africa's most democratic constitutions and then held one of Africa's freest and fairest elections. In March 1990, the Namibian government, headed by SWAPO leader Sam Nujoma, celebrated the end of seventy-five years of colonial rule and twenty-three years of guerrilla warfare.

Gorbachev's withdrawal from the Third World affected Angola as well, but the impact was delayed because of an unrelenting civil war. The conflict pitted the Soviet/Cuban-supported MPLA government, headed by José Eduardo dos Santos, against the US/South African–supported UNITA guerrilla forces of Jonas Savimbi, a former self-proclaimed Maoist who compared his military campaigns to Mao's "Long March." Washington turned a blind eye to Savimbi's brutality (Human Rights Watch reported incidents of witches burned alive) since he was engaged in fighting Soviet-backed Cubans. Indeed, he became the darling of the political and religious right in the United States. In 1986, President Ronald Reagan invited him to the White House and praised his struggle "for freedom." Once the Cold War was over and the belligerents exhausted, Portugal, the former colonial ruler, was able to serve as a peace broker. A precarious agreement was finally signed in May 1991, which called for the adoption of market-oriented economic reforms, the demobilization and integration of the two military forces into a national army, and an election by the end of 1992. The breakthrough promised to end the sixteen years of continuous and crippling warfare that had devastated the country, claimed more than 300,000 lives, and given Angola the morbid distinction of having the world's highest per capita of amputees.[16]

The new armistice held as both sides prepared for Angola's first free multiparty presidential election in September 1992, one relatively free of irregularities. The victor was dos Santos, but Savimbi charged election fraud and disputed the election even before the results were finally counted. Savimbi, by now an isolated international pariah, continued his armed resistance until February 2002, when government troops hunted him down and shot him to death. The civil war was over.

At the same time, a similar sequence of events unfolded in Mozambique, another former Portuguese colony in southern Africa. There, too, a long, bloody civil war between a Soviet-backed Marxist government and a South African–supported right-wing rebel force, Renamo (the Mozambique Nationalist Resistance), ended with a negotiated settlement. The peace agreement between Renamo and the government in September 1992 terminated an extraordinarily brutal war that had claimed nearly a million lives. It also set the stage for UN-supervised elections and opened the way for desperately needed foreign aid to reach the people of this blighted country. In 1990, Mozambique held the dubious distinction of being the world's poorest nation. Its per capita GNP stood at $80, refugees represented one-quarter of its population of 15 million, and over 3 million people faced starvation.[17]

Sudan, Ethiopia, and Somalia

The most war-ravaged and famine-stricken nations in Africa were Ethiopia and Somalia, where starvation, disease, and the displacement of peoples were endemic. In 1990, drought returned to Sudan and Ethiopia, causing crop failures and famine and forcing farmers to eat their remaining animals and seed grain. The main cause of misery, however, was the ceaseless civil wars.

In Sudan, war between the government in the north and the Sudan People's Liberation Army in the south had deep-seated ethnic and religious roots. In the heavily Muslim north, Arab and Egyptian influence was strong; in the south, darker-skinned Africans, many of them Christians, resisted northern domination. Prospects for a peaceful resolution of the conflict were set back in 1989 when a military junta, led by Omar al-Bashir, took power in the capital of Khartoum for the purpose of establishing an Islamic state. As the fighting continued, some 8 million Sudanese were in desperate need of food, many becoming wandering refugees in regions beyond the reach of overland food shipments. Additionally, the darker-skinned people in the south were subjected to slavery by northerners, even though the government in Khartoum denied it when it was brought to international attention.

In April 2003, five weeks after US president George W. Bush invaded Iraq, ostensibly to bring human rights to that nation, the world's largest human catastrophe began to unfold in Sudan. Between April 2003 and the summer of 2008, a UN estimate put the number of dead at approximately 300,000—mainly by disease and famine. Another 2.2 million became refugees.

The conflict took place in Darfur (literally, "the land of the Fur [people]"), the western provinces of Sudan. It pitted nomadic Arabs against the indigenous Fur who had long cultivated the land. The two had long coexisted; they had intermarried, and the Fur had become Muslims centuries ago. In the mid-1970s, however, as a prolonged drought ravaged Darfur accompanied by a population explosion,[18] farmers and herders began to engage in sporadic clashes.[19] The military regime in Khartoum, dominated by Arabs, took the side of the herders. In April 2003, the conflict took another bloody turn when Darfur rebels, organized as the Sudanese Liberation Army, alleging governmental discrimination and exploitation, attacked military garrisons, destroyed helicopters and airplanes, and killed about 100 soldiers. At the time, the government was still seeking to resolve a twenty-one-year-long conflict in the south that pitted northern Muslim Arabs against indigenous Christians. To complicate matters for the government, 40 percent of its armed forces came from Darfur; understandably, they were reluctant to fight against the rebels.

To solve this problem, the government turned to Musa Hilal, an Arab shaikh whose family had long been in conflict with blacks in Darfur. During the 1990s, the government had imprisoned Hilal for murder, armed robbery, and tax evasion. Now it released Hilal, who created an army of marauders, the *janjaweed* (literally, "evil horsemen" or simply "bandits"), who were supported by the government and given immunity to engage in ethnic cleansing and to plunder, murder, and rape throughout the countryside.

The conflict, however, was more than just a dispute over land. Since the late 1980s, under the influence of Muammar Qaddafi of Libya, Arabs had sought to establish an "Arab belt" south of the Sahara. The *janjaweed* argued that they—and not the black Africans—were the original settlers of the land, that Arabs had brought civilization to the region, and that they were hardly bandits but rather *mujahidin* (freedom fighters) protecting their own people.

By April 2004, the ongoing tragedy began to make headlines around the world, particularly at a time when the United Nations commemorated the ten-year anniversary of the slaughter in Rwanda (see below). In April 2004, US president Bush insisted that "the government of Sudan must not remain complicit in the brutalization of Darfur." Kofi Annan, the UN secretary-general, spoke of the possibility of "military action."[20] And in July 2004, the US Congress, under the influence of evangelical Christians who had long sought to drum up international support against Khartoum's atrocities aimed at fellow Christians in the south of Sudan, played a leading role in passing a resolution condemning "genocide" in Darfur. This marked the first time that the US Congress had used that word to discuss an ongoing massacre. The US State Department would not go so far as to call it officially genocide, but in September 2004, Secretary of State Colin Powell did for the first time speak of genocide. In August 2004, the UN Security Council gave Khartoum thirty days to disarm the *janjaweed*, threatening it with sanctions. Khartoum responded that the demand was unreasonable, comparing it to the inability of the United States to disarm militants in Iraq. After the thirty days had expired, neither the Bush administration—militarily overextended in Iraq—nor the United Nations had an answer to the violence in Darfur. Eventually, the United Nations and the African Union sent peacekeepers and relief workers into Darfur, but the violence continued unabated. Among the fatalities were now members of the peacekeeping troops.

In July 2008, the prosecutor at the International Criminal Court, the Spaniard Luis Moreno-Ocampo, issued an indictment against Bashir—charging him with crimes against humanity and war crimes. Bashir, ensconced in Khartoum beyond Moreno-Ocampo's reach, contemptuously dismissed all accusations.

* * *

In September 1974, the eighty-two-year-old Christian ruler in Ethiopia, Haile Selassie, who had governed his nation since 1916 (first as regent, then as emperor), once a symbol of African independence and resistance against European colonialism, was overthrown by a military junta, professedly Marxist, led by Haile Mariam Mengistu. By that time, the emperor—who many Ethiopians saw as the reincarnation of Jesus—had become a symbol of Ethiopia's medieval past. His reign was marked by economic backwardness, famine, and political repression.

The new government proved to be no better. In Moscow, Soviet leader Leonid Brezhnev saw a chance to extend Soviet influence in Africa and began to provide economic and military backing that eventually topped $11 billion.

Economic disarray, Mengistu's brutality, and continued ethnic strife ensured the further degradation of life in Ethiopia. Haile Selassie had done little to avert the famines and instead had gone to great lengths to suppress reporting of them. Mengistu's regime sought to carry out an extensive land reform program, only to reap another agricultural disaster that was the consequence not so much of the reforms as of many years of deforestation, overcultivation, and the impacts of nature.

Arrayed against Mengistu were ethnic-based rebel armies such as the People's Revolutionary Democratic Front in Tigre Province and the Eritrean People's Liberation Front. The Eritrean fight for independence, Africa's longest war, began in 1952, shortly after the United Nations had transferred Eritrea (previously an Italian colony along the shores of the Red Sea) to Ethiopia. Ironically, the Eritrean rebel leaders, too, were Marxists who fought the Marxist government in Addis Ababa; many of the Tigre rebels were Marxists as well.

In 1990, the Soviet Union shut off military aid to Ethiopia, and soon thereafter rebel forces gained the upper hand. In April 1991, as the rebels closed in on Addis Ababa and Eritrean forces liberated their homeland in the north along the coast of the Red Sea, Mengistu fled Ethiopia; the statues of Lenin came down in Addis Ababa. With the restoration of order, urgently needed international food relief and developmental aid began to arrive. The new Ethiopian government of Meles Zenawi and the Eritrean People's Liberation Front agreed to accept the results of an internationally supervised referendum on Eritrean independence held in May 1993. With the outcome of the referendum a foregone conclusion, Eritrea finally gained its independence.

* * *

In neighboring Somalia, Mohammed Siad Barre maintained a semblance of order for twenty-one years by force of arms (supplied first by the Soviet Union and then by the United States). In January 1991, opposing clans drove him from Mogadishu, where they fought for control of the capital. It was a clan feud, a fight for power by forces possessing arsenals of US- and Soviet-supplied weapons. Somalia became a lawless land wracked by savage fighting, fear, looting, and starvation. Jeeps roamed the streets of Mogadishu mounted with recoilless rifles, many of them manned by teenage soldiers. In a three-month period at the end of 1991, an estimated 25,000 people—mostly civilians—were killed or wounded in the fighting, and 250,000 residents of the capital were expelled.

Moreover, a combination of drought and warfare in Somalia produced a famine as severe as any in modern times. Nongovernmental relief agencies such as the Red Cross, CARE, and Save the Children (a British-based charity) managed to deliver thousands of tons of food each day, but many interior areas of Somalia and even some sections of Mogadishu were beyond reach. All too often, warring forces seized the food shipments. In mid-1992, the UN Security Council sent emergency food airlifts protected by a token UN force of 500 armed guards. The UN relief missions frequently came under armed attack at the airport, and ships laden with UN relief food were denied permission to unload at the docks. Finally, in December 1992, the United Nations sanctioned a request from US president George H. W. Bush to send a UN military operation, led by 28,000 US troops, to oversee the distribution of food and medicine. By the time the world's largest armed humanitarian rescue mission was launched, an estimated 300,000 Somalis had already died of starvation, and as many as one-third of the 6 million people of Somalia were in danger of succumbing to the same fate.

Bush envisioned a purely humanitarian mission of short duration; UN Secretary-General Boutros Boutros-Ghali, however, proclaimed a larger mission: to disarm the Somali warlords and establish political stability in the country. The new US president, Bill Clinton, accepted this expanded mission to eliminate the political source of mayhem and famine in Somalia.

Initially, the US-led intervention in Somalia was an admirable success, making possible the delivery of lifesaving food to hundreds of thousands of sick and starving people. But then President Clinton authorized US soldiers to engage in a manhunt for the Somali warlord considered most responsible for the continued violence, General Mohammed Farah Aidid. His capture was deemed all the more important after his troops had ambushed and killed twenty-four Pakistani UN soldiers in June 1993. Meanwhile, opposition to the extended military operations in Somalia was mounting in Washington. In October 1993, an unsuccessful US Army Ranger raid on Aidid's headquarters led to a furious daylong firefight that left eighteen US soldiers dead and eighty wounded. Worse yet was the spectacle of Aidid's troops dragging the corpse of a US soldier through the streets of Mogadishu. The Clinton administration quickly decided to cut its losses, and instead of fighting Aidid, it now considered him as someone who held one of the keys to restoring peace and order in Somalia. Sporadic warfare between Aidid's clan and various rivals continued, however, during the remaining year and a half of the UN operation in Somalia. In the end, the operation—which cost over $2 billion (30 percent of which was borne by the United States) and hundreds of casualties—was a political and military failure. The operation, coupled with a plentiful harvest in 1994, however, finally did end the famine.

Ethnic Violence in Burundi and Rwanda

The bloodiest confrontations between blacks in postcolonial Africa took place between the Tutsi and the Hutu in Burundi and Rwanda, in the Great Lakes region.

The origins of the two peoples are not clear. The Hutu arrived in the Great Lakes region well before the Tutsi, who came from around the Horn of Africa, perhaps from Ethiopia, 400–500 years ago. The Tutsi were cattle herders, and the Hutu were cultivators. By the mid-nineteenth century, when the first reliable records were kept, the two groups had developed a common culture (spirit faiths, cuisine, folk customs) and languages. Occasionally, they also intermarried. By that time, there were so few ethnic distinctions that one could not readily call them two different ethnic groups; the division was made mainly on the basis of class.

The Europeans helped to intensify the class and ethnic divisions between Tutsis and Hutus. Under Belgian colonial rule, differences between them were reinforced by issuing ethnic identity cards. The Belgians treated the minority Tutsis (15 percent of the population) as a separate, superior ethnic entity and favored them for educational, professional, and administrative opportunities. The majority Hutus (85 percent) were treated as an inferior group. By the time the Belgians withdrew in 1962, the divisions were deep. The colonial system of using ethnic identity cards remained in force.

Once the Belgians left, the Hutu and Tutsi began to jockey for power. In 1965, after Tutsi extremists assassinated the Rwandan Hutu prime minister only three days after he had been appointed, Hutu military officers attempted a coup. Tutsi reprisals were extremely brutal as they attempted to wipe out the first generation of postcolonial Hutu political leaders. In 1972, following another Hutu rebellion—this one in Burundi—Tutsis responded with what can only be called a genocidal fury. In a span of three months, they killed approximately 250,000 Hutus and purged the army, the government, and the economy of Hutu elements. Both sides practiced ethnic cleansing in an unambiguously genocidal manner. By this time, the Belgian myth of two different tribes had been turned into reality. Tutsis and Hutus feared each other and began to construct their own mythical versions of their pasts, which only further solidified division, fear, and hatred.[21]

In Burundi in 1987, the Tutsi general Pierre Buyoya attempted to reconcile the two peoples. But suspicion ran so deep that it proved impossible. In August 1988, a confrontation between Tutsi authorities and Hutus in northern Burundi sparked a renewal of violence. Hutu and Tutsi mobs once again began to slaughter each other indiscriminately. Tutsi control of Burundi continued until June 1993, when the country elected its first Hutu president, Melchior Ndadaye. Six months later, in December 1993, the Tutsi-dominated military assassinated him. This event touched off another round of bloodletting. In the first six months alone, the estimated death toll was between 50,000 and 100,000, and 600,000 refugees fled into neighboring countries.

Ethnic violence in Burundi was soon overshadowed by a far greater massacre in neighboring Rwanda. Under the banner of "Hutu Power," President Juvenal Habyarimana, who had ruled Rwanda since 1973, forced many Tutsis into exile in neighboring Zaire. In 1990, the exiled Tutsis formed the Rwandan Patriotic Front (RPF), whose aim was to reclaim political power in Rwanda. An RPF invasion of Rwanda in October of that year unleashed another round of violence against Tutsis.

The immediate cause for the most serious outbreak of violence was the assassination of President Habyarimana in April 1994, when his plane was shot down over Kigali, the Rwandan capital. Hutu soldiers blamed the assassination on Tutsis and immediately began to avenge Habyarimana's death with indiscriminate massacres of any and all Tutsis, as well as moderate Hutus—particularly those who had married Tutsis. The militants forced other Hutus to join in this orgy of murder or be killed themselves. Mobs conducted house-to-house searches, hunting down and killing victims with whatever weapons they had at their disposal—machine guns, machetes, spears, knives, and clubs. People were herded into buildings, including churches, which were then set ablaze. Hutus, in their genocidal fury, murdered an estimated 800,000 individuals, mostly Tutsis, over a period of three months. The Clinton administration—particularly its ambassador to the United Nations, Madeleine Albright—although well aware of the magnitude of violence, resolutely refused to be drawn into the conflict. Nor did the United Nations or any country take significant action.

In the end, Tutsis, true to their military tradition, fought back and took revenge. They rallied to the RPF, which fought its way into the capital and expelled the Hutu government and its army. In July 1994, RPF leader Paul Kagame set up a new government with a moderate Hutu as a figurehead president and himself as vice-president and defense minister. Kagame, who retained actual power, took effective measures to halt the violence. When the carnage ended in Rwanda, a country of 8 million people, between 800,000 and 1 million Rwandans lay dead, murdered in less than two months, the greatest-ever slaughter during such a short period.[22] In the capital city of Kigali alone, 100,000 had been slaughtered.

The refugee problem generated by the bloodletting was of immense proportions. Between 1.1 million and 1.5 million refugees—mainly Hutus fearing for their lives—streamed into neighboring Zaire, and another 350,000 poured into Tanzania. Besieged relief workers were overwhelmed. Donor nations and international relief agencies sent food and medicine, and even though a total of over $1.4 billion in aid was sent (one-fourth of total worldwide relief aid in 1994), it proved insufficient and tardy. Thousands of refugees died from hunger and disease inside refugee camps. The UN High Commissioner for Refugees negotiated a repatriation agreement with the new government of Rwanda, which again gave assurances to Hutu refugees that it was safe to return home, but few were persuaded to do so.

Only when the slaughter was complete did the United Nations act. At the end of 1994, it established in Arusha, Tanzania, a court of justice modeled after the international Nuremberg and Tokyo war crimes tribunals following World War II. The tribunal was commissioned to undertake the herculean task of trying more than 100,000 people suspected of genocide in Rwanda. In September 1998, after three years of taking testimony, it obtained its first convictions, including that of a small-town Hutu mayor, Jean-Paul Akayesu, for inciting fellow Hutus to kill Tutsis. It then convicted former Rwandan prime minister Jean Kambanda, who became the first head of any government to be convicted of genocide. (This also set the precedent for the 2008 indictment of President Bashir of Sudan. It also established a precedent in international law when it ruled that rape was an aspect of genocide.)

The judicial process in Arusha was maddeningly slow and limited in scope. Tutsis complained that the prosecutions took too long and that only sixty-three individuals had been charged with genocide; moreover, Tutsis refused to permit the tribunal to investigate its own Rwandan Patriotic Front for any crimes it may have committed.

Conflict in Zaire

In 1996, the Hutu-Tutsi war spilled beyond the borders of Rwanda and Burundi, notably into Zaire, where Rwandan Hutu militants linked up with the Zairean army in an effort to oust Tutsis indigenous to the eastern region of Zaire. The Zairean Tutsis, armed and supported by compatriots from Rwanda and Uganda, fought back. They routed the Hutu and in the process created another flood of desperate refugees. The violence in eastern Zaire soon became a full-scale civil war when Tutsis were joined by Laurent Désiré Kabila, who for more than thirty years had sought Mobutu's overthrow. As a young man, Kabila had been a Marxist and a supporter of Patrice Lumumba and had gotten to know the Cuban revolutionary Ché Guevara. Guevara, however, had come away disenchanted from their meeting, noting in his diary that Kabila's forces lacked discipline and that Kabila himself was "too addicted to drink and women."[23] After Mobutu's rise to power in 1965, Kabila fled to eastern Zaire, from where he launched a number of unsuccessful raids to overthrow Mobutu while receiving some support from the Soviet Union and Communist China. In the meantime, he became engaged in the trafficking of ivory, gold, diamonds, alcohol, and humans for the purpose of prostitution.

By the mid-1990s, the corrupt regime of the aged and ailing Mobutu had scant popular support. Under Mobutu, *The Economist* noted, Zaire had "experienced more than corruption. . . . It saw the systemic theft of the state, from top to bottom . . . his bank account [being] indistinguishable from the national treasury." Zaire, the size of Western Europe, had only 200 miles of paved roads; in the capital of Kinshasa 90 percent of the population was unemployed. In the spring of 1997, Mobutu's regime collapsed like a house of cards.

Kabila promised to bring freedom and democracy and disavowed his Marxist past. "That was 30 years ago," he said; the Russian leader, Boris Yeltsin, "was a Marxist 30 years ago." In May 1997, his troops entered Kinshasa, where he proclaimed a new order and a new name for the country: the Democratic Republic of Congo. The long-suffering people, expecting something better, welcomed the deliverance from thirty years of misrule. The joy did not last long, however. Kabila compared his long struggle against Mobutu to "spreading fertilizer on a field" and said that the "time to harvest" had come.[24] It was now the turn of Kabila's men to collect the spoils of victory and to engage in human rights violations. Within a year, Kabila faced a rebellion out of the eastern provinces. Congolese Tutsis, now supported by Uganda and Burundi as well as Rwanda, turned against Kabila. In Kinshasa, soldiers sympathetic to the rebels clashed with troops loyal to Kabila, who soon became dependent on troops from Angola, Namibia, and Zimbabwe to keep him in power. It became the most complicated of all African wars since independence, dubbed "Africa's first world war."

By the end of 2000, Kabila lost the eastern half of his nation to rebels and foreign invaders. The lion's share of partitioned Congo fell to Uganda. Rwanda, too, benefited financially; its capital, Kigali, became a market for gold and diamonds from Congo's Kivu Province.[25]

In January 2001, Kabila was assassinated by palace guards, and his son Joseph took over a divided nation wracked by a continuing civil war—accompanied by disease, dislocation, and famine—that, by 2008, took the lives of an estimated 5.4 million Congolese. UN peacekeepers proved to be ineffective, as they could barely manage to defend themselves. In October 2008, General Laurent Nkunda, a dissident Tutsi with a long history of atrocities, seized control of the province of North Kivu in eastern Congo; UN troops had no answer. Nkunda sought to protect Tutsis against Hutus, but he was also after the riches that Congo had to offer. (For instance, 80 percent of coltran, a valuable metal used in cellular phones and video-game players, comes from Congo.) The result was another round of massacres, refugees, hunger, and disease (mainly cholera).

Nigeria

In oil-rich Nigeria, General Sani Abacha seized power in a coup in June 1993, crushing all dissent. His greed knew no limit, his family's fortune estimated at between $3 billion and $6 billion. Political opponents languished in prison, some of them executed by firing squads or hanging. In November 1995, eleven activists, most famously among them the author and environmentalist Ken Saro-Wiwa, were hanged in defiance of vocal international protests. The men, members of the small Ogoni ethnic group (of about half a million people), had long criticized Abacha's dictatorship as well as the despoliation of their region by Nigeria's oil industry.

Nigeria was the world's sixth-largest exporter of oil, yet its people all too often lived in poverty. Most of its people were without clean water, adequate health care, and reliable electricity. Abacha's successor, Olusegun Obasanjo, vowed to restore democracy and end corruption, but this would be a tall order. Since independence, Nigeria had been under military rule for all but ten years, and the legacy of military rule was difficult to set aside. To complicate matters, Nigeria faced endemic poverty (approximately 90 percent of the population lived on $2 per day or less) and ethnic strife. In February 2000, violence in the northern province of Kaduna claimed 400 lives, mostly Christians, the consequence of the imposition of Islamic religious law—*sharia*—in the predominantly Muslim north by the cronies of the late dictator Abacha. The law provided for Islamic curricula in the public schools as well as the amputation of a hand for theft and public flogging for other crimes. It also forbade women from working outside the home or sharing public transportation with men.[26]

Zimbabwe

In the 1960s, under the leadership of Ian Smith, the whites of Southern Rhodesia resisted as long as possible the "wind of change" calling for independence. The result was a war of nearly twenty years' duration that claimed approximately 30,000 lives. In the end, the independence movement led by Robert Mugabe triumphed; a black majority government under Mugabe, after promising black-white reconciliation, took power in 1980 in what became known as Zimbabwe.

At the time of independence, the presidents of neighboring Mozambique and Tanzania told Mugabe, "You have the jewel of Africa in your hands. Now look after it." Zimbabwe had a fine railroad system, good roads, and a functioning hydroelectric system, and it produced vast amounts of food (maize, peanuts, pineapples, mangoes, apples) and raw materials (gold, chromium, platinum). Blacks had done fairly well economically, although they had no political power.[27]

After independence, the white settlers lost their political dominance, and their numbers dwindled from 278,000 in 1975 to 70,000 by 2000. Those who stayed retained their vast landholdings, however. An agreement in 1979 between the British government and Mugabe had stipulated that the white farmers were not to lose their lands without compensation, that all land transfers were to be based on the principle of a "willing buyer, willing seller," and that London would help finance the transfers of land to black farmers. It soon became apparent, however, that the transfer funds disappeared into the coffers of Mugabe and his allies.

Mugabe and his supporters enriched themselves at the expense of the economy at large, which by the end of the 1990s was in ruins from neglect. The telephone system, once the best in Africa, functioned only sporadically. The indigenous agricultural sector remained primitive. Thirty-six percent of the population lived in poverty—on an income of less than $1 per day. And 26 percent of people between the ages of fifteen and forty-nine years suffered from AIDS. Per capita GNP stood at $620; inflation ran at over 25 percent. Unemployment was at 30 percent, while wages fell by one-third during the

1990s.[28] In August 1998, Mugabe committed scarce resources to the conflict in Congo, with the number of Zimbabwe's troops eventually reaching 11,000.

To shore up his sinking popularity, Mugabe staged a referendum in February 2000 asking voters to give him additional powers, primarily to dispossess—without compensation—the remaining white farmers, who still controlled 4,500 large farms representing one-third of the nation's land. These farmers, however, also boasted the most productive segment of Zimbabwe's economy: They produced 70 percent of the nation's agricultural exports and employed approximately 300,000 black workers. When the predominantly black voters rejected the referendum, Mugabe declared the white farmers "enemies of Zimbabwe" and encouraged veterans of the war of liberation to seize white-owned farms, drive out their owners, intimidate the black workers, and, if need be, kill those who resisted. The veterans responded by murdering white settlers as well as Mugabe's black political opponents. By 2004, there were scarcely any white farmers left. The exodus led to a precipitous drop in agricultural output and with it foreign-currency earnings. The harvest of maize declined 67 percent, that of wheat 91 percent, and that of tobacco 75 percent.[29]

By 2008, the economy of Zimbabwe was in shambles. Inflation had destroyed the Zimbabwe dollar, trading officially at a rate of Z$30,000 to US$1. At the time of independence the currencies had been roughly at par. During the previous two decades life expectancy had dropped from sixty years to thirty-seven, the lowest in the world. The country faced a shortage of staples and supplies, including maize, cooking oil, gasoline, sugar, and salt. Unemployment was at 85 percent. One-third of the population had left the country, spilling mostly into South Africa, where they were unwelcome. Still, Mugabe repeatedly insisted that there was no crisis in Zimbabwe.

In March 2008, the eighty-four-year-old Mugabe lost the presidential election to Morgan Tsvangirai's Movement for Democratic Change. Initially Mugabe decided to step down and retire to his luxury villa, but the chief of the army, General Constantine Chiwenga, told Mugabe that the decision was not his alone. Mugabe's men would cling to power. After a month's delay came the announcement that Tsvangirai had not won an absolute majority—48 percent to Mugabe's 43 percent—and that a runoff election had to be held. In the meantime, the army worked out a plan ("Coercion, Intimidation, Beating, and Displacement"). First came the beatings of opponents; then in early May, Mugabe supporters rampaged through the streets of the remote farming village of Choana, whose residents had shown the effrontery of voting for Tsvangirai, leaving seven people dead. That pattern was repeated with increasing frequency elsewhere.[30] Hundreds of civilians and more than eighty members of Tsvangirai's party were murdered. Tsvangirai, who had been viciously beaten in the past, went into exile; when he returned he was arrested and rearrested several times. In the end, he stopped campaigning and sought refuge in the

Dutch embassy. In June, Mugabe won in a landslide and two days later took the oath of office for his sixth term.

The international community expressed outrage and eventually managed to broker a tenuous agreement after offering economic incentives, including a pledge to lift economic sanctions. By the agreement, in September 2008, Tsvangirai became prime minister, but Mugabe retained the all-important position of head of the army. It was far from a perfect solution, but it moved toward addressing the political deadlock.

Sierra Leone and Liberia

While the Western world's attention was riveted on the fate of a small number of white settlers in Zimbabwe, a more gruesome spectacle, largely ignored, continued in Sierra Leone. It began in 1991, when Foday Sankoh created the Revolutionary United Front (RUF). Sankoh, in the face of feeble resistance from the Sierra Leone government, gained control of lands rich in gold and diamonds. In January 1999, Sankoh torched one-third of the capital city of Freetown and massacred 6,000 people. A UN force of 8,700 soldiers failed to disarm the rebels; in fact, the RUF captured 500 UN peacekeepers before eventually releasing them. It was British paratroopers who stood between the rebels and Freetown.

Sankoh's forces engaged in systematic atrocities—torture, rape, arson, wholesale slaughter, and mutilation. The men under Sankoh, a visionary who claimed to have supernatural powers, hacked off the arms and legs of an estimated 10,000 children. They also pressed into military service children as young as ten years old. Fankoh even dubbed one of his campaigns Operation Pay Yourself, encouraging his men to loot anything they could find. By 2000, 100,000–200,000 people had perished in the conflict.[31]

None of that caused much of an outcry abroad. US president Bill Clinton—burned by the US military setback in Somalia in 1993 and now engaged in Kosovo—and most of the rest of Africa and the world showed little interest in Sierra Leone. It was up to Great Britain to see what it could do to restore order in one of its former colonies. In 2000, British troops with shoot-to-kill orders routed the RUF. Britain charged Fankoh with seventeen counts of war crimes, but before the trial began, Sankoh died of a stroke.

Sankoh had not acted alone in his murderous campaign. He had the support of a soldier of fortune, Charles Taylor of neighboring Liberia, a country with its own recent tragic history. In April 1980, a revolt led by Master Sergeant Samuel K. Doe overthrew the government of William Tolbert, a descendant of former slaves from the United States who had ruled Liberia since its formation in 1847. The former US slaves had become the colonizers and oppressors of the native majority. When Doe, a native Liberian (from the Krahn ethnic group), murdered Tolbert, it marked the first time that a native

Liberian had ruled the country. Doe quickly promoted himself to general and then launched a reign of terror, including mass executions and theft on a huge scale, as he and his Krahn supporters helped themselves to the spoils of war.

When, in 1989, Taylor, another Americo-Liberian, challenged Doe, Liberia was plunged into the bloodiest of civil wars, which included Doe's brutal torture and execution (at the hands of yet another rival faction). After that it became Taylor's turn to plunder and terrorize Liberia. There was no crime that Taylor's men did not commit with near-total impunity in Liberia (as well as in nearby Sierra Leone). An estimated 150,000–200,000 people died in Liberia, and one-third of the population became refugees. UN economic sanctions in 2001 and the advance of seven rebel factions steadily weakened Taylor's hand. In the end, Taylor fled, accepting political asylum from the generals in charge of Nigeria, leaving behind his devastated native land.

In response to brutality that took place in Yugoslavia at about the same time, the United Nations established in 2002 a new International Criminal Court, the first permanent war crimes tribunal. Its purpose was to bring to justice the worst of the worst if their native countries were "unable or unwilling" to do so. In July 2003, the court sought the extradition of Taylor, and—after nearly three years, in March 2006—the Nigerian government finally yielded to international pressure and handed him over to a Special Court for Sierra Leone in the capital of Freeport. Taylor became first sitting African former head of state to be indicted. (Slobodan Milošević of Yugoslavia was the first to be indicted by the ICC.) He was charged with eleven counts of war crimes and crimes against humanity committed in Sierra Leone. (The new government of Liberia, under Ellen Johnson Sirleaf, showed scant interest in putting Taylor on trial. Taylor still had a strong following in Liberia; besides, Johnson Sirleaf did not consider him a criminal, merely "someone who was human and who made some mistakes."[32]) Eventually, Taylor's trial was transferred to The Hague, where he did everything possible to drag out the process.

AIDS in Sub-Saharan Africa

During the 1990s, sub-Saharan Africa was ravaged by an epidemic of AIDS (acquired immune deficiency syndrome) reaching unprecedented proportions. Between the early 1980s and the end of 2000, more African people (19 million) had died of AIDS than in all the wars fought across the globe combined. About 6,000 Africans died from AIDS each day, and millions more were infected by HIV (human immune-deficiency virus), which weakens the natural immune system and is the root of AIDS. Sub-Saharan Africa, with 10 percent of the world's population, had 70 percent of the world's population infected with HIV (24.5 million out of 34.3 million total). Hardest hit were Zimbabwe, Zambia, Botswana, and South Africa. Botswana had the world's highest rate of infection—35 percent of the population.

South Africa was the last sub-Saharan African nation to be visited by AIDS. In the 1980s, the epidemic in South Africa was considered an illness that affected primarily white homosexuals. Within a decade, however, it had spread to more than a tenth of the population, and nearly all of the victims were black. By 2000, South Africa had more infected people than any nation in the world. During his five years as president, Nelson Mandela paid scant attention to the problem. When he finally did, in 1998, 20 percent of South Africa's pregnant women were already infected. Mandela's successor, Thabo Mbeki, as well as Mbeki's health minister, rejected the explanation that HIV caused AIDS and blamed it instead on drug and alcohol abuse, poverty, and underdevelopment. In the meantime, the disease spread. Among the breeding grounds for the virus were the communal residences of miners separated from their families for months at a stretch. There, sexual contact, the most common route of AIDS transmission, infected more than a third of the young adults—both men and women. When the men returned home, they spread the disease. HIV also contributed to the rapid spread of tuberculosis, particularly among miners, and a host of other illnesses. All the while, the topics of sex and AIDS remained taboo.

Mbeki's government refused to provide funds for AZT (Azidothymidin), a drug that suppresses the impact of the virus and that, in most cases, prevents the transmission of the disease to children borne by infected women. It is, moreover, an expensive drug that must be taken in combination with other expensive drugs to be effective.

In January 2000, AIDS became for the first time a topic at the UN Security Council, and that April the IMF linked its economic development programs with the fight against the disease. In May of that year, the US government declared it a potential threat to national security. The bitter truth was that AIDS threatened first and foremost the poorer countries where the workforces—those between the ages of fifteen and forty-nine—were most at risk. Ninety-five percent of individuals infected with HIV lived in underdeveloped nations. The International Labour Organization estimated that, unless the epidemic was checked, by 2020 sub-Saharan Africa would suffer from a shortage of at least 24 million workers. UN studies predicted that eventually half of all fifteen-year-olds in sub-Saharan Africa would die of the disease. The AIDS epidemic reduced life expectancy, raised mortality rates, lowered fertility, and produced millions of orphans. By the beginning of the twenty-first century, with the fate of the next generation at stake, AIDS education and preventive programs were finally becoming priorities for many governments in sub-Saharan Africa.[33]

Apartheid in South Africa

Between 1949 and 1994, South Africa stood apart from the rest of Africa, not only as the most economically developed nation but also as one ruled by an intransigent white minority. In defiance of world opinion and the demands of its black majority, the white National Party maintained political power by means of a racist policy known as apartheid, literally "apartness." It was a legal system that demanded the most rigid form of racial segregation anywhere. The laws forbade the most elementary contact among the four racial groupings in South Africa: blacks (also known as Bantus), whites (mostly of Dutch, French, and English descent), coloreds (of mixed black-white parentage), and Asians (largely Indians).

In 1948, the whites of Dutch (and in part French)[34] origin replaced another group of European settlers, the English, as the dominant political force in shaping the destiny of a country they considered to be theirs. The Dutch, having settled on the South African coast as early as 1652 for the purpose of establishing a new religious commonwealth, saw it as their native land and, in fact, called themselves "Afrikaners," Dutch for Africans. (They also called themselves "boers," or farmers, and are often referred to by that name.) They argued that their claim to the land rested on discovery, conquest, economic development, and, ultimately, the will of God.

Apartheid was steeped in the teachings of the Dutch Reformed Church, long in rebellion against the corrupt Old World and thus the exodus to Africa. The Afrikaners were God's chosen, a righteous people destined to dominate the land and others who inhabited it. The most fervent defenders of apartheid were ministers of the church. Apartheid was also based on the primitive principle of racial superiority. The Bantus, Afrikaners argued, had contributed nothing to civilization; their existence was one of savagery. The twin pillars of apartheid—religious determinism and racial superiority—grew out of the Afrikaners' long struggles against the Catholic Church and other heresies in the Netherlands, Western liberalism, and the black native population of South Africa.

By the end of the eighteenth century, the Dutch had established deep roots in the South African soil. In 1795, however, the British gained control of the South African cape and with it came a long struggle for political supremacy between the established Dutch and the newly arrived, victorious English. It was a contest the Afrikaners could not win, and it led to their decision to move into the hinterlands to escape once more the outside world closing in on them. In particular, the Afrikaners opposed the English ban of slavery, which in 1833 became the law of the British Empire. In 1835, the boers set out on the Great Trek northward into the high plains of Natal and Transvaal. The journey was filled with bitterness and determination, coupled with a deep religious fervor. The trek became a triumphant religious procession by which God's elect, a people with a very narrow view of salvation, set out to build a new Jerusalem.

And God's favor clearly seemed to shine on them when, on December 16, 1838—in a scene straight out of the Old Testament—470 boers decisively defeated a force of 12,500 Zulu warriors, killing 3,000 of them, on the banks of what became known as the Blood River.[35] After the Afrikaners came to power, December 16 became a national holiday, the Day of Covenant between God and His people.

Later in the century, when the British once again encroached on boer territory, the boers stood and fought two bloody and brutal yet losing wars that ended in 1902. From that day, they prepared for the day of liberation to redress their defeat and to reestablish the social and religious principles of the Great Trek. That day came in 1948, when their National Party, under the leadership of D. F. Malan—a minister of the Dutch Reformed Church—won a narrow electoral political victory. At this juncture, British efforts to maintain racial harmony in South Africa were abandoned, and the segregation laws came into being. The Afrikaners, driven by an intense sense of religious and cultural self-preservation, rejected all previous proposals for social and racial integration. Instead, they insisted that the races be kept apart by law and that no one had the right to cross the color line. It led to the eventual political isolation of South Africa. Yet, isolation only bred defiance and reinforced the outlook of a people long accustomed to adversity and determined to go it alone. A stiff-necked people, the boers had stood up to the British, the blacks, and the world.

The first of the segregation laws, enacted in 1949, forbade miscegenation—the marriage or cohabitation of persons of different color. Other segregation laws followed in rapid succession. Schools, jobs, and pay scales were all determined by the segregation laws. The Population Registration Act listed individuals on the basis of race; another law demanded residential segregation and limited the rights of blacks to remain in designated cities. Political organizations and strikes by nonwhites were outlawed. All public facilities—from hospitals to park benches and beaches—became segregated. Whites and nonwhites were not permitted to spend the night under the same roof. Every aspect of sexual, social, religious, and economic intercourse between the races was regulated, among both the living and the dead—even the cemeteries were segregated. The number of apartheid laws ran well over 300.

The issue of race and segregation became an obsession in South Africa. A classification board first had to assign a racial category for every individual, but the science of distinguishing skin color, facial features, and hair texture is not exact. Often the result was as follows:

> In one typical twelve-month period, 150 coloreds were reclassified as white; ten whites became colored; six Indians became Malay; two Malay became Indians; two coloreds became Chinese; ten Indians became coloreds; one Indian became white; one white became Malay; four blacks became Indians; three whites became Chinese.

> The official absurdity knew no end. Chinese were classified as a white
> subgroup and Japanese as "honorary whites."[36]

Apartheid turned the once oppressed Afrikaners into oppressors. In 1980, in this nation of 28 million, blacks outnumbered whites by a ratio of three to one, 18 million to 6 million. The coloreds numbered about 3 million, the Asians nearly 1 million. It was little wonder that a siege mentality permeated white society. And, in fact, white settlements were frequently referred to as *laagers*, literally "camps," a term taken from the Great Trek of the 1830s.

The segregation laws were also the linchpin of economic exploitation. The laws excluded nonwhites from the better-paying jobs and positions of authority. In the construction industry in the late 1980s, for instance, whites earned twice the salary of Asians, three times that of coloreds, and five times that of blacks. A white miner earned $16,000 a year, a black miner $2,500. The combination of rich natural resources, industrial planning, and cheap labor provided by the black workforce turned the nation into the African continent's only modern, industrialized state—but only for the white population. The defenders of apartheid pointed out that the wealth of the nation also trickled down to the black population, whose standard of living was the highest of any blacks in Africa. Blacks regarded this argument as irrelevant. Apartheid—a philosophy of psychological oppression, economic exploitation, and political domination—became a way of life that only force could maintain.

The Struggle Against Apartheid

In 1959, the National government set aside ten regions (Bantustans, or "homelands") for the black population that constituted 13 percent of the nation's land. The "homelands" were the official residences set aside for the native black population; accordingly, they were denied unrestricted access to the rest of South Africa. Blacks, who made up much of the nation's essential workforce, thus had no right to be in, say, the city of Johannesburg. It also meant that although black fathers could find work in areas set aside for whites, their families had to remain behind. In this fashion, many black families were divided, frequently for eleven months at a stretch. Blacks were but temporary visitors at the pleasure of the white hosts, aliens in their native land. The creation of the "homelands" signaled the completion of the system of apartheid. The South African government hoped to obtain international recognition of the Bantustans as the national homes of the blacks of South Africa, yet no country recognized them as independent. They acquired no legal international standing, for none of the "homelands" were ever viable; they remained financially dependent on the South African government.

The government's position became more rigid still in 1960, the official UN "Year of Africa," during which a number of sub-Saharan African nations

Nelson Mandela, leader of the African National Congress and first nonwhite president of the Republic of South Africa. *(Courtesy of the Embassy of the Republic of South Africa)*

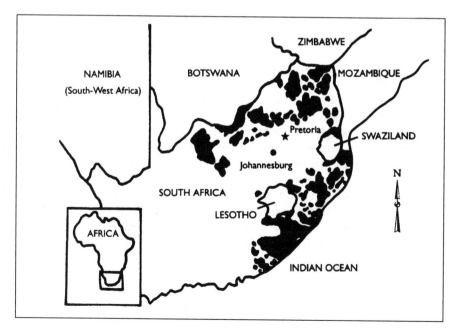

South Africa's "Homelands"

gained independence. In February, British prime minister Harold Macmillan went to Capetown to address the South African parliament, where he delivered his "wind of change" speech in which he warned that black nationalism was a force that had to be recognized, if only to prevent the newly independent African nations from being drawn into the Communist camp. The government of Hendrik Verwoerd ignored whatever winds were blowing through Africa and made clear that there would be no accommodation with African nationalism in South Africa. Six weeks later, on March 21, Verwoerd's government gave his reply to Macmillan. At Sharpeville, police gunned down sixty-nine demonstrators who had protested the creation of the Bantustans and the "pass laws" that required them to carry identification documents that restricted their right of movement.

The Sharpeville massacre had an extraordinary psychological impact on black Africans, who viewed it as a watershed. To many of them, the time had come to move from peaceful agitation to armed revolution. The laws left them two choices: either accept the status of second-class citizenship or rebel. In addition to Sharpeville, highly publicized disturbances took place in Soweto (short for South-West Township), a black ghetto of 1 million people thirty minutes from Johannesburg, the elegant financial capital of South Africa. In April 1960, the government banned the still moderate African National Congress (ANC) and the militant Pan-Africanist Congress.

It was at this juncture that South Africa's oldest and most influential civil rights organization, the ANC—an umbrella organization of blacks, whites, Asians, coloreds, and liberals—reassessed its strategy. Since its formation in 1912, the ANC had sought the peaceful establishment of a nonracial democracy. Its leader, Nelson Mandela, explained at his trial in 1964 that until the advent of apartheid his organization had "adhered strictly to a constitutional struggle."[37] But the events from 1959 to 1961 made clear that this approach had reached a dead end.[38]

In 1961, the ANC, having concluded that all legal venues were now closed, adopted armed struggle as one of the means to bring an end to apartheid and formed its armed wing, Umkhonto we Sizwe—the "Spear of the Nation." Mandela, one of the founders of Umkhonto, explained that "fifty years of nonviolence had brought the African people nothing but more and more repressive legislation, and fewer and fewer rights." On December 16, 1961, Umkhonto responded with its first acts of sabotage. The ANC marked that day as Heroes' Day to honor those who had lost their lives in the struggle against apartheid. The date was carefully chosen; it was the anniversary of the 1838 Afrikaner victory over the Zulus at the Blood River, the Afrikaners' Day of Covenant.

The armed conflict between Umkhonto and the National Party had the effect Macmillan had feared. The ANC made common cause with the Communist Party, and consequently South Africa was drawn into the global Cold War.

The Soviet Union provided money and weapons to the ANC, and the United States tilted toward the South African apartheid regime. The ANC, however, did not espouse Marxist economic theory; in fact, it advocated a capitalist South Africa in which private property was more equitably distributed.

A tip from the CIA led to the police arrest of Nelson Mandela in 1963. At his trial in 1964, Mandela justified the formation of Umkhonto by pointing to the repeated acts of violence by the government against the black population. The court rejected his argument and sentenced him to life in prison at hard labor.

Black Consciousness and Zulu Nationalism

The early 1970s saw the emergence of the "black consciousness" movement in South Africa, a trend influenced in part by the US civil rights movement. Its leading advocate was Steve Biko, who insisted that South African blacks must no longer rely on liberal whites to speak for them but must deal with all whites as equals. "Whites must be made to realize that they are only human, [and] not superior," he declared, and blacks "must be made to realize that they are also human, [and] not inferior."[39] The very thought of a black person demanding racial equality as his birthright made Biko a dangerous and marked man. The authorities arrested him on a pass violation—his refusal to carry a passbook. He died in police custody in September 1977, his skull repeatedly fractured. After Biko's death, the radical Azanian People's Organization (Azapo), the militant wing of the Pan-Africanist Congress, declared itself the heir of Biko's "black consciousness" and then went much farther than Biko ever did. It demanded the expulsion of all whites and declared war on them under the slogan "one settler, one bullet." Azapo also became engaged in an ideological—and soon bloody—conflict with the ANC and its allies, who promoted a nonracial democracy.

At the same time, the ANC faced opposition from still another black organization, the Inkatha Freedom Party, the political base of Zulu chief Mangosuthu Buthelezi. In their younger days, Buthelezi and Mandela had been comrades in their opposition to apartheid, but over the years Buthelezi had become the champion of narrow Zulu interests rather than broad national interests. He became a defender of the Zulu "homeland," KwaZulu, in the province of Natal. An integrated South Africa threatened Buthelezi's base of power, and thus he sought to perpetuate the continued existence of KwaZulu, either as a "homeland" or an entirely independent Zulu state. Biko and Mandela both had criticized Buthelezi for accepting the Afrikaner formula for a separation of the races.

The Dismantling of Apartheid

In the mid-1980s, the government slowly began to question the wisdom of continuing with apartheid. The financial, psychological, and human costs were becoming too high. June 1976 saw an uprising in Soweto, which the police were able to put down only by killing several hundred residents. In 1985, during demonstrations commemorating the twenty-fifth anniversary of the Sharpeville massacre, the police killed nineteen people at one demonstration alone, and scores of others died in other clashes. The funeral processions for those killed served as protest demonstrations and brought yet more violence. At summer's end, for the first time white residential areas became the scenes of racial confrontations. There were 1,605 outbreaks of political violence in January 1986, and the numbers kept climbing in subsequent months. The anti-apartheid uprising of the mid-1980s claimed 1,650 black lives and nearly 30,000 detainees.[40]

In 1985, as violence escalated, the government began to consider the unthinkable: the establishment of a political dialogue with the banned ANC and its leader. Mandela, however, refused freedom on the conditions that the ANC pledge to refrain from violent activity and that he live in the "homeland" set aside for the Xhosa, the Transkei. Another voice in opposition to apartheid came to national and international attention, that of Episcopalian bishop Desmond Tutu, who in 1984 received the Nobel Peace Prize in recognition of his attempts to work out a peaceful solution.

By 1985, President P. W. Botha came to acknowledge the reality of the permanence of blacks in "white" South Africa, a permanence that ultimately would have to be granted legality. His slogan was "adapt or die." Demographics alone, in a nation where the black population was growing much more rapidly than the ruling white population, demanded concessions. Within the government of South Africa, a split developed between the "enlightened" ministers and the conservatives fearful of any change.

Determined to quell disturbances and to put an end to worldwide press and television coverage of the carnage in the streets, Botha imposed a nationwide state of emergency on June 12, 1986. Under this decree, a black protester could be imprisoned without trial for up to ten years for statements meant to "weaken or undermine" confidence in the government. Botha, however, did scrap the hated pass laws and thereby abandoned the boer fiction that South Africa was a white-only preserve. He understood that the old days were over, without having a clear idea of what would come next.

International pressure began to have a telling effect. Under the aegis of United Nations leadership, the United States and most European governments imposed trade sanctions, and foreign corporations began withdrawing capital from South Africa. From 1986 to 1988, the country suffered a net capital outflow of nearly $4 billion; consequently, unemployment, inflation, and interest rates all increased and economic growth declined from a sturdy 5 percent to 2 percent. The price of apartheid had become too high.[41] A growing number of whites, especially in the business community, began urging change. Many whites also felt a sense of isolation from the world community. Since the late 1960s, South Africa, a nation proud of its world-class athletes, had been banned from the Olympic Games and other venues of international competition, such as the World Cup in soccer.

In response to these pressures, Botha gradually began to moderate the apartheid system. Some of the more superfluous apartheid restrictions were lifted. Certain public facilities—such as drinking fountains, movie theaters, and public parks and swimming beaches—were desegregated, and mixed residency was permitted in certain previously segregated urban residential areas.

De Klerk and Mandela

In September 1989, Frederik W. de Klerk succeeded Botha as president of South Africa. In his inauguration speech de Klerk pledged to work for "a totally changed South Africa . . . free of domination or oppression in whatever form."[42] He went on to declare his intentions of bridging the deep gulf of distrust and fear among the races and finding a "completely new approach" to negotiations with black leaders.

A major sign of the changing attitudes was de Klerk's remarkably conciliatory policy toward the outlawed ANC. Anti-apartheid protesters were permitted to hold a mammoth rally in Soweto at which released ANC leaders were allowed to address a throng of some 60,000 people. Even more surprising were the lifting of the political ban on the ANC and the unconditional release of its seventy-one-year-old heralded leader, Mandela, in February 1990. De Klerk also declared an end to Botha's state of emergency and promised to free all political prisoners. International investors responded swiftly by making money available to the South African economy, and the Johannesburg Stock Exchange industrial index rose 7.2 percent in two days.

As the newly freed Mandela began to take the first tentative steps to negotiate an end to apartheid with the de Klerk government, old issues came to the fore. One was the continued political rivalry between Mandela's ANC and Buthelezi's ethnic Zulu-based Inkatha movement. In contrast to Buthelezi, Mandela, although a descendant of Xhosa kings, had long since moved beyond ethnic politics and was committed to the abolition of the Bantustans.

Mandela's stature was greatly elevated after his release from prison, but he was unable to halt the black-on-black bloodletting. Between 1985 and 1996, ANC-Inkatha violence claimed 10,000–15,000 lives. Much of it was carried out by young radical blacks, the "Young Lions," who sought to gain control of the bases of economic and political power in the black townships. The Young Lions had gained notoriety by "necklacing" their victims (placing tires around their necks and setting them on fire) and proved to be impervious to pleas for moderation. Mandela's appeal to the Young Lions to throw their guns and knives into the sea fell on deaf ears.

In 1991, de Klerk took steps to abolish the apartheid laws (including the Population Registration Act, the legal underpinning of apartheid) to clear away obstacles to the negotiation of a new constitution. The ANC, as it had done in the past, insisted on "one man, one vote"—that is, majority rule. If implemented, it would mean the election of a black majority government and, therefore, would produce a strong reaction from the Afrikaner right wing, such as the Conservative Party and the Afrikaner Resistance Movement. Nonetheless, a national referendum by the white voters gave de Klerk an overwhelming mandate (68 percent in favor to 32 percent against) to continue negotiations with Mandela.

In 1992, the last obstacle, the "homelands," became a focal point of the ANC's political agenda. Pretoria still considered four of them—Ciskei, Bophuthatswana, Transkei, and Venda—independent entities. The ANC insisted they be reincorporated into South Africa and that they participate in the national political process. The leaders of these "homelands," where elections and opposition parties (including the ANC) had been banned, insisted on maintaining their autonomy and made clear that they would defend that autonomy by force if necessary. Only after repeated, bloody clashes with ANC supporters did they finally yield to incorporation into a unified South Africa. Buthelezi and KwaZulu remained defiant, however, holding out for independence for the Zulu population of 7.5 million, South Africa's largest ethnic group. Not until the very eve of the April elections did Buthelezi finally direct his Inkatha Freedom Party to participate.

Mandela's Victory

Meanwhile, the ANC and the National Party scheduled South Africa's first free multiparty and multiracial election, which, everyone knew, would mean the transition from white minority rule to black majority rule. April 27, 1994, was set as the date for electing a 400-seat National Assembly. At this point, Mandela joined de Klerk in calling for an end to international economic sanctions, stating that they had served their purpose.

Mandela's ANC, as expected, was the big winner in the historic election. It garnered 62 percent of the vote and won 252 seats in the National Assembly, whereas the National Party obtained but 20 percent of the vote and eighty-two seats. On May 27, 1994, the seventy-five-year-old Mandela, who had spent twenty-seven years of his life as a political prisoner, was elected by the National Assembly as the first nonwhite president of his country. "The time for the healing of wounds has come," he declared, "never, never, and never again shall it be that this beautiful land will again experience the oppression of one by the other. . . . Let freedom reign. God bless Africa!"[43]

This remarkable turn of events was the result of several coinciding factors: the South African government's inability to produce a stable society under apartheid; the enactment of effective international economic sanctions; the end of the Cold War, which ended deleterious outside meddling by the superpowers; and the roles of de Klerk and Mandela. For their efforts, de Klerk and Mandela shared the Nobel Peace Prize in 1993. Nor should the roles of old-guard National Party leaders, who had begun behind-the-scenes initiatives for change a decade earlier, be overlooked. At the time of the 1994 elections, several members of the former Botha government revealed that they had become convinced in the 1980s that apartheid could not be sustained for long and that they should strike a deal with the ANC to work out a peaceful transition to majority rule. It took another two and a half years after the election to reach an agreement on a permanent constitution. When the time came to sign this document in December 1996, it was only appropriate that the signing take place at Sharpeville in the presence of survivors of the 1960 massacre.

Mandela's inauguration, however, could not disguise the hard realities of unresolved divisive political issues and persistent economic and social inequalities. The dismantling of apartheid and the changing of the guard did not miraculously erase the miserable living conditions for the bulk of the black population or provide the education needed for their advancement.

One of the most difficult tasks was determining how to deal with those responsible for the political violence since 1960 (the year of Sharpeville and the banning of the ANC). Under Mandela's persistent demand, South Africa, which had one of the world's highest rates of capital punishment, abolished the death penalty. In July 1995, the government set up a Truth and Reconciliation Commission, which sought—as its name implied—not to punish the guilty but to try to bring about national reconciliation between peoples who only recently had been killing each other. The head of the commission was Tutu, the retired Episcopalian archbishop and recipient of the Nobel Peace Prize for 1984—a man whose life had been dedicated to the idea of peaceful reconciliation.

The commission operated on the principle of granting amnesty to all who acknowledged their past crimes. The families of the victims—understandably— were generally opposed to amnesty, but there appeared to be no workable alternative. If punishment were to be meted out, then to whom? The defense minister, Joe Modise, once the head of Umkhonto? Former defense minister Magnus Malan, who had organized anti-ANC death squads manned by Zulus? The guilty parties in the ANC-Inkatha violence that had claimed as many as 15,000 lives in a ten-year span and who continued to kill each other even as the commission was holding its hearings? Could the state, even if it wanted to, bring some of the Inkatha leaders—not to mention Buthelezi—into the dock? And what was one to do about the charges that directly implicated P. W. Botha in acts of violence?[44]

In October 1998, after two and a half years of hearings, the Truth and Reconciliation Commission issued its long-awaited final report. The 2,750-page document presented in gruesome detail thousands of instances of human rights violations perpetrated by both blacks and whites. Many whites, especially those associated with the National Party and right-wing organizations, denounced the report as biased against the white minority. Some blacks denounced the report for describing ANC abuses. The report did not implicate former president de Klerk for apartheid-era abuses, but it did implicate former president Botha, who denounced the commission as a witch hunt and repeatedly refused to testify. It offered recommendations, such as the creation of human rights bureaus in every government ministry, restitution for those who had suffered, apologies to those whose rights had been violated, as well as the prosecution of human rights violators who did not seek amnesty.

In the meantime, the new government had to tackle the mundane daily tasks of governance. Crime was one of the biggest problems. Police officers were often poorly trained and departments were affected by corruption, absenteeism, and lack of discipline. Many crimes were not properly investigated; only 32 percent of murder suspects were convicted—this in a country with the highest murder rate in the world. Another urgent problem was the AIDS epidemic. In 2000, the Health Ministry calculated that AIDS already had claimed 250,000 lives and that the nation faced 1,600 new AIDS cases daily. In December 1998, Mandela turned over the reins of the ANC to his old comrade-in-arms, Thabo Mbeki; six months later Mbeki succeeded Mandela as president of South Africa. The eighty-year-old Mandela thereby orchestrated a peaceful transfer of power in contrast to so many African leaders who had clung to power until they breathed their last. Mandela left behind an impressive legacy. He had led the fight against apartheid, achieved the transfer of power to the black majority, and laid the foundation for a free society: a critical free press, integrated universities, a working civil society, political pluralism, and a private economy. "We have confounded the prophets of doom and achieved a bloodless revolution," he said; "we have restored the dignity of every South African."[45] The revolution had by no means been bloodless, but there had been far less violence than thought possible. Mandela, however, also left behind a nation still troubled by great economic disparity and poverty, racial tensions, and unabated violent crime.

At the time of Mandela's ninetieth birthday celebration, in July 2008, he expressed fear that his legacy was eroding. His successors were in charge of what had become essentially a one-party state, the National Party having in effect ceased to exist. In August 2004, its leader announced he was joining the ruling ANC and advised his followers to do the same, explaining that "the real debate about the future of the country is within the ANC and not outside."[46] Absent an effective opposition party, the system of checks and balances in South Africa was breaking down. The upshot was increased massive political corruption and the failure to effectively deal with society's woes—the world's highest crime and AIDS rates, social inequality, a struggling economy (made all the worse by climate change)—even while South Africa was preparing to showcase the 2010 World Cup games, the first such awarded to an African nation.

Recommended Readings

Sub-Saharan Africa

Bayart, Jean François, and Stephen Ellis. *The Criminalization of the State in Africa.* London: Oxford University Press, 1999.
 A critical look at one of Africa's problems.
Gourevitch, Philip. *We Wish to Inform You That Tomorrow We Will Be Killed with Our Families: Stories from Rwanda.* New York: Farrar, Straus and Giroux, 1998.
 A reporter's account of the genocide in Rwanda.
Kapuscinski, Ryszard. *"The Shadow of the Sun": Africa, a Mosaic of Mystery and Sorrow.* New York: Knopf, 2001.
 The reminiscences of a veteran Polish journalist who covered Africa from the beginning of the independence movement until the end of the twentieth century.
Leys, Colin. *Underdevelopment in Kenya: The Political Economy of Neo-Colonialism.* Berkeley: University of California Press, 1975.
Mazrui, Ali A. *Africa's International Relations: The Diplomacy of Dependency and Change.* London: Heinemann, 1977.
 By a noted specialist who presents his case from the Africans' viewpoint.
Neuberger, Ralph Benyamin. *National Self-Determination in Postcolonial Africa.* Boulder: Lynne Rienner Publishers, 1986.
 An analysis of the impact of the colonial experience on postcolonial African nationalism and secession.
Soyinka, Wole. *The Open Sore of a Continent: A Personal Narrative of the Nigerian Crisis.* New York: Oxford University Press, 1996.
 By the Nigerian Nobel laureate for literature.

South Africa

Boraine, Alex. *A Country Unmasked: Inside South Africa's Truth and Reconciliation Commission.* New York: Oxford University Press, 2001.
 By the former president of the Methodist Church of South Africa and anti-apartheid activist who served as deputy chair of the commission.
Breytenbach, Breyten. *The True Confessions of an Albino Terrorist.* New York: Farrar, Straus and Giroux, 1984.
 An autobiographical account by a poet from a well-known Afrikaner family who became a revolutionary activist.
Lelyveld, Joseph. *Move Your Shadow: South Africa, Black and White.* New York: Times Books, 1985.
 A *New York Times* reporter explains the racial realities of South Africa.
Malan, Rian. *My Traitor's Heart: A South African Exile Returns to Face His Country, His Tribe, and His Conscience.* New York: Atlantic Monthly Press, 1990.
Mandela, Nelson. *The Struggle Is My Life.* New York: Pathfinder Press, 1986.
 A collection of Mandela's speeches and writings.
———. *The Long Walk to Freedom: The Autobiography of Nelson Mandela.* Boston: Little, Brown, 1995.
Shea, Dorothy. *The South African Truth Commission: The Politics of Reconciliation.* Washington, D.C.: United States Institute of Peace, 2000.
Thompson, Leonard. *The Political Mythology of Apartheid.* New Haven, Conn.: Yale University Press, 1985.
 An account of the origins of, and a justification for, apartheid.

Woods, Donald. *Biko.* New York: Paddington Press, 1978.
A white South African's sympathetic account of the anti-apartheid struggle, focusing on Steve Biko, founder of the black consciousness movement, who died in police custody in 1977.

Notes

1. *The World Bank Atlas, 1985* (Washington, D.C.: World Bank, 1985).
2. Cited in Arthur Agwuncha Nwankwo and Samuel Udochukwu Ifejika, *Biafra: The Making of a Nation* (New York: Praeger, 1970), p. 11.
3. The most notable exceptions include such rulers as Léopold Senghor of Senegal, Félix Houphouët-Boigny of the Ivory Coast, Jomo Kenyatta of Kenya, Julius Nyerere of Tanzania, Kenneth Kaunda of Zambia, Sekou Touré of Guinea, and Seretse Khama of Botswana—all of whom remained in power for fifteen years or more.
4. Reuters, "Ghana's Opposition Ahead in Early Election Returns," *New York Times*, December 8, 2000.
5. Moyibi Amoda, "Background to the Conflict: A Summary of Nigeria's Political History from 1919 to 1964," in Joseph Okpaku, ed., *Nigeria: Dilemma of Nationhood: An African Analysis of the Biafran Conflict* (New York: Third Press, 1972), p. 59.
6. "Proclamation of the Republic of Biafra," Enugu, May 30, 1967, in Nwankwo and Ifejika, *Biafra,* pp. 336–340.
7. David Lamb, *The Africans* (New York: Random House, 1982), p. 309.
8. Kwame Nkrumah, *Neo-Colonialism: The Last Stage of Imperialism* (New York: International Publishers, 1966), introduction.
9. Roland Oliver and Anthony Atmore, *Africa Since 1800* (New York: Cambridge University Press, 1981), p. 330.
10. World Bank, *Sub-Saharan Africa: From Crisis to Sustainable Growth: A Long-Term Perspective Study* (Washington, D.C.: World Bank, 1989). All data are from this source.
11. The figures are for all "reporting countries," which excluded the Soviet Union and most of its bloc—the inclusion of which, however, would not appreciably change the figures. See World Bank, *World Development Report, 1989* (Washington, D.C.: World Bank, 1989), p. 165.
12. Cited in "Democracy in Africa," *The Economist*, February 22, 1992, p. 21.
13. Cited in "Under Slow Notice to Quit," *The Economist*, July 6, 1991, p. 43.
14. Interview with the dissident journalist Charles Gnaleko from Ivory Coast, "Pressefreiheit gibt es nur in drei von 55 Staaten," *Frankfurter Rundschau*, April 13, 2000, p. 11.
15. Reinhard Muller, "Die Gruppe ist wichtiger: Die afrikanische Charta der Menschenrechte," *Frankfurter Allgemeine Zeitung*, May 24, 2000.
16. "Angola Moves to Put Aside the Devastation of War," *US News and World Report*, May 13, 1991, p. 50. During the sixteen-year war, Moscow had poured in 1,100 advisors, 50,000 Cuban troops, and between $500 million and $1 billion annually to prop up the leftist government; the United States provided at least $60 million per year to support Savimbi's guerrillas. Christopher Ogden, "Ending Angola's Agony," *Time*, June 3, 1991, p. 22.
17. World Bank, *World Development Report, 1992* (Washington, D.C.: World Bank, 1992), pp. 211, 218.
18. Sudan had one of the highest birthrates in the world; the CIA estimate for 2004 was 2.64 percent per year; CIA, *World Fact Book* (Washington, D.C.: CIA, 2004).

19. From 1987 to 1989, 2,500 Fur and 500 Arabs died in clashes. Samantha Power, "Dying in Darfur," *The New Yorker*, August 30, 2004, p. 61.

20. Ibid., p. 68.

21. Philip Gourevitch, "The Poisoned Country," *New York Review of Books*, June 6, 1996, pp. 58–60.

22. "Judging Genocide," *The Economist*, June 14, 2001.

23. "Laurent Kabila," *The Economist*, January 18, 2001.

24. Ibid.

25. Karl Vick, "Congo Looks for Leadership," *Washington Post*, October 30, 2000, pp. A1, A22.

26. Douglas Farah, "Islamic Law Splits Nigeria," *Washington Post*, August 31, 2000, pp. A24, A28.

27. Samora Machel of Mozambique and Julius Nyerere of Tanzania, cited in Doris Lessing, "The Jewel of Africa," *New York Review of Books*, April 10, 2003, p. 6.

28. "Poorer and Angrier," *The Economist*, August 15, 1998; Simon Robinson, "Power to the Mob," *Time*, May 1, 2000, pp. 42–46.

29. Samantha Powers, "How to Kill a Country," *The Atlantic*, December 2003, pp. 86–100.

30. Craig Timberg, "Inside Mugabe's Violent Crackdown," *Washington Post*, July 5, 2008, A1.

31. "Human Rights Watch Report 2000," letter to Kofi Annan, November 29, 2000; Udo Ulfkotte, "Kurzsichtigkeit ist die Amme der Gewalt," *Frankfurter Allgemeine Zeitung*, May 20, 2000, p. 1.

32. John Lee Anderson, "After the Warlords," *The New Yorker*, March 27, 2006, p. 64.

33. UN figures. Marion Aberle, "Sog des Verderbens," *Frankfurter Allgemeine Zeitung*, July 8, 2000. See also Brigitte Schwartz, "Fluch der Jungen," *Der Spiegel*, July 3, 2000. In contrast, North America and Europe combined had less than 1 percent of those infected.

34. In the late 1680s, French Calvinists, the so-called Huguenots, left France after their government revoked in 1685 the Edict of Nantes of 1598, a decree of religious toleration. The Huguenots were shortly absorbed into the Dutch Afrikaner community.

35. C. F. J. Muller, ed., *Five Hundred Years: A History of South Africa* (Pretoria: Academia, 1969), pp. 166–167.

36. David Lamb, *The Africans* (New York: Random House, 1982), pp. 320–321.

37. This and other statements by Mandela later in the chapter are from his defense from the dock in Pretoria Supreme Court, April 20, 1964, cited in *Nelson Mandela: The Struggle Is My Life* (New York: Pathfinder Press, 1986), pp. 161–181.

38. The Nobel Peace Prize committee acknowledged the peaceful nature of the ANC when in 1960 it awarded its medal to Chief Albert J. Luthuli, the ANC's president since 1952.

39. Biko, cited in Donald Woods, *Biko* (New York: Paddington Press, 1978), p. 97.

40. Rian Malan, *My Traitor's Heart: A South African Exile Returns to Face His Country, His Tribe, and His Conscience* (New York: Atlantic Monthly Press, 1990), p. 333. For black-on-black violence, see pp. 323–334.

41. World Bank, *World Development Report, 1989* (Washington, D.C.: World Bank, 1989), pp. 165, 167, and 179, has the following figures: The percentage of average annual growth rate, 1965–1987, stood at a mere 0.6 percent; the average rate of inflation, 1980–1987, was 13.8 percent. During 1980–1987, there was a decline in average annual growth rate in industry and manufacturing of –0.1 and –0.5, respectively. Gross domestic investment, 1980–1987, declined by 7.3 percent.

42. Peter Honey, "De Klerk Sworn in, Promises 'Totally Changed' S. Africa," *Baltimore Sun*, September 21, 1989.

43. "Mandela's Address: 'Glory and Hope,'" *New York Times*, May 11, 1994, p. A8.

44. Tina Rosenberg, "Recovering from Apartheid," *The New Yorker*, November 18, 1996, pp. 86–95.

45. Terry Leonard, "Mandela Has a Legacy of Peace," Associated Press, June 1, 1999.

46. Cited in "The Party of Apartheid Departs," *The Economist*, August 14, 2004, p. 44.

13 Latin America

Latin America embraces the thirteen countries of the South American continent, Mexico, the six countries that make up Central America, and the islands that dot the Caribbean Sea. Latin America is part of the Third World and shares many of its features: economic underdevelopment, massive poverty, high population growth rates, widespread illiteracy, political instability, recurrent military coups, dictatorial regimes, intervention by outside powers, and fervent nationalistic pride. A wide range of economic development exists, however, within Latin America. For example, several large nations such as Mexico, Brazil, and Argentina have sustained impressive industrial growth and attained GNP levels that may qualify them as middle-income nations.

The Colonial Heritage

Unlike most other parts of the Third World, the nations of Latin America are not newly independent states struggling to meet the challenges of nation-building. On the contrary, most had won their independence from Spain early in the nineteenth century and had by 1945 experienced more than a century of nationhood.

Although Latin America's colonial experience lies in the distant past, that history still conditions the present, much as other Third World nations are conditioned by their more recent colonial past. The legacy of Spanish rule has persisted over the centuries and is still embodied in the culture and social fabric. The countries inherited from their Spanish colonial experience complex multiracial societies with pronounced social cleavages between a traditional aristocracy and the underprivileged lower classes. The prosperous and privileged elite, mainly white descendants of the European conquerors later joined by newer immigrants from Europe, controlled the levers of economic, political, and military power and thoroughly dominated the remainder of the population, consisting mainly of *mestizos* (racially mixed peoples), native Indians, and descendants of African slaves.

The great gulf between the privileged class, who may be thought of as an oligarchy, and the dispossessed lower classes is best seen in the landholding patterns. Nowhere in the world was the disparity in landownership as great. Traditionally, over two-thirds of the agricultural land was owned by only 1 percent of the population. The *latifundios*, huge estates owned by the elite, were so large—often more than 1,000 acres—that they were not fully cultivated; as a result, much of that land remained fallow. A 1966 study, for example, revealed that in Chile and Peru, 82 percent of the agricultural land was *latifundio* and that the average size of the *latifundio* was well over 500 times larger than the *minifundios*, the small parcels of land held by most farmers.[1] *Minifundios* were often too small to provide subsistence even for small families. In Ecuador and Guatemala, for example, nine out of ten farms were too small to feed the owners' families. Moreover, in many Latin American countries the majority of the rural population owned no land; they were peons whose labor was exploited by the owners of the *latifundios*. Even after years of sporadic land reform efforts, the imbalance remained. Several Latin American countries (such as Mexico and Chile) enacted land reform programs, but they were seldom fully implemented; consequently, very little agricultural land was redistributed.

Many of Latin America's persistent economic problems stem from this inequity of landownership and its inherent inefficiencies. The wastefulness of the *latifundio* was a major cause of the failure of Latin American agriculture to meet the food needs of its people. Consequently, Latin America imported large amounts of foodstuffs, and the high cost of such imports had a baleful effect on the economies of the region. Moreover, the depressed state of agriculture and the impoverishment of the rural population militated against industrial development because the majority of the people were too impoverished to be consumers of manufactured products.

"Yanqui Imperialism"

The colonial heritage is but one major outside influence on the economic and political life of Latin America. Another one is the "colossus of the north," the United States. Since the 1820s, the United States began to cast its long shadow over its neighbors to the south. In many ways, the role played by the United States was analogous to the role the European colonial powers played in other parts of the Third World. Whereas the nationalism of Asian and African countries was directed against their former European colonial masters, nationalism in Latin America characteristically focused on "Yanqui imperialism," an emotive term referring to the pattern of US (Yankee) domination and interference in Latin America.

With the Monroe Doctrine of 1823, the United States claimed for itself a special role in the Western Hemisphere as the protector of the weaker countries to the south. In the 1890s, Washington extended its claim (notably with the Roosevelt Corollary of 1904) by which it asserted the right of direct intervention in Latin America. Washington began to prop up client governments and send the Marines to protect US investments. Inevitably, this intervention produced fear and resentment at Yanqui imperialism. The strains in US–Latin American relations were somewhat ameliorated, however, by President Franklin Roosevelt's "good neighbor" policy of 1933. This did not mean, however, that the United States rejected gunboat diplomacy; instead it would employ it only as a last resort.

After the war, Washington sought to strengthen its bonds with Latin American countries by plying them with military and economic aid, taking the lead in forming an organization for regional collective security, and creating bilateral defense agreements. Washington's increasing preoccupation with the Cold War gave its hemispheric relations a distinct anti-Communist ideological cast. It pressured Latin American governments to cut ties with the Soviet Union and to outlaw local Communist parties, and it altered US aid programs to give greater priority to bolstering the armies than to economic development.

President John Kennedy's ambitious 1961 Alliance for Progress program had two sides to it. The program was meant to take the steam out of leftist movements across Latin America by pledging $20 billion over ten years for economic investments. It also called for the establishment of democratic governments. Yet in the same breath it provided for increased military and police assistance, two of the pillars propping up right-wing Latin American dictatorships. Kennedy announced the Alliance for Progress in March 1961, during the final stages of preparation for the invasion of Fidel Castro's Cuba, a manifestation of gunboat diplomacy triumphing over the "good neighbor" policy.

The Alliance for Progress produced increased financial dependency and indebtedness among Latin American countries and caused confusion over priorities, for example, whether to focus on industrial projects, bolster the military to suppress leftist rebels, initiate social reform, or administer relief for the poverty-stricken.

Corporate US business interests added to US influence in Latin America. Businesses invested heavily, buying Latin American land, mines, and oil fields; establishing industries to take advantage of the cheap labor; and selling its manufactured products—automobiles, machinery, and weapons. In Brazil, for example, in the 1960s, thirty-one of the fifty-five largest business firms were owned by foreigners, mainly from the United States. In the 1970s, eight of the ten largest firms and 50 percent of the banks in Argentina were foreign-owned.[2] US business interests assumed that, as in the past, the US flag followed the dollar, and they lobbied for and expected Washington to protect their investments. Business interests usually dovetailed with Washington's ideological and strategic goals insofar as both gave priority to the maintenance of political stability and support to military strongmen—by US troops if necessary.

Economic and Political Patterns

After World War II, industrialization became an obsession for many Latin American countries, and the postwar industrial progress of several of the larger countries was indeed impressive. Governments began playing an important role in this endeavor, investing in heavy industry and erecting high import tariffs. Argentina particularly exhibited a strong economic nationalism aimed at ending foreign dependency. Industrial progress was, however, limited to only a few countries (Argentina, Brazil, and Mexico accounted for 80 percent of Latin America's industrial output in the late 1960s) and to just a few cities in those countries, such as Buenos Aires, São Paulo, and Mexico City.

Although industrial growth did produce higher GNP figures and contributed to a modest increase in the standard of living, it also produced frustration as it failed to meet expectations. It contributed to the growth of the middle class and an urban working class, both of which sought a larger share of the nations' wealth and a larger role in the political process. The emerging middle class, which found political expression through political parties, provided support for democratic movements. It remained, however, generally too weak politically to challenge the traditional landowning elite.

The new urban working class grew in size but remained largely impoverished. It sought to advance its cause for higher wages through both trade unions and political parties. The growing radicalism of organized labor, however, aroused fears of the middle class and caused it to side with the more conservative elements: the oligarchy and the military. The attempt to establish democratic governments was hampered by the frailties of the middle class, the entrenchment of the oligarchy, the lack of political involvement of the impoverished rural masses, and the potential radicalism of the growing labor class.

Military intervention in politics has a long history in Latin America. Since World War II, there have been scores of military coups, and in one short span (1962–1964) eight countries fell victim to military takeovers. The military, with few foreign wars to fight, assumed a domestic role as the guardian of the state. Officers, traditionally nationalistic and conservative, could be counted on to defend the status quo and maintain order. Military rule was reinforced by still another enduring colonial legacy: the rule by *caudillos*, charismatic strongmen with their cults of personality, such as Juan Perón in Argentina, Augusto Pinochet in Chile, Rafael Trujillo in the Dominican Republic, and Fidel Castro in Cuba. *Caudillos* first appeared in the early nineteenth century during the wars for independence. Their power was extraconstitutional, that is, outside the law and thus unchecked by law.

South America: Oscillation Between Military and Civilian Rule

The history of South America and its transformation during the twentieth century provides many examples of dictatorship, suppression, military domination, and nascent democracies.

Argentina

Postwar Argentina went through four distinct political phases: a decade of dictatorship under Juan Perón (1946–1955), a decade-long—largely unsuccessful—attempt to establish democratic governments (1955–1965), seventeen years of military dictatorship and the brief return of Perón (1965–1982), and a restoration of a semblance of democracy in 1983.

The rule of Juan Perón was distinctive, for it simultaneously contained elements of populism, dictatorship, capitalism, and national socialism. Perón, a former army officer, was elected to the presidency of Argentina in 1946 largely on the strength of votes from the working class, whose support he had cultivated in his previous post as labor minister. His nationalistic policies aimed at ridding Argentina of foreign domination and attaining self-sufficiency were initially successful, and as a result his popularity soared. He bought out foreign businesses, created a government board for marketing agricultural produce, subsidized industrial development, extended social services, expanded education, and strengthened labor's rights. All the while he took steps to increase greatly his personal power by impeaching the supreme court, enacting a new constitution that broadened his powers, and purchasing the support of the army by vastly increasing the military budget. He also benefited from the immense popularity of his young, beautiful wife, Eva Perón, who had at her disposal a large budget for building hospitals and schools and dispensing food and clothing to the needy.

Perón's economic program, however, began to sputter by 1950, and within a year Argentina was plunged into an economic crisis marked by falling agricultural and industrial production, wage reductions, worker layoffs, and runaway inflation. In response to protests, Perón became more dictatorial, silencing the press and political opposition. Frustrated by his loss of public support (occasioned in part by the death of Eva in 1952) and the mounting economic chaos, Perón became more erratic. His feud with the Roman Catholic Church, fueled in part by its refusal to canonize Eva, caused him to lose additional support. The church also opposed his efforts to require the teaching in schools of his ideology, which deified the state with Perón as its head. Perón responded by censoring Catholic newspapers, arresting priests, and forbidding church processions. Pope Pius XII retaliated by excommunicating him. Finally, in September 1955, the military, too, abandoned him and forced him into exile in Spain.

South America

The army sought—with limited success—to purge Argentina of all Peronista influence. It outlawed the Peronista constitution and the party itself and arrested its leaders. The election of February 1958 brought to power Arturo Frondizi, who inherited a politically fragmented country with a struggling, inflation-ridden economy. Although Perón himself remained in exile for the next seventeen years, he continued to cast a shadow over Argentine politics, since his Peronista Party—although officially outlawed—remained a force to be reckoned with. Frondizi's economic policies, specifically his invitation to foreign interests to take control of the stalled oil industry, provoked a nationalistic outcry. His relations with the military were strained, and when he began to look to the left for support, army leaders, known as the *gorillas*, began to stir. In desperate need of support during the 1962 election, Frondizi legalized the Peronista Party. After the Peronistas won a smashing electoral victory, the army intervened. It seized power once again, arrested Frondizi, and again banned the Peronistas.

The parade of military rulers was broken in 1972 by none other than Perón, whose regenerated party once again won an electoral victory. He died in office in July 1974, leaving power in the hands of his third wife, Isabel, who just happened to be his vice-president. She proved unequal to the immense task of governing a troubled nation, and in 1976, the army again stepped in— for the sixth time since 1930.

The new regime, headed by General Jorge Rafael Videla, was the most ruthless in Argentine history. Videla suspended congress, the courts, political parties, and labor unions and vested all power in a nine-man military commission. The army engaged in a witch hunt against any subversives and critics. Only several hundred of those killed were leftist guerrillas; the vast majority were peaceful activists. "We will kill all the subversives," the military governor of Buenos Aires declared, and after that the collaborators, sympathizers, those who were neutral, and, finally, the merely timid. The military murdered up to 30,000; many of them were tortured and some simply "disappeared," including victims who were pushed out of airplanes over the Atlantic Ocean. Beginning in April 1977, mothers of those who had disappeared began to protest at the Plaza de Mayo in the center of Buenos Aires. (At least three of the mothers themselves eventually disappeared.)

In 1982, the military took Argentina to war in an attempt to draw people's attention away from their economic woes and the "dirty war." The generals dusted off Argentina's historic claim to a group of islands, the Malvinas, a British possession better known as the Falkland Islands, some 300 miles off Argentina's coast. When Argentina's army and navy suffered a costly and decisive defeat at the hands of the British, the military junta was further discredited. It was forced to call elections and relinquish power to a civilian government in October 1983.

Argentina's new president, Raul Alfonsín, head of the Radical Party, was the first to defeat the Peronistas in an open election, and his election was considered a mandate to restore order and civility. Cautiously, Alfonsín set in motion criminal proceedings against his military predecessors. He put junta leaders on trial, and those convicted of various crimes committed in the "dirty war" were sentenced to long jail terms. Alfonsín also succeeded in retiring fifty generals. But a series of barrack revolts led to laws ending further prosecutions. Congress enacted a new law that granted the accused the right to argue that they only had been "obeying orders," a spurious defense used, unsuccessfully, by

Nazi war criminals at the Nuremberg trials. The next president, Carlos Menem, in what he called an "act of reconciliation," granted the generals a blanket amnesty and eventually, in October 1989, a blanket pardon. With a stroke of the pen he sought to undo any and all attempts to hold the military accountable for its crimes. Among those pardoned was the chief architect of the "dirty war," General Videla himself, who had been sentenced to life in prison.

But the issue would not go away. In June 1998, the courts overturned Menem's pardon, ruling that the pardons did not extend to officers such as Videla, who—among other crimes—had been charged with the abduction of children and the murder of their mothers. Survivors of the "dirty war"— mainly mothers and wives of the disappeared—continued through the years to demand justice as they sought to reclaim children who were stolen from them over thirty years earlier and then adopted by couples with connections to the military.[3]

Alfonsín had to face another challenge, an economy saddled with one of the world's highest rates of inflation and largest debts. At the end of Alfonsín's presidency in 1989, inflation had risen to 7,000 percent annually—and the debt crisis remained unresolved. Moreover, between 1976 and 1989, the income per person shrank more than 1 percent each year.[4]

A temporary economic turnaround came under Menem, who, following the advice of the International Monetary Fund, proceeded to peg the Argentine peso to the US dollar—backed by the country's hard-currency reserves—and sell off government property, such as the telephone system, airlines, railroads, electricity, water system, and even pensions. At the same time, Menem opened the Argentine economy to international investors. In return, the IMF provided new credits to help Argentina restructure its massive foreign debt. Between 1991 and 1997, the economy grew at an average rate of 6.1 percent, the highest in the region. Argentina became the poster child for globalization. Its economy, with IMF help, appeared to be on the right track.

The debt restructuring, however, had little effect because foreign debt increased to a whopping $155 billion in 1998. At the same time, public debt rose steadily. Entry into the global economy produced a raft of bankruptcies of Argentine companies that could not compete with foreigners, leading to a rising tide of unemployment. Although Menem had privatized the pension system, the state still had obligations to its remaining pensioners as well as the unemployed. But the state, hampered by an inefficient system of tax collection, eventually ran out of money. The peso began a precipitous drop in 2001, as it was no longer backed by hard currency reserves and as the government withdrew money from banks. By February 2002, the peso had lost half of its value against the dollar. The middle class lost much of its savings, unable to recover them from banks that did not have the means to fulfill obligations to depositors. Income per person dropped from $7,000 to $3,500 and unemployment rose to 25 percent. Among the consequences were a higher crime rate, the spread of *villas miserias* (shantytowns), higher divorce rates, and hunger. By February 2003, 58 percent of the population, according to the government's own figures, was designated as poor.[5] All this resulted in the biggest default on foreign debt in history.

Argentina, which in 1913 had ranked among the ten richest nations—ahead of France and Germany—had hit rock bottom. It was an economic calamity without parallel, one of the steepest declines in recent history.

Brazil

Brazil stands out among the nations of South America both because of its Portuguese (rather than Spanish) background and because of its vast natural resources and immense size, covering one-third of the continent and with a population, in 1990, of 150 million. Ever since Portugal formally accepted Brazil's independence in 1825, it has been a nation looking to the future.

Brazil experimented with democracy, but when democratically elected governments proved unable to cope with economic decline or attempted radical reforms, they gave way to military leaders. In the first decade after World War II, successive democratically elected presidents wrestled with inflation fueled by heavy government borrowing. A case in point was the administration of Juscelino Kubitschek, who aggressively pursued the goal of industrialization that depended on lavish government spending. His most extravagant project was the founding of a spectacular new capital city, Brasília, located in the interior of the country. Brasília—a proud symbol of the nation's future—was designed to spur the development of the interior region.

Kubitschek's successors continued to grapple with the economy, but, as they moved left of center, they raised hackles within Brazil's military and in Washington. João Goulart proposed extensive land reform, election reform to enfranchise the nation's illiterate (40 percent of the population), and tax reform to increase government revenues. In 1964, he ordered the expropriation of some of the nation's largest estates. This earned him the support of the peasantry and the working class but incurred the wrath of the landowning elite, the middle class, and the military. Goulart even antagonized Washington when he proclaimed a neutralist foreign policy, continued diplomatic relations with the Soviet Union (which his immediate predecessor had reestablished), legalized the Brazilian Communist Party, and began to woo that party's support. Goulart's free-spending policies, like those of Kubitschek, caused inflation, and this, in addition to Goulart's move to the left, eroded his support among the middle class. Army leaders, once they secured support from US president Lyndon Johnson, forced his resignation in April 1964. On the next day, Johnson extended his recognition and good wishes to the new military dictatorship.

This time the generals came to stay for twenty years. Blaming free-spending civilian politicians for Brazil's ills, they silenced all opponents and forced an austerity program on the nation. They banned the Communist Party and carried out mass arrests of Communists and suspected Communists. They then issued a series of "institutional acts" that incrementally restricted the powers of the congress, arrogated greater powers to the presidency, disenfranchised political parties, and sought to crush the labor unions.

The Brazilian economy responded to the generals' stringent austerity program. Indeed, during the twenty years of military rule, Brazil realized its highest economic growth rates. In 1966, Brazil's annual rate of growth of GNP was 4 percent; it rose steadily and reached 10 percent in the early 1970s. The growth of agricultural and industrial production made possible a favorable balance of trade for the first time since World War II. But economic success could not be sustained, partly because of the severe impact of the oil crises of the 1970s and partly because of the gigantic foreign debt the military leaders ran up. In addition, the growth of the GNP did not produce a higher standard of living for the majority of Brazilians. Industrial growth was tied to keeping wages low. All the while the rise in the cost of living exceeded the growth in wages. In addition, the military undertook no land reform and did nothing to improve the lot of the rural poor.

By the late 1980s, military rule gave way to free elections. Brazil's first such election in twenty-nine years, in March 1989, was won by Fernando Collor de Mello, a young, winsome, articulate, conservative politician who defeated the candidate of the left, Luiz Ignacio da Silva. Collor de Mello promised democratic reform and economic prosperity, but what he brought to Brazil, instead, was the largest scale of personal corruption the country had ever witnessed. In 1992, Collor de Mello was forced to resign.

The rule of the Brazilian military had been moderate by South American standards. The generals executed 200 people (as compared with up to 30,000 in Argentina) and forced hundreds into exile. It took more than a decade, but in 1995, the government of Fernando Henrique Cardoso finally offered compensation for the relatives of the victims.

In October 2003, Brazilian politics witnessed a shift to the left. Luiz Ignacio da Silva—commonly known as Lula—in his fourth bid for the presidency, won by a wide margin a runoff election. Lula's rise to power was literally from rags to riches. One of twenty-two children of an illiterate farmworker, he rose from shoeshine boy to the leader of São Paulo's militant car workers' union. He then organized the Workers' Party, Latin America's largest left-wing party.

Lula inherited an economy in deep trouble. In 2003, the *real*, Brazil's currency, had lost 40 percent of its value, and as a consequence the public debt spiraled upward. The international financial community feared that Brazil would follow Argentina and default on its foreign debt. Immediately after the election, however, Lula put on a tie and suit and stepped back from his previous pledge to renege on Brazil's heavy debt. He had already brought under control the radicals in his party and had made an alliance with the center-right Liberal Party. He agreed to work with the IMF to try to bring the debt under control, reminding the Brazilians that "there is no miraculous solution for such a huge social debt."[6]

Chile

Chile presents still another variation on the theme of oscillation between civilian and military governments. Chile, however, did not succumb to military rule until 1973. Chileans were proud that their army stayed out of politics. Between 1945 and 1973, Chile was the most orderly and democratic country in Latin America, its army exceptionally apolitical. Chile's fate was also to stand out as the most flagrant example of US interference in South America.

Nowhere in South America were US business interests more substantial than in Chile. Early in the twentieth century, Chile became the main source of copper for the United States, and its copper mines and many of its industries were owned by US firms. Thus, when Chilean politics moved to the left, it was not only conservative elements in Chile that were alarmed. Washington would not sit still as another Latin American country, especially one as economically important as Chile, edged closer to Communism.

Chile had received generous amounts of US Alliance for Progress loans to finance industrial expansion but, as a side effect, it also increased the nation's indebtedness. In the 1960s, Washington favored moderate conservative governments in Chile, such as that under Eduardo Frei, the head of the Christian Democratic Party. The Chilean elite, however, considered Frei's gradualist reforms—education initiatives to reduce illiteracy, expansion of social services, and a modest agrarian program—as too radical, while the working class and the parties on the left saw them as too modest. Only the middle class and Washington seemed happy with Frei.

The polarization of Chilean politics was evident in the 1970 election. The Marxist Salvador Allende, the candidate of a leftist coalition, Popular Unity, squeaked by with a narrow victory and became the world's first freely elected Marxist head of state. Allende, whose cabinet consisted mainly of socialists and Communists, called for a peaceful transition to socialism. To that end, he nationalized US and Chilean copper and nitrate companies and banks, extended the land reform begun by Frei, and placed a ceiling on prices while raising workers' wages. These measures were immensely popular with the majority of people in Chile, but they alarmed Allende's opponents, as well as the Nixon administration in Washington.

Chile was already in an economic depression when Allende took office. By the second year of his term, the economy was in a tailspin, with inflation running out of control. Allende's policies contributed to these problems, but the major blow to the Chilean economy was a drastic drop in the international price of copper. By mid-1972, Allende's base of support had dwindled to little more than the working class and the poor. Conservative elements—notably the

Chilean president Salvador Allende, who died in the presidential palace during the September 1973 coup. *(Organization of American States)*

General Augusto Pinochet, who led the military coup against Allende in 1973 and remained in power in Chile afterward. *(Organization of American States)*

military—began to organize against Allende and carried out actions such as a crippling, nationwide truckers' strike—a measure secretly supported by CIA funds. The polarization of the nation became extreme, and a violent clash seemed imminent. Allende and his Communist supporters began arming workers while the army began plotting a coup. In September 1973, the air force bombed the presidential palace, where Allende committed suicide as the army closed in on him.

The United States was deeply involved in Chilean politics, long before Allende's overthrow. In 1970, it had sought to prevent Allende from coming to power, and having failed that, it participated in the efforts to destabilize his government. Nixon's national security advisor, Henry Kissinger, regarded Allende as a threat to the entire region, famously declaring later that "I don't see why we have to let a country go Marxist just because its people are irresponsible."[7]

The Nixon administration funneled some $8 million through the CIA to Allende's opponents and cut off all loans, economic aid, and private investments to Chile. Speculation was rife of direct US involvement in the military coup, but Washington admitted nothing and kept its relevant documents classified until the late 1990s, when the Clinton administration declassified evidence supporting such speculation.[8] Moreover, a number of the Chilean military officers who led the coup—like many others from Latin American countries—had received training at the School for the Americas, a facility in Panama established by the US Army to train Latin American officers.

The new military government, headed by General Augusto Pinochet, swiftly carried out a relentless campaign against leftists and anyone suspected of having been associated with Allende. It crammed the jails, and initially even a huge stadium, with political prisoners, killing 3,000 of them and, over the years, at least 1,000 others. It formed a "Caravan of Death," with soldiers traveling throughout the country to carry out summary executions. It was under Pinochet that Latin America experienced the first cases of people simply "disappearing," a practice that subsequently spread through the region. Pinochet was the guiding force of Operation Condor, an effort on the part of military strongmen in six participating countries (Chile, Argentina, Brazil, Uruguay, Paraguay, and Bolivia) to track down opponents, not only in Latin America but also in Europe and the United States. In September 1976, Chilean operatives assassinated the former foreign minister, Orlando Letelier, in the streets of Washington. Kissinger knew of Operation Condor and, in fact, supported the campaign against leftist Chilean exiles in Argentina. He told the Argentine foreign minister that it should act "quickly" and then "get back quickly to normal procedure."[9]

Pinochet invited US copper companies back in, halted the land reform program, broke up labor unions, banned all leftist parties, and dissolved congress. All the while, Pinochet continued to enjoy the support of the United States, which preferred the secure climate for investment and the anti-Communist partnership that Pinochet provided to the political instability his overthrow might bring.

In the late 1980s, despite the ban against antigovernment demonstrations, thousands of protesters went into the streets to demand change. Finally, in 1990, Pinochet relented by allowing a referendum on whether military rule should continue. In the first free election in twenty years, the people voted overwhelmingly to restore civilian rule. Pinochet, however, remained in command of the army by virtue of a clause in the constitution he had written. The constitution also made the armed forces the "guarantor of institutionality,"[10] meaning that they had the right to step in whenever they felt their interests were threatened.

Pinochet relinquished his command of the army in March 1998 but then became "senator for life," a position that granted him immunity from criminal charges for atrocities committed under his seventeen-year rule. He returned to international attention when he was arrested in London, in October 1998, at the request of Spain, which wanted him extradited to be tried on charges of human rights abuses against Spanish citizens in Chile. The eighty-three-year-old former dictator languished in London under house arrest for over a year until January 2000, when a team of British physicians found him too ill to stand trial, thus clearing the way for his return to Chile.

In August 2004, Chile's supreme court, by a vote of 9–8, ruled that Pinochet was not immune from prosecution. Before he was brought to trial, he died in December 2006 at the age of ninety-one. The government denied him a state funeral (a custom for former heads of state), nor did it declare a national day of mourning. As a former commander-in-chief of the armed forces, Pinochet did receive a military funeral, however.

Colonel Manuel Contreras, the former head of the secret police, the Department of National Intelligence, was sentenced in 1993 to prison for his role in the 1976 murder of Letelier. The court did not accept Contreras's defense that he had only followed Pinochet's orders. By the end of the 1990s, some twenty soldiers and police officers were convicted of crimes committed after 1978, after the worst excesses had already been committed.

Peru

Perhaps nowhere in South America were social and economic inequities as wide as in Peru. A small, wealthy elite kept the Peruvian masses—mainly of native Indian stock—in dismal poverty. About 80 percent of the land was owned by a mere 1 percent of landowners, and the richest owned over 1 million acres. Landless Peruvian peasants sporadically rose in revolt, seeking to grasp some of the largely unused *latifundios* of the elite, only to be crushed by the Peruvian army. Neither the early postwar military regime in Peru (1946–1956) nor the civilian administrations that followed attempted land reform. All the while, the country was seething with peasant unrest, and a rural-based Communist movement began to spread. In October 1968, President Fernando Belaunde's government was floundering amid economic chaos and corruption scandals, when the military interceded and replaced him with one of their own.

The new leadership, headed by Juan Velasco, unlike the military governments generally in the rest of Latin America, became an agent of reform. In quick order, it introduced state planning and modest social and economic reforms enforced by the army. Most noteworthy was land reform, which within seven years expropriated and redistributed some 25 million acres—about 72 percent of Peru's arable land. The government also undertook a program of land reclamation to increase agricultural output and meet the needs of the land-starved Indians. Velasco also nationalized foreign properties, including US-owned copper, petroleum, and sugar companies. Private enterprise remained legal, but industries were required to share profits with their workers. Although a modest increase in agricultural production resulted from the agrarian reforms, the economy slumped badly, especially after the 1973–1974 oil crisis. Still, the military rulers, despite their reformist efforts, failed to achieve either a fundamental social transformation or a significant improvement in the standard of living for most Peruvians.

By 1980, the generals stepped back and permitted civilian rule once again. Belaunde, whom the generals had ousted in 1968, won the election, but he was no more capable of resolving Peru's economic problems than he had been twelve years earlier. The July 1990 presidential election was won by an unlikely candidate, Alberto Fujimori, an inexperienced politician of Japanese ancestry. When Fujimori took office, Peru had not made a payment for two years on its $23 billion debt; the inflation rate was over 40 percent per month; and the central government was unable to govern outlying areas, where hostile guerrillas stalked the countryside. Fujimori first attacked the economic problem. Through stringent measures such as slashing government payrolls and subsidies and overhauling the tax system, he managed to break the inflationary cycle within six months.

The unorthodox Fujimori then formed an alliance with the military. In April 1992, he carried out a political coup, suspending the constitution, closing the legislative assembly, and assuming emergency executive powers. For this he was denounced not only by the unseated Peruvian politicians but also by governments throughout the hemisphere. But Fujimori's bold housecleaning measures were, at first, popular with most Peruvians, even though they cost the country much-needed foreign aid and thus crimped economic development.

Fujimori also won acclaim at home and abroad by winning a surprising victory in Peru's twelve-year war against the Sendero Luminoso, or "Shining Path," a Maoist-Marxist movement that had combined violent revolution with drug trafficking. His government arrested and sentenced to life in prison the leaders of Shining Path, including its charismatic founder, Abimael Guzman Reynoso, a former philosophy professor. The Shining Path had organized poverty-stricken peasants to protect them against brutality at the hands of the police and the military, with the aim of ultimately bringing down the government. The result was a civil war with extraordinary brutality on both sides. It caused an estimated $22 billion in damages and caused the death of 69,000 Peruvians, killed outright or simply "disappeared," mostly impoverished native Quechuas in the high Andes.[11] Fujimori's stunning victory against the revolutionaries, combined with a measure of economic progress, won him considerable popularity within Peru. He handily won reelection in 1994.

But success came at a price. Fujimori's austerity program benefited only small segments of the population—among them the financial sector and international investors. One of Fujimori's first tasks had been to meet Peru's financial obligations as spelled out by the IMF, one of the pillars that sustained his regime. Meanwhile, real wages fell by 10 percent and the majority of Peruvians—about two-thirds of them—remained mired in poverty.

Still, Fujimori continued to present himself as the champion of "true democracy" and the common man, but all along he was doing the army's bidding.[12] In July 1992, a military death squad operating under the direct orders of the commander-in-chief of the army, General Nicolas Hermoza—and ultimately under Fujimori's orders—abducted and murdered nine students and a professor at La Cantuta University. When the courts eventually convicted and sentenced twelve soldiers for the crime, Fujimori pushed through the pliant congress a blanket amnesty for those convicted of human rights crimes between May 1980 and June 1995.[13] The amnesty cemented the symbiotic relationship between the president and the armed forces.

In December 1996, yet another leftist organization resurfaced, Túpac Amaru (which took its name from the last Inca ruler whom the Spanish hanged in 1572 and a namesake whom the Spanish tortured to death in 1781). Earlier, Fujimori had claimed that Túpac Amaru had been defeated. But at a Christmas party hosted by the Japanese ambassador, the group took approximately 400 hostages. It demanded the release of its imprisoned comrades, many of whom had been engaged in acts of violence and had been sentenced by Peruvian military tribunals. The hostage crisis continued unresolved into April 1997, in part because the Japanese government insisted on a negotiated settlement. In the end, Peruvian commandos stormed the building, killing all Túpac Amaru members inside while losing one hostage and two commandos. For Fujimori, it was another feather in his cap.

In 1996, the Fujimori majority in congress reinterpreted the constitution, which restricted a president to two five-year terms, and granted him another term. Judges who questioned the legitimacy of a third term were dismissed; newspapers turned into apologists for the Fujimori regime. Editors who refused to fall into line felt the wrath of Vladimiro Montesinos, head of the National Intelligence Service, who controlled the army as well as death squads operating out of his headquarters, the "Little Pentagon." Montesinos was on the CIA payroll, despite the agency's knowledge that he and Fujimori had long been engaged in extortion, larceny, drug trafficking, torture, and murder.[14] Fujimori's critics were slandered or, worse yet, stripped of their citizenship, blackmailed, tortured, or disappeared.

In the election of April 2000, Fujimori faced a surprisingly strong contender in the person of Alejandro Toledo. Toledo, of Indian descent, was another political novice whose party, Perú Posible, promised a new dawn. Toledo came in a strong second, forcing a runoff election. Toledo refused to participate in the runoff unless it contained safeguards against rigging it. Fujimori refused to oblige him and went ahead with his third term, despite daily protest demonstrations by the Toledo-led opposition and criticism from neighboring countries, the Organization of American States, and the United States, which heretofore had supported Fujimori.

Fujimori's grip on the nation slipped in September 2000, when his right-hand man, Montesinos, was caught on videotape attempting to bribe an opposition politician. Ten days later, Montesinos fled, hoping to find political asylum abroad. Unable to do so, he returning to Peru and went into hiding. Two weeks later, in November 2000, Fujimori fled to Tokyo, from where he resigned by fax. The Peruvian congress would not let him resign; instead, it accused him of dereliction of duty and declared him morally unfit to govern. The Peruvian government then launched an investigation leading to charges against Fujimori and Montesinos—the running of death squads (such as the La Cantuta University murders), embezzlement, and extortion. Montesinos was eventually arrested and got his day in court, where he was found guilty and sentenced to twenty years in the Callo maximum-security prison, which, ironically, he and Fujimori had built.

Fujimori began his political career by identifying with the nation's poor. He had emphasized his own humble origins, even campaigning in the garb of the rural Indians. During his ten years in power, however, endemic poverty remained unchanged; during the 1990s, the national poverty rate hovered around 50 percent, and 41 percent of the people lived on $2 or less per day.[15] Montesinos and Fujimori, however, had no difficulty in making ends meet. Transparency International concluded that the two had been engaged in "unprecedented looting of the resources" of Peru. Montesinos siphoned off an estimated $2 billion; Fujimori escaped with perhaps $600 million.[16]

For five years, Fujimori lived in luxury in Tokyo beyond the reach of Peruvian law, a celebrity, particularly in right-wing circles. Japan granted him citizenship, ensuring that he would not be extradited. It was unwilling to hand over one of their own like any common criminal. Inexplicably, in November 2005, Fujimori returned to Peru, ostensibly to run for president again. Quite possibly, the Japanese government found him an international embarrassment. Interpol (the 187-member International Criminal Police Organization) had him on its most wanted list, and the Peruvian government repeatedly demanded his extradition—this during an emerging global trend to hold dictators accountable for their crimes. The honorable thing for the now sixty-seven year-old Fujimori—"the last samurai," as he called himself—was to return to Peru and face the consequences. In December 2007, in the first of four scheduled trials, Fujimori, who denied all charges, was sentenced to six years in prison. In April 2009, after a lengthy second trial—based in part on declassified US documents—Fujimori was sentenced to a prison term of twenty-five years for political murders his security forces had committed.

The Shift to the Left

In the late 1990s, the political pendulum in Latin America began to move to the left—from accommodating Washington to resisting. The driving force was Hugo Chávez of Venezuela. In February 1992, he and 200 other army officers launched a failed coup for which they spent two years in prison. After his arrest, Chávez was permitted to address the nation on television, in which he denounced the corrupt politicians. The speech set the stage for his 1998 run for the presidency as the candidate of the dispossessed, the vast majority of the population. He campaigned as the fervid champion of a "Bolivarian revolution," a return to the ideals of "the Liberator," Simón Bolívar—including the grand union of the Spanish-speaking countries of South America. Once in office, Chávez erected billboards with the image of Bolívar replete with his 1829 quote: "The United States seems destined by providence to plague the Americas with misery in the name of liberty."

Chávez was popular among the forgotten. Many of them lived out of sight and out of mind in the barrios populating the fringes of the capital city, Caracas. He lavished on them large sums of petrodollars to set up schools, soup kitchens, small cooperative businesses, and medical centers. As a young man, Chávez was influenced less by Marxism than by nineteenth-century Venezuelan populists. Born into poverty at a time when oil money made others extremely rich, he now focused on the redistribution of land and oil wealth. Oil was the linchpin of the Venezuelan economy, its sale making up 80 percent of Venezuelan exports, nearly 30 percent of the country's gross domestic product (GDP), and 50 percent of the state's revenue.

Chávez's revolution produced the inevitable confrontation with Venezuela's elites—the "rancid oligarchs," Chávez called them—shocked by a "participatory democracy" that excluded them from power for the first time in their lives. Chávez also established close personal ties with Cuba's aged dictator, Fidel Castro, and provided Cuba with oil in exchange for at least 10,000 Cuban medical personnel who went into barrios that had never before seen a doctor. In the process, the charismatic Chávez followed in the footsteps of South America's *caudillos*, constantly seeking to expand his powers—by controlling the media, packing the courts, and drawing up blacklists. Chávez remained popular, however, winning seven national elections. But when he sought in December 2007, by way of a referendum, to amend the constitution designed to pave the way for unlimited presidential terms, the country voted against it. Chávez "wants a blank check," one of his supporters said, "and that's impossible." Nonetheless, in March 2009, the persistent Chávez won a second such referendum, which paved the way for the relatively young, fifty-four-year-old strongman to cling to power far into future.

In April 2002, the George W. Bush administration played a role in the unsuccessful coup to oust Chávez, thus increasing tensions between Washington and Caracas. When Chávez, in September 2006, addressed the General Assembly of the United Nations, a day after Bush had done so, he remarked that "the devil came here yesterday, and it smells of sulfur still today."

Chávez found a number of imitators in South America, although none of them was willing to go as far. The best known was Evo Morales, the first indigenous president of Bolivia, a forty-six-year-old Amaya Indian and former *cocalero*, or coca grower. It had taken the native Indians more than four centuries to put an end to serfdom (only as recently as 1952), and it took them another half-century to put one of their own at the political helm.

Between the early 1990s and the December 2005 victory by Morales's party, Movement Toward Socialism, Bolivia, the poorest of South American countries, had followed the dictates of the so-called Washington Consensus (see Chapter 17), which demanded cuts in social spending in exchange for private foreign investments and the promise of prosperity. The spending cuts were made (thus bringing hyperinflation under control) and the foreigners came, but prosperity was elusive. Corruption was rampant, per capita economic growth was a paltry 0.5 percent per year, and half of all Bolivians made do on less than $2 per day. In response to the privatization of the economy, the holy grail of the Washington Consensus, Morales nationalized enterprises, notably oil and natural gas, which existed primarily for the benefit of foreigners.

Other newly elected South American presidents (eight in all by 2006, representing Brazil, Chile, Bolivia, Uruguay, Argentina, and Nicaragua) took a more moderate approach, although they, too, owed their positions to campaign promises that they would invest heavily in social programs to close the wide gap between rich and poor. Once more, Latin American countries had to find the proper mix between state planning and the free market.

Mexico

The roots of the problems Mexico faced at the end of the twentieth century date back to the political and economic consequences of the extraordinarily bloody revolution of 1910–1917, during which 1.5 million people—approximately 10 percent of the population—lost their lives. Not until the late 1920s did the country begin to enjoy a measure of stability. It was then that a new party, the Partido Revolucionario Institucional (the Institutional Revolutionary Party, or PRI), came to power and began to organize diverse groups in support of the state. It encouraged workers, peasants, bureaucrats, big-business executives, owners of small enterprises, and teachers to bargain with the party, which then became the arbiter between the various interest groups. To maintain power, the PRI skillfully formed political alliances, doled out patronage jobs, co-opted its opponents, occasionally carried out reforms within the party, controlled the media, and, when necessary, resorted to fraud and violent repression. Incumbent presidents usually chose their successors behind closed palace doors. The PRI-dominated Mexican governments produced a surface calm, but they did not address the underlying causes of social discontent that periodically resurfaced.

The revolution of 1910 had begun as a liberal challenge to the dictatorship of Porfirio Díaz, but it soon became more radical when the *campesinos* (the peasantry), under the slogan "Land and Liberty," led by Emiliano Zapata and Pancho Villa, demanded the redistribution of land. At the time, 96 percent of the rural households owned no land, and fewer than 850 families owned 97 percent of Mexico's arable land.[17] The 1917 Constitution promised a redistribution of land, but prior to the presidency of the populist Lázaro Cárdenas

(1934–1940), only about 10 percent of the rural population had benefited from land reform.

Cárdenas distributed more land than any other Mexican president. During his tenure, the campesinos' irrigated landholdings increased fourfold,[18] but even under Cárdenas land distribution came to a halt after 1937. When army generals complained that his populist reforms had gone too far, Cárdenas, in March 1938, shifted his focus of attack to "imperialist intervention," that is, foreign—US and European—corporations in control of sectors of the Mexican economy, notably oil. The time was ripe, he declared, for the nationalization of these companies. There was a massive outpouring of public support; millions of Mexicans contributed to a national indemnity fund to help pay off the $200 million the oil companies eventually received in compensation.[19]

One of the PRI's functions was to oversee the development of state capitalism, which gave Mexico decades of sustained growth. Between 1940 and 1960, manufacturing rose by 365 percent, steel production by 934 percent, motor vehicle production by 451 percent, and agricultural output by 218 percent; during the same period, the population increased by 78 percent. Per capita government expenditures increased fourfold.[20] Yet the gap between the rich and the poor grew after World War II. Mexico witnessed a potentially volatile mix of economic growth, raised expectations, growing social inequalities, and dissent.

The economic downturn of the late 1960s had severe social and political repercussions. On October 2, 1968, tens of thousands of demonstrators—mostly young students—congregated in Mexico City's Tlatelolco Plaza to protest police brutality, political corruption, and economic hardship. The army promptly put an end to this challenge to the PRI by fatally shooting at least 300 civilians. Ten days later, the Olympic Games began in Mexico City, the first such showcase in a developing country. As the torch was lit in Aztec Stadium, troops and tanks continued to be deployed beyond the view of television cameras.

The massacre did not solve the PRI's problems; instead it triggered a crisis of legitimacy for the party. During the 1970s and 1980s, the government conducted Mexico's own "dirty war" against opponents, many of whom traced their anger back to the massacre. For thirty years, the PRI denied that this, and other massacres, had taken place. Eventually, Mexico began to come to terms with its past. In February 2002, pictures of the Tlatelolco Square massacre appeared in newspapers, and the courts began to grapple with the issue but were hopelessly divided on how to deal with Luis Echeverría, the interior minister at the time. It had not been a case of genocide, the courts ruled; moreover, the statute of limitations had expired.

In 1970, when Echeverría became president, dissidents—among them students, reporters, guerrillas, and practitioners of "liberation theology"—sought to build grassroots social bases in the barrios and among the campesinos. Echeverría, under pressure to create more jobs, borrowed both time and money. To save jobs, the government bought bankrupt enterprises to keep them running and borrowed increasing amounts of foreign money—without the revenue to repay it. When Echeverría took office, the nation's foreign debt stood at $5 billion; by the time his successor, José López (1976–1982), took office, it had risen to $20 billion. López came to power in the midst of the oil boom of the 1970s, which made it possible for Mexico—sitting on top of vast oil reserves—to borrow still more money. During López's presidency, the public and private sectors borrowed another $60 billion. By August 1982, Mexico was unable to pay off its massive foreign debt, a condition that triggered a Latin American debt crisis.

In the early 1980s, elections in northern Mexico—free of the usual tampering by PRI functionaries—showed the weakness of the PRI, which lost several local races to the Partido Acción Nacional (National Action Party, or PAN), a center-right, business-based party. In the mid-1980s, an environmental protest movement emerged partly in response to Mexico City's horrendous air pollution. Then came the massive earthquake of September 1985, which buried more than 10,000 people. In its aftermath, Cuauthemoc Cárdenas (the son of the revered Lázaro Cárdenas) broke with the PRI and became the candidate of a center-left coalition, and in the 1988 presidential election, he challenged the PRI candidate, Carlos Salinas de Gortari. Cárdenas had a substantial following, but two days before the election two of his key aides were murdered (crimes that were never solved), and a few hours after the voting ended, the computer counting the votes crashed. When the computers came back online, Salinas had won the election with just over 50 percent of the vote. A few months later, the PRI destroyed the ballots.

By now, Mexico's economy was treading water during what became the country's worst recession in sixty years. Between 1980 and 1993, annual output had declined by an average of 0.5 percent. Mexico worked out agreements with multilateral international lending institutions (such as the World Bank and IMF) that gave it access to additional credits; simultaneously, it negotiated with Canada and the United States the terms of the North American Free Trade Agreement (NAFTA). Lazaro Cárdenas's "anti-imperialist" campaign of the 1930s was now but a dim memory.

The social price of admission into the minefields of the global economy was high. It forced Mexico to carry out deep structural adjustments to satisfy creditors—the elimination of tariffs, deregulation of the economy, privatization of state enterprises, and labor "flexibilization" (literally, making labor more flexible, more amenable to the demands of factory owners)—to increase productivity and international competitiveness. In short, workers were expected to work harder for lower wages. The state took steps to deny unions the right of free association and repeatedly used police and the army against them. With economic restructuring and flexibilization, the unions lost both economic and political power.

Chiapas

On January 1, 1994, Mexico faced yet another crisis, this time a rebellion in the state of Chiapas, in the southeastern corner, along the Guatemalan border. Campesinos, mostly Indians, rose in rebellion, organized into the Zapatista National Liberation Army in memory of Emiliano Zapata, one of the heroes of the 1910 revolution. They seized control of several cities and *latifundios*, which they turned into communal farms, and insisted that the land they worked had been granted to them by the 1917 Constitution.

The Zapatistas of 1994 saw land as the core issue. Since the move toward privatization of the economy during the mid-1980s, the *campesinos*—who had little land to begin with—had been losing land to the *latifundistas*. When the Zapatistas seized the courthouse in San Cristobal de las Casas, they promptly burned the municipal archives that held the land titles. They denounced the government's electoral fraud,[21] demanded regional autonomy, and declared that they would no longer endure abuses at the hands of the police, the army, and the terrorist *guardias blancas* ("white guards") deployed by the *latifundistas*.

Chiapas was the poorest state in a poor country. The federal government spent less than half the amount of development money per capita in Chiapas that it did in the nation as a whole. Chiapas needed paved roads, adequate schools, electricity (the state contained large dams that exported energy to other states), and health facilities. A large percentage of the population was of Mayan Indian origin (26.4 percent, compared to the national average of 7.5 percent); a third of the people did not speak Spanish. The national minimum daily wage of workers in 1990 was $3.33; in Chiapas, nearly 60 percent earned less than that paltry amount. Nineteen percent of the labor force had no income, working as peasants and existing at a bare subsistence level. Food production barely kept up with a population that had doubled during the previous two decades, and prices for the main cash crop, coffee, had fallen drastically.

The rebellion broke out the very day NAFTA—the final indignity—went into effect. The Zapatistas saw the treaty with the United States and Canada as a "death certificate" for the Indians of Mexico, who would not be able to compete with manufacturers and food producers in the north. Led by the charismatic and mysterious Subcomandante Marcos, his face hidden by a ski mask, the Zapatistas declared that they spoke for all of Mexico in a struggle for democracy, land, economic change, and autonomy. The Salinas administration, hamstrung by repeated scandals and mistrusted by the majority of its people, deployed the army to end the rebellion. Estimates of those killed varied widely between 145 and 400. In the end, Salinas pursued a two-track strategy. He agreed to negotiate with the rebels, whose strength lay not so much in their military power but in their manifestos on the Internet, through which they rallied public support. But he also set up fifty-six permanent military bases from where the army continued to conduct deadly raids against the indigenous population and expropriate their land.[22]

The PRI Defeated

The Zapatistas were hardly alone in venting their anger against the system. Two million members of the middle class—small shopkeepers, merchants, and farmers, hard hit by the recession of the mid-1990s—formed their own resistance movement, El Barzon. They, too, had a program of legal action and civil resistance, such as showing up in large numbers to denounce foreclosure hearings. Another group, the Civic Alliance, sent election observers to polling stations to prevent the PRI's rampant election fraud. The National Episcopal Conference supported the Roman Catholic bishop in Chiapas, Samuel Ruíz García, who played the role of intermediary in talks between the rebels and authorities.

The PRI no longer fulfilled the functions for which it had been created—to arbitrate disputes among competing interest groups. Its political monopoly was crumbling. In 1996, PAN, the right-center party, elected four state governors and ruled about one-third of the population. Continued widespread corruption—including theft from the national treasury—and unresolved political murders in 1994 and 1995 further undermined the legitimacy of the PRI.

The Mexican people's growing dissatisfaction with the PRI was clearly expressed in the presidential election of July 2000. Vicente Fox, the National Action Party candidate and a businessman who campaigned for sweeping political and economic reforms, won a resounding victory against the PRI candidate, thus ending the PRI's seventy-one-year monopoly on power. For the first time, the presidential election was run by an independent commission that kept the PRI from rigging it.

Revolution and Counterrevolution in Central America

In Central America, political struggles, with origins in the nineteenth century, resurfaced with a vengeance during the 1970s. Fueled by deep social divisions, the conflicts quickly became part and parcel of the global struggle between the United States and Soviet Union. On one side were landowners, who enjoyed political power and had the backing of the army; on the other was the majority of the population, which possessed little land and even fewer political rights.

Direct US involvement in Central America began in the 1890s and increased after the Spanish-American War of 1898, when the United States took on the role of police officer of the Western Hemisphere, especially in the Caribbean. The United States, in the words of Teddy Roosevelt, would not

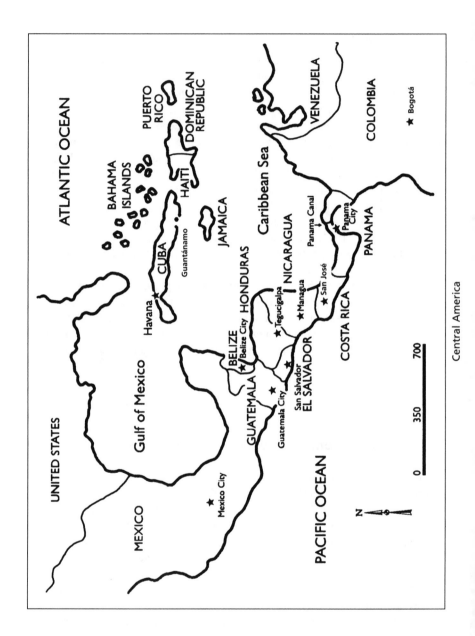

Central America

permit "chronic wrongdoing" in a region some in the United States considered its "backyard." The region became a US sphere of influence where the protection of US interests—political, economic, and military—was a paramount concern.

Officially, the US goal in Central America was to champion the blessings of democracy. In 1913, President Woodrow Wilson famously stated that he would "teach the South American republics how to elect good men."[23] The military regimes in Latin America, however, had other ideas. Moreover, US commitments to the cause of democracy often took a backseat to what became the primary quest: political stability and the protection of US interests. In the early 1960s, President John Kennedy described the US dilemma in Central America:

> There are three possibilities in descending order of preference: a decent democratic regime, a continuation of the Trujillo regime [a right-wing dictatorship in the Dominican Republic] or a Castro regime [a left-wing dictatorship in Cuba]. We ought to aim at the first, but we really can't renounce the second until we are sure that we can avoid the third.[24]

Washington's problem was the absence of Kennedy's "decent democratic regimes." Successive US administrations had to choose between the likes of a Trujillo and a Castro, invariably coming down on the side of the Trujillos, whom they then declared to be part of the "free world." Indeed, Washington even opposed democratically elected reformist governments such as that of Jacobo Arbenz in Guatemala in the early 1950s.

The Cuban revolution of 1959 provided the rationale for US policy in Central America. Fidel Castro, unlike other revolutionaries in Latin America, refused to accept the unequal relationship between Cuba and the United States, one that dated back to 1898 when the United States seized Cuba from Spain. The mafia, operating out of the United States, and US companies controlled large portions of the Cuban economy. Perhaps the most powerful man in Havana was the US ambassador. To rectify this unequal condition, Castro insisted on the nationalization (governmental takeover) of US property—with compensation[25]—and the reorganization of the Cuban economy along socialist lines. When talks stalled with Washington, Castro worked out a trade agreement with the Soviet Union, trading Cuban sugar for Soviet oil and machinery.

Unaccustomed to such a brazen show of defiance, Washington countered with an economic embargo and broke off diplomatic relations with Cuba. It then moved to overthrow Castro, an attempt that resulted in the fiasco at the Bay of Pigs in 1961 (see Chapter 4). Assassination attempts followed, but Castro survived and, with the help of the Soviet Union, consolidated his power. The Cuban missile crisis in 1962 led to a US pledge not to invade Cuba, but successive US governments, whether Democratic or Republican, were in no mood to tolerate other radical regimes in their "backyard." One Cuba was enough.

Nicaragua

The next serious outbreak of revolutionary violence in Central America began in Nicaragua during the late 1960s. It became more volatile after a devastating earthquake in 1972 that leveled much of Managua, the nation's capital. Nicaragua was ruled by the Somoza family, which had come to power in the early 1930s with the help of US Marines (an occupying force in Nicaragua, off and on, from 1911 to 1932). President Franklin Roosevelt once remarked that Anastasio Somoza García, the founder of the dynasty, was an "s.o.b., but [he is] our s.o.b."[26] The greed of the Somozas became legendary. When the last of the Somozas, Anastasio Jr. ("Tachito"), fled the country in 1979, he took with him an estimated $100–400 million, most of it from the national treasury.

The 1972 earthquake highlighted the greed of Anastasio Somoza Jr. and the National Guard, his private army. They had long been involved in the seizure of land and the control of many aspects of the economy—including construction kickbacks, prostitution, gambling, and taxation. When the devastation hit the capital, all discipline in the National Guard broke down. Its soldiers looted publicly while Somoza and his officers handled the foreign contributions for the relief of the earthquake victims, siphoning off large sums of money and selling relief supplies.

By 1974, Somoza had created powerful enemies, including the Roman Catholic Church and the middle class, neither of which had forgiven him for his conduct after the earthquake. In January 1978, Somocista hit men assassinated Pedro Joaquín Chamorro, an outspoken critic and the editor of the newspaper *La Prensa*. This act sparked the first mass uprising against Somoza. Once Jimmy Carter became president in 1977 and made human rights a priority, Somoza could no longer count on the United States to bail him out (although it continued to sell him arms). The National Guard executed thousands, but it was too late. The rebellion gathered in strength; no amount of bloodshed could save Somoza's regime.

The violence in Nicaragua was brought home to the US public in June 1979, when the National Guard arrested ABC newsman Bill Stewart, forced him to kneel, and executed him. Stewart's camera crew recorded the murder on film, and hours later the scene was reproduced on US television screens. Only then did the Carter administration cut off arms sales to Somoza. A month later, in July 1979—after having looted the national treasury—Somoza fled Nicaragua, leaving behind a devastated country. The death toll was between 40,000 and 50,000, 20 percent of the population was homeless, and 40,000 children were orphaned. The industrial base was in ruins; the Somocistas, having plundered the country, left behind a foreign debt of $1.5 billion.

In Somoza's place, the Sandinistas, a coalition of revolutionaries, seized power. The Sandinistas took their name from the revolutionary Augusto Sandino, whom the first Somoza had murdered nearly fifty years earlier. Carter did not like the leftist orientation of the Sandinistas yet provided a modest amount of foreign aid in order to retain a bit of leverage. But as the Nicaraguan revolution continued to shift to the left, a disillusioned Carter suspended all economic aid.

The Sandinistas established a new order that included nationalization of land, press censorship, political imprisonment, nationalization of segments of industry, a militarized government, and a restricted electoral process. But it also included extended health care, a fair measure of freedom of speech, a literacy campaign, the redistribution of land, and an economy of which half remained in private hands. In short, the Sandinista government became a typical example of a revolution consolidating its power while at the same time seeking to resolve the nation's most pressing social and economic problems.

The war of nerves between Washington and Managua escalated in 1981, after President Ronald Reagan took office. Reagan canceled all aid to Nicaragua and launched covert CIA actions against the Sandinistas, who had committed the unpardonable sin of becoming recipients of aid from the Communist states of Eastern Europe, and notably the Soviet Union (but also from West European states such as France and West Germany). Moreover, prior to March 1981, the Sandinistas had even sent a small amount of arms to the leftist rebels in neighboring El Salvador. In the eyes of the Reagan administration, the Sandinistas had become a spearhead of Soviet expansionism in Central America.

Daniel Ortega, Sandinista leader and onetime president of Nicaragua. *(Organization of American States)*

The CIA organized and armed the opponents of the Sandinistas, a group known as the Contras. Headed by former members of the National Guard—Somoza's army—the Contras were tainted by their past association with Somoza and therefore had little support in Nicaragua. Reagan had a difficult time selling his assistance to the Contras to Congress and the US public, who—after the Vietnam War—were leery of being drawn into another civil war in a land of which they knew little. But when Daniel Ortega, the dominant figure in the Sandinista government, flew to Moscow seeking economic aid, Congress approved financial assistance to the Contras, but that aid was to be used only for "humanitarian" rather than military purposes.

Reagan's policy was to tighten the screws on the Sandinistas until they "cried uncle." A number of Latin American countries, the so-called Contadora group—Mexico, Panama, Colombia, and Venezuela—called for a political settlement instead. It proposed a mutual disengagement of all foreign advisors and soldiers—Cuban, Soviet, and US—from Central America, in short, the political and military neutralization of the region. It pointed to the counterproductive nature of Washington's Central American military containment: The Sandinista army had doubled in size since 1981, and the Salvadoran revolutionaries had tripled their forces. Reagan brushed aside the Contadora plan and, instead, directed the CIA to arm and assist the Contras and conduct military exercises in nearby Honduras. Central America was now another Third World battleground in the East-West confrontation.

The Sandinistas proclaimed their willingness to abide by the Contadora solution; the Reagan administration, however, rejected this solution because it would permit the Sandinista regime to remain in power. In his address to Congress in April 1983, Reagan tied Nicaragua to the global Cold War:

> If Central America were to fall [to Communism], what would be the consequence for our position in Asia and Europe and for alliances such as NATO? . . . Our credibility would collapse, our alliances would crumble.[27]

The Contras made no significant military progress. They lacked popular support in Nicaragua, and had virtually no prospect of defeating the Sandinista army. The US Congress, in response to the public's distaste for becoming involved in Nicaragua, suspended further military aid to the Contras. Reagan resolved to find other ways to fund the Contras. Thus began the bizarre "Iran-Contra affair." Officials in Reagan's National Security Council worked out a complex scheme whereby profits from covert and illegal missile sales to Iran—through Israeli intermediaries—would be turned over to the Contras. Colonel Oliver North, who conducted this operation from the basement of the White House, also solicited money from private donors in the United States and from friendly foreign governments—all in violation of congressional laws prohibiting further military aid to the Contras and prohibiting trade with Iran as well. These illegal and covert operations, detected in November 1986, remained in the news for several years—much like the Watergate scandal in the Nixon era—for they raised many questions about ethics, law, and power. Congress, which earlier had vacillated on the issue of Contra aid, now firmly rejected any further military support, despite Reagan's persistent pleas. Another setback for Reagan came in June 1986, when the World Court (the International Court of Justice in The Hague, Netherlands) ruled—for the first time against the United States—that it had violated international law by mining Nicaraguan harbors in 1984 and by its attempts to overthrow the sovereign government of Nicaragua.

In 1987, Costa Rica's president, Oscar Arias, launched a new peace initiative that won the endorsement of the rulers of all five Central American nations—including Sandinista leader Daniel Ortega. The Arias plan committed the Central American nations to a cease-fire, a general amnesty, freedom of the press, free elections, the suspension of all foreign military aid, and a reduction in the level of arms. Ortega's unconditional acceptance of the Arias peace plan offered him a diplomatic victory over Washington and spelled doom for the Contras, who now stood isolated.

But Ortega's problems were by no means over. The Sandinistas now had to deal with a crisis more threatening to their survival than either the Contras or the United States: the failing economy. The looting of the treasury by Anastasio Somoza, the war against the Contras, the US trade embargo, the loss of foreign credits, hyperinflation, and their own mismanagement all had left their marks. Nicaragua's per capita gross national product had fallen from over $1,000 in 1980 to $830 in 1987 and to $340 in 1993.[28]

In February 1990, the Sandinistas took a calculated risk by holding a free and unfettered election. The result was not what they had expected. A coalition of fourteen anti-Sandinista parties led by Violeta Chamorro—the widow of the publisher of *La Prensa* whom Somoza had murdered in 1978—won fifty-two of the National Assembly's ninety seats. Nearly a dozen years of war and deprivation had taken their toll on the Sandinista revolution, and the voters cast their ballots for a change. Ortega grudgingly accepted the electoral defeat and agreed to transfer to the authority of the new government his movement's base of power, the 70,000 Sandinista troops.

Chamorro adopted a centrist and conciliatory policy, keeping a wary eye on both the army, which was still led by Sandinista officers, and the former Contras. Although peace—or at least the end of overt warfare—had its benefits, the incompetent Chamorro government showed little interest in economic reforms and, facing insurmountable difficulties, was unable to reverse the fortunes of the exhausted nation. Nicaragua remained heavily dependent on meager external financial aid. Meanwhile, incessant political violence continued as bands of retread revolutionaries—former Sandinista soldiers on the left and former Contras on the right—continued to fight each other. Nicaragua remained a blighted country with an estimated 60 percent of its people living in poverty. At the end of the century, it was among the poorest countries in the Western Hemisphere.

El Salvador

In El Salvador, a scenario similar to the one in Nicaragua unfolded in the early 1970s. A rebellion in the countryside threatened to oust the governing oligarchy, one composed largely of *las catorce familias*, the Fourteen Families. Jorge Sol Costellanos, an oligarch and a former minister of the economy, defined the class structure in El Salvador as follows:

> It's different from an aristocracy, which we also have. It's an oligarchy because these families own and run almost everything that makes money in El Salvador. Coffee gave birth to the oligarchy in the late 19th century, and economic growth has revolved around them ever since.[29]

Sol went on to say that the Fourteen Families (or, more accurately, clans) controlled 70 percent of the private banks, coffee production, sugar mills, television stations, and newspapers. In 1984, the annual per capita GNP of El Salvador was around $710 (with the poor receiving much less than that), about 6 percent of the US figure.

The revolution in El Salvador had its roots in events forty years earlier. In 1932, deteriorating economic conditions—brought about by the Great Depression and falling farm prices—and Communist activities under the leadership of Augustín Farabundo Martí led to peasant uprisings. A lack of organization and arms proved to be fatal for the peasants, for machetes were no match against a well-equipped army. In a matter of days, the armed forces, led by General Maximiliano Hernández, slaughtered 30,000 campesinos. Martí was captured and executed, thus ending the revolution. Its psychological impact, however, remained deeply etched into the collective memory of the nation. Hernández became the symbol of both deliverance and oppression, and his ghost continued to haunt El Salvador.

The 1932 massacre produced an uneasy stability until the 1972 national election. The civilian candidates of the Christian Democratic Party—José Napoleón Duarte and his running mate, Guillermo Ungo—calling for reform, particularly the redistribution of land, defeated the military candidates. The oligarchy and the generals responded by arresting Duarte, torturing him, and then sending him into exile.

The military deployed death squads on a rampage of indiscriminate violence, summarily killing thousands of men, women, and children. In March 1980, the Roman Catholic archbishop of San Salvador, Oscar Arnulfo Romero—a critic of the military—was gunned down at the altar while saying mass. The assassins, members of a death squad under the command of Roberto d'Aubuisson, were well-known in Washington. The CIA informed the Reagan administration that d'Aubuisson was the "principal henchman for wealthy landowners and a coordinator of the right-wing death squads that have murdered several thousand suspected leftists and leftist sympathizers during the past year." The agency went on to say that he was also involved in drug trafficking, arms smuggling, and the death of Romero—even providing details of how the men were selected to carry out the assassination.[30] The Reagan administration, although not condoning d'Aubuisson's crimes, continued to work with him as part of its strategy to deal with the insurgency.

Liberation Theology

The assassination of Romero put into sharp relief a major change in the political life of Latin America. Since the 1960s, the Roman Catholic Church, traditionally the champion of the status quo, had begun to reexamine its mission. Many of its clergy moved toward a renewed commitment to improve the lot of the faithful on this earth. Village priests in particular found they could not preach eternal salvation and at the same time ignore the violence visited upon their parishioners. The upshot was a split between the traditional wing of the clergy and those, such as Romero, who championed what became known as liberation theology. Liberation theology may be traced to the encyclicals of Pope John XXIII and Pope Paul VI and to the Second Vatican Council (1963–1965); it was subsequently embraced by the 150 Latin American Roman Catholic bishops in attendance at the Second General Conference in 1968 in Medellín, Colombia. The bishops criticized the "institutionalized violence" that condemned the lower classes to poverty and hunger. They also chastised foreign investors who benefited at the expense of the local population. The Catholic Church thus combined its spiritual mission with one for social change and justice. Marcos G. McGrath, archbishop of Panama, explained that the Catholic Church's mission was meant to "integrate eternal salvation and revolutionary action for a just order in this world."[31] The bishops, critics of both capitalism and Marxism, looked for a third way:

> The liberal capitalist system and the temptation of the Marxist system appear as the only alternatives in our continent. . . . Both these systems are affronts to the dignity of the human person. The first takes as a premise the primacy of capital, its power, and the discriminating use of capital in the pursuit of gain. The other, although ideologically it may pretend to be humanist, looks rather to the collective man, and in practice converts itself into a totalitarian concentration of state power.[32]

The Catholic Church began its work in the villages, where it established base communities and cooperatives in an attempt to ameliorate the consequences of police and army brutality, poverty, illiteracy, and the lack of medical facilities. When the Third Conference of Latin American Bishops convened in Puebla, Mexico, in 1979, a radicalized Catholic Church was already a fact of political life in much of Latin America. Church leaders repeatedly condemned state and guerrilla violence, capitalism, and Marxism. They directed their harshest criticism against corporations and their "stages of growth," which held that poverty in the Third World was but a temporary phenomenon and that capitalism would eliminate it.

Maryknoll Sister Ita Ford, shortly before she and three other nuns were murdered in El Salvador in 1980, understood that "the Christian base communities are the greatest threat to military dictatorships in Latin America," a view the military dictatorships—particularly that of El Salvador—readily shared. As early as 1972, Salvadoran death squads began to murder members of the clergy, at times leaving their bodies dismembered as a warning. The oligarchs denounced the clergy as Communists and urged citizens "to be patriotic—kill a priest!" In the years between the Medellín and Puebla conferences (1968–1979), military governments or their henchmen murdered, tortured, arrested, or expelled an estimated 850 nuns, bishops, and priests in El Salvador. The murder of Archbishop Romero was but the most dramatic act of violence visited on the champions of liberation theology.[33]

* * *

The Reagan administration ignored the social, economic, and political roots of Salvadoran revolutionary violence and insisted that it was inspired from the outside. It saw the rebels, organized as the Farabundo Martí National Liberation Front (FMLN), as a Communist threat linked to Nicaragua, Cuba, and, ultimately, the Soviet Union. It continued to strengthen the military and pretended to seek a political solution. Under US supervision, El Salvador went through the motions of holding presidential elections and, indeed, the 1979 election returned Duarte to power. Duarte, however, ruled as the cat's paw of the generals, because without him Washington could hardly justify its support of the military. Duarte's election enabled the Reagan administration to argue that reforms were taking hold and that the army's human rights record was improving. The violence, however, continued after the election of the hapless Duarte, who was powerless to stop it. The death squads went about with their grisly work.

By 1989, after nine years of fighting, some 70,000 Salvadorans had been killed. Despite $3.3 billion in US economic and military aid, little had changed. The guerrillas, regarded by one observer as "the best trained, best organized and most committed Marxist-Leninist rebel movement ever seen in Latin America,"[34] controlled about one-third of the country and made their military power felt through periodic attacks in the capital and elsewhere.

In November 1989, the army committed yet another atrocity. A right-wing death squad burst into the rooms of six Jesuit priests who taught at Catholic

University and murdered them, their cook, and her daughter. The newly elected president, Alfredo Cristiani, the candidate of the rightist National Republican Alliance party (ARENA), whose government still received US military aid, assured Washington that it would conduct a thorough investigation and bring the killers to justice. In January 1990, his government arrested and charged eight military men, including a colonel who allegedly had ordered the murder of the priests.[35]

Peace finally came to El Salvador. In March 1989, the FMLN agreed to participate in the electoral process. An FMLN offensive in November of that year showed the George H. W. Bush administration that military victory was beyond its reach. The end of the Cold War was another factor. ARENA could count on US military aid only so long as its army was seen as holding international Communism at bay. With the global Communist menace suddenly gone, Washington's threat to discontinue aid to El Salvador became more credible, and ARENA became more amenable to compromise.

In May 1990, Moscow and Washington agreed to back UN-arranged Salvadoran peace talks, which finally produced a peace agreement in January 1992. It ended a brutal war that had claimed approximately 80,000 lives over twelve years. In exchange for an agreement to dissolve their military forces, the rebels secured government pledges to legalize the FMLN as a political party and to reduce by one-half the size of the Salvadoran army within two years. The agreement also called for implementation of land reform, as well as judicial and electoral reforms and the creation of a UN Truth Commission to investigate cases of human rights violations.

The most appalling of these violations was the December 1981 massacre of more than 700 peasants—evangelical Christians who did not support the rebels—by the US-trained elite Atlacatl Battalion in the remote village of El Mozote. In 1982, the Reagan administration had angrily and repeatedly denied—although it knew better—that such a massacre had taken place. In El Salvador, El Mozote remained a metaphor for the army's ability to avoid responsibility for human rights abuses.[36] The Truth Commission's investigations produced reports, replete with damning evidence, of massacres by army officers and right-wing death squads, but the ARENA government did not carry out its recommendations. To the contrary, in 1994, it passed a law granting full amnesty to all army officers, despite the incontrovertible proof of massacres such as that of El Mozote. Civilian control of the military—a fundamental principle of democratic government—remained out of reach in El Salvador.

In May 1984, under pressure from the US Congress, which threatened to withhold aid, five enlisted members of the National Guard were convicted of the 1980 murder of four US nuns. It marked the first time in the nation's history that a member of the military had been found guilty of such a crime. Still, the officers who had given the orders, the director of the National Guard, Eugenio Vides Sasanova, and the minister of defense, José Guillermo García, escaped prosecution under a general amnesty. They retired to Florida, where they were tried under US law, but the prosecution was unable to establish a direct link between them and those who had committed the murders.

Latin American Drug Trafficking

Since the early 1970s, when US president Richard Nixon first committed his country to a war on drugs, every administration spent increasingly more money on a losing effort. The main focus was on the interdiction of the flow of narcotics from Latin America, notably from Colombia, famous for its powerful drug cartels, which in the 1980s were responsible for about 80 percent of cocaine entering the United States. Coca plants, from which cocaine is extracted, grow abundantly in the equatorial climate of Colombia, Bolivia, and Peru. Drug money provided a living for the *campesinos*. But coca production was also the source of corruption of law enforcement agencies by the fabulously wealthy criminal organizations. The powerful cartel in the city of Medellín operated like a large multinational corporation. US Drug Enforcement Agency officials estimated that during the 1980s its profits were as high as $5 billion a year and that tens of thousands of people were on its payroll—growers, processors, couriers, politicians, police, judges. When bribes failed to achieve their purpose, drug lords readily resorted to intimidation and violence.

In August 1989, the Colombian government launched its own highly publicized war on the drug cartels. President Virgilio Barco Vargas ordered the army into action, setting crops ablaze, destroying production facilities, and seizing the homes and properties of drug kingpins. The cartels responded in kind, gunning down politicians and judges. In November 1989, the Medellín cartel claimed responsibility for the bombing of a Colombian jetliner, killing all 107 aboard. In the following month, it blew up the headquarters of the Department of Security, the agency most involved in the effort to destroy their drug operations. Half a ton of dynamite destroyed the six-story building, killing fifty-two people and injuring about 1,000.

The drug lords' greatest fear was the extradition treaty with Washington, according to which they could be sent to the United States to stand trial. In February 1987, Carlos Lehder—one of the cofounders of the Medellín cartel and whose net worth was estimated at around $2.5 billion—was captured and extradited to the United States, where he was found guilty of an assortment of crimes and sentenced to life plus 135 years.

In June 1989, Pablo Escobar, the most powerful Medellín kingpin, surrendered to the authorities—but on his own terms. He did so in exchange for immunity against extradition to the United States, where he was under indictment. He was permitted to select his own "jail"—a comfortable rural villa in his home province replete with Jacuzzi, fax machines, cellular telephones, and computers—and was allowed to dictate the security arrangements, even selecting his own armed guards. This arrangement allowed him to continue to run his drug empire from "prison." Escobar's escape in July 1992, and his death during a shootout with Colombian police later that year, had little impact on the drug trade.

The apolitical cartels were not alone in the drug business. Leftist guerrillas, too, succumbed to the lure of this most profitable enterprise. The largest of the guerrilla groups was the Armed Revolutionary Force (FARC), 17,000 strong and in control of large areas of rural Colombia inhabited by several hundred thousand people—a state within a state. FARC was initially founded in 1964 as a movement seeking social change but since then had found a new calling: the sale of protection to growers of coca, marijuana, and poppy (the source of heroin) and the lucrative business of "miraculous fishing," that is, kidnapping for ransom. By the end of the 1990s, its activities netted an estimated $500 million annually.[37] Another, smaller guerrilla group with the same agenda was the National Liberation Army (known by its Spanish-language acronym ELN). Colombia's 11,000-man army proved generally ineffective against the well-financed guerrillas.

The early 1990s saw the emergence of another drug-running outfit, the Colombian Self-Defense Force, which deployed rightist paramilitary death squads between 5,000 and 7,000 strong. In their war against the left, they not only conducted their own reign of terror, murdering tens of thousands of individuals—mostly civilians—thought to be sympathetic to the guerrillas, but also were unable to avoid the temptation of the drug trade and kidnapping.[38] To add to Colombia's misery, the army, too, was engaged in the torture and murder of civilians as well as in the drug trade.[39] Colombia became one of the most dangerous places on earth.

In the late 1990s, the Clinton administration was drawn into the Colombian cauldron. In August 1999, Clinton, after obtaining bipartisan congressional support, traveled to Colombia to present the government there with an antidrug aid package of $1 billion that included 500 military advisors and transport and attack helicopters. During his visit, Clinton was careful to avoid the capital city of Bogotá; his eight-hour stay was limited to the coastal city of Cartagena under heavy military guard of 5,500 government troops, 350 US agents, four frigates, and eighteen patrol boats. He expressed confidence that this new round in the War on Drugs would succeed where previous efforts had failed.

The magnitude of the profits from the drug business spoke against this kind of optimism. At its source, 1 kilogram of coca paste already fetched $2,500; in Miami, after changing hands several times, the price was $20,000; by the time it reached New York City it was $80,000; and in Europe it was $120,000.[40]

In 2002, the George W. Bush administration introduced its ambitious Plan Colombia, and the following year the Colombian government—with US support—launched an offensive, the "Patriot Plan," against FARC. The defense minister announced a string of victories. "The tide has turned," he said, "and there is an end in sight," only to add that one "cannot expect a big [final] battle, a Waterloo."[41] That was putting it mildly. FARC continued its activities even after its founder, Manuel Marulanda, died in March 2008 at the age of seventy-seven.

Since the days of Richard Nixon, the War on Drugs accomplished nothing of substance, except to permit politicians to take the moral high ground and to contribute to the vast increase in the US prison population (the highest per capita in the world). Chemical spraying of coca fields and the destruction of labs were poor yardsticks by which to measure success. The fields were replanted and the labs rebuilt. "Colombia is the only country in the world where the problem of eradication has been resolved 10 times," a UN specialist on the drug war declared. "The problem is the replanting."

Success demanded a scarcity of illicit drugs, measured by a spike in prices. Prices, instead, steadily declined while the purity of drugs remained high. Cocaine prices in the United States fell from around $600 per gram in the early 1980s, to less than $200 in the mid-1990s, to around $100 by 2005. Global demand grew—notably in Europe—and the global drug traffickers—whether in Colombia, Guatemala, Mexico, or Afghanistan—met it.

In June 2008, the World Health Organization published its finding that the United States, despite draconian antidrug laws, led the world in per capita cocaine use—and by a wide margin at that—as well as that of marijuana. The per capita use of marijuana in the United States was twice as high as that in the Netherlands where its personal use was decriminalized.

The North American Free Trade Agreement of 1994 (see Chapter 17), intended to facility the flow of goods between Mexico and its neighbors to the north, was a boon to drug smugglers. Mexico became the center of transshipment and thus a battleground for cartels intent upon carving out their empires. From Mexico, drivers (in 5 million trucks and 92 million cars in 2005) took small packages across the border into the United States.

The war's cost during latter years may have been as high as $40 billion per year. Indeed, the United States appeared to have spent as much in this losing war as for that in Vietnam ($600–800 billion, in 2007 dollars).[42]

The Panama Connection

The first year of the George H. W. Bush presidency witnessed a bizarre war of words with Manuel Noriega, the military strongman of Panama. Noriega, previously an ally of the United States, was now suspected of being a conduit for Colombian drugs en route to the United States. Indeed, he had been on the payroll of the CIA, which had paid him $250,000 a year for Caribbean intelligence during the war against the Sandinistas. The Reagan administration turned a blind eye to Noriega's human rights abuses. Torture, murder, rape, plunder, prostitution, drug trading, and the theft of elections—such as that in 1984—did not faze Washington. It continued to fund Noriega's army as it contemplated US military withdrawal from the Canal Zone before 2000, as stipulated by the treaty of 1979. But in 1987, Washington became aware that Noriega had transgressed the bounds of propriety when it learned he was also offering intelligence to Castro's Cuba. Ambler Moss, President Carter's envoy to Panama, explained that Noriega was "dealing with everybody—us, the Cubans, other countries. We used to call him the rent-a-colonel." The betrayal became too much for President Bush to bear. He accused Noriega of being part of the international drug cartels. Bush's accusation was reminiscent of Claude Rains's discovery of gambling in Rick's place in the movie *Casablanca*. Knowledge in Washington of Noriega's drug connections went all the way back to the Nixon administration.[43]

Noriega resisted US pressure to step down, presenting himself instead as the champion of small Latin American nations bullied by the "colossus of the north." In 1987, grand juries in Tampa and Miami indicted him on drug-trafficking charges. Just before Christmas 1989, Bush sent a posse of 20,000 US soldiers to bring Noriega to justice. Operation Just Cause got its man, but the cost was high. Several hundred Panamanians—mostly civilians—and twenty-three US soldiers died in the fighting. In addition, the collateral damage of property and subsequent looting of stores in Panama City resulted in losses to small businesses totaling $1 billion.

The invasion of Panama was the first instance of US military intervention abroad since 1945 in which the anti-Communist theme was not central. It was a sign of the times that the Cold War was winding down. President Bush stood in direct contrast, however, to Soviet leader Mikhail Gorbachev, who had declared that no nation had a legal or moral right to interfere in the internal affairs of another.

In Miami, before a federal judge, Noriega—dressed in his general's uniform—presented himself as a "prisoner of war." The judge, however, thought that he was dealing with a common criminal. In April 1992, Noriega was found guilty on numerous charges, including the acceptance of millions of dollars in bribes from the Medellín cartel, and sentenced to a lengthy prison term. He became the first head of a foreign state to be convicted of criminal charges in a US court. He completed his sentence in September 2008, but his troubles were by no means over. France, where Noriega had already been sentenced in absentia to a ten-year prison for money-laundering, sought the extradition of the aging former strongman, who by then was in his seventies.

Recommended Readings

Latin America—General

Gill, Leslie. *The School of the Americas: Military Training and Political Violence in the Americas.* Durham, N.C.: Duke University Press, 2004.

Rosenberg, Tina. *Children of Cain: Violence and the Violent in Latin America.* New York: Penguin, 1991.

Wolf, Eric R., and Edward C. Hansen. *The Human Condition in Latin America.* New York: Oxford University Press, 1974.

South America

Blanco, Hugo. *Land or Death: The Peasant Struggle in Peru.* New York: Pathfinder Press, 1972.
A longtime revolutionary argues his case for radical land reform.

Burns, E. Bradford. *A History of Brazil.* 2nd ed. New York: Columbia University Press, 1980.

Valenzuela, Arturo. *The Breakdown of Democratic Regimes: Chile.* Baltimore: Johns Hopkins University Press, 1978.
Strongly critical of the militarist intervention in Chile.

Wesson, Robert. *The United States and Brazil: Limits of Influence.* New York: Praeger, 1981.

Whitaker, Arthur P. *The United States and the Southern Cone: Argentina, Chile, and Uruguay.* Cambridge, Mass.: Harvard University Press, 1976.

Central America

Berryman, Phillip. *Inside Central America: The Essential Facts Past and Present on El Salvador, Nicaragua, Honduras, Guatemala, and Costa Rica.* New York: Pantheon, 1985.
By the Central American representative of the American Friends Service Committee.

Chace, James. *Endless War: How We Got Involved in Central America and What Can Be Done.* New York: Vintage, 1984.
A brief, popular, but insightful historical analysis.

Danner, Mark. *The Massacre at El Mozote.* New York: Random House, 1993.

Diedrich, Bernard. *Somoza and the Legacy of US Involvement.* New York: Dutton, 1981.

LaFeber, Walter. *Inevitable Revolution: The United States in Central America.* Expanded ed. New York: Norton, 1984.
By a well-known revisionist historian on the role of the United States in the Cold War.

Langley, Lester D. *Central America: The Real Stakes, Understanding Central America Before It's Too Late.* New York: Crown, 1985.

Lopez Vigil, José Ignacio. *Rebel Radio: The Story of El Salvador's Radio Venceremos.* Willimantic, Conn.: Curbstone Press, 1995.
An oral history of the "Voice of the Voiceless," which broadcast from the mountains of El Salvador each night from 1981 until the peace accord of 1992.

Montgomery, Tommie Sue. *Revolution in El Salvador.* Boulder: Westview Press, 1982.
Schlesinger, Stephen, and Stephen Kinzer. *Bitter Fruit: The Untold Story of the American Coup in Guatemala.* Garden City, N.Y.: Doubleday, 1982.
The best-seller on the CIA's 1954 coup in Guatemala.

Notes

1. Paul Harrison, *Inside the Third World: The Anatomy of Poverty,* 2nd ed. (New York: Penguin, 1984), cites a survey by the Inter-American Commission for Agricultural Development, pp. 108–109.
2. E. Bradford Burns, *Latin America: A Concise Interpretive History,* 3rd ed. (Englewood Cliffs, N.J.: Prentice-Hall, 1982), p. 214.
3. Luis Marcus Ocampo, "Beyond Punishment: Justice in the Wake of Massive Crimes in Argentina," *Journal of International Affairs* (Spring 1999); "The Challenge of the Past," *The Economist,* October 22, 1998.
4. "A Decline Without Parallel," *The Economist,* February 28, 2002.
5. Ibid. Also, "Argentina's Bottomless Pit," *The Economist,* August 8, 2004, and Peter Greste, "Argentina's Poor Hit New Record," *BBC News,* February 1, 2003.
6. "From Pauper to President: Now Lula's Struggle Really Begins," *The Economist,* October 31, 2002.
7. Cited in Walter Isaacson, *Kissinger: A Biography* (New York: Touchstone Books, 1993), p. 290.
8. Between 1998 and 2004, sixteen thousand documents in the US Archives relating to Pinochet's reign were declassified. See Peter Kornbluh, director, "Chile Documentation Project," www.gwu.edu/~nsarchiv/.
9. Knight Ridder/Tribune, "Pinochet Is Not Immune, Chile's High Court Rules," *Baltimore Sun,* August 27, 2004, p. 18A.
10. Tina Rosenberg, "Force Is Forever," *New York Times Magazine,* September 24, 1995, p. 46.
11. "The Shining Path Revisited," *The Economist,* September 4, 2003.
12. Guillermo Rochabrun, "The De Facto Powers Behind Fujimori's Regime," *NACLA Report on the Americas* (July–August 1996), pp. 22–23. For the impact of economic reform on the population at large, see Manuel Castillo Ochoa, "Fujimori and the Business Class: A Prickly Partnership," ibid., pp. 25–30.
13. Enrique Obando, "Fujimori and the Military: A Marriage of Convenience," *NACLA Report on the Americas* (July–August 1996), pp. 31–36; also "Anatomy of a Cover-Up: The Disappearances at La Cantuta," a summary of a report by Human Rights Watch/Americas, ibid., pp. 34–35.
14. Kevin G. Hall, "CIA Paid Millions to Montesinos," *Miami Herald,* August 3, 2001.
15. *World Bank Development Report 2000/2001: Attacking Poverty* (New York: Oxford University Press, 2000), p. 281.
16. Press release, "Transparency International Calls on Japanese Government to Extradite Fujimori," August 27, 2003; "Cleaner-Than-Thou," *The Economist,* October 7, 2004.
17. Judith Gentleman, "Mexico: The Revolution," in Barbara A. Tenenbaum, ed., *Encyclopedia of Latin American History and Culture,* vol. 4 (New York: Charles Scribner's Sons, 1996), p. 15; Alma Guillermoprieto, "Zapata's Heirs," *The New Yorker,* May 16, 1994, p. 54.

18. James W. Wilkie, *The Mexican Revolution: Federal Expenditure and Social Change Since 1910* (Berkeley: University of California Press, 1970), pp. 193–194.

19. James D. Cockcroft, *Mexico: Class Formation, Capital Accumulation, and the State* (New York: Monthly Review Press, 1983), pp. 136–138.

20. Wilkie, *The Mexican Revolution*, pp. 222–225, 128–129, 195–197.

21. Paco Ignacio Taibo II, "Images of Chiapas: Zapatista! The Phoenix Rises," *The Nation*, March 28, 1996, pp. 407–408.

22. Naomi Klein, "Zapatista Code Red," *The Nation*, January 7/14, 2008, p. 9.

23. From a conversation with Sir William Tyrell, a representative of Britain's Foreign Office, November 13, 1913. Arthur S. Link, *Wilson, II, The New Freedom* (Princeton, N.J.: Princeton University Press, 1956), p. 375.

24. Quoted in Arthur M. Schlesinger Jr., *A Thousand Days: John F. Kennedy in the White House* (Boston: Houghton Mifflin, 1965), p. 769.

25. Castro offered to pay for US property, but only on the basis of a low assessment the companies themselves had submitted for tax purposes. The US companies, however, had other figures in mind. Stephen E. Ambrose, *Rise to Globalism: American Foreign Policy, 1938–1970* (New York: Penguin, 1971), p. 269n.

26. "I'm the Champ," *Time* cover story on Somoza, November 15, 1948, p. 43.

27. Reagan to a Joint Session of Congress, *New York Times*, April 28, 1983, p. A12.

28. World Bank, *World Development Report: Workers in an Integrating World* (New York: Oxford University Press, 1995), p. 162.

29. Paul Heath Hoeffel, "The Eclipse of the Oligarchs," *New York Times Magazine*, September 6, 1981, p. 23.

30. Clifford Krauss, "US Aware of Killings, Kept Ties to Salvadoran Rightists, Papers Suggest," *New York Times*, November 9, 1993, p. A9.

31. Marcos G. McGrath, "Ariel or Caliban?" *Foreign Affairs* (October 1973), pp. 85, 87.

32. From the bishops' "Document on Justice," ibid., p. 86.

33. Walter LaFeber, *Inevitable Revolutions: The United States in Central America*, expanded ed. (New York: W. W. Norton, 1984), pp. 219–226; Tina Rosenberg, *Children of Cain: Violence and the Violent in Latin America* (New York: Penguin, 1992), pp. 219–270.

34. James Le Moyne, "El Salvador's Forgotten War," *Foreign Affairs* (Summer 1989), p. 106.

35. One month later, however, a witness to the murders complained to church officials of "coercive interrogation" by Salvadoran and US officials, who were attempting to get her to change her story. Neither Cristiani nor the Bush administration wanted the Salvadoran army to be found responsible for the atrocity, which threatened to bring about congressional suspension of further military aid to the country.

36. Mark Danner, "The Truth of El Mozote," *The New Yorker*, December 6, 1993, pp. 50–133; eventually published in book form as *The Massacre at El Mozote* (New York: Random House, 1994).

37. Almo Guillermoprieto, "The Children's War," *New York Review*, May 11, 2000, p. 37; Patrick Symmes, "Miraculous Fishing: Lost in the Swamps of Colombia's Drug War," *Harper's* (December 2000), p. 64.

38. "Colombia's Overdose," *Harper's* (February 2000), p. 100. The paramilitaries committed an estimated 78 percent of Colombia's human rights atrocities. Serge F. Kovaleski, "Widespread Violence Threatens Colombia's Stability," *Washington Post*, March 1, 1998, p. A22; "Colombia in the Long Shadow of War," *The Economist*, July 17, 1999, p. 31.

39. "US Issues Rights Report Criticizing Colombia," *Baltimore Sun*, February 26, 2000, p. 1A; "Colombia's President Vows to Crack Down on Death Squads," *Baltimore Sun*, July 25, 2000, p. 12A.

40. Richard Wagner, "Kolumbien's illusionsloser Kampf gegen das Kokain," *Frankfurter Allgemeine Zeitung*, May 30, 2000, p. 4.

41. "Victories, but No Waterloo," *The Economist*, July 15, 2004.

42. Juan Forero, "Colombia's Coca Survives U.S. Plan to Uproot It," *New York Times*, August 19, 2006; Ken Dermota, "Snow Fall," *The Atlantic*, July/August 2007, pp. 24–25; Jordan Smith, "U.S. Ranks #1 in Consumption of Pot, Cocaine, Smokes," *Austin Chronicle*, July 23, 2008.

43. Tim Collie, "Noriega Played All Angles in Ascent," *Tampa Tribune*, December 25, 1989, pp. 22A, 25A.

14 The People's Republic of China and Taiwan

In the mid-1990s, many of the countries of Asia were Third World nations, and several—such as Bangladesh, Cambodia, Myanmar (Burma), and Laos—were among the world's poorest. The two giant Asian nations, the People's Republic of China and India, each with a per capita GNP under $400 in 1990, also qualified as Third World nations. Other countries in Asia, however, all on the Pacific Rim, had far higher GNPs and growth rates and could by no means be classified as Third World or underdeveloped nations. Japan immediately comes to mind, but other Asian countries followed in Japan's footsteps in the 1970s, and by the 1990s China too was rapidly becoming a highly industrialized nation.

The twentieth century was an age of social and political experiments and upheavals, and China, the world's most populous nation, had its share of both. The Chinese Communist government's efforts to transform and modernize China warrant an examination, not only because of the magnitude of the task but also because of the great lengths to which the Chinese Communists went to achieve a Marxist society. The endeavor to put Marxism into practice in this huge country, however, caused enormous political and economic upheavals. Only after the death of Mao Zedong in 1976 did China attain a significant measure of both political stability and economic growth.

India, the other Third World giant in Asia, maintained a democratic form of government and enjoyed a greater degree of political stability than China, but its economic performance was no better. India, too, engaged in social and economic experimentation, mixing elements of capitalism and socialism while avoiding radical shifts in policy. In their own ways, India and China struggled to come to terms with a massive population and massive poverty. Not until the 1980s were they able to register substantial economic gains, and since then China has decidedly outpaced India.

Mao Zedong's Quest for a Communist Utopia

The enormity of China is the starting point of any inquiry into China's economic progress, for its size alone sets the country apart. Never before in history has there been a nation of more than 1 billion people. China has always been an agrarian nation with a mass of poor peasants. The Communist government of China stressed industrialization, agrarian growth, and improvement in the standard of living. At the same time, it devoted itself to building a revolutionary Communist society. The interplay of the economic and political objectives is the key to understanding revolutionary China and its efforts to achieve economic growth.

First, one must note the objective conditions in China and the country's past efforts to deal with those conditions. China's overriding problem in modern times (for at least the previous two centuries) has been how to feed itself. The population continued to grow rapidly both before and after the Communists came to power in 1949. At that time, it was about 535 million; by 1970, it was 840 million; and in the early 1980s, it passed the 1 billion mark. Traditionally, about 90 percent of the people were peasants engaged in subsistence agriculture. Despite the country's great size, there was hardly enough arable land to support the people. Only about 20 percent of the land is arable, with the remainder either too mountainous or too arid. China's huge population, therefore, was heavily concentrated in the areas with arable land, mainly the coastal regions. In the past, because of the unequal distribution of land, the bulk of the peasants either owned too little land or none at all. This set of conditions—the plight of the impoverished peasants and their exploitation by the landowning class—gave rise to Mao Zedong's Communist movement, which was committed to putting an end to these conditions.

China had made little progress toward industrialization prior to Communist rule. The Nationalist regime in the 1930s attempted to industrialize, but this endeavor was cut short by the eight-year war with Japan. In 1949, the Communists inherited a country that had suffered the destruction of that war, as well as three subsequent years of civil war. The country had only very meager industrial development, was wracked with uncontrolled inflation and economic chaos, had an impoverished and illiterate peasantry, and saw its cities swollen with jobless, desperate people. Moreover, China lacked many of the basic elements for modernization: capital, technology, and an educated working class.

Under the rule of Chinese Communist Party chairman Mao, politics—which is to say, Marxist ideology—had greater priority than economic growth. Mao's often-quoted dictum "politics take command" meant that every activity in China was to be defined in Marxist terms. Thus, to study economic development in Mao's China was to study the Marxist politics of Mao and his comrades in the CCP.

Upon coming to power in 1949, the Communists stressed economic rehabilitation and then focused on their socialist objectives. In the first three years,
they managed to establish economic and political order, control inflation, and
restore production in the existing industries to their prewar level. Major industries were nationalized, foreign enterprises were confiscated, and private enterprise was gradually eliminated as state control of the economy was increased. The new regime also addressed the peasant question—an issue that
could not wait—by instituting wholesale land reform. The redistribution of
land was carried out swiftly and ruthlessly, resulting in the transfer of millions
of acres to over 300 million peasants and the elimination of the "landlord
class." Estimates of the loss of life vary greatly, but possibly several million
Chinese met their deaths during this revolutionary upheaval.

By 1953, the Chinese government was ready to institute its First Five-
Year Plan, which was modeled on that of the Soviet Union and guided by Soviet economic advisors. Economic assistance from the Soviet Union was of
great importance to China—the technical aid more than the monetary loans,
which were rather meager. As in the Soviet Union, the First Five-Year Plan
stressed rapid development of heavy industry. It was implemented successfully, and as a result China's production of steel, electricity, and cement increased remarkably.

The Great Leap Forward

As the Second Five-Year Plan was about to be launched, Mao questioned the
effect this method of economic modernization was having on the Chinese revolution; he feared it would result in the entrenchment—as in the Soviet
Union—of a powerful bureaucracy, a new elite that would exploit the Chinese
masses. In early 1958, Mao suddenly called a halt to the Second Five-Year
Plan, thereby rejecting the Soviet model for development, and called instead
for a "Great Leap Forward." This plan called for tapping the energies of the
masses of people—China's greatest resource—to industrialize and collectivize
at the same time. In the countryside, the agricultural collectives, which had
been formed in the mid-1950s, were to be reorganized into large communes
that were to embody the basic Marxist principle "from each according to his
abilities, to each according to his needs." Mao's approach was to mobilize the
masses through the use of ideology to develop and sustain a revolutionary fervor. This frenzied pace could not be maintained, however, and an excess of
zeal, a lack of administrative ability, and poor planning soon produced an economic disaster. Matters were made worse by Soviet premier Nikita
Khrushchev's withdrawal of all Soviet technicians from China in 1960, as well
as by three consecutive years of crop failures (1959–1961). The Great Leap
Forward was, in fact, a disastrous leap backward, and it cost China dearly—

crippling the economy, causing untold hardship, and taking a huge toll in lives. It is impossible to know the number of Chinese who died as a result of this revolutionary experiment, and the violence and famine it caused, but it may have been as high as 10 million.

From this point, we can clearly detect the contention between two conflicting strategies in Communist China. One we can label Maoist or radical, the other moderate. The radical approach was reflected in the manner in which Mao had built the Communist movement in China in the 1930s, in the Great Leap Forward, and later in the Great Cultural Revolution. This approach stressed the "mass line," meaning the power of the people and their active engagement in the revolution. It called for intense ideological training of the CCP cadre, the dedicated party activists who served as a model for the masses. The cult of Mao was also an important tool for politicizing the masses. It was not an end in itself but a means to an end: a thoroughly revolutionary society that was egalitarian and free of exploitation of the masses.

The moderate line deemphasized ideology and revolutionary zeal and instead stressed state planning and development of the skills and expertise necessary for the advancement of China. Its main feature was pragmatism—a rational, problem-solving, do-what-works approach. It was less political, ideological, and emotional than the Maoist line, and it gave higher priority to bureaucratic management and economic modernization than to ideology.

The Great Cultural Revolution

After the Great Leap Forward fiasco, the moderates took charge of cleaning up the mess Mao had made. Gradually, during the first half of the 1960s, the economy recovered under the guiding hand of such moderate leaders as Liu Shaoqi and Deng Xiaoping. But once again, Mao was perturbed about the trend toward bureaucratic elitism. Using his immense prestige as "the Great Helmsman," Mao bypassed the party structure and in July 1966 initiated a new political movement aimed at purging the CCP of its elitist leaders: the "Great Proletarian Cultural Revolution."

Mao was determined once and for all to eradicate bureaucratism in the Chinese revolution. He charged his opponents not only with elitism, meaning they were guilty of selfishly guarding and advancing their own personal power and privilege, but also with revisionism, meaning they were guilty of revising (distorting) Marxism-Leninism, just as Mao felt recent Soviet leaders had done. He claimed that many party leaders were taking the "capitalist road" and thus destroying the Communist revolution. Mao enlisted the active support of the youths of China, who were dismissed from colleges and schools en masse, organized into the "Red Guards," and instructed to go out and attack all those who were guilty of selfish elitism. "Serve the people" was the slogan, and

Mao's writings were the guidelines. Throughout China, the Red Guards pressured people high and low—officials, soldiers, peasants, and workers—to reform themselves through the arduous study of the thought of Mao Zedong as presented in capsule form in the "Little Red Book," and they severely rebuked and punished all those found wanting.

Mao's Cultural Revolution was a unique event—a revolution within an ongoing revolution, a people's revolt against the revolutionary party ordered by the head of that party. Mao called upon the masses to purge their leaders—even in his own Communist Party—to put the revolution back on track. This upheaval was an embodiment of Mao's theory of "permanent revolution"—that is, continuing class struggle and use of revolutionary violence to purge the enemies of the revolution and thereby prevent any backsliding toward capitalism.

Coercion, Mao contended, was necessary to rid people of wrong ideas, just as "dust never vanishes of itself without sweeping." Mao's own Revolutionary Committee was to do the sweeping. Even though his Cultural Revolution was proclaimed in the name of lofty ideals, to bring about a utopian, egalitarian society utterly free of class exploitation, it would produce unimaginable mayhem—terror, death, and destruction. Mao's Red Guards, motivated by Mao's revolutionary charge, rampaged throughout the country as on a crusade—wreaking havoc, destroying property, and capturing, condemning, brutalizing, and sometimes killing those deemed to be less than ideologically pure. Their excessive fervor soon rendered the Cultural Revolution a terrifying witch hunt that not only destroyed the political order in China but also disrupted the economy and caused untold torture, suffering, and death for countless people—probably in excess of 1 million. (After the death of Mao in 1976, the CCP condemned his Cultural Revolution and its excessive violence and encouraged the Chinese people to testify to its cruelty, but the party remained reticent to reveal the number of lives the violence had claimed.)

When Red Guard radicals met resistance, clashes occurred. In time, even opposing bands of Red Guards, each claiming to possess the correct Maoist line, engaged in pitched battles against each other with weapons secured from the police or army units. As the violence mounted, Mao had to call in the military, the People's Liberation Army, to restore order.

Two other victims of Mao's Cultural Revolution were the economy and education. Unchecked political violence caused disruption of the economy: work stoppages, decreased production, shortages, and inflation. In the long run, however, education, science, and technology may have suffered the greatest damage. High schools and universities were shut down for about five years; teachers and professors were taken to the countryside for political reeducation consisting of forced labor and the study of Mao's writings. Books and laboratory equipment were destroyed. When schools reopened, academic standards were replaced with ideological standards—that is, students and teachers were evaluated not on the basis of measurable knowledge but on their dedication to Mao's version of Communism. This was political correctness to the extreme. The disruption in Chinese higher education probably retarded China's economic development by more than a decade.

It took several years for the Cultural Revolution to wind down. Although never repudiated or terminated until after Mao's death in 1976, it was being quietly abandoned by the early 1970s. By then, Mao was aged and ill, and leadership passed into the hands of the very able Zhou Enlai. Zhou, a moderate and pragmatic politician, had managed to dodge the attacks by the Maoists and now, more than ever, Mao trusted and relied on him. Gradually, Zhou reinstated moderates who had been expelled from the CCP and led them to put China back on the track toward economic development. It was Zhou who engineered the new foreign policy of rapprochement with the United States in the early 1970s.

But tensions between Maoists and moderates were mounting under the surface of calm maintained by Zhou and Mao. They erupted in 1976, the eventful "Year of the Tiger," during which both Zhou and Mao died. Mao's designated successor, Hua Guofeng, was able to quash an attempt by the radicals to regain control of the CCP and the government. Hua arrested the ringleaders, the so-called Gang of Four. One of the principal culprits was none other than Mao's wife, Jiang Qing. For the next several years, Hua and the resurrected moderate leader Deng Xiaoping conducted a political campaign of denunciation of the Gang of Four as a means of attacking the radicalism that the departed Mao had embodied. By the end of the 1970s, Deng was in full control of the party. He gently nudged Hua aside, and the Gang of Four was put on trial for its crimes. Cautiously, the new leadership undertook the de-Maoization of China, and even the once adored and infallible Mao was denounced for his "mistakes" during the Cultural Revolution. It was now the moderates' turn to reorganize Chinese society.

Deng Xiaoping's Modernization Drive

Under Deng's leadership, the march toward economic development gained momentum. China normalized relations with the United States and Japan with the objectives of developing trade relations, attracting foreign capital, and purchasing technology. These and other programs, such as providing bonuses as material incentives for production and restoring a capitalistic market mechanism, stimulated economic growth and modernization. In their drive to close the technology gap, Chinese leaders welcomed foreign visitors—especially scientists, technicians, and industrialists—and began sending large numbers of Chinese students abroad, especially for the study of technology, computer science, and business management.

In 1979, Deng instituted a new agrarian program called the "responsibility system." Under it, the peasants contracted for land, seeds, and tools from

Chinese leader Deng Xiaoping, chairman of the Chinese Communist Party Central Advisory Commission, December 14, 1985. *(Embassy of the People's Republic of China)*

the state; at harvesttime, they met their contract obligations and were allowed to keep as personal income all they had earned over and above what they had contracted for. They then sold their surplus production on the newly created open market. The incentive for personal profit led to more efficient farming and served to increase overall agricultural production. An able farmer could rent land to others, and even hire workers, and thus become an entrepreneur.

The new system, which greatly increased production and personal income, struck observers as more like capitalism than Communism. It surely represented a radical departure from Mao's brand of Communism, with its emphasis on egalitarianism. But Deng, the dauntless pragmatist, remained determined to pursue whatever course would speed China's modernization and strengthen its economy. The new pragmatism was promoted by Deng's two slogans: "practice is the sole criterion of truth" and "seek truth from facts."[1] Deng also said, "It doesn't matter what color the cat is, as long as it catches mice." Soviet leaders, who once had criticized Mao for moving too far left, condemned Deng's programs as going too far right. A Soviet visitor to China is said to have remarked, "If this is Marxism, I must reread Marx."[2] The following commentary, which appeared in the authoritative *People's Daily*, the official party organ, in December 1984, made it abundantly clear that the Chinese leaders had indeed adopted a new view of Marxism:

> [In addition to Marx] we must study some modern economic theories, as well as modern scientific and technological know-how. We can never rigidly adhere to the individual words and sentences or specific theories [of Marx]. His works were written more than 100 years ago. Some of his ideas are no longer suited to today's situation, because Marx never experienced these times, nor

did Engels or Lenin. So we cannot use Marxist and Leninist works to solve our present-day problems.[3]

Economic liberalization transformed China from a drab proletarian society, in which individual expression was suppressed, into a lively new consumer society in which individuality was expressed much more freely. In Deng's China, private enterprise, profit-seeking, capital investment, consumerism, and the pursuit of private wealth were no longer taboo but instead were encouraged. Enterprising Chinese became successful in business ventures and displayed their newfound wealth in conspicuous ways, purchasing large homes and automobiles and taking trips abroad. Although authorities were concerned about the jealousy this behavior caused, they nonetheless encouraged people to seek their fortunes in the belief that doing so was for the betterment of both the individual and the economic development of the nation. Deng went so far as to proclaim, as a new credo for the Chinese people, that "to get rich is glorious," an utterly outlandish notion by Maoist standards but one welcomed by the new entrepreneurs.

Deng's economic reform program represented a bold attempt to restructure the economy of the world's largest nation, and it proved to be remarkably successful. By 1987, eight years after Deng's ascent to power, the nation's GNP grew by leaps and bounds; rural incomes tripled and urban incomes doubled; foreign trade doubled, reaching $10 billion; and direct foreign investment in China rose dramatically. Between 1978 and 2007, China sustained an average annual growth rate of nearly 10 percent. The rapid rise in agricultural output in the first half of the 1980s resulted in self-sufficiency and even a modest surplus in food production, feats previously considered impossible for this nation of 1.1 billion people.

A major persistent problem in modern China remained overpopulation, but the Communist regime addressed this problem effectively. It instituted a stringent birth control program that rewarded families with no more than one child (e.g., with increased food rations and employment and education benefits) and penalized families with more than one child by limiting those benefits. This policy and its related family-planning program, including coerced abortions, resulted in a significant reduction of the rate of population growth. It served to hold in check a population explosion that threatened to swallow up any increased economic output. One of its social consequences, however, was an increase in infanticide—with parents killing unwanted female newborns.

The Tiananmen Square Massacre and Its Aftermath

The program of economic liberalization ended the Marxist economic experiment in China. It became a nation of class division where even the pretense of common ownership of the means of production was abandoned, particularly since much of it was in the hands of foreign capitalists. The transformation of the economy, however, was not accompanied by a sustained program of political liberalization. Deng's regime did offer, however, a greater degree of openness and accountability in reporting on governmental affairs. It introduced legal reforms aimed at replacing arbitrary and personal power with the rule of law and began to pay heed to public opinion through such means as opinion polling. It permitted freer access to information and ideas, reduced censorship, and allowed greater freedom of personal expression—with the party, however, remaining the arbiter of what was permissible.

The reforms were attended by considerable rhetoric about "democratization." The reforms were never intended, however, to introduce a democratic political system characterized by free elections contested by rival political parties vying for power. Deng strongly rejected the notion that "bourgeois liberalism" was appropriate for China. He stressed that there were limits to democratization. Nonetheless, the rhetoric of democratization, as well as the greater political and personal freedoms already permitted, whetted the appetites of many Chinese for a greater measure of political liberalization. Since the early 1980s, hundreds of thousands of Chinese had gone abroad to study and were exposed to institutions, ideas, and social values that gave greater import to individual rights and liberties. By the mid-1980s, however, the government began a crackdown on the new wave of Western-styled popular culture (such as rock music), condemning it as "spiritual pollution."

The growing desire for change was suddenly made manifest by university students in large political demonstrations starting in December 1986. First in Shanghai and then in Beijing, students turned out by the hundreds of thousands to register their calls for political reforms. The demonstrations continued for almost two weeks before being broken up by the government, which nevertheless showed considerable restraint and offered vague promises to address the students' concerns.

The movement for reform erupted again in the spring of 1989. Students and intellectuals chafed not only at growing repression but also at increased economic hardships. They were also perturbed by the increasing evidence of widespread corruption among high-ranking government officials and their families. Furthermore, they were repulsed by a ruling party that had, in effect, abandoned Marxism and the ideals of Mao and offered nothing worthy of commitment in their place. For many disillusioned youths, state ideology had become irrelevant and the party had lost its moral authority to govern China. At the very least, the students demanded accountability from government leaders and an unfettered press, without which accountability could not be achieved.

The occasion that triggered the student demonstrations in late April 1989 was the death of the party chief, Hu Yaobang, the most outspoken advocate of political reform. Students from several Beijing universities defied government orders by marching on Tiananmen Square in the heart of Beijing, first to commemorate Hu, whom they heralded as a champion of the democratic cause, and then to call for political reforms. On their posters they called for increased respect for human rights, the release of political prisoners, a new democratic constitution, greater freedom of speech and press, and the right to hold demonstrations.[4]

The student leaders exploited Western press coverage but deluded themselves by thinking that the government would not risk its international prestige by using force against them. By early May, their numbers in Tiananmen Square grew to more than 100,000, and the movement spread to other cities. Government leaders considered it too dangerous to use force against the demonstrations, partly because of the scheduled arrival of Soviet leader Mikhail Gorbachev on May 15. Gorbachev's visit had enormous diplomatic significance in its own right, for Chinese leaders were eager to ratify the end of the Sino-Soviet feud. Beijing could not afford to jeopardize good relations with the new Soviet leader by using brutal force against the students on the eve of, much less during, his visit. Two days before Gorbachev arrived, 2,000 student protesters began a public hunger strike in Tiananmen Square, and the next day hundreds of thousands flocked to the square in their support, ignoring the deadline the government had issued for clearing the area.

The students hailed Gorbachev as a true champion of democratization and lampooned Deng, the dauntless author of the post-Mao reforms, as a stodgy old hard-liner. Gorbachev deftly managed neither to support nor discourage the students, and he gave faint praise to Chinese leaders for "opening a political dialogue with the demonstrators."[5]

No sooner had Gorbachev left Beijing than the government declared martial law. The protests continued nevertheless. The students took heart when the soldiers deployed at Tiananmen Square seemed disinclined to use force against them. Emotions were heightened after students erected on Tiananmen Square a "goddess of democracy" statue (resembling the Statue of Liberty in New York) as a symbol of their cause and then escalated their demands. No longer satisfied with a dialogue with party leaders, they began to call for the dismissal of some of them.

Finally, under the cover of darkness in the early hours of June 4, columns of tanks rumbled toward the square, and the dreaded massacre began. The extent of the carnage may never be known, but estimates range from several hundred to several thousand deaths. The Chinese government took the position that no unarmed students were killed in Tiananmen Square, that no more than 300 people died in the clashes between the soldiers and the rebels on the avenues approaching the square, and that most of the dead were soldiers.[6]

No sooner was the shooting over than the Chinese government employed the controlled mass media to broadcast to the nation—and the world—its version of what had taken place and to block any other version. First came the denial of a massacre and then the rationalization of the crackdown. The Chinese were told that the army had heroically defended the nation against an armed counterrevolution. Then came the reprisals, as dissidents were hunted down, arrested, and pronounced guilty of treason. Of the thousands arrested after the massacre, about forty were executed and eighteen were given long prison sentences.

When a US State Department official inquired into possible violations of the dissenters' human rights, Beijing countered with charges that such inquiries constituted a violation of China's sovereignty and lectured that those in jail were not "dissidents" but "offenders."

Cowed by state power, Chinese citizens who had witnessed the events in or near Tiananmen Square denied having witnessed anything at all. Indeed, the party outlawed all talk of the massacre, a ban it extended to the families of those killed. Many Chinese reverted to the style of mutual self-protection that they had learned in earlier Maoist times.

Meanwhile, Beijing sought to repair the damage the Tiananmen massacre had done to its international prestige and its commerce. It sought foreign investors and buyers to continue to do business with China. The crackdown had cost China an estimated $2–3 billion in investments and developmental assistance and resulted in a decline in the economy's growth rate, but by the second anniversary of the event, Beijing had succeeded in wooing most major industrial democracies back into normal diplomatic and economic relations. A reason for the return to business as usual was the desire for foreign companies to resume their profitable activities in China. China also gained international respectability through such diplomatic moves as supporting UN resolutions against Iraq during the Gulf War, signing the Nuclear Non-Proliferation Treaty, and playing an active role to bring an end to the decade-long civil war in Cambodia.

China in the 1990s and Beyond

A festering debate between reformers and hard-liners among the Chinese Communist leaders over economic policy came into the open in early 1992. Chief among the ideological hard-liners was Prime Minister Li Peng, widely known as "the most hated man in China," a leader who remained critical of the market reforms Deng Xiaoping had instituted. Deng, however, was able to override Li's objections to the reforms. In January 1992, the eighty-seven-year-old Deng reemerged from retirement to make a trip to southern China to inspect the most advanced special economic zones there and witness firsthand the spectacular progress of these commercial boomtowns, where foreign capital and technology were concentrated to build modern, world-class industrial plants. In Shenzen, near Hong Kong, Deng declared that henceforth "everything should serve economic construction."[7] *People's Daily* trumpeted Deng's command: "Seize the opportunity to speed up reform and opening up to the outside world to improve the economy."[8] Li and the hard-liners in Beijing initially were stunned by Deng's strong pronouncements, but within a month all members of the ruling Politburo jumped on Deng's bandwagon, publicly endorsing his campaign for accelerated economic liberalization.

Deng's full-speed-ahead policy remained in force through the 1990s and produced spectacular results. In 1993, China's GNP grew by 13 percent, industrial output by 21 percent, and foreign trade by 18.2 percent; during that single year China received $27 billion in foreign capital—the largest sum for any nation—and 140,000 new foreign-funded businesses were created.[9] Consumerism swept the country, a stock market was created, and old, inefficient state enterprises gave way to privately owned businesses. China was on a building binge as modern high-rises sprouted in cities large and small and new high-speed railroads and highways were built. All the while, China's foreign trade was soaring. By the end of the 1990s, China had a surplus of over $60 billion in its bilateral trade with the United States, surpassing that of Japan. Shanghai's modern transformation was especially spectacular. By 1993, it had more than 2,000 new projects, involving more than $3.5 billion in foreign investments, and more than 120 new multinational corporations had begun operations there.[10] Although it is true that China's economic boom benefited primarily the new economic zones and major cities in eastern China, it is also true that there was a significant improvement in most of the Chinese people's standard of living. By the end of the decade, the people were generally wealthier, freer, and better fed, dressed, and housed than at any time in the past. China's robust economy was able to withstand the financial crisis that caused havoc in Asian nations in the late 1990s and continued to grow at a rate of over 7 percent while annual trade surpluses continued to grow.

The economic surge served to drive out the legacy of Tiananmen and to divert attention away from politics. But there were problems attendant with such rapid economic development. Beijing's leaders—especially the hard-liners—feared that unrestrained growth would lead to gross inequality in wealth, as well as corruption, social instability, and discontent among restless youths. The new economic forces also unleashed a flood of over 100 million rural migrants who flocked to China's cities in search of economic opportunity, but only some of them were successful in securing employment. Rapid industrialization also brought with it a serious environmental problem: Pollution levels, especially from coal-fired power plants, were so severe that by the late 1990s many Chinese cities were the most polluted in the world.

The party's legitimacy rested on its success in maintaining unprecedented economic progress and the political stability necessary for sustaining it. Reform was to be limited to the economic arena. Dissenters who dared to call for radical democratic reforms were arrested and given long prison terms. Brushing aside criticism of human rights violations, the authorities continued such crackdowns periodically throughout the 1990s. Their anxiety about instability was reflected in their reaction to Falun Gong, a popular movement that arose in the early 1990s and quickly attracted millions of followers. The movement, which combined elements of meditative religion and physical and spiritual training, was based on traditional martial arts disciplines. The party viewed it as a potential source of instability, since its members had a higher allegiance to their leader, Li Hongzhi, than to the state. Li claimed to possess supernatural healing powers and the gift of prophecy, even predicting the doom of the current immoral Chinese civilization. When, at the gates of the government leaders' compound in Beijing in April 1999, some 10,000 Falun Gong members staged a defiant, silent protest against their treatment by authorities, the government broke up the gathering, denounced Falun Gong as an "evil force," outlawed the group, and arrested thousands of its members.[11]

As long as Deng lived, political stability held, but by the mid-1990s he had reached the age of ninety and was becoming feeble. But even in infirmity, Deng retained authority as China's "paramount leader" until 1996, when he designated a successor, Jiang Zemin, who by then already had held the offices of president and general secretary of the party. When Deng, who had ruled about as long as Mao had, died in March 1997, the transition to Jiang was a smooth one. Jiang, formerly an engineer, was determined to press forward with economic modernization while maintaining political order under strong party control.

In the 1990s, China's leaders were also confronted with several persistent foreign policy issues, particularly its relations with the United States. After Tiananmen Square, Washington pressured China—albeit only perfunctorily—about its human rights record. It threatened to deny China most-favored-nation treatment (trade terms equal to those enjoyed by other nations), thus restricting virtually unlimited access to the huge US market, unless China took measures to safeguard the civil rights of political dissenters. Beijing contended that such demands constituted unwarranted encroachment on China's sovereignty. In the end, the Chinese won the argument. In 1993, President Bill Clinton sided with Wall Street investors when he separated human rights and economic issues and renewed most-favored-nation status to China. International rebukes of China on human rights persisted. Beijing, however, rebuffed criticism on this and on such issues as its suppression of Tibet, its atmospheric testing of nuclear weapons, and its sale of missiles and nuclear technology to Pakistan. Trade relations with the United States remained contentious as China built up an enormous trade surplus at US expense and came under attack for pirating intellectual property (computer software, videos, and compact disks). Beijing voiced its own list of grievances such as continued US military support of Taiwan, including the sale of advanced jet fighters, and it strongly denounced US plans to shelter Taiwan under a proposed missile defense system.

In 2002, the rule of the aging Jiang Zemin ended with his passing the baton to another predetermined successor, Hu Jintao, who in November became the secretary-general of the Communist Party, the most powerful position in the political system. Five months later he took control of the government bureaucracy as president of China. Hu made no departure from his predecessor's economic policy; rapid industrialization and integration with the world would continue. China's GDP continued to grow at a rate of 8–10 percent. In 2006, China surpassed Britain to become the world's fourth largest economy (after the United States, Japan, and Germany). Its gigantic surplus in foreign trade (in 2007, over $250 billion with the United States alone) signified that it was fast becoming the world's factory. A case in point: Its most industrialized province, Guangdong (adjacent to Hong Kong), employed a workforce of approximately 18 million industrial workers, which is larger than that of the entire United States (14 million). One particular industrial firm in Guangdong—the Taiwan-based Foxconn, the world's largest manufacturer of electronic components—employed over 200,000 workers, its kitchens requiring 3,000 pigs to be slaughtered each day to feed its workforce. From Guangdong Province, in 2007 alone, as many as 40 million cargo containers left for destinations abroad.[12]

Small towns and fishing villages suddenly morphed into boomtowns with large factories on newly cleared lands surrounded by towering apartment buildings for workers newly arrived from the distant countryside. The enormous scale of China's industrial leap was epitomized by the nearly completed Three Gorges Dam on the Yangtze River, the world's largest man-made structure, five times larger than the Hoover Dam, holding back a reservoir 410 miles long (approximately 600 kilometers).

China, with one of the world's fastest growing economies, became a driving force of the global economy. According to one journalist, writing in mid-2007, China has "dislodged the United States from its long reign as the main engine of economic growth" in the world.[13] Although its GDP remained considerably smaller than that of the United States, China has challenged it as the world's leading manufacturer, exporter, consumer, and borrower of international capital.

Historical transformations of this scale and speed cannot be the result of a single cause; invariably, a number of factors are involved. The leadership and vision of Deng Xiaoping, especially his opening of China to foreign trade and investment, played a major role. China's rise could not have been possible without the normalization of relations with the United States, entry into the vast US market, and the timely admission of China to the World Trade Organization (WTO) in December 2001. In addition, foreign corporations provided models for industrialization, capital investment, technology, and financial institutions. (For details of China's economic rise within the context of globalization, see Chapter 17.)

Once Deng opened China's door to outside capital, multinationals (i.e., foreign global corporations) began to take advantage of conditions in China, notably a disciplined workforce willing to work for little pay. Foxconn, for instance, the largest private employer in China, is of Taiwanese origin. US corporations—one after another—pulled up manufacturing stakes at home and planted them firmly on Chinese soil. The by-products were soaring multinational corporate profits and depressed industrial wages back home—and the industrial boom in China.

For three decades the global companies drove Chinese industrial growth. During 1995–2007, for instance, they were responsible for 66 percent of the increase in China's overall exports and for 60 percent of goods shipped to the United States. For the companies to maximize profits, however, wages had to be kept low, and to that end they lobbied vigorously with the Chinese National People's Congress to keep wages low. When, in 2006, a new labor law made it more difficult for employers to cheat workers of their already meager wages, the American Chamber of Commerce in Shanghai and the United States–China Business Council resolutely opposed the law and threatened to relocate enterprises to other countries. Predictably, the Chinese legislature accommodated them.

Relocations were beginning to take place nonetheless. In 2007, a shortage of labor led to a rise in assembly-line wages of 10–30 percent depending on skills. Vietnam, with an average wage of one-quarter of that in China, became a favored destination for foreign capital. As in China, a one-party state promised stability and greater profits. Still, China remained the main destination for foreign capital, $83 billion in 2007. Vietnam, with but one-sixteenth the population of China, drew $17.86 billion.[14]

Taiwan—the Other China

After arriving on the island of Taiwan in 1949 with 2 million soldiers and civilian supporters, Nationalist ruler Jiang Jieshi (Chiang Kai-shek) created the political myth that the Nationalist government (the Republic of China), now firmly established on Taiwan, remained the only legitimate government of China. Although lauded for many years by the United States as the "democratic" alternative to the oppressive Communist regime on the mainland, the "free China" under Jiang was anything but free or democratic. When the Nationalist Army took control of Taiwan from the Japanese after World War II, it was met with resistance by native Taiwanese, who were brutally suppressed. In February 1947, the Nationalist Army crushed an anti-Nationalist demonstration with enormous violence, killing between 5,000 Taiwanese (the Nationalist figure) and 20,000 (the Taiwanese figure). For four decades, Jiang's decree of martial law forbade anyone from speaking of this massacre on punishment of death.

Jiang maintained a one-party dictatorship. The National Assembly became a rubber-stamp legislature, made up entirely of Nationalist Party politicians who had been elected on the mainland in 1948, and it remained without Taiwanese representation until the 1980s. The Taiwanese majority of about 13 million people in the 1950s had no political voice. Until his last breath, Jiang remained ever vigilant against any and all challenges, and he ruthlessly suppressed all opposition, including a nascent Taiwanese independence movement. When he passed away in April 1975, he was succeeded by his son, Jiang Jingguo (Chiang Ching-kuo), who continued his father's anti-Communist and undemocratic policies.

Taiwan suffered a major diplomatic setback in 1972, when the United States normalized relations with the People's Republic of China, and again in 1979, when Washington broke off official relations with the Nationalist government. Economic ties with the United States, Japan, and other industrial countries remained intact, however, and the people of Taiwan directed their attention to developing a strong export economy.

Throughout the 1960s, 1970s, and 1980s, Taiwan was undergoing a remarkable economic transformation. Taiwan's GNP rose from $8 billion in 1960 to $72.5 billion in 1986, and for most of the 1970s it maintained double-digit growth rates. Taiwan's annual volume of foreign trade increased from $2.2 billion to $100 billion between 1969 and 1988. By virtue of its burgeoning exports, Taiwan by 1988 had accumulated a foreign exchange reserve in excess of $70 billion, second in the world only to Japan. (See Chapter 16 for Japan's economic performance.)

Taiwan, together with South Korea, Singapore, and Hong Kong, East Asia's "Four Tigers," followed in the footsteps of Japan in achieving rapid industrialization and stunning GNP growth rates. Among the four, the two most successful, South Korea and Taiwan, had several common characteristics that set them apart from the other two. Both countries were highly militarized, with each facing threats to its security—from Communist North Korea and from the Communist mainland, respectively. Like South Korea, Taiwan thrived on adversity. The maintenance of large military establishments and the burden of large military budgets seemed to have the effect of spurring economic development instead of dragging down the economy. Moreover, the presence of an outside threat produced a sense of national urgency and purpose that was useful to these governments as well as government-supported industrialists.

Taiwan's economic success can also be attributed to other factors unique to the island, including the infrastructure the Japanese had built in Taiwan before 1945, the influx of highly educated Chinese from the mainland in 1949, a quarter-century of US economic aid, an open US import policy for Taiwanese goods, the growth-oriented economic policies of the Nationalist government, and Taiwan's industrious people. In the 1950s, a sweeping land reform was carried out and agricultural production grew steadily, paving the way for capital accumulation and the investment necessary for industrial development. By the 1960s, Taiwan's industries began shifting from production for domestic consumption to export-oriented production. Lured by Taiwan's cheap, high-quality labor, US and Japanese companies made substantial investments, and Taiwanese industrialists and workers rapidly absorbed modern technology. In the late 1970s, Taiwan gravitated toward capital-intensive and knowledge-intensive industries, a shift that paid huge dividends in the 1980s. By the end of the 1980s, electronics replaced textiles as the leading export, and Taiwan became one of the world's leaders in microcomputers and computer parts.

It was not until the 1980s that Taiwan's economic modernization engendered political modernization. Liberalization became possible by the passing of the old guard, the lowering of Cold War tensions, the challenge of a modernizing Communist China, the new prosperity in Taiwan, the spread of education, and the government's increased confidence in the nation's security. In 1986, a newly formed opposition party, the Democratic Progressive Party (DPP), whose platform called for full implementation of democracy, welfare, and self-determination for Taiwan, was permitted to run candidates in the National Assembly election and won a surprising 25 percent of the vote. In July 1987, the government finally lifted the martial law decree, which had been in effect for thirty-eight years, granted freedom of the press, and legalized opposition parties. It also dropped the ban on travel to Communist China, for the first time permitting its people to visit families on the mainland. By 1993, over 1.5 million Taiwanese quickly took advantage of this new opportunity.

President Jiang Jingguo died in January 1988, thus ending the sixty-year Jiang dynasty. His successor was Vice-President Lee Teng-hui, who was not from mainland China but from Taiwan. Although Lee did not advocate independence for Taiwan, the fact that a native Taiwanese was now president encouraged those who did. Moreover, Lee, without a strong power base of his own, could hardly revert to the strongman rule characteristic of the Jiang dynasty. Instead, he continued the political liberalization begun by Jiang Jingguo. The December 1989 National Assembly election was the first free, multiparty election in Chinese history. The result of this election, in which 78 percent of eligible voters cast ballots, was an assembly far more representative than the previous one. Another major step on the road to democracy was the first direct election of the president of the republic, held in April 1996. The incumbent Lee, the head of the ruling Nationalist Party, was reelected as president, but his party's share of the vote decreased while the opposition parties made substantial gains. The Nationalist Party's rule finally ended in March 2000, when the DPP candidate, Chen Shui-bian, won the presidential election.

Divided China: Taiwan and the People's Republic

Democratization in Taiwan not only carried the risk of the Nationalist Party being voted out of power; it also raised serious questions about the very status of the Republic of China and its relations with the People's Republic of China. Taiwan's liberalization movement, especially the growing independence movement it unleashed, was of great concern to Beijing, which was vehemently opposed to even the idea of a permanent separation of Taiwan from China. Beijing had consistently maintained that Taiwan was merely a renegade province of China that sooner or later must be reunited with the mainland.

Prior to the deaths of Jiang Jieshi and Mao Zedong in the mid-1970s, relations between the mainland and Taiwan had been extremely hostile, but the 1980s saw the beginnings of a thaw in those relations. This was fostered, on the one hand, by Deng Xiaoping's policy of liberalization and openness on the mainland and, on the other, by the political liberalization taking place in Taiwan. Moreover, Deng eagerly sought Taiwanese investments as much as Taiwan's financiers and manufacturers sought profitable investments. Trade and contact between the two Chinas increased vastly after Taiwan lifted the ban on travel to China in 1987. That year, the two contending regimes cautiously opened a formal diplomatic channel, the so-called cross-strait talks, for negotiating economic and social issues. Although both governments professed the goal of reunification, they remained far apart on the terms. Beijing offered assurances that Taiwan, upon reunification, would become an autonomous region within the People's Republic of China, retaining its capitalist economy. The Taiwan government insisted that as a first step the PRC must renounce the use of military force to coerce reunification. This Beijing refused to do. Moreover, Taiwan argued that reunification would not be possible until genuine democratization was achieved in China.

The growth of the Taiwanese independence movement brought a new sense of urgency to these talks. They brought Beijing and the Nationalist government closer together, since both opposed Taiwanese independence. But Beijing expressed concern that President Lee, as a Taiwanese, might succumb to political pressure to endorse the independence movement. It remained wary of any action or assertion by Lee suggesting Taiwan's independent status, such as Taiwan seeking membership in the United Nations.

Beijing was not content merely to register protests; it attempted to intimidate Taiwanese voters by threatening the use of force, by engaging in military exercises near the coast of Taiwan. In April 1996, just prior to Taiwan's first presidential election, the PRC carried out large-scale military maneuvers—including missile tests with live ammunition—dangerously close to Taiwan's main port cities. It was not clear what effect this show of force had on Taiwan's voters, since President Lee was reelected by a comfortable margin. However, it did provoke a strong response from the United States, which warned Beijing against any attack on Taiwan.

The return of Hong Kong by the United Kingdom to China in July 1997 (see below) and the reversion of the tiny Portuguese colony of Macao in 1999 served to quicken Beijing's insistence on the return of Taiwan. Beijing offered Taiwan the Hong Kong reversion formula of "one-country, two systems" that would reunite Taiwan under the PRC but allow it to retain its capitalist economy and a degree of autonomy. Taiwan flatly rejected this offer, arguing that its own situation was utterly different from Hong Kong's, for it was not a foreign-controlled colony and had a much larger population and much greater economic and military power compared to Hong Kong.

The feud between the two Chinese governments heated up in July 1999, when President Lee Tung-hui stated explicitly that negotiations between them must be conducted on a state-to-state basis, that is, two sovereign governments negotiating on equal terms. Beijing vehemently rejected the notion of two separate and equal Chinese governments and warned that any step by Taiwan toward separation would be met by force. An alarmed President Clinton warned against the use of force while strongly cautioning President Lee against abandoning the "one China" position. At the same time, there was talk in Washington of increasing military assistance to Taiwan and providing it with an antimissile defensive shield.

In March 2000, Chen Shui-bian, the candidate of the pro-independence DPP, won the election. Once in office, however, Chen cautiously shied away from his party's independence agenda and chose a safer course: maintaining the status quo (i.e., de facto independence). In Beijing, the new leader, Hu Jintao, held fast to the position of his predecessor: "peaceful reunification" of Taiwan with the mainland if possible, but with the proviso that "we shall by no means . . . forsake the use of force."[15]

Hong Kong

The former British crown colony of Hong Kong, which emerged after World War II as a budding mecca of Asian capitalism, also experienced phenomenal economic growth in the post–World War II era. Britain's "gunboat diplomacy" had pried Hong Kong away from China in the nineteenth century, and it remained in British control even after the Communists came to power. In its early years, the PRC was militarily too weak to attempt to recover Hong Kong by force, and Beijing eventually took a pragmatic, rather than a doctrinaire, view of the British presence there, deciding that it represented not a threat to China but an opportunity for maintaining profitable economic relations with the West.

The British governors of Hong Kong had presided over a docile populace (6 million in 1990) and a prospering economy. Hong Kong steadily developed as a major financial, trade, and insurance center, and in the 1980s it also became highly industrialized. The thriving business environment attracted huge investments from Western countries and Japan, further stimulating Hong Kong's economic growth (averaging 5.5 percent between 1980 and 1992). Although Hong Kong had a large number of poor people—mainly recent arrivals from the PRC—its per capita GNP reached $15,360 in 1992. The central section of the city-state became resplendent with wealth, the gleaming skyscrapers soaring above Mercedes-Benz automobiles and free-spending shoppers crowding the streets below.

In the 1970s, the British and Chinese governments began to discuss terms for returning Hong Kong. International business interests became nervous about their investments, and to head off a flight of capital and the attendant financial chaos, the British government was eager to secure an early agreement for an orderly transition. Similarly, it was in the PRC's interest to maintain the financial strength of Hong Kong, since the city-state played an important role in China's international trade and economic development plans.

In 1984, London and Beijing signed a joint declaration that provided a framework for Chinese takeover in 1997. The agreement stipulated that Hong Kong would retain its capitalist system while maintaining "a high degree of autonomy" as a "special administrative region" of the People's Republic for fifty years after the reversion. With this formula, the Chinese and British sought to preserve political and economic stability. The agreement also stipulated that the ethnic Chinese citizens of Hong Kong (98 percent of the population) would become citizens of China at the time of reversion but that they were free to leave the colony prior to that time.

The reversion agreement produced mixed results as the years ticked away. Economic growth did not decline appreciably, and, in fact, foreign and domestic investments increased dramatically. Even in 1996, with reversion to China only a year away, the Hong Kong government was pumping record amounts ($21 billion) into a series of new projects, including a new international airport, a high-speed rail line to link the airport to the inner city, new superhighways, a new harbor tunnel, and the world's longest suspension bridge.

But if investors remained confident about Hong Kong's future, many of its residents were less so. In the late 1980s, about 50,000 people emigrated from Hong Kong annually (mainly to Canada, Australia, and the United States). This exodus of residents—largely wealthy, well-educated elites—reflected a real fear of the Chinese regime.[16] It caused consternation in Beijing, which sought to reassure those living in the colony and avert the hemorrhage of wealth and talent. The bloody suppression of the prodemocracy movement in Tiananmen Square in June 1989 and the subsequent political repression had damaged the Chinese government's credibility in Hong Kong. Within five years, however, the annual rate of emigration leveled off, and about 12 percent of those who had previously emigrated decided to return.

As the date neared for handing over Hong Kong, its economy was still growing (at a steady 5 percent annually), and plans for the transition were being worked out with improved cooperation. All involved—the Chinese, the British, and the residents of Hong Kong—seemed to recognize the importance of Hong Kong's future as the dynamic economic capital of southern China and Southeast Asia. Yet apprehension and uncertainty remained palpable, especially for residents, because of the enormous gulf between Hong Kong's economic system—

said to be the freest economic system in the world—and the politically controlled economy of the PRC.

The long-awaited date for the return of Hong Kong to China came on July 1, 1997. The colorful ceremony marking the event mixed nationalistic celebrations by China, nostalgia on the part of Britain (witnessing the end of its long imperial presence in Asia), and uneasiness on the part of Hong Kong residents. For the most part, the transition from British crown colony to Special Administrative Region went smoothly, and Hong Kong continued to prosper.

The PRC then started counting down to the reversion of the Portuguese colony of Macao at the end of 1999; having achieved that, it turned to Taiwan expectantly yet patiently.

China and Tibet

With the assistance of its expanding economy, the Beijing government was able to fulfill the dreams and aspirations it had nurtured for decades. In the summer of 2008, it successfully staged, to worldwide acclaim, the Olympic Games, another symbol that China now played a major role in the affairs of the world.

In 2006, China completed a railroad link into Lhasa, the capital of Tibet, the highest railroad in the world, a marvel of engineering that traversed hundreds of miles of permafrost at elevations exceeding 13,000 feet. On July 1, 2006, on the eighty-fifth anniversary of the birth of the Communist Party, the first train left Golmund for its 700-mile journey to Lhasa. The railroad tied the "roof of the world" ever closer to Beijing and increased the pace of economic development in the region. With it, however, came a further influx of ethnic Chinese, who were already the majority population in Lhasa and, indeed, all of Tibet (whereas in 1950 there had been virtually none).

China heralded the railroad as a symbol of progress; Tibetans, who resented Beijing's control ever since Tibet's annexation in 1950, saw it as another assault on their ancient culture and a means of further economic exploitation that served first and foremost the dominant Chinese. Massive deforestation and strip mining—for the world's largest reserves of uranium, borax, and lithium as well as copper, chromite, copper, bauxite, gold, silver, tin, and oil—for the benefit of China produced a trickle-down economic effect but also bitterness. Tibetans charged that the Chinese had brought only vulgar materialism, as manifested in the dance halls at the foot of the Potala Palace, the former residence of the Dalai Lamas, the spiritual and political leaders of Tibet.

China's actions in Tibet were strikingly similar to those of Western colonial powers in their far-flung colonies (and Japan in Korea) during previous centuries. That was precisely the problem. The colonizers, with their modern weapons, forced the colonized into submission, exploited them, and then extracted wealth from their lands. They also brought superior technology and were thus able to rationalize their mission as one of civilizing the "backward" natives, the lesser breed. The French called it their *mission civilisatrice*, the British spoke of carrying the "white man's burden," and the Japanese claimed to be establishing a "co-prosperity sphere." Such language masks the racial and exploitative aspects of the violent process of colonization. So it was with the Chinese in Tibet.

China claimed it was bringing modernization to backward Tibetans. And, indeed, China poured huge investments into Tibet's infrastructure construction and new industries. This included improvements to electrification, communications and transport, agriculture, commerce, public education, and health (replete with modern medicine and hospitals). The educational reforms were designed to redress the widespread illiteracy of Tibetans, to prepare them for employment in the new economy, and thus make possible their escape from poverty. The main benefactors of restructuring in Tibet were the Chinese residents, however. Tibetans remained marginalized, and the trickle-down effect was slow. Moreover, the changes were imposed by force and disrupted traditional Tibetan society.

In line with their tradition, Tibetans continued to worship their aged Dalai Lama, in exile in India, and looked toward the reincarnation of the next Dalai Lama—the transfer of the rarified mindstream of Buddha to a new mortal body. The Chinese response was a curious law, passed in August 2007, that sought to deny the Tibetan Buddhist monks the right of the reincarnation of the next Dalai Lama without government permission.

During the mid-1980s, the Dalai Lama, a firm champion of nonviolence, conducted negotiations with Beijing and was even willing to acknowledge that Tibet was part of China, provided that Tibet's ancient culture was protected. Negotiations led nowhere, however. The reformer Hu Yaobang—who upon returning from a 1980 fact-finding mission to Tibet had urged economic development coupled to a respect for Tibetan culture—died in 1989, and then came the Tiananmen massacre. In 2008, Communist Party chief Hu Jintao, who once had served as party secretary in Tibet (and who, in 1989, had not hesitated to use force), was in no mood to negotiate with a people he considered uncultured and dangerous.

Over the years, young Tibetans lost faith in the efficacy of nonviolent means. In March 2008, the mood among Tibetans turned ugly. First came the indiscriminate massacre of Chinese civilians in Lhasa, and then the inevitable crackdown by the authorities, something they had sought to avoid, since it came just five months before the opening ceremonies of the Olympic Games in Beijing. The news media abroad were universally critical of Beijing's handling of the crisis, but the Olympic torch completed its journey around the globe under tight security and even made a scheduled visit to Lhasa.[17]

Similar to Tibet, other outlying non-Chinese regions faced a rapid influx of huge numbers of Han immigrants, particularly after the completion of the railroad system designed to tie the western regions ever closer to the center, first to Urumqui (2000)—the capital of the Xinjiang Uygur Autonomous Region, the ancestral home of Turkic Sunni Muslim Uygurs—and then to the city of Kashgar (2003), at the far western frontier of China. The arrival of the Chinese was a contributing factor to the rise of militant Islam in western China, particularly among the Uygurs. China's distant frontiers were brought closer to the center. In 2008, only Taiwan remained outside the fold.

Recommended Readings

Bergston, C. Fred. *China: The Balance Sheet: What the World Needs to Know About the Emerging Superpower*. Washington, D.C.: Public Affairs, 2006.

Copper, John. *A Quiet Revolution: Political Development in the Republic of China*. Lanham, Md.: University Press of America, 1988.

Eichengreen, Barry, Charles Wyplosz, and Yung Chul Park, eds. *China and the New World Economy*. New York: Oxford University Press, 2008.
A collection of essays arguing that China has emerged as the most significant global economic factor at the outset of the twenty-first century.

Evans, Richard. *Deng Xiaoping and the Making of Modern China*. London: Penguin, 1992.

Fishman, Ted C. *China Inc.: How the Rise of the Next Superpower Challenges America and the World*. New York: Scribner, 2006.

Hsu, Immanuel C. Y. *The Rise of Modern China*. 6th ed. New York: Oxford University Press, 2000.
An excellent, evenhanded, and comprehensive history.

Kristoff, Nicholas, and Sherl Wudunn. *China Wakes*. New York: Random House, 1994.
A readable account of the early phase of China's economic surge by *New York Times* correspondents.

Lardy, Nicholas R. *China's Unfinished Economic Revolution*. Washington, D.C.: Brookings Institution, 1998.
One of the leading experts on China's economy examines China's emergence as the fastest growing economy in the world.

Meisner, Maurice. *Mao's China and After: A History of the People's Republic*. New York: Free Press, 1986.
Assesses Chinese politics on its own Marxian terms.

Overholt, William. *The Rise of China: How Economic Reform Is Creating a New Superpower*. New York: Norton, 1993.

Perkins, Dwight. *China: Asia's Next Economic Giant*. Seattle: University of Washington Press, 1986.

Schell, Orville. *In the People's Republic*. New York: Random House, 1977.
A lucid eyewitness account of the PRC shortly after Mao's death.

———. *Mandate of Heaven: The Legacy of Tiananmen and the Next Generation of Chinese Leaders*. New York: Simon and Schuster, 1994.
A superb analysis of China in the wake of Tiananmen and its economic takeoff in the early 1990s.

Zhang Liang, Perry Link, and Andrew J. Nathan. *The Tiananmen Papers: The Chinese Leadership's Decision to Use Force Against Their Own People—In Their Own Words*. New York: New York Review of Books, 2003.

Notes

1. Immanuel C. Y. Hsu, *The Rise of Modern China* (New York: Oxford University Press, 1983), p. 804.
2. Quoted in John F. Burns, "Canton Booming on Marxist Free Enterprise," *New York Times*, November 11, 1985, p. A1.
3. Deng Xiaoping in a front-page commentary in the December 7, 1984, edition of *People's Daily*, quoted in "China Calls Rigid Adherence to Marxism 'Stupid,'" *New York Times*, December 9, 1984.
4. John Schidlovsky, "Strike Gains Momentum in China," *Baltimore Sun*, April 25, 1989.
5. Scott Shane, "Gorbachev Praises China for Dialogue with Demonstrators," *Baltimore Sun*, May 18, 1989.
6. Orville Schell, *Mandate of Heaven* (New York: Simon and Schuster, 1994), p. 154.
7. Quoted in ibid., p. 343.
8. Cited in *Baltimore Sun*, March 13, 1992, p. 3.
9. Schell, *Mandate of Heaven*, p. 433.
10. Ibid., p. 433.
11. "Why the Exercisers Exercise China's Party," *Economist*, July 29, 1999; "China's Trial of Faith," *The Economist*, November 4, 1999.
12. James Fallows, "China Makes, the World Takes," *The Atlantic*, July/August 2007.
13. Patrice Hill, "China Driving the World Economy," *Washington Post*, July 26, 2007.
14. Keith Bradsher, "Investors Seek Asian Options to Costly China," *New York Times*, June 18, 2008; Brendan Smith, Tim Costello, and Jeremy Brecher, "Chinese Heat Is on US Sweatshop Lobby," *Asia Times Online*, April 5, 2007, www.atimes.com.
15. Cited in Richard Halloran, "How Will Hu Change China's Foreign Policy?" *Baltimore Sun*, September 29, 2004, p. 17A.
16. "New Record Set in Exodus," *Free China Journal*, December 22, 1988.
17. Pankaj Mishra, "The Quiet Heroes of Tibet," *New York Review of Books*, January 17, 2008, 39–40; Jonathan Mirsky, "How He Sees It Now," *New York Review of Books*, July 17, 2008, pp. 4–6; Peter Hessler, "Tibet Through Chinese Eyes," *The Atlantic*, February 1999, 56–66; Jim Yardly, "Trying to Reshape Tibet, China Sends in the Masses," *New York Times*, September 15, 2003; International Committee of Lawyers for Tibet, "Human Rights and the Long-Term Viability of Tibet's Economy," November 1997.

15 The Indian Subcontinent and Southeast Asia

The Himalayan Mountains separate the two Third World giants— China and India. After World War II, India shared many of China's problems, not the least of which was a burgeoning population. About one-fifth of the world's population lives on the Indian subcontinent, which consists mainly of India, Pakistan, and Bangladesh. In the postwar era, India and the other heavily populated nations of this region struggled to hold population growth in check and to elevate the standard of living, but only recently has India met with success. Although they shared many problems, the nations of the Indian subcontinent have not lived in peace with one another. Hostility between India and Pakistan has flared up several times, and both countries have confronted violent internal disorders. The maintenance of large armies to deal with these problems has drained their limited resources.

To speak of India after World War II is to speak of population and poverty. At the time of the partition of India in 1947, its population was about 350 million, and it has grown steadily ever since at a rate of almost 3 percent a year. This meant an average annual increase of about 5 million people in the 1950s, 8 million in the 1960s, and 13 million in the 1970s. An electronic display in New Delhi reminded Indians that in mid-July 1992, the country's population stood at 868 million and was increasing by 2,000 people per hour, 48,000 per day, or 17.5 million per year.[1] By the year 2000, the population reached 1 billion, almost triple that of 1947; in 2008 it stood at 1.15 billion. Moreover, about 40 percent of the Indian people are concentrated in the Ganges River basin, where the population density is among the highest in the world. Although in the mid-1980s India had eight cities with over 1 million inhabitants, over 80 percent of the people still lived in rural villages.

India's primary task was to feed its huge population. The twin aims of the Indian government, therefore, were population control and increased food production. Its birth control program, however, had minimal effect in rural areas. The largely illiterate villagers were suspicious of the purpose and methods of birth control, and they clung to the age-old ideas that a large family was a blessing and that it represented wealth and security. Moreover, one way Indians combated the high infant mortality rate was simply to have more children in the hope some would survive. But even where birth control had some effect, it did not produce a significant decrease in population growth. Offsetting the slight decrease in the birthrate was a declining death rate; thus, the pressure of overpopulation on India's economy remained undiminished.

Indian food production increased steadily following independence, but it remained barely adequate. In general, the rate of increase of output was slightly higher than the rate of population growth, but this was offset by occasional years of crop failure caused by droughts or flooding. Moreover, the increased food production was unevenly distributed. Indian agriculture consisted largely of subsistence farming and was one of the world's least efficient in terms of yield per acre. Among the reasons for this inefficiency were the small size of farms, a shortage of farming machinery, a general lack of irrigation, a tradition-bound social system, and widespread malnutrition. The last of the reasons suggests a cruel cycle of cause and effect: Malnutrition and disease contributed to low agricultural productivity, which in turn led to greater poverty and hunger.

In India, as in the other agrarian nations in this part of the world, a wide gulf existed between the wealthy landowners and the far more numerous poor peasants, many of whom were landless. This great discrepancy between well-to-do farmers and the rural poor was an age-old problem that was inherent in the traditional society and the farming system. The practice of dividing land among sons contributed to making the average farm so small that it did not support the family; thus, the farmer was often forced to borrow money at high rates of interest to make ends meet. All too often, he was unable to repay the loan without selling what little land he had left. The result was a steady increase in the number of landless peasants and an increase in the size of farms owned by the wealthy.

More recent developments—the so-called US-sponsored Green Revolution (introduced in 1965) and agricultural mechanization—produced an increase in agricultural output in India and thus increased food supply. The Green Revolution introduced newly developed plants—high-yield varieties of wheat and rice—and new farming techniques (with considerable emphasis on irrigation) to grow the new types of grain.[2] In certain areas of India, wheat production doubled between 1964 and 1972, and the new rice strains had a similar effect. The Green Revolution, however, turned out to be a mixed blessing. It benefited mainly the minority of India's farmers—the wealthy landowners who could afford the new seeds and the additional irrigation works, fertilizers, and labor required to grow the new high-yield grain. The majority of the rural population—small landholders, landless peasants, and dryland farmers—lacked the capital or the means to borrow enough money to grow the new crops. Not only were they unable to reap the benefits of the increased food production, but they were actually hurt by it; the increased yield lowered the market price for grain crops, which meant a lower income for peasants who still followed traditional modes of farming. The Green Revolution thus tended to make the rich richer and the poor poorer.

The mechanization of farming, meaning primarily the increased use of tractors, had a similar effect. On the one hand, it contributed to a rise in food production; on the other, mechanization benefited only those who could afford the expensive new equipment. Furthermore, the use of tractors greatly reduced the need for farm laborers and, by eliminating many jobs, increased the ranks of the unemployed. More and more impoverished villagers of India were reduced to collecting firewood and animal droppings to sell as fuel. Even progress can breed poverty.

One of the consequences of dislocating the landless in the countryside was overcrowding in Indian cities. Many of those who migrated to the cities found life little better there than in the villages they had just left. Cities such as Calcutta and Bombay (Mumbai) were teeming with hungry and homeless people, many of whom literally lived and died in the streets. In the mid-1980s in Calcutta—which had a population of about 11 million—around 900,000 people were living in the streets with scant shelter.

India's Economic Development

India's efforts to modernize its economy and increase industrial production met with moderate success in the first two decades after independence. India opted for a mixed economy, whereby major industries such as iron and steel, mining, transportation, and electricity were nationalized—that is, owned and operated by the government. The government instituted its First Five-Year Plan for economic development in 1951. The plan's relatively modest goals for increased industrial output were attained, and they were followed by a sequence of similar Five-Year Plans. In 1961, at the conclusion of the second plan, Prime Minister Jawaharlal Nehru admitted that his country "would need many more five-year plans to progress from the cow dung stage to the age of atomic energy."[3] Although some impressive large-scale, modern industrial plants were built, most of India's industry remained small in scale and lacked modern machinery.

The overall growth rate of India's economy was steady but not particularly high. Following independence, India maintained an average annual GNP growth rate of between 3 percent and 4 percent.[4] A large gap existed between the incomes of the educated elites, technicians, and skilled laborers in the industrial sector and those of the unskilled laborers and peasants in the traditional sector—not to mention the many unemployed or underemployed city-dwellers.

India was handicapped by most of the problems of Third World countries: a lack of capital, difficulty in attracting foreign capital, illiteracy, and a lack of technology. To this list one might add India's unique social conservatism—the weight of tradition, especially a Hindu religious tradition in which much of Indian life was centered. The remnants of the ancient caste system militated against social mobility and the advancement of all members of society. Ethnic and linguistic diversity was also an obstacle to economic modernization. Still another factor retarding India's economic growth was the continual "brain drain" the country experienced. Many of India's best foreign-trained scientists and engineers chose not to return and remained in Western countries that provided career opportunities, modern technology, and creature comforts unattainable in their native land.

One important prerequisite for economic development is the existence of a market, either domestic or foreign. In India, the poverty of the masses meant a lack of purchasing power and thus the lack of a strong domestic market. India strived to increase its exports of raw materials and manufactured goods to pay for its large volume of imports—a substantial portion of which consisted of petroleum, foodstuffs, and industrial equipment. The impact of the oil crisis in the 1970s and global inflation and recession made it virtually impossible to maintain a favorable balance of trade. India was unable to match the increased cost of its imports with its substantially increased exports. Over the years, its trade deficit, its need of capital to finance continued industrialization, and its periodic food shortages forced India to rely heavily on foreign loans. In the 1950s and 1960s, India received huge shipments of food grains, mainly from the United States. However, with the increase in food production, a consequence of the Green Revolution, India needed less food relief, and in fact it became a net exporter of food in the early 1980s. After US developmental aid was terminated in 1971, the Soviet Union became India's primary source of foreign aid. In the decades since the First Five-Year Plan (1951), India received more foreign aid (from the World Bank, the Asian Development Bank, and Japan) than any other developing country. Its per capita income, however, remained among the world's lowest.

Political stability is an important asset for developing nations, and India possessed a degree of stability—at least at the beginning. The nation had a functioning parliamentary system based on the English model. It also had prolonged rule by one dominant party—the Congress Party—and continuity of leadership in the persons of Jawaharlal Nehru, who ruled from independence (1947) until his death in 1964; his daughter, Indira Gandhi, who ruled (except for one brief interlude) from 1966 to 1984; and her son, Rajiv Gandhi, who ruled until 1989.

After independence, India's leaders were confronted with the monumental task of binding together in nationhood the numerous subgroups of diverse ethnic, religious, and linguistic identities. Ethnic tensions were punctuated

Indian prime minister Rajiv Gandhi, a former pilot who succeeded his mother, Indira Gandhi, as prime minister in October 1984. *(Embassy of India)*

time and again by violent clashes between one or another of the ethnic groups and the Hindu majority. In the mid-1970s, the Indian political consensus, guided by Nehru and then by Gandhi, began to fray at the edges. The economy had suffered from the steep rise of oil prices in the early 1970s, dissent increased as railroad workers threatened to paralyze the vast railroad system, and popular agitation spilled into the streets. To forestall impeachment, Gandhi, in June 1975, responded with a twenty-one-month-long "National Emergency," accompanied by the suspension of the constitution, stringent press censorship, and the arrest of her political opponents. The emergency ended when Gandhi called for elections that she then lost, Congress's first electoral defeat. The emergency cast a long shadow, for it weakened India's commitment to constitutional principles. The chief beneficiaries were the Hindu far-right groups, which until then had carefully been kept out of politics. Among the Hindu jingoists arrested in 1975 were members of what became the rightist ruling political coalition of the late 1990s, including the future prime minister, Atal Bihari Vajpayee.[5]

India, Pakistan, and Bangladesh

In foreign affairs, India sought to follow Nehru's dictum of "live and let live." Nehru refused to be drawn into the Cold War and, instead, sought to exert the moral influence of India as a neutral peacemaker. It gained him considerable international prestige from some quarters, although John Foster Dulles, President Dwight Eisenhower's secretary of state, thought it was the height of immorality to stay neutral in the global struggle between good and evil. Nehru's neutrality, however, did nothing to mitigate India's troubles with its immediate neighbors, Pakistan and China. An ongoing border dispute with China, in particular, undermined India's Cold War neutrality and necessitated huge military expenditures.

Indian-Pakistani relations were strained from the time of partition and worsened as the two countries feuded over disputed territory. Both claimed the remote mountainous state of Kashmir. In 1948 and 1949, Indian and Pakistani forces clashed over Kashmir, despite UN efforts to keep the peace. India managed to secure control of most of Kashmir and turned a deaf ear to Pakistan's continual demands for a referendum there. The Pakistani claim to sparsely populated Kashmir was based on the fact that the majority of its people were Muslim, which explains why Pakistan wished to settle the matter with a plebiscite. India's claim rested mainly on the expressed will of the local Hindu ruling elite (from which Nehru himself descended) of Kashmir to remain within India.

China and India laid claim to the remote southern slopes of the Himalayan Mountains north of the Assam Plain, each staking its claim on different boundaries drawn by nineteenth-century British surveyors. India took the position that its claim was non-negotiable and turned down repeated diplomatic efforts by Beijing to settle the issue. In 1962, India's forces suffered a humiliating defeat by China in a brief border war. It led to a reassessment of India's neutrality. With Washington tilting toward Pakistan, there was little left for Nehru but to move closer to Moscow.

While India was still recovering from this setback, and not long after the death of Nehru, Pakistan decided to seek a military solution to the Kashmir issue. Tensions had mounted as skirmishes along the disputed border occurred with increasing frequency. Pakistan's forces then crossed the cease-fire line in August 1965, and the conflict quickly escalated into a brief but fierce war.

At this point, the Indian-Pakistani conflicts took on important global dimensions. Immediately after its 1962 war with China, India tilted toward Moscow, which was more than willing to provide support to a new client and thus extend its influence into South Asia. Washington responded by increasing its long-standing military support to Pakistan. The Pakistani air force relied on US-made F-86 Sabre and F-104 Starfighter jets; the Indians relied on Soviet-made Antonov-12 bombers and MiG-21s. Pakistan, meanwhile, found another source of support, the People's Republic of China. Ironically, the supporters of Pakistan—the United States and China—were bitter Cold War foes during these years.

During the 1960s, Pakistan faced economic problems similar to those in India. It was beset by an additional problem stemming from its peculiar situation as a nation with two separate parts. West Pakistan, where the capital was located, was separated from East Pakistan by nearly 1,000 miles of Indian territory. The distance between the two parts was even greater culturally and politically. The people of East Pakistan were Bengalis who, except for their Muslim religion, had little in common with the West Pakistanis, who are made up of several ethnic groups—the largest of which is the Punjabi. Political and military power was concentrated in West Pakistan, despite the fact that the more densely populated East Pakistan contained more than half of the nation's population. According to the constitution, however, East Pakistan comprised only one of the nation's five provinces and thus had only 20 percent of the seats in parliament. Only about 35 percent of the national budget was earmarked for East Pakistan, which was, moreover, a captive market for West Pakistani goods.

Bengali frustration mounted until it erupted in late 1970, when East Pakistan was hit, first, by a terrible natural catastrophe and then by a man-made disaster. In November, a powerful cyclone was followed by an enormous tidal wave and widespread flooding, leaving approximately 200,000 people dead and 1 million homeless. The lack of effective government relief was further evidence for the Bengalis of their government's indifference toward their problems and thus fed the flames of Bengali separatism. While still suffering the prolonged effects of the flooding, East Pakistan fell victim to the second disaster, an assault by the military forces of West Pakistan.

The military regime of General Yahya Khan had called for an election in December 1970 for a national assembly to draft a new constitution for Pakistan in the hope of ending thirteen years of military rule. In the election, Sheikh Mujibur Rahman, the Bengali leader and head of the Awami League, a political party that stood for elevating the status of East Pakistan, won a large majority. General Khan and Zulfikar Ali Bhutto, head of the leading West Pakistan–based party, were shocked by the election results. Instead of accepting them, they initiated a military crackdown and the imposition of martial law. In March 1971, General Khan unleashed a military attack on East Pakistan, striking first at the leaders of the Awami League, placing Mujibur under arrest. Thus began the bloody suppression of the Bengali people in which, ultimately, some 3 million people met their deaths at the hands of a Pakistani army of 70,000 troops. The indiscriminate brutality, in turn, led to resistance by the Bengalis, who now demanded independence. Meanwhile, roughly 10 million of the terrorized Bengali people fled their ravaged homeland, crossing the borders into India.

The assault on East Pakistan was met by Bengali armed resistance, mainly in the form of guerrilla warfare, and the conflict soon escalated into a full-fledged civil war. In December 1971, India, under the leadership of Indira Gandhi, seized the opportunity to deliver a blow against West Pakistan (it never had a quarrel with East Pakistan) and entered the fray. After two weeks of intensive combat, India drove West Pakistan's army out of East Pakistan.

The upshot was that, after nine months of bloodshed and casualties in the millions, India scored a decisive victory over West Pakistan and with it came the birth of a new nation, Bangladesh.

During the war, the Nixon administration supported Pakistan, despite its widely reported brutality, and went on record opposing the independence of Bangladesh. During the war, it denounced India for its aggression and terminated US economic aid. This, combined with China's support of Pakistan, caused India to strengthen its ties with the Soviet Union, and they signed a twenty-year pact of friendship in August 1971.

Nixon and his national security advisor, Henry Kissinger, saw the crisis in purely geostrategic terms, denouncing India as a "Soviet stooge." Nixon and Kissinger ignored the local causes for the war, preferring to see it as one between proxies of Moscow and Washington. They also downplayed reports of genocide on the part of the West Pakistani army (even while other White House officials acknowledged a "reign of terror").

In a supreme act of recklessness, Nixon and Kissinger went so far as to urge China to intervene on the side of Pakistan. Such a step had the potential of touching off a war across South Asia, something Nixon and Kissinger were well aware of (the Soviet Union would have been obliged to support India, and the United States to support Pakistan and China). The India-Pakistan war gave Nixon, who suffered from an incurable fear of appearing weak, the opportunity to show his mettle. In the midst of extricating the US military from Vietnam, Nixon wanted to show the Vietnamese—in Saigon and in Hanoi—his toughness and his resolve to stick with allies.[6]

Washington and Beijing balked at extending diplomatic recognition of independent Bangladesh, but eventually they did so, setting the stage for its entry into the United Nations in 1975. With US recognition came shipments of economic aid, something Bangladesh desperately needed.

For Pakistan, the 1971 war had a sobering effect. Now limited to what had been West Pakistan and with a population reduced by more than half, Pakistan turned to the tasks of rehabilitation and reorganization. Military government was ended when General Yahya Khan resigned and transferred power to Bhutto, whose Pakistan People's Party had come in second in the December 1970 election. One of Bhutto's first acts was to release Sheikh Mujibur from prison and arrange his return to Bangladesh, where he became its president. Bhutto also saw the wisdom of reducing tensions with India, and for that purpose he agreed to meet with Indira Gandhi in 1972. Indian-Pakistani relations were substantially improved until May 1974, when India successfully tested what it called a "nuclear device." By demonstrating its nuclear capacity, India established even more conclusively its position as the dominant military power in South Asia, but at the same time it aroused Pakistani fears.

Bangladesh, born of disaster, learned that independence produced no significant improvement in the lives of its people. After the war, India ordered the return of the 10 million Bengali refugees to their ravaged homeland. The catastrophic flood damage and war destruction had left the country devastated and unable to cope with the continuing waves of starvation and disease. Mujibur's government confronted not only a destitute people but also crime, corruption, and general disorder. The government declared a state of emergency in 1974, and in 1975 the once popular Mujibur was killed in a military coup. In the years that followed, political instability was prolonged by feuds between military factions contending for power.

Bangladesh, one of the most densely populated nations in the world, became synonymous with poverty. No larger than the US state of Georgia, it was the home of 154 million people in 2008, with an annual per capita GDP of $1,300. There was simply too little land to support its swollen population. About 90 percent of the people lived in the countryside, and about half of them owned less than an acre of land—an amount insufficient to feed the average household of six. Since the mid-1990s, however, it was able to sustain an annual GDP growth rate of about 5 percent. Nevertheless, in 2004, half of its people still lived below the poverty line, its incidence of malnutrition remaining among the highest in the world.[7]

South Asia Since 1980

India

The 1980s brought to the Indian subcontinent a modest improvement in the standard of living. In India and Pakistan, one could witness the slow but steady growth of industry, increased urban construction, greater agricultural output, and the expansion of the middle class. Yet, because of continued population growth, both countries remained among the poorest in the world in terms of per capita GNP, which in 1994 was $320 for India and $430 for Pakistan. Both countries endeavored to control population growth, which threatened their economic futures. Family-planning programs in past years had witnessed scant success. Activists were hoping for a feminist revolt against the grain of societies dominated by men.[8]

Another problem in India was the Sikh separatist movement in the northern state of Punjab and the repressive measures Indira Gandhi used in response to that movement. The Sikhs, whose religion is a mixture of Hinduism and Islam, made up about 2 percent of India's population, but they constituted the majority in Punjab. A brutal raid by government security forces on the Sikhs' Golden Temple in Amritsar in June 1984 left 1,200 dead and as many taken prisoner (the number of fatalities remaining in dispute). The Sikhs became relentless in their demand for an independent state—to be called Khalistan—and the Indian police were equally relentless in their effort to ferret out Sikh militants,

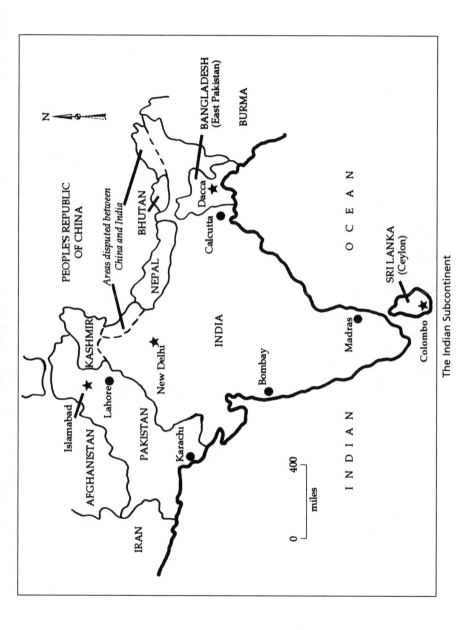

The Indian Subcontinent

sometimes taking the law into their own hands by torturing and murdering suspects. Thousands of Sikhs became political prisoners, held with neither charges nor trials. In October 1984, two of Gandhi's bodyguards, both Sikhs, shot her to death. Riots across India claimed the lives of thousands of Sikhs.

Indira Gandhi was succeeded by her son, Rajiv, who continued the repression of Sikhs. In May 1987, after four months of escalating violence during which security officers killed more than 500 Sikhs, he imposed direct federal rule over Punjab and ousted the elected state government of the Sikh moderates.

In November 1989, the Congress Party was narrowly defeated in the parliamentary elections, and Rajiv Gandhi resigned as prime minister. His administration was followed by two caretaker governments that wrestled with India's faltering economy and divisive religious/ethnic disputes. While campaigning for reelection in May 1991, Rajiv Gandhi was assassinated, the victim of a terrorist suicide bomb, one of the first ever. It was the work of the Tamil Liberation Tigers, who felt Gandhi had betrayed them in their war for independence against the Singhalese majority on the island nation of Sri Lanka. He died as his mother had, the victim of an ethnic movement seeking independence.

In the early 1990s, India was burdened with a foreign debt of $71 billion and dwindling foreign reserves. Moreover, it could no longer count on the Soviet Union for support, as the latter itself was disintegrating. India thus took the historic step of abandoning its centrally planned economy, which Jawaharlal Nehru had established four decades earlier.

The first move was to reverse India's balance-of-payments crisis by securing emergency loans from the International Monetary Fund and World Bank. In return, India slashed government spending, cut red tape, reduced import duties, invited foreign capital, and loosened interest rates to encourage private business and increase exports. The upshot was sustained economic growth.

India was less successful, however, in reining in its religious zealots. In December 1992, the nation suffered a renewal of religious violence. Fighting between Hindus and Muslims erupted in Ayodhya, where Hindu zealots tore down a Muslim mosque built in 1528 by the Mogul emperor Babur at the birthplace of the Hindu god Ram. This was the first time Hindus had razed a mosque since the 1947 partition. The violence spread to numerous Indian cities. Before order was restored, the casualty toll reached over 1,200 dead and 4,600 injured in the worst Hindu-Muslim clashes since 1947.

In March 1998, Congress lost its political monopoly to the Hindu nationalist Bharatiya Janata Party (BJP) under the leadership of Atal Bihari Vajpayee. The BJP—a linear descendant from the Hindu extremists of 1947—stood for making India a Hindu state and curbing the rights of India's Muslims and other religious and ethnic minorities. Its most extreme supporters expressed open admiration for Adolf Hitler.

The BJP program called for a break with the tolerant political tradition established by Congress Party rulers—Nehru and Gandhi—and enshrined in the Indian constitution stipulating that India was a secular state. In short, India, with its overwhelmingly large Hindu majority, would tolerate religious and ethnic diversity. It was something that Nehru, who did not want a "Hindu Pakistan," had been able to achieve only with great difficulty and in the face of opposition that insisted on denying the remaining Muslims full rights of citizenship. That opposition was now in power, setting out to rewrite with a vengeance the history of India.

BJP historians insisted that India was a Hindu nation, that the Vedas—the sacred, primary texts of Hinduism—were the only source of Indian culture, and that the Indus Valley was the birthplace of its civilization more than 5,000 years ago. Islam, they declared, came to India by force, only recently at that, and Muslims—and other religious groups, including Christians—should be reconverted to the Vedas. Moreover, they insisted, the caste system, steeped in Hinduism, was the natural order of things.

The greatest blot on the Vajpayee tenure in office became the Gujurat riots of 2002, worse than the religious violence in Ayodhya a decade earlier. After fifty-nine Hindus perished on a train, apparently the result of an accident, Hindu extremists went on a rampage. They raped hundreds of women and girls, looted stores, killed approximately 2,000 Muslims, and left a flood of refugees estimated at 200,000. Human Rights Watch accused the government of providing the Hindu killers the addresses of Muslim families and the police of participation in the pogroms.[9]

Vajpayee advocated a tougher line against Pakistan and declared openly that India possessed a nuclear weapons arsenal—something all previous Indian governments had been careful not to do. The Pakistani government, which had been working on its own nuclear arsenal for many years, responded in kind, telling India and the world that it, too, had joined the nuclear club.

In May 1998, India put on display its nuclear prowess by setting off five underground nuclear explosions. Pakistan responded with six of its own. For a while, it appeared that a nuclear war in South Asia was a distinct possibility. In the end, both sides backed off and Vajpayee, in fact, was able to mend fences with Pakistan after he stunned his nation in April 2003 by calling for a dialogue with Pakistan over Kashmir. He also established closer ties with Beijing, no mean feat, and with Washington.

Under Vajpayee, India continued to tie its economy to that of the world at large. He continued to break down trade barriers, dismantle state monopolies, and sell off state assets to private investors. A rising middle class found employment in information technology, business-processing outsourcing, and biotechnology. Still, despite the growth of per capita income—from $370 to $480 in four years—it remained one of the world's lowest.

In the spring of 2004, Vajpayee, confident of winning reelection, suffered a surprising defeat. All the experts were caught off guard when the Congress Party returned to power. Its leader, Sonia Gandhi, the Italian-born widow of Rajiv Gandhi, however, rejected the post of prime minister after Hindu nationalists bitterly complained about a foreign-born premier. The party then turned to Manmohan Singh, a Sikh, who became the first prime minister from a religious minority. Singh, who as finance minister during 1991–1996 had begun the reform program, continued to open the economy to the outside world.

The election outcome was largely the result of the anger of those left behind, particularly the rural poor. Privatization had thrown many out of work, had reduced the number of government jobs, and had been accompanied by rising prices. The BJP slogan, "Shining India," was popular with the monied classes at home and abroad, but neoliberal policies caused havoc among the rank and file. Unchecked greed was responsible for stock market and banking scams, drug trafficking, and political corruption. There were nearly 35 million unemployed in 2002, and their numbers continued to rise. Even the educated had trouble finding jobs. The suicide rate—particularly among farmers who could not compete in the global market and were falling into debt—was rapidly increasing. Forty percent of the population lived below the poverty line; 47 percent of children suffered from malnutrition; clean water was scarce; and the UN Human Development Index showed India slipping from 115th place in 1999 to 127th in 2001. Of the world's 800 million people living below the starvation line—defined as 1,960 calories a day—223 million lived in India.[10]

At the same time, however, another trend was in the making, the growth of a large middle class, estimated at 300 million people in 2008, between one-quarter and one-third of the population. With their disposable income they were increasingly able to purchase durable goods—appliances, electronic goods, and motorized vehicles. They were the beneficiaries of an economy that had been able to sustain an annual growth rate above 6 percent since the early 1990s. By 2007, India's per capita income had risen to an estimated $2,700—admittedly unevenly distributed.

Pakistan

Pakistan, too, witnessed swings of the political pendulum in the late 1980s and the 1990s. Until 1988, it remained under the rule of military strongman General Mohammed Zia ul-Haq, who disregarded critics who called for a return to civilian rule, citing the national emergency caused by the ongoing war in Afghanistan on Pakistan's northwestern border. The influx of hundreds of thousands of refugees from that war-ravaged country strained the economy and threatened internal security. Zia also pointed to the perceived threat of Indian aggression, which remained a Pakistani obsession.

Military rule ended abruptly in August 1988, however, when General Zia died in an airplane explosion—an apparent assassination—and parliamentary elections were held in November to return the country to civilian rule. The election produced a stunning victory for Benazir Bhutto as the new prime minister. The thirty-five-year-old Bhutto became the first female head of government of a Muslim nation. She was the daughter of Zulfikar Ali Bhutto, Pakistan's last civilian ruler, who had been deposed in 1974 and executed in 1979 by the same General Zia she now succeeded. After returning from extended exile early in 1988, the British-educated Bhutto had led a national movement against Zia.

Bhutto's grip on power was tenuous from the beginning because she had only a slight parliamentary plurality, and the opposition parties, the military, and the conservative clergy were watchful lest she make a slip. Her task was nothing less than ruling a nation beset with all the problems of Third World nations and at the same time satisfying its military leaders, who remained distrustful of her. Bhutto endeavored to steer a careful course between delivering promised increases in social spending and implementing an austerity program required by international lending agencies for desperately needed loans. During her first year in power, Bhutto's government played a key role in negotiating the terms by which the Soviet military withdrew from neighboring Afghanistan, while officially maintaining Pakistani support for Afghan rebels based in Pakistan.

Although Bhutto appeared on Pakistan's political scene as an angel of democracy and enjoyed popular support among younger Pakistanis, she was confronted by formidable political foes. Military leaders, suspicious of her popular appeal, were eager to find a pretext for her removal, lest she become too popular. Corruption and ethnic violence, although not new to Pakistan, proved cause enough to overthrow Bhutto in August 1990. She and her husband were charged with abuse of power and misconduct. The real force behind her demise was General Mirza Aslam Beg, who resented Bhutto's attempts to rein in the military.

The winner of the parliamentary elections held in October 1990 was Nawaz Sharif, who immediately set out to make good on his campaign pledge to establish an Islamic state in which the Koran became the supreme law and all aspects of life were subjected to its ultimate authority. Sharif's government, however, was ineffective in dealing with endemic corruption, recurrent violence (such as kidnapping for ransom), a mounting foreign debt, and worsening relations with India. Moreover, Pakistan suffered a major diplomatic and economic setback when the United States withdrew an annual $500 million in aid in protest of Pakistan's program to develop nuclear weapons.

Meanwhile, Benazir Bhutto was again waiting in the wings. When elections were held in 1993, Bhutto narrowly defeated Sharif in a bitter contest. As had been true during her previous stint as prime minister, Bhutto's government was insecure. Although she defended Pakistan's position on the two key foreign policy issues—the territorial dispute over Kashmir and Pakistan's development of nuclear weapons—her military and political adversaries faulted her for her lack of diplomatic toughness. Her position was made more difficult when opposition party leader Sharif declared publicly in August 1994 that Pakistan had produced nuclear weapons and even threatened their use against India in another war over Kashmir. In doing so, Sharif broke Pakistan's long silence regarding its nuclear capability and inflamed relations with India and with the United States, its erstwhile ally.

Bhutto's second term was beset with scandals and accusations. Corruption was so rampant that neither her vehement denials, her personal charisma, nor her family name were sufficient to save her from the wrath of her political opponents and the general public. She was forced to resign. Sharif, the militant Muslim, was returned to power in 1997 with a strong electoral victory, but his administration soon proved to be no less afflicted by corruption. When the supreme court began hearings on corruption charges against Sharif, he directed mobs to surround the court and then sacked the chief justice. He used similar methods to silence the press and control the police. Meanwhile, much of the country was in chaos because of violent feuds among rival ethnic, religious, and political groups beyond the pale of law and order. Sharif neglected the nation's infrastructure, and with that came a steep decline in such basic services as health care, education, and public transportation. Matters got worse as the economy slumped in mid-1998, partly as a result of punitive economic sanctions imposed on Pakistan for its nuclear weapons testing in May of that year.

To draw attention away from his own corruption and the chaotic social situation, Sharif allowed Islamic militants to pick a fight with India high up in the Himalayas. In early 1999, Pakistani "freedom fighters" made an incursion across the Line of Control in Kashmir into the Indian side. The result was the most pointless of wars imaginable as Pakistani and Indian soldiers engaged in sporadic combat high in the Himalayas at an elevation of 19,000 feet, even in the dead of winter on the Siachen Glacier, a region so desolate it was known as the "third pole." Sharif insisted that the Pakistani guerrillas were volunteers outside his government's control; the Clinton administration insisted that they withdraw from Kashmir. The militants, however, insisted on fighting in Kashmir "until the last drop of blood."

Finally, the army, which Sharif failed to control, had had enough. In October 1999, it arrested Sharif and thereby ended twenty-two years of ineffective and corrupt civilian rule. The army chief of staff, General Pervez Musharraf, who headed the coup, was roundly criticized worldwide for having sacked a democratically elected ruler. Many Pakistanis, however, expressed relief. Now it was once again the army's turn to attempt to make Pakistan governable.

Southeast Asia

In their quest for security, and particularly in response to the perceived threat of Communism, five of Southeast Asia's non-Communist nations—Indonesia, Malaysia, Thailand, Singapore, and the Philippines—formed the Association of Southeast Asian Nations (ASEAN) in 1967. ASEAN's founders proclaimed that its purpose was "to promote regional peace and security" as well as to foster regional economic cooperation.

ASEAN was a loosely organized group of nations whose leaders talked ardently of regional cohesion and cooperation. Nationalism remained an inhibiting force, however, as each of ASEAN's member states tended to be preoccupied with its own national interests and internal affairs. Antipathy toward Communist Vietnam was the glue that initially kept ASEAN together and gave it meaning in the 1970s. The US withdrawal from Indochina in 1973 and the Communist victories in Vietnam and Cambodia in 1975 increased ASEAN members' fears of Communist expansion. It served as the impetus for building stronger diplomatic ties and for strengthening their respective armies, albeit without taking steps to establish a regional military alliance. ASEAN denounced Vietnam for its invasion of Cambodia at the end of 1977 and turned down requests from the warring parties there—Vietnam and the Khmer Rouge—for economic assistance and better relations.

Once the Cold War ended, ASEAN membership was expanded to ten—including Cambodia and Vietnam, the former locus of concern. Its concentration was now on greater regional economic coordination. The countries made substantial progress toward industrializing their economies while shifting to an export-oriented pattern of economic growth. Increased cooperation, such as tariff reductions, contributed to remarkable new economic growth for the region, especially in Indonesia, Thailand, and Malaysia.

Indonesia

After a long and difficult struggle for independence in the late 1940s, Indonesia faced the daunting task of bringing its large, ethnically diverse population (the fifth largest in the world), which is spread over thousands of islands, into a functioning national entity. Its many ethnic groups had little in common except that they had been under Dutch colonial rule for three centuries. Indonesia's revolutionary leader and new president, Achem Sukarno, continued to provide nationalistic and charismatic leadership in the first two decades after independence. After experimenting with parliamentary democracy for several years, Sukarno in the 1950s turned to "guided democracy," which was a barely disguised dictatorship. His regime failed to stimulate economic growth, but he sought to quiet the growing discontent by harping on the theme of nationalism. Meanwhile, many disenchanted Indonesians joined the rapidly growing Communist Party of Indonesia (known by the acronym PKI). Before long, Sukarno himself turned to the PKI for support of his faltering government. To make matters worse, as far as Washington was concerned, Sukarno also accepted assistance from Moscow.

It was then, in September 1965, that a military coup led by a general named Suharto deposed Sukarno and place him under house arrest. The army claimed that it had carried out a countercoup against an attempted coup plotted by leftist army officers and the PKI. Suharto's determination to exterminate the PKI resulted in what the CIA called "one of the worst" mass murders of the twentieth century when the army slaughtered, within a year, hundreds of thousands of Indonesians—Communists and suspected Communists. Suharto's military dictatorship then ruled Indonesia for the next three decades.

For years, a succession of US administrations had sought the overthrow of Sukarno. The CIA provided covert aid to anti-Sukarno elements in the army (notably the Suharto faction) and cut off economic aid. It did not help when, in March 1964, Sukarno told Washington to "go to hell with your aid." US involvement was a scenario the CIA recommended "as a model for future operations" (one it followed, notably in Chile during the early 1970s).[11]

To legitimize his rule, Suharto created a "government party," which leading military and administrative officers were required to join, and an election system in which his party always managed to handily defeat the two opposition parties allowed. Having settled into this pattern of "guided democracy," Suharto decreed that Western-style liberal democracy was inappropriate for a nation with Indonesia's traditions, diverse makeup, and needs.

In his quest for national integration, Suharto readily resorted to armed force to suppress an independence movement on the island of East Timor on the southeastern fringe of the archipelago. East Timor, never part of Indonesia, had been a Portuguese colony for more than 400 years and had been granted independence in 1974. In December 1975, as rival leftist revolutionary groups were fighting for power in East Timor, Suharto—with the apparent support of Washington—sent in his army to claim the territory as Indonesian. In the meantime, the administration of Gerald Ford provided the Indonesian army with an array of weapons, with the congressional stipulation that they be used for "defensive" purposes only. In December 1975, Ford and his secretary of state, Henry Kissinger, met Suharto in Jakarta, where, with a wink and a nod—referred to as the "big wink" in State Department circles—they gave him the green light for an invasion, which began the day after *Air Force One* left Indonesian airspace. Kissinger gave Suharto the same advice he gave the assassins of Latin America's Operation Condor: "It is important that whatever you do succeeds quickly."[12] For the next twenty-three years, every US president—from Ford to Clinton—armed Indonesia's armed forces and consistently backed its brutal occupation of East Timor.

The invasion of East Timor touched off a long and bitter war. The resilience of the revolutionaries and the massive force applied by Suharto's army to defeat them resulted over the next two decades in a death toll of more than 200,000 people. Insofar as this was about one-third of the population of East Timor and most of the dead were noncombatants, the slaughter may well be considered genocide.

Suharto was more successful in achieving economic development, a major goal of the "New Order" he had proclaimed in 1966. With the help of his Western-educated bureaucrats, he embarked on an ambitious program of economic growth. He courted foreign investment, especially from oil companies, which greatly increased Indonesia's production of petroleum. Oil export earnings increased still more with the international increase in oil prices in the 1970s, and this windfall fueled continued economic development. By the early 1980s, oil accounted for 78 percent of the country's export earnings. Steady, though not spectacular, economic growth continued until oil prices tumbled in the mid-1980s. The government then introduced reforms that called for a reduction in government expenditures, diversification, less reliance on oil revenues, and even more foreign investment and joint ventures. These reforms were generally successful, and Indonesia's GNP continued to climb.

If Suharto's record as ruler of Indonesia were to be based on GNP alone, he would receive decent marks, but the economic figures masked a grim reality of the military dictatorship's unbridled corruption, unabashed nepotism, and gross inequities in the distribution of wealth. Under Suharto the flow of money went mainly to the island of "imperial Java," specifically Jakarta, the capital city, at the expense of the rest of the country. Indeed, hundreds of millions of dollars of the new wealth flowed into the hands of Suharto himself and his family members.[13] Still, even as the financial crisis (which began in Thailand) hit his country in late 1997, Suharto (now seventy-six years old) was confident that his handpicked consultative assembly would elect him in March 1998 to his seventh five-year term as president. But by that time the economy was in a meltdown. Indonesia's currency, the *rupiah*, had lost 70 percent of its value against the dollar, and, according to the World Bank, no nation in recent history "has ever suffered such a dramatic reversal of fortune" in such a short time.[14] (In contrast, the decline of the Russian economy had taken place over several years.) Inflation reached 70 percent a year; widespread unemployment meant that an estimated two-thirds of the population were now living in poverty, unable to purchase the 2,000 calories of food necessary for a minimum diet. This led to looting and violence, particularly against ethnic Chinese scapegoats, who were blamed for the financial disaster.

Student protesters, demanding Suharto's ouster and democratic reforms, took to the streets day after day, clashing with police and army troops. As the crisis worsened, Suharto's own privileged military, which had benefited handsomely during his tenure, abandoned him to save its own skin. Suharto stepped down and turned the reins over to an old crony, B. J. Habibie.

Habibie introduced political reforms aimed at mollifying the protesters and foreign critics and held parliamentary elections in June 1999, which brought to power Abdurahman Wahid, an elderly, moderate Muslim scholar. His first task was to take the US-trained and -equipped military out of politics. He placed Jakarta under the command of generals loyal to him and then, in February 2000, dismissed the army chief (and defense minister) Wiranto, the man largely responsible for the "dirty war" of 1999 in East Timor.

Early in 1999, the government agreed to a referendum on independence to be held in East Timor under UN auspices in August of that year. But this did not prevent the Indonesian army commander in East Timor from declaring that in the event of independence "everything will be destroyed, so that East Timor will be worse off than it was 23 years ago."[15] Despite such threats and brutal assaults on civilians by heavily armed "militias" (instruments of the Indonesian army), nearly 80 percent of the East Timorese voted for secession. The "militias," as promised, went on a rampage that destroyed much of East Timor's infrastructure, killing an estimated 3,000–7,000 people and deporting to West Timor another 150,000–200,000. They also killed several unarmed UN workers, the remainder fleeing to nearby Australia. Indonesia's National Human Rights Commission later placed the blame squarely on the shoulders of General Wiranto, who had done nothing to stop the massacres and thus was "morally responsible." When a helpless United Nations was unable to stop the violence, Australia finally decided to act. Its troops landed on the island, expelled the military and its militias, and restored order. Then came the difficult task of rebuilding devastated East Timor, the newest UN member.

Wahid then turned to another pressing problem, the growing restlessness in other regions, notably Aceh and Irian Jaya. He offered them federalism, that is, a share of local control, a concession hitherto unthinkable. The greatest challenge was Aceh, the westernmost outpost of the far-flung archipelago. It was here, in "Mecca's verandah," where the first contacts with Islam had been established in the eighth century; its people remained particularly religious and resistant to outside control. It had taken the Dutch more than a quarter-century to conquer Aceh at the end of the nineteenth century, and even then it was never fully pacified. In 1945, its people were particularly enthusiastic for independence and thus their disappointment was much the greater when the heavy hand of Sukarno, and later of Suharto, came down on them. Aceh's wealth from its lucrative oil industry did not go to its people, schools, and hospitals, but instead to Jakarta. In 1976, the Free Aceh Movement (FAM) declared independence and the military reacted predictably, and in the 1990s the army tortured and murdered an estimated 5,000 people there.

In December 2004, an earthquake in the Indian Ocean—at 9.0 on the Richter scale one of the largest ever recorded—triggered a massive tsunami that caused havoc in several nations. Aceh took the full brunt of it. The devastation has been compared to that of Hiroshima. In the wake of the tsunami, in August 2005, a new Indonesian government and the FAM worked out a cease-fire that ended a twenty-nine-year civil war. Jakarta granted Aceh a high degree of autonomy; the FAM, in its turn, agreed to disarm.

Irian Jaya, the western half of the island of New Guinea, on the eastern fringe of the archipelago, nurtured its own dreams of secession that dated back to 1961 (when it was still under Dutch rule). After the Netherlands handed over the region to Indonesia in 1969, Suharto suppressed its independence movement there. Irian Jaya holds substantial natural resources, including the world's most lucrative copper and gold mines. The mines, however, employed a scant 300 of the indigenous population; the other 11,000 workers came from other parts of Indonesia and from abroad. Wahid was not alone in believing that, particularly after East Timor, the loss of another province would mark the beginning of the end of Indonesia. Wahid, who earlier had spoken of federalism, backtracked in December 2000, when the army launched a crackdown in Irian Jaya, killing and jailing demonstrators who had hoisted the illegal separatist flag.

Decades of exploitation and misrule by Suharto greatly weakened the idea that the 200 million people of Indonesia had a common heritage, something they had believed as they fought to rid themselves of Dutch rule. The centrifugal forces at the end of the twentieth century were severely testing the commitment to Indonesian nationhood.

Thailand

Having escaped colonization, Thailand was spared the pains and devastation of a revolutionary war for independence in the postwar period. This, in addition to political stability, contributed to Thailand's economic growth, facilitated by increased agricultural production and foreign investments, the latter making possible Thailand's emerging industrial base.

The new prosperity was by no means enjoyed by all elements of society; indeed, the hard-suffering, underpaid working class saw precious little of the national earnings its labor helped to generate. Moreover, Thailand's political tradition of deference to authority and patron-client relationships was more conducive to military rule than to democracy. In the 1930s, the military had entrenched itself in power and only occasionally had given way to civilian rule, which usually proved unstable. Thus, when the generals took control of the government in February 1991, events followed a traditional pattern. The leader of the 1991 coup and strongman of the new regime, General Suchinda Kraprayoon, arrested the prime minister, established martial law, abolished the constitution, and dissolved parliament. After a brief civilian interlude, Suchinda and his generals reclaimed ruling power. Their intervention touched off angry antimilitary demonstrations in the capital of Bangkok. Soon, over 100,000 protesters—mainly students—took to the streets. As the demonstrations grew larger and more riotous, the highly revered Thai king, Bhumibol Adulyadej, who had occupied the throne since 1946, intervened, calling on leading parties to amend the constitution (intended to protect the country against military rule) as the protesters demanded.

General Suchinda, however, refused to give in to the protesters, and in May 1992 he unleashed a ruthless assault against them. For three days, 50,000 troops scattered the unarmed civilians, firing live ammunition and killing over 100. The bloody spectacle was seen on television screens around the world—except in Thailand, where the military controlled the media. Once again, King Bhumibol interceded to put an end to the massacre.[16] Business leaders condemned the army's resort to brute force, warning that such measures damaged Thailand's international image and drove away much-needed foreign investors.

This time, Suchinda was forced to resign and was replaced by former prime minister Anand, who, bolstered by the king's mandate and public support, sought to break the military's sixty-year hold on power. He commissioned an investigation of the recent massacre and, on the basis of its findings, sacked four leading military officers. Meanwhile, the parliament enacted amendments to the constitution intended to ensure civilian rule in the name of democracy.

The military influence was curtailed but by no means eliminated, for it retained control of many levers of power, including the police and important state industries (e.g., telecommunications, airlines, shipping, and trucking). When Prime Minister Thaksin Shinawatra, Thailand's richest man, first elected in 2001, used his office to enrich himself and his cronies even further, the army once again intervened. This time, in 2006, it acted on behalf of the king, wearing the monarchy's traditional colors. The army may have done the nation a service in removing a dictator, but it also shredded the provision of the 1997 constitution designed to keep it out of politics.[17] Thaksin, convicted in absentia of corruption, remained nonetheless popular among those less well off. His supporters came from the ranks of those who benefited from the cheap health care, microcredit, and patronage network he had introduced and that now challenged the established order. The king's meddling in political affairs (largely on behalf of the military) over the years had undermined the rule of law. The political tug-of-war in 2008 once again took to the streets, with Thaksin's "red shirt" supporters demonstrating against the royalist "yellow shirts." Eventually Thaksin's demonstrators even directed their protests against the once revered king (but now feeble and aged) for having repeatedly backed military coups. Thailand faced a future with the illusion of a universally adored monarchy shattered, a weak parliamentary system, and an army standing in the wings.

Malaysia

Once Malaysia gained its independence in 1957, it gradually became a poster child for Third World economic progress. Blessed with natural resources—agricultural products of all sorts, tin, and gas and oil reserves—it also took pains to develop its manufacturing base, which in 1960 made up a scant 10 percent of GDP but rose to nearly 50 percent by 2008.

Malaysia's economic development was all the more remarkable in light of its ethnic and geographic diversity. The main part of the nation is on the Malay Peninsula south of Thailand; the other two parts, Sabah and Sarawak, are on the island of Borneo, over 1,000 miles to the east. Malaysia reorganized in 1963 into a federation composed of those three parts and Singapore, and as such it had an ethnic Chinese majority. But in 1965, Singapore—with its predominantly Chinese population—seceded and became independent. The population of the remainder of the federation, renamed Malaysia, then consisted of 50 percent Malay, 36 percent Chinese, and 9 percent Indian.

At the time of independence, Malaysia's economy was overwhelmingly agricultural, typical of a Third World nation. Half a century later, with the industrial sector providing up to 50 percent of the nation's GNP and with its per capita GNP at around $14,000, Malaysia joined the ranks of the newly developing nations.

With the exception of a two-year interval of military rule (1970–1972), Malaysia maintained stable civilian rule under a peculiar parliamentary system designed to maintain the Malays in power and to keep the Chinese and other ethnic minorities satisfied with economic growth and limited representation in parliament. The first prime minister, Tuanku Azlan Muhibbudin, the founder of the Malay-dominated Alliance Party, won successive rigged elections. But when the Alliance Party lost its majority in the 1969 election, it led to four days of bloody clashes between ethnic Chinese and Malays. The government proclaimed a state of emergency, disbanded parliament, and brought in troops to restore order. The result was the implementation of a "New Economic Policy," which granted special rights and privileges to Malays while excluding Chinese and other ethnic groups. The government also enacted "sedition acts" prohibiting criticism of "sensitive issues," meaning the special rights granted to Malays.

During the 1970s, the economy—driven largely by petroleum and natural gas exports—grew at a rate of nearly 8 percent annually. The new wealth offered advantages for many educated Malays and Chinese and thus served to reduce ethnic tensions. The lower class benefited from trickle-down economics that included new schools, electrification projects, piped water, and paved roads.

Malaysia, like other export-oriented countries, became increasingly integrated into the global economy. Prime Minister Mahathir Mohamad (1981–2003) privatized public utilities and was able to attract increasing foreign investments. Mahatir, a vocal critic of Western values, also initiated a "Look East" policy, an Asian approach to solving Asian problems (which included emulating the Japanese and Korean industrial models). The result was continued robust economic growth (8 percent annually) in the late 1980s. By the 1990s, manufactured goods accounted for half of the country's exports, and Malaysia became the world's largest exporter of semiconductors. The showpiece of Malaysia's economic success was its gleaming capital city, Kuala Lumpur, which boasted the world's tallest building.

Singapore

Singapore, an island nation at the southern tip of the Malay Peninsula, is a city-state and a former British colony that gained its independence from Malaysia in 1965. Unlike the other ASEAN nations, its population was overwhelmingly ethnic Chinese. Moreover, Singapore's economic liftoff came in the 1960s, about a decade earlier than the other ASEAN members. Under its authoritarian ruler, Lee Kuan Yew, Singapore became one of the most prosperous countries in the world, with a per capita GNP of approximately $50,000 in 2008. A combination of political stability, population growth control, high standards of education, a disciplined and skilled workforce, efficient economic management, export-oriented planning, and a free-market system worked miracles for its 4.6 million people. Strategically situated at the center of the Southeast Asian sea-lanes, Singapore was a conveyor belt for the shipment of goods from outside the region to neighboring ASEAN countries, as well as a major regional financial center.

Singapore's remarkable economic development was largely a result of the stewardship of Prime Minister Lee, whose authoritarian rule extended well beyond the bounds of conventional politics. He endeavored to make Singapore a spotless, crime-free, morally upright, and austere society. Toward that end, he took it upon himself to dictate social and moral standards and to enforce them with strict laws and strong penalties. He decreed, for example, that men could not grow their hair long, and offenders were subject to arrest, fines, and even imprisonment. Possession of drugs, even small amounts, was punishable by death. Nor did Lee, who had exercised unlimited authority in Singapore since the late 1950s, allow dissent. He maintained that the curbs on individual freedoms were not regimentation but rather paternalistic guidance that made for a more disciplined and productive people whose work habits contributed to ever higher productivity and the betterment of society.

Dictatorship and Revolution in the Philippines

While ASEAN members Thailand, Malaysia, and Singapore registered impressive economic growth in the 1970s, the Philippines failed to do so. This nation of many islands, once a Spanish dominion (1571–1898) and then a US colony (1898–1946), struggled to sustain economic growth and to maintain a semblance of democratic institutions after gaining independence in 1946. Under a succession of dictators, the Philippines lost ground on both fronts, especially during the twenty-year rule of Ferdinand Marcos. When Marcos came to power in 1965, the country was developing apace with Taiwan, Singapore, and Thailand. When Marcos was driven from power in 1986, however, those nations had per capita incomes three to four times higher than that of the Philippines. By then, the country had a foreign debt of $27 billion and had been unable to make payments on the principal of that debt since 1983. The GNP declined during the years 1978–1990.

At the center of mismanagement and corruption was Marcos himself. He had been elected president in 1965 as a social reformer, but he soon succumbed to the pattern of patron-client corruption common to Philippine political tradition, and he proved to be the master. Governing the Philippines became so lucrative for Marcos that he made certain he would stay in power despite a constitution that permitted only two four-year terms. As the end of his second term approached, Marcos declared martial law, citing a mounting Communist insurgency as the justification for canceling elections, suspending the constitution, and writing a new constitution that gave him a new term and broad powers. He also rounded up and jailed political opponents and critical journalists. Marcos and his wife, Imelda, became very wealthy by schemes such as demanding kickbacks from businessmen and pocketing foreign aid.

Marcos—who promoted himself as the nation's indispensable leader— claimed to be a lawyer who had never lost a case, a heroic military officer who had never lost a battle, a lover who had won the heart of the nation's beauty queen, a great athlete and marksman, a good father, a good Catholic, and an honest and modest man. The popularity of his wife, Imelda, the former Miss Philippines, was an added attraction to his cult of personality. Successive administrations in Washington turned a blind eye to what was taking place in Manila and instead honored Marcos as a stalwart opponent of Communism and a champion of democracy. When US vice-president George H. W. Bush visited the Philippines in 1981 after nine years of martial law, he told Marcos, "We [the United States] love your adherence to democratic principles and to the democratic processes."[18]

Washington remained tolerant as long as Marcos provided the political stability considered necessary to protect substantial US financial investments in the Philippines and to retain the two mammoth US military installations on the islands—Subic Bay Naval Station and Clark Air Base—considered vital to US strategic interests in East Asia. Marcos skillfully traded assurances regarding the military bases for ever larger economic and military aid packages from Washington.

In the early 1980s, however—around the time of Vice-President Bush's visit—the Marcos regime began to unravel. In 1981, he released from prison his foremost political opponent, Benigno Aquino, to allow him to go to the United States for heart surgery. Aquino, the likely winner of the 1973 presidential election had it taken place, decided to end his exile in August 1983 to return home to lead a movement to unseat Marcos. Upon arriving at Manila's airport, before even setting foot on the tarmac, he was shot to death. Responding to the outrage among Filipinos, Marcos appointed a commission to investigate the murder. After lengthy deliberations, the commission reported that evidence pointed to a military conspiracy reaching all the way to chief of staff General Fabian Ver, a cousin of Marcos. The verdict of the eight-month trial that followed was predictable: Ver and the twenty-four other military defendants were acquitted. Meanwhile, a vigorous opposition movement developed that regarded the fallen Aquino as a martyr and his wife, Corazon, as a saint. While Marcos was losing credibility at home and abroad, the economy was deteriorating rapidly, largely because of the flight of capital triggered by Aquino's assassination. In the hinterlands, a Communist-led New People's Army stepped up its insurgency.

In response to mounting pressure, in November 1985, the undaunted dictator, who had won every election he had entered thus far, announced his decision to hold a presidential election in February 1986. Corazon Aquino had already stated she would run against Marcos should he allow an election. The stage was set for a showdown that had all the makings of a morality play. Although the sixty-eight-year-old Marcos was visibly ill, suffering from kidney disease, and was roundly attacked by the press, he remained confident of victory and appeared unfazed by the enormous throngs of people who rallied in support of his opponent. Aquino, who presented herself as Cory, a humble housewife, sought to redeem the legacy of her murdered husband and called for a return to democracy, decency, and justice. Moreover, she did not hesitate to charge that "Mr. Marcos is the No. 1 suspect in the murder of my husband."[19] As election day approached, it appeared that Cory's "people power" would surely sweep her to victory—if the elections were fair. Big business and the middle class were abandoning Marcos, and the Roman Catholic Church openly supported Aquino. Many feared, however, that the cagey Marcos, who paid people to attend his political rallies, would find ways to rig the voting to ensure his reelection.

No clear winner emerged from the election, as each side claimed victory and charged the other with fraud. Despite indisputable evidence of election interference and fraudulent vote counting by the Marcos-appointed election commission, Marcos proceeded to plan for inauguration ceremonies. He was emboldened by US president Ronald Reagan's acceptance of the election results.[20] Meanwhile, at the encouragement of Roman Catholic leader Jaime Cardinal Sin, hundreds of thousands of people went into the streets to express support for Aquino and to demand that Marcos step down. At this point, Marcos's defense minister and several high-ranking army officers switched sides. The climax came when pro-Marcos troops, advancing toward the rebel encampments, were stopped by the human wall of Aquino supporters and Catholic nuns kneeling in prayer in front of stalled tanks. At that juncture, Reagan, who had steadfastly supported Marcos, bowed to the manifest will of the majority of the Filipino people and arranged for the fallen dictator to be airlifted to Hawaii. Marcos and his wife fled the country with the billions of dollars they had amassed. With the help of people power, the church, and her new military allies, Cory Aquino proclaimed victory for a democratic revolution.

After the exultation over Aquino's triumph against dictatorship and corruption, the new and inexperienced president had to face the hard realities of governing the nation and restoring its shattered economy. Aquino moved swiftly to restore civil rights, free political prisoners, eliminate pro-Marcos elements from the government, and enact political reforms. Aquino, whose family owned large stretches of land, had promised land reform during her campaign, but afterward she showed little interest in it. The power of the old oligarchy and the old economic system remained intact. The Philippines was still saddled with a large foreign debt, the payment of which consumed about one-third of the country's export earnings. In 1988, the country was granted a $10 billion developmental grant from the combined sources of the IMF and several European and Asian nations, but to little avail. Affluence for the few and misery for the many remained the dominant trend. On the eve of Aquino's fourth anniversary in power in February 1990, people power was but a distant memory. She had lost support in virtually all segments of the population.

One of the major issues she faced was the status of the two large US military facilities, Subic Bay Naval Station and Clark Air Base. Nationalist groups saw them as an affront to Philippine sovereignty, a social blight, and potential targets in a nuclear war. Aquino promised not to abrogate the agreement on the bases, which was due to expire in September 1991, but she placed clauses in the new Philippine constitution that forbade nuclear weapons on Philippine territory and required that any extension of the lease agreement beyond 1991 be approved by a two-thirds majority of the Philippines senate.[21]

Two events in 1991 intervened to cause an unanticipated resolution of the issues surrounding the military bases: the sudden end of the global Cold War and a powerful volcanic eruption. The former caused the United States to reconsider its Asian security needs, and the latter provided sufficient cause to vacate the two bases. In June, Mount Pinatubo, a volcano dormant for 600 years, erupted, sending a towering plume into the air and blanketing the surrounding region—including the two bases—with a thick layer of powdery ash. With Clark Air Base buried under volcanic ash, US authorities decided to abandon the base rather than spend the estimated $500 million to dig it out. Soon afterward, when the Philippines senate rejected a ten-year extension of the lease on

Crouch, Harold A. *The Army and Politics in Indonesia.* Ithaca, N.Y.: Cornell University Press, 1988.

Diamond, Larry, Juan Linz, and Seymour Martin Lipset, eds. *Democracy in Developing Countries: Asia.* Boulder: Lynne Rienner Publishers, 1989.

Kulick, Elliot, and Dick Wilson. *Thailand's Turn: Profile of a New Dragon.* New York: St. Martin's Press, 1992.

Neher, Clark D. *Southeast Asia in the New International Era.* 2nd ed. Boulder: Westview Press, 1994.

Palmer, Ronald D., and Thomas J. Reckford. *Building ASEAN: 20 Years of Southeast Asian Cooperation.* New York: Praeger, 1987.

Taylor, John G. *Indonesia's Forgotten War: The Hidden History of East Timor.* London: Zed Books, 1991.
An exposé of Indonesia's ongoing effort to suppress the Timorese nationalist movement.

Wurfel, David. *Filipino Politics: Development and Decay.* Ithaca, N.Y.: Cornell University Press, 1988.

Notes

1. "Population Commentary," *Baltimore Sun*, July 12, 1992, p. 2A.

2. The development of new plants producing more grain and less stem per plant was the result of years of scientific work financed by the Rockefeller and Ford Foundations. Under ideal conditions, the new rice plants produced twice as much grain per acre and reduced the growing period by half, so that two crops could be grown in one growing season.

3. Quoted in Stephen Warshaw and C. David Bromwell, with A. J. Tudisco, *India Emerges: A Concise History of India from Its Origins to the Present* (San Francisco: Diablo Press, 1974), p. 132.

4. World Bank, *World Development Report, 1984* (New York: Oxford University Press, 1984). India's average annual rate of growth of GNP between 1955 and 1970 was 4.0 percent; during the 1970s, it fell to 3.4 percent. The rate of growth of GNP per capita for these two periods was 1.8 percent and 1.3 percent, respectively.

5. P. N. Dhar, *Indira Gandhi, the "Emergency," and Indian Democracy* (New Delhi: Oxford University Press, 2000).

6. "Nixon/Kissinger Saw India as 'Soviet Stooge' in 1971 South Asia Crisis," *National Security Archive*, June 29, 2005.

7. World Bank, "The World Bank in Bangladesh," September 2004.

8. Steve Coll, "Burgeoning Population Threatens India's Future," *Washington Post*, January 21, 1990, p. H7.

9. Human Rights Watch, April 2002 report, *"We Have No Orders to Save You": State Participation and Complicity in Communal Violence in Gujarat,* http://www .hrw.org/en/news/2002/04/30/state-supported-massacres-gujarat.

10. Pankaj Mishra, "India: The Neglected Majority Wins!" *New York Review of Books*, August 12, 2004, pp. 30–37.

11. Peter Dale Scott, "The United States and the Overthrow of Sukarno, 1965–1967," *Pacific Affairs* (Summer 1985), pp. 240, 253, 263, passim.

12. Jeffrey A. Winters, "US Media and Their Ignorance Partly Blamable for E. Timor's Misery," *Jakarta Post Online*, May 28, 2002. Also, John Pilger, "Journey to East Timor: Land of the Dead," *The Nation*, April 25, 1994. Kissinger here, perhaps un-

consciously, drew upon Macbeth's contemplation of the murder of Duncan: "If it were done when 'tis done then 'twere well it were done quickly."

13. "Indonesia to Probe Riches Amassed by Suharto Since '66," *Baltimore Sun*, June 2, 1998, p. 10A. Estimates of the personal riches he and his family amassed vary greatly, but one estimate puts it at about $40 billion.

14. Floyd Norris, "In Asia, Stocks Melt Faster Than in '29," *New York Times*, January 11, 1998, p. BU1; wire service reports, "Indonesia Falls Rapidly from Riches to Rags," *Baltimore Sun*, October 8, 1998, p. 2A.

15. Colonel Tono Suratnam, cited in Erhard Haubold, "Verraten und verkauft?" *Frankfurter Allgemeine Zeitung*, September 18, 1999, p. 12.

16. The king learned about the massacre from his daughter in Paris, where she saw it on the TV news. "Months of Grace," *The Economist*, June 20, 1992, p. 32. The king summoned the general and members of the opposition for an audience. As they knelt before him, he demanded an immediate restoration of order—a scene seen on television screens around the world and this time in Thailand as well.

17. Joshua Kurlantzick, "Tanks Roll in Thailand," *Washington Post*, September 24, 2006, p. B3.

18. Cited in William J. vanden Heuvel, "Postpone the Visit to Manila," *New York Times*, September 8, 1983, p. A23.

19. Cited in "A Test for Democracy," *Time*, February 3, 1986, p. 31.

20. William Pfaff, "The Debris of Falling Dictatorships," *Baltimore Sun*, February 17, 1986, p. 9A.

21. The constitutional provision outlawing nuclear weapons on Philippine territory begged the question of enforcement, because the US government's position was that it would neither confirm nor deny the presence of nuclear weapons on its ships or bases.

Part 5

The Emergence of a New Landscape

During the 1980s, the Cold War took the world on a roller-coaster ride, escalating in the first half of the decade and descending rapidly at the end. In the United States, the Reagan administration stepped up its confrontation with the Soviet Union while in the Kremlin the old guard dug in. All the while, the pace of the nuclear arms race was quickening.

The combination of the continued East-West conflict and the widening gulf between North and South produced a host of dilemmas. Many Third World countries were politically unstable, and the superpowers continued to battle each other through proxies, as in Nicaragua and Afghanistan. The rise of militant Islam in Iran and other Islamic nations produced a powerful third ideological force in the Middle East and beyond. As the global standoff between East and West continued, other power centers emerged. Japan and the European Community sustained remarkable economic growth and became new economic forces to be reckoned with. Once the Cold War ended, international economic issues became more nettlesome.

At the end of the decade came a series of momentous events that, taken together, signified the disappearance of the forty-five-year post–World War II world order. The Soviet Union, under a dynamic new ruler, Mikhail Gorbachev, began a program of restructuring that not only resulted in the transformation and then the demise of the Communist system, but also had an explosive effect on its East European satellites.

We begin with the emergence of Japan as an economic superpower and South Korea's remarkable economic development, the main topics of Chapter 16. One of the premier postwar success stories is the rise of Japan from the ashes of war to become the world's second-largest economic power in the 1980s. We discuss Japan's "economic miracle," the friction that developed in its economic relations with the United States, and Japan's downturn in the 1990s. Also presented in this chapter are South Korean industrialization and democratization, as well as the ongoing Cold War contention between South Korea and North Korea, where a Stalinist regime continued to hold power.

Chapter 17 examines the economic and political integration of Western Europe under the aegis of the European Union. Its success spurred economic regionalism in other parts of the world, namely, the creation of the North American Free Trade Agreement and regional economic blocs in Latin America and Asia. The issues of protectionism, economic interdependence among nations, and globalization are also discussed, with particular emphasis on the impact of globalization on Third World nations. Also examined are the impact of the Organization of Petroleum Exporting Countries (the oil cartel), the problem of Third World debt, and the issue of climate change.

We turn in Chapter 18 to the incredible cascade of events in the Soviet Union at the end of the 1980s. Our focus first is on Mikhail Gorbachev, the architect of the Soviet empire's radical transformation and eventual dissolution. We examine the various aspects of his program of restructuring—perestroika—and his call for openness—glasnost—which touched off a wave of nationalistic unrest among the non-Russian Soviet republics and soon disrupted the cohesion of the Soviet Union. We then analyze the sudden fall of Gorbachev and the collapse of the Soviet Union, after which Boris Yeltsin endeavored to steer the new Russian Federation toward capitalism and democracy while struggling to maintain political and social order—and to stay in power—and the politics of his successor, Vladimir Putin.

We then examine the breakup of the Soviet empire, beginning with the 1979 Soviet invasion of Afghanistan, its impact on the Cold War, and its aftermath: the withdrawal of Soviet troops leaving behind a shattered nation. We then turn to Poland, where in the early 1980s a dramatic showdown between Solidarity, the Polish labor movement, and the Communist government took place. Next, we examine the political upheavals in Eastern Europe triggered by Gorbachev's call for reforms and his pledge of noninterference. For more than forty years, Poland and other Soviet satellites in Eastern Europe had been ruled by Communist regimes that answered to Moscow, but suddenly in 1989, when it became clear that Moscow would not intervene to prop up faltering governments, these regimes soon crumbled. Included in the account of the dismantling of East European Communism is the dramatic story of the fall of Communism in East Germany and the reunification of Germany. The chapter closes with an examination of the breakup of Yugoslavia and the subsequent turmoil in the Balkans.

In Chapter 19, we turn to one of the gravest issues facing the world since 1945: the nuclear arms race. As both cause and effect of the Cold War, the arms race continued unabated for over forty years. The deadly logic of deterrence compelled both sides to build ever more weapons and continually upgrade them. We review earlier efforts at nuclear disarmament and then turn to the Strategic Arms Limitation Talks, the controversy over the Strategic Defense Initiative, and the Strategic Arms Reduction Talks. The next major concern is nuclear proliferation, which is the focus of attention in the last section in this chapter.

Beginning in the late 1970s, the world felt the impact of the revival of Islam and its political militancy. Although long one of the world's great religions, Islam is little known by Westerners; for that reason, we have seen fit to devote the first section of Chapter 20 to an exposition of the tenets of Islam and its political dimensions. It is necessary to see that within Islam, religion and politics are inseparable and that an Islamic state is not merely one in which the predominant religion is Islam, but one in which politics are rooted in that religion. The political power inherent in Islam became evident most dramatically in the Iranian revolution of 1979 when leaders of the Shiite branch of Islam overthrew the shah and brought a new order to the country. In Chapter 20, we also turn our attention to the Iran-Iraq War and the problem of Middle East terrorism. We conclude the chapter with an account of the Gulf War, ignited by Iraqi ruler Saddam Hussein's attack on Kuwait in August 1990.

In Chapter 21, we turn to the dramatic events of September 11, 2001, and its consequences: US president George W. Bush's war on terror and his invasions of Afghanistan and, inexplicably, of Iraq.

16 Japan and South Korea as Economic Powers

In the early 1940s, the United States and its allies were at war with Germany and Japan. Less than a half-century later, those two countries again posed a challenge—this time an economic one. After World War II, the United States, the world's only economic superpower, assisted West Germany and Japan in their economic recoveries and provided security. By the 1980s, however, the European Community, in which West Germany was economically the strongest member, and Japan became major economic powers. We discuss Germany's postwar resurgence and the development of the European Community in Chapter 17; here we examine the remarkable postwar economic development of Japan, the strains in its economic relations with the United States, and its economic slump since the 1990s. About a decade after Japan's "economic miracle" of the 1960s, four Asian nations followed Japan's path in rapid economic development. The so-called Four Tigers were South Korea, Taiwan, Hong Kong, and Singapore. Among the four, South Korea, which was most closely connected to Japan historically and economically, will also be treated in this chapter.

Japan's "Economic Miracle"

Between the late 1940s and the late 1970s, Japan underwent an incredible transformation. This nation, no larger than the state of California, gutted by bombs in World War II and lacking in virtually all the raw materials needed for modern industry, grew in the space of thirty years to become the second-largest economic power in the world.[1] Only the United States had a larger GNP. But Japan's industrial productivity—in terms of output per person—was already as efficient as that of the United States.

Japan's recovery was rapid, but it did not occur immediately after World War II. It was not until 1953 that Japan's economic output reached its prewar level. This resulted from US assistance, Japan's own assets and hard work, and some good luck as well. The luck was the timely outbreak of the Korean War in 1950, which provided Japanese the opportunity to sell their light industry goods to the UN forces in Korea and thereby earn capital to invest in the rebuilding of Japan's industries.

US assistance came in various forms. In addition to a total of about $2 billion in direct economic aid (spread over a span of five years), the United States (1) persuaded its Western wartime allies to drop their demands for reparations from Japan, (2) pressured Japan to curb inflation and regain fiscal solvency, (3) provided modern technology by making US patents available cheaply, (4) opened the US market to Japanese goods, (5) persuaded other countries to resume trade with Japan, (6) tolerated Japan's protective tariffs for its industries, and (7) took up the burden of Japan's defense. This assistance was not mere kindness to a former enemy but instead the strengthening of a new, strategically located Cold War ally. The Japanese appreciated the generous US assistance and took full advantage of it. Without the diligent work of the Japanese themselves, however, the economic recovery would not have been possible.

Japan's economy began its skyrocket growth in the late 1950s, and it kept on zooming upward through the 1960s. The average annual growth rate of Japan's GNP in the 1960s was about 11 percent, far higher than other industrialized nations. The double-digit growth rate continued into the 1970s, until Japan's economic drive was thrown off track in 1974 by the global oil crisis. Detractors were quick to point out the fragility of Japan's economy because of its resource dependency, and some declared that Japan's miracle had ended. But the Japanese made adjustments, reducing their oil consumption and diversifying their energy sources, and were back on track by 1976. Until the late 1980s, Japan's average annual growth rate was about 4.5 percent, still the highest among the world's industrialized nations.

Japan surged past most European industrial leaders—Italy, France, and Britain—in the 1960s, and then in the early 1970s it surpassed West Germany, whose postwar economic recovery was also impressive. By 1980, Japan ranked first in production in a number of modern industries. It had long been first in shipbuilding; in fact, it has built more than one-half of the world's ships by tonnage in the last quarter of the century. It outpaced the United States in the production of electronic equipment such as radios, televisions, and video recorders. Japanese automobiles captured an increasing share of the world's markets, so that in 1980, Japan became the world's leader in automobile production. In the 1970s, it had the world's most modern and efficient steel industry. By 1980, Japan was poised to mount a challenge to US leadership in the new, all-important high-tech industries, especially in the computer and microelectronics fields.

Many in the West tended to belittle Japan's success and explained it away with self-serving excuses or outdated, if not entirely erroneous, notions—for example, Japan's cheap labor. Japan, they argued, was competitive because its people were willing to work for very low wages. Such an assertion may have been accurate during the 1950s and early 1960s, but by the early 1970s Japan's wages had reached the level of most industrial nations. Another notion was that Japan's prosperity was a consequence of its free ride on defense spending because the United States guaranteed its security. Japan surely benefited from having a much lower level of defense spending than the United States.[2] However, other factors were more important in explaining Japan's economic growth. Scholars specializing in Japan studies have adduced a host of factors or sources of Japan's remarkable economic advance, most of which focus on factors unique to Japan. The following are seven of these factors.

1. The government-business relationship in Japan was complementary and cooperative rather than antagonistic. The government, particularly the Ministry of International Trade and Industry (MITI), charted a course for the economy and coordinated its industrial growth. Government and industrial firms engaged in long-term planning, which made for policy continuity. It guided industrial development not only by targeting specific industries for growth but also by designating declining industries to be scaled down or dismantled. It also targeted foreign markets on which the Japanese would concentrate their attack.

2. The labor-management system in Japan stressed mutual harmony between the workers and management rather than confrontation. Japan's "lifetime employment" system, with its built-in rewards for worker seniority, provided job security to the workers, who in turn developed strong identity with and dedication to their firms. The companies, in their turn, were able to count on the services of a well-trained and loyal workforce. Worker morale and motivation were increased by various management programs, such as a generous bonus system, educational benefits, housing, insurance, and recreational facilities. There were labor unions in Japan, but they were rather weak, being only local as opposed to national trade unions, and their relations with management tended to be cooperative rather than confrontational. Worker participation in management decisionmaking and in quality-control circles also contributed significantly to the mutual benefit of employer and employee.

3. The Japanese educational system, which is controlled by the central government, maintained uniform, high standards and was extremely competitive. In Japan, university entrance examinations determined a person's future, and only the best of the best were admitted to the best universities, whose graduates obtained the best jobs. Therefore, students at all levels studied intensely in preparation for entrance examinations or, as they were called in Japan, "examination hell." The result

was a highly educated society with well-developed work habits. On the whole, the Japanese students received more, if not better, education than their counterparts in other countries. The Japanese school year was sixty days longer than in the United States, and Japanese schoolchildren typically studied many hours a day after school with tutors or in private schools. The education system was centralized under the Ministry of Education, which stressed high standards, especially in math and science. This and the fact that Japanese universities turned out more engineers (even in absolute terms) than the United States help to explain Japan's technological progress.

4. The Japanese aggressively sought new technology in quest of industrial rationalization and greater productivity. They were swifter than their foreign competitors to modernize their steel plants with the most recent, efficient, and cost-saving technologies. When the oxygen-burning type of steel furnace was developed in Austria in the early 1960s, the Japanese quickly purchased the patents and invested a vast amount of capital to rapidly convert their plants to the new technology. This explains, in part, why the Japanese were able to compete with US-made steel in the United States, even though they had to import their iron ore and ship their finished steel across the Pacific Ocean. Japan swiftly gained the lead over the rest of the world in robotics and in automating the production line. By the late 1980s, Japan had twice as many industrial robots in operation as the rest of the world combined.[3]

5. The high rate of personal savings by the Japanese and Japan's financial and banking practices were beneficial to capital formation for economic growth. Japanese workers saved a remarkable 18 percent of their salaries, compared to about 6 percent for US workers.[4] The banks then invested this surplus capital in industry and commerce. Although Japanese firms were also financed by selling stock, a great portion of their capital came from banks, which, unlike stockholders, did not insist on quarterly profits. Instead, the banks financed long-term business enterprises, which at times operated in the red for several years before they began to turn a profit. The ready availability of capital made possible continuous plant modernization.

6. Japan developed superior mechanisms for marketing its products abroad. Japanese comprehensive trading companies set up branch offices around the world collecting data, conducted thorough market research, and in numerous other ways facilitated Japanese trade. They also worked with MITI to arrange the most advantageous trade agreements, secure long-term supply of vital raw materials, and direct Japanese investment abroad. Although Japan was vulnerable because of its lack of natural resources, it made itself much less so by becoming indispensable to resource-supplying nations, both as a reliable buyer

and as a supplier of technology and capital. Other nations had nothing comparable to Japan's comprehensive trading companies for conducting a large volume of foreign trade.

7. There were also certain intangible factors unique to Japan—and to other East Asian countries—that contributed to economic growth. The Japanese were served well by historically conditioned cultural traits, such as acceptance of authority, paternalism, an emphasis on group harmony, loyalty, discipline, and a sense of duty and sincerity. Group consciousness prevailed over individualism. Without these traits, Japan's labor-management system would hardly have been possible. Additionally, there were certain historical circumstances that fortuitously benefited Japan, such as the timing of its industrial development during a period of global economic expansion. It may also be argued that Japan thrived on its own deprivation. Japan's dearth of raw materials, for example, necessitated hard work and planning to attain, conserve, and use them efficiently. By necessity, the Japanese came to excel in industry and foreign commerce.

There were, no doubt, other factors involved in Japan's economic performance, such as industrial rationalization or efficient organization of the industrial workplace and the rapid growth of Japan's domestic market. Japan's relatively low level of defense spending also worked to Japan's economic advantage, but it was important only in the first two decades after World War II[5] (when the United States saw fit to protect the nation it had just demilitarized). But from the 1970s, Japan's military spending steadily increased, and eventually it had one of the world's largest military budgets. A more important explanation for Japan's economic success was the preferential treatment Japan received from the United States throughout the Cold War years. Japan was strategically important to the US policy of containment, and for that reason the United States tolerated Japan's protectionist policies and threw its doors wide open to Japanese products. However, as Japan's industrial competitiveness improved and its trade surpluses increased sharply in the 1970s and 1980s, its trade partner across the Pacific became less tolerant—and still less tolerant when the Cold War ended in the late 1980s. By that time, another explanation for Japan's economic miracle became commonplace: its unfair trading practices.

Strains in US-Japanese Economic Relations

In the late 1970s, people in the United States were caught by surprise by Japan's seemingly boundless economic growth and began to wonder about the contrast between Japan's economic success and the recession in their own country. Many of those disaffected by the latter, especially the unemployed, blamed their problems on Japan. They saw a direct relationship between the growing volume of Japanese imports and rising US unemployment.

The 1980s: Japan's Economic Boom

Bilateral trade between the United States and Japan in the 1980s became the largest volume of overseas trade between any two nations in history. (Only US-Canada trade, which is not overseas commerce, was larger.) Japan had a deficit in its commodity trade with the United States until 1964; that is, it exported less than it imported from the United States. From that point, it has been the reverse, with the US deficit in the bilateral trade rising to $1 billion in 1972, $12 billion in 1978, $25 billion in 1984, and then soaring to an astronomical $56 billion in 1987.[6] This was, by far, the largest trade imbalance ever between two nations; Communist China eventually broke all records in the first decade of the twenty-first century.

In the 1980s, when unemployed US workers increasingly blamed Japan for their joblessness, "Japan bashing" became one of Washington's favorite pastimes, even though economists and government officials recognized that declining US industrial competitiveness was an important cause of the trade imbalance. Consumers found Japanese products, especially cars and electronic equipment, superior and less expensive than US-made products. Japan did, however, engage in trade practices such as "dumping" (selling its products abroad at a loss or at lower prices than in Japan) while protecting its own market from foreign imports by instituting high tariffs, import quotas, and various nontariff barriers. Politicians in the United States gained political points by calling for "get-tough" trade policies and economic sanctions against Japan. If the Japanese did not lower their trade barriers, they argued, then the United States must erect barriers against the flood of Japanese products. In the 1980s, President Reagan, like his immediate predecessors in the White House, opposed taking this protectionist route, knowing that it could lead to a mutually damaging trade war. Instead, he put pressure on Japan to open its markets to US goods.

Generally, Washington joined Tokyo in accentuating the positive aspects of US-Japanese relations, which the US ambassador to Japan, Mike Mansfield, liked to call "the most important bilateral relationship in the world, bar none."[7] But despite the talk of partnership and cooperation, Washington maintained pressure on Tokyo, which grudgingly and gradually gave in to some of its persistent demands. On the one hand, Tokyo agreed "voluntarily" to various trade limitations and quotas on its exports to the United States; on the other, Washington endeavored to pry open Japan's doors to US products by removing Japan's trade barriers. In the 1960s, Japan agreed to quotas on its textiles exports to the United States, in the 1970s to limitations on steel exports, and in 1981 to a voluntary ceiling on US-bound automobiles. Japan also began building auto-manufacturing plants in the United States, partly to reduce the volume of Japanese automobile imports and partly to quiet the argument that Japanese cars robbed US workers of their jobs. Moreover, since the late 1960s, Tokyo had, in fact, steadily reduced its own tariffs and quotas to make foreign goods more competitive in Japan.

Japan, however, persisted in the continued protection of its farmers from foreign suppliers of such foodstuffs as beef, oranges, and especially rice. After years of hard bargaining, the two sides managed only to achieve interim agreements on beef and oranges. But Tokyo continued to hold out on rice, even if it meant that the Japanese would continue to pay as much as seven times the world price for their precious homegrown staple. Still, Tokyo could respond to US charges by pointing out that Japan was already by far the world's largest importer of US agricultural commodities.

Washington became convinced that Japan kept US goods out of its market through various nontariff barriers such as restrictive licensing, burdensome customs-clearing procedures, rigid safety standards, a uniquely cumbersome distribution system, and nettlesome purchasing regulations. It particularly targeted *keiretsu*, Japan's informal but powerful corporate network that controlled the distribution system and excluded foreign suppliers. These were complicated matters involving peculiarities of the Japanese business system as well as cultural patterns, and in any case they proved difficult to change or adjust.

The Reagan administration hoped that a weak dollar (which lowered the prices of goods produced in the United States) would make US goods more attractive in Japan. The weak dollar, however, also lowered the cost of Japanese investments in the United States. This, as well as high interest rates in the United States, attracted Japanese investors. As a result, the Japanese, who had accumulated a tremendous amount of capital, recycled these profits by going on a buying spree, purchasing US banks, businesses, and real estate. Most conspicuous were the highly visible real estate acquisitions of Japanese investors in Hawaii, California, and New York City. US senator Ernest F. Hollings, an advocate of retaliatory sanctions against Japan, noted that the effect of Reagan's monetary approach was to transform the United States "into a coast-to-coast yard sale, with our assets available to foreigners at cut-rate, foreclosure-sale prices."[8]

By 1982, Japan had gained an edge on US competitors in the production and sale of microchips (particularly the 64K RAM chips—which at the time were cutting-edge).[9] In the early 1980s, Japan found a booming market in the United States for VCRs (video cassette recorders), a product that, ironically, had been invented in the United States but abandoned as commercially impractical. The Japanese also won increased shares of the US market for other industrial products such as precision tools, musical instruments, and power tools. Meanwhile, Japan surpassed the United States in nonmilitary technological research and development expenditures, and its research programs either gained the lead or challenged the US lead in a number of new and important fields, particularly in robotics, magnetic levitation, fiber optics, and superconductivity.

Japan pulled ahead of the United States in several other ways during the decade. In the mid-1980s, the United States swiftly fell from the status of the leading creditor nation in the world to the largest debtor. Japan just as swiftly became the world's leading creditor. Japan's assault on the money market in the United States in the late 1980s was breathtaking. By the end of the decade, eight of the ten largest banks in the world were Japanese, and 20 percent of US government bonds were purchased by Japanese financial firms. The Tokyo Stock Exchange surpassed the New York Stock Exchange in capital value, while the Osaka Exchange surpassed the London Stock Exchange.[10]

The 1990s: Japan's Long Economic Downturn

Two major developments at the outset of the 1990s greatly affected Japan's relations with other nations: the end of the Cold War and the collapse of Communism in the Soviet Union and Eastern Europe, and the Gulf War in 1991. The Cold War had tied Japan and West Germany to the United States for over four decades, and when it ended, these ties loosened—if only ever so slightly. With the Cold War over, Japan could no longer freely rely on US favors, and Washington began to take a harder line against Japan on trade issues.

Japan's relations with the United States and other nations were also affected by the Gulf War of 1991. Its constitution barred it from sending military forces to the Persian Gulf, but this did not shield it from criticism in the United States and in Europe, where many were unhappy by Japan's unwillingness to engage in a war fought to protect its main source of oil. After months of parliamentary debate, the Japanese government finally pledged $13 billion toward the cost of the war, and it offered a token contribution to the post–Gulf War peacekeeping effort by sending a fleet of minesweepers for duty in the Gulf. The Persian Gulf conflict touched off a heated debate in Japan over permitting its Self-Defense Forces to participate in UN peacekeeping operations. Within a year the Japanese Diet passed legislation allowing it to do so, preparing the way for Japan to play a leading role in the UN operation in Cambodia aimed at ending the decade-long civil war there. This marked the first time since World War II that Japanese military forces had been deployed abroad.

US criticism of Japan persisted into the early 1990s, when polls showed Japan's popularity in the United States plummeting.[11] Contributing to the growing acrimony were US media coverage of the fiftieth anniversary of Pearl Harbor in December 1991, President George Bush's twice-postponed and—as it turned out—ineffective visit to Japan in February 1992, and several tactless (actually racist) remarks by Japanese political leaders critical of the US work ethic. A best-selling novel (and later movie) by Michael Crichton, *Rising Sun*, painted a strongly unfavorable portrait of a Japan covertly seeking to destroy the US economy. Moreover, a new "revisionist" view of US-Japanese economic relations was finding favor in the United States. Writers such as Karel van Wolferen, Lester Thurow, James Fallows, and Clyde Prestowitz argued that the Japanese political economy was fundamentally different from the Western market economies and operated in ways that gave it distinct advantages in international economic competition. Japanese international business activity, they argued, was driven primarily by national considerations, as if in a war with the rest of the world. It was not enough for Japanese businesses merely to make a profit; they sought, instead, to control the market. Predictably, the revisionists called for strong countermeasures against Japan. Such sentiments reinforced the impression that international trade was becoming national cutthroat competition.

However, the acrimony in US-Japanese relations over trade in the early 1990s suddenly vanished as Japan fell into an economic recession by late 1992. The economic bubble—the overheated economy—had burst. The real estate and stock markets that had soared to dizzying heights declined sharply, leaving Japan's financial institutions with a massive debt problem, which is to say billions of dollars' worth of "nonperforming" (i.e., uncollectible) loans. The annual growth rate of GDP fell sharply from over 5 percent to below 2 percent, where it remained for most of the decade; industrial production and plant spending declined, as did savings and interest rates; businesses tightened their belts and reduced their payrolls; and unemployment rose above 3 percent, which was unusually high in Japan.

As serious as the prolonged recession was for the Japanese, it had surprisingly little effect on Japan's trade imbalance with the United States. In fact, Japan's bilateral trade surplus crept further upward. As Japanese cut back on purchases of goods—foreign as well as domestic—the US appetite for Japanese goods remained strong. And while Japan's doldrums continued, the US economy began a period of sustained growth in the early 1990s. This reversal, which now saw Japan headed downward and the United States upward, had the effect of silencing the voices of trade-war rivalry of the previous decade. Japan virtually disappeared from the pages of US newspapers, in part because the United States was running up a new record trade deficit, this one with the People's Republic of China.

Just how bad was Japan's decade-long recession? By one estimate, businesses and households suffered a combined capital loss of $7.2 trillion between 1992 and 1996.[12] The government shelled out some $802 billion in economic stimulus packages between 1992 and November 1998. As bad as it was, however, Japan's economy was not in a meltdown, as some alarmists outside the country seemed to think. Its economy was quite different from those of other Asian nations in recession in 1997, such as Indonesia, Thailand, and South Korea, for it had a huge current account surplus and foreign currency reserves, a far larger industrial capacity, and world-class technology. Throughout the recession, the value of the yen against foreign currency held fairly steady; there was only a marginal decline in living standards; and Japan remained the world's largest provider of overseas development aid.

Japan also faced an increasingly urgent demographic issue: its aging population. It had the world's largest proportion of people over age sixty-five and the smallest under fifteen. The aging of Japan's population was the result of both a declining birthrate—the lowest in the world, in 2007 down to 1.25 children for every female, with 2.1 needed to keep the population steady—and increasing longevity, the highest in the world at eighty-two years. The former was caused mainly by decades of birth control as well as a rise in the age of marriage, females tending to delay marriage until their late twenties—or not marrying at all. The result was a shrinking workforce, a detriment to continued economic growth. The impending crisis of labor shortage might be remedied by opening the doors to immigration, but Japan's political leaders—in the thrall of inertia and procrastination—and the majority of the people, determined to safeguard their ethnic purity, remained loath to do that.

The Four Tigers of Asia

By the 1980s, four other prospering nations had emerged along the Asian shores of the Pacific Ocean: South Korea (the Republic of Korea), Taiwan (the Republic of China), Hong Kong, and Singapore. These nations, sometimes referred to as the Four Tigers of Asia, followed in Japan's footsteps in the 1970s and 1980s to produce their own economic miracles. Their economic performance, especially their vigorous export-oriented industrial development, together with that of Japan, gave rise in the 1980s to such notions as the coming "Asian century" and to the concept of the "Pacific Rim" as the arena of the world's fastest economic growth and largest international trade flow. The Four Tigers became the source of a flood of imports into the United States and a major source of its mounting trade deficit. The US trade gap with the four countries grew from $3.6 billion in 1980 to over $35 billion in 1987.

The Four Tigers all shared with Japan certain common features that accounted for their remarkable economic performance (see Table 16.1). They shared a Chinese historical and cultural heritage, particularly the historically ingrained Confucian value system. It appears that this philosophy—long ridiculed by the West (and by Westernized Asians) as antiquated and a barrier to modern progress—was a major source of such traits and attitudes as discipline, loyalty, respect for authority, paternalism, desire for harmony, sincerity, a strong sense of duty, and respect for education, which fostered the high productivity of Asian workers and the efficiency of Asian management. The Confucian legacy became a vital ingredient for making capitalism work in East Asia.

Other factors were no doubt involved in the economic success of the Four Tigers, including the model of Japan and the investments and technology

Table 16.1   **Growth Rates of the Four Tigers (by percentage)**

	1977–1981	1982–1986	1987	1988
South Korea	7.3	8.5	12.2	10.3
Taiwan	9.0	6.9	12.3	7.4
Hong Kong	10.8	5.9	13.5	7.1
Singapore	7.1	4.4	8.8	9.1

Sources: Bank of Japan, *Comparative International Statistics*, 1988; International Monetary Fund, *International Financial Statistics*, 1988, Tokyo; and *Wall Street Journal*, Washington, D.C., November 1, 1988, p. A24.

flowing from abroad. Another major cause of the economic boom in these countries was their ready supply of relatively cheap labor. Moreover, each of these countries had authoritarian governments that curbed democratic development but made economic development their highest priority and marshaled the power of the state toward that end. Their rulers centralized power and economic planning, enforced political stability, and effectively mobilized human resources. They also emphasized public education, the development of technology, and birth control.[13] Like Japan, all four nations, as newly industrializing countries, stressed export-oriented industrial development and took advantage of the global free-trade system established by the industrialized nations of the West after World War II.

South Korea and Taiwan, the two most successful of the Four Tigers, had several additional characteristics in common that contributed to their economic growth and eventual democratization. Both countries seemed to have thrived on adversity. Both were "divided nations" that shared the experience of having been separated in two in the 1940s as a result of bloody Cold War conflicts, and both faced continuing serious threats to their security by Communist opponents—North Korea and the People's Republic of China, respectively. The persistent threat fostered a sense of urgency and national purpose that facilitated the mobilization of people and resources to strengthen the military and the economic base. In both cases, these Cold War exigencies fostered dictatorships, but after a couple of decades of strong economic growth and modernization, a prosperous middle class emerged and began to assert itself, demanding political liberalization.

South Korea

South Korea catapulted from the level of a miserably poor, war-torn, Third World nation in the 1950s to the status of a rapidly industrializing nation by the early 1990s. Both North and South Korea suffered from the division of the Korean nation after World War II because most of the minerals and electric power were located in the north and most of the agricultural land was in the south. At that time, Korea, as a whole, had a better economic infrastructure—particularly in terms of transportation and communications—than most Third World countries, owing to construction done by the Japanese before World War II. Nonetheless, Korea was an impoverished nation, and the devastation it suffered in the Korean War made matters still worse. North Korea, with Soviet-style political regimentation, attained economic recovery sooner than did the south, which was less stable politically.

South Korea began its economic takeoff in the mid-1960s, about a decade after the end of the Korean War. Its annual rate of economic growth rose above 14 percent in the early 1970s, and after a brief slowdown in the early 1980s, it climbed again to the rate of 12 percent in 1986 and 1987. In 1964, the per capita GNP of South Korea had been a mere $103, but by 1994 it had soared to $8,260.

South Korea's economic resurgence occurred mainly during the nineteen-year dictatorship of General Park Chung Hee. Park, who came to power as a result of a coup in 1961, made economic growth his highest priority. He planned a strategy for a government-led industrialization drive led by large state-supported industrial firms, financed by generous development loans from the United States and Japan. Park, having been trained in the Japanese army, was familiar with Japanese organizational methods, and he assiduously employed the Japanese model for economic development. By the 1970s, Korea was rapidly becoming an industrialized nation.

Park's assassination in 1979 did not end military rule, as he was replaced by another military man, General Chun Doo Hwan. When Korean students protested vehemently against the continuation of dictatorship, Chun expanded martial law, closed universities, dissolved the national assembly, banned all political parties, and for good measure threw student leaders into prison. The most vicious act of repression came in the city of Kwangju in May 1980, where perhaps as many as 3,000 civilian protesters were gunned down by security forces. The event transpired with the implicit approval of President Jimmy Carter's administration, which knew the military's heavy hand was about to come down. The aim of the United States at the time was to prevent South Korea from becoming another Iran, where demonstrations had brought down another US-supported dictator the year before (see Chapter 20).[14] Throughout the 1980s there was no letup in student agitation. All the while, as the police and army cracked down on the protesters, South Korea's economic modernization continued on its rapid course. Its industries were churning out quality goods competitive in the world market.

Halting Steps Toward Korean Democracy

The showcase of South Korea's emergence as a modern nation was the Olympic Games in Seoul in September 1988. In anticipation of the event, there was great concern over the possible disruption of the event either by acts of terrorism by North Korea or by violent student demonstrations. After President Chun rejected the pleas of opposition parties for reform of election laws—to allow the direct election of the president—he faced still larger and more volatile demonstrations, spearheaded by university students now joined by many of the country's new middle class. Finally, to head off a bloody confrontation that could result in the cancellation of the Olympics, Chun backed down. In June 1987, he appointed his military academy classmate, Roh Tae Woo, as his successor, and Roh announced a general election to be held in December in which he would run as candidate for president. In that election, the first free presidential election in Korean history, Roh won a narrow victory, but only because the two popular opposition candidates, Kim Dae Jung and Kim Young Sam, had split the opposition vote.

A political lull prevailed during the summer and fall of 1988 as South Korea basked in the international limelight of the Olympics. But the political rancor resumed soon afterward. In the national assembly Roh's political opponents demanded that his predecessor, General Chun, be put on trial for corruption. And in the streets students cried for Chun's head for having been responsible for the Kwangju massacre and protested the continued presence of US forces in Korea. President Roh achieved some startling breakthroughs on the diplomatic front—establishing diplomatic and economic relations with both the Soviet Union and China—but he encountered new problems on the home front in the early 1990s: a series of political scandals and an economic downturn.

The presidential election of December 1992 established a precedent when two civilian candidates—Kim Dae Jung and Kim Young Sam—competed for the office. The winner was Kim Young Sam, who, as president, took bold steps to reform South Korean politics, including purging corrupt politicians from the legislature, curbing the power of the internal security agency, and arresting military officers charged with corruption. He also sought to pacify the student protesters by pledging a full-scale investigation of the 1980 Kwangju massacre in addition to compensation for its victims. The students, however, kept the pressure on; 50,000 marched in May 1993, demanding that former presidents Chun and Roh be punished for the massacre and for corruption. In November 1995, Roh was arrested after he had admitted receiving huge contributions from business tycoons and operating a $653 million slush fund. High-ranking military officers and industrial leaders of the most powerful business groups (Hyundai, Samsung, and others) were also implicated. Kim Young Sam brought indictments against Chun and Roh for their role in the Kwangju massacre; in a sensational trial, Chun was found guilty and sentenced to death (subsequently commuted to a lengthy prison term) for his role in the 1979 military coup and the 1980 Kwangju massacre. Roh was sentenced to a twenty-two-month prison term for accepting a half-million dollars in bribes.

It was finally the other Kim's turn. Kim Dae Jung, long the country's leading dissident and democracy's most fervent advocate, won the presidency in December 1998. (Kim had previously been kidnapped by the Korean CIA, imprisoned on sedition charges, and sentenced to death; he was later exonerated and freed by his predecessor.) Kim pledged to rid the country of corrupt, authoritarian rule and to revive its economy. South Korea had been hard hit by the economic depression that had swept across Asia in 1997. In that year the value of Korean currency against the dollar fell 54 percent, GDP fell by 5.8 percent, several of its largest companies went bankrupt, and some of its banks were unable to collect on loans and became insolvent.

The first step to recovery was a huge bailout of $57 billion put together by the IMF, World Bank, and eight donor nations. Kim then took some difficult steps, including regulating the financial industry, holding down inflation, legalizing foreign investment, and liquidating weak businesses. Within two years the reforms succeeded in reviving the economy, more so than in any of the other East Asian nations. In 1999, for example, South Korea achieved its largest surge in industrial production in twenty years.

Divided Korea: North Versus South

For decades after the Korean War, Korea remained the site of the Cold War's most intense confrontation, as South Korea and North Korea sought reunification on their own terms and armed themselves against attacks by the other. In the North, Kim Il Sung consolidated his power over a Stalinist regime, which by the early 1960s had achieved an impressive economic and military recovery. In the 1960s, Kim occasionally sent commandos across the DMZ, and in 1968 he went so far as to send agents on a mission to assassinate President Park. The shots fired at Park missed their target but killed his wife.

North Korean policy toward the south was marked by a bewildering fluctuation between threats and provocations, on the one hand, and appeals for talks on the other. Examples of the former were the digging of tunnels under the 2.5-mile-wide DMZ wide enough to infiltrate large numbers of North Korean troops into the south; attacking US border guards and killing two of them with hatchets at Panmunjom in 1978; an attempted assassination of President Chun on a state visit to Burma in 1983 in a bomb attack that killed seventeen South Korean officials, including four cabinet members; and, in 1987, the bombing of a South Korean airliner in flight from Africa to Seoul, killing all 115 people onboard. Such reckless provocations brought talk of war in the south and assurances of support from Washington. One of North Korea's longstanding major objectives was the removal of US troops from South Korea. These forces, about 40,000 strong through the 1980s, were armed with tactical nuclear weapons, which Washington made clear it would use in the event of a North Korean attack on the south.[15]

After Mikhail Gorbachev came to power in the Soviet Union in March 1985, the international climate improved drastically as he sought to end the Cold War. With it came opportunities to resolve the Korean conflict. Both the Soviet Union and the People's Republic of China became interested in lowering tensions in Korea and were less willing to support the dangerous and impoverished Communist regime in Pyongyang, North Korea's capital. Moreover, they sought to do business with the prosperous south. South Korean president Roh met with Soviet leader Mikhail Gorbachev in June 1990 and secured an agreement establishing diplomatic and trade relations between their countries. He also won Gorbachev's support for South Korea's admission to the United Nations. North Korea had consistently opposed the entry of either of the two Koreas into the United Nations and had been able to count on a Soviet veto, but now it had to acquiesce. In September 1991, both Koreas were admitted.

Roh increased diplomatic pressure on the North Korean ruler, Kim Il Sung, to join negotiations for the peaceful reunification of Korea. Later, in 1990, direct talks between the two Koreas produced some surprising results when they signed a nonaggression pact and an agreement banning nuclear weapons from the Korean peninsula. The latter agreement was especially remarkable, since North Korea's clandestine nuclear bomb project had become a major bone of contention. Washington and Seoul insisted that Pyongyang submit to inspections by the International Atomic Energy Agency (IAEA), but Kim steadfastly denied that he was building a bomb and refused to comply.

Throughout this period, North Korea's diplomatic isolation and economic stagnation worsened, and the economic disparity between it and the south—already vast—increased further.[16] Then, in August 1992, Kim reversed himself and agreed to open its nuclear facilities to inspections. IAEA inspectors determined that North Korea had built a plutonium-reprocessing plant but had not produced enough material to make an atomic bomb. Pyongyang, however, refused to allow inspectors to see all of its nuclear facilities and was thus able to perpetuate uncertainty in Seoul and Washington.

In July 1994, Kim Il Sung, the eighty-two-year-old dictator and the world's longest-surviving ruler, died. He was succeeded by his fifty-two-year-old son, Kim Jong Il, about whom little was known outside of North Korea. Like his father, Kim Jong Il was made the object of the state-promoted ideology or cult, the omniscient and infallible "Dear Leader."

This unproven and mercurial leader was soon to be tested by a cluster of dilemmas, not the least of which was a failing economy. North Korea's economy had stagnated for decades, and by the 1980s the disparity between it and the industrialized south had become vast. For years its frail economy had been propped up by economic assistance and preferential trade arrangements with the Soviet Union, but in the mid-1980s Gorbachev slashed that support and terminated it altogether at the end of the decade. The North Korean economy took a nosedive, shrinking by one-half in the 1990s.

Next came a natural disaster. In 1995, North Korea was inundated by a deluge of floods of biblical proportion. Torrents of water destroyed reservoirs, farms, livestock, roads, bridges, schools, and more than 1 million metric tons of food reserves. UN officials declared the food situation the worst in the world. Rations were set at 450 calories per day, but not everyone had access to even that meager amount.[17] North Korea was reduced to accepting a donation of 150,000 tons of rice from South Korea, but it took pains not to reveal to its people the source of the handout. In the spring of 1996, the United States, South Korea, and Japan provided an additional $15 million in food. For the next several years Pyongyang swallowed its pride and accepted these badly needed food shipments, as well as fertilizer and other material aid, even from its erstwhile capitalist enemies.

Still, the feisty Kim Jong Il was not ready to abandon his belligerence toward South Korea and continued thumbing his nose at the United States and Japan. In August 1999, he tested a medium-range missile that made its way over Japan. He declared that it was not a military missile but rather a rocket for launching satellites that had "inadvertently" flown off course.

In South Korea, the newly elected president, Kim Dae Jung, was determined to find a way to make peace with the north. From the day he took office, he pledged to conduct a "sunshine policy" toward North Korea, a policy of engagement aimed at bettering relations and ultimately the peaceful reunification of Korea. He persisted in that policy undeterred by continued provocations by the north. In February 1998, the north suddenly responded to Kim Dae Jung's "sunshine policy" with a surprising peace overture of its own, calling for the promotion of "co-existence, co-prosperity, common interests, mutual collaboration, and unity between fellow countrymen."[18] Soon afterward, the diplomatic ice between the United States and North Korea was broken when Pyongyang agreed to receive a visit from a special envoy from the United States in May 1999 and also agreed to send a high-ranking diplomat for talks in Washington. South Korea sent ever larger amounts of food relief, fertilizer, and other aid to the north, where the famine was worsening. To negotiate and administer the food aid program, South Korean officials and businessmen traveled into North Korea, something that had been impossible before. Contacts among North Korean, US, and Japanese officials, as well as officials from other nations involved in famine relief, also increased.

The major breakthrough, however, came with a historic summit meeting of the rulers of North and South Korea in Pyongyang in June 2000. After almost a half-century of Cold War enmity that had continued more than a decade after the Cold War had ended, the democratically elected South Korean president Kim Dae Jung and the reclusive dictator Kim Jong Il of North Korea met face-to-face and mutually declared their commitment to bury the hatchet. At their meeting, the two discussed the whole range of issues that separated them and, while not resolving those issues, signed an agreement to work toward the eventual reunification of Korea. The agreement also called for reuniting thousands of families that had been divided by the closed border since the Korean War, promoting South Korean investment in the north, and holding another summit in Seoul. The meeting proved to be more than diplomatic theater, for it was followed by a series of confidence-building gestures by both sides, such as conducting the first exchange of visits by separated families, the first meeting of the respective defense ministers, the preparation to open highways and railroads across the heavily armed border, and the mutual cessation of propaganda attacks against each other.

The Kim-meets-Kim 2000 summit in Pyongyang paved the way for further negotiations between the two Koreas as well as the north's talks with Japan and the United States, which included a diplomatic visit to Pyongyang by US secretary of state Madeleine Albright. The visit was hailed as a great diplomatic success, but both sides acknowledged that it was but a first step and that the road to reunification would be a long and difficult one. It helped Kim Dae Jung garner the Nobel Peace Prize, but that honor was diminished greatly when, in 2003, investigations confirmed that he had secretly delivered a sum of $186 million to the other Kim to bribe him to attend the heralded summit.[19]

But the tentative negotiations between Pyongyang and Washington ran into a roadblock when George W. Bush was inaugurated president in January 2001. Bush ordered a 180-degree turnabout in US–North Korean relations. He wanted no part of the "sunshine policy," nor of President Bill Clinton's negotiations with Kim Jong Il. In the wake of the September 11 terrorist attacks on the United States, Bush lumped North Korea together with Iraq and Iran into something he labeled the "axis of evil." He asserted the right to wage a preventive war against North Korea (the so-called Bush Doctrine of preemption), just as he was about to do against Iraq. Kim Dae Jung, chagrined at having his peace efforts chopped off at the knees, was at pains to make certain that President Bush understood that a war with North Korea was the last thing the South Korean government wanted. Its capital, Seoul, was highly vulnerable to attack, within easy range of North Korea's massive array of howitzers and rocket launchers, a scant 30 miles from Seoul across the DMZ.

In the North, Kim Jong Il responded by playing the only card he held. In October 2002, he made the stunning announcement that he was not only restarting North Korea's plutonium-processing program but had launched a uranium production program as well. President Bush, preoccupied in Afghanistan and Iraq, had no meaningful answer except to shrug off the significance of this sensational disclosure. Moreover, Bush steadfastly rejected Kim's call for bilateral talks with Washington at which Kim hoped to secure, among other things, a peace treaty officially ending the Korean War and a mutual nonaggression pact. Bush insisted instead on multilateral talks with six nations (the United States, North Korea, South Korea, China, Japan, and Russia), which he felt certain Kim would reject. In October 2006, North Korea exploded its first nuclear weapon, a plutonium bomb. That got the attention of President Bush, and he agreed to resume the talks that the Clinton administration had initiated over a decade earlier. The new round of talks led to some successes. In June 2008, the North Koreans blew up the cooling tower of their reactor in Yongbyon that produced the country's plutonium. (For details, see Chapter 19.) In February 2009, however, North Korea provoked additional criticism by threatening to test-launch a new model rocket capable of reaching Alaska and Hawaii under the cover of launching a scientific satellite.

Recommended Readings

Japan

Christopher, Robert. *The Japanese Mind.* New York: Fawcett, 1983.
    One of the most readable of the many books on Japan's "economic miracle."
Dower, John. *Embracing Defeat: Japan in the Wake of World War II.* New York: Norton, 1999.
    A definitive study by a first-rate scholar of modern Japanese history.
Johnson, Chalmers. *MITI and the Japanese Economic Miracle: The Growth of Industrial Policy, 1925–1975.* Stanford: Stanford University Press, 1982.
    A superb analysis of the role of government in Japan's economic growth.
Lincoln, Edward. *Japan's New Global Role.* Washington, D.C.: Brookings Institution, 1993.
    A critical analysis by a noted expert on the Japanese economy.
Nakamura, Takafusa. *The Postwar Japanese Economy: Its Development and Structure.* Tokyo: University of Tokyo Press, 1981.
Reischauer, Edwin O. *The Japanese Today: Change and Continuity.* Cambridge, Mass.: Harvard University Press, 1986.
    A masterful survey of many facets of modern Japan by one of the foremost Japanists in the United States.
Vogel, Ezra. *Japan as Number 1: Lessons for America.* Cambridge, Mass.: Harvard University Press, 1979.
    Not only offers an explanation for Japan's economic success, but also suggests ways in which the United States can learn from the Japanese.

US-Japan Relations

Buckley, Roger. *US-Japan Alliance Diplomacy: 1945–1990.* London: Cambridge University Press, 1991.
    Provides an evenhanded historical survey of the recently troubled US-Japanese relationship.
Forsberg, Aaron. *America and the Japanese Miracle: The Cold War Context of Japan's Postwar Economic Revival, 1950–1960.* Durham: University of North Carolina Press, 2000.
    Stresses the US role and the importance of the Cold War in Japan's postwar economic recovery.

Green, Michael J., and Patrick M. Cronin, eds. *The US-Japan Alliance: Past, Present, and Future*. New York: Council on Foreign Relations, 1999.

Johnson, Chalmers. *Blowback: Costs and Consequences of American Empire*. New York: Henry Holt, 2001.
In this expansive and provocative study, the author offers a sharply critical analysis of both US and Japanese economic policies.

Kuttner, Robert. *The End of Laissez-Faire: National Purpose and Global Economy After the Cold War*. New York: Knopf, 1991.
Argues that since Japan and the European Union have close government-business cooperation, strategic economic planning, and managed trade, the United States must also develop a national strategy.

LaFebre, Walter. *The Clash: A History of US-Japanese Relations Throughout History*. New York: Norton, 1997.
An excellent survey by a seasoned diplomatic historian.

McCraw, Thomas K., ed. *America Versus Japan*. Boston: Harvard Business School Press, 1986.
Topical essays offering a comparative analysis of economic policies and an excellent overview and conclusion by the editor.

Prestowitz, Clyde V. *Trading Places: How We Are Giving Our Future to Japan and How to Reclaim It*. 2nd ed. New York: Basic Books, 1989.
A revisionist interpretation of the twin causes of Japan's rise to economic power: Japan's strategic, long-range program and the US "flight from reality."

Thurow, Lester. *Head to Head: The Coming Economic Battle Among Japan, Europe, and America*. New York: Morrow, 1992.
A revisionist treatment of the nature of the Japanese economy and the consequences of European economic integration.

Korea and East Asia

Amsden, Alice. *Asia's Next Giant: South Korea and Late Industrialization*. New York: Oxford University Press, 1989.
Examines South Korea's economic surge in the 1960s, 1970s, and 1980s.

Cumings, Bruce. *Korea's Place in the Sun: A Modern History*. New York: Norton, 1997.
A comprehensive and critical survey of modern Korean history focusing on the postwar period.

Keon, Michael. *Korean Phoenix: A Nation from the Ashes*. Englewood Cliffs, N.J.: Prentice-Hall, 1977.

Oberdorfer, Don. *The Two Koreas: A Contemporary History*. Rev. ed. New York: Basic Books, 2001.

Vogel, Ezra. *The Four Dragons: The Spread of Industrialization in East Asia*. Cambridge, Mass.: Harvard University Press, 1991.
Explains the common causal factors for economic growth in the Four Tigers.

Notes

1. The size of the GNP of the Soviet Union was not known for certain, but it was generally believed in the West that Japan's GNP was as large and probably larger by 1980. Its per capita GNP was certainly much larger.

2. From the 1950s, Japan steadily increased its defense spending; by the 1980s it was about 6 percent of the annual budget, or 1 percent of its GNP, compared to US defense expenditures of approximately 6–8 percent of its GNP.

3. Robot Institute of America, *Japan 1989: An International Comparison* (Tokyo: Keizai Koho Center, 1988), p. 27.

4. This remarkably high rate of savings was accounted for in part by the government taxation laws and the relatively low pensions for Japanese workers, but other factors included the huge lump-sum biannual bonuses Japanese workers received and traditional habits of saving for future security. Similar saving habits were found in other Asian countries, such as South Korea and Taiwan.

5. Chalmers Johnson, *MITI and the Japanese Miracle: The Growth of Industrial Policy, 1925–1975* (Stanford: Stanford University Press, 1982), argues that because of Japan's high rate of capital formation "the effect of low defense expenditures was negligible" (p. 15). He points out that for a nation with a very low rate of investment, such as China, a large defense expenditure does retard economic growth, but for nations where investment rates were high, such as Japan, South Korea, and Taiwan, "very high defense expenditures have had little or no impact on economic performance" (p. 15).

6. Japan also built up a large surplus—$20 billion in 1987—with its trade with the European Community, where the demand for protection against Japanese imports was even stronger than in the United States. Japan also had large trade surpluses with most Asian nations.

7. John E. Woodruff, "Veteran Envoy Mansfield to Retire from Tokyo Post," *Baltimore Sun*, November 15, 1988.

8. Ernest F. Hollings, "We're Winning the Cold War While Losing the Trade War," *Baltimore Sun*, December 17, 1989, p. 4N.

9. See Clyde V. Prestowitz, *Trading Places: How We Are Giving Our Future to Japan and How to Reclaim It*, 2nd ed. (New York: Basic Books, 1989), chapter 2. By August 1982, the Japanese had captured 65 percent of the world market for microchips. In 1980, when the United States was still trying to get its 64K chip out of the lab, the Japanese had already produced prototypes of the 256K chip.

10. Richard W. Wright and Gunter A. Pauli, *The Second Wave: Japan's Global Assault on Financial Services* (New York: St. Martin's Press, 1987.)

11. Edwin Reischauer, Center for East Asian Studies, *The United States and Japan in 1992: A Quest for New Roles* (Washington, D.C.: Johns Hopkins University Press, 1992), pp. 51–58. A *Washington Post*–ABC News poll on February 14, 1992, reported that US respondents who felt that anti-Japanese feelings were increasing rose from 33 percent in November 1991 to 65 percent in February 1992.

12. Shigeyoshi Kimura, "Japan Blames Inaction for Economy," Associated Press, December 12, 1998.

13. The World Health Organization rated Taiwan's birth control program first among developing nations in 1989. Singapore rated second, South Korea third, and Hong Kong fifth. The PRC was fourth. "ROC Rated Top for Birth Curbs by World Group," *Free China Journal*, December 21, 1989.

14. See Chalmers Johnson, *Blowback: The Costs and Consequences of American Empire* (New York: Henry Holt, 2000), pp. 112–116. Johnson bases his account on the work of US journalist Tim Shorrock. The South Korean government admitted to only 240 deaths.

15. David Rees, *A Short History of Modern Korea* (New York: Hippocrene Books, 1988), p. 168. In 1975, US secretary of defense James Schlesinger stated explicitly that in the event of a North Korean attack the United States would not become involved in "endless ancillary military operations" but would "go for the heart" of its opponent.

16. "Placing Bets on a New Korea," *Economist*, December 21, 1991, pp. 27–28. In 1990, South Korea had over five times higher per capita income and twenty times more foreign trade than the north; the north spent more than 20 percent of its meager GNP on its military, whereas the south spent only 4 percent of its burgeoning GNP on its military.

17. Walter Russell Mead, "More Method Than Madness in North Korea," *New York Times Magazine*, September 15, 1996, p. 50.

18. "North Korea Makes Overture to South," *Baltimore Sun*, February 26, 1998, p. 14A.

19. Anthony Faiola, "As Tensions Subside Between Two Koreas, US Strives to Adjust," *Washington Post*, July 25, 2004, p. A16.

17 The Globalization of the Economy

The modern age—that is, since the days of European exploration— witnessed the expansion of trade across the globe. By the beginning of the twentieth century, a global, interconnected economy was a long-established fact. The central question was always over the nature of the organization of international trade.

Should commerce be regulated according to the principles of mercantilism, that is, for the benefit of the state? This school of thought coincided with the rise of the European nation-states and their absolute monarchs who sought to control trade to fill royal treasuries. Mercantilism called for a favorable balance of trade as exemplified by the flow of gold and silver to capital cities such as Lisbon, Paris, and London.

Or should commerce be relatively free to serve primarily the interests of individual enterprise, as Adam Smith (*The Wealth of Nations*, 1776) proposed? This school gave rise to the argument that the economic activity of individuals and nations should be engaged in unfettered competition, or "free" trade, with the premise that it was beneficial for all involved. Gradually, the European world (i.e., Europe and its extensions overseas, such as the United States, Australia, etc.) in fits and starts moved toward this free-trade paradigm.

The central debate between the proponents of free trade and those of mercantilism, however, was never resolved. Free trade was never absolutely free; it always had its national restrictions as countries repeatedly sought protection behind economic barriers—mainly tariffs—to keep out competitors who all too often were demonized as exploiters.

Nowhere was this more evident than in the US response to the stock market crash of 1929. To protect the nation's economy, Congress passed the Smoot-Hawley tariff (1930), which raised tariffs by 50 percent. The trading partners of the United States responded in kind, and a trade war resulted with grave consequences all around. It was this, rather than the dramatic collapse of the overvalued stock market, that brought about the Great Depression of the

1930s. Before World War II came to an end, the Western Allies took steps to ensure that history would not repeat itself. They expected an economic downturn after the war, but they resolved to deal with it without resorting to national solutions. In July 1944, at Bretton Woods, New Hampshire, the representatives of forty-four Allied nations met for the purpose of facilitating the resumption of international trade after the war. They established the International Monetary Fund, which was designed to restore the system of multinational international payments that had broken down during the Great Depression. By 2008, nearly every one of the United Nations' 193 members had joined the IMF.[1]

The IMF fund consists of a pool of money provided by member states, of which the United States is the largest contributor. For that reason, Washington is in a position to determine how IMF money is spent. When a debtor nation proves unable to meet its international obligation, the IMF takes on the role of financial savior and steps in to eliminate the specter of "nonperforming" (i.e., failing) loans and the subsequent breakdown of the international system of payments. As the lender of last resort, particularly for the poorest nations, the IMF lends money and lines up banks willing to extend additional credit. But the IMF also insists that borrowers remain in compliance with the lending terms. In this way, therefore, the IMF shores up the international system of debt obligations and trade. Its most potent weapon is its ability to carry out the threat of withholding additional funds necessary to keep impoverished and indebted nations afloat. In time, such heavy-handedness created much resentment within the Third World, as the IMF appeared to be more interested in bailing out private lending institutions in wealthy nations than in helping borrowers who were desperate.

The IMF was not alone in dealing with Third World nations, but it was the most visible institution and thus became a lightning rod for populations and politicians who felt victimized by the developed, capitalist First World. The IMF's defenders replied that it provided much-needed capital and was merely demanding a reasonable regimen to restore ailing patients to financial good health. Such was the love-hate relationship between desperate nations that needed assistance and a Western capitalist agency; part of the lending bargain was an authority to interfere in the internal affairs of nations. For the IMF, it was a short path from hero to whipping boy and back again.

Another Bretton Woods institution was the World Bank, which in 1946 began operations to finance specific projects across the world. Its original working capital came from members' contributions, but the bulk of its current capital now comes from borrowing in the world's money markets. It operates as any bank, that is, it borrows money (frequently at high rates) and then lends it at a markup.

Shortly after World War II, the Allied victors created yet another international organization, the General Agreement on Tariffs and Trade (commonly abbreviated as GATT), initially a small club of twenty-three members.[2]

Through eight rounds of lengthy negotiations (the last one, the Uruguay Round, taking place between 1986 and 1994), GATT was remarkably successful in managing to reduce the average tariff on the world's industrial goods from 40 percent to 5 percent of market value. It marked the first multilateral agreement to reduce trade barriers since Napoleonic times.

GATT was created as a temporary expedient but lasted for nearly a half-century. In 1995, it voted itself out of existence to be replaced by the World Trade Organization, a body designed to take the case of trade liberalization even farther. (In 2009, its membership stood at 153; at that time, the most important nation still outside the WTO was Russia.) WTO was established as a permanent institution with much greater powers to arbitrate trade disputes. Its rules demand that countries restricting free trade change their behavior or face sanctions. When China applied to join the WTO, the argument favoring admission was that if China became a WTO member it would have to reduce its extraordinarily high tariffs, which ran as high as 100 percent on certain commodities.

The European Union

The best example of free trade in practice is the European Union. It is the outgrowth of the European Coal and Steel Community, founded in 1952, designed to facilitate international trade in those commodities, the building blocks of postwar reconstruction. Its members were France, West Germany, Italy, Belgium, the Netherlands, and Luxembourg. In 1957, by the Treaty of Rome, these nations created the European Community—also known as the Common Market—the purpose of which was to eliminate all trade barriers.

The founding fathers of the EC were two Frenchmen, the foreign minister Robert Schuman and the economist Jean Monnet. They sought more than efficient trade; they hoped that an interdependent Western Europe would lead to nothing less than a change in the psychological makeup of its citizens, to change Europe, which had just undergone the most devastating war in history. Schuman's emphasis was on preventing war more than on economics. When Schuman presented his historic proclamation of May 9, 1950—five years to the day after the end of World War II—he underscored that the Coal and Steel Community's purpose first and foremost was to establish a lasting peace, particularly between Germany and France.

Schuman's proclamation became the day of birth of what eventually became the European Union. For more than a half-century it not only kept the peace in Western Europe among former bitter enemies but also created a genuine peace of mutual understanding. Perhaps it should not have been surprising, therefore, that in September 2003—upon the fortieth anniversary of Schuman's death—the Roman Catholic bishop of Metz submitted to the Vatican a stack of documents to support a request for the beatification of Schuman. For Schuman to enter the pantheon of Catholic saints, however, the church would have to show that Schuman had worked a miracle. The mitigation of centuries-old national hatred would qualify as such.

In March 1985, the European Council, whose members included the heads of the governments of the twelve member states at the time,[3] announced its intent to establish a single integrated market by the end of 1992, which would fulfill the goal set in 1957. In its 1985 white paper, "Completing the Internal Market," the European Council called for the removal of national rules and regulations in areas such as banking, transportation, and border controls in favor of supranational regulations. It was a mammoth task encompassing 279 subject areas, from the rights of labor and women to banking and insurance, agricultural subsidies, border controls, immigration, pollution, health standards, transportation, and communications. It even called for the creation of a common currency, the euro, to put an end to the eleven different national currencies. The euro was meant to streamline commerce and do away with the fact that a traveler on a journey to all EC member nations would lose 47 percent of his money changing it into local currencies.[4]

Within a few years after its creation in 1957, the European Community—by then known as the Common Market—broke down many of the formidable trade barriers among the nations of Western Europe. Many remained in place, however. Moreover, some nations at times turned to "national solutions" to solve economic problems. But in the early 1980s, several factors came together: The French and Spanish socialists, who in the past had favored governmental regulations and control of the economy, acknowledged the superiority of the market over a planned economy. They began to extol the virtues of competition and the deregulation of the economy. The EC of 1992 was the logical result of this trend of deregulation.

The first nation to take the road to 1992 was France, which at the time was no longer ruled by the nationalist Charles de Gaulle but by the "European" François Mitterrand. In January 1984, Mitterrand became the president of the Council of Ministers of the EC, and in this capacity he became a convert to European economic and social integration. His term as president of the council, a French diplomat noted, became his "road to Damascus."[5] The chancellor of West Germany, Helmut Kohl, felt that the strong German economy could only benefit from the removal of national economic barriers. Margaret Thatcher, the prime minister of Britain, long an apostle of laissez-faire capitalism, had no reason to object to a free market.

One of the goals was to strengthen the competitiveness of the EC against the other great players—the United States, which in 1989 created its own free-trade zone with Canada, and particularly Japan, the primary target. The Europeans resented Japan's aggressive economic expansion and its continued protection of its own domestic market. To European eyes, competition with Japan had turned into economic war.

The driving force behind European economic unification was the business elite; it was not a popular mass movement. Many, in fact, viewed the full integration process with misgivings. West Germans, for example, feared the influx of immigrants from southern Europe. In the 1960s, West German industry had recruited a large number of "guest workers" from Turkey, Yugoslavia, and Greece, many of whom had not returned home. The EC had its own north-south division. Northern workers feared competition from immigrants from countries in the south such as Portugal, Spain, and Greece, where the standard of living was less than half that in the north. Labor also feared that the removal of barriers could mean relocation of businesses to countries with lower wages and few social benefits.

At the end of the 1980s, the EC's competitors, including the United States and Japan, increasingly took notice of the emerging structure. The EC sought to allay fears abroad that it was creating a "Fortress Europe" by stressing its commitment to international trade. After all, total exports of EC member nations (including exports to each other) amounted to 20 percent of international trade, compared to the United States with 15 percent and Japan with 9 percent. To forestall the impact of future protectionism, US and Japanese companies

US president Bill Clinton received by Jacques Delors, president of the EU's European Commission, Brussels, January 1994. *(European Commission)*

invested heavily in EC countries. Toyota invested $1 billion in an auto factory in Great Britain; AT&T bought into Italtel in Italy to circumvent the rules of origin. For the Japanese the central problem was access. Should the walls go up, Japan's global companies hoped to qualify as insiders by building industrial plants within EC nations. For this reason, Japan's direct investments in EC countries increased from $1 billion in 1984 to about $9 billion in 1989.

After 1987, the EC cracked down on "dumping" by Asian firms, particularly against Japanese companies, but also other countries of East Asia. It drew up "rules of origin" and "local-content regulations" to determine the national origin of goods. These were meant to prevent the establishment of Asia's so-called screwdriver plants built in Europe.

The Europeans remained divided over the issue of Japanese investment. Margaret Thatcher's government particularly welcomed Japanese investment to shore up the economy of Britain, where in 1989, 100 Japanese-owned factories employed over 25,000 workers. But many European industrialists feared that unrestricted Japanese investments could lead to Japan's domination of entire sectors of the European economy.

During the late 1980s, the four leading members of the EC—West Germany, France, Italy, and the United Kingdom—ranked third through sixth in the world in GNP. West Germany alone, with one-half the population of Japan and one-quarter that of the United States, had become the world's leading exporter in 1988, surpassing the United States for the first time and extending its lead in 1989. West Germany's 1989 commodity trade surplus of $61 billion equaled that of Japan and exceeded it in 1990.[6]

The 1980s: Three Economic Superpowers

In the 1960s, the United States accounted for 33 percent of world GNP, but by 1989 its share had slipped to 20 percent. The US current account trade deficit—that is, trade in goods and services *plus* income from US investments abroad *minus* payments to foreigners on their US investments—reached $125 billion that year, while Japan's surplus rose to $72 billion, Taiwan's to $70 billion, and Germany's to $53 billion. Japan and West Germany began to take on the role of the world's bankers. Throughout the 1980s, Japan and the Asian newly industrializing countries, on the one hand, and West Germany and the EC, on the other, were gaining momentum while the United States was struggling (see Table 17.1). Its massive domestic debt was a recurring symptom that the nation was living beyond its means, consuming too much and unable to pay its bills.

During the 1980s, Japan ran up annual trade surpluses with the United States in the neighborhood of $50 billion, and such a large trade imbalance was bound to cause friction. Many of the economic problems that plagued the

Table 17.1   Comparative Data on the EC, the United States, and Japan, 1987

	Population	Per Capita GNP (US$)
European Community	322,871,000	10,730
West Germany	61,200,000	14,400
United States	243,800,000	18,530
Japan	122,100,000	15,760

United States were of its own making: a huge defense budget (around $300 billion annually), the quest for short-term gain at the expense of investment and planning for the long haul (which frequently led to shoddy craftsmanship and the attendant loss of market share, especially in automobiles), and the opening of its markets to many competitors.

The oil crises of the 1970s hit the US automobile industry particularly hard as US makers produced a host of gas-guzzling behemoths when the world demanded smaller, more fuel-efficient cars. Germany and especially Japan benefited handsomely because they already produced the smaller cars and efficient diesel automobiles now much in demand. Japan also profited from the production of other sought-after, relatively inexpensive consumer goods of high quality—cameras, television sets, stereo equipment, and VCRs.

The open US market also served Japan well. It was in part the product of the Cold War. The US foreign policy establishment in Washington—the Pentagon and the State Department—continued to favor a strong Japan allied with the United States, while the Commerce Department and Treasury Department fretted over the trade imbalance and the outflow of the nation's wealth.

For international trade to work smoothly, there must be an even flow of goods. An imbalance inevitably leads to friction. A case in point was the imbalance of trade between the United States and East Asia. During the early 1980s, US trade with China was still negligible, but since 2001, China's trade surplus grew at an astonishing, unprecedented rate (see Table 17.2).

Table 17.2   China's Current Account Balance, 1996–2007 (in US$ billions)

	China's Balance
1995	1.6
1996	7.2
1997	29.7
2003	45.9
2004	68.7
2005	160.8
2006	249.9
2007	371.8

Source: State Administration of Foreign Exchange, People's Republic of China, www.chinability .com/CurrentAccount.

As the US economy continued to be the locomotive pulling other economies of the world by purchasing vast amounts of goods from abroad, it was not merely Japan and China that ran up huge trade surpluses with the United States. US current account trade deficits kept setting new records (see Table 17.3). In 1998, the deficit stood at $166 billion; in 1999 it jumped to $265 billion; in 2003 it reached $495 billion only to surpass $753 billion in 2006. (The figures for 2007 showed a slight improvement, down to $700 billion,[7] because of a global economic slowdown and the weakening of the US dollar, which made US manufactured goods cheaper—and thus more attractive abroad.)

In the 1980s, when "Japan-bashing" became a fashionable trend in the United States, many blamed declining US economic performance on Japanese trade barriers. These barriers tended to be informal, "nontariff" constraints (including currency devaluation that made Japanese goods artificially cheaper abroad) that made it frustratingly difficult for US businesses to crack the lucrative Japanese market (more than 120 million buyers with deep pockets). The EC, too, complained about the restricted access to the Japanese market. Europeans showed even less compunction to charge the Japanese with unfair trading practices. In 1989, the leading West German news weekly, *Der Spiegel*, launched a broadside of articles in which it charged that the Japanese were not interested in trade but in ambushing their competitors, not merely to gain a share of the market but to dominate certain sectors completely—and all this by unfair means such as dumping, stealing technology, and excluding foreign competitors from their shores. The Japanese Ministry of International Trade and Industry, *Der Spiegel* charged, not only organized trade; it was the headquarters of an economic war machine on a mission to dominate the world.[8]

During the early 1990s, a rift began to emerge in the United States between those who pushed for ever greater integration of the world's economies and those who argued for measures against unfair competition. But interdependence was too deeply entrenched, and the proponents of the second argument were fighting an uphill battle. Several examples illustrate the extent of interdependence. General Motors no longer saw itself as a US corporation but

Table 17.3 US Current Account Trade Deficit with Its Most Important Trading Partners (in US$ billions)

	2001	2003	2005	2007
China	83	123	201	256
Japan	68	65	82	82
Canada	53	54	76	64
Mexico	29	40	50	74
Germany	29	39	50	44

Source: US Census Bureau.

as an international corporation. The Chrysler Corporation held 50 percent ownership in a joint venture with Mitsubishi Motors to produce cars in the United States and a 15 percent interest in Mitsubishi of Japan, which produced cars in Japan for Japanese and foreign markets. General Motors, Ford, and several British corporations entered into similar joint ventures with Japanese car producers. In 1998, Chrysler merged with the venerable German automobile manufacturer Daimler-Benz, the head of the new conglomerate being a German national. Many "US-made" or "British-made" cars had a large component of Japanese parts produced in Japan. Honda, the Japanese car maker, shipped some cars that were manufactured in Ohio by US workers to Japan.

Regional Trading Blocs

In Europe as well as North America, South America, and Asia, nations banded together to improve their competitive positions within the globalizing economy by negotiating and entering into regional trade agreements that would affect regional economies for decades.

The Deepening and Widening of the European Union

In Europe, the EC member states continued to pursue the goal of full economic integration. In December 1991, in line with the white paper of 1985, representatives of the twelve EC nations worked out a treaty in the Dutch city of Maastricht committing the EC to a "deepening" process, including the creation of an economic and monetary union with a single currency as well as a common central bank. In addition, border controls were to come down, and foreigners were to be cleared at whatever border (or airport) they arrived. Maastricht also called for standard environmental, labor, and social laws such as minimum wages, vacations, and maternity leave. All citizens would be free to work and live anywhere they chose and even be able to vote in local elections.

The Maastricht Treaty, before it could go into force, had to be ratified. In nine of the nations, the governments quickly did so. But in Denmark, Ireland, and France it would be the voters, by way of a referendum, who would decide. In June 1992, the voters of Denmark, the third-smallest member of the EC, rejected Maastricht by a narrow majority (barely above 50 percent). French voters ratified the treaty but only by a scant majority of the vote, and Irish voters did so by a comfortable margin.

The Danish vote underscored a general uneasiness with the Maastricht plan. The deepening process, the handiwork of business and governing elites, clashed with the skepticism of the public, who felt that politicians had gone too far, too fast along the road to political, social, and economic integration by insisting, to an unprecedented degree, on the subservience of national sovereignty to a supranational community. The Danes were not necessarily against a unified Europe, but they were against granting bureaucrats in Brussels authority to decide, for example, on the maximum speed of a Danish moped.[9] There was also the danger of the EC being dominated by a resurgent Germany, and on this the Danes were not alone in their fears. The plans for 1992 had been drawn up before German reunification, something no one had predicted, at a time when Germany was first among equals (but equal nevertheless) and not as dominant as it once was during the early 1990s. Earlier, the French had used the metaphor of the French rider controlling the German horse. With German reunification, however, the horse threw its rider and galloped off to the east to reclaim its former sphere of influence.[10]

The Maastricht Treaty finally went into effect in November 1993 (after Danish voters approved a modified version of the treaty in a second referendum in May 1993). At this juncture, the European Community took a new name that reflected its commitment to integration; henceforth it would be known as the European Union (EU).

Despite the ratification of the Maastricht Treaty, a measure of pessimism over the deepening process remained. How deep should integration become? Britain's leaders, in particular, were having second thoughts about further EU integration. Moreover, the enlargement of the European Union (to twenty-seven members in 2007) made the intergovernmental process more unwieldy. In the years after the implementation of the ambitious Maastricht Treaty, public expressions of "euro-pessimism" became widespread. Many, particularly in Germany and Britain, wanted no part of a single monetary system—"esperanto money," as it was called derisively—preferring instead to retain their national currencies. But for politicians there was no alternative to further integration. The deepening of the EU—that is, the granting of additional powers to the European Parliament at the expense of national legislatures—might slow down its accelerated pace, but it would continue nonetheless.

A case in point is the acceptance of the EU currency, the euro. With the exception of Britain, Sweden, and the ever skeptical Denmark, the EU committed itself to embracing the euro on January 1, 2002. The new banknotes featured open doors and windows and bridges, symbolic of the EU mission to integrate a continent that only recently had witnessed unprecedented bloodshed.

Even before the Maastricht Treaty's ratification, the EU took steps to widen membership. The first to seek admission was Austria in July 1989— months before the Berlin Wall, the symbol of European division, came crashing down. Austria's 1955 treaty with its former occupying powers had prevented it from joining any sort of association with Germany—economic or military. The major Western powers (the United States, Britain, and France) had no objection to Austria's membership in the EU. It was primarily the Soviet Union that did not want to see another German *Anschluss*, or annexation, of Austria, creating another *Grossdeutschland*, or Greater Germany. Earlier,

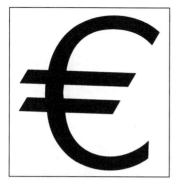

The symbol for the euro. The symbol was chosen after extensive public opinion research across the European Union. A cross section of EU citizens between the ages of eighteen and seventy-five gave their evaluations of eight different symbols. This one was chosen for its stability, combination of modern look and classic lines, and because it projects a strong image.

however, Mikhail Gorbachev had spoken of a culturally and economically unified Europe, "our common home." He, too, raised no objections to Austrian membership in the EU.

Sweden sought membership in July 1991, and Finland and Norway followed suit in March 1992. Finland had close trade and defense arrangements with the Soviet Union based on the treaty of 1948. But Finland suffered from an unemployment rate of 20 percent—the highest since World War II—and it saw the EU as a potential life raft. Membership in the EU also offered Finland the window of opportunity to formally become a part of Western Europe. Again, Moscow did not object.

In June 1994, Austrian voters approved EU membership by a wide margin. In Scandinavia, however, the votes were much closer. There, many farmers opposed opening their markets to imports from the south. Voters in Sweden and Finland ratified EU membership by narrow margins; in Norway, however, the voters (as they had done twenty years earlier) narrowly rejected EU membership, preferring to go it alone. Norway was self-sufficient in agriculture and energy (by virtue of North Sea oil), and its fishers did not relish the thought of vessels from Portugal and Spain gaining entry into their coastal waters.

When the three new members officially joined the EU on January 1, 1995, the total population for EU member countries increased from 349 million to 370 million, and total GNP increased by 7 percent. The EU economy was now 10 percent larger than that of the United States. And still more applicants—mostly in Eastern Europe—were waiting in the wings. The projected expansion raised questions even among previous champions of the EU. For one, the EU operated on the principle of unanimity, something much more difficult to achieve in a greatly expanded organization. Then there was the question of whether new applicants could meet the stringent entrance requirements on environmental standards, low unemployment, low state operating deficits, a viable private economy, and solid democratic institutions. Moreover, financial assistance to new nations would strain the budgets of EU governments that were in the process of curtailing social programs for their own citizens.

Former champions of the EU were beginning to ask whether it should not concentrate on integration (i.e., the "deepening" of the union) before focusing on the uncertain consequences of "broadening." Among them were Helmut Schmidt, the former chancellor of West Germany, and Jacques Delors, the former president of the European Commission. Delors feared that with expansion into Eastern Europe the EU would become nothing more than a free-trade zone at the expense of the common social and political ideals, particularly as spelled out in the Maastricht Treaty. The skeptics, however, lost the battle. In May 2004, the EU accepted ten additional members—Poland, the Czech Republic, Slovakia, Lithuania, Latvia, Estonia, Slovenia, Hungary, Malta, and the Greek part of Cyprus; and in 2007, Romania and Bulgaria. Turkey had sought membership for decades, but its application was always on hold, in part because of the requirement that EU members be genuinely democratic. Moreover, many Europeans raised the question whether Turkey, with its Muslim population and location primarily in Asia Minor, was a suitable candidate to join a *European* union.

The new members brought the EU population to 490 million (as compared to 305 million in the United States). Because of the relative poverty of its newest members, the overall per capita GDP among the EU membership dropped slightly to $32,900 (as compared to $45,800 in the United States).[11]

After "broadening" its membership in May 2004, the EU returned to the complex task of "deepening" the integration of members. In October 2004, the heads of the twenty-five EU member states signed the European Constitution, which would be scheduled for ratification by a vote within two years. The first such transnational entity in history, this became in effect an attempt to create the "United States of Europe." Many Europeans, particularly among younger generations, already saw themselves as Europeans first and only second as citizens of their respective countries.

The newly proposed constitution was steeped in the tradition of the Enlightenment and social democracy. It granted a host of civil liberties that closely represented the guarantees found in the Bill of Rights of the US Constitution. Yet there were differences, since the Europeans defined rights differently. The European Constitution specifically stressed the need for "peace, justice, and solidarity throughout the world." A right-to-life clause rejected the death penalty. In the United States, the future of Social Security and social assistance was widely debated, but the Europeans saw it as an inalienable "right," as was universal health care, yet a distant dream across the Atlantic.

Once more, the "deepening" of European integration ran into skepticism. In the spring of 2005, voters in France and the Netherlands refused to ratify the constitution. The result was a redrawn, "streamlined" treaty (no longer called a constitution), signed in Lisbon in December 2007. Irish voters rejected it in June 2008. The "deepening" of the European Union remained a work in progress.

NAFTA: North American Free Trade Agreement

During the early 1980s, the United States, to improve its global competitive position, took the lead in negotiating the North American Free Trade Agreement with Canada and Mexico. Its aim was to establish a free-trade zone encompassing more than 400 million consumers.

The roots of NAFTA may be traced back to the mid-1980s, when Mexico decided to join the global economy and began to open its economy to foreign goods and investors. The movement toward that end began after Mexico had accrued a staggering foreign debt of over $100 billion. At that point its creditors, among them US banks, urged the privatization of Mexico's state enterprises, some of which were sold off to creditors. In 1986, Mexico joined GATT, and as a result protective tariffs as high as 100 percent dropped to 20 percent or less. Foreign investments in Mexico began to increase. Between 1986 and 1991, US investments increased from $5 billion to $11.6 billion, and US exports to Mexico rose from $12 billion to $33.2 billion. NAFTA was meant to eliminate all tariffs among Mexico, the United States, and Canada (which already had a free-trade agreement with the United States, effective January 1, 1989). NAFTA was also designed to protect the rights of North American investors in Mexico, open it to foreign capital, lock it into the global economy, and foreclose radical options in the future.

In June 1990, President George H. W. Bush of the United States and President Carlos Salinas de Gortari of Mexico first proposed NAFTA, hailing it as a "powerful engine for economic development, creating new jobs and opening new markets." From the outset, an intense debate ensued over NAFTA's pros and cons. The business elites in all three countries, as well as all five living former US presidents and all former secretaries of state, favored the agreement. Three hundred of the best-known US economists signed a letter of support. In corporate boardrooms across Mexico, the United States, and Canada, support for NAFTA was nearly unanimous. To obtain congressional ratification of the agreement,[12] President Bill Clinton needed to persuade the US public of its benefits. He repeatedly promised that NAFTA would produce hundreds of thousands of new jobs in the United States—and high-skilled, well-paying ones at that.

There were those, however, who had misgivings about NAFTA. The rebellion in the state of Chiapas in Mexico began on the very day—January 1, 1994—that NAFTA went into effect, precisely because the agreement made it possible for foreigners to purchase ever more Mexican lands. Canadian and US workers expressed concern that competing with lower-paid Mexican workers could lower their standards of living. Between 1989 and 1993, even before NAFTA, the free-trade agreement with Mexico had already cost more than 360,000 US manufacturing jobs. The American Federation of Labor–Congress of Industrial Organizations (AFL-CIO, the major US union) estimated that the

United States would lose 500,000 manufacturing jobs to Mexico, where the average wage was one-seventh of that in the United States. An AFL-CIO official correctly predicted:

> What is unstated . . . is that you are adding 50 million low-wage Mexican workers, many of them skilled, to the United States labor force. They are not located across the Pacific, but in a country that is attached to ours, as if it were another state.[13]

The concerns of US workers were not alleviated when, in October 1993, President Clinton asked large corporations to pledge that they would not outsource jobs to Mexico and found he had no takers. This came at a time when the Mexican state of Yucatan advertised that workers there could be hired for less than $1 per hour (including fringe benefits), an annual savings of $15,000 for every worker hired.

NAFTA went into effect on January 1, 1994, at a time when the Mexican economy already suffered from the effects of a deep recession and when the government of President Ernesto Zedillo introduced drastic measures to pay off Mexico's obligations. Mexicans had to swallow a very bitter pill. Zedillo raised taxes; clamped down on wages to make Mexican goods more competitive in the world economy (labor unions meekly accepted an 8 percent cut in real wages); raised interest rates to retain the capital of foreign investors; cut back on state-subsidized prices for basic items such as food, bus transportation, and gasoline; cut spending on social programs (such as pensions); and sold off state-owned enterprises—often at bargain prices—to cronies of politicians. These measures, however, went a long way toward addressing the concerns of international investors. When Zedillo raised taxes in March 1995, Wall Street received the news enthusiastically, the US stock market rose, and the peso gained 18 percent in value. These steps also produced a deeper recession in Mexico during which 1 million workers lost jobs. Unemployment, fiscal austerity, and the decline of the value of the peso drove down the purchasing power of many Mexicans by as much as 50 percent. The middle class, which had hoped for a better day, was particularly hard hit.

In the *maquiladoras*, the assembly plants established by foreign companies across the Mexican border, NAFTA also drove down the wages of workers. The *maquiladoras* were "restructured"—that is, wages were lowered and workers were dismissed—to become more competitive in the global economy. (After all, they were not merely competing with US workers but with Chinese workers as well.) Mexican farmers also felt the impact of NAFTA when they suddenly faced competition from the efficient farms in the United States and Canada that sent large amounts of processed meat, powdered milk, corn, and other commodities across the border.

NAFTA was an experiment that had never been tried before. It marked the first time that fully developed economies had agreed to eliminate all trade barriers with a low-wage, developing country that had a minimum daily wage of $4.20, and in this regard it was very different from the EU.

Primarily, NAFTA benefited investors, who were granted a set of new rights and privileges that promoted the relocation of factories. NAFTA was first and foremost *not* a free-trade agreement but rather a free-investment agreement. It worked to the advantage of employers who, in a deregulated global market, could move from country to country and purchase labor essentially as a commodity at the lowest possible price.

After ten years under NAFTA, workers had little to cheer. Investment in Mexico quintupled in size from 1994 to 2001, but the influx of money had not translated into jobs. Moreover, the wages of Mexican manufacturing workers had dropped 13.5 percent. The Mexican government's minimum daily wage of $4.20 had not changed since 1994. In the United States, NAFTA was a contributing factor to the loss of nearly 880,000 jobs.[14] NAFTA also contributed considerably to the record-setting US trade deficits with Mexico and Canada (see Table 17.3).

Mercosur: Economic Regionalism in South America

In 1991, four nations in the southern part of South America—Argentina, Brazil, Uruguay, and Paraguay—established a trade bloc known as Mercosur (using the Spanish acronym for Common Market of the South). Over the years nearly all South Americans showed interest in joining. Among its objectives were the elimination of tariffs among its members and the creation of a common external tariff for nonmembers. In 1994, Mercosur began negotiations with NAFTA in the hope of creating a free-trade zone encompassing the thirty-four nations in the Western Hemisphere. In 1995, it began discussions with the European Union to establish an interregional trade agreement. Meanwhile, Hugo Chávez of Venezuela appealed to other leftist leaders in South America, calling for Mercosur to take a firm stand against neoliberalism and for anti-imperialism in order to curb Washington's influence on the continent.

ASEAN: Economic Regionalism in East Asia

ASEAN, the Association of Southeast Asian Nations, was formed in 1967—during the Vietnam War—by Indonesia, Malaysia, the Philippines, Singapore, and Thailand, primarily for political and security purposes. Brunei joined in 1968; after the conflicts in Indochina were over, Vietnam, Cambodia, Laos, and Burma were admitted. The diplomatic solidarity created by ASEAN in the 1970s served as a platform on which to build regional economic coordination designed to reduce tariffs and to facilitate joint industrial ventures. With the exception of the Philippines, each of the original ASEAN nations registered steady economic growth in the 1970s and early 1980s by shifting to the manufacture of export-oriented goods.

Globalization: Remedy or Curse?

In the mid-1990s, *globalization* became a buzzword to describe the growing integration of the international economy. For its proponents it was a call for free trade to facilitate the flow of goods and services throughout all parts of the world. Globalization was the new reality, and the general feeling was that every country had better get onboard or be left behind. US president Bill Clinton was particularly fond of globalization and became its leading champion. It became a gospel to be preached and practiced as if it were a cure-all: The removal of national barriers to free trade produces economic growth, makes more goods available at cheaper prices, and thus ultimately benefits everyone—consumers as well as businesses, poor nations as well as rich ones. "A rising tide," the promoters of globalization argued, "lifts all boats."

Globalization called for deregulation (reduction of government controls of the economy), privatization (putting more state-owned property and operations under private ownership and management), austerity (reduction of government budgets), and trade liberalization (lowering of tariffs and other barriers to free trade). This formula, known as the "Washington Consensus," was adopted by the IMF and World Bank as the basis for their financial-assistance operations. It meant that nations applying for assistance had to meet stringent conditions and were required to undertake a stipulated set of painful reforms. In those nations, many politicians and the public at large often complained, but they were assured that the pain was only temporary.

A series of events in Asia provides a case in point. In 1997, several Asian countries (South Korea, Indonesia, Thailand, and Malaysia) saw the value of their currencies drastically decline (caused by currency speculation). The IMF, World Bank, and various industrialized nations came quickly to their rescue with massive loans totaling over $100 billion to shore up the currencies. This was not a matter of generosity, for the loans were intended to keep the financial disaster from spreading beyond Asia. With the bailouts came the famous IMF "discipline," calling for recipient nations to undergo economic liberalization. The IMF's view was that these Asian economies had suffered from overvalued currencies, heavily indebted banks, excessive government control, and "crony capitalism" (close ties among politicians, big business, and bankers). Thus, it called for a strong dose of deregulation, privatization, and market liberalization. The harsh medicine worked, and these nations gradually pulled themselves out of recession.

Globalization did not always bring benefits, however. Its impact in Latin America was more negative than positive. In the case of Mexico, demands for deregulation and privatization called for an economy entirely free of government involvement. The globalists (also known as neoliberals) sought a balanced budget, and to achieve it they slashed government spending by cutting out "expendable" items, which consisted all too often of social programs such as health care, education, and welfare. In the last two decades of the twentieth century, many Latin American countries employed this approach to stimulate economic growth, but poverty was not reduced. In Latin America and the Caribbean, the percentage of those who lived on an income of $1 per day remained constant in the years between 1987 and 1998.[15]

The persistence of poverty was not unique to Latin America. The World Bank spoke of poverty as "a global problem of huge proportions." It acknowledged that, between 1990 and 1998, the number of people who lived below the international poverty line (less than $2 per day) had risen from 2.1 billion to 2.8 billion—nearly half of the world's population—and that 1.2 billion lived on less than $1 per day.[16] In Africa, the most impoverished continent, many countries had an incredible 80–90 percent of the population living on less than $2 per day. And in the three most heavily populated Asian countries, India, Indonesia, and China, the percentages of people living on $2 per day or less were 86 percent, 66 percent, and 53 percent, respectively. The report also pointed out that the combined wealth of the world's richest 200 *individuals* was greater than the combined incomes of the poorest 2 billion people. These shocking facts made it abundantly clear that a serious maldistribution of wealth existed; two decades of aggressive globalization had not solved the problem but, instead, had often contributed to it.

One of the strongest opponents of globalization was organized labor. Unions protested against it on two fronts: On one hand, they lamented the loss of jobs for workers in their own country (after large firms relocated abroad to take advantage of cheap labor); on the other hand, they decried the exploitation of workers abroad and their lack of union rights. Labor leaders charged that globalization was most destructive in countries where independent unions did not exist and organizing was suppressed.

The wrath of various antiglobalization groups—among them environmentalists, organized labor, human rights activists, and the so-called G-77 (i.e., the world's poorest nations)—became manifest in huge protest demonstrations in November 1999 in Seattle on the occasion of a WTO conference. The protesters disrupted the conference and grabbed headlines in attempting to attract a global audience and thereby publicize their cause.[17]

At the beginning of the twenty-first century, the Washington Consensus was under increased criticism. There were those who continued to believe in the missionary work of the World Bank and IMF, namely, that economic growth will eventually solve the problems of widespread human misery and the inequality of wealth distribution. And there were those who argued that globalization had been responsible for unequal distribution of wealth, a major cause of poverty. The solutions offered by the World Bank and IMF only compounded the problem. The once solid World Bank–IMF consensus began to break down. Joseph Stiglitz, the World Bank's chief economist, who had served as an economic advisor to President Bill Clinton, broke ranks when he criticized austerity programs, deregulation, and privatization as the standard panacea for the developing world. The market alone, he insisted, would not abolish poverty. He advocated, instead, a "third way" between the "free market fundamentalists" and outright governmental planning. He saw the 1997 East Asian economic crisis as the consequence of reckless decisions by private investors pressured by World Bank and IMF bureaucrats:

> The older men who staff the fund [IMF] . . . act as if they are shouldering Rudyard Kipling's white man's burden. . . . [They] believe they are brighter, more educated, and less politically motivated than the economists of the countries they visit. In fact, the economic leaders of those countries are brighter or better-educated.[18]

Stiglitz, along with several coworkers at the World Bank and other leading orthodox economists, was moving toward the ideological camp of the protesters in the streets. Lawrence Summers—who had been the World Bank's chief economist and who played a role in Stiglitz's ouster there and later became President Clinton's treasury secretary—began to have his own doubts about globalization. In 2007, he expressed the heretical view that "it is not even altogether clear that [globalization] benefits America in aggregate."[19]

In 1998 and 2001, the Nobel Prize for Economics, which had gone to the champions of the free market, now went to its critics, Amartya Sen and Joseph Stiglitz. In awarding it to Sen, an Indian economist who specialized in social welfare, the Nobel committee explained that Sen, by pointing out how little of the resources were allocated to the poorest members of society, "had restored an ethical dimension to the discussion of vital economic problems." Sen, instead of relying on complicated computer-generated formulas, presented a simple thesis: Poverty, not food shortages, caused famines. During the famine of 1974 in Bangladesh, for example, workers simply did not have the money to purchase the food available to feed their families.[20] Sen pointed to one of the great challenges for the twenty-first century: how to distribute as equitably as possible the astonishing volume of wealth that the world's economies produced.

OPEC: Organization of Petroleum Exporting Countries

The apostle of free trade, Adam Smith, argued that the free market worked best when regulated by the benevolent "invisible hand" of the market. This theory of a well-meaning, self-regulating market, however, often ran aground on the shoals of capitalist practice, which has traditionally sought to regulate the market on its own behalf. The oil shocks of the 1970s were a case in point. In the fall of 1973, the world suddenly woke up to find that the supply of petroleum products did not meet the demand. The unprecedented oil shortages of the 1970s had an immediate and long-term destabilizing effect on economies all over the world, which since 1945 had become increasingly reliant on oil as the energy source for industry, transportation, and heating.

The Organization of Petroleum Exporting Countries (OPEC)—the association (some would say cartel) responsible for the shortages—argued that there existed only a finite amount of fossil fuel (particularly petroleum) and that it was being consumed much too fast. Politicians across the globe hastened to legislate remedies such as conserving energy, diversifying energy sources, and reducing dependence on foreign oil. A second shortage in 1979 was not as shocking or severe as the first, but it nevertheless fed raw feelings of uncertainty and insecurity.

The oil shortages had been artificially created by OPEC, led by Saudi Arabia and the shah of Iran, and by the Western oil companies. In the 1970s, OPEC encompassed the oil-exporting states of the Middle East (Saudi Arabia, Iran, Iraq, United Arab Emirates, Qatar, and Kuwait) as well as four African states (Algeria, Libya, Nigeria, and Gabon), two South American nations (Venezuela and Ecuador), and Indonesia. Equally important were the oil-exporting nations that did not belong to OPEC but had the best of reasons to follow OPEC's lead: the Soviet Union (among the world's leading exporters of oil in the 1970s and 1980s), Mexico, Great Britain, the United States, and Canada.

When OPEC conspired to limit the supply of oil, the result was a fifteen-fold increase—from $2 to about $30 per barrel (at one point even to $40)—in the price of crude oil by the end of the decade. During the 1970s, OPEC managed to dictate the price of oil by virtue of the fact that in 1979 it controlled 63.4 percent of the world's market.

OPEC dominance, however, began to weaken during the early 1980s, when a global oil glut was in the making and the bottom of the oil market began to drop out. The surplus was the result of conservation, a worldwide economic recession (which lessened the demand for all fuels), the discovery of new deposits (on the North Slope of Alaska and in the North Sea, as well as in Mexico), a worldwide increase in oil production once prices rose, and the cold, hard fact that even during the shortages at the pump there had always been a surplus of oil. By 1984, OPEC's share of oil on the global market dropped to 42.8 percent; by 1985 it fell to 30 percent. In 1985, as OPEC's market share continued to decline, its members, desperate for oil revenues, began to break ranks by surreptitiously selling more than their allotted quotas. The artificial shortages that OPEC had created gave way to competition based on the laws of supply and demand.

For years, Mexico (although not a member of OPEC) sought to follow OPEC's pricing levels, but in the summer of 1985, it began to establish its own pricing policy in direct confrontation with OPEC. It lowered the price of a barrel of crude oil to about $24. The Soviet Union followed Mexico's lead, thus placing additional pressures on OPEC. OPEC, in its turn, tried to cut back on production to reestablish an artificial scarcity, but this had little impact on prices. OPEC output declined to about 14.5 million barrels per day, the group's lowest level of production in twenty years. Saudi Arabia, the linchpin of OPEC, in order to shore up the price of oil, dropped its production to 2.3 million barrels per day (almost half of its quota allotted by OPEC), its lowest level since 1967. At the meetings of OPEC oil ministers in the summer of 1985, the debates centered on whether to cut prices or production. In the end, OPEC wound up doing both. No event underscored OPEC's dilemma as sharply as Ecuador's defection in September 1992, when it became the first member to leave the organization. For Ecuador, membership in OPEC, with its quotas for members, had become pointless. Without OPEC restraints, Ecuador's oil industry expected to double its output.

In June 1998, the price for a barrel of oil dropped to rock bottom, to $10, the result of a number of factors such as overproduction and a steep decline in demand caused by the Asian financial crisis of the year before. OPEC's income in 1998 of $80 billion—in real terms—was its lowest ever. To recover its losses, OPEC, supported by such nonmembers as Norway, Russia, and Mexico, cut production at a time of renewed rising demand and thus managed to drive up the price for a barrel of oil to $38 by the fall of 2000. Still, in real terms, the price per barrel was less than half of what it had been during the 1970s.

Insurmountable Debts

As the price of oil declined in the 1980s, it deeply affected the economies of oil-exporting nations such as Mexico, Venezuela, and Nigeria. Not only did they receive less for their once precious commodity; they now had to deal with large foreign debts that they had incurred when times were good, when they were flush with "petrodollars"—money that oil producers had invested in Western banks. That money made it possible to borrow additional money, which now became more difficult—indeed, impossible—to repay. Western banks, with their surfeit of petrodollars, then made them available as well to poor Third World nations that, ultimately, did not have the means to repay. By the mid-1980s, the combined debt of Africa and Latin America rose to more than $500 billion—Mexico and Brazil owing around $100 billion each. A default by any one of the major nations threatened to trigger an economic crisis with worldwide repercussions: failures and the contraction of credit as well as a slowdown of international trade, perhaps even a global recession. Such a train of events was certain to produce an extraordinary economic and political fallout, particularly in the regions hardest hit, the Third World.

Third World countries at times raised the specter of default, but they were at pains to avoid such a drastic measure and sought, instead, to meet their obligations. When, in early 1987, Brazil announced a halt to foreign debt payments, its government was careful to spell out that this was a temporary emergency measure and that it eventually hoped to find a solution. Similarly, in March 1987, after Ecuador was hit with a devastating earthquake that cut its main oil pipeline from the interior to the coast, it also suspended foreign debt payments, albeit temporarily. Third World leaders well understood that a declaration of bankruptcy was no solution. It would cut their nations adrift, make them incapable of borrowing additional funds, and even lead to economic retaliation.

The staggering Latin American debt gave the Communist Fidel Castro of Cuba the opportunity to take center stage as the region's elder statesman. In 1985, Castro spoke of the need to create a "debtors' cartel" to resolve Latin America's debt obligations. Oddly, Castro, the revolutionary, urged a resolution of the crisis, with the help of the US government and the Western capitalist banks, for the purpose of avoiding widespread unrest. Indeed, Castro sought the mitigation of debts to prevent revolution. He pointed to the example of the Soviet Union, which repeatedly had written off the assistance it gave to Cuba.[21]

In the summer of 1985, Peru's newly elected president, Alan García, declared that his nation would limit its foreign debt payments to 10 percent of export earnings. This was the first time a debtor nation had tried to link payments to the ability to export. When, in early 1987, Brazil and Ecuador temporarily suspended payments, they looked to Peru as their model. This approach was an attractive alternative to the impossible payments and domestic austerity measures that the IMF demanded.

Donor nations had to grapple with the prospect that some debts could not be recovered no matter what. In the late 1980s, a number of nations (including Canada, Finland, Germany, the Netherlands, Norway, Sweden, and Great Britain) converted some loans to grants (meaning the money did not have to be paid back). France decided to write off $2.4 billion in loans to the thirty-five poorest African countries, and Belgium canceled debts of $200 million to thirteen African nations. The amount of money involved, however, was relatively small and affected only government-to-government loans.[22] In June 1999, Japan wrote off $3.3 billion of its $8.2 billion in loans to some of the world's most impoverished countries. Several months later, at a global summit in Cologne, Germany, world leaders pledged to forgive some of the debts of at least twenty nations. Private banks, however, were in no mood to write off their massive—and unrecoverable—loans to Third World nations.

The debt crisis demanded a reevaluation of what had gone wrong with international monetary lending practices, why some countries were showing little (if any) economic growth and were therefore unable to repay their debts. In

1991, a World Bank study, "Managing Development: The Governance Dimension," concluded that dishonest and inefficient governments were at the core of the problem. Britain's Ministry of Overseas Development came to a similar conclusion and as a result began to shift substantial amounts of money to train efficient local officials in Commonwealth nations such as Zambia, Ghana, and India in an effort to eliminate widespread corruption, a by-product of the Cold War when officials were permitted to skim off aid in exchange for loyalty to the donor. The ministry also increased its funding of private nongovernmental organizations (NGOs) in an attempt to bypass corrupt government officials. It gave as an example the British Red Cross's contributions to health care on the local level. The World Bank considered the NGOs to be "eyes and ears" capable of providing a system of checks and balances over corrupt governments and for monitoring the effective uses of aid.[23]

To repay the debts meant putting one's economic house in order. In meant swallowing bitter medicine. It meant first and foremost the raising of taxes, which could be achieved by various means: the elimination of subsidies on food, sales taxes on fuel, a limitation on imports (particularly luxury items), and the devaluation of money. Such steps, however, promised inevitable political repercussions, for they entailed lowering standards of living across the board. Resentment was particularly great when the price of meeting international debt obligations—as demanded by the IMF—produced an increase in the cost of food. It frequently led to riots in the streets, as in Sudan, Tunisia, the Dominican Republic, Jamaica, Bolivia, and Argentina. It was little wonder that Egyptian president Hosni Mubarak famously referred to the IMF as the "International Misery Fund."

The Third World was caught between two unpalatable choices: either default and then risk the potential economic repercussions—and the attendant political unrest—or undertake compliance and risk potential political unrest. Either way, the Third World was not a place to look for political stability, which goes hand in glove with economic progress.

The mid-1980s witnessed another phenomenon that compounded the debtors' plight: the flight of capital from the Third World. A case in point is Mexico, where a high rate of inflation undermined the value of money on deposit in Mexican banks. Depositors, therefore, sought safer havens—Western Europe and the United States—where inflation rates were under control. Since the mid-1980s, the Third World changed from a net importer of capital to a net exporter, a trend that only served to widen the gap between the rich nations and the poor nations, the North and the South.

The reassessment of reckless lending practices to poor nations scarcely able to repay the loans brought the bankers back to the fiscal conservatism of earlier days. The World Bank's second president, Eugene Robert Black (1949–1962), had insisted that in the struggle against Communist influence investments would have their greatest impact only if they made "the greatest possible contribution, raising living standards and opening opportunities for further investment." Black was not interested in providing money for questionable projects simply to bring a leader of a Third World nation into the Western ideological camp. He insisted that money must be lent for projects that created income, which then would be used to repay the loans. Black's fiscal conservatism made possible the lending of billions of dollars by the World Bank without a default, a basic lesson that the lending spree of the 1980s forced international lending institutions to relearn.[24]

Throughout the 1990s many developing nations sank deeper into debt, and the mounting debt continued to be a drag on their economic development (see Table 17.4). Between 1970 and 1980, their debt grew more than tenfold, from $59 million to $603 billion; by 1990 it had more than doubled, and in the period 1990–1997 it grew at an average annual rate of over $100 billion to reach $2.1 trillion. Moreover, in the years between 1985 and 1999, the Third World's share of world GNP declined steadily: In 1985 it was 31 percent; in 1989, 28 percent; and in 1999, 21 percent.[25]

Zambia became a textbook case of a poor nation trying to repay its external debt. The IMF and World Bank worked out a program for Zambian debt relief under the international Heavily Indebted Poor Countries (HIPC) initiative. Under this plan the IMF and World Bank would restructure a nation's debt, providing an additional infusion of money, but only on strict conditions, namely, the implementation of "structural adjustments," which meant that the Zambian government drastically cut its expenditures.

Under the HIPC initiative, Zambia was required to increase its debt payments from $70 million per year to $200 million. The additional outflow of $130 million meant the curtailment of vital social services. The World Bank

Table 17.4   Foreign Debt Increase of Selected Nations, 1990–1998 (in US$ billions)

Country	1990	1998	Percentage of 1998 GNP
Algeria	27	30	66
Argentina	62	144	52
Brazil	119	232	29
China	55	154	15
Indonesia	69	150	169
Malaysia	14	44	69
Mexico	104	159	39
Nigeria	33	30	74
Philippines	30	47	66
Russia	59	183	62
South Korea	34	139	43
Turkey	49	102	49
Thailand	28	86	79

Source: World Bank, *World Development Report, 2000/2001,* pp. 314–315.

then praised Zambia's "reformed" health care system as a model for the rest of Africa. The "reforms," however, consisted of slashing state subsidies, which did eliminate long lines in the hospitals but only because people who could not afford admission were dying at home. The reforms also meant the reduction of government payrolls and the privatization of state enterprises. The result was increased unemployment. Children, particularly girls, were withdrawn from school and put to work to augment their families' incomes. Primary-school enrollment dropped from 96 percent to 77 percent. The reforms also contributed to malnutrition, an increase in preventable disease, and a decrease in life expectancy. In Zambia, 20 percent of the children died before they reached the age of five.[26] (The social disaster, one should add, was not the making of the IMF and World Bank alone. Zambia's dilemma was compounded by government corruption, political instability, and human rights abuses.)

Global Environmentalism

Toward the end of the twentieth century, industrialized nations increasingly became concerned with climate change caused by global warming. Records showed that the planet's temperature had been steadily rising in the twentieth century, the warmest on record. The 1990s, in particular, set new records. The chief cause was the emission of carbon dioxide, mainly from the exhaust pipes of the ever increasing number of motor vehicles, as well as other "greenhouse gases" that were polluting the atmosphere and trapping heat. A number of scientists forecast a temperature increase of 6 degrees Fahrenheit by 2100. Some speculated that the effects could be catastrophic, leading to widespread droughts and desertification, more frequent devastating storms, and a rise in ocean levels by as much as 3 feet, submerging heavily populated and cultivated lands.

The environmentalists were among the most persistent opponents of globalization and its drive for ever greater expansion. They faulted industrialists for their voracious consumption of the earth's raw materials and their unrestricted pollution (particularly in the Third World) of the land, water, and air. A good example is China, which after three decades of rapid industrialization had seven of the world's ten most polluted cities. The environmentalists insisted that business leaders make a commitment to environmentally sustainable growth.

In the past, environmentalists and union workers were generally on opposite sides, the former seeking to limit industrial growth and the latter seeking to preserve jobs. Now they were being drawn closer in a loose "blue-green" coalition that combined the interests of blue-collar workers with those of green activists.

In 1988, the United States, by far the world's largest polluter and responsible for one-quarter of global carbon dioxide emissions, proposed an international panel to investigate scientific evidence of climate change. The Netherlands, Germany, the United Kingdom, and Japan took the next step by setting targets for reducing carbon dioxide emissions, something the United States opposed. The first agreement to cut emissions came out of the international conference on climate change in Kyoto, Japan, in October 1997, where 150 nations were represented.

The Kyoto Protocol called for reducing emissions by at least 5 percent below 1990 levels by 2010, with demonstrable progress to be achieved by 2005. Developing countries received exemptions from the mandatory emissions cuts. Over European objections, the Kyoto Protocol also included the US-sponsored plan for international trading of emission quotas. This scheme allowed US factories to obtain the right to continue emitting pollutants by "buying the rights" from countries that did not fully use their quotas. Europeans and environmentalists objected to this as a giant loophole allowing the United States to escape its obligations. French president Jacques Chirac scolded the United States for ducking its responsibility, adding that "no country can elude its share of the collective effort."[27]

Meanwhile, environmentalists wrung their hands and lamented the meager progress toward slowing global warming. But the news soon got worse. The newly elected US president, George W. Bush, bluntly announced in April 2001 his administration's flat rejection of the Kyoto Protocol, claiming that its provisions would be harmful to the US economy. The world's number-one polluter simply checked out of the process, leaving all the other global players aghast. Nonetheless, Kyoto went into effect when Russia ratified it in November 2004, becoming the 127th nation to do so. Still, the world's insatiable appetite for machines driven by internal-combustion engines was undiminished. China (as a developing nation) was granted an exemption, and the world's leading polluter stood on the sidelines. There was little hope that global warming could be slowed. As China prepared to host the 2008 Olympic Games, there was fear that the heavily polluted air in Beijing would negatively impact the competition, especially endurance events. The Chinese authorities resolved the problem by shutting down smokestacks in and around Beijing and banning many vehicles from the streets. As a short-term solution it worked, but the root of the problem remained after the competitors returned home.

The Economic Fallout from the Rise of China

In the 1990s, while the three established economic superpowers were jostling for dominance in world trade, a fourth player—China—was nudging its way into the ring of economic behemoths. The Chinese industrial revolution, over a period of thirty years, was more impressive than the German and Japanese "economic miracles" of the 1950s and 1960s, respectively. Indeed, at no time in history had a nation undergone such an industrial transformation in so short a time. The German and Japanese achievements consisted of rebuilding their industrial infrastructures from the damage incurred during World War II and then going from there. The Chinese, in contrast, had to begin from a very low base. China had a factory system, but it was rather small, organized along inefficient Stalinist lines where production was dictated not by demand but by decree from the top; it was rather old and inefficient by late-twentieth-century standards. Thirty years later—between 1978 and 2008—China had become a wealthy nation, its per capita GNP having risen from around $300 to (an exchange rate–based) $2,458 in 2007.[28]

China's economic success came within the context of globalization. Two trends converged. In 1978, the Chinese government removed restrictions against foreign investments; in turn industrialized nations, notably the United States, removed any and all restrictions against doing business in China. Once China agreed to accept foreign investments, the economy began to take off. Foreign capital did what it had done in the past and followed the labor market. US capital had gone south of the border into Latin America, then later to the Pacific Rim (Japan, South Korea, the Philippines, etc.). As wages in those places rose, US investors looked for new opportunities and found them elsewhere, particularly in China, where wages were only a small fraction of what they were at home. China became the recipient of a massive, record-setting infusion of foreign direct investment as well as money in the form of loans. This infusion of capital was historic in its proportion; no other even came close. In all, between 1984 and 2007, China contracted $1.8 trillion in the form of "direct" investments (which gave rise to "foreign control" of domestic assets) as well as loans. It was a question of supply and demand. The Chinese demand was met by the motivations and capabilities of multinational corporations.[29]

There was money to be made by relocating operations to China. The money went primarily to investors—the stockholders—who financed the transfer of industry. Not only did the US government stand aside during the transfer of capital to China; it encouraged the players, going so far as to provide tax credits for companies that relocated abroad. The multinational corporations—joined by successive US administrations, whether Republican or Democratic, it did not matter—became apologists for China. They argued, against clear evidence, that economic growth and the development of democracy go hand in hand. (The critics of this line of reasoning point to the examples of Japan and Germany before World War II, where economic growth did not foster democracy.)

As US corporations shifted operations abroad and as the US manufacturing sector became hollowed out, the lessons of the past were forgotten, namely, that a strong manufacturing class is necessary for the nation's economic well-being. The workers who built the cars have to be able to purchase them. But as the number of these workers shrank, and as companies like General Motors relocated to China, the thirty-year rise of China coincided with the largest gap between the very rich and the poor in US history. Increasingly, consumer spending depended on the purchasing power of fewer and fewer individuals.

The Chinese, as they were brought into the global economy, took a page from the Japanese economic miracle and developed an economy geared for exports. They were quick learners. As in Japan, China's currency, the yuan, was kept artificially devalued against the US dollar, which made Chinese goods artificially cheap abroad and artificially expensive at home. The yuan, devalued by an estimated 40 percent, thus provided a subsidy to China's exporters and a tax on imports by making them more expensive. (Currency manipulation is in violation of WTO rules and, under pressure, China promised currency reform without, however, carrying it through.) Moreover, the PRC government provided tax incentives for exporters, and in late 2008, as the global recession hit China particularly hard, it offered export tax rebates.

Multinationals' thirst for cheap labor, coupled with US consumers' insatiable appetite for cheap Chinese imports, undermined the industrial base of the United States. The US-China trade deficit in 2007 was more than $250 billion in China's favor. Trade deficits have to be financed either by foreign investments (which took care of 10 percent of the deficit) or by borrowing from foreigners. The result was a $6.5 trillion US foreign debt (most of it to China), part of a federal deficit of more than $10 trillion altogether. A major contributing factor to the huge debt became Chinese exports to the United States, which exceeded imports by a ratio of 4.3:1. US trade deficits consisted of approximately 4.8 percent of GDP, which was a drag on the US economy and became one of the causes of increasing unemployment. During 2000–2008, the US lost 3.8 million manufacturing jobs. The foreign debt was also responsible for depressing US economic growth from 4 percent to 3 percent.[30]

The race to the bottom of the wage structure affected wages across the globe. Between 2001 and 2007, the global economy grew at 4 percent. Wages, however, grew at only 1.9 percent. The lion's share of profits was distributed among investors (stockholders) rather than workers. This trend was facilitated by what one economist called the "great doubling" of the workforce, from 1.5 billion to 3 billion, after India, China, and the countries of the former Soviet bloc joined the capitalist system. This unprecedented widening of the labor pool in such a short time led to competition among workers against other workers and thus depressed wages overall.[31]

Otherwise, China's industrial expansion paralleled that of other nations as they underwent a similar process. It was accompanied by the exploitation of workers, an uneven distribution of wealth, endangering of consumers, industrial waste (on a scale never seen before) that gave China the filthiest air on the planet, and the problem of controlling a restless population.

The Return of Expensive Oil?

In 2004, the price per barrel of crude oil pushed past the $50 benchmark. That price, however, was still 62 percent—in constant dollars—of the price in

1979–1980. The subsequent spike during 2007–2008 (at one time reaching nearly $150 per barrel) reflected a belief that the world's oil production and reserves might have reached their plateau, promising permanently high prices in the future.[32]

The primary reason for the spike in oil prices was growing demand across the globe, not only in the industrial world but also in the former Soviet bloc and developing nations. This was especially true for China and India, which, combined, made up one-third of the world's population and whose economies were rapidly industrializing.

As demand grew and so long as the price of energy remained relatively low, conservation was an afterthought. Vice-President Richard Cheney, a longtime oilman whose hand was at the helm of US energy policy during the George W. Bush administration, infamously declared in April 2001 that "conservation may be a sign of personal virtue" but it was "not a sufficient basis . . . for sound, comprehensive energy policy."[33] The sum total of the Bush-Cheney energy position consisted of maintaining the status quo and continuing US reliance on fossil fuels.

Uncertainty also played a role in the rise of oil prices. With war and threats of war (including piracy on the high seas) promising to disrupt oil supply lines, purchasers of future deliveries were willing to pay ever higher prices. Speculators in the futures markets, betting that prices would continue to go up, also played a part in driving up prices (adding perhaps 10 percent to the price for a barrel of oil).[34] Adding to the uncertainty was the belief, generally absent in the 1970s, that the world was finally *beginning* to run out of oil, that peak oil production was about to be reached.[35]

The precipitous decline of the price of a barrel of oil—from its high mark of $150 to below $50 by March 2009—came from an unexpected, and unwelcome, quarter: the global recession of 2008, which greatly lessened the demand for energy.

The Global Economy and Recession

The full-blown and multifaceted global crisis that gripped worldwide markets in 2008 was long in the making. It came at a time when the US economy—the engine that drove global consumption—was already in recession. The sins of the past (overlending, speculation, and subprime mortgages that led to a portfolio of toxic assets) caught up with Wall Street and the financial markets. The financial crisis, in its turn, produced a deeper global recession accompanied by a decline in productivity, employment, and purchasing power. The result was a vicious cycle with no clear route for escape.

The roots of the 2008 crisis went back at least three decades. Beginning in the early 1980s, a new economic orthodoxy gradually replaced that of the

New Deal, a series of massive federal programs that had been cobbled together during the Great Depression of the 1930s. Whereas the New Deal had stressed a regulated economy, the new approach, which became firmly established during the 1980s, argued that a market free of cumbersome restrictions—and placed in the expert hands of global banks and money managers—would govern itself for the benefit of all. This policy, known as monetarism, insisted that the money supply, not macroeconomic government planning, must regulate the economy. The politicians most closely identified with monetarism were British prime minister Margaret Thatcher and US president Ronald Reagan. Government was not the solution, Reagan repeatedly insisted, but was instead the problem. Indeed, some wanted government to get out of people's lives altogether, to see it shrunk "down to the size where we can drown it in the bathtub." Inexorably, these "free-market fundamentalists," as critics called them, became deeply entrenched in the corridors of power.

In the process, many financial institutions were unregulated, where too many risky and unsupervised transactions were approved on a massive scale. Extending credit to even the riskiest applicants (those who had no income or no job, or simply lied about incomes on their loan applications) became business as usual. These "liar's loans" were quickly repackaged by the originating institutions and resold to Wall Street investors under the process of "securitization." It was easy money, and it created an unsustainable bubble in the US housing market. In the end (and as many had predicted), overextended borrowers, unable to make house payments, walked away from their mortgages and defaulted en masse; overextended banks (unable to collect on the mortgages and holding unsalable houses) and investment firms (now possessing worthless or toxic assets) went bankrupt. Capital markets (i.e., the availability of money) were drying up with severe consequences, undermining the capitalist system, which cannot function without the rational circulation of capital. The specter of deflation across the globe—the contraction of money in circulation—not seen since the Great Depression, became a real possibility. In the United States, the markets plummeted as unemployment skyrocketed.

During the age of unrestrained globalization, the United States had witnessed an unprecedented imbalance of wealth, greater than during the era of robber barons and monopolies and, later, the unrestrained prosperity of the Roaring Twenties. The shift of US manufacturing plants to underdeveloped countries, where wages were dramatically lower, in the proverbial race to the bottom meant that wages remained depressed at home and abroad. As workers in manufacturing sectors saw their share of the nation's wealth decline, the economy increasingly depended on the purchasing power of the well-to-do. But now, even the beneficiaries of globalization, the multinational corporations that had moved operations abroad and the institutions that financed global investments, were being hammered on the balance sheet. A decade later, the optimism of the 1990s was a distant memory.

US firms facing bankruptcy included some of the most venerable investment, banking, and insurance companies. The crisis started on Wall Street but soon spread across the globe, and many governments scrambled to save (and to reregulate) their own financial institutions and stock markets. The French president, Nicolas Sarkozy, who had won his recent election as the darling of the political right, now lurched to the left, famously declaring that "laissez-faire is finished, the all-powerful market that is always right, that's finished."

The most dramatic aspect was seen in the meltdown of international financial institutions, overextended to such a degree that they were unable to meet their obligations to stockholders as well as to customers in need of capital. US treasury secretary Henry Paulson, the point man in George W. Bush's last-ditch effort in the fall of 2008 to stave off economic catastrophe, singled out some of them as "too big to fail" and insisted that they be shored up with massive sums of public money to preserve their ability to extend credit within the faltering global financial system. The US government, first under George W. Bush and then under President Barack Obama, thus approved bailout packages reaching trillions of dollars—all underwritten by US taxpayers.[36] At first, the beneficiaries of this largesse were told that they had to accept regulation and oversight.

The big financial institutions were happy to accept the money but chafed at any restrictions. Paulson, a former head of Goldman Sachs, an investment firm with its own severe financial problems, saw little reason to impose undue hardships on the companies and their officers. Six weeks after Congress voted for an initial $700 billion bailout, and after Paulson had allocated nearly $300 billion to various firms, the rules and regulations were yet to be written. Paulson was adamant that the officers of the companies responsible for the global financial meltdown be given a free pass. He reminded Congress that since "no playbook" existed to deal with such an unprecedented crisis, he was free to act on his own volition. Nor did he bother to reveal who received what and how much. Whatever strings were attached to the bailout were frayed, and much of the money handed over to these huge financial institutions was unaccounted for.

The Bush and Obama administrations had no clear idea of how to deal with the financial meltdown. A telling example was their approach to American Investment Group (AIG), the world's largest insurance company. Since 2000, one of AIG's subdivisions, the Financial Products Group, had taken full advantage of the lack of regulations and had insured banks and investment houses—foreign and domestic—against reckless lending practices. Its chief officer, Joseph Cassino, boasted as late as August 2007 that it was "hard for us . . . to even see a scenario within any kind of realm of reason that would see us losing $1 in any of those transactions."[37] Within twelve months, however, AIG had to make good for more than half a trillion dollars in credit insurance—money it did not have—to cover the toxic loans of venerable financial institutions in the United States and Europe (such as Bank of America, Citibank, Goldman Sachs, Société Generale, Deutsche Bank, and Barclay).

AIG's bankruptcy threatened to bring down the institutions it had insured against losses. It had an obligation of $307 billion to European banks alone. In September 2008, France's finance minister, Christine Legarde, pleaded with Paulson to shore up AIG—and with it France's banking system. The result was AIG's first bailout of $85 billion (a figure that ballooned to $173 billion by March 2009). When AIG made public the extent of its first payouts, billions of dollars went to European and US investment houses.

With AIG's bailout, the US government owned 80 percent of AIG's depreciated assets, yet the company continued to operate as an independent, private entity—throwing lavish parties and extending even more lavish bonuses to the same people who had brought it to ruin. The Obama administration, particularly its secretary of the treasury, Timothy Geithner (similar to Paulson), had no answer to the crisis except to shovel more money into the coffers of AIG and hope that the company somehow would right its ship before it sank under the wave of deregulation, recklessness, and greed—and before the attendant maelstrom did further harm to the international capitalist system.

A more important problem was the overall US economy. US automakers (General Motors and Chrysler) had received a bailout of $25 billion, and in November 2008 they asked for another $25 billion. It did not help that the auto executives, hats in hand, came to Washington in corporate jets and had no specific answers for how they would spend the money. The board of General Motors also expressed full confidence in its management team, as if the company had just set record sales. In the meantime, the market for new autos plummeted to near-record lows.

With the global recession in full force and with banks loath to lend money to stimulate the economy, stock markets across the globe lost much of their value. Unemployment rose everywhere, discretionary spending by jittery consumers slowed, and the crisis grew more severe. In Detroit, automakers laid off tens of thousands of workers; in Moscow, construction stopped on Europe's tallest building; and in China, factories closed their doors. Indebtedness (both public and private) and massive job losses throughout 2008 and into 2009 further eroded confidence in the economy. Emerging economies, their debt estimated at $4–5 trillion, were unable to repay. It had taken the Great Depression three years to bottom out after the stock market crash of 1929. The "free-market fundamentalists," once certain of their understanding of the economy, had no idea when—or under what conditions—this recession would end.

Recommended Readings

Dinan, Desmond, ed. *Encyclopedia of the European Union.* Updated ed. Boulder: Lynne Rienner Publishers, 2000.
A comprehensive reference work on the European Union.

Frank, Thomas. *One Market Under God: Extreme Capitalism, Market Populism, and the End of Economic Democracy*. New York: Doubleday, 2000.
A critical view of the negative consequences of globalization.
Galeano, Eduardo. *Upside Down: A Primer for the Looking-Glass World*. New York: Henry Holt, 2000.
By a Guatemalan writer who tells the story of globalization from the perspective of the South.
Garten, Jeffrey E. *A Cold Peace: America, Japan, Germany, and the Struggle for Supremacy*. New York: Oxford University Press, 1992.
Grubb, Michael, et al. *The Kyoto Protocol: A Guide and Assessment*. London: Royal Institute of International Affairs, 1999.
Harrison, Paul. *Inside the Third World: The Anatomy of Poverty*. 2nd ed. New York: Penguin, 1981.
An English journalist's introduction to the realities of the Third World.
Kuttner, Robert. *The End of Laissez-Faire: National Purpose and Global Economy After the Cold War*. New York: Knopf, 1991.
An argument on behalf of a US national economic strategy.
Reich, Robert B. *The Work of Nations: Preparing Ourselves for 21st Century Capitalism*. New York: Knopf, 1991.
A call for a seamless global economy in which national competition is no longer of importance.
Reid, T. R. *The United States of Europe: The New Superpower and the End of American Supremacy*. New York: Penguin, 2004.
Sampson, Anthony. *The Sovereign State of ITT*. 2nd ed. New York: Fawcett, 1974.
The history of an international corporation and its reach across the globe.
Sen, Amartya. *Inequality Reexamined*. Cambridge, Mass.: Harvard University Press, 1995.
One of several books by the recipient of the 1998 Nobel Prize for Economics; its focus is on the downside of globalization, that is, on its impact on those left behind.
Stiglitz, Joseph E. *Globalization and Its Discontents*. New York: Norton, 2002.
By the former chief economist at the World Bank, a critique of how the major institutions of globalization failed many of the developing nations.
Stiglitz, Joseph E., and Shahid Yusuf, eds. *Rethinking the East Asian Miracle*. New York: Oxford University Press, 2000.
A collection of articles on the pitfalls of globalization.

OPEC

Blair, John M. *The Control of Oil*. New York: Pantheon, 1976.
Emerson, Steven. *The American House of Saud: The Secret Petrodollar Connection*. Danbury, Conn.: Franklin Watts, 1985.
An account of the link between the US oil companies and Saudi Arabia.
Lacey, Robert. *The Kingdom: Arabia and the House of Sa'ud*. New York: Avon, 1983.
Yergin, Daniel. *The Prize: The Epic Quest for Oil, Money, and Power*. New York: Simon and Schuster, 1990.
The definitive history of the geostrategic quest to control the world's supply of oil.

Notes

1. The sole major exceptions were Cuba and North Korea (as well as the principalities of Andorra, Monaco, Liechtenstein, Tuvalu, and Nauru).

2. By the time of its dissolution in 1995, GATT membership stood at 125 nations.

3. The twelve members of the European Council and their years of admission, listed in order of size of GNP in the early 1990s, are West Germany (1958), France (1958), Italy (1958), Great Britain (1973), Spain (1986), the Netherlands (1958), Belgium (1958), Denmark (1973), Greece (1981), Portugal (1986), Ireland (1973), and Luxembourg (1958).

4. Belgium and Luxembourg had a common currency. Stanley Hoffmann, "The European Community and 1992," *Foreign Affairs* (Fall 1989), p. 28.

5. Andrew Moravcsik, "Negotiating the Single Act: National Interests and Conventional Statecraft in the European Community," Cambridge, Mass., Harvard University, Center for European Studies, Working Paper Series 21, n.d., pp. 14–15.

6. Organization for Economic Cooperation and Development (OECD), December 1989; Hobert Rowen, "Bonn Next in Line as Power Center," *Washington Post*, January 7, 1990, pp. H1, H8.

7. US Census Bureau, Foreign Trade Division, "FT 900: U.S. International Trade in Goods and Services," March 13, 2009, www.census.gov/foreign-trade; see Exhibit 1.

8. "Der Krieg findet längst statt" ("The War Began Long Ago"), *Der Spiegel*, December 6, 13, and 20, 1989.

9. *Berliner Zeitung*, June 5, 1992, in "Pressestimmen zum dänischen EG-Referendum," *Deutschland Nachrichten*, June 5, 1992, p. 3.

10. Conor Cruise O'Brien, "Pursuing a Chimera: Nationalism at Odds with the Idea of a Federal Europe," *Times Literary Supplement*, March 13, 1992, pp. 3–4.

11. "European Union Economy 2008," *CIA World Factbook*, 2008.

12. NAFTA was not a treaty (which the Senate would have to ratify by a two-thirds vote) but a "trade agreement," which needed a majority vote from both houses of Congress.

13. Cited by Clyde N. Farnsworth, "What an Earlier Trade Pact Did Up North," and Louis Uchitelle, "NAFTA and Jobs: In a Numbers War, No One Can Count," *New York Times*, November 14, 1993, p. 1E.

14. David Bacon, "NAFTA's Legacy—Profits and Poverty," *San Francisco Chronicle*, January 14, 2004; James Cox, "10 Years Ago, NAFTA Was Born," *USA Today*, December 30, 2003.

15. World Bank, *World Development Report 2000/2001: Attacking Poverty* (New York: Oxford University Press, 2000), p. 23.

16. Ibid., pp. vi, 3–6, 23, 280–282; Joseph E. Stiglitz, *Globalization and Its Discontents* (New York: Norton, 2002), p. 259.

17. G-77 is in contrast to another group, the G-7, representing seven of the leading capitalist nations. (With Russia's addition, it became the G-8.)

18. Stiglitz, cited in Doug Henwood, "Stiglitz and the Limits of Reform," *The Nation*, October 2, 2000, pp. 20, 22.

19. Clive Crook, "Beyond Belief," *The Atlantic*, October 2007, pp. 44–47; Lawrence Summers, "The Global Consensus on Trade Is Unravelling," *Financial Times*, August 24, 2008.

20. Wire reports, "Expert on Welfare Who Studied Famine Wins Economic Nobel," *Baltimore Sun*, October 14, 1998, p. 14. See also Amartya Sen, *Poverty and Famines: An Essay on Entitlement and Deprivation* (New York: Oxford University Press, 1981).

21. Joseph B. Treaster, "Cuban Meeting Stokes Emotions on Latin Debt," *New York Times*, August 1, 1985, p. D1.

22. *Sub-Saharan Africa: From Crisis to Sustainable Growth: A Long-Term Perspective Study* (Washington, D.C.: World Bank, 1989), pp. 176–179.

23. Barbara Crosette, "Givers of Foreign Aid Shifting Their Methods," *New York Times*, February 23, 1992, p. 2E.

24. "Eugene R. Black Dies at 93; Ex-President of World Bank," *New York Times*, February 21, 1992, p. A19.

25. Tahir Beg, "Globalization, Development, and Debt-Management: A Third World Perspective," Spring 2000, www.balanced-development.org.

26. World Bank, *World Bank Development Report, 2000/2001*, p. 315; Oxfam International, press release, September 18, 2000, "HIPC Leaves Poor Countries Heavily in Debt: New Analysis," www.oxfaminternational.org; Mark Lynas, "Letter from Zambia," *The Nation*, February 14, 2000.

27. Matt Daily, "US Offers to Break Deadlock in Climate Talks," Reuters, November 20, 2000.

28. US State Department, Bureau of East Asian and Pacific Affairs, "Background Note: China," January 2009 update, www.state.gov.

29. Ministry of Commerce, "People's Republic of China," www.chinability.com; Yasheng Huang, *Selling China: Direct Foreign Investment During the Reform Era* (New York: Cambridge University Press, 2003), pp. 1–10.

30. Peter Morici, "The Trade Deficit and Job Losses," *CounterPunch*, August 15, 2008, www.counterpunch.org.

31. International Labour Office, *Global Wage Report 2008/09: Minimum Wages and Collective Bargaining* (Geneva: International Labour Office, November 2008), pp. 59–60; for the "great doubling," see the writings of Richard Freeman.

32. Matt Piotrowski, "Oil Sets New Records: 'This Is Not a Speculative Bubble,'" *Oil Daily*, Energy Intelligence Group, October 11, 2004.

33. Cited in Michael T. Klare, "Anatomy of a Price Surge," *The Nation*, July 7, 2008, p. 6.

34. "Are Speculators Sending the Right Signals?" *Petroleum Intelligence Weekly*, June 30, 2008.

35. Michael T. Klare, "Beyond the Age of Petroleum," *The Nation*, November 12, 2007, pp. 17–21; US Census Bureau, Foreign Trade Division.

36. *Bloomberg News*, a financial publication, calculated that the US government, at the end of November 2008, pledged $7.7 trillion (equivalent to $24,000 for every US resident) to bail out the financial sector; Mark Pittman and Bob Ivry, "U.S. Pledged Top $7.7 Trillion to Ease Frozen Credit (Update 2)," *Bloomberg.com*, November 24, 2008, www.bloomberg.com.

37. From a tape obtained by ABC News. Jay Shalor, Lauren Pearle, and Tina Babarovic, "AIG's Small London Office May Have Lost Big," March 10, 2009, www.abcnews.go.com.

18 Russia: The Legacy of Soviet Empire

After Leonid Brezhnev came to power in the Soviet Union in 1964, he showed little taste for reform. Innovations in the economic sector that his predecessor, Nikita Khrushchev, had introduced were quickly shelved and the Soviet Union entered a seventeen-year-long "era of stagnation" that only a change in leadership could reverse. In 1979, the Soviet ministries ceased publishing statistics in order not to reveal the fact that the country was falling farther behind the West in productivity, health care, and the standard of living. In March 1985, the Communist Party elected as general secretary Mikhail Gorbachev, who immediately took a number of highly publicized steps to transform the Soviet Union.

Gorbachev advocated a new openness, called "glasnost," giving Soviet citizens and officials alike the freedom to discuss not only the nation's strengths but also its weaknesses. *Pravda*, the newspaper of the Communist Party, began to cover disasters such as the nuclear accident at Chernobyl, floods, collisions between ships in the Black Sea, corruption, cover-ups, shoddy workmanship, police abuse, Stalin's impact on society, and so on. Motion pictures never before shown to the public played to sold-out crowds. The Gorbachev revolution was on its way.

Gorbachev's "New Thinking"

When the Communist Party turned to Mikhail Gorbachev, the Soviet public and the West knew little about him, although in December 1984 he had made a successful appearance on the world stage during a visit to London, where he had behaved unlike previous Soviet visitors. Khrushchev's visit in 1955 had turned sour when he reminded his hosts ominously of the Soviet Union's potentially devastating nuclear arsenal. Gorbachev spoke, instead, of the need to disarm and reminded the British of their wartime alliance with the Soviet

Union and their losses at Coventry. Instead of the customary visit to Karl Marx's grave at Highgate Cemetery, Gorbachev visited Westminster Abbey. Margaret Thatcher, Britain's conservative prime minister, concluded: "I like him. We can do business with him."

Gorbachev soon caused another stir with his speech in February 1985, in which he declared that the Soviet Union was in need of a radical transformation. "Paper shuffling, an addiction to fruitless meetings, windbaggery and formalism" would no longer do.[1] He proved to be a reformer who understood that politics is the art of the possible. In his first speech as general secretary of the party, he placated the right wing with his reaffirmation of the old values. As time went by, however, he showed that he intended to carry through a radical restructuring, called "perestroika." To that end, "new thinking" was required.

Among Gorbachev's targets were the centrally planned industrial system and the collective farms Stalin had introduced beginning in the late 1920s. He also ended the long and debilitating conflict between the state and organized religions, ended the isolation of his country's intellectuals, invited those who had been expelled from the Soviet Union to return to their native soil, sent an unprecedented number of Soviet citizens abroad, permitted the sale of Western publications, forced the Soviet Union's conservative historians to come to grips with the past, and broke the party's monopoly on political power. He also redefined the Soviet Union's position vis-à-vis China, Eastern Europe, the West, and the Third World and took the Soviet army out of Afghanistan. In sum, Gorbachev turned the science of "Kremlinology" on its head; he did what had been thought no leader in the Kremlin could or would even try to do.

Gorbachev called for an open and honest discussion, "to call things by their name." To this end, he had to give society, not just the party, a voice. Glasnost, from the Russian word for "voice," therefore, became the first order of business. The most severe test of glasnost came in April 1986, when an atomic reactor in Chernobyl, in the Ukrainian Republic, suffered a meltdown and an explosion, spewing radioactive matter into the Belorussian Republic, Scandinavia, down into Germany, and as far south as Italy. Soviet technology was contaminating what Gorbachev earlier had called "our common European home." The recognition of mistakes, he said, was the "best medicine against arrogance and complacency." But for the first nineteen days after Chernobyl, no acknowledgment of the disaster came out of Moscow. When Gorbachev finally spoke on national television, he admitted that a nuclear plant—a symbol of Soviet technological prowess—had burned out of control.

Gorbachev used Chernobyl to weaken the conservative wing of the party, the chief obstructionists to perestroika. Gorbachev would go on to repeatedly use political, natural, and man-made disasters—on the surface, setbacks—to his advantage.

Artists and writers quickly tested the limits of glasnost. The consequence was a veritable flood of works that had been created years before "for the drawer," waiting to see the light of day. Among them were Anatoli Rybakov's *Children of the Arbat*, a novel set in 1933–1934 at the beginning of Stalin's terror, and films such as *Our Armored Train*, a critical analysis of the legacy of the Stalin era.

The acid test of glasnost would be how the Kremlin treated the writings of the exiled Alexander Solzhenitsyn, whose novel *One Day in the Life of Ivan Denisovich* had been the literary sensation of 1962. Khrushchev had used this exposé of the prison system to discredit Stalin. In his later writings, however, Solzhenitsyn, in his three-volume *Gulag Archipelago*, laid the blame for the prison system squarely at the feet of the revered Lenin—whose stature in the Soviet Union was no less than that of a saint. Gorbachev and his Politburo initially opposed the publication of *Gulag Archipelago* on the grounds that it undermined "the foundation on which our present life rests." But public pressure, expressed in thousands of letters and telegrams, had an unprecedented impact on Soviet cultural history. In June 1989, Gorbachev told his Politburo that the decision whether to publish Solzhenitsyn should be made by editors, not the party. After an absence of twenty-five years, Solzhenitsyn was reintroduced to Soviet readers.[2]

Soviet historians generally wanted no part of Gorbachev's "new thinking." Early 1988, however, saw the purge of the editorial boards of the leading historical journals. The lead article in the February 1988 issue of *Voprosy istorii* (Problems of History) announced that the time had come to discuss events hitherto taboo, including Stalin's purges of the party, the "tragedy" of collectivization in Kazakhstan, and the nationality problem. Historical journals began to participate in the political rehabilitation of Khrushchev and victims of Stalin's purges and went so far as to publish Leon Trotsky's essay, "The Stalin School of Falsification of History." In the huge Lenin Library in Moscow, "new" books were made available to readers—books that had been published decades earlier and then suppressed.[3]

Most intellectuals, freed from the constraints of the past, expressed distinctly liberal, Western values. They supported Memorial, an organization honoring the memory of those who had fallen victim to Stalin's purges. But glasnost also gave writers of an anti-Western, anti-liberal persuasion a voice and showed that the nativist tradition still ran deep. Their organization, Pamiat (Remembrance), recalled history differently from Memorial. The Russian National-Patriotic Memory Front, Pamiat's formal name, did not consider the Stalinist legacy to be the nation's source of difficulty; instead it blamed Zionists. In its view, Stalin had played the role of the good tsar, terrible but righteous, who had punished the wicked and brought the nation to its military and industrial power.

Industry

When Gorbachev first began to speak of an economic perestroika, he expected an orderly process. It became clear, however, that reconstruction would be

Soviet leader Mikhail Gorbachev and US president Ronald Reagan in Geneva for their first summit meeting, November 19, 1985. *(AP/Wide World Photos)*

extraordinarily difficult, compounded by the fact that many workers and managers of factories and collective farms looked upon the Gorbachev revolution with skepticism, even resentment. They had learned to fulfill the plan on paper and saw few reasons to embrace a new approach that threatened to punish those who failed. In the mid-1960s, Premier Alexei Kosygin had sought to reorganize the economy so that factories would have to sink or swim on their own. In 1965, "accountability" became the watchword of the Kosygin-led reforms. The conservatives, however, who had their hands on the political levers, soon brought this experiment to a halt.

The majority of the population expected the state to solve their problems; this was an attitude that had seeped into their blood. When Gorbachev suggested that government subsidies—for bread, milk, apartments, education, health care, transportation, and so on—come to an end and spoke of closing down inefficient factories and raising prices, he hit a raw nerve. His comments produced a resistance to an economic perestroika that promised not only higher prices but also unemployment. The relative security of the past began to give way to an uncertain future.

Farming

In his speech on November 3, 1987, commemorating the seventieth anniversary of the October Revolution, Gorbachev—under pressure from conservatives—

still defended the necessity of Stalin's collectivization. In October 1988, however, in a televised address, he proposed radical changes. Farmers, he insisted, must once again become "masters of their land." Five months later, in March 1989, he took his case to the party's decisionmaking body, the Central Committee, where he summarized the failure of Soviet agriculture. Between 1946 and 1953, he argued, Stalin had bled the farmers by setting low farm prices. Khrushchev and Brezhnev subsequently had spent huge sums to improve the productivity and eliminate waste on the collective and the state farms, but to little avail. The time had come to abandon decisionmaking at the top and to learn from experimentation, and even from the United States, China, India, and the Green Revolution.[4]

Gorbachev's conservative opponents in the Politburo were strong enough to prevent such a drastic measure. But on April 9, 1989, the government did pass a law permitting private individuals and collectives to lease land, buildings, mineral deposits, small factories, and machines from the state "for up to 50 years and more." TASS, the Soviet news agency, underlined that the law was intended to promote the establishment of family farms.

The Role of the Party

When Gorbachev established a new legislature, the Congress of People's Deputies, which held its first session in May 1989, not only were the majority of the delegates freely elected but many were non-Communists. The weakness of the party became glaringly apparent when many of their candidates failed to receive a majority of votes, even though they ran unopposed.

Gorbachev, however, did not yet go so far as to support the abolition of Article 6 of the 1977 Constitution, which granted the Communist Party a monopoly of political power. He still lacked the votes in the party's Central Committee to do so. Yet, the sentiment to scrap Article 6 ran deep. During his January 1990 visit to Vilnius, Lithuania, where the republic's Communist Party had already legalized a multiparty system and elections, Gorbachev stated that "we should not be afraid [of a multiparty system], the way the devil fears incense."[5] In early February 1990, during an extraordinary session of the party's Central Committee, after three days of debates, the party did the unthinkable when it legalized opposition parties. Lenin's legacy, the Communist Party as the sole driving force in the Soviet Union, became the casualty of the "February Revolution" of 1990.

The Nationality Question

Gorbachev's emphasis on glasnost set into motion a discussion of the Soviet Union's nationality question. The Russians made up 145 million of the total population of 282 million people; of the other Slavs, 51 million were Ukrainians, and 10 million were Belorussians. Over centuries, Ukrainians and Belorussians had developed their own national consciousness, and many among them sought independence from Moscow.

The Communist revolution of 1917 had taken place in an empire that consisted of well over 100 nationalities. Many had only one thing in common: They had been conquered by the dominant Russians. According to the official interpretation, the revolution had forged a new social consciousness among the varied ethnic groups that now voluntarily resided in the new Soviet state. The fact that none had requested to secede from the Soviet Union—as permitted under the constitution—was offered as proof that the new Communist consciousness had obliterated national antagonisms, that the Soviet citizens made up one happy family.

Glasnost blew the official theory apart. Discussions revealed deep-rooted grievances among national minorities, and they were directed not necessarily against the dominant Russian majority but against each other.

The fourteen non-Russian republics sought, at a minimum, substantial economic and political autonomy. This demand envisioned strong republics with a strong center, something on the order of the Swiss model—a nation of four nationalities with four official languages. Gorbachev favored this approach, as it would keep the nation together and fit into the framework of his plan for "democratization."

The radicals, however, called for the dismemberment of the empire, a 180-degree reversal of Russian history. It was no coincidence that the Russian monarchs who had been granted the appellation "Great"—Ivan III, Peter I, and Catherine II—had earned it by virtue of expanding their empire's borders. All this was now in jeopardy.

The most serious challenge came from the Baltic states—Lithuania, Latvia, and Estonia—where radicals began to test the limits of Gorbachev's "democratization." First, they demanded economic autonomy, stating they were merely supporting perestroika—that is, the decentralization of the top-heavy economy. Then they insisted on—and gained—the right to fly their old flags, openly practice their religions, and rewrite their histories. They spoke of fielding their own teams for future Olympic Games and declared their Communist parties to be independent of the party in Moscow. Then came the inevitable talk of secession.

The reason for the radicalism in the Baltic states can be found in their recent history. They had been part of the Russian empire for over 200 years, but after the 1917 revolution they had managed to establish their independence—which, however, lasted only until 1940. On the eve of World War II, Hitler and Stalin agreed on a nonaggression pact and for good measure decided, on the basis of a secret protocol, to divide Eastern Europe. The Baltic states fell to the Soviet Union, and Stalin deported or murdered hundreds of thousands of suspected nationalists. Glasnost's critical reassessment of the Stalin era could not ignore the infamous Hitler-Stalin pact. After much soul-searching and hesitation, official Soviet historians finally admitted that, yes, there had been a secret protocol in violation of international law.

In December 1989, the Communist Party of Lithuania voted to establish its independence from Moscow. The mass movement Sajudis demanded (1) "freedom and independence" and the repeal of the Hitler-Stalin pact, (2) removal of the "occupant Soviet Army," (3) compensation for "the genocide of Lithuanian citizens and their exile" and for environmental destruction, and (4) the establishment of friendly relations between Lithuania and the Soviet Union on the basis of the 1920 peace treaty.

In January 1990, Gorbachev took a highly publicized trip to Lithuania in an attempt to convince the people there of the dangers of secessionism. He pleaded, cajoled, and issued thinly veiled threats, all to no avail. As his limousine departed for the airport, the crowd jeered him. In Moscow, the spokesman for the foreign ministry, Gennady Gerasimov, remarked that the divorce between Lithuania and Russia must follow an orderly course. Lithuanians quickly replied that there had been no marriage, only an abduction and rape, and that there was nothing to negotiate. On March 11, 1990, the newly and freely elected parliament of Lithuania unilaterally declared its independence.

Not all nationalist grievances were directed against the Russians. As Lithuanians demonstrated against the Russians, the Polish minority in Lithuania demonstrated for incorporation into Poland. Nearly every Soviet republic had territorial claims against a neighbor. The bloodiest clash among Soviet nationalities was between the Christian Armenians and the Turkic-speaking Shiite Muslims of Azerbaijan. When Gorbachev gave the Armenians a voice, they immediately demanded the return of a piece of their historical territory, Nagorno-Karabakh, which Stalin had placed under Azeri administration in 1923.

Armenian national consciousness is deeply affected by the 1915 massacre at the hands of the Turks, in which 1.5 million Armenians died.[6] The Turks then drove the Armenians from their historic territory in what today is eastern Turkey. As a result, the symbol of Armenian nationalism, biblical Mount Ararat, is in Turkey, just across the border from Armenia's capital, Yerevan.

Tensions rose in February 1988, when up to 100,000 people demonstrated in Yerevan over a period of several days against Azerbaijan but also against Moscow and Communism. At the end of the month, Azeris staged a pogrom in Sumgait, a city north of Baku, the capital of Azerbaijan, where thirty-two Armenians were murdered.

In June 1988, the Communist Party of Armenia voted to reconquer Nagorno-Karabakh, and the Communist Party of Azerbaijan voted to defend it. For the first time, Communist parties of the Soviet Union split along national lines and went to war against each other. Only Moscow's intervention minimized further bloodshed, but the fear and hatred remained. When, in December 1988, an earthquake destroyed much of eastern Armenia, killing tens of thousands, Azeris rejoiced over the misery of their neighbors.

On January 13, 1990, Azeri-Armenian violence erupted anew—this time in Baku, where Azeris murdered at least sixty Armenians in a replay of the Sumgait pogrom. Gorbachev decreed a state of emergency in the region; when it had no effect, he sent the Soviet army and troops of the Interior Ministry into Baku, explaining that he had no choice because "neither side listened to the voice of reason."[7]

*   *   *

Gorbachev's revolution was the product of historical processes. The social conditions that had produced support for Lenin and Stalin had undergone significant changes since 1917. The number of Soviet citizens, for example, who had a high-school education or better had increased from 25 million to 125 million between 1964 and the mid-1980s.[8] When de-Stalinization began with Khrushchev's 1956 speech, more than half of the nation's population still lived in the countryside; that figure was down to about one-quarter by the late 1980s. Gorbachev inherited a nation with a sizable and largely urbanized middle class. His generation (he was born in 1931) came to political maturity during Khrushchev's "thaw" and his attacks on Stalin. Perestroika became a battle between reformers and the dead weight of history, the legacy of centralization and intolerance bestowed on the nation by generations of tsars and commissars.

In December 1988, the West German news weekly *Der Spiegel* named Gorbachev its "Man of the Year: Man of the Hour"—the first time it had bestowed such recognition on anyone. It compared him to the Westernizer Peter the Great, the Protestant reformer Martin Luther, and the emancipator Abraham Lincoln. In January 1990, *Time* magazine named him "Man of the Decade." The applause, however, was for a tightrope walker who had not yet reached the other side.

The End of the Soviet Union

Gorbachev's perestroika alienated those on the right, who thought he was irrevocably disrupting Soviet society, as well as those on the left, who felt the reforms were not going far enough. By autumn 1990, both the left and the right wanted him out.

After years of hesitation, Gorbachev and his economic advisors eventually concluded that the freeing of prices (determined by supply and demand) and the right to make a private profit were not merely necessary evils but positive economic forces. In other words, the Soviet Union would legalize capitalism. By autumn 1990, Gorbachev was about to accept a radical proposal by Stanislav Shatalin, an economist long opposed to the Soviet centralized economy. The Shatalin Plan called for a sudden transition—during a period of a scant 500 days—from centralization to what was still called a "market" economy, a pseudonym for capitalism. But Shatalin was unable to answer questions regarding the economic, social, and political consequences of his bold proposal.

At this juncture, Gorbachev moved to the right. He feared the so-called democratic opposition on the left, led by Boris Yeltsin, a fellow Politburo member, who sought to topple him and then dismantle the Soviet Union. In July 1990, Yeltsin staged a dramatic exit from the party. Abandoned by former allies such as Yeltsin, Gorbachev began to surround himself with conservatives uncomfortable with perestroika.

But then Gorbachev moved back to the left. In April 1991, he and Yeltsin worked out the "9-plus-1" formula, which called for a decentralized Soviet Union: The republics would be able to exercise virtually unlimited power on the local level, while Moscow would continue to handle matters such as currency, diplomacy, and the military.

In June 1991, Yeltsin won a historic victory at the polls when he was elected president of the Russian republic, the largest component of the Soviet Union, becoming Russia's first popularly elected head of state. At the same time, Gorbachev, being forced to move to his left, commissioned the economist Grigorii Yavlinskii, with the help of economics professors from Harvard and the Massachusetts Institute of Technology, to launch the capitalist experiment.

These events triggered a military coup by desperate party members who saw their power slipping away. On August 19, 1991, as Gorbachev vacationed in the Crimea, the leaders of Soviet military and paramilitary organizations—Defense Minister Dmitrii Yazov, the chief of the secret police (the KGB) Vladimir Kriuchkov, and Minister of the Interior Boris Pugo—sent tanks into the streets of Moscow and declared a state of emergency. Two of Gorbachev's recent appointees, Gennadii Yanaev and Valentin Pavlov, presuming to speak for the nation, declared that Gorbachev had fallen ill and would be relieved of his duties as president. At a live news conference later that day, Yanaev stated that "his good friend Gorbachev" would someday return to political life in another capacity. Virtually no one believed his account, particularly as neither Gorbachev nor his physician was present to confirm Gorbachev's illness. A subversive camera operator instead focused on the trembling hands of Yanaev.

Since the days of Lenin, Communist ideology had always stressed unity of action. During the attempted coup, however, there was none. The conspirators had acted in desperation and haste, without planning or coordination.[9] They never managed to enlist a unified military or KGB. Some commanders were deeply unhappy with the state of affairs to which perestroika had brought them, but even they were unwilling to use force against fellow citizens. Other commanders openly opposed the coup. A similar division was apparent in the press and on television, the diplomatic corps, the KGB, and the party. The coup collapsed with scarcely a shot fired. The conspirators had but one hope:

that Soviet society would tacitly accept the transfer of power. Back in 1964, when the party had changed leadership, the KGB was surprised to find out that not a single demonstration or voice of support was heard on behalf of Khrushchev. This time it was different. President Yeltsin, standing on top of a renegade tank in front of the "White House," the parliament building, denounced the coup and demanded Gorbachev's return. The conspirators had gone after Gorbachev, the head of both the party and the Soviet government, without taking into account the fact that political power had already become diffused throughout the Soviet Union. Yeltsin's election as president of Russia in June 1991 had already created a situation of "dual power": Yeltsin and Gorbachev were in effect coequals. Had Yeltsin been arrested and had Gorbachev accepted the transfer of power (as he was pressured to do for three days), the coup might have succeeded.

Yeltsin held the Communist Party—and indirectly Gorbachev, the party's general secretary—responsible for the coup and suspended the party's activities indefinitely. The conspirators had hoped to preserve the Soviet Union; instead, they hastened its demise. The 9-plus-1 formula no longer served a purpose. Instead, Yeltsin and the radicals dissolved the Soviet Union. By the end of 1991, the red flag with its golden hammer and sickle, the symbol of the Bolshevik seizure of power in 1917, came down from the buildings of the Kremlin and was replaced with the old flag of imperial Russia.

The Former Soviet Republics

Yeltsin and the presidents of the now independent republics inherited a disintegrating economy. By 1990, the Soviet Union was already in a depression as severe as that the West had experienced in the 1930s. It was in the midst of this depression that Yeltsin committed Russia to the full embrace of capitalism. The movement toward a market economy, however, further disrupted the network of resource allocation, and factories had to fend for themselves to obtain necessary supplies. Suppliers asked for hard—that is, Western—currency, which factories simply did not have. Ethnic tensions added to the economic chaos. Armenians no longer provided parts to machine-tool factories in Moscow, and Russians refused to deliver steel to the huge truck factories of independence-minded Tatarstan on the Volga River. The result was increased idleness in factories, empty stores, and a continued decline in the standard of living.

The collapse of the Communist regimes in Eastern Europe brought an end to COMECON, the Kremlin-imposed system of economic integration. It meant, for instance, that the former Soviet Union, which had obtained about half of its medicines from COMECON trading partners, saw a drastic decline in its already perilous health care. Hungarians were still willing to sell buses to Russia, but now only for hard currency (see below).

To cushion the shock of higher prices, Yeltsin's government printed ever more money. The result was an inflation rate of 2,000 percent and a government budget deficit reaching 25 percent in 1992. Wages declined relative to the newly freed prices to the point where, during winter 1991–1992, 90 percent of Russians lived below the official subsistence level.[10]

Yeltsin and his economic advisors were committed to a "grand bargain," the entrance into the global market economy and membership in the International Monetary Fund. It was predicated on obtaining aid from the capitalist nations, which were basking in the glow of their ideological victory over the Soviet Union. Unfortunately, the money markets had dried up. US president Ronald Reagan's push for military superiority had produced a binge of borrowing. A worldwide economic recession and the collapse of the Japanese stock market—a decline of approximately 60 percent of its value since 1986—ended the era of cheap capital. The German government provided more assistance to the former Soviet Union than did any other nation, but it, too, had little money to spare because of the heavy cost of German reunification.

The former Soviet republics turned to the IMF for assistance. In turn, the IMF demanded from the recipients a balanced budget, the repayment of debts, a convertible currency to permit foreign investors to take their profits out of the country, the freeing of prices (notably of energy), letting unprofitable businesses fail, and protecting the sanctity of foreign investments. Once the price of oil—previously sold to the Soviet Union's consumers at $3 per barrel—was raised to the world market's price of $19, Western investments and technology arrived.

The transition to capitalism produced a class of private entrepreneurs (who only recently had been called capitalist exploiters), as well as an impoverished, humiliated, and increasingly embittered mass of people who could not understand how their great nation had reached this juncture in its history. When the Communist Party went on trial in fall 1992, the Russian people were more concerned with their economic lot. A political commentator remarked that even to dream of such a trial in the past could have led to arrest—but now no one cared.[11]

The Fragmentation of the Soviet Union

After the dissolution of the Soviet Union, the nationality problems remained. Armenia had the most homogeneous population, as approximately 90 percent of its citizens were Armenians. But in Latvia, 34 percent were Russian, as were 38 percent in Kazakhstan and 13 percent in Ukraine; in Moldova, 14 percent were Ukrainian and 13 percent Russian.[12]

Georgia witnessed the most serious political problems among any of the former Soviet republics. Abkhazia in western Georgia and South Ossetia (which Stalin had separated from North Ossetia, located inside Russia proper), provinces with their own history and languages distinct from Georgian, declared their independence. It was a problem that a succession of Georgian governments failed to resolve.

In May 1991, the anti-Communist Georgian nationalist Zviad Gamsakhurdia became the first democratically elected president of a former Soviet republic; he was also the first dissident to come to power. In the past he had expressed admiration for Western political ideals. Within months, however, Gamsakhurdia began to arrest political opponents, whom he denounced—in language reminiscent of his countryman Joseph Stalin—as spies, bandits, and criminals, "enemies of the people" all. In a fit of chauvinism and paranoia, he sought to ban interracial marriages, by which, he charged, the Russians sought "to dilute the Georgian race."[13] In September 1991, he declared a state of emergency. In the ensuing civil war between Gamsakhurdia loyalists and his opponents, heavy fighting destroyed the center of the capital, Tbilisi. After Gamsakhurdia fled, the victorious faction turned to Eduard Shevardnadze, Gorbachev's former foreign minister, to bring stability to Georgia.

Yeltsin, who had frequently criticized Gorbachev for refusing to grant the Baltic states their independence, had to face his own secessionists in Russia when the Muslim Chechen-Ingush (in November 1991) along the Georgian border and the Tatars (in March 1992) along the Volga River declared their independence.

An even more ominous development began to appear: the call for "ethnic cleansing." Russians demanded the expulsion of Jews and Azeris from Moscow, Chechen-Ingush were driven out of Volgograd, and in Stavropol attempts were made to force out Armenian families. In the Kuban, north of the Caucasus Mountains, Russian Cossacks appeared in their traditional dress, insisting upon the ouster of Turkic-speaking Meskhetians.[14]

The Yeltsin Presidency

Yeltsin's embrace of capitalism was accompanied by the transfer of state property to individuals with connections to his government. The oil and gas industry, once the Soviet Union's chief source of Western currency, fell into private hands. Politicians began to milk state-owned properties, and their managers paid themselves generous salaries. The situation was corrupt even by Soviet standards.[15] In the struggle for the spoils of victory, theft, extortion, and even murder became widespread while the devil took the hindmost. Those left behind found that the former Soviet safety net contained increasingly larger holes as state subsidies were eliminated. Inflation wiped out the savings of millions of citizens. The capitalist experiment did not turn out as many had hoped. Cynics remarked that "we thought the Communists were lying to us about [the glory of] socialism and [the evils] of capitalism, but it turns out they were lying only about socialism."[16]

The economic disaster triggered a rebellion by Russia's parliament. By early spring 1993, Yeltsin began to talk of dissolving the parliament and holding new elections. Parliament countered with an attempt to impeach Yeltsin. The issue was settled with violence. On September 22, 1993, Yeltsin—already accustomed to ruling by fiat—issued Decree No. 1,400, ordering the dissolution of parliament. Parliament refused to go quietly, and its building—the so-called White House—soon became a defiant armed camp surrounded by concertina wire. In early October, 10,000 anti-Yeltsin demonstrators overwhelmed the police and then marched to the state television complex (which was heavily biased in favor of Yeltsin) in an attempt to seize it. Yeltsin declared a state of emergency and dispatched troops, who were soon shelling the White House—the same building that had served as a symbol of democracy and resistance to the Communists in August 1991. Russia's short-lived democratic experiment was over.

Yeltsin disbanded parliament, suspended the Constitutional Court, and banned the opposition press and television. A total of 144 Russians lay dead, and the top half of the once gleaming White House was charred by tank artillery fire. Throughout, the Western powers refused to condemn Yeltsin and continued to refer to him as a "democrat," declaring that the radicals had forced his hand. The new constitution promulgated later in 1993 gave Yeltsin the power to rule virtually without the legislature.

The First Chechen War

Then came the violence in Chechnya. It began at the end of 1994, when Yeltsin decided he could no longer tolerate claims of independence by Chechnya, one of Russia's eighty-nine regional subdivisions. Yeltsin, the chief architect of the dissolution of the Soviet Union, now stood fast against a breakup of the Russian Federation.

The Muslim Chechens, along the northern slopes of the Caucasus Mountains, had been brought under Russian control in the mid-nineteenth century, but it took another quarter-century for the army to finally subdue them. During World War II, as the Germans pushed into the Caucasus, a number of Chechens—acting on the time-honored principle that "the enemy of my enemy is my friend"—collaborated with them. The Chechens paid a heavy price for it. Stalin meted out collective punishment and in 1943–1944 deported the Chechens (along with other ethnic groups in that region) to Central Asia and Siberia. In his Secret Speech of 1956, Nikita Khrushchev listed the deportation of the Chechens as one of the crimes Stalin had committed, and in 1957 he permitted the Chechens' return to their ancestral home. But the Chechens never forgot what the Soviet state had done to them, and at the first opportunity they declared their independence.

For three years, Yeltsin ignored Chechen claims to independence. But then Dzhokhar Dudayev, the leader of the Chechen rebels, reminded the Russians that the northern Caucasus is one of the great fault lines where the Christian and Muslim worlds meet. He predicted that all Muslims in the Caucasus would rebel, Siberia would secede, and the Russian far east would align itself with East Asia, adding ominously that "Russian racism in the Caucasus will not go unpunished."[17]

Yeltsin decided to act. Instead of quickly reasserting control, however, Russian troops walked into deadly ambushes set by Chechen rebels, particularly in Grozny, the capital city. The heavy-handed Russian response reduced the city to ruins; by the end of 1996, an estimated 45,000 people had died in Chechnya, and almost 2 million had become refugees.[18] Television images from Grozny reminded Russians of the devastation of World War II.

When the Chechen resistance proved to be much tougher than anticipated, Yeltsin sought a negotiated solution on the political future of Chechnya. The best he was able to obtain, in August 1996, was an interim five-year cease-fire. In the meantime, Aslan Maskhadov, the Chechen chief of staff, flatly declared, "No Chechen has ever signed any kind of document saying that Chechnya is part of Russia and there will never be such a Chechen."[19]

The Election of 1996

Early in 1996, few gave Boris Yeltsin much chance of winning the presidential election. Opinion polls showed that a scant 10 percent of voters planned to cast their ballots for him. The unpopular war in Chechnya, a drastic increase in the crime rate, Yeltsin's poor health, and money and political power in the hands of the *nouveaux riches*, commonly known as the "mafia," all took their toll. The Communist Party candidate, Gennadi Zyuganov, appeared the likely winner.

Yeltsin and his advisors, however, would not accept defeat. In March 1996, when Yeltsin's prospects for a victory were dim, he leaned toward a so-called forceful option by which, under the pretext of a bomb threat, he would dissolve parliament and cancel the election. In the meantime, he followed the "softer option": television controlled by the government (running footage of Communist atrocities) and money spent to curry favor with the voters. As one of Yeltsin's advisors bluntly declared, "If Yeltsin loses, he will not give power to the Communists. He has said that more than once."[20] Either way, Zyuganov would not win.

But in April 1996, Yeltsin overtook Zyuganov in the polls and in the end won the election by a comfortable margin. Voters—even those who suffered hardships because of the new economic order—ultimately proved reluctant to place their future in the hands of a Communist who unabashedly praised Stalin and promised a return to economic policies that had been tried and had failed. Zyuganov offered no new ideas; he did not even bother to change the name of his party.

In the ten weeks before the election in June, Yeltsin unabashedly used the power of the incumbent. He issued decrees that doubled the minimum pension—effective immediately—and compensated those who had lost their savings because of hyperinflation. He singled out students; teachers; war veterans; single mothers; small businesses; and the agro-industrial, military, and aviation complexes; and one region after another; for special treatment and subsidies—from the heart of Russia to the farthest reaches of Siberia.

A woman who worked for a coal mine in Vorkuta asked for and received from Yeltsin a car, an event carried on national television. Yeltsin's aides blatantly handed out cash. Yelstin's largesse cost the hard-strapped Russian treasury the astonishing sum of $11 billion. It became the most expensive political campaign ever conducted. The IMF—which had a stake in keeping the capitalist reforms of Yeltsin on track—underwrote his spending spree with a new $10.2 billion loan.[21]

Throughout, Bill Clinton's US administration turned a blind eye to the political and economic conditions in Russia, arguing that they were part of the growing pains of the transition from a planned to a market economy. By the end of the decade, approximately one-half of the population was living below the official poverty line of $30–35 a month, and perhaps another 25–30 percent were close to it. The political scientist Stephen Cohen concluded that "in modern peacetime, never have so many fallen so far."[22]

The Putin Presidency

In 1999, the once-again unpopular Yeltsin, now physically ailing and prohibited by law to serve a third term, began to look for a way to retire and at the same time avoid a criminal investigation of his finances and sundry other transgressions. After dismissing one prime minister after another, he finally found, in August, a man to his liking, the obscure Vladimir Putin, a product of the KGB, the Soviet Union's secret police organization. Under Yeltsin, Putin had risen to head the KGB's successor, the FBS, as well as a government commission formed to combat terrorism. One of Yeltsin's earlier prime ministers, Evgeny Primakov, had refused to grant Yeltsin and his corrupt clan immunity from prosecution. Putin, however, had no such qualms. Thus, on New Year's Eve 1999 came the stunning announcement that Putin had replaced Yeltsin and had become the acting president until the election in March 2000. Yeltsin obliquely apologized for past "mistakes," for which, however, he would not be punished.

The Second Chechen War

After the first Chechen war, the Chechen rebels behaved as if they governed an independent—although scarcely functioning—state, now a training ground for criminal activities—trading in slaves, smuggling drugs, operating stolen-car rings, counterfeiting, and taking hostages, ranging from a general of the Russian Interior Ministry to foreign aid workers.

Putin came to power two days after a radical fringe group of Chechens launched an attack on neighboring Dagestan to establish the "independent Islamic state of Dagestan" in hopes of sparking an Islamic anti-Russian uprising. Putin responded to the challenge. Five days later the Russian fighter jets came, an omen of things to come.

Three weeks later a series of explosions shook Moscow. There was no question in the minds of most Russians that the bombings had been the work of Chechen terrorists. Although it remained unclear who was responsible for the bloody deeds, Putin had his justification to go to war, to avenge not only the recent bombings but also Russia's defeat in the first Chechen war.

This time, the Russian military did not simply walk into Grozny in the expectation of a quick victory. It prepared, instead, a massive assault. The war left tens of thousands of Chechens dead, mostly civilians. Little was left standing of Grozny and other rebel strongholds. The world stood by idly, wringing its hands but not daring to challenge a power in decline—economically, militarily, and morally—but one that still possessed approximately 7,000 strategic nuclear warheads. After the Russian army took Grozny, the rebels retreated into the mountains, vowing to continue the fight. In the end, the conflict became more than merely a war of secession: It took on ethnic and religious connotations, with Russians against Chechens and Christians against Muslims.

Putin had no discernible foreign policy except to argue repeatedly that Russia must once again play the role of a great power. With that in mind, he emphasized the need for a strong state and patriotism. The stress was on executive power and discipline, not democracy. He offered his people, instead, a "dictatorship of the law," adding later, "as I choose to rewrite it."[23]

Putin never solved the Chechen issue. In October 2002, forty-one Chechen terrorists, including several "black widows" (women who had lost relatives to the Russian terror), seized 700 hostages in a Moscow theater. The rescue attempt went terribly awry when 129 hostages perished (as well as the terrorists who were summarily executed). In the months to come, Chechens bombed a train in southern Russia, Moscow's military command base in Grozny, and a subway station in Moscow. At the end of summer 2004, "black widows" on suicide missions brought down two Russian airliners, and then in September 2004 came the shocking spectacle of Chechens seizing a school in Beslan in southern Russia. Putin, who had always refused to negotiate with renegade Chechens, sent the army to carry out what became another ill-fated rescue attempt. Among the 335 dead, most were children. Immediately thereafter, Putin issued a decree ending popular elections of regional governors to establish a "single chain of command" to strengthen the "unity of the country and prevent further crises."

Under Yeltsin the news media had been left alone. Putin, however, quickly declared war on the independent voices in Russia. When Andrei Babitsky, a reporter for Radio Free Europe/Radio Liberty, reported honestly on the brutality of the second Chechen war, Putin arranged Babitsky's kidnapping. Babitsky was "on the side of the enemy," Putin charged; what he did was "much more dangerous than firing a machine gun."[24] It was largely because of an international outcry that Babitsky was eventually released. Other journalists were less fortunate. In October 2006, Anna Politkovskaia, a scathing critic of the Chechen warlords and Moscow's brutality in Chechnya, was—after receiving a number of death threats—finally gunned down. Putin also turned against Media-Most, a company that published a daily newspaper and owned a radio station and NTV, the only Russian television network not controlled by the government. In June 2000, the company's owner, Vladimir Gusinsky, was arrested and briefly jailed. His exposure of corruption in the Kremlin had hit too close to home; moreover, Gusinsky's television station had satirized Putin. Public criticism of Putin came to an end after the October 2003 arrest—on charges of tax evasion—of Mikhail Khodorkovsky, the chief executive of the YukosSibneft oil company and one of the world's richest men, with an estimated personal fortune of $8 billion. Not even the high and mighty were able to escape Putin's wrath. The arrest of Khodorkovsky—who had used his wealth to challenge Putin, the real reason for his arrest—achieved its purpose. Other tycoons quickly took pains to show their loyalty to Putin.

In November 2006, a former KGB-FSB officer, Alexander Litvinenko, suffered an agonizing death, succumbing after twenty-two days to Polonium-210 radiation poisoning. Years earlier, Litvinenko had become a vocal dissident in the ranks of the FSB. He was fired, briefly jailed, and then made his way to London, where he received political asylum and subsequently became a citizen of the United Kingdom. From what he considered a safe haven, Litvinenko continued to criticize Putin, charging him and the FSB of having ties to the al Qaeda terror network, masterminding violent acts in Russia, and then blaming the Chechens. Scotland Yard determined that Litvinenko's assassin was Andrei Lugovoi, who in the meantime had made his way back to Moscow, where he became a hero in the eyes of ultranationalist circles, even winning election to the Duma. London sought Lugovoi's extradition; Moscow denied that he had played any role in Litvinenko's murder.

One of Putin's priorities was to rebuild the military. He was photographed flying an Su-27 fighter jet into Grozny and aboard the ill-fated submarine *Kursk*. His point was clear: Russia must once again be respected as a military power. But in August 2000, seismologists in Norway noted two powerful blasts in the Barents Sea. *Kursk*, Russia's state-of-the-art, nuclear-powered, missile-launching submarine, commissioned only five years earlier, had been ripped apart (by its own torpedoes, it was later learned). Putin reacted slowly to the catastrophe. Surviving sailors continued to hammer on the hull until they ran out of oxygen. The disaster, the slow official response, and the inability of Russian divers to open the hatch put into sharp detail the sorry state of Russia's once vaunted military forces. At first, Putin refused to accept foreign assistance (particularly from NATO), but in the end he had to swallow his national pride and ask for help from Britain and Norway.

The subsequent years were kinder to Putin and Russia. The economy began to recover—thanks largely to the phenomenal rise of the cost of energy—and the Kremlin began to play a more confident—at times belligerent—role in international affairs. In neighboring Georgia, it supported a secessionist movement in Abkhazia, the westernmost part of Georgia.

The Russian constitution limited the popular Putin to two five-year terms as president. Unwilling to go gently into retirement, he simply switched jobs with his protégé, Prime Minister Dmitri Medvedev, who in March 2008 was elected president as the candidate of the United Russia political party. Putin then moved into Medvedev's former office of the prime minister—from where he expected to continue to exercise his enormous influence.

The Non-Russian Successor States

A number of Soviet republics—notably Estonia, Latvia, and Lithuania—managed to establish functioning democracies. But in most instances, the road to democracy proved to be difficult. The Caucasus and Central Asia were plagued by ethnic strife and wars for political supremacy. When elections were held, they were often tampered with or fixed outright. The president of Uzbekistan, Islam Karimov, for instance, was reelected in September 1996 with 99.6 percent of the vote—in a country that had neither freedom of speech nor freedom of the press.

Belarus was another case where things did not go according to plan. In July 1994, its voters had elected a conservative, Alexander Lukashenko, a Communist functionary who had no taste for change. Instead, he called for a return to the not-too-distant past. He saw privatization as stealing from the state and insisted on retaining collective farming as well as state control of factories. Among his heroes were Felix Dzherzhinski, the legendary founder of the Soviet secret police.

Belarus, Lukashenko stated, should be ruled by "one strong man." He fired the editor of the country's largest newspaper and demanded that citizens seeking to travel abroad register with the proper authorities. He called demonstrators "enemies of the people" and blamed a strike by subway workers in Minsk, the capital, on the US State Department. In October 2004, in a rigged referendum, he gained the right to amend the constitution to run for a third presidential term.

In 2003, manipulated elections were held in Azerbaijan, Armenia, and Georgia. In November 2003, Georgian president Eduard Shevardnadze, who had come to power as a champion of democracy in 1991, rigged the parliamentary election. After twelve years in power, Shevardnadze had overstayed his welcome; corruption and the violation of the rule of law had taken their toll. When he faced large, hostile demonstrations, neither the army nor the police backed him. In January 2004, Georgia's bloodless "Rose Revolution" brought to power Mikheil Saakashvili, a thirty-five-year-old US-trained lawyer, who, as it turned out, was another Georgian with a penchant for unlimited power.

The Retreat from Empire

A cursory glance at the Soviet Union's position in the world in the early 1980s revealed a powerful presence in Europe and Asia. Yet a restless population in Eastern Europe showed no signs of coming to terms with their status subordinate to Moscow's interests. Along its other borders, the Soviet Union had its hands full. A hostile Communist China tied down more than one-third of the Soviet army at the Sino-Soviet border. The Ayatollah Khomeini's Islamic government in Iran did not hide its distaste for the secular, atheistic government in Moscow, and Afghanistan, governed by a socialist regime since the early 1970s, remained torn asunder by a bloody civil war that threatened to topple the Kremlin's clients in the Afghan capital of Kabul.

The Afghan Crisis

In December 1979, in an act that stunned the world, the Soviet Union sent 80,000 troops into Afghanistan. For the first time since the end of World War II, the Soviet Union had sent troops into a territory beyond its sphere of influence.

Since 1973, the political orientation in Afghanistan had been toward the left, yet it was generally considered a neutral nation, a part of the Third World outside the spheres of any of the world powers. Until 1973, both the United States and the Soviet Union jockeyed inconclusively for influence in Afghanistan, one of the poorest nations on earth, with an annual per capita GNP in 1979 of $170.[25]

The US Reaction

The Soviet invasion came at an unfavorable time for the United States. For one, the country's recent defeat in Vietnam did not sit well with many citizens.

Second, 1979 saw the second oil shortage of the decade. Third, the traumatic hostage crisis had just begun in Iran, where the takeover of the US embassy in Tehran pointed to the limitations of US power. One setback after another produced frustration and belligerence among the populace.

The US response to the Soviet invasion of Afghanistan was swift. Domestic political pressure forced President Jimmy Carter to act. On the eve of the 1980 presidential election, Carter could ill afford to be blamed for "losing Afghanistan." Afghanistan, a country of extraordinary poverty and of little significance in the international balance of power, suddenly took on an importance unmatched in its modern history.

There was scarcely a debate in the United States of the motives behind the invasion. The CIA explained that the Soviet Union faced an "extremely painful" decline in oil supplies and that the invasion of Afghanistan was intended to move the Soviet army closer to the lucrative oil fields in the Persian Gulf region. "Moscow is already making the point," said CIA director Stansfield Turner, "that Middle Eastern oil is not the exclusive preserve of the West." (The CIA later retracted its statement when it acknowledged that the Soviet Union was not likely to suffer from oil shortages in the near future.)[26] A Soviet thrust through Afghanistan directed at the oil refineries near the Gulf, however, made little sense. Why take a 500-mile detour through rugged terrain and at the same time tip off your enemy?

Carter's options were limited. A direct military challenge to the USSR was out of the question. He refused to permit US athletes to participate in the Soviet showcase, the 1980 Olympic Games in Moscow, unless the Soviets withdrew from Afghanistan. The Soviets were stung by the boycott, for they had envisioned the Olympics as validating their country as one of the world's two great powers. They ignored Carter's ultimatum and held the Olympics without the participation of the United States and other Western nations. Carter also halted US grain sales to the Soviet Union. The glut on the world market in agricultural commodities, however, meant that the Soviets shifted their orders to more reliable sources. Last, Carter began to look for clients willing to help him contain the Soviet Union in Asia. Communist China and the United States were drawn a bit closer, and both began in secret to provide weapons to Afghans fighting the Soviets, with Saudi Arabia underwriting much of the cost. The Soviets responded by beefing up their forces, which soon numbered more than 100,000.

The invasion of Afghanistan finished off détente. The Soviets could not expect a thaw in the Cold War and at the same time intervene in the internal affairs of another nation. The Soviets replied that détente would not prevent the Kremlin from playing the role of a great power, insisting that détente and throwing one's weight around in the Third World—as the United States had done in Vietnam—were not antithetical.

Soviet Objectives in Afghanistan

The reason the Soviet Union intervened in the internal affairs of Afghanistan was to bring order to a chaotic political situation in a neighboring socialist country. Moscow did not want to lose Afghanistan because, according to the simple arithmetic of the Cold War, a setback for one side meant a victory for the other. The purpose was to avoid a sense of loss of prestige and image rather than rational analyses of the needs of national security. It rested on what conclusions others might draw from one's own misfortune.

Political instability has long been endemic in Afghanistan; coups and countercoups often followed in rapid succession. In 1973, the leftist Prince Muhammad Daoud had exiled his cousin, King Zahir Shah. In April 1978, Daoud himself was ousted and killed in a coup by the Marxist People's Democratic Party under the leadership of Nur Muhammad Taraki, who established closer ties with the Soviet Union. Taraki in turn was ousted and murdered in a third leftist coup carried out by Hafizullah Amin, who was in power in Kabul at the time of the Soviet invasion. All this bloodletting took place within Afghanistan's Marxist Party.

It is here that one can find another clue to the Soviet Union's decision to invade Afghanistan. Taraki and Amin had a falling-out, with Taraki looking to Moscow for support and Amin looking to Washington. Amin had met a number of times with the US ambassador, Adolph Dubs. What transpired between these two men was not clear, but the Soviets feared the worst. To them, Amin was at the threshold of following in the footsteps of Anwar Sadat, the Egyptian head of state who, in 1972, had ousted the 20,000 Soviet advisors in Egypt and then invited in the US military. More than anything else, the fear of an Afghan diplomatic revolution—from Moscow to Washington—prompted the Soviet invasion.

The Kremlin's concerns were not unfounded. Washington had shown interest in Afghanistan even before the Soviet invasion. CIA director Robert Gates confirmed in his memoirs that the United States had begun to assist Afghan rebels six months earlier. In 1998, President Carter's national security advisor, Zbigniew Brzezinski, acknowledged that Carter, on July 3, 1979, had signed the first directive providing assistance to the rebels in the hope that this provocation would lead to a Soviet invasion.[27] The Carter administration did not have to wait long.

In March 1979, when Taraki initially asked for Soviet intervention to deal with his opponents, Leonid Brezhnev and his prime minister, Alexei Kosygin, were resolutely opposed to such a drastic step. Brezhnev told Taraki: "We must not do this. It would only play into the hands of enemies—both yours and ours." But after Taraki's murder at the hands of Amin, the Kremlin, against its better judgment, sent the Soviet army into Afghanistan to restore order.[28] Soviet commandos killed Amin and replaced him with his rival, Babrak Karmal.

The Kremlin then announced that it had acted upon invitation from the government of Afghanistan.

In the name of freedom, Islam, and anti-Communism, the *mujahidin*—or freedom fighters, as they referred to themselves—rose against a succession of Marxist governments in Kabul, which were increasingly being isolated. Resistance against the center has long been a central feature of Afghan politics, with local rulers in outlying regions jealously guarding their authority and freedom of action. This time they had other grievances, the social and economic transformation of their tradition-bound society, untouched even by colonial rule. Resentment of social reforms—such as the establishment of coeducational schools (which touched off the rebellion in western Afghanistan in March 1979), as well as the elimination of the veil and bridal dowries, particularly when carried out with brutality and in direct opposition to popular will—ran deep.

The Kremlin also feared the spread of radical Islam into Central Asia, where most of the Soviet Union's 50 million Muslims lived. As the Soviet army crossed into Afghanistan, it mobilized recruits from Central Asia, a step in line with the standard procedure of using the most readily available reserves. But this policy soon ran into trouble when Muslim soldiers showed little inclination to fight their ethnic and religious counterparts. Some deserted, while others went over to the rebels. Within three months, the Soviet army began to bring in politically more reliable Slavic troops.

Unlike guerrilla movements in other parts of the world, the Afghan rebels had no program of social, political, and economic reform. There was no literacy campaign (in 1979, primary-school enrollment stood at 30 percent, mostly in the cities; the adult literacy rate was 15 percent), no declaration of the rights of women, no medical programs (life expectancy at birth was thirty-six years; in the industrial nations of the West it was twice that), and no political experiments such as elected village councils. Gerard Chaliand, a French specialist on Third World guerrilla movements, concluded: "The current Afghan resistance movement looks [more] like a traditional revolt [against the capital] . . . than like modern guerrilla warfare. Among contemporary guerrilla movements, only the Kenyan Mau Mau [of the early 1950s] are less sophisticated in their strategy and organization."[29] The *mujahidin* represented the preservation of a traditional society to the exclusion of the industrial revolution and all it entailed. In a strange twist of fate, the United States, the standard-bearer for the industrial revolution and parliamentary democracy, became the main arms supplier for the Afghan rebels, who drew their inspiration from seventh-century Arabia.

Soon Islamic fundamentalist foreign *jihadists* began to flock to Afghanistan, recruited largely through the efforts of Saudi Arabia. The CIA and US State Department looked with favor upon their arrival and, in fact, sought ways to increase it, despite warnings of their anti-US sentiments.[30]

The Soviet Exodus from Afghanistan

Mikhail Gorbachev, upon coming to power in March 1985, inherited a war his army was unable to win. The determined rebels were too well equipped. Their deadly, effective, US-made Stinger ground-to-air missiles, for example, brought down numerous Soviet aircraft (including passenger planes). At first, Gorbachev was unwilling to accept a defeat along the southern flank of the Soviet Union, and for that reason he escalated the war. But Gorbachev soon realized if he wanted to end the Cold War, his army would have to retreat from Afghanistan. When the Soviet army finally did so, Gorbachev stated that the invasion had not been merely another one of Brezhnev's many mistakes; it was also a sin.

But the Soviet retreat would not be unilateral. Gorbachev insisted—and Ronald Reagan agreed—that Afghanistan must not be allied with the West. On February 15, 1989, the last Soviet troops marched out of Afghanistan, leaving behind a client government led by President Mohammad Najibullah in power in Kabul.

Earlier, Gorbachev had declared several times his opposition to the Brezhnev Doctrine, Moscow's right to interfere in the internal affairs of other Communist countries. The retreat from Afghanistan in February 1989 marked the end of that doctrine. The war had claimed the lives of approximately 1 million Afghans (out of a population of 15 million). Between 5 million and 6 million people had become refugees in Pakistan and Iran; another 2 million had been displaced within Afghanistan. The estimated physical damage—to agriculture, industry, power stations, schools, and hospitals—was $20 billion.[31]

The Aftermath: Civil War

Weapons and ammunition, from a variety of sources, continued to pour into Afghanistan. The government in Kabul managed to survive the Soviet army's withdrawal—if only for the time being—because of the extraordinary fragmentation among the Afghan resistance. In December 1991, however, Moscow stopped supplying arms to Najibullah, and Washington ended its arms deliveries to the *mujahidin*, who were nevertheless able to obtain weapons from Iran, Pakistan, and Saudi Arabia. Najibullah was on his own, and when he proved unable to suppress a local army mutiny in January 1992, his generals, sensing vulnerability, began to switch sides. By April 1992, Najibullah negotiated the transfer of political power to the *mujahidin* and then took refuge inside a UN compound in Kabul. As the *mujahidin* closed in on Kabul, the doomed Najibullah prophetically told reporters:

> We have a common task—Afghanistan, the U.S.A., and the civilized world
> to launch a joint struggle against fundamentalism [that, if it] comes to

Afghanistan, will continue for many years. Afghanistan will turn into a center of world smuggling for narcotic drugs. Afghanistan will be turned into a center for terrorism.[32]

No one in the West, however, paid attention to Najibullah's warning.

Kabul fell to the Islamic fundamentalist Shiite, Gulbuddin Hekmatyar, who had been the chief recipient of US aid. In April 1992, a coalition led by the ethnic Tadzhik, Ahmad Shah Masoud, entered Kabul from the north and expelled Hekmatyar. Hekmatyar, now supported by Shiite Iran, continued to fight from entrenched positions in the hills south of Kabul. In August 1992, he launched a deadly artillery barrage in which over 1,200 residents lost their lives. The war intensified between rival warlord armies, and Kabul suffered greater death and destruction in the single year after the fall of Najibullah than during the previous fourteen years of revolution, foreign invasion, and civil war. Continued bombardments over the next three years turned the city of 1 million inhabitants into rubble, killing as many as 10,000 and sending over half the population into flight.

Between January and September 1992, a succession of corrupt and brutal Islamic governments vied for control of Kabul. But then the country witnessed the emergence of yet another—the most extreme—Muslim movement, the Taliban. The Taliban ("student" in Pushtun) was created in August 1994 (with the help of Pakistan's Inter-Services Intelligence, the country's military intelligence arm) by former Islamic seminary students (many from across the border in Pakistan). Led by its supreme leader, the one-eyed Mullah Muhammad Omar, the Taliban had become disgusted with the corruption and factional fighting and demanded an Afghan government subject to the laws of the Koran. It quickly gained popular support and began to rule wide stretches of the country, where it applied stern measures against those who transgressed the laws of Islam. It closed girls' schools, confined women to their homes, punished thieves by cutting off their hands, and carried out public executions.

In September 1996, the Taliban—already in control of more than half of Afghanistan—began its final push toward Kabul. Upon taking the city, its first act was to seize Najibullah inside the UN compound, beat him, shoot him, and then finally hang him and his brother from a traffic post as a warning to any and all who opposed it.

The Taliban's second act was to forbid women to work in offices, hospitals, and so on and to demand that they wear the traditional burqa, a garment that covers the wearer from head to toe. It also ordered government officials to grow beards, closed Kabul's sole television station (because Islam equates the reproduction of images of humans with idolatry), and banned Western music and other amusements such as flying kites.

The Taliban controlled more than three-quarters of Afghanistan, but the fighting was not over. The history of Afghanistan—a struggle between the center and the provinces—continued. When the Taliban moved into the Panjshir Valley, ninety miles north of Kabul, Uzbek and Tadzhik forces blocked their way.

Poland and Solidarity

In December 1970, the Polish Communist Party elected Edward Gierek to lead an increasingly radicalized country. Gierek's tenure coincided with Willy Brandt's *Ostpolitik*, which was marked by an easing of tensions between East and West. With détente came a considerable increase in East-West trade, underwritten by Western bankers who made available increasingly larger amounts of "petrodollars"—money deposited by the oil-rich nations. Gierek, unlike his frugal predecessor, Wladyslaw Gomulka, began to borrow heavily. In 1973, Poland owed $2.5 billion to the West; by 1982 the debt had risen to $27 billion. With the influx of Western capital and goods—machinery, grain, and consumer items—the standard of living rose, but the day of financial reckoning had to come.

That day came in July 1980, when the Gierek government, in order to pay off Poland's large foreign debt, decreed an increase in food prices. The

Polish Solidarity leader Lech Walesa, surrounded by supporters, Warsaw, Poland, November 11, 1980. *(AP/Wide World Photos)*

General Wojciech Jaruzelski, prime minister, defense minister, and first secretary of the Polish Communist Party, addressing the UN General Assembly, September 27, 1985. *(AP/Wide World Photos)*

announcement at first led to illegal strikes and demonstrations and then to the emergence of Solidarity.

In the past, the government had bought off striking workers with economic concessions. This time, however, the workers refused to take the bait. Instead, workers at the mammoth Lenin Shipyard in Gdansk insisted on concessions from the government that were nothing short of revolutionary. They demanded that any settlement would have to cover the country's workers as a whole, rather than merely with this single group of workers. This demand gave rise to Solidarity, a union that at one point represented 10 million people in a country of 35 million. Lech Walesa, the head of Solidarity, became one of the most powerful men in Poland.

Solidarity, with the support of the vast majority of the population as well as the Roman Catholic Church, was able to wring concession after concession from the government. During the next sixteen months, the attention of the world was riveted on Poland, where the impossible was taking place. According to Marxist ideology, Polish workers were striking against themselves, for, in theory at least, they were the owners of the "means of production," the factories. Strikes by workers against their places of employment were, therefore, both illogical and illegal. Yet this right to strike was the first and most important concession that Solidarity wrenched from the state. In this way, Solidarity established its independence from the state and thus became the only union in Eastern Europe not controlled by government.

Solidarity then demanded additional concessions. It broke the government's monopoly of the information media. It received the right to put out an uncensored daily newspaper as well as access to radio and television. It then wrested from the state the materials necessary to erect monuments in honor of workers that the state had gunned down during the riots of 1956 and 1970. Finally, Solidarity managed to obtain free local parliamentary elections with a secret ballot.

The Polish Communist Party was paralyzed in the face of Solidarity's demands. It was also deeply split. Some members openly supported Solidarity; others even quit the party to join Solidarity. The party began to look for a savior, a Napoleon Bonaparte, to bring the revolution under control. It turned to a man of considerable moral authority, General Wojciech Jaruzelski, who in 1970 and 1976 as minister of defense had refused to use force against workers, declaring that "Polish troops will not fire on Polish workers." In rapid succession, the party promoted him to prime minister in 1980, and then first secretary of the party in October 1981.

Jaruzelski well understood the precariousness of his position. He now held the three paramount positions in Poland and yet was unable to govern effectively. Lech Walesa, the head of Solidarity, who held no government position, was his coequal.

Party hard-liners resented the concessions granted to Solidarity; Solidarity hard-liners felt there could be no coexistence with the party. One of them, Jacek Kuron, long a bitter critic of the party, put it succinctly: The regime either "must die, or it must destroy Solidarity. There is no other solution."[33]

On December 12, 1981, a radicalized Solidarity called for a popular referendum—one it was sure to win—on the fate of the Communist Party. The government and TASS, the Soviet news agency, warned against an attempt by Solidarity to seize political power.

Brezhnev's Politburo hesitated, for it knew that the cost of intervention would be high; the result could be war between the two most important members of the Warsaw Pact, at a time when the Soviet army was already bogged down in Afghanistan. When, in November 1980, the Soviet army attempted to mobilize troops along the Polish border in order to intimidate Solidarity, it proved to be a disaster when reservists could not be found; others failed to answer the call, and so many deserted and went home that the authorities gave up trying to punish them.[34]

The day after Solidarity's call for the referendum, Jaruzelski's security forces arrested its leadership and declared martial law—effectively outlawing Solidarity and reestablishing the primacy of the party. The commonly held view in the West was that the Soviet Union bore direct responsibility for Jaruzelski's actions. But there was no clear proof of this. No doubt, Jaruzelski did what the Soviet Union had demanded all along, the restoration of order. But he also knew that either he would do it or the Kremlin would do it for him.

Solidarity's extraordinary gains of the previous sixteen months were now largely erased. Jaruzelski's security forces acted with remarkable efficiency in restoring order, which astonished most observers, including Solidarity itself. Jaruzelski and the party, however, did not manage to win the hearts and minds of the nation. But this chapter of Polish history was far from closed.

Annus Mirabilis

In Europe, 1989 became known as *annus mirabilis*, the "year of miracles." When the year began, all of Moscow's satellite Communist parties appeared firmly in control. By year's end, however, the ring of Communist states along the Soviet Union's western borders, which Stalin had created in 1945, was no more.

The events of 1989 underscored the fact that the governments of Eastern Europe had little popular support. In the past, whenever a Communist party had shown signs of being overwhelmed by its own people, Moscow had always intervened—in East Germany in June 1953, in Hungary in 1956, and in Czechoslovakia in 1968. Intervention and threats had maintained a deceptive calm.

Eastern Europe (1995)

Early in his reign, Gorbachev announced that the Brezhnev Doctrine was dead, that no nation had the right to impose its will on another people. He restated this position several times, including in his address to the United Nations in December 1988. The Communist parties in Eastern Europe now stood alone, and they had to face their people without Moscow's support.

Economic factors played a major role in the events of 1989. The economies of Eastern Europe had done tolerably well in the first decade or so when the Communist parties had organized large factories. The test was whether the Communist system could sustain productivity, absorb new technology, and produce a wider range of sophisticated products. When it could not, the result was that in 1989 every East European country was much poorer compared to the West than it had been in the 1970s. In 1987, per capita gross national product for Poland and Hungary, for example, was 14 percent of that of either West Germany or Sweden.[35] Moreover, the Iron Curtain had long ceased to be a barrier to the flow of information. Many East Germans regularly watched West German television—via cable, no less. That and the steady flow of visitors from the West gave the East Europeans a clear picture of how far they had fallen behind.

Poland

The dam began to crack first in Poland. After Jaruzelski had declared martial law, he found out that he could not rule Poland without Solidarity, particularly as the economy continued to deteriorate. In January 1989, Jaruzelski resumed talks with Solidarity, leading to its relegalization in April and to elections in June. The Communist Party proposed that Solidarity's representation in parliament be limited to 35 percent of the seats. Solidarity balked at this offer. The deadlock was broken only after the government agreed to create an upper house, or senate, that would be elected democratically.

The free and competitive elections sealed the fate of the party. The senate elections gave Solidarity 99 of the 100 contested seats and became what Poles termed "the only known crucifixion in which the victim has nailed himself to the cross."[36] After Solidarity's smashing victory in the senate elections, the Peasant Party, which during the previous forty years had been little more than a front for the Communists, suddenly bolted and joined the opposition. Solidarity and the Peasant Party now controlled a majority of seats in the lower house and formed the government. In August 1989, they elected Tadeusz Mazowiecki as prime minister, the first non-Communist leader in Eastern Europe since shortly after World War II.

Mazowiecki flew to Moscow to assure Gorbachev that his non-Communist government did not plan to leave the Warsaw Pact, as the Hungarian Communists had attempted in 1956. Moreover, Solidarity would not make the mistake it had made in 1981; it refrained from language suggesting the abolition of the Communist Party, which, in any case, was on its way to becoming irrelevant. Gorbachev replied that he had no intention of invoking the Brezhnev Doctrine; instead, he welcomed the events in Warsaw.

The Mazowiecki government now had to manage an economy deeply in debt and run aground on the shoals of central planning. On New Year's Day 1990, it abolished numerous subsidies to which Poland's citizens had long become accustomed. Immediately, the price of bread rose by 38 percent and that of coal, which many used for heating, went up 600 percent. A drastic increase in gasoline and auto-insurance prices forced some Poles to turn in their license plates.[37] The primary advocates of such "shock therapy" were the Western banks and governments and the IMF, all of which insisted that Poland put its fiscal house in order to be eligible for aid.

Poland's plan for dismantling its centralized economy was the boldest in Eastern Europe. By the summer of 1991, however, the government began to roll back some of its free-market policies to stave off a popular rebellion. It intervened to check the rising rate of unemployment by preventing state-owned factories from going bankrupt and introduced protective import tariffs on certain goods. Economists who had envisioned a "big-bang" transformation to capitalism began to speak of an evolution taking place over ten years. Poland's problems were but a microcosm of those facing all East European economies seeking a break with the centrally planned economies of the past.

East Germany

In the summer of 1989, Hungarian soldiers went to work to dismantle the fortifications along the Austro-Hungarian border, the first example of the physical demolition of the Iron Curtain. The Communist Hungarian government already had granted its citizens the right to a passport and with it the freedom of travel and emigration. Moreover, Hungary made no effort to keep East Germans from taking the same road to the West. Hungary, officially still a Communist country, became a hemorrhaging wound that threatened to bleed Communist East Germany, which for the first time since 1961—when the Berlin Wall was built—was losing tens of thousands of its citizens. In September 1989, 12,000 East Germans crossed into Austria in the span of three days. Other East Germans left through Czechoslovakia and Poland. East Germany's Warsaw Pact allies had become the road by which East Germans abandoned what they considered a sinking ship.

East Germany's rigid Communist Party chief, Erich Honecker, declared that he would ride out the storm. But in May 1989, after the party had rigged the results of local elections, the voices of protest grew louder. Church leaders, in particular, grew increasingly critical of the regime; they were joined by civic groups such as New Forum. Then came the summer exodus. But more important, summer 1989 saw repeated demonstrations in many cities, notably in Leipzig, where increasingly larger crowds demanded change and insisted "we're staying here." Honecker promised "another Beijing" (in reference to the massacre of protesters in Tiananmen Square in June 1989) and ordered the security police, the despised and dreaded Stasi, to use "any means" to put down the "counterrevolution."

The showdown came in Leipzig on the night of October 9, 1989, one month after Hungary had become an unimpeded escape route and the day after Gorbachev's visit to East Berlin to commemorate the fortieth anniversary of the East German state. Gorbachev made clear that he had not come to support Honecker but to say good-bye to him. He reminded the East German Politburo that a leadership that isolates itself from its people loses the right to exist. During the demonstration on October 9, the party backed down and did not use force. Nine days later, the Politburo forced Honecker to step down in favor of his protégé, Egon Krenz.

Krenz's first trip as head of the party was a visit to Moscow, where he took pains to describe himself as a disciple of Gorbachev's "new thinking." Mass protests, Krenz now insisted, were a healthy sign of change. The demonstrators wanted "better socialism and the renovation of society."

The demonstrations continued nonetheless. On November 6, 1989, 500,000 people demonstrated in Leipzig on a cold, rainy night. There were

Between November 9 and 12, 1989, more than 1 million East Germans walked or drove into West Berlin, where they received a joyous reception. *(German Information Service)*

also rallies in Dresden, Erfurt, Schwerin, Halle, Cottbus, and Karl-Marx-Stadt. The Dresden march was sanctioned by authorities and led by the mayor and the reformist local party chief. The march was the first officially approved antigovernment demonstration in that city. What only a short time ago would have been sensational concessions by the government were no longer enough. On November 9 came the historic announcement that East Germans wishing to emigrate to the West could do so by applying for passports. Moreover, East Germans who wanted to visit West Berlin would be able to pass through the checkpoints along the Berlin Wall. The Berlin Wall was crumbling.

The logic of revolution, however, demands that halfway measures are not enough. Dissidents now demanded the abolition of Article I of the constitution, which granted the party its political monopoly. The party caved in and scuttled Article I on December 1, 1989. This cleared the way for free elections.

German Reunification

The breach in the Berlin Wall put the unification of Germany on the agenda. Washington, Moscow, and the nations of Europe were bracing themselves for the inevitable.

After the creation of the West German government in May 1949 and that of East Germany in October 1949, the division of Germany had taken on an aura of permanence. Officially, however, the West German government rejected the notion of a divided Germany that, moreover, had been divided not just into two but into three parts; there was still the issue of Silesia, Pommerania, and East Prussia—under Polish and Soviet "administration" since 1945.

When West German chancellor Helmut Kohl began to speak of unification in November 1989, Moscow declared that just because East Germans had been granted unrestricted access to West Germany, this did not mean the automatic unification of the two Germanies. Kohl's statements also received a cool reception in the West. The wartime allies and most Europeans did not relish the re-creation of a strong and unified Germany in the heart of the continent. Such an eventuality dredged up unpleasant memories of Germany's past.

The unification of Germany in October 1990 and the decision to move the capital from Bonn to Berlin was taken by the West German government without much consultation with its allies. In the end, Germany did calm the fears of its neighbors, particularly Poland, when it officially accepted the borders the victors of World War II had drawn up and, concomitantly, the loss of East Prussia and the lands beyond the Oder and Neisse Rivers.

With the decline of the Soviet empire, the economy of a united Germany became the most powerful in Europe. Immediately after the failed coup in Moscow in August 1991, it was Germany that took the lead in recognizing the independence of the Baltic states. In Yugoslavia, Germany broke ranks with the European Community (EC) and the United States when it recognized the breakaway republics of Slovenia and Croatia and convinced its reluctant EC partners to do the same. During the Gulf War, Germany sent troops abroad for the first time since 1945, an air squadron to Turkey. In the summer of 1992, the German navy showed its flag in the Adriatic Sea off the coast of Yugoslavia to help the UN enforce its embargo against Serbia, a matter-of-fact step the government did not even deem worth discussing in the parliament.

Germany also took the lead in providing economic assistance to Eastern Europe. It was in part designed to prevent the dreaded consequences of a collapse of the East European economies—a flood of refugees westward. West Germany was already grappling with the unpopular fact that approximately 10 percent of its population consisted of foreigners. As residents—whether as workers or refugees—they were entitled to services from a government whose resources were stretched to the limit. The result was an antiforeigner backlash; in 1992, there were 2,000 assaults—including a number of fatalities—against Turks, black Africans, and Jews. The attackers were generally young males who unabashedly proclaimed themselves neo-Nazis. By the end of 1992, the euphoria and promise of German reunification had given way to bitterness, violence, and economic stagnation.

After unification, nearly all physical traces of the Berlin Wall were immediately erased. But the psychological gulf between the Easterners and the Westerners remained. The Easterners had lived since 1933 under two consecutive dictatorships, first the Nazis and then the Communists. Their past experience was different from those in the West. Many recoiled from the open democratic political discourse. Unification also meant the East German economic enterprises were thrown into a marketplace in which they had little chance of surviving. Economic recovery in East Germany came slowly, assisted by the infusion of massive sums—raised by drastic, unpopular tax increases.

Hungary

At the time that Solidarity in Poland conducted its noisy challenge to the Communist Party, events in Hungary, though quieter, brought similar results.

János Kádár had come to power in 1956 after the Soviet army crushed the Hungarian rebellion. By the late 1960s, Kádár and his party began a cautious program of domestic innovation that, by East European standards, was remarkable. While gradually moving away from the Soviet model, Kádár remained at pains to assure the Soviets that he had no intention of threatening their East European empire.

Kádár's innovations produced experiments in small-scale capitalism. The result was a mixed economy. The "commanding heights" of the economy—heavy industry, transportation, and banking—remained in the hands of the state. At the same time, however, small private enterprises—such as small shops, restaurants, bars, food stands, artisan shops, and garages employing no more than three persons—were permitted. Western journalists called it "goulash Communism." Hungarians spoke of "Communism with a capitalist facelift."

From a rigid Marxist point of view, the Hungarian innovations were acts of heresy. But at no time did Karl Marx waste his time discussing the malfeasance of the man who owned a barbershop or the peasant woman selling flowers at a street corner. When Marx wrote *Das Capital*, he denounced, instead, what the poet William Blake had called the "dark Satanic mills" of the early industrial revolution.

On June 8, 1985, Hungarian voters cast their ballots for representatives to parliament and local councils, in which at least two candidates ran for nearly all seats. This was the first election under a 1983 law that demanded a choice for the voters, something unique for a Soviet bloc country.

In May 1988, the reform wing of the Communist Party nudged the seventy-six-year-old Kádár aside as party leader. It paved the way for the political, posthumous rehabilitation of Kádár's victims. For the first time since 1956, it became possible in Hungary to mention the names of Imre Nagy, Hungary's party chief at the time of the 1956 revolution, and Pal Maleter, the general who had fought the Soviet army. They had been among those Kádár had executed and dumped, with their faces down and hands still tied behind their backs, in an unmarked mass grave. Their names had disappeared from the official histories but not from the collective memory of the nation. Their rehabilitation culminated in the solemn June 1989 reinterment of Nagy and his associates, a ceremony broadcast live on national television.

In September 1989, the Communist Party renamed itself the Socialist Party, and parliament rewrote the constitution to permit multiparty elections the following spring. On October 23, 1989, the thirty-third anniversary of the beginning of the 1956 uprising, parliament declared Hungary no longer a "People's Republic." It became the Republic of Hungary, and the red star on top of the parliament building came down. Two rounds of elections, in March and April 1990, shattered whatever illusions the Socialist Party still had of clinging to power. The voters gave the Hungarian Democratic Forum, a populist, nationalist umbrella organization with a right-of-center orientation, a plurality of the seats in parliament; its leader, Jozsef Antall, set out to create a coalition with the other conservative parties. The Socialist Party won but 8 percent of the parliamentary seats. The Communist experiment in Hungary was over.

Czechoslovakia

The fourth Communist domino to fall in 1989 was Czechoslovakia. The revolutionary vanguard against the old Communist regime initially consisted of intellectuals and students. In the center of the opposition stood Charta 77, a loose union of 1,600 individuals who in 1977 had signed a petition demanding civil rights. Their leaders were Jiri Hajek, the country's foreign minister during the Prague Spring, and the dissident writer Vaclav Havel. Since June 1989, a petition demanding the release of all political prisoners, freedom of expression and assembly, and an independent news media had circulated throughout the nation, and 40,000 citizens had signed it. Czechoslovakia's "Velvet Revolution" was under way.

As long as the demonstrating crowds remained relatively small—2,000 in January 1989 and still only 10,000 at the beginning of November 1989—the police were able to maintain a semblance of order by arrests and occasional beatings. The workers who enjoyed a relatively high standard of living were slow to join. When they did join the demonstrators on Saint Wenceslas Square in Prague, the end had arrived for the Communist regime. At the end of November 1989 it folded like a house of cards.

Nearly the entire nation stood in opposition to the Communist Party. Not even a bloodbath could save it. Once the party agreed to abandon its ruling monopoly on November 29, 1989, events moved quickly. The opposition established a provisional government until the voters were able to choose the country's first freely elected government since 1948. Havel, who earlier in the year had been arrested and jailed for antistate activities, became the new prime minister. Alexander Dubček, one of the architects of the Prague Spring, became the country's new president.

At a Warsaw Pact meeting in December 1989, the five participants in the 1968 invasion of Czechoslovakia—the Soviet Union, East Germany, Poland, Hungary, and Bulgaria—formally declared that the invasion had been "illegal" and pledged in the future strict noninterference in each other's internal affairs. The declaration marked the formal repudiation of the Brezhnev Doctrine. The Soviet government issued a separate statement admitting that the reasons for intervention had been "unfounded" and that its decision to intervene had been "erroneous."[38]

Havel, in a pointed reminder that Czechoslovakia was a part of Central and not Eastern Europe, went on his first official state visit to Berlin and then to Warsaw. "It's not good-bye to Moscow," a foreign ministry official explained, "but it's a new orientation toward West and Central Europe."[39]

In the summer of 1992, militant Slovaks in the eastern part of the country decided to secede from their Czech cousins. Czechoslovakia had come into existence in 1918 as a federation of Czechs and Slovaks under the leadership of the Czech Tomas Masaryk. From the outset, Slovaks resented Czech domination, particularly the fact that they never received the autonomy the Czechs had promised. Remarkably, there was little sentiment among Czechs to preserve the union with their ungrateful cousins. The breakup became official on New Year's Day 1993.

Bulgaria

Next in line was Bulgaria, the most loyal member of the Warsaw Pact. The seventy-eight-year-old boss of the Communist Party, Todor Zhivkov, in power since 1954, at first showed no signs of stepping down. But his long rule had bred widespread opposition. He had been responsible for reviving the ancient quarrel between Bulgarians and Turks in 1984 when he forced the 1-million-strong Muslim Turkish minority to adopt Slavic names. In May 1989, he pressured 310,000 Turks to emigrate. Not only did he damage Bulgaria's international standing, but the exodus also wrought havoc with the nation's economy. When Zhivkov promoted his son to the Central Committee's Department of Culture in 1989, even his old allies deserted him. In the end, the Politburo demanded his resignation.

The charges against Zhivkov consisted of corruption and nepotism. But the ouster of Zhivkov was too little, too late. Increasingly larger and more defiant crowds focused on the party's monopoly on power.

On January 15, 1990, the Communist Party caved in to popular pressure and agreed to give up its leading political role and to hold free elections. In September 1992, after an eighteen-month trial, the now eighty-one-year-old Zhivkov was found guilty of embezzling nearly $1 million and sentenced to seven years in prison (commuted to house arrest due to ill health and old age). Zhivkov here became the first former Soviet bloc leader to be judged by a post-Communist court.

Romania

The last and least likely of the Communist dictators to be toppled in 1989 was Nicolae Ceauşescu, who had come to power in 1965. Ceauşescu carved out a foreign policy independent of Moscow without, however, leaving the Warsaw Pact. He reserved Romania's right not to join in the pact's annual war exercises, continued to recognize Israel after the 1967 Six Day War, and refused to participate in the invasion of Czechoslovakia in 1968. In 1984, he did not honor the Moscow-led boycott of the Olympic Games in Los Angeles, where the Romanian team received a standing ovation at the opening ceremonies. The West rewarded maverick Romania with most-favored-nation treatment, and US presidents Richard Nixon and Jimmy Carter paid highly publicized visits to Bucharest. They spared no words in heaping praise on the Romanian dictator, ignoring the fact that Ceauşescu's regime was by far the most repressive within the Warsaw Pact.

Ceauşescu decided what few dictators dared to contemplate. Romania would pay off its $10 billion foreign debt, never mind the social consequences. The result was a sharp drop in the standard of living. Large amounts of food were exported, the workweek was increased to six days, the price of gasoline was raised, apartments were kept at about 50 degrees Fahrenheit in the winter, and electricity was rationed; even hospitals lacked supplies. The 24 million people of Romania, an agrarian land, were reduced to a meager diet. Pigs' feet, commonly known as "patriots," remained in abundance; they were the only parts of the pig that stayed behind after the rest had been exported.

Ceauşescu's style was a combination of that of Stalin and the fascist Benito Mussolini of Italy. He dropped the label "comrade" and began to call himself "Conducator," or leader. Ceauşescu ruled not through his party but, similar to Stalin, through the secret police, the Securitate. The party existed merely to legitimize Ceauşescu's rule. The most prominent feature of Romanian television was the glorification of Ceauşescu and his wife, Elena, the nation's second-most-powerful figure. Their son, Nicu, was groomed to follow in his father's footsteps. Forty other relatives were on the government payroll.

In June 1989, Ceauşescu sent a congratulatory message to Deng Xiaoping for crushing the Chinese student demonstrations. He promised to respond likewise should dissidents take to his streets. A party official explained the Ceauşescu method of governance: "All the systems of the world are based on reward and punishment. Ceauşescu works only with punishment. It is a reward that there is no punishment."[40]

After the foreign debt was largely repaid, economic conditions in Romania did not change. Ceauşescu continued to bleed his people by initiating a massive building program, a monument to his megalomania. Fifteen thousand workers began work on the thirteen-story, 1,000-room House of the Republic, of white marble, on the Avenue of Socialist Victory. To make room for this palace, nearly 40,000 people were moved and many historic buildings were destroyed—among them the sixteenth-century Monastery of Michael the Brave, the ruler who in 1600 had unified Wallachia, Moldavia, and Transylvania into modern Romania. Ceauşescu personally supervised the project, visiting it two or three times per week. His other projects included the razing of entire towns in Transylvania, many inhabited by ethnic Germans and Hungarians whose ancestors had built them over the span of seven centuries.

The city of Timişoara, in Transylvania, lit the spark that brought down the seemingly impregnable Ceauşescu dictatorship. In early December 1989, the government decided to deport from Timişoara a little-known Hungarian Protestant priest, Laszlo Tokes. The decision touched off demonstrations, forcing the government to reconsider. The concession was a victory of sorts for the people in the streets and produced an even greater demonstration on December 16. Economic considerations also played a part. In October, additional food had been rationed—this in a city that contained large food-processing factories and bakeries. Workers who knew nothing of Tokes, but who handled the food destined for export, joined the ranks of the demonstrators.

The fall of the other East European Communist parties had taken place without a single fatality; Romania was destined to be different. Ceauşescu took a page from the Chinese book by sending the Securitate into Timişoara. The Conducator, the "hero of the nation, the brilliant son of the people," began murdering his own people.[41] The uprising might have been contained by the police had it not continued the practice of refusing to return the bodies of those killed, who instead were dumped into a mass grave on the outskirts of the city. "Give us our dead," the demonstrators demanded.

In a speech in Bucharest, Ceauşescu vowed to win the war against the "terrorists and hooligans." That speech—before what appeared to be a traditionally docile crowd assembled by the authorities—became a disaster as it turned into an anti-Ceauşescu demonstration. Ceauşescu never finished it and fled the presidential palace. At that point, he also lost control of the army. He had never trusted the military, and for good reason. After initially firing into the crowd, soldiers turned their guns on the police. Ceauşescu and his wife fled, only to be captured.

The Ceauşescus were put before a military tribunal and charged with genocide—the murder of 60,000 Romanian citizens—theft, and looting the state treasury for personal profit. Elena Ceauşescu termed the last accusation a "provocation." The unrepentant Conducator denied all charges and still claimed to be the leader of Romania. A firing squad ended the discussion on Christmas Day 1989. Romanian television showed a tape of the trial and the elegantly dressed corpses of the Ceauşescus.

The new provisional government was headed by Ion Iliescu, Gorbachev's classmate in Moscow in the 1950s and party boss in Timişoara in the late 1960s, who had become popular with many party members for speaking out against Ceauşescu's economic measures. On the surface, the new government followed the precedents established in other East European countries. It declared that Romania was no longer a socialist state, stocked the stores with food, reduced the workweek to five days, cut the price of electricity by more than half, permitted each farm family an acre of land for private cultivation, abolished the death penalty after the Ceauşescus' execution, dissolved the Securitate, and promised free elections in April 1990. The government also arrested Ceauşescu's closest associates, including the entire Politburo and ranking officers of the Securitate, promising punishment for "all evildoers from the old regime."

What had taken place in Romania, however, was neither a political nor a social revolution. The Ceauşescus were executed by their own henchmen, among them Iliescu, who now tried to save their own necks. Their aim was to eliminate the dictator but not the dictatorship. The "red aristocrats," as the party leaders were known, then made sure to stress the myth of a political revolution.[42]

The conspirators produced the trappings of parliamentary democracy yet continued Ceauşescuism without Ceauşescu. Their task was facilitated by the fact that Romania never had known a modern party system, a responsible political intelligentsia, or an autonomous church. Romania's political culture was steeped in intrigue, conspiracy, and subservience to authority.

Six months after the death of Ceauşescu, the Marxist Iliescu found solace in fascism. He announced the formation of a national guard reminiscent of the fascist Iron Guard of World War II, and he proceeded to arrest opposition leaders, insisting all along that he was defending democracy.[43]

By the beginning of the twenty-first century, Romania remained at best a society in transition to democracy. It was plagued with widespread economic and political corruption. It sought to join the European Union, but that organization always insisted that its members follow the rules of democracy.

Then came the brutal economic collapse. Forty percent of the population lived on less than $35 per month, that is, below the international poverty line of $2 per day. The Craiova giant heavy machine and tool complex, for instance, which once had employed 7,000 workers, ten years later employed but 800.[44]

The presidential election of 2000 pitted the discredited Ion Iliescu against Corneliu Vadim Tudor, once Ceauşescu's court poet, the head of the ultra-nationalist Greater Romania Party. Tudor declared that Romania could be governed only at "the point of a machine gun" and promised to end corruption "with a Kalashnikov." He continued to call Ceauşescu a "great patriot" and filled his publications with racist articles and cartoons railing against "dirty Jews," "fascist Hungarians," and "criminal Gypsies." Iliescu handily defeated Tudor, who had become an embarrassment to many voters who had to choose between the lesser of two evils. With Tudor, Romania had no choice of joining the EU; with Iliescu its chances improved a little. Still, when the EU added ten new members in 2004, Romania was not among them. The country had to wait until 2007, after it had instituted several rounds of reforms.

Albania

The Communist state of Albania, the creation of Enver Hoxha in 1944, became the next casualty. Hoxha's regime, a fusion of the worst features of Stalinism and Maoism, was even more oppressive than that of Ceauşescu. Poverty-stricken and isolated, Albania was the world's only official atheist state. Defendants were often executed without trials or simply disappeared; their relatives were punished for good measure. After Hoxha's death in April 1985, Ramiz Alia continued his policies. After 1989, however, Alia introduced reforms to an increasingly restless population. He rescinded, for example, the "crime" of religious propaganda and granted free elections, which ended Communist rule in March 1992.

Yugoslavia

Yugoslavia, although under Communist one-party rule, had remained outside the Soviet orbit since the Tito-Stalin split in 1947. Under its politically savvy leader, Josip Tito, Yugoslavia remained neutral in the Cold War. The country was a patchwork of eight major ethnic regions. They consisted of six republics—Bosnia, Croatia, Macedonia, Montenegro, Serbia, Slovenia—and two officially autonomous provinces within Serbia, Kosovo and Vojvodina. As long as Tito lived, Yugoslavia retained a remarkable degree of cohesion. After World War II, the Croat Josip Tito established a federation in which no one people would dominate another, particularly the numerically and historically dominant Serbs. Tito understood the potential danger that ethnic strife posed for Yugoslavia—literally "South Slavia"—an artificial nation formed in 1918 after the collapse of Ottoman Turkish control. To appease the competing nationalities, the 1974 Constitution granted the ethnic regions a measure of autonomy. The Serbian nationality, because of its size, remained first among equals but an equal nevertheless. However, after Tito's death in 1980, the new Communist Party leader, the Serb Slobodan Milošević, stripped the Albanian majority in Kosovo Province of its autonomy. Milošević gave notice that he sought a Greater Serbia dominating the other nationalities. On June 28, 1989, he added fuel to the fire when he led a Serb demonstration of 1 million people into Kosovo during the commemoration of the 600th anniversary of the Battle of Kosovo Field, in which the Muslim Turks (with the help of Muslim Albanians) had defeated the Christian Orthodox Serbs. The time had come, Milošević declared, to restore Serbia to its former greatness.[45]

Although most Yugoslavs were of Slavic origin, there were serious divisions among them. Slovenes and Croats in the west had fallen under the influence of Roman Catholicism, while the Slavs farther to the east, including Serbs and Macedonians, belonged to the Eastern Orthodox Church. The country, moreover, contained a sizable Muslim population—Albanians and Bosnians—the legacy of centuries of Turkish control. To complicate matters, the diverse populations were interspersed. Yugoslavia consisted of an uneasy fusion of Western and Eastern Christianity and Islam.

Assertive Serbian nationalism produced a fearful reaction from other nationalities. Taking their cue from the independence movements in the Soviet Union, they began to demand independence. The first to do so, in June 1991, was Slovenia—with a population of 2 million—in Yugoslavia's northwestern corner. At the same time, the larger and more powerful Republic of Croatia (4.8 million people) also seceded. Bosnia followed suit in 1992. These events triggered a bloody conflict—the first on the European continent since 1945—when the Serbian-dominated Yugoslav army invaded Croatia.

At this point, the United Nations intervened. It brokered a cease-fire that took effect in January 1992. Blue-helmeted UN troops—14,400 from thirty-one nations—became the first such deployment on the European continent. But the troops did not have a combat role; they merely served to keep the belligerents apart. Germany became the first nation officially to recognize Slovenia and Croatia in January 1992, and the other members of the European Community

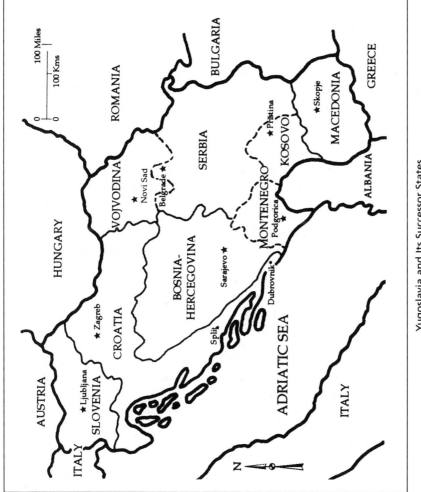

Yugoslavia and Its Successor States

followed suit. The United States continued to hold out hope that a united Yugoslavia could somehow remain a viable option. But in April 1992, the administration of George H. W. Bush came into line with the European Community when it simultaneously recognized Slovenia, Croatia, and Bosnia.

Bosnia

The ethnic makeup of Bosnia was the most complex of all the regions—92 percent of its people were of Slavic origin, but 44 percent were Muslim, 31 percent were Orthodox Serbs, and 17 percent were Catholic Croats.[46] Milošević, stymied in Croatia, turned against Bosnia, ostensibly to protect the threatened Orthodox Serb minority. He provided weapons for Serbian militia forces in Bosnia, who proceeded to lay siege to Bosnia's capital, Sarajevo. The siege lasted more than 1,000 days, one of the longest in history.

The conflict in Bosnia became a war of extraordinary brutality. Serbs established concentration camps and undertook "ethnic cleansing" in parts of Bosnia—including a frightful series of rapes, tortures, massacres, and forcible deportations of civilians in freight cars. These actions were reminiscent of crimes last committed in Europe by Stalin and Hitler. Serbian perpetrators were well aware that they faced potential charges as war criminals, and for that reason they often masked their faces. The violence in Yugoslavia produced approximately 2.5 million refugees by 1992, the first on such a scale in Europe since 1945.

By 1992, what had once been Yugoslavia was reduced to five separate entities: a rump state of Yugoslavia (Serbia, the once autonomous provinces of Kosovo and Vojvodina, and the Republic of Montenegro), Slovenia, Croatia, Bosnia, and Macedonia. The Serbian chauvinist Milošević had become the destroyer of Yugoslavia, including its peoples, cities, villages, the economy, as well as the currency (inflation, at 25,000 percent per year, rendered the Yugoslav *dinar* worthless). As recently as 1989, many Europeans had exulted in the spiritual rebirth of the continent. Yet in 1992, the European Community, the United Nations, and the United States were stymied by a defiant, virulent Serbian chauvinism.

The Muslims in Bosnia received little help from the outside world because of a UN weapons embargo. The Bosnian Serbs, in contrast, were able to obtain large quantities of arms from their kinsmen in Serbia. Led by their president, Radovan Karadžić, and the commander of their forces, General Ratko Mladić, the Serbs of Bosnia proclaimed the creation of an ostensibly independent Serbian Republic.

The homicidal Mladić saw himself as the vindicator of Serbian history. To him, there was hardly a difference between the past and the present; the violence of the 1990s was part of the continuum of Serbian history. Serbs were again fighting to save Europe from an Islamic tide.[47]

It became increasingly difficult for the United Nations and NATO to stand by idly as the evidence of atrocities began to mount. In February 1994, as Serbs made gains in eastern Bosnia, the United Nations declared several regions there as safe havens and threatened NATO air strikes to maintain them. But when NATO carried out its first air strikes against Serb forces near Goražde in April 1994, the Serbs responded with their own attacks on the "safe areas." In 1995, they seized 270 UN peacekeepers and shackled them to potential bombing targets. French general Bernard Janvier, whose troops made up more than one-half of the hostages, arranged their release through Mladić, but the price was a halt to further air strikes on the Serbs. The deal left the United Nations powerless, and the 40,000 Bosnian Muslims in Srebrenica—officially still under UN protection—were now defenseless.

By early summer 1992, the US government had gathered evidence that the Serbs were conducting widespread massacres of Muslims. Its spy satellites showed that in the northern town of Brčko, Serbs had herded 3,000 Muslim men into an abandoned warehouse, then tortured and murdered them. It had even intercepted telephone conversations in which Mladić spoke of his intentions to cleanse Goražde and Žepa.[48] In July 1995, Serbs carried out yet another massacre, this one in Srebrenica, of 6,000–8,000 Muslim men and boys. According to eyewitnesses, Mladić was present at the killings. This time, Madeleine Albright, who at the time was US ambassador to the United Nations, revealed photographs of fresh graves taken from US spy planes.

In May 1993, the UN Security Council established the International Criminal Tribunal for the Former Yugoslavia, the first such court since the Nuremberg and Tokyo trials in the aftermath of World War II. In May 1996, a young Croat, Dražen Erdemović, who had fought for the Serbs, became the first person to plead guilty to war crimes—confessing he had murdered scores of unarmed Muslim men at Srebrenica. His defense was that, fearing for his life, he had only followed orders.[49]

At the end of summer 1995, the tide turned against the Serbs when Croatian forces wrested control of southeastern Croatia, causing more than 170,000 Serbs to flee in fear. In October 1995, the three warring sides—by now thoroughly exhausted—agreed to a cease-fire and to hold talks in the United States.

Bosnian Muslims hoped a settlement of the conflict would not recognize the partition of Bosnia and the consequences of "ethnic cleansing." "Bosnia is the place to draw the line against ultranationalism on the march," a Bosnian journalist pleaded; "appeasement of Serbian conquests and ethnic partition of Bosnia would encourage such forces."[50] But it was to no avail. The Dayton Agreement of November 1995 (negotiated in Dayton, Ohio) divided Bosnia between a Serbian-controlled Serbian Republic and the Bosnian Federation (Croats and Muslims) by a ratio of 49:51, respectively. In effect, the split rewarded Serb aggression. A small NATO force was left behind to monitor a precarious cease-fire.

Officially, Bosnia remained a single country but one divided into two republics. As of June 1996, 1,319,250 Bosnian refugees had made their way to European nations that did not want them. They were unable to return to their former domiciles, which—as likely as not—had been "ethnically cleansed."[51] Muslims in Bosnia remained bitter that the world had done little to protect them, and Serbs in Croatia, who had been put to flight, dreamed of retribution.

Kosovo

After the partition of Bosnia, the focus shifted to the Yugoslav province of Kosovo. Its population, 90 percent Albanian, was ruled by the Serb minority there and by Milošević in Belgrade. Early in 1999, violence between an Albanian Kosovo Liberation Army (KLA) and the Serbian authorities began to escalate. By March 1999, the number of dead was estimated at between 1,500 and 2,000.

This time, the Clinton administration—prodded primarily by Secretary of State Madeleine Albright—decided to act. It would not stand by idly as it had in the recent Balkan wars. Moreover, Third World leaders had criticized the West for doing nothing while Hutus had gone about their business of exterminating Tutsis in Rwanda. This time the West took action.

Clinton knew that he would not be able to act through the United Nations, as President George Bush had done during the Gulf War, because Russia was certain to exercise its veto in the Security Council. Russia has historic ties to Serbia: Russians and Serbs are Slavs, they tend to be of the Orthodox faith, and in the not-too-distant past Russia had come to the assistance of Serbia against the Turks, Austrians, and Germans. Moreover, the Kremlin, unhappy with NATO's recent eastward expansion, had no intention of facilitating the expansion of US military might farther into the Balkans.

It took the Clinton administration some doing to persuade its NATO allies to join the fray in Kosovo, but in the end they came onboard, agreeing that the Western alliance could not ignore another case of genocide, this one in Europe.

After Milošević rejected Clinton's demand that he withdraw his army from Kosovo, NATO began an air war that lasted for seventy-eight days (March 24 until June 9, 1999). Here NATO went into combat for the first time, even though the war had nothing to do with a threat against one of its members. At best, this was a war to defend the self-esteem of NATO's member nations.

The immediate consequence of the war was precisely what the West had feared and had sought to avoid, the brutal ethnic cleansing of Albanians—accompanied by rapes, mass executions, and arsons. A stream of 850,000 refugees headed across the Albanian and Macedonian borders.

The air war involved the deployment of 1,100 airplanes flying 38,000 sorties, the largest concentration of airpower in history. Serb forces in Kosovo were subjected to a hail of thousands of "smart" bombs and cruise missiles.

NATO did not suffer a single combat fatality in the first war ever won solely by airpower. It was dubbed the first "telecommunications war" waged by remote control, the first "virtual war" with pilots viewing sophisticated computer displays to guide and follow the bombs heading for their targets.

NATO repeatedly insisted that it was not waging a war against the Serbian people, only against the government of Milošević. "Collateral damage" among Serb civilians was relatively small, particularly when one considers the scale of the sustained air attacks—about 500 dead caused by approximately 100 sorties gone astray.

Meanwhile, towns were divided, both sides vowing to make them eventually theirs. It was now the turn of the Albanians, particularly the KLA, to exact revenge. In the eight months after the war, 250,000 Kosovo Serbs were driven from their homes. The fighting ended, but peace remained a distant mirage. In the end, Milošević agreed to withdraw from Kosovo. After three wars in the span of less than a decade, in addition to an international economic boycott, Yugoslavia's economy was in shambles.

Milošević, under political pressure at home, agreed to hold a presidential election in September 2000. The winner, to his surprise, was the candidate of the Socialist Party, Vojislav Koštunica. At first Milošević refused to acknowledge defeat, but when street demonstrations became uncontrollable, he finally stepped down.

Koštunica was no more inclined than was Milošević to accept the loss of Kosovo and the continuing expulsion of Serbs from lands they considered to be theirs. In December 2000, the two sides were trading mortar rounds across the three-mile buffer between Kosovo and Serbia. Koštunica warned that a declaration of independence by ethnic Albanians in Kosovo would touch off yet another Balkan war.

Officially, NATO had not gone to war to create a separate state of Kosovo. Once the Serbs had been brought to heel, however, an independent Kosovo was a matter of time. Until 2006, an interim civilian government of a de facto independent Kosovo, headed by Ibrahim Rugova, was able to counterbalance the KLA, an army with a proclivity for violent and illegal behavior—including the smuggling of drugs and guns, extortion, and murder. After Rugova died in January 2006, the KLA seized power. The new prime minister was Hashim Thaçi, a former KLA guerrilla leader known for his ruthlessness. Western leaders took the curious position that the sporadic violence in Kosovo could spread out of control unless the region was granted de jure independence. With virtually no public debate, George W. Bush's administration—joined by Germany, France, and Britain—crossed its fingers and, in February 2008, extended diplomatic recognition to the poorest and most unstable nation of Europe, now known as the Republic of Kosovo. Predictably, Serbians—who had long considered Kosovo to be part of their patrimony and portrayed Thaçi as a war criminal—denounced the United States, some of them going so far as to torch several rooms of the US embassy in Belgrade. The dismemberment of what since 1919 had been the patchwork of Yugoslavia was now complete.[52]

Of the three men primarily responsible for the violence, only one was relatively quickly apprehended. In 2001, after he had lost the election, Milošević became the first head of state since World War II to face charges of war crimes and genocide. At the International Criminal Tribunal for the Former Yugoslavia, Milošević, acting as his own lawyer, managed to drag out the proceedings for years. His death of a heart attack, in March 2006, put an end to the judicial process. The Bosnian Serb leaders, Karadžić and Mladić, indicted in 1995, continued to live quite openly in Belgrade as long as Milošević remained in power. After that they went into hiding. When Karadžić was finally apprehended in July 2008, he made clear that he would follow Milošević's example and try to tie up trial proceedings for years.

Recommended Readings

Brown, Archie. *The Gorbachev Factor.* New York: Oxford University Press, 1996.
  On Gorbachev's role in the perestroika of the Soviet Union.
Cohen, Stephen F. *Failed Crusade: America and the Tragedy of Post-Communist Russia.* New York: Norton, 2000.
  A critical assessment of the US role in urging the Yeltsin government to accept capitalism and to dismantle Soviet institutions.
Goldman, Marshall I. *Gorbachev's Challenge: Economic Reform in the Age of High Technology.* New York: Norton, 1987.
  A discussion of the magnitude of Gorbachev's economic problems.
Gorbachev, Mikhail. *Perestroika: New Thinking for Our Country and the World.* New York: Harper and Row, 1987.
———. *The August Coup: The Truth and the Lessons.* New York: HarperCollins, 1991.
Hollander, Paul. *Political Will and Personal Belief: The Decline and Fall of Soviet Communism.* New Haven, Conn.: Yale University Press, 2000.
  Focuses on the lack of faith in Communism as an all-encompassing ideology.
Karny, Yoav. *Highlanders: A Journey in Quest of Memory.* New York: Farrar, Straus and Giroux, 2000.
  By an Israeli journalist who discusses the complexities of the Caucasus.
Matlock, Jack F., Jr. *Autopsy of an Empire: The American Ambassador's Account of the Collapse of the Soviet Union.* New York: Random House, 1995.
Medvedev, Zhores A. *Gorbachev.* New York: Norton, 1986.
  By a dissident Soviet historian.
Putin, Vladimir. *First Person: An Astonishing Frank Self-Portrait: Interviews with Nataliya Geborkyan, Natalya Timakova, and Andrei Kolesnikov.* London: Hutchinson, 2000.
  Putin's black-and-white view of the world.
Reddaway, Peter, and Dmitri Glinski. *The Tragedy of Russia's Reforms: Market Bolshevism Against Democracy.* Washington, D.C.: United States Institute of Peace, 2000.

Schmidt-Häuer, Christian. *Gorbachev: The Path to Power.* Boston: Salem House, 1986.
A Moscow-based West German journalist's account of how the party elected Gorbachev as its chief.
Smith, Graham, ed. *The Nationalities Question in the Soviet Union.* London: Longman, 1990.

Afghanistan

Bradsher, Henry S. *Afghanistan and the Soviet Union.* 2nd ed. Durham, N.C.: Duke University Press, 1985.
A detailed account of the events leading up to the Russian invasion.
Chaliand, Gerard. *Report from Afghanistan.* New York: Penguin, 1982.
An introduction to the history, geography, and politics of Afghanistan.
Garthoff, Raymond L. *Détente and Confrontation: American-Soviet Relations from Nixon to Reagan.* Washington, D.C.: Brookings Institution, 1985.
Argues that the Soviets feared that Amin would expel their advisors and bring in US personnel.

Eastern Europe

Ascherson, Neal. *The Polish August: The Self-Limiting Revolution.* New York: Viking, 1982.
A survey of the political climate in Poland that set the stage for the rise of Solidarity.
Ash, Timothy Garton. *The Polish Revolution: Solidarity.* New York: Charles Scribner's Sons, 1984.
A British journalist's account of the rise and fall of Solidarity.
———. *The Magic Lantern: The Revolution of '89 Witnessed in Warsaw, Budapest, Berlin, and Prague.* New York: Vintage, 1993.
An eyewitness account of the historic events of 1989.
Behr, Edward. *Kiss the Hand You Cannot Bite: The Rise and Fall of the Ceauşescus.* New York: Villard Books, 1991.
Political biography that focuses on the deep social and cultural roots of the dictatorship.
Brumberg, Abraham, ed. *Poland: Genesis of a Revolution.* New York: Random House, 1983.
A collection of essays by Polish activists.
Carre d'Encausse, Helene. *Decline of an Empire: The Soviet Socialist Republics in Revolt.* New York: Harper and Row, 1978.
An introduction to the ethnic complexity of the Soviet empire.
Djilas, Aleksa. *The Contested Country: Yugoslav Unity and Communist Revolution, 1919–1953.* Cambridge, Mass.: Harvard University Press, 1993.
An analysis of why Tito's concept of a unified Yugoslavia eventually failed.
Gati, Charles. *The Bloc That Failed: Soviet–East European Relations in Transition.* Bloomington: Indiana University Press, 1990.
Brief history of the Soviet bloc in Eastern Europe, with an emphasis on the impact of Gorbachev's reforms.
Glenny, Misha. *The Balkans: Nationalism, War, and the Great Powers, 1804–1999.* New York: Viking, 2000.
By a BBC correspondent who covered the disintegration of Yugoslavia.

Stokes, Gail. *From Stalinism to Pluralism: A Documentary History of Eastern Europe Since 1945.* New York: Oxford University Press, 1996.

Sullivan, Stacy. *Be Not Afraid, for You Have Sons in America: How a Brooklyn Roofer Helped Lure the US into the Kosovo War.* New York: St. Martin's Press, 2004.

Notes

1. "On a Course of Unity and Solidarity," *Pravda*, February 21, 1985; *Current Digest of the Soviet Press*, March 20, 1985, p. 7.

2. David Remnick, "Solzhenitsyn—A New Day in the Life," *Washington Post*, January 7, 1990, p. B3.

3. B. Minonov, "'Otkryvaia dver' v 'spetskhran,'" *Pravda*, September 10, 1988, p. 6.

4. "On the Agricultural Policies of the Communist Party of the Soviet Union Under Present Conditions," *Pravda*, March 16, 1989.

5. Cited in Ester B. Fein, "Gorbachev Hints He Would Accept Multiparty Rule," *New York Times*, January 14, 1990, p. 1.

6. The exact number is unknown. The Turkish government bitterly resents any mention of a massacre, denying it ever took place, merely admitting to Turkish-Armenian violence in which both sides suffered fatalities.

7. Esther Schrader, "Baku Refugees Celebrate Deaths of Azerbaijanis," *Baltimore Sun*, January 23, 1990, p. 4A.

8. Jerry F. Hough, "Gorbachev's Politics," *Foreign Affairs* (Winter 1989–1990), p. 30.

9. See the interrogations of the conspirators in V. A. Zatova and T. K. Speranskaia, eds., *Avgust-91* (Moscow: Politizdat, 1991), pp. 253–271.

10. Leslie Gelb, "The Russian Sinkhole," *New York Times*, March 30, 1992, p. A17; Steven Greenhouse, "Point Man for the Rescue of the Century," *New York Times*, April 26, 1992, section 3, pp. 1, 6.

11. Aleksandr Pumpianskii, "Sud na partiei, kotoraia byla pravitel'stvo," *Novoe vremia*, no. 42 (1992), p. 5.

12. *Baltimore Sun*, April 28, 1991, p. 11A; based on *Europa World Yearbook*, 1989 Soviet Census, and *World Almanac*.

13. Joe Murray in an interview with Gamsakhurdia, "Outside the Stronghold," *Baltimore Sun*, October 30, 1991, p. 9A.

14. Galina Kovalskaia, "Kavkaztsam v Stavropole doroga zakazana," *Novoe vremia*, no. 28 (1992), pp. 8–9.

15. Zhores A. Medvedev, "Property Rights," *In These Times*, April 19, 1993, p. 29; Stephen F. Cohen, "American Policy and Russia's Future," *The Nation*, April 12, 1993, p. 480.

16. Cited by Stephen F. Cohen, *Failed Crusade: America and the Tragedy of Post-Communist Russia* (New York: W. W. Norton, 2000), p. 115.

17. Cited in Michael Specter, "From Mother Russia with Brute Force," *New York Times*, January 21, 1996, p. 6E.

18. The estimated fatalities vary widely. Among the highest, eighty thousand, is that of Michael Specter, "The Wars of Aleksandr Ivanovich Lebed," *New York Times Magazine*, October 13, 1996, p. 44.

19. "Chechnya Will Never Be Part of Russia, Top Rebel Leader Says," *Baltimore Sun*, October 7, 1996, p. 7A.

20. Comment by Sergei Karaganov to David Remnick, "The War for the Kremlin," *The New Yorker,* July 22, 1966, p. 50. In October 2000, Yeltsin, in his third book of memoirs, confirmed this scenario.

21. Remnick, "The War for the Kremlin," p. 49. Daniel Treisman, "Why Yeltsin Won," *Foreign Affairs* (September–October 1996), pp. 64–77.

22. Cohen, *Failed Crusade,* p. 49. According to World Bank figures, about one-third lived in poverty; *World Development Report 2000/2001: Attacking Poverty* (New York: Oxford University Press, 2000), p. 281.

23. Andrew Meier and Yuri Zarakhovich, "Putin Tightens His Grip," *Time,* May 29, 2000, p. 24.

24. Cited by Amy Knight, "Hit First and Hit Hard," *Times Literary Supplement,* June 9, 2000.

25. World Bank figures for Afghanistan in 1979 put it among the "low-income developing countries . . . with incomes below about a dollar per person per day." World Bank Atlas, www.worldbank.org.

26. Associated Press, "Soviets Facing Oil Crunch, CIA Director Says," *Baltimore Evening Sun,* April 22, 1980, p. A5. In September 1981, the CIA announced that the Soviet Union's energy prospects looked "highly favorable for the rest of the century." Bernard Gwertzman, "Soviet Is Able to Raise Production of Oil and Gas, US Agency Says," *New York Times,* September 3, 1981, pp. A1, D14.

27. Raymond L. Garthoff, *Détente and Revolution: American-Soviet Relations from Nixon to Reagan* (Washington, D.C.: Brookings Institution, 1985), pp. 887–965; Chalmers Johnson, "Abolish the CIA!" *London Review of Books,* October 21, 2005, p. 25.

28. Michael Dobbs, "Secret Memos Trace Kremlin's March to War," *Washington Post,* November 15, 1992, pp. A1, A32. Also the memoirs of KGB colonel Alexander Morozov, the deputy of intelligence operations in Kabul during 1975–1979, "Kabul'skii rezident," *Novoe vremia,* nos. 38–41 (1991); and "KGB i afganskie lidery," *Novoe vremia,* no. 20 (1992).

29. Gerard Chaliand, *Report from Afghanistan* (New York: Penguin, 1982), p. 49.

30. Steven Coll, *Ghost Wars: The Secret History of the CIA, Afghanistan, and bin Laden, from the Soviet Invasion to September 10, 2001* (New York: Penguin, 2004), pp. 155–156.

31. "Spravka 'NV,'" *Novoe vremia,* no. 17 (1992), p. 26.

32. Coll, *Ghost Wars,* p. 234.

33. Michael Dobbs, K. S. Karol, and Dessa Trevisan, *Poland, Solidarity, Walesa* (New York: McGraw-Hill, 1981), p. 70.

34. Andrew Cockburn, *The Threat: Inside the Soviet Military Machine,* 2nd rev. ed. (New York: Random House, 1984), pp. 111–114, 178–180; Michael T. Kaufman, "Bloc Was Prepared to Crush Solidarity, a Defector Says," *New York Times,* April 17, 1987, p. A9.

35. World Bank, *World Development Report, 1989* (Washington, D.C.: World Bank, 1989), p. 165.

36. "A Survey of Eastern Europe," *The Economist,* August 12, 1989, p. 10.

37. Craig Whitney, "East Europe Joins the Market and Gets a Preview of the Pain," *New York Times,* January 7, 1990, p. E3.

38. For the statements, see *New York Times,* December 5, 1989, p. A15.

39. Diana Jean Schemo, "Soviet Troops to Leave Czech Soil," *Baltimore Sun,* January 6, 1990, p. 2A.

40. Cited in William Pfaff, "Change in a Vulnerable Land," *Baltimore Sun,* December 22, 1989, p. 17A.

41. The death toll in Timişoara ran into several hundreds, not the 4,500 initially reported. Mary Battiata, "State's Violence Sparked Rebellion," *Washington Post*, December 31, 1989, p. A1.

42. Edward Behr, *Kiss the Hand You Cannot Bite: The Rise and Fall of the Ceauşescus* (New York: Villard Books, 1991), chapter 13, pp. 251–268. Behr cites a Romanian proverb: "A change of rulers is the joy of fools." Antonia Rados, *Die Verschwörung der Securitate: Rumäniens verratene Revolution* (Hamburg: Hoffmann und Campe, 1990); Bartholomäus Grill, "Revolution der Funktionäre," *Die Zeit*, January 11, 1991, p. 30.

43. William Pfaff, "Romania Moves Forward to the Past," *Baltimore Sun*, June 21, 1990, p. 11A; Associated Press, "Iliescu Inaugurated with Pledge to Defend Democracy," *Baltimore Sun*, June 21, 1990, p. 4A.

44. New York Times News Service, "Romanian Voters Look Both Left and Right," *Baltimore Sun*, November 26, 2000, p. 29A.

45. June 28 is St. Vitus' Day. It was on that day in 1914 that Gavrilo Princip, a member of the Serb nationalist group the Black Hand, assassinated the heir to the Austrian throne, Francis Ferdinand, touching off World War I.

46. Helsinki Commission on Security and Cooperation in Europe, *The Referendum on Independence in Bosnia-Herzegovina, February 29–March 1, 1992* (Washington, D.C.: US Government Printing Office, 1992), p. 3.

47. Robert Block, "The Madness of General Mladić," *New York Review of Books*, October 5, 1995, pp. 7–9.

48. Charles Lane and Thom Shanker, "Bosnia: What the CIA Didn't Tell Us," *New York Review of Books*, May 9, 1996, pp. 10–15.

49. Commission on Security and Cooperation in Europe, "Prosecuting War Crimes in the Former Yugoslavia: An Update," *CSCE Digest* (May 1996), pp. 13, 21–27.

50. Kemal Kurspahic, former editor-in-chief of the Sarajevo daily *Oslobodjenje*, ". . . And Don't Divide Bosnia," *Washington Post*, September 8, 1995, p. A25.

51. Figures by the United Nations High Commissioner for Refugees, "Doors Slam," *The Economist*, September 28, 1996, p. 64.

52. Mark Kramer, "Welcome to Kosova, the Next Failed State?" *Washington Post*, March 2, 2008, p. B3.

19 The Proliferating Nuclear Arms Race

The Cold War of the 1950s and early 1960s produced an unchecked deadly nuclear arms race in which neither the United States nor the Soviet Union dared fall behind the other. Each advance in size of nuclear arsenals or weapons technology had to be matched by the other side. Various studies in the first three decades of the nuclear arms race concluded that 200–300 nuclear warheads could utterly destroy the Soviet Union or the United States. The strategic arsenals had thus taken on fantastically destructive dimensions. Nuclear weapons were useful only as defensive deterrents, but they could not be used offensively in a first strike without inviting certain retaliation. "Overkill," the ability to destroy the enemy several times over, had become institutionalized—and thus rationalized.

The deployment and stockpiling of nuclear weapons became the goal. In 1964, Secretary of Defense Robert McNamara acknowledged that a nuclear force of 400 megatons (the equivalent of 4,000 million tons of TNT) was enough to sustain a balance of terror known as Mutually Assured Destruction (also known by its acronym, MAD). Yet, at the time, the United States possessed 17,000 megatons, or more than forty times the amount deemed necessary to destroy its superpower enemy. The irony of the nuclear arms race was that the fear of destruction called for a continuing strategy of building ever larger and better—more powerful and more accurate—weapons.

Another factor that drove the nuclear escalation was that nuclear weapons were relatively cheap, as compared to the costs of maintaining, equipping, and deploying large armed forces. Atomic bombs, it was often argued, provided "more bang for the buck." The bombs themselves, indeed, were relatively cheap to produce. In 1998, a Brookings Institution study showed, however, that the stages leading to nuclear deployment—research, development, manufacture, deployment itself, command and control, defense, and dismantlement—had cost the United States since 1940 a staggering $5.8 trillion, an average of $21,646 per citizen.[1]

Throughout the nuclear arms race, the United States maintained the lead despite political rhetoric depicting bomber and missile gaps favoring the Soviet Union. Presidential candidate John F. Kennedy charged that the Eisenhower administration had been asleep at the helm and permitted the Soviets to forge ahead in the missile race. It was an argument laid to rest shortly after Kennedy's election, when the Pentagon announced in 1961 that the United States possessed a second-strike capability—that is, the ability to retaliate—that was more powerful than a potential Soviet first strike. The hard cold fact of US ascendancy, coupled with the Soviets' humiliation during the Cuban missile crisis the following year, put two items on the Kremlin agenda: closing the gap favoring the United States, and negotiating with Washington to establish nuclear parity between the two superpowers. The immediate consequence of the Cuban missile crisis, however, was actually a gradual improvement in East-West relations. Détente during the late 1960s and the early 1970s then produced a number of US-Soviet treaties to limit escalation of the nuclear arms race. The first such treaty was a partial Nuclear Test Ban Treaty in 1963, which prohibited nuclear testing in the atmosphere, in outer space, and on the high seas. The United States and Soviet Union then took nuclear weapons tests underground, thus limiting environmental contamination. More than 100 other nations also signed the treaty. Notable exceptions were France, already a nuclear power, and Communist China, soon to become one (it exploded an atomic bomb in 1964). Both countries signed this treaty in 1992.

Additional agreements soon followed. These included the Outer Space Treaty (1967), which banned nuclear weapons in space and in Earth orbit; the Nuclear Non-Proliferation Treaty (1968), by which the Soviet Union, United States, Great Britain, and eighty-three other nations pledged to prevent the spread of nuclear weapons and technology; the Seabed Pact (1971), which prohibited nuclear arms on the ocean floors beyond a nation's twelve-mile limit; and the Biological Warfare Treaty (1972), which outlawed the development, production, and stockpiling of biological weapons.

The SALT Treaties

Nonetheless, the superpowers continued to add to their nuclear arsenals by developing and testing new weapons and by adding warheads. Toward the end of the decade, the governments of the United States and Soviet Union, seeing the need for renewed efforts to control the open-ended arms race, initiated the negotiations known as the Strategic Arms Limitation Talks (SALT). Their purpose was to limit—and eventually abolish—a costly and potentially catastrophic nuclear arms race. When negotiations began during the late 1960s, both sides had more than enough weapons to destroy the other side many times over. SALT negotiations were meant to bring an element of control and rationality to the arms race.

President Richard Nixon and Communist Party chief Leonid Brezhnev signed the first SALT Treaty (known as SALT I) in Moscow in May 1972. Its aim was modest: a limit on the deployment of strategic weapons that have a range of 6,000 miles and include the intercontinental bomber forces, intercontinental ballistic missiles (ICBMs), and submarine-launched ballistic missiles (SLBMs). SALT I, however, did not put a dent in either side's nuclear arsenal; it merely placed a ceiling on the destructive power that each side possessed. But SALT I marked the beginning of a process of mutual consultation. The negotiators expressed hope that subsequent treaties would address the more difficult problem of actually *reducing* the numbers of weapons in the superpowers' nuclear arsenals.

GLOSSARY

ABM antiballistic missile; a defensive missile to destroy incoming enemy missiles

ASAT antisatellite missile; a missile to neutralize satellites in Earth orbit; a central component of Star Wars

ICBM intercontinental ballistic missile

INF intermediate-range nuclear forces; see "theater weapons," below

IRBM intermediate-range ballistic missile (such as the Pershing II and the SS-20)

MIRV multiple independently targeted reentry vehicle; a missile carrying several smaller missiles, each capable of reaching a different target

NMD National Missile Defense; US program for an antimissile defense system; a scaled-down version of SDI

NPT Nuclear Non-Proliferation Treaty

payload destructive power of a warhead, measured in megatonnage (1 megaton equals 1 million tons of TNT; 1 kiloton equals 1,000 tons of TNT); a bomb with an explosive force of about 12 kilotons destroyed Hiroshima, where at least 70,000 people died; in the 1970s, US strategic warheads carried an average payload of more than 4 megatons, or more than 300 times the Hiroshima bomb; the warheads of the Soviet Union were even larger

SALT Strategic Arms Limitations Treaty; the emphasis is on strategic and limitations

SDI Strategic Defense Initiative; the official name of Star Wars

SLBM submarine-launched ballistic missile

START Strategic Arms Reduction Treaty; the emphasis is on reduction rather than limitation

strategic weapons warheads carried over long distances (usually over 3,000 miles); they include intercontinental missiles, bombers, and submarine-launched missiles

tactical weapons short-range nuclear battlefield weapons (such as artillery shells)

theater weapons intermediate-range weapons for use in a specific global region, or theater (such as Europe or the Far East); also known as INF

warhead a nuclear bomb

SALT I froze the existing number of land-based ICBMs, leaving the Soviet Union with a numerical advantage in ICBMs: 1,398 to 1,052. The Nixon administration, to appease domestic critics, argued that the agreement had prevented the buildup of the Soviet Union's latest surface-to-surface missile, the powerful SS-9.[2] Moreover, the treaty offered the United States several advantages. It ignored the questions of US intercontinental bombers (in which the United States always enjoyed a marked superiority), US intermediate-range missiles in Europe (which became a major issue during the early 1980s), and the French and British arsenals. The Soviets also accepted, if only for the time being, a US advantage in the number of strategic warheads, with the United States having twice as many as the Soviets.

But the treaty did not limit MIRVs (multiple independently targeted reentry vehicles), which gave missiles the capability to carry several warheads, each of which could destroy a separate target. When MIRVed, the missile—the expensive component—carries multiple warheads, the less expensive components. During the SALT I negotiations, the United States had refused to discuss the Soviet proposal of banning MIRVed missiles, as it saw no reason to give up its most significant nuclear weapon advantage. US negotiators soon had reasons to regret this decision, however.

SALT I was not expected to halt the arms race. For one thing, it did not prevent improvement in the quality of weapons, which continued to become increasingly more sophisticated and destructive. The emphasis on limiting launchers (bombers, missiles, and submarines) made less and less sense, since such launchers, especially missiles, were beginning to carry more warheads, the component that actually causes the damage. By the mid-1970s, the Soviet Union had deployed its own MIRVed missiles. MIRV technology thus began to work to the Soviet Union's advantage, because its ICBMs were larger and much more powerful compared to US ICBMs. Soviet missiles were able to carry up to thirty warheads; in contrast, the heaviest US ICBM, the Minuteman III, carried only three. SALT II, which negotiators hammered out by 1979, therefore attempted to limit not only launchers but also the number of warheads by placing a ceiling on the number of missiles that could be MIRVed.

Leonid Brezhnev and Jimmy Carter met in Vienna in June 1979 to sign SALT II. It created a ceiling for each side, 2,400 missile launchers each, of which only 1,320 could be fitted with MIRVs. It also limited the number of warheads that an ICBM could carry to ten. SALT II thus created a cap to blunt the Soviet Union's strategic strength, its land-based ICBMs. But it also perpetuated the Soviet Union's 5:2 advantage in ICBM warheads. US advocates of SALT II argued that the gap in this category would have been much wider had it not been for the treaty. Nevertheless, SALT II gave Washington the decided advantage in other categories, particularly submarine-launched ballistic missiles (SLBMs).

The signing ceremony proved to be the last act of détente. By that time a climate of mutual suspicion had already set in. US critics of negotiations with the Soviet Union were becoming increasingly vocal. They argued that the Soviet Union could not have it both ways: It could not maintain normal relations with the West while also supporting revolutionary movements in Africa and Asia. Détente, these critics insisted, must be tied to improved Soviet behavior, especially abroad. The international climate worsened when, in November 1979, the US hostage crisis in Iran shocked the world. Some even blamed the Soviet Union for this event. Moreover, in December the Soviet Union invaded Afghanistan.

Even more important than Soviet behavior abroad was the allegation that détente and the SALT treaties had made it possible for the Soviet Union to surpass the United States in the arms race. The most vocal critic of détente by 1980 was the Republican presidential hopeful Ronald Reagan, who declared that the SALT treaties had opened a "window of vulnerability" and that only one side, the Soviet Union, was engaged in the arms race. The United States, he declared, had in effect disarmed itself unilaterally. Reagan gained considerable traction with this political argument, but, in fact, during the 1970s the United States had doubled its strategic arsenal. By the time of the 1980 presidential election, the Soviet Union had narrowed the nuclear weapons gap, but the United States continued to lead. It had never been a race with only one contestant.

Nuclear arms negotiations became a casualty of the renewed Cold War. The US Senate never ratified SALT II, in part because critics such as Reagan had hammered home the point that it favored the Soviet Union. Once Reagan became president, however, he gave tacit recognition to the fact that SALT had, after all, placed a limit on the Soviet Union's strategic strength, a fact the Joint Chiefs of Staff acknowledged when it urged the treaty's ratification, calling it "a modest but useful step."[3] Reagan agreed to abide by the unratified terms of SALT II for the next five years.

The Correlation of Forces

By the mid-1980s, the United States and Soviet Union had roughly the same number of deliverable nuclear warheads. The configurations of their delivery systems, however, were different. The Soviet Union placed its faith in a nuclear "triad" that consisted of 65 percent of warheads in land-based missiles, 27 percent in submarines, and a scant 8 percent (an amount sufficient to destroy the United States, however) in intercontinental bombers.

The Soviet Union relied largely on powerful land-based ICBMs, equipped with up to ten warheads. US missiles were smaller and contained less powerful, but more accurate, warheads. The Soviet Union, because its missiles were less accurate, relied on larger missiles and thus enjoyed an advantage in "payload," or "megatonnage." As missiles became increasingly accurate, however, both sides reduced their respective megatonnages. The United States, because of its more accurate missiles, did not need to build large warheads. Thus, if one focused on payload, then the Soviet Union was ahead in the arms race; but if one took into account accuracy, then the advantage went to the United States.

In contrast to the Soviet Union, the United States had a more balanced (and thus sensible) strategic "triad": 51 percent of warheads were deployed in submarines, 30 percent in its intercontinental bomber force, and only 19 percent in land-based missiles. Should the Soviets choose to knock out any single leg of the US nuclear triad, the retaliatory power of one or the other two provided a credible and powerful second-strike deterrent. Moreover, unlike Soviet warheads, most US warheads were not stationary targets on land, whose location was known to spy satellites in orbit, but instead were constantly on the move in the world's oceans.

All of this caused problems for determining an equitable formula in the attempt to stem the arms race. The Soviet Union, with its massive land-based force, was not about to negotiate away its strength.[4] Yet missiles deployed in the ground were inviting targets, as they were most vulnerable. Although powerful and deadly once they were launched, the Soviets' ground-based ICBMs used liquid fuel and were thus slow to fire. US missiles, in contrast, used a solid-fuel propellant and thus could be fired virtually at will. For this reason, the Soviet Union moved toward deploying smaller, mobile, solid-fuel ICBMs. Mobile ICBMs promised to add new elements to the arms race: increasing difficulty in verification and the ability to respond quickly.

During the first half of the 1980s, there was no progress toward nuclear disarmament; instead, both sides produced greater numbers of ever more accurate nuclear weapons at a furious pace. In December 1981, the Soviet Union walked out of arms-reduction talks in Geneva when it failed to halt the deployment of US intermediate-range missiles (Pershing IIs) as well as cruise missiles. Talks were not resumed until March 1985. During the intervening forty months, both sides added approximately one new warhead every day to their strategic arsenals—not including intermediate-range weapons, which both sides continued to deploy. In all, during the first half of the 1980s, each side added more than 2,000 strategic warheads to already bloated arsenals.

In the mid-1980s, the United States possessed the capability of destroying the Soviet Union fifty times with its strategic arsenal alone (see Table 19.1). US strategic planners ran out of targets. The surfeit of atomic warheads made possible the luxury of targeting grain elevators in Ukraine as well as open fields that Soviet bombers could conceivably use—their airfields having been destroyed—on their return trips from the United States.[5] The Soviet Union's ability to destroy the United States was no different. The pointlessness of continu-

Table 19.1   US and Soviet Strategic Arsenal, 1985

Weapon Carrier	Number of Warheads	Percentage of Strategic Arsenal
United States		
1,025 ICBMs	2,125	19
36 submarines with 640 missiles	5,728	51
263 B-52 bombers, 98 of which carry		
12 cruise missiles each	3,072	27
61 FB-111 bombers	366	3
Total	11,291	100
Soviet Union		
1,398 ICBMs	6,420	65
62 submarines with 924 missiles	2,688	27
173 bombers, 25 of which carry		
10 cruise missiles each	792	8
Total	9,900	100

Source: *New York Times,* October 4, 1985. All figures are estimates of classified information. They were compiled from Pentagon publications, the International Institute for Strategic Studies, the Arms Control Association, and the Center for Defense Information.

ously adding to the nuclear arsenals led Henry Kissinger to ask in 1974: "What in the name of God is strategic superiority? . . . What do you do with it?"[6]

Intermediate-Range Weapons

The late 1970s saw the end of détente. The reasons for the deterioration of relations between the Soviet Union and the West were many. One factor, however, was the lack of understanding by the Soviets of the US definition of détente. In the US state of mind, détente was always linked to a change in Soviet behavior. For Soviets, however, détente meant Western acceptance of the Soviet Union as a major power, an equal of the United States—and with it an acceptance of the global role that a great power traditionally plays. After all, the Soviets argued, they had normalized US-Soviet relations at a time when the United States was engaged in a war against "international Communism" in Vietnam. From the US viewpoint, however, the cessation of Soviet aggression, particularly in Afghanistan, was a precondition to maintaining détente. The Soviets complained that, for them, détente had been more important than Vietnam; but for the United States, Afghanistan was more important than détente.[7] With détente at an end, the arms race began to take more ominous turns. The introduction of an increasingly sophisticated generation of intermediate-range nuclear weapons added to the complexity of the debate on how to limit these weapons.

The Europeans, and the Soviets in particular, with their record of suffering and defeat, had a better understanding than most people in the United

States that history is all too often tragedy. The destruction wreaked by World War II, a conventional war fought with primitive weapons by modern standards, remained a recent memory. Berlin, Stalingrad, and many other cities contained the ruins of enemy firepower, only now they were memorials and museum displays depicting that war and the attendant suffering. The persistence to negotiate, if only to limit the arms race, was a mute tribute to the uncomfortable fact that a nuclear war could have no winners. The ruins of the Soviet Union and Germany in 1945 did not reveal which country had won the war and which had lost the war.

From the early 1960s, both sides accumulated an ever larger arsenal of intermediate-range nuclear arms. Military strategists saw Europe as the most likely theater where such weapons might be used. To deal with this eventuality, the Soviets put into place their most sophisticated medium-range missiles—the mobile SS-20s—capable of reaching, and devastating, every capital city in Europe.

The SS-20 was a significant improvement over the older, single-warhead, liquid-fuel SS-4s and SS-5s. It had a range greater than 3,000 miles, it was mobile, it could house three independently targeted warheads, and it used a solid-fuel engine that could be fired quickly. This new addition to the Kremlin's military might produced a psychological shock among Western military strategists. The SS-20 did not change the nuclear balance, but it did give the appearance of a Soviet escalation of the arms race, a perception that was largely correct.

The United States responded, predictably, with its own intermediate-range weapons in Europe, the Tomahawk cruise missile and the Pershing II ballistic missile. Slow-moving, cruise missiles hug the ground during target approach and are therefore difficult to detect and destroy in flight. With a range of perhaps 2,000 miles at that time, cruise missiles were capable of reaching the Soviet Union from West European soil. The Pershing II was a fast-flying missile with a range greater than 1,100 miles. Its mobility, range, accuracy, and speed made it one of the premier weapons in the US arsenal. It was a potential first-strike weapon suitable for the elimination, or "decapitation," of Soviet command structures. The distinction between "strategic" and "theater" missiles became increasingly blurred. What was the difference, for example, between a Minuteman missile fired from Wyoming (thirty minutes' flying time to a Soviet target) and a Pershing II missile fired from West Germany (six minutes' flying time)?

This leg of the arms race was filled with such irony, something all participants in this dangerous game realized. The United States was first to understand this strange twist of logic. The atomic bomb had given the United States the "ultimate weapon," only to subject the country to the prospect of nuclear annihilation within ten short years. Similarly, the SS-20 briefly gave the Kremlin an advantage in case of a nuclear exchange in Europe—provided the contest could be limited to Europe, a most unlikely prospect. When the United States countered with the deployment of increasingly dangerous weapons, the Soviet Union became less secure.

To be effective, US intermediate-range missiles had to be stationed on European soil. Presidents Carter and Reagan had their work cut out in selling their deployment to their NATO allies. The Europeans understood all too well that both the Soviet and US arsenals threatened to turn Europe into a nuclear shooting gallery—particularly after President Reagan said, "I could see where you could have the exchange of tactical weapons in the field [in Europe] without it bringing either one of the major powers to pushing the [strategic] button"[8] and unleashing a full nuclear exchange. The very mention of fighting a limited nuclear war in Europe split apart NATO. Still, the United States was able to convince several European allies to accept 464 cruise missiles and 108 Pershing IIs.[9]

This round of escalation produced a series of discussions at Geneva beginning in spring 1981. Each side sought to eliminate the other's missiles while also holding on to what it had. It was a prescription for deadlock. Negotiators, instead of seeking compromises, played to larger audiences, notably the people back home and the nervous Europeans. Propaganda and accusations of bad faith became the order of the day.

The two chief negotiators, Yuli Kvitsinsky for the Soviet Union and Paul Nitze for the United States, did manage to agree to a compromise, the so-called walk-in-the-woods proposal. It called for a rough balance between the Soviet Union's seventy-five SS-20s (each carrying three warheads) and the United States' seventy-five Tomahawk cruise missiles (each with four warheads). By this agreement, the Soviets would have had to curtail, but not scrap, the deployment of their SS-20s, while the United States would have had to forgo the deployment of its Pershing IIs. Hard-liners in Moscow and Washington quickly denounced this attempt at compromise. In December 1981, the Soviets left the conference table when the United States proceeded to deploy on schedule the first cruise missiles and Pershing IIs in Great Britain and West Germany, respectively. The deadlock lasted three and a half years; in the meantime, missile deployment accelerated.

In April 1985, about a month after the Soviet and US negotiators had resumed talks in Geneva, the new Soviet leader, Mikhail Gorbachev, announced a freeze on further deployment of SS-20s until November 1985, provided that the United States halt deployment of missiles in NATO countries. Yet there was nothing in Gorbachev's proposal suggesting a reduction of the Soviet arsenal—its deployment largely completed. The Soviet gesture was too little, too late. Instead of facing seventy-five slow-moving cruise missiles, as proposed during the "walk in the woods," the Soviets now faced fifty-four deadly Pershing IIs and forty-eight cruise missiles, with the prospect of more to come. Western Europe faced 250 of the Soviet Union's 414 SS-20s.

Star Wars: The Strategic Defense Initiative

In March 1983, the arms race took another twist when President Reagan went public with a military research program long on the drawing board. It was a missile defense system officially called the Strategic Defense Initiative (SDI), commonly referred to as "Star Wars." Its purpose was to protect US land-based missiles in the event that the Soviet Union struck first with its powerful and accurate land-based ICBMs, notably the SS-18s. With this pronouncement, Reagan officially committed the United States to creating an entirely new and futuristic kind of defense system. The research program was now no longer a scientific quest for a hypothetical defensive weapon. Instead, the United States committed its resources to finding a technological breakthrough to disarm—if only partially and indirectly—the Soviet nuclear arsenal.

Thus far, the avoidance of all-out nuclear war had been based on deterrence—the balance of terror—based on the assumption that neither side wanted to commit suicide. The deterrence strategy (MAD) had, in fact, worked to prevent nuclear war. This balance of terror had kept the peace.

In the late 1960s, the Soviets had entertained the idea of creating a defensive shield, which, however, was unacceptable to the United States. US officials warned that a Soviet deployment of such a shield would lead to the deployment of US countermeasures. The United States could simply increase its number of warheads to overwhelm the Soviet protective shield. This would mean a new round of escalation in the nuclear arms race, one that promised no security for anyone. The United States prevailed upon the Soviet Union to abandon its missile defense program. The resultant accord, the Anti-Ballistic Missile (ABM) Treaty (1972), permitted both sides to create two *limited* defensive systems each, which neither bothered to develop fully.

The ABM Treaty became part and parcel of SALT, without which SALT I would have been impossible. The United States was not about to sign any agreement whereby it agreed to freeze its missile strength while sitting by idly as the Soviets took unilateral steps to put in place a defensive shield designed to neutralize the US strategic arsenal. Once the Soviets understood this fact, the door was opened for the ratification of SALT I and the limited ABM Treaty. The simple, brutal deterrent of Mutually Assured Destruction remained intact.

In March 1983, eleven years after the superpowers had agreed to limit their nuclear firepower and antimissile defenses, Reagan announced plans to build a highly complex defensive system within the next twenty-five years. Reagan had never been comfortable with arms agreements that accepted Soviet parity with the United States. That and his unlimited faith in US ingenuity and know-how led him to opt for a program that, he argued, would protect the United States and its allies and not cause an escalation of the arms race.

Reagan's proposal challenged the underlying strategy of MAD. It was immoral, he insisted, to rely on a military strategy predicated on the potential annihilation of the United States. A high-tech barrier that could shoot down missiles before they reached their targets, he argued, would make nuclear war impossible. In fact, he went so far as to suggest that once US scientists had solved the riddle of how to intercept incoming Soviet ICBMs, the US government would hand over the secret to the Soviets. Nuclear war would then become impossible and peace would prevail. The ultimate goal, President Reagan said, was "to eliminate the weapons themselves."[10]

Star Wars played to mixed reviews. Its theoretical underpinnings could not be faulted. But there were serious problems in implementing a missile defense of such staggering complexity. First, to be effective it would have to be nearly perfect. Since merely 2 percent of the Soviet Union's existing strategic arsenal could destroy the United States, a 90 percent efficiency in the Star Wars defense system—which, according to some scientists, was the best that could be gained—would not do. Mutually Assured Destruction, therefore, would continue to prevail, for 10 percent of 10,000 Soviet warheads would destroy the United States several times over. Nevertheless, even if only 90 percent effective, Star Wars threatened to bring about the unilateral neutralization of a sizable portion of the Kremlin's arsenal, something it could not abide.

Second, Star Wars promised to contribute to another escalation of the arms race, for the Soviets threatened to produce an ever-increasing number of warheads. In short, the Soviets were being given the alternative of accepting US nuclear superiority or of deploying enough weapons capable of overwhelming the Star Wars defense.

Third, there was the staggering cost. Reagan requested a budget of $30 billion ($3.7 billion for fiscal 1986) for research and development during the first five years. There was doubt whether the US government, already running a record deficit of more than $200 billion per year, could readily afford the program.

Fourth, there was the complexity of the system. Star Wars called for a new generation of sensors for the surveillance, tracking, and destruction of enemy missiles. They would have to work flawlessly to discriminate among thousands of incoming warheads and decoys. The program also envisioned the deployment of energy weapons, consisting primarily of powerful lasers, based either on the ground (and deflected by huge mirrors circling the planet) or in orbit. The most crucial part of the entire program, "systems concepts and battle management," called for an error-free computer system that instantaneously linked the system's diverse elements.[11]

Fifth, ways had to be found to protect the system from destruction by hostile elements. Mirrors and spy satellites in orbit would be inviting targets that could be neutralized easily. They would have to be defended somehow.

And finally, Soviet scientists were sure to work overtime to find ways over, under, around, and through any missile defense envisioned by their US counterparts.

In light of these obstacles, it was little wonder that Pentagon officials told Congress, which had to finance all of this, that this was a long-range program of at least twenty-five years' duration. There was soon talk, however, of an "interim deployment" to protect land-based missiles. This put first things first; civilians would have to wait. Former defense secretary Harold Brown admitted that "technology does not offer even a reasonable prospect of a population defense."[12]

Some domestic critics of Star Wars feared that it would militarize space and add little security. Its deployment promised an open-ended contest in space. *Pravda* repeatedly warned that the Kremlin would not accept the existence of Star Wars. Instead, the Kremlin threatened to join the race into space. Reagan's secretary of defense, Caspar Weinberger, when asked how he would view a unilateral deployment of a Soviet version of Star Wars, replied that such an act "would be one of the most frightening prospects I could imagine."[13]

Gorbachev's Peace Offensive

Mikhail Gorbachev, upon coming to power in March 1985, launched a "peace offensive." He was determined to bring about not only domestic perestroika but one in foreign relations as well. "We will rob you of your enemy," he told the West. His proposal to freeze the deployment of Soviet SS-20 intermediate-range missiles was but his first move.

Soon the world witnessed a number of summit meetings between Gorbachev and Reagan, who had previously resolutely refused to sit down with his Soviet counterparts. Brezhnev, Andropov, and Chernenko were clearly dying men; moreover, Reagan felt there had been nothing to talk about with the leaders of what he had called early in his presidency the "evil empire." The first meeting between Reagan and Gorbachev was a successful get-acquainted session in November 1985, in neutral Geneva. Several factors played a role in Reagan's turnabout. He had been criticized at home as being the first president since 1945 who had not met with Soviet leaders. He also came to realize he was dealing with a new type of Soviet man. The Reagan-Gorbachev summits led to negotiations that, in the end, produced the first reduction of nuclear armaments.

The first order of business was the recent escalation of the nuclear race in the heart of Europe: the deployment of intermediate-range nuclear forces (INF) such as US Pershing IIs and cruise missiles and Soviet SS-20s. Gorbachev surprised the Reagan administration when he suddenly dusted off an old US proposal, the zero-option: If the Soviet Union did not deploy its missiles, the United States would not counter with the deployment of its own

Radioactive substances released in the US nuclear bomb test, boiling skyward—taken from a plane directly above the blast, July 12, 1948. *(National Archives)*

rockets. Gorbachev would undo Brezhnev's error; he would take Soviet INF forces out of Europe if the United States did the same. Gorbachev had called Washington's bluff: If Reagan rejected Gorbachev's proposal to eliminate all INFs, the US position would be exposed as just another example of Cold War propaganda.

Reagan responded positively. The result—after a year of difficult negotiations—was the INF Treaty of May 1988, which eliminated an entire category of nuclear missiles, those with a range between 310 and 3,400 miles. Under the watchful eyes of onsite inspectors, the superpowers proceeded to dismantle their costly weapons—1,752 Soviet and 867 US missiles.[14]

Reagan was then able to turn to one of his favorite programs, namely, the Strategic Arms Reduction Talks (START). Early in his presidency, he had argued—correctly—that SALT had accomplished little. SALT merely kept the nuclear arms race within broad parameters, making it possible, nevertheless, for both sides to increase their strategic arsenals. When the INF Treaty was signed, the US arsenal still contained 13,134 strategic warheads, and the Soviet arsenal contained 10,664.[15] The time had come to reduce both. Reagan found a responsive partner in Gorbachev. Earlier, in October 1985, Gorbachev had already proposed a 50 percent reduction of strategic nuclear forces, which would lessen the Soviet threat to US land-based missiles. In October 1987, at their summit in Reykjavik, Iceland, Gorbachev went so far as to offer Reagan the elimination of all strategic nuclear weapons. A surprised Reagan was on the verge of accepting before his suspicious advisors interfered. They feared that a world free of nuclear weapons would leave Western Europe at the mercy of superior Soviet conventional forces.

Gorbachev was not finished with his surprises, however. On December 7, 1988, he launched another volley in his peace offensive. He announced—unilaterally and without precondition—the reduction in the Soviet armed forces by 10 percent (500,000 soldiers), as well as the elimination of 800 airplanes, 8,500 pieces of artillery, and 5,000 tanks within two years. Included in the offer was the promise to dissolve six of the fifteen divisions in East Germany, Hungary, and Czechoslovakia by 1991. But most important, Gorbachev pledged the withdrawal from central Europe of Soviet assault troops and mobile bridges for crossing rivers. Gorbachev's speech marked a 180-degree turn in Soviet military doctrine as it had existed since the early 1960s. The Soviet conventional military threat against Western Europe was scheduled to be dismantled. The East German party chief Erich Honecker recognized immediately what he called the "immense historical significance" of the Soviet troop withdrawal.[16] Gorbachev's speech also shocked many in the US defense community; some saw it as a propaganda offensive designed to disarm the West, even comparing it to Pearl Harbor.

The critics of Gorbachev's speech of December 7, 1988, were partly correct. The first casualty of that speech was the US program of "modernizing" the short-range Lance missile, a tactical nuclear weapon. The Lance II, a new weapon with a range of just under the 310-mile limit stipulated by the INF Treaty, made possible the circumvention of the spirit, if not the letter, of that treaty. The Lance II would give the United States a backdoor route to maintaining an INF arsenal.

West German politics torpedoed the Lance II "modernization" program. The powerful Social Democratic opposition party insisted that the shorter-range rockets, too, must go. "The shorter the rockets, the deader the Germans" became the West German catchphrase. In February 1989, Egon Bahr, the national security expert of the Social Democratic Party, explained to Brent Scowcroft, US president George Bush's national security advisor, that the United States had no chance of deploying the Lance II. If the conservative government in Bonn capitulated to US pressure and accepted the weapons, his party would win the next election and take them out.[17] West German foreign minister Hans-Dietrich Genscher, who was born in Halle, East Germany, and whose relatives still lived there, declared: "I have sworn an oath to avert harm from the German people and that includes East Germany."[18]

East German scientists joined the debate. Even in case of conventional war, they argued, Europe would still be contaminated with nuclear fallout. The continent contained 220 civilian nuclear reactors that, if damaged, would turn into radioactive infernos. Because of the type of fuel they used, they would emit greater doses of radiation than would atomic weapons. The large concentrations of chemical plants—along the Rhine River in Western Europe and in cities such as Halle and Leipzig in East Germany—would spew deadly poisons upon humans, plants, and animals. Even a conventional war would turn Europe into an "atomic, chemical and genetically contaminated desert." It would lead to the "destruction of what the aggressor would seek to conquer."[19]

Gorbachev stood in stark contrast to the cautious Bush, who was slow to accept the idea that he, too, could play a role in affecting the course of history in a major way. Gorbachev had been the engine of change, Bush a mere spectator. The demise of the Communist parties in Eastern Europe led to demands, in January 1990, in Czechoslovakia, Hungary, and Poland that the Soviet army leave those territories by the end of 1991. It had become a question of when, not if, Eastern Europe would live without Soviet forces. It was at this point that Bush took the initiative and proposed the reduction of US and Soviet forces to a level of 195,000 each in Central Europe. "New thinking" finally came to Washington. Even the most hawkish officials in the Pentagon had to admit that in the fourteen months since Gorbachev's speech of December 7, 1988, the Soviet Union had dismantled its capability to invade Western Europe. Bush's speech was welcome news in Warsaw, Budapest, Prague, and Moscow because it facilitated the Soviet army's withdrawal from its forward positions in Eastern Europe. The military confrontation in the heart of Europe was coming to an end.

After the last Russian combat troops stationed in Poland pulled out in October 1992, Polish president Lech Walesa declared: "Polish sovereignty has finally been confirmed." Problems related to logistics, and a lack of adequate housing at home for Russian troops and their dependents, produced a longer timetable for withdrawal from the newly independent Baltic states and East Germany. The troop departures from those two locations were finally completed by 1993 and 1994, respectively.

START

The START negotiations, begun in 1982, proceeded at a snail's pace for eight years, during which the intricacies of attaining balanced reductions in Soviet and US arsenals were debated in twelve rounds of formal negotiations, thirteen foreign ministers' meetings, and six summits. It was not until July 1991 that the treaty was ready to be signed by the heads of state.

Ironically, the signing of the treaty in Moscow was attended with little fanfare—certainly not what had been expected for the signing of one of the most important nuclear disarmament treaties, one that had reversed the forty-five-year-old strategic nuclear arms race. START seemed anticlimactic because it had been so long in coming and its main features had long since been known. Moreover, the deteriorating situation in the Soviet Union and the fading of the Soviet military threat made the treaty seem less significant. START, however, broke new ground by calling for a reduction rather than merely a limit on the growth of strategic weapons. The US arsenal would be cut from 12,646 warheads to 8,556 and the Soviet Union's from 11,012 to 6,163 by 1999. To the distinct advantage of the United States, START reduced the Soviets' heavy ICBMs by 50 percent, yet it allowed the United States to retain a three-to-one advantage in SLBMs. The treaty, however, did not place limits on nuclear weapons modernization. Thus, it left unhampered the development of weapons systems such as the US B-2 bomber and the Trident submarine, not to mention Star Wars.

By the end of 1991, the Soviet Union ceased to exist, and Washington now had to deal with Boris Yeltsin, the president of the new Russian Federation, and with the heads of the other fourteen successor states of the former Soviet Union. Yeltsin proclaimed his commitment to stand by START and the disarmament pledges made by Gorbachev. In addition to Russia, however, three of the new sovereign republics—Belarus, Ukraine, and Kazakhstan—had nuclear weapons stationed on their soil. All three announced their intention to get rid of them. Confident that Russian security was not threatened by the United States, and greatly needing to slash military costs and attain Western economic assistance, Yeltsin declared his intentions to scrap even more nuclear weapons.

At the first US-Russian (as opposed to US-Soviet) summit, in Washington in February 1992, Yeltsin joined Bush in signing a "Declaration of Friendship" and agreed to begin new negotiations for further nuclear disarmament. Four months of negotiations produced another startling agreement, one that promised far deeper cuts in strategic nuclear forces than the yet-to-be-ratified START had called for. Yeltsin, given to grandstanding, made offers that Bush could hardly refuse, and the result was a spectacular agreement. START II called for the reduction of strategic nuclear weapons on each side to 3,000–3,500 by the year 2003. This was approximately one-half of what START I allowed and amounted to a reduction of 73 percent of the existing strategic nuclear warheads. The most extraordinary feature of the Bush-Yeltsin agreement was its call for banning all MIRVed land-based missiles, leaving each side with only 500 single-warhead, land-based strategic weapons. This represented a Russian abandonment of its long-held advantage in heavy land-based missiles, which Washington had regarded as Moscow's first-strike capacity. In announcing this concession, Yeltsin stated that Russia needed only a "minimum-security level" of nuclear forces and that it was abandoning the concept of nuclear parity, which had caused Russia "to have half its population living below the poverty line."[20] In return for this concession, Bush agreed to a ceiling on SLBMs of 1,744, a 70 percent reduction.

It remained to be determined which delivery systems were to be destroyed. By the end of 1992, a compromise was reached. Russia agreed to the conversion of US strategic bombers (including the new B-2 stealth bomber) to conventional use, rather than destroying them. The United States, in its turn, agreed that Russia, as a cost-cutting measure, could keep 90 of its SS-18 silos for conversion to be used by single-warhead SS-25 missiles as well as 105 of its 170 MIRVed SS-19s (with six warheads each), provided they were refitted with single warheads. Similarly, the United States would convert its Minuteman III missile to carry but a single warhead. The compromise became possible only after each side accepted unprecedented verification procedures. Bush and Yeltsin signed START II in Moscow in January 1993, pledging their nations to return by 2003 to where they had been in the early 1970s, before the MIRVing of their missiles. As such, it was a tacit admission of the mindlessness of the nuclear arms race. Table 19.2 provides comparative data on the size of the arms reductions called for in START.

The implementation of these agreements proved to be a difficult matter, however. The ratification of START I was delayed mainly by complications caused by the breakup of the Soviet Union. Both Washington and Moscow wanted to be certain that all four former Soviet republics with strategic weapons abided by the treaty. In May 1992, the four successor states to the Soviet Union—Russia, Belarus, Ukraine, and Kazakhstan—signed a protocol making them parties to START I. They agreed to place their strategic weapons under Russian control, to remove them in accordance with the terms of START I, and then to sign the Nuclear Non-Proliferation Treaty as non-nuclear nations. Satisfied with these arrangements, the US Senate finally ratified START I in October 1992, and one month later the Russian parliament did so as well.

Table 19.2   Strategic Warhead Levels and Reduction Proposals

	Land-Based (ICBMs)	Sea-Based (SLBMs)	Air-Launched (bombers)	Totals
Levels in 1991				
US	2,450	5,760	4,436	12,646
USSR	6,612	2,804	1,596	11,012
				23,658
START I, to be implemented by 1999; a reduction of 38% from the 1991 levels				
US	1,400	3,456	3,700	8,556
USSR	3,153	1,744	1,266	6,163
				14,719
START II, to be implemented by 2003; a reduction of 73% from the 1991 levels				
US	500	1,728	1,272	3,500
Russia	500	1,744	752	2,996
				6,496

Ukraine, in contrast to earlier professed intentions of becoming a nuclear-free nation, had second thoughts about giving up its nuclear weapons without something in return, namely, substantial financial assistance for its struggling economy. The Ukrainian wish to be paid to disarm pointed to an additional, unforeseen problem accompanying the removal and destruction of thousands of missiles: its high cost. The former Soviet republics (Russia included) could ill afford the cost of dismantling so many missiles. In order to facilitate the process, Washington pledged some $800 million to that end.

But it was only a down payment. There was still the cost of environmental cleanup. One estimate to clean up the nuclear weapons environmental mess in the United States alone was $300 billion.[21] In the former Soviet Union, environmental pollution and safety hazards at many of its nuclear weapons sites had reached crisis proportions. Once these costs were factored in, nuclear weapons did not turn out, after all, to be the financial bargain their defenders had claimed.

The US Senate ratified START II in January 1996; in Russia, however, the treaty ran into opposition. Nationalists and Communists stressed that START II sold out Russian interests. The ultranationalist Vladimir Zhirinovsky, leader of the Liberal Democratic Party—the second largest in the Duma (parliament)—glossed over the fact that the treaty called for parity between the United States and Russia and charged that the reduction of nuclear weapons "makes Russia a secondary state." His party would not ratify an agreement that would "humiliate, insult or limit Russia as a great nation."[22]

It was not until shortly after Vladimir Putin's election as president in March 2000 that the Duma ratified START II. Putin also managed to obtain the ratification of the Comprehensive Nuclear Test Ban Treaty.

The Expansion of NATO into Eastern Europe

When Mikhail Gorbachev agreed to withdraw Soviet troops from Eastern Europe, he insisted—and George H. W. Bush agreed—that the region remain a neutral buffer between the NATO powers and the Soviet Union. NATO was not to expand into a military vacuum once occupied by the Warsaw Pact. But then came the sudden end of the Soviet Union, after which Poland, Hungary, and the Czech Republic asked for membership in NATO as insurance against renewed Russian military ambitions.

Washington and its NATO allies tried to present the expansion into these formerly Soviet bloc nations as benign, meant largely to shore up democracy in Eastern Europe and somehow "strengthen European security." But the Russians well remembered the numerous invasions of their land from the west—through Germany and Poland. In June 1996, at a Berlin meeting of the foreign ministers of the sixteen NATO nations, Russian foreign minister Yevgeny Primakov warned that NATO expansion was "unacceptable."

Table 19.3   Estimated Nuclear Warheads, Select Countries

	Early 1990s	2008	2012
United States[a]	9,680	3,575	1,700–2,200[b]
Russia[a]	10,996	3,340	1,700–2,200[b]
Britain	260	160	160
France	100–200	348	300
China	100–200	200	modernizing
India	not available	50–60	building more
Pakistan	not available	30–50	following India's example
Israel	100–200	100–200	never officially declared
Iran	none	2–10 years away from capability	
North Korea	1–2	up to 10	pledged to giving them up

Sources: Bulletin of the Atomic Scientists; International Institute for Strategic Studies; Stockholm International Peace Research Institute; *The Economist*, "Just How Low Can You Go?" March 27, 2008.

Notes: a. Strategic warheads only.

b. Maximum permitted under the Strategic Offensive Reductions Treaty (SORT), signed by Vladimir Putin and George W. Bush in May 2002; ratified in 2003.

Gorbachev joined the debate by pointing out that the agreement regulating the Soviet withdrawal from East Germany had demanded that East German troops not be integrated into the unified German army. The "borders" of NATO must not expand. Such a move could only have one meaning—namely, the isolation of Russia from Europe, resulting in "highly unpredictable consequences."[23]

US president Bill Clinton paid no heed to these warnings, however, and in 1999 he helped complete the first expansion of NATO into the former Soviet bloc when it offered full membership to Poland, the Czech Republic, and Hungary. There was not much Moscow could do except to put on hold the ratification of START II. NATO's ambitious move came at a time when Russia still suffered from severe economic problems, much of its military-industrial complex was dismantled, and its conventional forces were severely reduced.

NATO, which had been created to check the Soviet military across the Iron Curtain, now had a new, amorphous mission, despite the fact that there was no longer an Iron Curtain, a Soviet military in Eastern Europe, or a Soviet Union. It created a new military line dividing Europe, this one farther to the east. Yeltsin (as well as Gorbachev) bitterly complained, but with Russia still suffering from the consequences of a historic economic meltdown, he was unable to check NATO's ambitions. All he managed to obtain was a pledge from Clinton that NATO would not expand all the way to the borders of Russia.

The critics of NATO expansion were not given a hearing. In June 1997, the conservative Arms Control Association sent an open—and prescient—

letter to Clinton warning that an expansion of NATO was "a policy error of historic proportions." Russia did not "pose a threat to its western neighbors"; moreover, an enlargement could draw NATO into "countries with serious border and national minority problems."

The next US administration, under George W. Bush, heedless of the consequences, pushed for another round of NATO expansion in March 2004, which would reach to Russia's border by bringing in the former Soviet republics of Lithuania, Latvia, and Estonia (as well as Slovenia, Slovakia, Romania, and Bulgaria).

One of the arguments used to justify NATO's eastward expansion was that it would shore up the newly formed democratic institutions in Eastern Europe. The European Union, however, with its insistence that its members be democracies (never a criterion for NATO membership), was a better vehicle to that end. Putin had no choice but to swallow this bitter pill since there was nothing he could do about it. But then came a further attempt, by the Bush administration, to push NATO ever farther eastward when it offered membership to Georgia and Ukraine. By this time, Russia's economic and military fortunes had undergone a recovery. Putin announced that he would take measures— unspecified—to prevent further NATO expansion.

The Bush administration took yet another step the Kremlin looked on with great misgiving when he proposed placing in the Czech Republic and Poland an anti–ballistic missile system, ostensibly directed against Iran. It was an argument, however, that Russia's leaders were unwilling to accept. Instead, they saw it as another NATO initiative directed at them.

Once Bush had pushed the enlargement of NATO up to Russia's borders, his next aim was to go even deeper into Eastern Europe—into Ukraine and into the Caucasus region, along Russia's southern border. Simultaneously, he scuttled the Anti-Ballistic Missile Treaty (without which there could have been no strategic arms limitation and reduction treaties). Moscow ominously spoke of consequences.

Russia had other grievances. In 1999, Clinton had managed to wrest the province of Kosovo from the control of Serbia, historically an ally of Russia, and in February 2008, under the prodding of the Bush administration, the West recognized Kosovo as a sovereign state. In 2008, a resurgent Russia (primarily thanks to climbing energy prices) repeated the warning that Russia would not tolerate NATO expansion into the Caucasus (or Ukraine). If the trans-Caucasus was destined to be someone's security zone, it would be Russia's. In May 2008, even Mikhail Gorbachev accused the Bush administration of deliberately undermining hopes for a permanent peace with Russia. He recalled the pledges of the past that NATO would not expand beyond Germany. "What happened to their promises?" he asked, suggesting that it appeared that "every US president has to have a war."[24]

Georgia, led by its US-educated president, Mikheil Saakashvili, sought entry into NATO but was blocked—primarily by Germany and other West European NATO members—at the Bucharest NATO meeting in April 2008. This did not prevent the Bush administration from continuing to press for Georgian and Ukrainian membership. Saakashvili—who treated Vladimir Putin with disdain, a feeling Putin openly reciprocated—insisted that Georgia needed NATO protection to prevent it from suffering the same fate as Czechoslovakia in 1938.

The issue was put to the test by the Russo-Georgian war of August 2008. The immediate issue was South Ossetia and Abkhazia, the de facto independent breakaway provinces of Georgia openly backed by Russia. For reasons difficult to fathom, Saakashvili, the president of a country of 4.6 million people—and fewer yet if one excludes the residents of Abkhazia and South Ossetia—sent his army into South Ossetia. The Russian tanks had little difficulty in scattering the Georgian army, in part trained by US special forces. After the war, the Russians declared that Abkhazia and South Ossetia were now independent nations, adding that they were only doing what NATO had done in Kosovo.

The Bush administration complained but—tied down in Afghanistan and Iraq—was unable to act. Washington faced a choice: bring Georgia into NATO and with it bring the United States into a state of war with Russia, or accept the reassertion of the Kremlin's power in what had for centuries been Moscow's sphere of influence. The recent expansion of US military power across the globe had not taught the Russians the lessons US geopoliticians had wanted them to learn. The relative stability during the Cold War was not replaced by a genuine peace but with another round of superpower confrontations.

National Missile Defense

With the end of the Cold War, Star Wars appeared to be dead, although successive administrations continued to fund the research project at about $3–4 billion per year. But then a coalition of political conservatives, the aerospace industry, and the Pentagon sought to deploy a more modest version of it, now dubbed the National Missile Defense (NMD) system. The cost of NMD, projected at about $60 billion, was not cheap, yet it was a far cry from the estimated price tag for SDI, up to $1 trillion. Its aim was also more modest; it was designed to intercept a few dozen warheads launched by such "rogue" states as North Korea, Iran, and Iraq. As Clinton's term in office came to an end, he left the decision of whether to go forward with the controversial weapons system to his successor.

There were a number of problems with the system, however. In tests, it did not perform as well as advertised. Then there was the fact that the costly system's interceptor missiles, as in the case of SDI, could be fooled by inexpensive decoys. It also violated the 1972 Anti-Ballistic Missile Treaty with the Soviet Union, without which nuclear arms reduction treaties would be put into jeopardy. The Russians warned that they would not reduce their arsenal while the United States further "disarmed" them via the NMD system. China, too, declared that it would not accept a US system capable of intercepting "tens of warheads" in light of the fact that it possessed a nuclear deterrent of only eighteen to twenty single-warhead ballistic missiles.

None of that made an impression on President George W. Bush. He declared that the United States would deploy the system, the main purpose of which was to guard against North Korean missiles. In December 2001, Bush gave Russia notice of US withdrawal from the ABM Treaty. Reaction from Russia and the People's Republic of China was relatively mild. Neither wanted a renewal of tensions with Washington; moreover, both had more than enough weapons to counter a US attack.

Nuclear Proliferation

Among the different types of weapons of mass destruction (WMD), nuclear weapons remain by far the most dangerous. Chemical and biological weapons instill a particular horror because of their nature. The very idea of such weapons arouses a deep revulsion. When US president George W. Bush went to war against Saddam Hussein in Iraq, ostensibly to eliminate his chemical and biological arsenals as well as nuclear weapons—the WMD that were not there—he struck a responsive chord among his fellow citizens, despite the fact that in the past, conventional weapons have produced by far much greater "mass destruction."

Chemical weapons are not well suited for the battlefield. In World War II, Germans used poison gas, but they did so against defenseless prisoners, not enemy soldiers, as part of the Nazis' "final solution," the Holocaust of the Jews. Saddam Hussein also used it against defenseless civilians—75 percent of them women and children—in Halabja in March 1988, but he had less success with poison gas against Iranian troops.

On the field of battle, however, conditions have to be just right. When the Germans launched their devastating poison gas attack at Ypres in April 1915, killing 5,000 French soldiers, it was the fifth such attack during World War I, but the first to succeed. The Germans had to wait six weeks for the wind to blow in the right direction. Moreover, it could not be over seven miles per hour, otherwise it would quickly disperse the poison's effectiveness. Among the Western allies in that war, chemical weapons caused fewer than 1 percent of all battlefield deaths. They quickly learned that protective clothing could readily negate the impact of chemical weapons. Biological weapons are even more difficult to employ effectively against enemy forces.[25]

Atomic bombs remain by far the most potent WMD. As the superpowers rushed to eliminate thousands of nuclear weapons, other countries were working surreptitiously to develop such weapons of their own. Suddenly, in the early 1990s, nuclear proliferation began to replace superpower confrontation as the leading potential threat to international security.

The 1968 Non-Proliferation Treaty required signatory nations *without* nuclear weapons not to produce or receive them and to open their nuclear power facilities to inspection by the UN's International Atomic Energy Agency. Signatory nations *with* nuclear weapons were treaty-bound not to make such weapons available to non-nuclear nations and to negotiate in good faith toward nuclear disarmament. Only in 1992 did China and France sign the NPT, bringing all five declared nuclear powers under its regime. By that time, 149 nations had signed the treaty. There were several holdouts, however—notably India, Pakistan, Israel, Argentina, Brazil, and Algeria, all of which had nuclear weapons programs in various stages of development. These nations were thus beyond the pale of IAEA inspectors. Other nations that had signed the NPT, such as Iraq, North Korea, South Africa, Iran, and Libya, had nonetheless managed to acquire nuclear materials and had begun nuclear weapons programs.

Several nations halted their programs and permitted external inspections. South Africa, which had begun its nuclear weapons project in secret in the 1970s, closed its nuclear plants in 1990, signed the NPT, and opened its nuclear facilities to IAEA inspectors, thus becoming the only nation to abandon its nuclear weapons program voluntarily. In March 1993, South Africa admitted that by 1989 it had built six nuclear bombs, which, however, it had destroyed prior to the signing of the NPT. Brazil and Argentina both built large uranium-enrichment facilities in the 1980s and thus had the potential for making nuclear weapons. In December 1990, they too accepted inspection of their nuclear materials and facilities and permitted full IAEA monitoring.[26]

The danger of nuclear proliferation increased with the collapse of the Soviet Union and the prospect that its critical nuclear material, technology, and technicians might become available to the highest bidder. In 1991, the Soviet Union had over 40,000 nuclear weapons; about 700,000 people worked at its nuclear weapons plants, over 2,000 of whom had access to key technical information; and since the 1940s it had produced some 100–150 tons of weapons-grade plutonium and 500–700 tons of enriched uranium, only a pound of which is needed for a Hiroshima-size bomb. The problem was how to keep nuclear fuel and technology out of unauthorized hands or the hands of rulers with past records of, or the propensity for, military aggression.

Although Israel never confirmed that it had nuclear weapons—estimated at well over 100 warheads, the product of an effort that began in the early

1960s—it made sure that no Arab country acquired them. In 1982, Israeli fighter planes destroyed a nuclear reactor that Iraq had purchased from France, the centerpiece of Saddam Hussein's nuclear weapons program; in September 2007, Israel destroyed a nuclear reactor in Syria, a facility that apparently had the potential of producing atomic bombs. When the United States invaded Iraq in 2003, ostensibly to rid the country of "weapons of mass destruction," which included atomic weapons, it found that Saddam had not rebuilt what the Israelis had destroyed twenty-two years earlier.

Pakistan's Role in Nuclear Proliferation

In December 2003, the United States and Libya ended their twenty-year-long confrontation, which had begun during the Reagan administration and then reached crisis proportions when Libyan agents blew up a TWA airliner over Lockerbie, Scotland, killing all 259 onboard as well as 11 on the ground (see Chapter 20). The settlement between the United States and Libyan strongman Muammar Qaddafi included the opening up of Libya to inspections by the IAEA.

The inspections revealed that Qaddafi was in possession of a primitive nuclear bomb program. For a paltry sum—estimated at between $60 million and $100 million—Libya had purchased from Pakistan enriched uranium, plutonium, centrifuges to enrich uranium, and warhead designs. One US official called it "the complete package." It was all useless, however, because Libya did not know how to use it.

Libya's nuclear project had come courtesy of Abdul Qadeer Khan—the chief of the Khan Research Laboratories, the father of the Pakistani bomb, and a national hero. In addition to Libya, Khan had provided nuclear assistance to more technologically sophisticated nations, such as Iran and North Korea. Nuclear proliferation was suddenly on the IAEA's busy agenda.

The head of IAEA spoke of Khan's operation as "a veritable Wal-Mart." Khan did it mostly for money, but in the case of North Korea, he traded nuclear know-how for missile technology. These were not private transactions, however. None of this could have been arranged without the assistance of Pakistan's military, which provided cargo planes for transport.

Pakistan's role in nuclear proliferation had long been suspected in the West. Still, there was little that President Bush could do when he heard the stunning news. He had enlisted Pakistan in his war against the Taliban and al Qaeda and was still looking for Osama bin Laden in Pakistan's rugged North-West Frontier Province. He did not challenge, therefore, the explanation of Pakistan's military dictator, General Pervez Musharraf, who claimed that his military, too, had been shocked by the deeds of a lone wolf. Musharraf, however, was more annoyed by the duplicity of his Libyan "Muslim brothers." Without a word of public rebuke, Musharraf then pardoned Khan.[27]

The Case of North Korea

Another severe challenge to the NPT system was North Korea's nuclear weapons project, another beneficiary of Khan's black-market operation. In the 1980s, North Korea had built nuclear reactors and a plutonium-processing plant capable of turning spent nuclear fuel into weapons-grade plutonium. Not known to the West was whether it had succeeded in producing plutonium and, if so, how much. North Korea's dictator, Kim Il Sung, remained tight-lipped, denying possession of a bomb or the intention of building one, yet skillfully creating uncertainty by playing on the fears of others. There was indeed much to fear. A nuclear-armed North Korea could threaten South Korea and Japan, both of which had forsworn nuclear weapons (but were under US nuclear protection). Moreover, the prospect of North Korean nuclear bombs, missiles, or technology exported to other nations posed a danger to global nonproliferation efforts.

The possibility of a North Korean nuclear bomb became an international crisis in 1994. North Korea had signed the NPT in 1985, but then, in September 1993, Kim barred all further monitoring by IAEA inspectors. In exchange for a promise of direct high-level talks with the United States, he agreed in January 1994 to allow the international inspectors to continue their work. Yet two months later, when the inspectors returned to North Korea, they were prevented from entering the key plutonium-processing plant and from testing samples.

Tensions escalated rapidly. The Clinton administration sounded the call for UN sanctions and began talks with China and others to rally support for such a move. North Korea warned that sanctions were tantamount to an act of war. A visit by former US president Jimmy Carter to Pyongyang in June 1994 served to cool things off. Carter secured from Kim Il Sung a pledge not to expel IAEA inspectors as long as good-faith negotiations continued between the United States and North Korea. Clinton demanded that talks could resume only if North Korea would "freeze" its plutonium weapons program and accept international safeguards. Kim agreed and a new round of high-level talks began. These talks had barely opened when Kim Il Sung, the eighty-two-year-old Stalinist who had ruled North Korea since 1945, died. The negotiations were suspended while the North Korean government regrouped under its new ruler, Kim Jong Il, son of the long-lived dictator.

In August 1994, the negotiations resumed. They soon produced an outline of an agreement whereby North Korea pledged to freeze its plutonium production and the United States promised to replace North Korea's graphite rod nuclear reactors with light-water reactors, which have far less potential for producing plutonium. The new reactors were to be produced jointly by the United States, Japan, and South Korea at an estimated cost of $4 billion. The same three nations would also provide North Korea with fuel oil to meet its energy needs until the new reactors were in operation. The agreement, which in effect rewarded North Korea handsomely for ceasing its violations of the NPT, was finally signed in October 1994.

The agreement, however, was silent on the question of processing uranium as a fuel for nuclear weapons. In 1998, Kim Jong Il began to circumvent the spirit, although not the letter, of the agreement when he acquired from Pakistan the means to build several uranium bombs. After September 11, 2001, President Bush pronounced his "axis of evil" by lumping together Iraq, Iran, and North Korea as terrorist nations without making much of a distinction among them; Kim Jong Il's uranium bomb became his ace in the hole. In an act of defiance, in October 2002, the Dear Leader volunteered the stunning news that North Korea had joined the select nuclear club, that it had successfully built its first nuclear weapon. Bush, already stretched thin in Afghanistan and Iraq, had no answer. Kim, as his father had proposed, wanted bilateral talks with the United States with the purpose, among other things, of obtaining a nonaggression treaty (i.e., a US pledge not to attack North Korea, thus officially ending the Korean War). Bush, however, resolutely refused to sit down with a man he loathed. Instead, he insisted on six-party, multilateral negotiations—including South Korea, China, Japan, and Russia—and threatened Kim with preventive war. Bush's secretary of defense, Donald Rumsfeld, already had declared that the United States had the military means to fight a two-front war, against Iraq and North Korea, two nations the Bush administration had singled out as possessing WMD. Events in Iraq, however, belied Rumsfeld's confident claim. There was little option left for Bush but to change course and pretend that North Korea hardly posed a problem.

Meanwhile, North Korea proceeded with its uranium and plutonium weapons projects. In 2005, Kim Jong Il proposed to end his nuclear weapons program in return for economic assistance and improved relations with Washington. When Bush was slow to respond, Kim went ahead, in October 2006, with an underground test of a plutonium bomb. That got the attention of the Bush administration, which quickly reestablished negotiations with Kim. Bush accepted an agreement similar to the one the Clinton administration had hammered out, an arrangement he once had treated with unconcealed contempt. In return for economic assistance and North Korea's removal from the US State Department's terror list, Pyongyang agreed to end its plutonium enrichment program and did so by blowing up the cooling tower of its plutonium reactor in Yongbyon. The agreement, however, left a number of problems unresolved, such as the amount of processed plutonium still in North Korea's possession (estimated at 30–50 kilograms), as well as a full accounting of its uranium-processing capabilities.

The Cases of India and Pakistan

India, which had developed and tested a "nuclear device" as early as 1974 but never admitted to possessing a nuclear bomb, refused to sign the NPT. Pakistan, seeking a deterrent to India's bomb, finally succeeded in the mid-1990s, with some assistance from China, in developing its own nuclear bomb, but it kept it a secret. This all changed in May 1998, when in rapid succession India and Pakistan conducted successful tests of their nuclear weapons. Shortly after coming to power, India's nationalist government, headed by Prime Minister Atal Bihari Vajpayee, flexed its nuclear muscle by exploding five thermonuclear bombs in underground tests. Vajpayee explained that the tests were purely defensive in character. The events caused jubilation in India but caused strong rebukes around the world. The major nuclear powers, as well as other nations, called upon India to halt its nuclear program. Having carried out its tests, India declared a moratorium on further testing. The major powers warned Pakistan against matching India with tests of its own nuclear weapons, but Pakistan was in no mood to listen. Within two weeks, Pakistan answered with six underground nuclear bomb tests. It was the Pakistanis' turn to rejoice. Pakistan officials, too, spoke of national defense needs.

With India and Pakistan brandishing their nuclear arsenal, there was fear that the low-intensity warfare still going on in Kashmir might trigger a South Asian nuclear war. Animosity between India and Pakistan was deep-seated, and their nuclear face-off created a sense of urgency, particularly since both nations had missiles capable of delivering weapons. Yet the tests had a sobering effect. They revealed an Indian-Pakistani balance of terror that demanded confidence-building measures that, indeed, gradually led to an improvement in their relationship.

The Case of Iran

Iran began a nuclear weapons program in the early 1970s, during the days of the shah, and in 1970 it joined the NPT, thus permitting inspections without prior notice. The Islamic revolution of 1979 briefly suspended the program. In 1984, Khomeini's government resumed it in secret. With the assistance of the Soviet Union (and later Russia), North Korea, and Pakistan, Iran began to develop its secret weapons program. It would admit to a civilian nuclear program but not to working on a bomb. After September 11, 2001, Bush immediately declared Iran—with which the United States had no diplomatic or economic relations since 1979—as part of the "axis of evil" and repeatedly threatened preemptive war. Despite a potential attack by the United States and economic sanctions imposed by the UN and European Union, Iran remained defiant. In October 2004, Hasan Rowhani, Iran's chief nuclear negotiator, declared that "no other country can stop us exploring technology, which is the legal right of Iran."[28]

Toward the end of the Bush presidency, Iran had a nuclear weapons program of indeterminate quality. In December 2007, the US National Intelligence Estimate concluded that Iran had suspended its program in 2003, but that did not stop the administration's constant drumbeat that Iran still sought to build a nuclear arsenal. During the presidential campaign of 2008 all the major candidates took a hard-line position on Iran, repeating the Bush administration's position that Iran was a threat that had to be confronted. Bush kept repeating that "all options"—including a military attack—were "on the table." It was the generals in the Pentagon, however, more than anyone else, who took steps to scotch this idea. Tied down in Iraq and Afghanistan, the military showed scant enthusiasm for another war in the Middle East, one with unknown consequences, one that was bound to complicate the US mission in Iraq. Iran had allies in Gaza (Hamas), Lebanon (Hezbollah), and even Iraq (the Mahdi Army, the Badr Organization, and the Maliki government). It had the capability of disrupting the shipping lanes out of the Persian Gulf, at a time when the price of fuel at the pump in the industrial world had reached—if only briefly—record levels. The generals who had meekly followed Bush into Iraq in 2003, seduced by the promise of a short war, now paid closer attention to the truism that even the most meticulous military plans fall by the wayside once the shooting starts.

Admiral William Fallon, chief of Central Command, went public with his insistence that a war with Iran "isn't going to happen on my watch." Consequently, in March 2008, Secretary of Defense Robert Gates announced Fallon's "voluntary" retirement. Gates and the chairman of the Joint Chiefs of Staff, Admiral Mike Mullen, although publicly supporting Bush's stance on Iran, nevertheless repeatedly urged a political solution. It was a remarkable departure from the voices in the Pentagon on the eve of the war against Iraq.[29]

The Quest for a Comprehensive Nuclear Test Ban Treaty

As a result of the partial Nuclear Test Ban Treaty of 1963, three of the five declared nuclear powers—the United States, Britain, and Russia—took their tests underground. The other two—China and France—however, continued to test their weapons in the atmosphere. The tests were crucial in giving a nation its first reliable nuclear weapons or the ability to reconfigure them (although computer simulations were becoming increasingly accurate). To curtail nuclear proliferation, a comprehensive test ban treaty was needed to end all tests by declared as well as undeclared nuclear powers. To that end, in 1996 the United Nations worked out the Comprehensive Nuclear Test Ban Treaty (usually abbreviated as CTBT).

India repeatedly resisted such an agreement and presented two arguments against the CTBT: It preserved the division between nuclear haves and have-nots, and it did not commit the haves to getting rid of their weapons. When the vote came before the UN General Assembly in September 1996, India voted against the treaty (along with Libya and Bhutan). For the treaty to become international law, the legislatures of all forty-four countries possessing nuclear reactors had to ratify it.[30] Still, the vote (158–3 in favor) henceforth meant that all future nuclear testing would fly in the face of world opinion.

By September 2004, 116 nations had ratified the treaty, including Russia. The US Senate, however, rejected it in October 1999 after the Senate Foreign Relations Committee, headed by the conservative Republican senator Jesse Helms of North Carolina (often derided as "Senator No"), denounced it, citing the potential need for future testing and problems with verification. President George W. Bush showed no interest in taking up the treaty's ratification, another piece of unfinished business his successor, Barack Obama, inherited.

As of September 1996, the nuclear powers had conducted 2,045 tests of nuclear weapons. To these figures must be added the more recent tests by India, Pakistan, and North Korea (see Table 19.4).

Table 19.4   Known Nuclear Tests, 1945–1996

	US	USSR	France	Britain	China	India
Atmospheric	215	219	50	21	23	0
Underground	815	496	159	24	22	1
Total	1,030	715	209	45	45	1

Sources: UN; Physicians for Social Responsibility; Barbara Crosette, "U.N. Endorses a Treaty to Halt All Nuclear Testing," *New York Times,* September 11, 1996, p. A3.

Recommended Readings

Bottome, Edgar M. *The Balance of Terror: A Guide to the Arms Race.* 2nd rev. ed. Boston: Beacon Press, 1986.

Broad, William J. *Teller's War: The Top-Secret Story Behind the Star Wars Deception.* New York: Simon and Schuster, 1992.
> How Edward Teller, the "father" of the US hydrogen bomb, sold SDI to the Reagan administration.

Bundy, McGeorge. *Danger and Survival: Choices About the Bomb in the First Fifty Years.* New York: Random House, 1988.
> John Kennedy's national security advisor on how successive US governments worked out a "tradition of nonuse."

Cockburn, Andrew. *The Threat: Inside the Soviet Military Machine.* New York: Random House, 1983.
> A sober assessment of Soviet capabilities and weaknesses.

Cox, Arthur Macy. *Russian Roulette: The Superpower Game.* New York: Times Books, 1982.

FitzGerald, Frances. *Way Out There in the Blue: Reagan, Star Wars, and the End of the Cold War.* New York: Simon and Schuster, 2000.
> An analysis of a program that, after $60 billion, had little to show for it.

Freedman, Lawrence. *The Evolution of Nuclear Strategy.* New York: St. Martin's Press, 1981.

Gervasi, Tom. *The Myth of Soviet Military Supremacy.* New York: Harper and Row, 1986.

Challenges the claim that the Soviet Union had overtaken the West in the arms race in the 1980s.

Holloway, David. *Stalin and the Bomb: The Soviet Union and Atomic Energy, 1936–1956.* New Haven, Conn.: Yale University Press, 1994.

Matlock, Jack F. *Reagan and Gorbachev: How the Cold War Ended.* New York: Random House, 2004.
By Reagan's ambassador to the Soviet Union.

Mazarr, Michael J. *North Korea and the Bomb: A Case Study in Non-Proliferation.* New York: St. Martin's Press, 1997.
Discusses the 1994 nuclear weapons issue between North Korea and the United States.

McDougall, Walter A. *The Heavens and the Earth: A Political History of the Space Age.* New York: Basic Books, 1984.

Newhouse, John. *Cold Dawn: The Story of SALT.* New York: Holt, Rinehart and Winston, 1973.

Office of Technology Assessment. *SDI: Technology, Survivability, and Software.* Princeton: Princeton University Press, 1988.
Reprint of a study for the House Armed Services Committee and Senate Foreign Relations Committee that concluded that SDI would fail in case of war.

Rhodes, Richard. *Dark Sun: The Making of the Hydrogen Bomb.* New York: Simon and Schuster, 1995.
A definitive study of the first two decades of the nuclear arms race.

Schell, Jonathan. *The Fate of the Earth.* New York: Knopf, 1982.
The best-seller on the consequences of nuclear war.

Sigal, Leon. *Disarming Strangers: Nuclear Diplomacy with North Korea.* Princeton: Princeton University Press, 1999.
A study of North Korea's nuclear weapons project, arguing that the crisis in 1994 came dangerously close to war.

Smith, Gerard. *Doubletalk: The Story of SALT I.* Garden City, N.Y.: Doubleday, 1980.
By the chief US arms negotiator at the talks.

Soviet Military Power. Washington, D.C.: US Government Printing Office, six editions, 1981–1987.
The Pentagon's exaggerated assessments of the Soviet threat.

Spector, Leonard S. *Nuclear Ambitions: The Spread of Nuclear Weapons, 1989–1990.* Boulder: Westview Press, 1990.
The fifth in a series providing a detailed country-by-country analysis.

Talbott, Strobe. *Endgame: The Inside Story of SALT II.* New York: Harper and Row, 1979.
———. *Deadly Gambits: The Reagan Administration and the Stalemate in Nuclear Arms Control.* New York: Knopf, 1984.
This and the previous book, by a former correspondent for *Time*, are among the most detailed and lucid accounts of arms negotiations during the 1980s.

Union of Concerned Scientists. *The Fallacy of Star Wars.* New York: Vintage, 1984.

Zuckerman, Solly. *Nuclear Illusion and Reality.* New York: Random House, 1982.
A critical view of the nuclear arms race by a former scientific advisor to the British Ministry of Defence: Neither side can gain nuclear advantage.

Notes

1. Walter Pincus, "US Has Spent $5.8 Trillion on Nuclear Arms Since 1940, Study Says," *Washington Post,* July 1, 1998, p. A2.

2. SS (surface-to-surface) is the US designation of Soviet missiles. As soon as a Soviet missile was tested, the Pentagon assigned it a number.

3. George McGovern, "SALT II: A Political Autopsy," *Politics Today* (March–April 1980), p. 64.

4. This was the basis of Ronald Reagan's "window of vulnerability": The increasingly accurate Soviet land-based arsenal was capable of overwhelming the US missiles in their silos and thereby threatened the very existence of the United States. It ignored the fact that US submarines and bombers were more than enough to keep the Soviets honest. Reagan promised that, if elected president, he would close this window. In 1984, he declared that he had closed it—without, however, having done anything to protect US land-based missiles.

5. Thomas Powers, "Nuclear Winter and Nuclear Strategy," *The Atlantic*, November 1984, p. 60.

6. Kissinger, cited in Lawrence Freedman, *The Evolution of Nuclear Strategy* (New York: St. Martin's Press, 1981), p. 363.

7. Georgy Arbatov, director of the Institute of US and Canadian Studies of the Academy of Sciences of the Soviet Union, in Arthur Macy Cox (with a Soviet commentary by Georgy Arbatov), *Russian Roulette: The Superpower Game* (New York: Times Books, 1982), pp. 177–178, 182.

8. Leonid Brezhnev and Ronald Reagan, "Brezhnev and Reagan on Atom War," transcripts of statements, *New York Times*, October 21, 1981, p. 5.

9. Great Britain accepted 160 cruise missiles; West Germany, 108 Pershing II and 96 cruise missiles; Italy, 112 cruise missiles; Belgium and Holland, 48 cruise missiles each.

10. Ronald Reagan, quoted in "President's Speech on Military Spending and a New Defense," *New York Times*, March 24, 1983, p. A20.

11. Wayne Biddle, "Request for Space Weapons Reflects Early Goals," *New York Times*, February 4, 1985, p. A10. The fate of the world would be in the hands (or the chips and software) of computers with a computer-driven system. "Perhaps we should run R2-D2 for president in the 1990s," Senator Paul Tsongas (D-MA) quipped at a congressional hearing. "At least he'd be on line all the time. Has anyone told the President that he's out of the decision-making process?" George Keyworth, President Reagan's science advisor, replied, "I certainly haven't." Philip M. Boffey, "'Star Wars' and Mankind: Consequences for Future," *New York Times*, March 8, 1985, p. A14. In January 1987, the Office of Technology Assessment concluded that the software would have to be written "without the benefit of data or experience from battle use," that is, it could not be properly tested. It would have to rely on theoretical "peacetime testing," which, however, would offer "no guarantee that the system would not fail catastrophically . . . as a result of a software error . . . in the system's first battle." Office of Technology Assessment, *SDI: Technology, Survivability, and Software* (Princeton, N.J.: Princeton University Press, 1988), p. 249.

12. Harold Brown, December 1983, quoted in Boffey, "Star Wars," p. A14.

13. Caspar Weinberger quote, ibid., p. A14.

14. The Soviet SS-20 rockets carried three warheads each; thus the Soviet Union gave up more than three times as many warheads as the United States.

15. Arms Control Association, from data supplied by the US Defense Department, the Joint Chiefs of Staff, and the Arms Control and Disarmament Agency, *New York Times*, May 26, 1988, p. A12.

16. "Wir werden euch des Feindes berauben," *Der Spiegel*, December 12, 1988, p. 22.

17. Christian Schmidt-Häuer, "Die Armee gerät unter Beschuss," *Die Zeit*, November 11, 1988, p. 8.

18. "Unsere Antwort wird Nein sein," *Der Spiegel*, May 1, 1989, p. 21.

19. Wolfgang Schwarz of the Institute for International Politics and Economy in East Berlin, in a report to the East German Council of Ministers, "DDR-Wissenschaftler warnt vor Atomverseuchung Europas," *Frankfurter Rundschau*, June 21, 1989, p. 2.

20. John F. Cushman Jr., "Senate Endorses Pact to Reduce Strategic Arms," *New York Times*, October 2, 1992, pp. A1, A6.

21. George Petrovich, "Counting the Costs of the Arms Race," *Foreign Policy* (Winter 1991–1992), p. 87.

22. Cited in David Hoffman, "Russian Says Arms Treaty Vote Should Follow Election," *Washington Post*, February 1, 1996, p. A17.

23. Mikhail Gorbachev, "'Geroi' razrusheniia Sovetskogo Soiuza izvestny . . . ," *Novoe vremia*, nos. 2–3 (1995), p. 27.

24. Adrian Blomfield and Mike Smith, "Gorbachev: US Could Start New Cold War," *Daily Telegraph*, May 7, 2008.

25. William K. Blewett, "Chemical and Biological Threats: The Nature and Risk," *HPAC Engineering* (September 2004), pp. 2–4; William Blewett, "75 Years of Chemical Warfare," *Baltimore Sun*, April 20, 1990.

26. Leonard S. Spector, "Repentant Nuclear Proliferants," *Foreign Policy* (Fall 1992), pp. 26–27.

27. Seymour M. Hersh, "The Deal: Why Is Washington Going Easy on Pakistan's Nuclear Black Marketers?" *The New Yorker*, March 8, 2004, pp. 32–37. Khan was released from house arrest in February 2009.

28. Associated Press, "Iran Threatens to End Nuclear Talks with Europeans," *Baltimore Sun*, October 28, 2004, p. 14A.

29. Thomas Powers, "Iran: The Threat," *New York Review of Books*, July 17, 2008, pp. 9–11.

30. "A Nice Red Afterglow," *The Economist*, March 14, 1992, p. 43.

20 The Emergence of Political Islam

The Cold War was largely a bipolar struggle between Western liberalism and the Soviet variant of Communism, with much of the world simply trying to stay out of harm's way. In the 1970s, however, a new political force took center stage: militant Islam. It sought to resurrect the world of Islam, to free it from the debilitating and overbearing influence of outside forces such as Communism, secularism, and above all the pervading Western presence. Militant Islam left its mark on Islamic societies, stretching, with few interruptions, from the Atlantic shores of Africa to the easternmost tip of the Indonesian archipelago in Asia, encompassing nearly a billion people in the 1980s.

Islam: Theory and Practice

Islam is the third of the world's great religions to come out of the Middle East. It represents to Muslims the third and last of the "true revelations" by a divinity whom the Jews call Jehovah, the Christians call God, and the Muslims call Allah.

This final revelation came in the seventh century of the Christian era when Allah spoke to his prophet, Mohammed of Mecca, Islam's holiest city, in what today is Saudi Arabia. Mohammed was born into a society of idol worshipers, Jews, and Christians, and he fell under the influence of Arabia's two dominant monotheistic faiths, Judaism and Christianity. In fact, these were the starting point of Mohammed's teachings. He was always at pains to acknowledge that God had revealed himself to his prophets of another age—Abraham, Moses, and Jesus Christ among them. In fact, Islam recognized that Jews and Christians were "people of the book," that is, God's revelations in the Old and New Testaments. Mohammed held the view that uncorrupted Judaism and Christianity were early manifestations of Islam, literally "submission" to God, and that, indeed, Abraham had been the first Muslim. Mohammed also insisted, however,

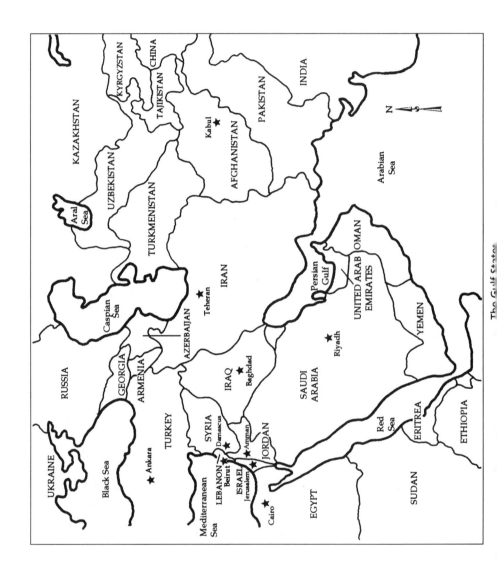

The Gulf States

that Christians and Jews had gone astray and had ignored God's commandments and corrupted the original scriptures. Since Jews and Christians had strayed from God's word, God then revealed himself to the last in the long line of prophets, Mohammed. The links between Islam and Christianity were such that some seventh-century Christian theologians believed that Islam was a heterodox Christian doctrine, similar to Nestorianism, a deviation that attributed to Jesus two natures—divine and human—a heresy that had been suppressed but continued to have adherents in the Middle East.[1]

Islam is an offshoot of Judaism and, to a lesser degree, Christianity. Its linear relationship to Judaism resembles Christianity's link to Judaism. At one time, Muslims, including Mohammed, faced Jerusalem while in prayer. All three religions stress justice and compassion. Islam has a heaven and a hell; God spoke to Mohammed through the Archangel Gabriel (as he did to the Virgin Mary); Islam has its Day of Resurrection and Judgment, "and the hour is known to no one but God." Believers who are created "from an essence of clay . . . shall surely die hereafter, and be restored to life on the Day of Resurrection," a "day sure to come."[2]

Arabs and Jews both claim Abraham as their ancestor. The Jews descended from Abraham's second son, Isaac, born of his wife Sarah; the Arabs descended from the first son, Ishmael, born of Hagar, Sarah's Egyptian maid. The Bible prophesied that great nations would descend from the two sons of Abraham. The biblical account, however, also stresses that God renewed with Isaac the covenant he had made with Abraham, while the Muslim account makes no distinction between the sons of Abraham. Islamic scholars argue that it is inconceivable that God would favor one son over the other. In Islamic teachings, the conflict between Jews and Muslims, therefore, becomes a family divided against itself. Since both Muslims and Jews trace their religious ancestry to Abraham, it was not surprising that both sought to control the West Bank city of Hebron, which contains the tombs of Abraham and his family (notably his wife Sarah and his son Isaac). Some Jews consider Hebron their second-holiest city.

The revelations to Mohammed were codified in the Koran (literally "recitation" of the word of God), the holy, infallible book of the Muslims, which contains God's commands to the faithful. The Koran is God's word, last in time and the completion and correction of all that had been written before.

A deviation from established religions is no trifling matter; it is nothing less than an attempt to replace established faiths with one that claims to be the only true revelation from God. The consequences of such an attempt have been religious conflicts, which began in Mohammed's day and have lasted centuries down to our time. Neither Judaism nor Christianity has ever recognized the validity of Islam. Western scholars have often used the label "Mohammedanism" to describe Islam, a term insulting to Muslims because it suggests that it is an invention of one man rather than God's final word. And

Islam, in its turn, has denied the Holy Trinity, and thus the divinity of Jesus Christ, which amounts to a demand for "the unconditional surrender of the essence of Christianity."[3] Islam does, however, recognize Jesus as one of God's revered prophets.

A Muslim is someone who submits to the will of God. Islam is thus a religion that encompasses the totality of one's existence. It is a complete way of life, both secular and religious. There can be no separation between one's spiritual and secular existence. In an Islamic nation, therefore, a believer cannot make a distinction between secular and religious laws. All laws must be based on the Koran; it cannot be otherwise. Muslim societies must be governed according to the word of Allah. Islam, the Koran makes clear, is a religion of laws.

There is an elemental simplicity to the fundamental laws, the "five pillars" of Islam. They include, first and foremost, an affirmation that is one of the shortest credos of any religion in the world: "There is no god but God and Mohammed is the Prophet of God." All that a convert to Islam has to do is to state this credo in the company of believers. No other rite or ceremony is required. (The very simplicity inherent in the act of conversion explains in part why Islam was the fastest-growing religion in Africa at the end of the twentieth century.) Second, a Muslim is obliged to pay an alms tax (the *zakat*) of around 5 percent. Islam emphasizes the importance of charity: "Whatever alms you give . . . are known to Allah . . . and whatever alms you give shall be paid back to you in full."[4] In an Islamic state, the alms tax is also a source of revenue for the government. Third, a Muslim must say five daily prayers while facing toward Mecca. The *muezzin* (crier) calls the faithful to prayer from the minaret (a slender tower) of a mosque at various times during the day: at sunset, during the night, at dawn, at noon, and in the afternoon. Fourth, Islam demands abstention from food, drink, and sexual intercourse from dawn to sundown during the lunar month of Ramadan, which commemorates Allah's first revelation of the Koran to Mohammed. Fasting here becomes a spiritual act of renunciation and self-denial. Last, a Muslim must attempt to make at least one pilgrimage, or *haj*, to the holy city of Mecca.

In the seventh century, following the death of Mohammed, Islam spread quickly throughout the Middle East and North Africa. With Islam came the establishment of some of the world's great civilizations, centering on the cities of Damascus and Baghdad. Yet, ultimately, this golden age of Islam gave way to a European ascendancy, which may be dated to the Crusades of the Middle Ages. In more recent times, Western powers (notably Great Britain, France, and Italy) managed to establish their presence in the Muslim lands of the Middle East, only to find their grip weakening after World War II. Militant Islam seeks to free the Muslim countries from the centuries-old overbearing influence of the Christian West and to reassert the sovereignty and dignity denied them over the past centuries. Militant Islam is a potent political and revolutionary weapon that seeks the restoration of a golden age.

The Shiites and the Sunnis

In the 1970s, the most visible and radical advocates of resurgent, militant Islam were the Shiites, the smaller of the two main branches of Islam. The other wing, the Sunnis, represents what is generally called the mainstream of Islam and, in fact, makes up approximately 90 percent of all Muslims. Shiites are little known in Africa among the Arabs in the north or among the blacks in sub-Saharan Africa. The same is true of southern Asia, in countries such as Indonesia, Malaysia, Bangladesh, India, Turkey, and Pakistan. The keepers of the holy places in Mecca and Medina, the Saudi royal family, and their subjects are mostly Sunnis. In Iran, however, nearly all Muslims belong to the Shiite branch; in fact, Shiism became a state religion there. The majority of the Muslims of Iraq and of the former Soviet Republic of Azerbaijan are Shiites. Shiites may also be found in large numbers in all the other states of the Persian Gulf, as well as Syria, Lebanon, Yemen, and Central Asia.

The split in Islam came two decades after the prophet's death in A.D. 632. A line of *khalifa*, or caliphs, took Mohammed's place as his deputies and successors. The first four caliphs, the Rightly Guided, were selected from the ranks of Mohammed's associates, and after that the line became hereditary. From the very outset there were strains in the Muslim community over the question of succession. As the caliphs became more tyrannical, they increasingly appeared as usurpers. There were those who insisted that Ali, the husband of Mohammed's daughter Fatima, was the true successor. The assassination of the reigning caliph in 656 set off a civil war between two contending branches within Islam. The faction in support of Ali, the Shiites (in Arabic, *shia* means "party"), and the Sunni branch, representing the caliphs (in Arabic, *sunna* means "practice" or "custom"), fought each other until the Battle of Kerbala in 681, in today's Iraq. During the fighting, Ali died a martyr's death. It was here that the Sunnis established their domination and the Shiite resistance went underground. The struggle was both political and religious in nature. Its political content lay in the fact that the Shiites became the champions of the oppressed and the opponents of privilege and power. The Shiites found their inspiration in the actions of Mohammed in Mecca, where the Prophet first made his mark as the advocate of the downtrodden. As such, the Shiites in Iran, for example, have always been in conflict with the throne in their quest to re-create a social and political order in line with the teachings of the Koran.

Politics and religion, in the Shiites' eyes, cannot be separated. Obedience to civil authority has never been a hallmark of Shiite behavior. Shiites, in their challenges to entrenched political power, time and again have elevated political disobedience to a religious duty. When, in 1963, the shah of Iran offered his uncompromising critic, the Ayatollah Ruhollah Khomeini, his freedom on condition he leave politics to the politicians, Khomeini replied: "All of Islam is politics." Khomeini became the shah's most vocal opponent, accusing him of having sold his country into bondage on behalf of US interests. In 1964, Khomeini was briefly detained for having publicly refused to recognize the government, its courts, and laws. Ten days after his release, Khomeini delivered the first of his political sermons. In one of them, he denounced a law, passed in October 1964, that had granted US citizens in Iran the right of extraterritoriality, that is, the right to be tried according to US law instead of Iranian law. Khomeini called the law "a document for the enslavement of Iran" that "acknowledged that Iran is a colony; it has given America a document attesting that the nation of Muslims is barbarous." At the end of 1964, he was rearrested and then exiled.[5]

Sunnis and Shiites both accept the Prophet's promise of the return of one of his descendants who will "fill the world with justice and equity."[6] For the Shiites, however, the spirit of messianism is central to their creed. They look to an *imam*, a divinely appointed descendant of Mohammed, whose purpose is the spiritual—as well as political and at times insurrectional—guidance of the faithful.

The Sunnis, the party of custom and practice, stand—as a rule—for the continuity of the social, political, and religious order. They emphasize consensus and obedience to civil and religious authority. In contrast to the Shiites, they look for inspiration to Mohammed's work in Medina, where he created the first Muslim state and ruled as a military commander, judge, and teacher to whom Allah's word was revealed.

Radicalism in the name of Islam, however, is not a Shiite monopoly. The Shiites have a lower boiling point when it comes to dealing with corruption and oppression. The militant Muslims in Iran, Iraq, Lebanon, and Saudi Arabia are generally Shiites; the Islamic radicals in Algeria, Hamas in Gaza, the Taliban in Afghanistan, and members of al Qaeda are Sunnis. What militant Islam—whether Shiite or Sunni—sought to achieve was the elimination of foreign influences that humiliated and degraded their societies. The militants in Algeria fought a military dictatorship still heavily dominated by French culture; those in Iran combated Western (at first largely British and later US) influence; and the Soviet Muslims (whether Shiite Azeris or Sunni Chechens or Uzbeks) sought to free themselves of Moscow's rule and dreamed of a restoration of their once glorious civilizations.

The Revolution in Iran

During the twentieth century, Iran was buffeted by world war, colonialism, and instability and division within. And once the guiding hand of the US-backed shah weakened, the gates to Islamic revolution were flung open. The implications for world history were manifold.

The Shah and the United States

From the end of World War II until the late 1970s, Iran stood in sharp contrast to its Arab neighbors. Shah Mohammed Reza Pahlavi and his country appeared to be a rock of stability in the turbulent Middle East, a bulwark against political radicalism, Islamic fundamentalism, and Soviet expansionism. It was little wonder that, even after the shah's internal position had been shaken by violent protests, US president Jimmy Carter could still praise him for his stabilizing influence in the Middle East. Surely, there was no solid reason to believe that the shah, still apparently a vigorous man in middle age, would not continue to rule Iran as he had in the past. Moreover, he was preparing his young son to succeed him on the Peacock Throne.

But Iran turned out to be another case of US involvement in a foreign land of which few people in authority in Washington had an adequate understanding. The outward stability of the nation only masked the volatile undercurrents, which had deep historic roots. The shah had ruled for a long time, since 1941, but his reign had often been unstable, an uncomfortable fact that too many US policymakers often conveniently overlooked. The militant clergy were a nuisance, they reasoned, but they certainly appeared to be no threat to the shah.

Successful resistance to Iran's shahs by the militant Shiite clergy over the centuries was a constant thread running through Iranian history. This was particularly the case with shahs who made deals with foreigners, granting them favorable concessions at the expense of the nation. In 1872, for example, Nasir ed-Den Shah granted Paul Julius de Reuter, a British subject, such comprehensive monopolies that the shah, in effect, had sold him the country. De Reuter received monopolies in the construction of railroads, canals, and irrigation works; the harvesting of forests; the use of all uncultivated lands; and the operation of banks, public works, and mines. The British leader Lord George Curzon called this "the most complete and extraordinary surrender of the entire industrial resources of a kingdom into foreign hands that has ever been dreamed of, much less accomplished."[7] In 1892, the shah faced an angry mob demanding the repeal of a monopoly granted to a British firm in the production, sale, and export of tobacco. The demonstrators were able to bring about the repeal of these concessions. The shah's troubles persisted, however, and in 1896 he was assassinated. Nasir ed-Den Shah's reign points to a recurring pattern of Iranian politics: royal complicity with foreign powers, the power of the mobs in the streets, and the inability of most shahs to maintain their power. During the previous 360 years, only four shahs died natural deaths while still in possession of the throne. The rest were either dethroned or assassinated. Shiite Iran was not a likely place to look for political equilibrium.

After Nasir ed-Den Shah's assassination, the practice of selling favors to foreigners—British, French, and Russian—continued nonetheless. In 1906, the Iranian parliament, the *majlis*, took away this privilege from the shah. But despite the prohibition, the practice continued, contributing to a legacy of bitterness and resentment directed toward the ruling Qajar dynasty (1779–1925) that ultimately led to its demise. In its place, a usurper pronounced the creation of his own ruling house. He was Colonel Reza Khan, who subsequently crowned himself Reza Shah Pahlavi.

Years later, Reza Khan's son, Mohammed Reza (who ruled from 1941 to 1979), attempted to identify his ruling house, the Pahlavi dynasty, with the glories of Persia's past. In 1971, he staged an elaborate ceremony in Persepolis, the ancient city of Cyrus the Great. Guests from far and wide attended the gala celebration. The shah then proceeded to date the calendar from the reign of Cyrus, symbolizing over 2,500 years of historic continuity. In March 1976, a dutiful parliament created the "monarchy calendar" (dating from the coronation of Cyrus the Great, 2,535 years prior), replacing the Islamic calendar based on the date of the *hegira* (flight) of Mohammed from Mecca to Medina in A.D. 622.[8] The shah became the Shahansha (King of Kings), the Light of the Aryans, who ruled by divine right, a man who claimed to have experienced religious visions.[9]

This spectacle impressed the world, but many Iranians, particularly the Shiite clergy, saw the shah in a different light. They considered the shah merely a usurper—only the second in the short line of the Pahlavi dynasty—who had been educated in the West and who had sent his own son to study there.

Reza Shah did not act appreciably differently from the previous monarchs when it came to dealing with foreign powers. In 1933, he granted new favorable concessions to the Anglo-Iranian Oil Company, an enterprise that was largely controlled by the British. His close association with the British continued until World War II, when he shifted toward Nazi Germany at a time when it threatened to take the Soviet Union's oil fields north of the Caucasus Mountains along the western shores of the Caspian Sea, notably around the city of Baku. A successful German drive in that direction would have linked German-occupied territory with Iran. The upshot was the joint occupation of Iran by the Soviets (who took control of the northern part) and the British (who occupied the southern regions). The shah was then sent packing when the British and Soviets forced him to abdicate in favor of his young son, who turned out to be the second and last of the Pahlavi dynasty.

The greatest source of wealth for the Pahlavi dynasty was the country's oil. By 1950, Iran was one of the largest producers of oil in the Middle East. By that time Iran's own share of the oil profits had increased, but many nationalists, including many of the clergy, were not satisfied. For one thing, the Arab-American Oil Company, a US concern operating in Saudi Arabia, had offered the Saudis more favorable terms. More important, the lion's share of the profits from Iran's natural resources still went to the foreign investors, mostly British.

The result was that in 1951 the parliament, under the direction of Prime Minister Mohammed Mossadegh, challenged the shah and voted for the nationalization of the oil industry. The British, predictably, declared such an act illegal. US president Harry Truman sought to mediate the dispute, eventually siding with the British, but refused to become involved in Iraq's internal affairs. The new US administration under Dwight Eisenhower, however, had no such qualms; its secretary of state, John Foster Dulles, and his brother, Allen, the chief of the CIA, decided to act. Truman had thought that Mossadegh was a barrier against the aspirations of the Communist Tudeh Party; the Dulles brothers thought that Mossadegh was contributing to an eventual Communist takeover.

Mossadegh's challenge to the West struck a responsive chord in Iranian society. As tensions rose, the CIA and British intelligence were plotting to oust Mossadegh. Washington also put economic pressure on Iran by cutting off aid and refusing to buy Iranian oil. The use of an economic weapon only inflamed the militants in the capital of Tehran. In August 1953, street riots forced the shah to flee to Rome. There he came to the conclusion that his reign had ended.

The CIA moved quickly and decisively. With the help of elements in the Iranian army and others opposed to Mossadegh, the United States and Great Britain managed to return the shah after only three days in exile. Demonstrations in the streets had ousted the shah; counterdemonstrations in these same streets created a political climate permitting the shah to return.

The shah now owed his throne to a foreign power, something he always resented. But his ties with the United States continued to grow. Oil production and export to the West continually increased, and in the process the shah became one of the United States' best overseas customers. He took steps to modernize Iranian society by launching his conservative "White Revolution." Such a transformation, however, came at a price. It created a gulf between a new privileged class, which benefited from the shah's close link with the West, and much of the rest of the country. The influx of Western technicians, engineers, military advisors, and sales representatives disturbed many Iranians. The uneven distribution of the country's enormous wealth and the attendant Westernization led to a distortion of traditional Iranian social patterns. Too many were left out, and it was inevitable that the shah's actions would breed resentment. Traditional Iranian self-sufficiency became a thing of the past. By the 1970s, Iran became greatly dependent on foreign imports; it even bought food from abroad. And since Iran based much of its wealth on a one-product economy (80 percent of its export earnings came from the sale of oil), its dependency on the West appeared to be total.

Much of the money the shah spent abroad went for the purchase of modern military equipment, most of it US-made. Between 1972 and 1978, he ordered $19.5 billion in US arms. The greater the oil revenues, the more weapons he bought. After 1973, about one-third of the government's spending went for armaments. This proved to be a boon for US arms manufacturers, for by the end of the 1970s, one-third of all US arms sales went to Iran.

Richard Nixon's administration applauded such a course: Iran, armed to the teeth, would preserve stability in the Middle East, particularly in the Persian Gulf, the waterway through which passed much of the oil on which the industrial powers depended. It was here that the "Nixon Doctrine" appeared to work best. Nixon had first formulated his doctrine toward the end of the war in Vietnam. The doctrine called for client states to be armed (and at times financed) by the United States to do the actual fighting in support of US interests. In South Vietnam the doctrine collapsed like a house of cards in 1975, when its army took to its heels. In Iran the doctrine seemed to be working to perfection.

In the early 1970s, it was not clear how Iran would pay for the massive military equipment the shah demanded. But good fortune intervened. October 1973 saw the fourth Arab-Israeli conflict, the Yom Kippur War, which led to an oil embargo by the Arab members of OPEC and a doubling of oil prices. The shah took the lead in demanding this increase in the price of oil. The Nixon administration, however, saw a silver lining in all of this. The United States was now able to supply Iran with military equipment without raiding the US treasury. Henry Kissinger, Nixon's secretary of state, explained in his memoirs: "The vacuum left by British withdrawal [from Iran during the early 1950s], now menaced by Soviet intrusion and radical momentum, would be filled by a power friendly to us . . . And all of this was achievable without any American resources, since the Shah was willing to pay for the equipment out of his oil revenues."[10]

This scenario began to fall apart in a most unexpected way when militant Islam drove the shah, whom it denounced as a servant of the "Great Satan" (the United States), from power.

The Return of Khomeini

The best-known practitioner of militant Islam in the 1970s was the Ayatollah Ruhollah Khomeini. He identified Western civilization as Islam's enemy; an Islamic society, therefore, must be purged of it. The shah, with the trappings of Western civilization all around him, was little different from the tens of thousands of Western technicians he had invited to Iran. In the eyes of the *mullahs*, the Muslim clergy, the shah stood in direct violation of the history and religion of Islam.

Khomeini's denunciations of the shah at first had little effect. They were regarded merely as the raving and ranting of an old man in exile. But as dissatisfaction with the shah's rule increased, Khomeini's sermons, distributed on audiocassette tapes smuggled into Iran, began to have an effect. By January 1979, it became apparent that the shah could maintain his throne only if the notoriously brutal SAVAK (the secret police established in 1957 with the help of the CIA) and the army were willing to suppress all manifestations of discontent. Civil war loomed on the horizon. The shah, unsure of the loyalty of the army and unable to obtain a clear-cut US commitment from the Carter administration, decided to leave the country. Corruption, favoritism, police brutality, poverty and luxury side by side, the lack of justice, the influence of foreigners—all contributed to the fall of the shah.

The events of the late 1970s showed that the shah had merely maintained an illusion of power. In February 1979, Ayatollah Khomeini returned in triumph from exile in Paris, where he had been the most visible symbol of righteous Islamic resistance to a ruler who had betrayed both his religion and his people. Iran, under the leadership of the Muslim clergy, would now undergo a spiritual and national rejuvenation. There was little doubt that the support for Khomeini's regime was massive in those heady days when the shah was put to flight.

But the shah had not officially abdicated. When he left in January 1979, he emphasized that he and his family were going abroad for an unspecified period. In effect, he promised to return.[11] It was clear that the United States preferred the shah over the anti-US militants who now governed Tehran. The militants, for

Shah Mohammed Reza Pahlavi, monarch of Iran, with US secretary of defense James Schlesinger, Washington, D.C., July 26, 1973. *(AP/Wide World Photos)*

Ayatollah Ruhollah Khomeini, Shiite leader of the Iranian revolution, 1979. *(Embassy of Iran)*

their part, feared a repetition of the events of 1953, when the CIA had returned the shah to power from his brief exile in Rome. Radicals, bitterly hostile to a US government on which they blamed all of Iran's ills, were able to stir up deep emotions. Anti-US street demonstrations became daily affairs, and two weeks after Khomeini's return from exile, the first attack by militants on the US embassy took place. The organizers of the attack claimed—correctly—that the embassy housed the CIA. Khomeini's police at this time dispersed the attackers.

The Khomeini government, instead of concentrating on the consolidation of power, sharpened its differences between his revolution and Washington when it repealed the 1947 law authorizing a US military mission in Iran. Tensions were already high when, in October 1979, the shah arrived in New York for medical reasons. To the militants, this marked the first step of what to them was a US attempt to bring the shah back to power. They refused to believe the shah was in need of treatment.

On November 4, a group of radical students decided to take matters into their own hands. They climbed over the walls of the US embassy compound in Tehran and seized its diplomatic personnel, demanding that the United States extradite the shah to Iran to stand trial. Only then would they release their fifty-two hostages, who were kept bound and blindfolded in the embassy. There was no evidence that Khomeini had ordered them to engage in an act that clearly violated international law. Still, it suited his political position, since it further drove political sentiments in Iran to a radical extreme. The huge crowds who gathered daily in the square in front of the embassy in support of the students limited Khomeini's options.

The hostage crisis came at a time when memories of helicopters lifting off the rooftop of the US embassy in Saigon were still fresh in the US public's mind. And, eight weeks after the onset of the hostage crisis, the United States was hit with yet another jolt when the Soviet Union sent 80,000 troops into Afghanistan—a country bordering Iran—to bail out a bankrupt Communist government. The hostage crisis and the Soviet invasion of Afghanistan had a dramatic impact on US public opinion. The United States had lost a sphere of influence in Iran, and the Soviets had sent troops outside their postwar sphere for the first time. The US loss and what appeared to be the Soviet Union's gain in Afghanistan gave President Jimmy Carter a foreign policy headache that ultimately played a major role in his defeat in the presidential election of 1980. He was unable to do anything about Afghanistan except to refuse to sell the Soviets grain and to lead a boycott of the 1980 Olympic Games in Moscow.

Carter did manage to obtain the release of the hostages, but only after the 1980 election, following 444 days of captivity and a failed rescue attempt. Because Carter could not shake the damaging public perception that he was indecisive and a "wimp," voters decided to give the tough-talking Republican Ronald Reagan the chance to handle the nation's foreign policy.[12]

Khomeini's government set out to transform Iran according to the strictures set down in the Koran. The Islamic revolution transferred sovereignty from the shah to the clergy. The secular parties, however, had a different vision of the future of the Iranian republic. The upshot was a bloody conflict between the Shiite clergy and its opponents. The challenge to the revolution came mainly from the numerous splinter groups on the left—Marxists, Maoists, and socialists—who feared the replacement of one dictatorship by another. When the bloodletting was over, the Islamic revolution had consolidated its power. Waves of revolutionary terror had brought about the execution of approximately 10,000 Iranians, and another half million, many of them of the professional classes, went into exile. The revolution swept aside all remnants of the Pahlavi dynasty and many of the Western influences it had introduced, and it denied the United States a client in the Middle East.

Khomeini's revolution brought a redistribution of land and gave the nation a new constitution based on Islamic laws. In addition, it threatened to spread beyond the confines of Iran. Large Shiite communities in Lebanon, Iraq, the Gulf states, and Saudi Arabia began to look to Iran for guidance. Khomeini's revolutionary message in support of the downtrodden masses and his virulent opposition to the West added a new and dangerous element to the Middle East. The shah, until the very end, had always felt that Communism posed the greatest danger to his throne. But with the Iranian revolution, the conflict in the Middle East ceased to be primarily a contest between Western democracy and Communism. Militant Islam, in direct challenge to the Soviet Union and the West, became another force to be reckoned with.

Revolutionary movements have a tendency to run their course. The fervor that makes a revolution possible cannot be sustained indefinitely. As long as Khomeini was alive and was able to inspire his followers, the revolution appeared secure. After his death in June 1989, however, many Iranians were ready for change. After 1979, Shiite-led Iran was isolated diplomatically, economically, spiritually, and intellectually from the rest of the world. It was branded a "terrorist state," and some of its officials were sought to stand trial abroad for criminal complicity in terrorist acts. The clergy exercised great power in the application of religious laws, regulating private affairs and imposing strict press censorship. (The newspaper editor Abdullah Nouri, for example, was declared a heretic and sentenced to a five-year prison term after he had enraged the religious hierarchy by questioning their absolute power.) It was a country in which the majority of the young people—and in particular women, who were now second-class citizens—faced an uncertain future.

The Iran-Iraq War

With Iran in the throes of a revolution, the government of Saddam Hussein of Iraq availed itself in September 1980 of the opportunity to invade Iran. Hussein had three objectives. He sought (1) to destroy Khomeini's revolution, which he feared might spread to his subjects, most of whom, although Arabs, were Shiites; (2) to secure disputed territory at the confluence of the Tigris and Euphrates Rivers, the Shatt el-Arab; and (3) to emerge as the paramount leader in the Arab world.

Hussein's plan called for securing the Shatt el-Arab, capturing Iran's oil ports on the other side of the river, and crippling Iranian forces in a drive eastward into Iran. He calculated that Iran was unprepared for war because of extensive losses to the officer corps and to its pilots due to purges and desertions during the revolution. Iran, however, still had many loyal middle-grade officers and pilots, and it rallied its people quickly to a conflict that it saw as the resumption of the ancient wars between Persians and Arabs.

Because Iraqi forces moved too cautiously, Iran gained time to rapidly build up its Revolutionary Guard (regular forces) from 7,000 to 200,000 men and to create a new militia of more than 350,000 men to fight a "holy war." Iran was thus able to offset Iraq's initial advantage of a better-trained and better-equipped army. With the two sides evenly matched, neither side was able to score a decisive victory. The war became a stalemate after Iran's counteroffensive in 1982 regained lost territory and captured almost 60,000 Iraqi troops on the battlefield.

The United States and the Soviet Union, as well as the European powers, declared their neutrality in the conflict. But as the war dragged on, over forty nations supplied weapons to one side or the other, and several nations, including the United States, sold weapons to both sides. Israel and the United States both sold weapons covertly to Iran to keep the war going. Israel's defense minister, Yitzhak Rabin, stated frankly, "We don't want a resolution of this war."[13] Iran was supported also by Libya and Syria. Iraq received financial support from Saudi Arabia and the other oil-exporting Arab states near the Gulf, all of which feared Iran's ideological revolution.

Both sides understood the importance of oil in financing the war, and each targeted the other's oil-producing and -shipping facilities in the Gulf. The United States, however, was determined to keep the Gulf open as the passageway through which much of the Western world's and Japan's oil flowed. It accepted, in December 1986, a request by the Kuwaiti government to protect its oil tanker fleet. Kuwaiti tankers were then "reflagged," that is, they were placed under the US flag and escorted by US naval vessels.

The war also saw the first extensive use of chemical weapons—by both sides—since World War I. In March 1988, Iraq launched a chemical weapons attack on its own city of Halabja, which was populated by Kurds, a non-Arab Islamic people hostile to Hussein's regime. The lethal chemicals killed as many as 5,000 of the city's residents. Iraq's use of chemical weapons brought strong worldwide rebuke, for it underscored the new potential danger the world faced, "the poor man's atomic bomb," as some in the Third World called it.

The long war of attrition left its mark on both sides. In the summer of 1987, Hussein accepted a UN Security Council resolution calling for an armistice. Khomeini held out for another year, demanding that Hussein first step down and that Iraq pay $150 billion in reparations. But after suffering a series of military setbacks and a decline in oil profits, Khomeini reversed himself, announcing in July 1988 that he must take "the bitter drink of poison" and accept the UN peace formula.[14]

There was no winner of the absurd eight-and-half-year-long war. Each side suffered almost a million casualties and enormous economic losses. Iraq emerged from the war with the stronger military forces. But Iran was not defeated, and its Islamic revolution remained very much intact.

Terrorism in Lebanon and Libya

In Lebanon, Arabs and pro-Iranian extremists, inspired by Islamic fundamentalism and frustrated by setbacks at the hands of Israel, resorted to desperate, sometimes suicidal, acts of violence against Israeli troops in Lebanon. They considered terrorism as a moral act, whatever the cost to themselves, their enemy, or, for that matter, innocent parties. In some instances, they acted to redress specific grievances or to gain specific ends, such as the return of prisoners taken by Israel. Israeli forces responded in kind with bombing raids and kidnappings.

The United States, by its military intervention on behalf of the Phalangist government of Lebanon in 1983 and its naval bombardment of Muslim strongholds in the mountains, made itself the target of terrorism. In retaliation, terrorists took Westerners in Lebanon as hostages. In March 1984, in Beirut, the Islamic Jihad, a pro-Iranian Shiite group, kidnapped CIA agent William Buckley and later killed him. In the following two years, at least twenty others—college teachers, journalists, businessmen, and priests from the United States, Britain, France, and several other countries—were taken hostage by the Islamic Jihad and other revolutionary groups in Lebanon. Lacking knowledge of the specific identity of the kidnappers or the location of the hostages, Western governments were unable to rescue them. In January 1986, Terry Waite, an envoy of the Church of England, went to Beirut in an effort to negotiate the release of foreign hostages, only to be kidnapped himself by the Islamic Jihad. Although most of the hostages were eventually released, at least ten were killed.[15]

Exasperated by the continuing wave of terrorism and determined to stop it, the Reagan administration vowed to retaliate. It found a likely target for retaliation in Muammar Qaddafi, dictator of Libya. Qaddafi, a strident Arab extremist, had already raised President Reagan's ire for his support of the Palestine Liberation Organization and for his brash threats against the United States for trespassing in what he proclaimed to be Libya's territorial waters, the Gulf of Sidra. Moreover, Qaddafi had maintained terrorist training camps in Libya and had provided financial support for Lebanese extremist groups suspected of terrorism.[16] In April 1986, a terrorist bomb ripped through a discotheque in West Berlin, killing two people, among them a US soldier, and leaving 204 injured. Reagan blamed Qaddafi and ordered a punitive air attack on the Libyan cities of Tripoli and Benghazi. One bomb landed yards away from Qaddafi's residence, leaving him unharmed but, Qaddafi claimed, killing his adopted infant daughter. The US attack, which was not supported by its European allies, was little more than an act of frustration and vengeance and was of questionable value as a deterrent to terrorism, which, in any case, continued unabated.

Two years later, in December 1988, one of the most savage of terrorist attacks occurred when a US jetliner, Pan Am flight 103, exploded in flight over Lockerbie, Scotland, killing all 259 people aboard and 11 on the ground. After three years of masterful detective work, investigators were able to identify two suspects, agents in the Libyan secret service. In the interim, Qaddafi sought improved relations with the West by renouncing and apparently refraining from terrorism. He refused, however, to hand over the suspects to be tried, no doubt fearing that in a trial the two defendants might point the finger at him. Britain and the United States sought his extradition, later joined by France, which itself was investigating an explosion of a French airliner over Niger in September 1989 that killed 170.

The cornered Qaddafi made the best of a bad situation. UN economic sanctions and diplomatic isolation had their impact. After stalling for nearly a decade, he agreed to hand over the two men involved in the Lockerbie bombing to be tried in the Netherlands under Scottish law. Two years after their conviction, Qaddafi admitted, in August 2003, responsibility for the bombing and agreed to pay compensation totaling $2.7 billion to the families of the 270 victims. Later that year, in September, Qaddafi also agreed to pay compensation to the families of those killed over Niger. The settlements set the stage for Libya's reestablishment of normal relations with other nations.

The Gulf War

In 1990 the Persian Gulf—long a site of Western colonialism, internecine conflict among Muslims, and now one of the world's wealthiest regions—became a flash point of violence when Iraq's Saddam Hussein threatened and then invaded a neighboring country.

A War of Nerves

On August 2, 1990, the Iraqi dictator Saddam Hussein launched a full-scale invasion of Kuwait and quickly conquered this small, virtually defenseless, oil-rich nation. The ruler of Kuwait, the Emir Sheikh Jabir al-Sabah, his cabinet, and his family fled to Saudi Arabia. International reaction was swift. Four days later, the UN Security Council voted unanimously to impose a worldwide trade embargo and three weeks later approved the use of armed force to execute it. US president George H. W. Bush responded to a request from Saudi Arabia for protection by ordering Operation Desert Shield, a massive airlift of US ground troops, aircraft, and naval vessels, to guard that country and its oil fields from further Iraqi aggression. Meanwhile, Arab League nations held an emergency meeting at which twelve of its twenty-one members, including Egypt and Syria, voted to send troops to protect Saudi Arabia.

In speeches full of bravado, Hussein promised a "holy war" against whatever "aggressive invaders" dared attack his forces in Kuwait. In the weeks prior to the invasion, he had accused Kuwait of cheating on its OPEC-approved quota of oil production; of dumping large quantities of oil on the market to keep prices low, thus depriving Iraq of badly needed revenue; of stealing oil from the Ramaila oil field, which straddled the Iraqi-Kuwaiti border; and of refusing to cancel the billion-dollar loans it had granted Iraq during its long war against Iran. Hussein ordered his massed troops into action three days after Kuwait rejected his demands for some $14 billion compensation for lost oil revenue and for the cession of two Kuwaiti islands to Iraq. Hussein then revived old Iraqi claims to the entire territory of Kuwait and proclaimed it Iraq's nineteenth province. He ordered the foreign embassies in Kuwait closed and took many of their diplomatic personnel hostage, removing them to military sites in Iraq.

When Bush decided to move against what he called Hussein's "naked aggression," virtually no government took Iraq's side. Instead, statesmen recalled Hussein's unsavory past, his political beginnings as an assassin, his summary execution of political opponents, and his use of poison gas in his earlier war against Iran and his own Kurdish population. They charged him with violations of international law for annexing Kuwait, committing acts of brutality against its people, and taking diplomats hostage. Bush even equated Hussein with Adolf Hitler.

Bush decided not only to expel Hussein's army from Kuwait but also to remove the dictator from power. To that end he took the lead in building a powerful international military coalition and ambitiously spoke of creating a "new world order." He projected a vision of a new era in which the United Nations—led by the United States—maintained international peace and order. Bush also came to see the Gulf crisis as a means of restoring the honor of the US military and of purging the United States of its "Vietnam syndrome."

Bush's outrage against Hussein masked concerns about the failure of his policies toward Iraq prior to the attack on Kuwait. In September 1990, Baghdad released a transcript of US ambassador April Glaspie's final talk with Hussein, on July 25, one week before he attacked Kuwait. In the transcript, which the US State Department confirmed as 80 percent accurate, she was quoted as saying: "I know you need funds. We understand that and . . . you should have the opportunity to rebuild your country. But we have no opinion on the Arab-Arab conflicts, like your border disagreement with Kuwait."[17] The ambassador not only had failed to read Hussein's aggressive intentions; she also had failed to object clearly to his explicit threats against Kuwait.

Revelations after the Gulf War also indicated that the Bush administration had been far less than candid about its pre–August 1990 relations with Hussein. It had consistently pursued a policy of providing substantial economic, military, and intelligence support to Hussein, a policy begun by the Reagan administration early in the 1980s when Iraq was at war with Iran. In 1983, Reagan had sent a special envoy, Donald Rumsfeld, for the purpose of reestablishing diplomatic relations—which had been broken off in 1967—and offering economic and military assistance.[18] Washington here ignored Hussein's record of human rights violations, took Iraq off the State Department's list of terrorist nations, offered Hussein intelligence secrets, and suppressed warnings regarding Iraq's atomic bomb project.

Bush rejected economic sanctions to get Hussein out of Kuwait. At his urging, the UN Security Council, on November 29, 1990, passed (by a 12–2 vote) Resolution 678 authorizing the use of military force if Iraq did not leave Kuwait by January 15, 1991. It now became a forty-eight-day countdown during which allied forces readied for a war already sanctioned by the United Nations. By mid-January 1991, a thirty-one-member coalition massed in the Gulf region, led by more than 530,000 US, 35,000 Egyptian, 25,000 British, 22,000 Saudi, 19,000 Syrian, and 5,500 French fighting forces—in all nearly 700,000

Saddam Hussein, former president of Iraq. *(Iraqi Office, Embassy of Algeria)*

troops. Hussein responded that if war occurred, it would be a horrible "mother of all wars" with "columns of dead bodies that may have a beginning but which would have no end."[19]

A Most Unusual War

The Gulf War, code-named Desert Storm, was fought almost exclusively from the air. Iraqi pilots chose not to engage attacking coalition aircraft in battle and instead flew their planes on a one-way trip to Iran, apparently for safekeeping. As a result, coalition sorties were able to strike at Iraqi targets at will. In the first fourteen hours they flew more than 2,000 unimpeded sorties, and the round-the-clock bombing of Baghdad and other parts of Iraq continued until the end of the war. Television coverage of the war provided viewers with an impressive display of the new, seemingly pinpoint-accurate high-tech weaponry deployed against defenseless Iraqi targets.

Iraq answered the air attacks with Scud missile attacks against Israel. On the first day of the war, it fired eight missiles, with two hitting Tel Aviv and three more exploding near Haifa. Although no one was killed by these Scud attacks, they caused great fear and anger in Israel. Especially frightful was the prospect that the next Scuds might be armed with chemical weapons. Hussein hoped that this diversionary attack would draw a military response from Israel, which might cause Arab nations to withdraw from the coalition. Washington was able to restrain Israel with promises of destroying the Scud missile sites and providing Israel protection with US Patriot antimissile batteries.

The air war produced only a small number of coalition casualties, but the anticipated, potentially bloody ground war against Hussein's armies had yet to be fought. When it finally came, the ground war lasted only 100 hours because the coalition forces, carrying out a well-laid battle plan under the command of US Army general Norman Schwarzkopf, met far less resistance than expected in liberating Kuwait and entering Iraq. Iraq's vaunted Republican Guard forces retreated from the battle, leaving the weaker, poorly trained, poorly fed, and exhausted regular troops to absorb the brunt of the invasion.

In compliance with UN Resolution 660, which called for a cease-fire and Iraqi withdrawal to the pre-invasion lines, Hussein withdrew from Kuwait. Nevertheless, his retreating, demoralized army was massacred on the "highway of death," a stretch of road running sixty miles from Kuwait to Basra. US airplanes trapped the long retreating convoy by disabling the vehicles at the front. One US pilot likened it to "shooting fish in a barrel." Tens of thousands of Iraqis perished.[20]

At the United Nations on March 3, Iraqi foreign minister Tariq Aziz stated that Hussein accepted the UN terms for a cease-fire, including the requirement that it make reparation payments for damage to Kuwait, but not before opening oil pipeline valves in Kuwait to create in the Gulf the largest oil spill in history and torching some 700 Kuwaiti oil wells, creating an environmental catastrophe.

Despite the decisiveness of the coalition military victory, the war's outcome was ambiguous. Before and during the war, Bush spoke of liberating Kuwait but also of removing Hussein from power, of trying him as a war criminal, and of completely destroying Iraq's military forces, including its weapons of mass destruction. Only the first of these objectives was achieved. Removing Hussein would have meant a march into Baghdad. As Bush later explained in his memoirs:

> Trying to eliminate Saddam . . . would have incurred incalculable human and political costs. . . . We would have been forced to occupy Baghdad and, in effect, rule Iraq. . . . There was no viable "exit strategy" we could see. . . . Had we gone the invasion route, the United States could conceivably still be an occupying power in a bitterly hostile land.[21]

Another unusual feature of the war was that the militarily powerful United States did not have to carry the entire cost of the war. For the first time, a superpower sought contributions from other nations to pay for a military operation it had already undertaken. Several Gulf nations and wealthy nonparticipants (Germany and Japan) ended up paying nearly the entire bill. The UN victory was obtained at a low price in allied lives. The coalition lost fewer than 300 on the battlefield, the United States alone losing 148 troops, two-thirds of them from "friendly fire."

The Aftermath

The single indisputable accomplishment of the Gulf War was the liberation of Kuwait, but this was no victory for democracy. Two weeks after the war, the ruling emir, his family and government, and the wealthy Kuwaiti elite returned from their seven-month exile to reclaim their devastated homeland, now darkened by the smoke from the oil wells on fire. But there would be no significant postwar political change in Kuwait. When the emir formed a new cabinet in April 1991, it included no members of political opposition groups; it was, as before, composed almost entirely of members of the ruling Sabah family. His government was mainly concerned about rehabilitation and security. Initial estimates for reconstruction costs ranged as high as $110 billion, with the most serious problem being the sabotaged oil wells, which took nine months to cap.

In Iraq, a spontaneous rebellion by Shiites, who made up 55 percent of the nation's population, threatened the battered Hussein regime. Shiites briefly took control of the bombed-out city of Basra. In northern Iraq, Kurds fought to take control of the region where they were the majority. During the war, Bush had openly encouraged such uprisings, only to betray them later when he stated that he would not support or protect them. Hussein quickly moved his remaining troops against them. He flew his helicopters unimpeded, and within less than three months he crushed the insurrection in the south, killing perhaps as many as 30,000 Shiites and driving more than 1 million into Iran.

The Kurds

The Kurds in the north suffered a similar fate. Kurdish leaders claimed that the "whole of Kurdistan [in Iraq] had been liberated," but they spoke too soon. In the following week, Iraqi forces using helicopter gunships drove Kurdish forces out of their strongholds. Ultimately, Hussein's troops killed about 50,000 Kurds and turned more than 1 million of them into refugees. Bush followed the lead of British prime minister John Major in sending food and supplies and implementing a plan to create a "safe haven" for the refugees in northern Iraq, to be policed by US, British, French, and Dutch troops. In June, the United Nations assumed responsibility for humanitarian aid and protection of the Kurds.

The defeat of the Kurds was but another chapter in the long and tragic history of an ancient people whose Indo-European language and distinct culture set them apart from their neighbors. At the end of World War I, US president Woodrow Wilson proclaimed in his Fourteen Points that the ethnic minorities of Ottoman Turkey should have "absolutely unmolested opportunity of autonomous development." The Treaty of Sèvres (1920), by which the Ottoman Empire was carved up, called for an independent Kurdish state, but the Turkish government of Kemal Ataturk refused to accept it. In 1990, there were approximately 10 million Kurds in eastern Turkey, 5 million in western Iran, 4 million in northern Iraq (about 20 percent of the population), and 1 million in northeastern Syria. These nations were always able to agree on one thing: that there must be no independent Kurdistan. Since 1961, Kurds fought the authorities in Baghdad and Tehran whenever the opportunity availed itself, only to be defeated repeatedly by one or the other and sometimes both. In the 1970s, the United States supported the Kurds, only to drop them after the shah and Hussein worked out an agreement to bring the Kurds to heel. In 1971, when the Kurds asked for continued US aid, Secretary of State Henry Kissinger ignored the request, explaining that "covert action should not be confused with missionary work."[22] Turkey wanted no part of a successful rebellion of Kurds in Iraq. In the past, Turkish Kurds had been prevented from speaking their language in public and their very existence was denied by their government. Turkish politicians and newspaper publishers were sentenced to long prison terms for even mentioning the Kurds. Predictably, Bush obliged Turkey, a NATO ally and participant in the Gulf War, by delivering the Kurds into the arms of Hussein.

The Sunni Arabs of Iraq, who live mainly in the central region, fared only somewhat better than the Shiites and Kurds, for they, too, suffered from deprivation and disease. Tens of thousands of Iraqis died during and in the aftermath of the war due to allied bombing of electric power plants and transport facilities, which affected water purification, sewage treatment plants, and the distribution of food and medicine. Subsequent UN sanctions, which continued until George W. Bush's war, claimed an even larger number of lives. US secretary of state Madeleine Albright, when asked (on the CBS program *60 Minutes* in 1996) whether the death of half a million Iraqi children had been worth the price of the continued containment of Saddam Hussein, she said, "Yes, we think the price is worth it."

* * *

The UN-brokered cease-fire was accompanied by severe economic sanctions. Under its terms, Iraq agreed to destroy its chemical, biological, and nuclear weapons and production facilities. For the next seven years UN weapons inspectors endeavored to gain Iraq's compliance with the 1991 cease-fire weapons inspection regimen. Some weapons-producing facilities were opened to them and some of these were dismantled, but Hussein continued to thwart full inspection. The issue of inspections was brought to a head in December 1998, when Hussein ordered all US members of the inspection teams out of Iraq. As a result, still another test-of-wills crisis was played out, with President Bill Clinton launching a series of bombing attacks in an unsuccessful attempt to force the defiant Hussein into compliance. In October 1998, a frustrated US Congress went so far as to pass the Iraq Liberation Act, calling for the overthrow of Hussein by "the Iraqi opposition." President Clinton, however, upon signing it, made no mention of a US invasion.

Recommended Readings

Islam

Dawood, N. J., trans. *The Meaning of the Glorious Koran.* New York: Penguin, 1956.
    A translation of the Koran for Western readers, as well as a valuable introduction to the early history of Islam, by Muhammad Marmaduke Pickthall, an English convert to the faith.
Guillaume, Alfred. *Islam.* 2nd rev. ed. New York: Penguin, 1956.
    The classic analysis of the theological basis of Islam by one of the West's recognized scholars in the field.
Jansen, G. H. *Militant Islam.* New York: Harper and Row, 1979.
    Explains to Western readers the philosophic foundations of Islam and the reasons for its militant form in Iran.
Kedourie, Elie. *Islam in the Modern World.* New York: Holt, Rinehart and Winston, 1980.
    Focuses on the link between Islam and Arab politics.

Iran and Its Revolution

Bakhash, Shaul. *The Reign of the Ayatollahs: Iran and the Islamic Revolution.* New York: Basic Books, 1984.
Kapuscinski, Ryszard. *Shah of Shahs.* San Diego: Harcourt Brace Jovanovich, 1985.
By a veteran Polish journalist, an eyewitness to the Iranian upheaval.
Rubin, Barry. *Paved with Good Intentions: The American Experience and Iran.* New York: Oxford University Press, 1980.
A discussion of what went wrong with the US scenario for the shah's Iran.
Said, Edward W. *Covering Islam: How the Media and the Experts Determine How We See the Rest of the World.* New York: Pantheon, 1981.
A critical analysis, by a US citizen of Palestinian descent, of how the US press handled the Iranian hostage crisis.
Salinger, Pierre. *America Held Hostage: The Secret Negotiations.* Garden City, N.Y.: Doubleday, 1981.
By a US journalist directly engaged in settling the crisis.
Sick, Gary. *All Fall Down.* New York: Random House, 1985.
A member of President Carter's National Security Council offers a firsthand account of the hostage deliberations.

Iraq and the Gulf War

Arnett, Peter. *Live from the Battlefield: From Vietnam to Baghdad: 35 Years in the World's War Zones.* New York: Touchstone, 1994.
By a New Zealand correspondent, the voice of CNN in Baghdad during the Gulf War.
Bush, George, and Brent Scowcroft. *A World Transformed.* New York: Knopf, 1998.
The memoirs of the US president and his national security advisor.
Gordon, Michael R., and Bernard E. Trainor. *The General's War: The Inside Story of the Conflict in the Gulf.* Boston: Little, Brown, 1994.
Schwarzkopf, H. Norman. *It Doesn't Take a Hero.* New York: Bantam, 1992.
The memoirs of the commander of US forces in the Gulf War.

Notes

1. Some Western scholars have even argued that Muhammad did not believe he was "founding a new religion" as much as bringing to "fullness . . . divine revelation . . . granted to earlier prophets." Richard Fletcher, *The Cross and the Crescent: Christianity and Islam from Muhammad to the Reformation* (New York: Viking, 2004), cited in William Dalrymple, "The Truth About Muslims," *New York Review of Books*, November 4, 2004, p. 32.

2. N. J. Dawood, trans., *The Koran*, 4th rev. ed. (New York: Penguin, 1974), p. 220, Surah 23:14–16; p. 375, Surah 4:87.

3. Alfred Guillaume, *Islam*, 2nd rev. ed. (New York: Penguin, 1956), p. 38.

4. Dawood, *The Koran*, pp. 362–364, Surah 2:261–265, 270–277.

5. Khomeini citations in Bernard Lewis, "How Khomeini Made It," *New York Review of Books*, January 17, 1985, p. 10.

6. The basis of the Shiite creed, in Bernard Lewis, "The Shi'a," *New York Review of Books*, August 15, 1985, p. 8; Shiites point to Allah's will "to favour those who were oppressed and to make them leaders of mankind, to bestow on them a noble heritage and to give them power in the land." Dawood, *The Koran*, p. 75, Surah 28:5.

7. Robert Graham, *Iran: The Illusion of Power* (New York: St. Martin's Press, 1979), p. 33.

8. Ibid., p. 61.

9. "Aryans" here is in reference to the Farsi- (Persian-) speaking peoples of Iran, originally from northern India. It was an attempt to identify the shah with the nation's earliest history.

10. Henry Kissinger, *The White House Years* (Boston: Little, Brown, 1979), p. 1264.

11. After the shah's death in 1980, his son became the claimant to the throne, and many Iranian exiles pinned their hopes on him.

12. It came as a surprise to the US public, therefore, when in November 1986, it was revealed that Reagan, who for six years had bitterly denounced any and all terrorists and had vowed never to deal with any of them, was found to have paid ransom to terrorists in Lebanon who were holding US hostages and then went so far as to ship weapons to the government of the Ayatollah Khomeini, at that time engaged in a long and bloody war with Iraq.

13. Quoted in Mansour Farhang, "Iran-Iraq Conflict: An Unending War Between Two Despots," *The Nation*, September 20, 1986.

14. Graham E. Fuller, "War and Revolution in Iran," *Current History* (February 1989), p. 81.

15. Seventy hostages were finally released between August 1991 and June 1992; some had been in captivity for more than ten years.

16. In October 1989, Qaddafi admitted to having bankrolled terrorist groups but added: "When we discovered that these groups were causing more harm than benefit to the Arab cause, we halted our aid to them completely and withdrew our support." "Kadafi Admits Backing Terrorists, Says He Erred," *Baltimore Sun*, October 26, 1989.

17. Cited in Jim Hoagland, "Transcript Shows Muted US Response to Threat by Saddam in Late July," *Washington Post*, September 13, 1990, p. A33. In March 1991, before the Senate Foreign Relations Committee, Glaspie refuted the Iraqi version of her conversation with Hussein; the State Department, however, refused to make public its transcript of the meeting or its correspondence with Glaspie.

18. In April 1984, the Reagan administration gave the Bell Helicopter Corporation the green light to sell helicopters to the Iraqi ministry of defense, provided that they "can not be in any way configured for military use." National Security Archive online, www2.gwu.edu/~nsarchive.

19. Cited in Robert Ruby, "Security Council OKs Military Force," *Baltimore Sun*, August 26, 1990, p. 1A.

20. Joyce Chediac, "The Massacre of Withdrawing Soldiers on 'The Highway of Death.'" From her report at the New York Commission hearing, May 11, 1991, www.deoxy.org/wc/wc-death.

21. George Bush and Brent Scowcroft, *A World Transformed* (New York: Knopf, 1998).

22. Quoted in Raymond Bonner, "Always Remember," *The New Yorker*, September 28, 1992, p. 48.

21 September 11, Afghanistan, and Iraq

On September 11, 2001, nineteen young Arabs, fifteen of them from Saudi Arabia, under the leadership of the Egyptian Mohamed Atta, hijacked four US airliners. Two of them slammed into the twin towers of the World Trade Center in New York City, bringing the skyscrapers down within minutes. Another airplane plowed into the Pentagon across the Potomac River from the White House. A passenger revolt caused the crash of the fourth airplane in a field near Shanksville, Pennsylvania. In all, almost 3,000 individuals perished, nearly all of them civilians.

Within hours, the US government identified the hijackers as members of al Qaeda, a shadowy organization under Osama bin Laden, an exile from Saudi Arabia living in Afghanistan under Taliban protection. This was not al Qaeda's first attack against US targets: In February 1993, it had sought to topple the twin towers for the first time, and in August 1998 it carried out simultaneous suicide bombings of US embassies in Nairobi, Kenya, and Dar-es-Salaam, Tanzania, killing 224 and injuring over 5,400 (mostly Africans, many of them Muslims, as well as 12 US citizens).

After the attacks on the US embassies, the administration of President Bill Clinton quickly identified al Qaeda as the perpetrator and then lashed out with cruise missiles against targets in Afghanistan that did not hit their targets. Clinton was at that time embroiled in the Monica Lewinsky scandal, which severely restricted his freedom of action; besides, there was little public outcry for more drastic action. Then came a suicide attack against the USS *Cole* in October 2000 in the harbor of Aden, Yemen, which claimed the lives of seventeen US sailors; eleven months later the September 11 attacks rocked the United States.

In his first speech after the September 11 attacks, US president George W. Bush vowed to find the perpetrators and bring them to justice. The United States, he declared, was now engaged in a "global war on terror." He called upon all nations to join the fight, adding that "you are either with us or against us."

It was difficult to understand what drove nineteen young, educated Arabs to commit mass murder in the course of a suicide mission. Bush could offer nothing better than "they hate us for our freedoms." Bush here came down squarely on the side of those who saw the Islamic militants as individuals driven by resentment, hate, irrationality, and a flawed religion. Others spoke of a "clash of civilizations."

Israeli intelligence tried for years to come up with a typical profile of suicide terrorists, only to conclude that they could not establish one. Not surprisingly, then, every statement about suicide terrorists is speculative. Moreover, attempts to comprehend the motives of the terrorists ran into a taboo against trying to understand them and, thus, did not last long. Comprehension, it was argued, only dignified the terrorists. In the United States, publishers of the collected works of bin Laden were accused of promoting "al Qaeda's evil."[1]

Some terrorists have personal problems, while others are deeply affected by the deaths of relatives or friends at the hands of the enemy. The majority—55 percent—of Palestinian suicide bombers, for example, had witnessed their father's humiliation by Israelis. They often mentioned a specific event for which they sought revenge. Once life becomes unbearable, suicide becomes an option.

When a conflict becomes cloaked in religious arguments—absolute and dogmatic—killing and dying become easier. The struggle for Palestine, for instance, initially a secular conflict between socialist Zionists and the secular Palestine Liberation Organization (also in part socialist), became a holy war on both sides that made it easier for true believers to kill and die for.

Geographic displacement, and the resultant alienated existence in a foreign land, affect many of the terrorists. Terrorists are frequently engaged in the struggle for land, their people's rightful place in the sun, and the redemption of history—the return of territory and to a golden age, particularly glorious when compared with the current unbearable situation.[2] Such struggles frequently lead to ethnic cleansing accompanied by massacres.

Suicide bombings are part of what became known as "asymmetric warfare," the weapon of last resort by the poor and weak. They are cheap to produce and—guided by human intellect—highly accurate. Between 1980 and 2003, suicide attacks accounted for 48 percent of those killed in terror attacks, even though they made up only 3 percent of the attacks launched.[3]

Militant Islam

The September 11 attacks were the consequence of militant Islam's conflict with Western imperialism, which, in the eyes of the militants, had brought its "filth of disbelief" and "moral bankruptcy" to the House of Islam. As a graduate student in urban planning in northern Germany, Mohamed Atta had ded-

September 11, 2001: Smoke
and debris erupt from the
South Tower of the World
Trade Center as it collapses
after terrorists crashed two
passenger airliners into the
twin towers. *(AP/Wide World
Photos)*

icated his master's thesis to the preservation of the ancient, vast market, the
souk, in Aleppo—perhaps the world's oldest continuously inhabited city—a
living symbol of the Arab world. Despite the Syrian government's best efforts
to preserve the *souk*, it was dying, under siege by the Western imprint, such as
fast-food restaurants and concrete tourist hotels. In Cairo and Aleppo, Atta fell
under the influence of the Muslim Brotherhood. In Hamburg, living among the
prostitutes and heroin dealers in the city's red-light district, an alienated Atta
came to accept the noble obligation of martyrdom.[4]

George W. Bush was in part correct when he asserted that Islamic terrorists hated what US society represented. Al Qaeda's war against the West, however, was not against the Bill of Rights but against the West's presence in the
House of Islam. Islamic militants singled out the West's support of apostate
and corrupt, tyrannical governments. They also decried support for Israel; US
troops on the Arabian peninsula; support for Russia, India, and China in their
suppression of Muslims (in Chechnya, Kashmir, and Central Asia); and the
pressure on Arab oil suppliers (notably Saudi Arabia) to keep prices low.

Terrorism is the choice of last resort by the weak against the powerful—
in Vietnam, Algeria, Chechnya, Iraq, Sri Lanka, and elsewhere. In the 1965
motion picture *The Battle of Algiers*, a terrorist in the dock is asked: "Isn't it
cowardly to use your women's baskets to carry bombs that have killed so
many innocent people?" To which he replies: "And you? Is it less cowardly to
drop napalm on defenseless villages, killing thousands more? With planes, it

would have been easier for us. Let us have your bombers and you can have our women's baskets."[5]

Islam does not permit suicide. A Muslim's life belongs to Allah and only Allah has the right to take it. But it does encourage martyrdom. A Hamas official explained the difference between suicide and martyrdom: "If a martyr wants to kill himself because he is sick of being alive, that's suicide. But if he wants to sacrifice his soul in order to defeat the enemy and for God's sake—well, then he's a martyr."[6]

The hijackers came from established, well-to-do families and had grown up in the shadow of the culture, wealth, power, and overbearing presence of the West. Their resentment of the West eventually turned into the conviction that the West sought to destroy Islam, that little had changed since the days when the Crusaders first arrived at the end of the eleventh century. After the 1991 Gulf War, bin Laden denounced the US occupation of "the most sacred lands of Islam: the Arab Peninsula . . . stealing its resources, dictating to its leaders, humiliating its people."[7] History must not repeat itself. Ayman al-Zawahiri, bin Laden's chief lieutenant, declared that "we will not accept [in Palestine] the [repetition of the] tragedy of Al Andalus," that is, the 1492 traumatic expulsion of Arabs after 700 years from Andalusia, in modern Spain.[8]

Bin Laden's aim was to rearrange the unequal relationship between the West and the Islamic world. Five weeks after the deadly bombings of Madrid railway stations in March 2004 (which claimed the lives of 191 people and injured another 1,800), he offered the Europeans reconciliation that "will start with the departure of the last soldier from our country."[9] In late October 2004, he made the same offer to the United States. Predictably, his offers were rejected.

After World War II, as the Arab states gained their independence from France and Britain, Arabs looked to a new beginning, a renaissance that would restore the Arab world to its previous grandeur. In most Arab nations, socialist movements came to power with the promise of such a revival. In fact, the Ba'ath Party, which seized power in Syria and Iraq, took its name from the Arabic word for "rebirth." But the rebirth was not to be. Arab governments—whether socialist or monarchist—became corrupt, propped up by either oil money, secret police, or armies equipped by infidel nations such as the United States and Soviet Union. This was true across the board, from Morocco in North Africa to the very heart of the Arab world—to Syria, Lebanon, Iraq, and Saudi Arabia.

The disenchantment, particularly among young Arabs, was heightened by the fact that they had limited professional opportunities at home. Some went abroad, some sought solace in religion, and some joined terrorist organizations. The problem was especially acute in Saudi Arabia. Between 1980 and 1998, it had the highest population growth in the world, at the phenomenal annual rate of 4.4 percent. By 2002, its population had swollen from 6 million to 22 million, 43 percent being fourteen years of age or younger. The number of princes, widely viewed as hypocrites who feigned piety while serving foreign interests and engaging in foreign vices (pornography, alcohol, prostitution), rose from 2,000 to 7,000. At the same time, oil revenues declined from $227 billion in 1981 to $31 billion in 1986. Saudi Arabia's per capita income peaked at $19,000 in 1981, only to drop to $7,300 in 1997 (in constant US dollars). As the universities produced far more graduates than the economy needed, it was not surprising that Saudi Arabia became a hotbed for Islamic militancy. Saudi Arabia is, after all, the only modern Muslim state created by Wahhabi warriors who espoused a particularly strict interpretation of Islam, with an emphasis on *jihad*, an aspect of which is the sacred struggle against infidels. It was also one of but a handful of Muslim countries that had escaped European imperialism, Afghanistan being another. The Saudi royal family's dilemma was that, having come to power with the assistance of the Wahhabi clergy, it spent lavish sums on the clergy in the vain hope of tempering its anti-Western militancy.[10]

Militant Islam's quest to purify society and return it to its former glory has a long history. In the recent past, it was the Muslim Brotherhood that played the leading role in the revival of Islam. Founded in Egypt in 1928, the Brotherhood was the response to the calamity of the destruction of the caliphate, which had ruled the House of Islam since after Mohammed's death, and the return of the European powers. The Brotherhood rejected nationalism, Communism, socialism, and liberalism and dreamed, instead, of the creation of an Islamic system that provided divine instruction for politics, laws, and daily behavior. The Brotherhood's founder, Hassan al-Banna, railed against the West's corruption of Islam with "their half-naked women . . . their liquors, their theaters, their dance halls." The Brotherhood's credo was "God is our objective, the Koran is our constitution, the prophet is our leader, the struggle is our way; and death for the sake of God is the highest of our aspirations."[11] By the late 1940s, the Westernized Egyptian government and the Brotherhood were in a deadly embrace; after the Brotherhood assassinated the prime minister in 1949, the police shot Banna to death.

The mentor of the late-twentieth-century Arab radicals was the Egyptian Sayyid Qutb. In his magnum opus, *Milestones* (1964), Qutb popularized the view that the Arab world lived in the state of *jihaliya*, a darkness that had existed before Mohammed's revelations. The prevailing apostasy must—and will—give way to a true Muslim state after the purification of "the filthy marsh of the world." Qutb developed his views in part as the consequence of a two-year stint among the *kuffar*, the unbelievers, at the Colorado State College of Education. A student of US literature and popular culture, Qutb became repulsed by aspects of US society, such as dances in church recreation halls—organized by ministers no less—and by a people who attended the numerous churches in Greeley, Colorado, yet appeared uninterested in spiritual matters.[12]

The quest to return to the Prophet's teachings led to a vicious war between the militants and the socialist/militarist government of Egypt. President Gamal

Abdel Nasser arrested members of the Brotherhood and in August 1966 had Qutb hanged. Upon hearing his death sentence, Qutb replied: "Thank God. I performed jihad for fifteen years until I earned this martydom."[13] In October 1981, the Brotherhood, after infiltrating the Egyptian army, assassinated the "pharaoh" Anwar Sadat for having signed a peace treaty with Israel.

Sadat's successor, Hosni Mubarak, introduced a permanent state of emergency. Tens of thousands of Islamicists and other political dissidents filled prisons, where they were subjected to systematic torture. The Brotherhood responded with assassinations that ended only after a crackdown following the murder in 1997 of sixty-two people in Luxor—mostly foreign tourists—at the hands of the Brotherhood. By that time, however, Arab Islamic militancy— born in the mosques and coffeehouses and nurtured in the prisons of Egypt— had already begun its migration to the far corners of the earth.

In the 1980s, the attention of the Islamicists was diverted to Afghanistan. After the Soviet invasion, Ayman al-Zawahiri, a member of one of the most prominent Egyptian families, deeply affected by Qutb's worldview, was one of the first Arabs to arrive in Afghanistan. There he linked up with the charismatic Osama bin Laden, the scion of one of the most prominent—and wealthy—Saudi families. Their organizations merged into one. Zawahiri was vital to bin Laden's plans because of his organizational abilities. He had helped to form an underground cell at the age of fifteen and had experience in secret work. It was Zawahiri who plotted the attacks on US targets, including that of September 11. Zawahiri was also responsible for bin Laden's new focus on corrupt Arab governments. An Egyptian lawyer for the Brotherhood explained that, in the early 1980s, bin Laden already "had an Islamic frame of reference, but he didn't have anything against the Arab regimes."[14] Zawahiri would change that.

Bin Laden spent much of his time shuttling between Saudi Arabia and Peshawar, Pakistan, raising money for the anti-Soviet cause. He imported bulldozers for civilian and military projects, and in April 1987 he became engaged in a battle against Soviet troops. It was here that he earned the public reputation as a jihadist warrior. There is no evidence that he worked directly with the CIA, but US officials looked favorably on his recruitment of Arabs. In fact, the CIA sought ways to increase the jihadists' participation in the war, ignoring rumors of their anti-US sentiment among the Arabs.

In Afghanistan, the United States, with considerable help from its jihadist proxies, won a historic Cold War victory over the Soviet Union. After the last Soviet soldier departed in 1989, the CIA's station chief at the US embassy in Islamabad, Pakistan, Milt Bearden, cabled Washington, "WE WON," turned out the lights, and joined the celebration at the embassy.[15] But it was a costly victory. The CIA left behind in Afghanistan a network of jihadists—stronger and wealthier than ever—who now trained their gun sights on the US presence in the Islamic world.

The Arab-Israeli conflict was also a contributing factor to the rise of Arab resentment against the West, particularly against the United States for its role in backing Israel, even though Washington professed to be an honest broker in the conflict, something no Arab believed. In the Yom Kippur War of 1973, the Nixon administration openly sided with Israel, and in 1983 Reagan sent the Marines into Lebanon, ostensibly in the capacity of neutral peacekeepers, only to have guns from the battleship *Missouri* shell Arab targets. In his videotape of October 2004, bin Laden stated that it had been this event, the destruction of "towers in Lebanon," that made him determined to give the United States a taste of its own medicine.

Al Qaeda began its work shortly after the Gulf War of 1991, when bin Laden began to criticize sharply the Saudi royal family for granting the United States a permanent military base in Saudi Arabia. Eventually, bin Laden crossed the line in his criticism and he was ordered to leave. He went first to Sudan, at that time a haven for terrorists. In 1996, after he wrote an open letter to King Faud of Saudi Arabia, once again denouncing the US presence in the land of the Prophet, he left for Afghanistan, where the Taliban had just come to power.

Al Qaeda's first attempt to challenge the West came during the Serbian-Bosnian conflict. Militant Arabs arrived in Bosnia to fight the Orthodox Christian Serbs, bringing with them the military expertise acquired in Afghanistan, as well as money they laundered with the help of cultural and benevolence societies set up in places such as London, Milan, Chicago, Hamburg, and Saudi Arabia. Their engagement in Bosnia proved to be a failure, however, since the Bosnians resented them for their viciousness.

Afghanistan: The War Against al Qaeda

Before September 11, Bush had not been all that concerned about al Qaeda, although the outgoing Clinton administration—notably the national security advisor, Sandy Berger, and terrorist expert Richard A. Clarke—had warned Bush's national security team that they would spend more time on terrorism than on anything else. Four days into the Bush administration, Clarke wrote a memo to Bush's national security advisor, Condoleezza Rice, that a review of al Qaeda was needed most "*urgently*" (emphases in original). Al Qaeda, Clarke tried to explain, was an international, "active, organized, major force," a "first order issue" for the administration.[16] Rice ignored the warning. Clarke stayed on as terrorist expert, but he lost his cabinet-level status and now reported to Rice, who showed little interest in what he had to say.

On July 10, 2001, the director of the CIA, George Tenet, briefed Rice on al Qaeda, a meeting she was unable to recall in 2006. Shortly after his inauguration, Bush appointed Vice-President Dick Cheney to chair a task force on terrorism, one that never met, however. The attorney general, John Ashcroft, on

July 5, 2001, rejected a request from the acting head of the FBI, Thomas Pickard, for another $59 million to combat al Qaeda, adding that he was tired of hearing about it.[17]

Even after Bush received the CIA's now famous Presidential Daily Brief ("Bin Laden Determined to Strike in US") of August 6, 2001, warning of an al Qaeda attack using airplanes against government buildings, he continued his vacation in Texas. In the meantime, beginning in late March 2001, in the words of Clarke, the "system was blinking red." In the summer, Clarke cancelled all vacation leave for his staff in a desperate attempt to stave off an attack. As a member of the Clinton staff, he had participated in the successful disruption of the "millennium plot" against the Los Angeles international airport by "shaking the trees"—pursuing every lead and working with various US as well as foreign authorities, notably in Canada and Jordan.[18] This time, however, despite repeated warnings, the White House showed little concern.

September 11 called for an immediate and forceful response. President Bush, rallying a stunned and angry nation, vowed to go after Osama bin Laden, to pursue him to the four corners of the earth, and to find him "dead or alive." A CIA agent requested a box with dry ice in anticipation of bringing home the supreme war trophy, the head of bin Laden. Bush dismissed Clinton's earlier response to al Qaeda, the "launching [of] a cruise missile into some guy's . . . tent," as a "joke."[19] He would do it right.

Global support for the United States was nearly universal; for the first time, NATO declared September 11 as an attack on one of its members. Bush demanded that Mohammed Omar, the head of the Taliban, hand over bin Laden. When Omar refused, Bush took the fight into Afghanistan on October 7, 2001. First came the bombs, dropped by state-of-the-art jet fighters from nearby carriers and B-2 bombers from as far away as Missouri. Then came a highly mobile, efficient contingent of special forces supported by the latest computers, CIA agents, air force personnel, soldiers, sailors, and NATO forces. The United States, however, initially relied on too small a number of "boots on the ground," 110 CIA officers and 316 special forces.[20]

The US contingent was assisted by Afghan warlords who made up the Northern Alliance—primarily Tadzhiks and Uzbeks—who had held out against the Pushtun Taliban during the previous five years. It was an uneven contest—one between the richest and strongest nation with powerful allies on its side and the poorest. By early December 2001, the Taliban and al Qaeda were beaten, their surviving forces streaming toward the Pakistani frontier from where the Taliban had originally come.

Bush's secretary of defense, Donald Rumsfeld, held a series of press conferences where he basked in the adulation of a grateful nation. Yet it was at this point that things began to go sour. The enemy had been mauled, but when the United States and its NATO allies reached bin Laden's redoubt in the caves in the steep mountains of Tora Bora, they did not have a sufficient number of

Osama bin Laden, spiritual and operational chief of al Qaeda, was the inspirational leader of the September 11 terror attacks. *(FBI)*

troops available to trap and capture him. Omar and bin Laden disappeared into the rugged terrain along the Afghan-Pakistani border, surviving to fight another day.

Bin Laden was not captured because General Tommy Franks, the US commander in Afghanistan, relied on Afghans to do the job—who were either not up to the task or, worse, collaborated with the fleeing al Qaeda fighters, something Franks—already hard at work planning the invasion of Iraq from his command center in Tampa, Florida—grasped too late. Still, Bush proclaimed victory. Bin Laden, he explained on March 14, 2002, had "met his match" and had been "marginalized," that he "may even be dead," adding that "I truly am not that concerned about him."[21] After that, administration references to the still-at-large bin Laden became fewer and fewer.

Early in the war in Afghanistan, General Franks told Pakistani president Pervez Musharraf that "we won't stop until we get" bin Laden.[22] Yet two months into the war, with Osama bin Laden still at large, Franks shifted his resources to Iraq, leaving behind a scant 4,000 US troops in Afghanistan, augmented by 5,000 NATO soldiers. In his memoirs, Franks spoke of a "historic victory" in Afghanistan, ignoring the fact that the perpetrators of September 11 remained at large.

In all likelihood, the Taliban and al Qaeda escaped to Waziristan, across the border from Tora Bora, in Pakistan's North-West Frontier Province. The Waziris, ethnic Pushtuns who claim to be descendants of King Saul, have held off since 600 B.C. any and all invaders—among them Alexander the Great,

Genghis Khan, and Great Britain—to keep their realm "pure and clean." When the Pakistani army—at the urging of the Bush administration—entered Waziristan in March 2004, it ran into a wall of silence and came away empty-handed, despite the FBI's $50 million bounty on the head of bin Laden.

During the Soviet invasion of Afghanistan, Waziristan fell under the thrall of radical Islam, becoming the home of at least ninety schools—*madrasas*—preaching a radical strain of Islam for which the Taliban were known. Before the invasion, the Waziris had considered themselves primarily Pushtuns; afterward, they increasingly saw themselves as Muslims and Pushtuns. In October 2003, an exclusively Islamist government took power in Waziristan, a region that by this time had become an exporter of heroin, which, by Islamic law, was *haram* (forbidden). But if heroin killed a single non-Muslim, it was defensible.[23]

Detour to Iraq

Even before September 11, the Bush administration had its eyes on Iraq and, before the smoke even cleared in Afghanistan, began to prepare an invasion of Iraq. Richard Clarke, the White House expert on terrorism under Clinton and Bush, warned that an invasion of Iraq just might fulfill al Qaeda's "dream" of a "Christian government attacking a weaker Muslim region," allowing it "to rally jihadists from many countries to come to the aid of the religious brethren."[24] Prominent government officials and military officers tried to warn Bush about the pitfalls awaiting him in Iraq, including his own father and his father's foreign policy advisors (Brent Scowcroft and James Baker), Republican leaders in Congress, top military officers (Eric Shinseki and Anthony Zinni), CIA analysts, and foreign heads of state. The venerable diplomat and historian George Kennan warned that "if we went into Iraq . . . you know where you begin. You never know where you are going to end."

Bush paid no attention to the voices of caution; instead, he obliged bin Laden with the invasion of Iraq. As for the jihadists, he famously challenged them in July 2003: "bring 'em on." Predictably, jihadists from across the Middle East began to descend on Iraq. "If Osama bin Laden believed in Christmas," a CIA intelligence official declared, "this is what he'd want under his Christmas tree." In October 2003, seven months after the war began, the London-based International Institute for Strategic Studies concluded that al Qaeda, despite having suffered considerable losses in Afghanistan, was now "fully reconstituted," with an estimated strength of 18,000 members and with a "new and effective modus operandi," operating in as many as ninety countries.[25] Al Qaeda–sponsored acts of terrorism spread beyond Iraq to Spain, Morocco, Indonesia, Tunisia, Pakistan, Kenya, Turkey, and Saudi Arabia.

In the months prior to the September 11 attacks, Bush and his cabinet focused on Iraq and its vast oil reserves. In February 2001, when Vice-President

Cheney convened his secret sessions on energy, maps of Iraq, with its oil fields marked, were rolled out. Immediately after the invasion of Iraq, Cheney's office, the Pentagon, the CIA, and Iraqi exiles pushed for the privatization of the Iraqi oil industry. The *Wall Street Journal* called the quest for Iraq's oil "one of the most audacious hostile takeovers ever." Much of the determined Iraqi resistance came from the oil workers, so strong that it soon became evident that, in the words of the satirist P. J. O'Rourke, it was "much cheaper to buy oil than to steal it."[26]

In the early 1990s, Dick Cheney, secretary of defense at the time, issued a document, "Defense Planning Guidance," that called for the permanent expansion of US power abroad. After he returned to power in January 2001, Cheney and others, in the span of two months, drew up plans for war against Iraq without, however, knowing how to implement them. September 11 gave them the opportunity to put those plans into action. Six hours after the attacks, Rumsfeld drew up orders for his generals to prepare for war against bin Laden and Saddam Hussein, Iraq's dictator. "Sweep it all up," one of Rumsfeld's aides wrote in the margin of the orders, "things related and not."[27]

Bush was aided and abetted by his foreign policy advisors, a group collectively known as the neoconservatives, or "neocons." Its leading members were Cheney, Rumsfeld, Deputy Secretary of Defense Paul Wolfowitz, and Condoleezza Rice. Many of them had gotten their start in the 1970s as members of the Committee on the Present Danger and the CIA's B Team under George H. W. Bush, committees that persistently had exaggerated the Soviet threat.

The neocons had a Cold War frame of reference, and for them defeat in Vietnam had been a central event. They advocated preemptive war, were optimistic about US power, and tended to dismiss warnings about an overextension of US forces. They showed no great inclination to consult with either allies or the United Nations. They disdained the realpolitik of Richard Nixon and Henry Kissinger, who had pursued détente and had negotiated with both the Soviet Union and Communist China. They embraced a highly ideological and idealistic view of US influence that, they were certain, was capable of bringing progress and morality to a world wracked by evil. They believed in the moral superiority of the United States, still the "city on the hill," the shining—Christian—beacon for other nations, an idea their hero Ronald Reagan had frequently expressed. The neocons were certain that in Iraq they would be received with open arms, sweets, and flowers. In March 1917, the British general Stanley Maude had suffered from the same delusion when he told the Iraqis: "Our armies do not come into your cities and lands as conquerors or enemies, but as liberators." Until the end of his presidency, George W. Bush was unable to understand why the ungrateful Iraqis had not thanked him personally and publicly for their liberation.[28]

After September 11, the neocons worked overtime to argue that Hussein had been part of the September 11 conspiracy and that he possessed weapons of mass destruction that could arrive any day on US territory, even in the shape of a nuclear mushroom cloud. Yet in the months before September 11, Bush's secretary of defense, Colin Powell, and Condoleezza Rice had publicly stated that Hussein had lost his war-making capacity of a decade earlier and that he had not rebuilt his military. Richard Clarke's conclusion that there was no link between bin Laden and Hussein fell on deaf ears.

As the neocons prepared for war, they convinced the public—as well as the press whose job it was to ask questions[29]—that the war on terror demanded regime change in Baghdad. They drummed home the argument that Hussein possessed chemical and biological weapons, the capability to produce nuclear weapons, and the will to use them. They repeatedly emphasized that in the 1980s Hussein had used poison gas against Iranian troops and then against the Kurds in Iraq. Moreover, they insisted, Hussein was about to make his WMD available to al Qaeda.

This argument shunted aside the fact that bin Laden and Hussein were mortal foes. When bin Laden spoke of apostate Arab governments, he also had Hussein in mind, something Hussein well understood. When in 1991 the United States went to war against Hussein for the first time, bin Laden sought—unsuccessfully—Saudi backing to unleash a jihad against Hussein.[30] It was no secret to Hussein that the greatest domestic threat he faced was militant Islam, whether of the domestic Shiite or al Qaeda Sunni variety. In 2004, the *9/11 Report* destroyed one of the rationales for the war when it pointed out that Hussein had not responded to a bin Laden request to establish terrorist camps in Iraq. (In 2005 and 2006, reports by the CIA and the Senate Intelligence Committee offered the same conclusion.) The report went on to say that other countries had provided assistance to al Qaeda—either officially or unofficially—notably Afghanistan but also pro-US nations such as Pakistan, Saudi Arabia, and the United Arab Emirates.

To prepare public opinion for war, the neocons turned to Ahmed Chalabi, a US-educated Iraqi whose family, once one of Iraq's wealthiest, had been dispossessed by the Ba'athist revolution of 1958. In the early 1990s, Chalabi joined a conservative think tank, the American Enterprise Institute, created the Iraqi National Congress (INC), and began to lobby for a US invasion to return him to Iraq. Chalabi's INC was the primary force behind a 1998 US congressional resolution calling for "regime change" in Baghdad. Chalabi charmed high-level officials in Washington to the degree that between 1992 and 2004 three administrations funneled at least $100 million to his organization. The CIA and State Department, however, considered him a charlatan, and a court in Jordan sentenced him to twenty-two years at hard labor for the embezzlement of large sums of money. None of that prevented him from cultivating powerful patrons in high places in Washington—Rumsfeld, Wolfowitz, and Cheney. The Bush administration used Chalabi's disinformation—channeled through the Pentagon—to sell the war. When US officials thought that Hussein might have mobile chemical and biological laboratories, it was Chalabi who provided the story that Hussein did in fact have them and that he could provide their location. He also circulated stories of al Qaeda terrorist camps in Iraq and stated that it would take but 1,000 US troops to topple Hussein.

The commander of the US Marine Corps, Anthony Zinni, called Chalabi's plan a "pie-in-the-sky fairy tale." Bush was told of the State Department's and CIA's doubts about Chalabi but sided with the neocons nevertheless. In March 2003, Chalabi had his war, and when his Free Iraqi Fighters arrived in Baghdad, they joined the looting in progress, except that they focused on villas, SUVs, and the like. When the time came to establish an interim government, the UN opposed Chalabi's candidacy. The Bush administration subsequently dropped Chalabi, who by now had done his duty; besides, it had discovered that Chalabi had sold intelligence to Iran.

At first, Bush sought UN approval for an invasion, but all he was able to obtain was a resolution authorizing the return of UN weapons inspectors, whom Hussein had kicked out in 1998. The UN commissioned Hans Blix, a Swedish diplomat, to scour Iraq for WMD. After Blix's team issued intermediary reports that they had found no evidence of WMD, Bush started the war before they could complete their task.

During his State of the Union address in January 2003, Bush gave a hair-raising appraisal of the threat emanating from Iraq. He accused Hussein of having enough biological and chemical weapons (500 tons of sarin, mustard, and nerve gases) "to kill several million people" as well as enough botulinum toxin "to subject [an additional] million of people to death." The final argument for war was offered by Bush's respected secretary of state, Colin Powell. Before the United Nations—and the world—Powell offered "incontrovertible" proof of the existence of these weapons. Powell, who initially had refused to read the report,[31] swallowed his pride and, as a good soldier, came onboard. In the process, he converted many doubters. His "evidence" consisted of photographs and specific addresses where the weapons were allegedly produced and stored, and he even held up a small vial, the contents of which, he claimed, could kill thousands. Yet nearly everything Powell said that day was incorrect as he spun a tale of half-truths and outright misrepresentations.

The neocons piled "evidence" on top of "evidence." They stated that Hussein's son-in-law, Hussein Kamal, who had defected to Jordan, had alleged in August 1995 the existence of WMD. In his speech before the UN, Powell invoked Kamal's name. Only after Kamal's testimony found its way to the Internet did it become evident that he had made no such claim. Instead, Kamal had told the CIA that Hussein had destroyed his WMD in 1991. The professed certainty that Hussein had WMD trumped the evidence that he did not. The war was launched on the basis of Rumsfeld's famous rationale that "the absence of evidence is not evidence of absence."

The *New York Times* journalist Thomas Friedman, who had originally beaten the drums for war, stated that the invasion had been the handiwork of twenty-five individuals who worked within "a five-block radius" of Friedman's office in Washington. "If you had exiled them to a desert island a year and a half ago," Friedman went on to say, "the Iraq war would not have happened."[32]

No one ever found evidence of a Hussein–bin Laden connection or WMD. David Kay, the Pentagon's chief weapons inspector in Iraq, after scouring the country with 1,500 agents on behalf of the Pentagon's Iraq Survey Group, failed to come up with the evidence the neocons hoped to find.

When the United Nations—led by France, Germany, Russia, and China—insisted that containment of Hussein continue, instead of resorting to force, Bush decided to go it alone. Of all the major nations, only Great Britain—whose government, too, had hyped the imminent threat from Iraq—offered meaningful assistance by sending 10,000 troops. British prime minister Tony Blair thought that by supporting Bush he would be able to assert a measure of influence in Washington. Blair wanted Bush to engage in the Palestinian-Israeli conflict as an honest broker, but he did not, however, tell Bush that British support depended on that issue being addressed. In the end, Blair had nothing to show for his efforts except a disillusioned electorate, which increasingly saw him as "Bush's poodle." In May 2005 came the revelation of the existence of the so-called Downing Street memo, a firsthand report by British intelligence—written as early as July 2002, eight months before the invasion—that warned Blair that Bush had already decided on war. The memo explained that "intelligence and facts were being fixed" to provide the rationale for war. It also pointed out what later became painfully obvious, that "there was little discussion in Washington of the aftermath after military action."

No one doubted that the United States would be able to make short shrift of Hussein's depleted army, which had been mauled in 1991 and had not been rebuilt. Hussein had virtually no air force and approximately one-third the troops, artillery, and armor as in 1991. His inventory contained Soviet T-55 tanks nearly fifty years old.

After Vietnam, the Pentagon had concluded that the next war would have to be fought differently. The result was the Powell Doctrine, named after Colin Powell, at that time the chairman of the Joint Chiefs of Staff: In the next war, US leaders must define their objectives clearly—including an "exit strategy"—and the military must marshal all its resources to achieve victory here and now. In the 1991 Gulf War, the Powell Doctrine worked to perfection. The UN-sanctioned coalition consisted of more than 530,000 US troops—accompanied by a vast array of airpower—and another 160,000 allied soldiers. After the initial aerial bombardment, the ground war lasted 100 hours. The United States lost 148 troops in combat, two-thirds by "friendly fire"; its allies lost another 150. Moreover, the United States had an "exit strategy." Hussein would be driven out of Kuwait and after that the UN would keep an eye on his armed forces, particularly their arsenal of WMD.

In 2002, Colin Powell, this time as secretary of state, warned the administration that if it intended to occupy Iraq, it must not go in "light." It must not repeat the mistakes of Vietnam. The army chief of staff, Eric Shinseki, and the former commander of the US Marine Corps, Anthony Zinni, too, spoke of the need for 400,000 troops, not the 75,000 the civilian leadership at the Pentagon (notably Rumsfeld and Wolfowitz) had in mind. (The 150,000 troops ultimately deployed were the result of a compromise between the military and the civilians in the Pentagon.) The academician Wolfowitz publicly ridiculed Shinseki, whose estimates, Wolfowitz declared, were "wildly off the mark"; moreover, "it's hard to conceive that it would take more forces to provide stability . . . than it would take to conduct the war itself." It marked the first public dressing-down of a four-star general since the Harry Truman–Douglas MacArthur clash more than fifty years earlier. Zinni fared even worse, being called a traitor in meetings in the Pentagon.

Many of the problems the United States subsequently faced in Iraq stemmed from the fact that it did not have sufficient "boots on the ground." The comparison with the 1991 Gulf War is instructive. There, a coalition force of 690,000 troops was given but one task: to drive Hussein out of Kuwait. In 2002, in contrast, a force less than one-quarter that size was deployed to defeat the Iraqi army, dismantle it, occupy a resentful nation the size of Texas containing 25 million people, and administer and rebuild it.

Powell also warned that the United States was responsible for the destruction it caused, invoking the "Pottery Barn rule"—if you break it, you own it. Powell's admonition was dictated not only by common sense but also by international law: The occupier is responsible for the well-being of the citizens it controls, something that could not be done by going in "light." The first casualty of this war, as always, was truth; the second was the Powell Doctrine.

Events quickly proved Powell, Shinseki, and Zinni correct. Hussein's army did not stand and fight; instead, it melted away to fight another day. Determined to sweep away the symbols of the old order, US troops pulled down statues and portraits of Hussein, and US "ambassador" Paul Bremer went so far as to disband the 400,000-strong Iraqi army, dissolve the police, dismiss Ba'athist bureaucrats, and begin to privatize the state sector of the Iraqi economy. In one fell swoop, Bremer not only threw hundreds of thousands of Iraqis out of work but also tore apart the complex fabric of Iraqi society that the Ba'ath Party had stitched together over thirty-five years.

As the United States dismantled the old order, Iraqis were no longer under any sort of constraint, and they began to loot stores, museums, hospitals, all of the government ministries, and—most important—army depots, carting off vast stores of weapons and explosives. US forces made no effort to stop the looting. At first, plundering was confined to eastern Baghdad, as US tanks striding the Tigris bridges prevented it from spreading. When the tanks withdrew after two days, western Baghdad was looted as well.[33] Rumsfeld dismissed reporters' concerns by declaring that "free people are free to make mistakes and commit crimes and do bad things."

"Mission Accomplished"

Bush announced that the United States would withdraw as soon as its objectives—never spelled out—were accomplished. In the meantime, however, the Pentagon began to build permanent military bases. On May 1, 2003, three weeks after the fall of Baghdad, President Bush, donning an aviator's suit, was dropped off on the aircraft carrier USS *Lincoln*. Standing under a banner proclaiming "MISSION ACCOMPLISHED," he declared that "major combat" in Iraq had ended. The number of US dead at that point stood at 139.

Policymakers in Washington expressed the hope that the political and economic reconstruction of Iraq would follow the lines of the postwar occupations of Germany and Japan. In those countries, however, the people well understood why they were under foreign occupation. The neocons sold the invasion of Iraq as an act of liberation, but many Iraqis, with the exception of the Kurds in the north, generally did not see it as such. Even the Shiites, who were finally free of Saddam Hussein's brutality, saw the permanent US bases as symbols of a permanent occupation. Iraqis, with their keen sense of history, well remembered other occupations of their country—most recently by the Ottoman Turks and the British. They saw the US invasion as the first step leading to recolonization by foreigners who pursued their own interests and who neither understood nor respected their language, customs, or religion.

In postwar Germany and Japan there had been no resistance to occupation. Their people focused, instead, on clearing the rubble and on rebuilding their cities and factories. Equally important, the Western Allies during World War II did not dismantle the efficient bureaucracies of these nations. In Japan, in particular, the government in power during the war scarcely skipped a beat as it continued to run the country under the US occupation.

Bush's first envoy to Iraq, General Jay Garner, was a pragmatist who saw the country as "our coaling station in the Middle East," on the model of Cuba and the Philippines. Garner thought the United States should fix the economic infrastructure, hold quick elections, and leave economic shock therapy to the International Monetary Fund. Garner lasted but three weeks. The neocons wanted more than a coaling station. Their mission called for the transformation of Iraq's economy and political structure from the ground up. Iraq was to become the poster child for free markets and democracy in the Middle East. On May 12, 2003, Bush replaced Garner with Paul Bremer, who began to hand out contracts to US companies poised to establish their control of the Iraqi economy. Every economic sector, with the exception of oil (for the time being), was now up for grabs by foreigners who assumed the right to take any and all profits out of the country.

Iraq now belonged to the true believers, who initiated the most drastic economic shock therapy anywhere. *The Economist* called Iraq "a capitalist's dream." US businessmen drooled over an economic climate that would permit a well-stocked 7-Eleven store to knock out thirty Iraqi family-owned stores. Yet all this was illegal. The Geneva Conventions of 1907 and 1949 stipulated that an occupier must abide by the nation's laws and has no right to its assets. As early as October 2003, an Iraqi political backlash emerged over that issue.

Because of escalating violence, US companies were slow to set up shop in Iraq. One of the problems was that few of the individuals the Bush administration recruited had the requisite expertise in either running Iraq or rebuilding its economy, being chosen, instead on the basis of political loyalty. In 2003, the US Congress appropriated nearly $20 billion for reconstruction, yet whatever money was spent went to Western corporations at the exclusion of Iraq's state-owned enterprises, which were now operating at 50 percent capacity. The ubiquitous concrete barriers (derided as "Berlin walls" or "Bremer walls"), for example, were available from Iraqi contractors for $100 each; instead, they were imported at $1,000 each. Iraqi popular resistance was largely in response to the economic shock therapy. Workers, out of a job, joined the ranks of the unemployed—and the resistance. Estimates of the number of unemployed in the summer of 2004 ranged between 50 percent and 70 percent.

The resistance targeted foreign business interests—US, South Korean, Japanese, Italian, Turkish, and others—by kidnapping, ransoming, and killing hostages. By November 2004, more than 170 foreigners had been kidnapped; more than three dozen of them were murdered or "disappeared." Iraq, the neocons' dream laboratory, became the most dangerous place to do business.

The resistance came from many quarters, including an indeterminate number of foreigners, the most important of whom was Abu Musab Zarqawi, a Jordanian who appeared to have been personally responsible for the decapitation of two US contractors in September 2004 and who, the US military claimed, led the foreign contingent in the city of Fallujah. Zarqawi, the head of his own organization that previously had caused bloodshed in Europe and the Middle East, was both a rival and an ally of al Qaeda. As with so many of the Islamic militants, he had cut his teeth in Afghanistan, where he first made contact with bin Laden's al Qaeda and where he began to construct a distinct network, called Monotheism and Jihad. Zarqawi was particularly effective in the conservative Sunni city of Fallujah, where he called for resistance against the United States as well as a sectarian war against the heretic Shiites.

Shiite clergy were among the early critics of the occupation. The most vociferous of them was Moqtada al-Sadr, a young ayatollah who had inherited the mantle of his revered father, who had been assassinated in 1999, presumably by Hussein's agents. The Shiite sector of Baghdad, home to more than

2 million impoverished residents, formerly known as "Saddam City," became "Sadr City" (renamed in honor of the father). In March 2004, Bremer padlocked the offices of Sadr's weekly newspaper after it had charged that "Bremer Follows the Steps of Saddam."[34] He issued a warrant for the arrest of the "outlaw" Sadr for his alleged complicity in the (unresolved) April 2003 murder of a rival Shiite cleric, Abdel Majid al-Khoei, the son of a grand ayatollah, whom the CIA had brought back from exile.

Sadr's resistance movement, the Mahdi Army, was a classic example of "blowback." Its members were the young, the unemployed, the disillusioned. "Sadr took Bremer's economic casualties," a Canadian journalist explained, "dressed them in black and gave them rusty Kalashnikovs."[35] The US military considered Sadr a priority because of his stature and uncompromising militancy. Repeated flare-ups of pitched battles between the Mahdi Army and US troops ended in a stalemate after a final round of fighting in the Shiite holy city of Najaf, the burial place of the founder of the Shiite branch, Mohammed's son-in-law, Ali. Grand Ayatollah Ali al-Sistani, the most influential ayatollah in Iraq, brokered a truce under the terms of which US troops withdrew from Najaf and the militia agreed (without doing so) to give up their weapons.

The troubles in Fallujah, the "city of mosques," a conservative Sunni religious center of approximately 300,000 inhabitants thirty-five miles west of Baghdad, began early, at the end of April 2003, after US troops commandeered a local school to use as a military base. During the confrontation, US troops killed thirteen residents, several of them children. The resistance in Fallujah began as an act of revenge for the killings.

A year later came the disturbing images on television and the Internet of four US "contractors" working for the Pentagon who had been trapped in Fallujah and were killed, their dismembered bodies strung up from one of the city's bridges. US forces sought to retake the city with the help of a US-trained militia—the "Fallujah Brigade"—only to see it go over to the other side. Fallujah became a symbol of national and religious resistance and a haven for jihadists, many of them foreigners—from Saudi Arabia, Jordan, Egypt, and Syria—under the command of Zarqawi.

In November 2004, immediately after the US presidential election, 10,000 US Marines, augmented by 5,000 Iraqi soldiers, took Fallujah after a bloody, weeklong battle, leaving behind thousands of casualties, a flood of civilian refugees, and much of the city in ruins. Once again, the United States proclaimed victory, but many of the resistance fighters had escaped.

The US cause in Iraq was not helped when, in late April 2004, photographs on the Internet proved that US troops had been engaged in systematic torture of Iraqis at the Abu Ghraib prison, just west of Baghdad. Amnesty International and the International Red Cross had already reported on the abuses, but their complaints had been ignored. Rumsfeld had dismissed the initial reports of torture as "isolated pockets of international hyperventilation." This time the shocking photographs could not be readily dismissed. Ironically, the Abu Ghraib prison had first gained notoriety for torture, rapes, and executions under Hussein. The Pentagon and the White House feigned shock at such behavior and immediately placed the onus on a few low-ranking "bad apples." It soon became evident, however, that the decision to use torture had been made at the highest levels within the Bush administration.

In other parts of the world, the United States had long been engaged in torture, but it had generally done so surreptitiously through intermediaries, such as South Vietnamese forces and the Latin American military, using lessons learned at the School of the Americas in Fort Benning, Georgia. After September 11, torture began in Afghanistan when the Bush administration lumped the Taliban and al Qaeda together in a new category of "enemy combatants," not enemy soldiers, and thus not subject to the provisions of the 1949 Geneva Convention that prohibited the torture of any and all prisoners "at any time and in any place whatsoever."

Beginning in February 2002, White House counsel Alberto Gonzales declared that the Geneva Conventions had become "irrelevant" and that the president, acting as commander-in-chief, was not bound by any law—US or international. The inflicting of pain on prisoners, Gonzales went on to say, was permitted as an act of "self-defense" or the result of "superior orders." In the Pentagon, Donald Rumsfeld signed off on several similar such directives. After the Bush administration withdrew the Geneva protection from the Taliban and al Qaeda in Afghanistan, torture migrated to the Guantánamo Bay Naval Base, to which the Taliban and al Qaeda prisoners had been taken, and from there to Iraq.

In the summer of 2003, as the Iraqi resistance grew in strength, US forces became desperate to gain information about the ubiquitous insurgents. Soldiers began to arrest civilians at the site of attacks, often raiding homes, wrecking furniture, and dragging people out. Eventually the number of detainees reached 50,000, guarded by understaffed, ill-prepared National Guard troops. Few of the detainees had information to give; fewer still were released.

At the end of August 2003, torture in Iraq became institutionalized when Major General Geoffrey Miller, commander of the detention camp at Guantánamo, arrived in Baghdad. Miller demanded "actionable intelligence" any way possible—by beatings, sexual humiliation, "waterboarding" (near-drowning of detainees), and the use of dogs. All this was sanctioned by the commander of US forces in Iraq, General Ricardo Sanchez. The system was self-defeating, however, since it merely created more hostility. In June 2004, at Friday prayers in Baghdad, imams charged that the only freedom the United States had brought to Iraq was the freedom to abuse Iraqis, "the freedom of rape, the freedom of nudity and the freedom of humiliation."[36]

At Guantánamo, just as the "enemy combatants" were about to be tried by novel "military commissions," US federal courts intervened. By way of these "commissions" the US government, despite its ratification of the Geneva Convention of 1949, denied for the first time enemy soldiers prisoner-of-war status. In November 2004, however, US district judge James Robertson declared that the "commissions" were neither lawful nor proper. Defendants were entitled to hear the charges against them and to challenge their imprisonment in US federal court.

Iraq's ethnic complexity proved to be another vexing problem. When Bremer began to draw up the first transitional laws, he stated that ethnicity had no place in the new Iraq, that the country's citizens were all Iraqis. It was a tall order. The Kurds did not see themselves as Iraqis; 75 percent of Kurdistan's adult population had signed a petition demanding independence. Even before the invasion, Kurdistan had become de facto independent. Kurds flew their own flag, paid no Iraqi taxes, controlled their own borders, and had their own army. To complicate matters, most Shiites—60 percent of the population—wanted an Islamic state, and the Sunnis saw the Shiites as heretics and believed that it was their right to govern Iraq. The potential for ethnic and religious violence was particularly great in the northern oil center of Kirkuk, a city of 850,000 people, roughly evenly divided among Kurds (35 percent), Sunni Arabs (35 percent), and Turkomen (26 percent), the latter being ethnic Turks hostile to both Kurds and Arabs. Each of them had their own historic claims to the city and its oil.[37]

None of the neocons expected that by the end of 2008 the number of US military dead in Iraq and Afghanistan would total more than 4,200 and another 30,000 seriously wounded. In addition, more than 1,000 civilian contractors also died in Iraq. As for Iraqi civilian casualties, the Pentagon did not bother to count them. "We don't do [civilian] body counts," General Tommy Franks declared. By the end of 2008, a conservative tally put the number at around 100,000.[38]

As regular and National Guard units had their tours of duty extended, US forces were stretched to the breaking point. The cost in dollars, once estimated at a paltry $30 billion, shot past $850 billion by the end of 2008. Estimates for the final cost—after everything was added up, including veterans' benefits and health care, interest on borrowed money, and so on—ranged between $2 trillion and $3 trillion. President Clinton's budget surplus was a distant memory wiped out by September 11, homeland security, the wars in Afghanistan and Iraq, and tax cuts—the first in history, anywhere, in time of war. The wars were conducted on borrowed money (largely from Japan and China) down to the last cent.

When the United States went to war against the Taliban, the world, including many Muslims and even Arabs, believed that its cause was just. Iraq, however, quickly drained the reservoir of goodwill. Clerics at Cairo's Al-Azhar University, an esteemed center of Muslim thought, who had condemned the attacks of September 11, now preached that every Muslim had an obligation to defend Iraq.[39]

The Bush administration sought an Iraqi government that would accept a permanent US presence. Once elections were proposed, Iraq's most revered Shiite cleric, Ali al-Sistani, insisted on a direct election—one person, one vote—in contrast to an indirect election that the United States hoped to manipulate. Under Sistani's proposal, the Shiite majority was destined to gain control of the national government. Indeed, one of their own, Nouri al-Maliki, became prime minister. By necessity he had to work with the Bush administration, which provided money and trained his army. But there was another winner. The Islamic Republic of Iran obtained what it had always wanted: a Shiite Islamic government in neighboring Iraq. The head of Iran's powerful Guardian Council thought that the "election results are very good."[40] Iran's influence in Baghdad was evident in numerous ways. It provided assistance to all the Shiite militia. And it was Iran that brokered the cease-fire between Sadr's and Maliki's armies in May 2008.

Indeed, the new Iraqi government had close ties to Tehran. Maliki headed the Islamic Dawa Party, a sworn enemy of Saddam Hussein going back to the 1960s. But the party was also opposed to the West's presence in the Arab world. (In 1983, for instance, Dawa bombed the US and French embassies in Kuwait.) In 1980, Hussein had sentenced Maliki to death; in December 2006, it was Maliki who gladly signed Hussein's death warrant. Iran also had close ties to another Shiite bloc, the Badr Organization, which had been founded in Tehran during Hussein's war with Iraq. Its godfather was the Ayatollah Khomeini. Upon the Badr Organization's return to Iraq, it became a powerful militia outside Maliki's control, notorious for its vicious campaigns against Sunnis. Another Shiite militia that Iran supported was the Mahdi Army under the direction of the nationalist Moqtada al-Sadr, whose family was proud of the fact that, even during the darkest days of Hussein's reign of terror, it had stayed in Iraq. Keeping its hand in the game, Iran supported all of them, even though the Mahdi Army periodically clashed with Maliki's troops. Iran's influence went a long way to explain why Maliki was in no position to cut deals with the United States. All-important issues—such as the proposed fifty-eight permanent bases, control of oil, and immunity from prosecution of US troops—were subject to parliamentary ratification by the Shiite majority.

In the meantime, a civil war between Sunnis and Shiites threatened to spin out of control. It was fanned, in part, by the nihilistic brutality of Zarqawi, who was responsible for the death of an estimated 6,000 Iraqis. In February 2006, Zarqawi poured additional gasoline on the fire by blowing up one of Iraq's holiest Shiite shrines, the golden dome of the Al-Askari Mosque in Samarra, the burial place of two revered ninth-century Shiite imams. The savage Shiite retaliation convinced many Sunnis that Zarqawi was leading them down the path of destruction. Zarqawi's violence appalled even bin Laden and his lieutenants. Can Zarqawi's men "kill all the Shia in Iraq?" Zawahiri asked; "has any Islamic state ever tried that?"[41] Residents of the "Sunni triangle," the region to the north and west of Baghdad, on whose behalf Zarqawi was fighting, began to turn against him. In June 2006, acting on a paid informer's tip, US troops finally tracked him down and killed him.

The Sunni "Awakening"

Sunni insurgents concluded that their best chance of survival against the US-supported Shiite tide was cooperation with the US military. The result was the Sunni "Awakening." The US military, under the command of General David Petraeus, gained a new ally in the war against al Qaeda. More than 100,000 so-called Sons of Iraq—who until then had been killing US troops—were put on the Pentagon's payroll and entrusted to guard checkpoints, set up barriers to prevent roadside bomb explosions and suicide car attacks, and patrol neighborhoods.

Three years after Bremer's disastrous decision to dismantle the Sunni-dominated Ba'athist state, many of Saddam Hussein's men now returned to power and respectability. Under the Awakening, the city of Fallujah gained a new police chief, Colonel Faisal Ismail al-Zobaie, once a member of Hussein's Republican Guard and, after the invasion, a supporter of al Qaeda. After al Qaeda murdered members of his family, he joined the Awakening. The Marine Corps website touted Fallujah's newly found stability as a success, but it came at a heavy price. Zobaie was more than the new police chief. He became the law in Fallujah—judge, juror, and jailer—who arrested, convicted, tortured, and killed suspects. One of his interrogators, who had honed his methods under Hussein, saw no need to change them. "Since Saddam Hussein until now," he explained, "Iraq obeys only force." What Zobaie ultimately wanted was for the United States to leave, giving him full control of the city. Then "I'll be tougher with the people."[42]

The Awakening solved one problem—the drastic reduction of US fatalities—but created another one. The Sunni leaders—rehabilitated, financed, and armed by the Pentagon—posed a direct challenge to the Shiite-dominated government in Baghdad. Petraeus now found himself in the difficult position of serving two antagonistic masters at the same time. His counterintelligence advisor obliquely spoke of "balancing competing armed interest groups." However, as a former senior member of President Clinton's national security staff pointed out, by virtue of this "balancing" act "we're midwifing the dissolution of the country."[43]

The Maliki regime dreaded the thought of a revival of Sunni power nurtured by dreams of the restoration of a Sunni-dominated political order, the ultimate goal of the Awakening. "Once Anbar [Province] is settled," one of the province's tribal leaders explained, "we must take control of Baghdad, and we will."[44] In response to explicit threats, in the summer of 2008, an alarmed Maliki government began to round up prominent members of the Awakening.

The "Surge"

The Awakening came at a time when Iraq appeared to be flying apart and when US casualties reached record levels. To continue to sell an increasingly unpopular war, Bush announced a temporary increase in troop deployment. This escalation—prudently called a "surge" so as not to invoke unpleasant memories from the Vietnam War—added another 30,000 troops (bringing the total to 146,000). The troops would be able to "clear and hold" (a concept inherited from the latter stages of the Vietnam War) neighborhoods and thus prevent the insurgents from regaining control. The additional troops would be brought home once stability was achieved. Yet in September 2008, with violence down and US fatalities at record lows, Bush announced that the troops would remain in Iraq, thus kicking the issue down the road for his successor, Barack Obama, to deal with.

There were additional factors—other than the Awakening and the surge—that led to a reduction of violence. By 2008, ethnic cleansing had been largely completed and neighborhoods were divided by concrete barriers. More significant, US troops were no longer engaged in large operations against Shiite militias. Moqtada al-Sadr, in the face of Maliki's army backed by US firepower, had ordered his troops to stand down. But as the leader of the largest

Barack Obama declared his candidacy. It was a historic moment—an African American started his successful run for the presidency in Springfield, Illinois, Lincoln's burial place. *(Photograph courtesy of Steve Grimes)*

political bloc in the parliament, Sadr remained well placed to bide his time and wait for political and military events to play out. At the end of 2008, the most pressing—and unresolved—question was the duration of the US military occupation of Iraq.

Kurdistan

In the north of Iraq, the status of Kurdistan remained unresolved. In September 2008, the *pesh merga*, soldiers of Kurdistan's regional government, autonomous since 2005 under the Iraqi constitution, advanced along a 300-mile front into territories claimed by Arabs and Turkomen. In the process, they seized control of the cities of Kirkuk and Mosul and their adjacent oil fields. Kurdistan's autonomy had never been popular with Iraqi Arabs, and now the Kurdish state, in one fell swoop, had increased its territory by 70 percent.

The Kurdish seizure of territory had been going on for some time. Previously, the relatively weak Maliki government had been unable to challenge the *pesh merga,* who manned checkpoints as far as 75 miles south of the official Kurdish border. In the regions the Kurds controlled, Saddam Hussein's policy of "Arabization" was replaced by "Kurdification," replete with ethnic cleansing, torture, and killings. Kurds justified their actions as self-defense against the Maliki government, which, they claimed, had its eyes on Kurdish lands. They insisted that history was on their side since the lands they had seized had always been Kurdish territory. Arabs replied they would not permit the Kurds and their "Gestapo" to "steal" their land and oil.

The United States, by virtue of the 1991 and 2003 wars against Saddam Hussein, had made possible an independent Kurdistan. The Bush administration looked with considerable favor and satisfaction upon Kurdistan's reasonably democratic government, its economic recovery, and even its powerful army. Paradoxically, Washington was officially committed to a unified Iraq under the Maliki government that sought to reclaim Kurdistan. Kurdistan's neighbors— Syria, Iran, and Turkey (already in a sporadic war with Kurdistan)—remained hostile to the idea of an independent Kurdistan. The Kurds countered with a rapid military buildup of their own.

Afghanistan

In December 2001, on the eve of the Taliban's overthrow, the UN convened an Afghan council in Bonn, Germany, to choose an interim head of state. The Bush administration engineered the selection of Hamid Karzai, a royalist who had gone into exile after the Soviet invasion and who had established close ties to the CIA and the US oil giant Unocal. When Karzai returned to Kabul, he came courtesy of Washington, a president who had no army of his own and little authority beyond the capital. Unable to rely on his military to protect him, his safety was ensured by US "contractors" paid by the Pentagon.

After the Taliban were driven to the periphery of Afghanistan, an economic recovery of sorts took place. In three years, the annual per capita GDP doubled from $123 to $246 and daily wages rose from $2.70 to $6.25. Primary-school enrollment, a more significant measure of progress, increased from 1 million to 3.5 million. Progress, however, was limited largely to Kabul.

Much of the new wealth came from the production of opium, the raw material for heroin. Banned by the Taliban and virtually nonexistent in 2001, opium production now increased drastically. Among the chief beneficiaries were the Taliban and the other militias still operating in Afghanistan. In 2006, the UN reported that Afghanistan provided 95 percent of the world's poppy crop. Washington now had another front in its global "war on drugs," one it had little chance of winning. Instead, the opium trade threatened to turn Afghanistan into a narcostate on the Colombian model.

In the meantime, the Taliban and al Qaeda were rebuilding their strength. Mohammed Omar, the head of the Taliban still at large, smuggled seditious "night letters" into Kabul urging Afghans to resist the infidel foreigners and their Afghan lackeys—"dog washers," in popular parlance, individuals who looked after the dogs (considered dirty creatures in the Muslim world) of the infidel occupiers. Afghanistan, upon which Bush had once turned his back, demanded increasingly greater resources in a war for which there was no end in sight. In September 2008, the number of allied troops—mostly from NATO countries—had risen to 47,600. The US contribution consisted of 17,790 troops at the cost of $171 billion (through fiscal year 2009). In February 2009, US president Barack Obama authorized the dispatch of another 17,000 troops to Afghanistan. The Brookings Institution's "index of state weakness" ranked Afghanistan just ahead of Somalia, the poster child for failed states. And in the index's "annual corruption perceptions index," Afghanistan ranked near the bottom.[45] It was not surprising that US military officers spoke of a war that was being lost.

Pakistan

The Taliban's revival was tied directly to the unstable political situation in Pakistan. After the US invasion of Afghanistan, the Taliban and al Qaeda made their way into Pakistan's North-West Frontier Province, where they were able to reconstitute their organizations. They were greatly assisted by the fact that Pakistan's military and its intelligence branch, the Inter-Services Intelligence (ISI), showed little zeal in joining the Bush administration's war on terror. For years, it was more concerned about the Indian threat and thus put the Taliban–al Qaeda problem on the back burner.

More significant, however, was the close relationship between the Pakistan military and radical Islamicists, one that went back to the days of the Soviet invasion of Afghanistan. At the time, Pakistan's strongman, General Zia ul-Haq, became a hero to Washington when he fully supported the US effort in Afghanistan and then, with the blessing of the CIA, cemented the relationship between the anti-Soviet conservative military and the reactionary mullahs. Pervez Musharraf, who seized power in a military coup in October 1999, saw no reason to go to war against the Taliban; indeed, in September 2006, he signed a peace treaty with the Taliban in North Waziristan, the rugged frontier bordering Afghanistan. Officially, Musharraf was part of Bush's war on terror, but he did little to warrant the largesse that Washington bestowed upon his military.

Popular pressure eventually forced Musharraf into retirement. The pressure came from the middle and professional classes (in the form of protesting lawyers), Islamic radicals (who railed against Western cultural pollution in Pakistani society), and the landowning classes (the traditional *zamindars* who owned vast stretches of land and traditionally exercised considerable political powers).

Once it became clear that Musharraf's days in power were numbered, the old guard returned from exile. Among them was Benazir Bhutto, a woman from the wealthy landowning class who was educated at Harvard and Oxford, previously had served two terms as prime minister, and was still under investigation for corruption (along with her husband, Asif Ali Zardari, known as "Mr. Ten Percent," after the kickbacks he allegedly received for government contracts). Before they could return home, however, Bhutto and Zardari were granted immunity from further prosecution. In December 2007, as Bhutto campaigned for president, she was assassinated by assailants unknown. Her death was but one of a number of unsolved political murders in recent Pakistani history. In the West, the tendency was to blame groups associated with al Qaeda that saw her as a supporter of Bush's war on terror and who had returned to Pakistan at the prodding of the Bush administration. But she was also a threat to the military establishment. Before her death, she had stated publicly that she considered General Musharraf as the major threat to her safety. It was also possible that she was murdered by ISI agents with Islamist ties.

Zardari completed the family's political comeback, and in September 2008 he was sworn in as president. His first test came soon, in November, after an Islamic suicide squad of ten men launched an audacious assault in India's financial center, the city of Mumbai (formerly known as Bombay). It began at a railway station and then shifted to two luxury hotels and a restaurant catering to foreigners, a Jewish center, and even a hospital, the primary targets being US and British citizens and Jews. The terrorists killed more than a dozen policemen (including the city's chief counterterrorism official), more than 170 people in all.

This was the eighth Islamic attack in Mumbai since 1993, when terrorists set off thirteen bombs, killing more than 250 people. This attack, however, was of such sophistication that, so Indians argued, it had to have been organized with foreign assistance. Indeed, the evidence pointed to Pakistan, where several terrorist groups had ties to al Qaeda, which in the past had threatened strikes against India.

After India demanded the extradition of twenty terrorists from Pakistan (including the mastermind behind the 1993 bombings), Zardari at first promised cooperation. But the ISI intervened, making clear that there would be no handover of Muslims to India, thereby underscoring the fact that Pakistan's powerful army, which had played a role in creating these terrorist organizations in the first place, was beyond the control of a civilian president, particularly one whose family had long been engaged in a deadly feud with the military. All Zardari managed to extract was a promise to shut down the terrorist camps, a tall order indeed, since any such move would touch off violent civil strife.

Pakistani politicians of every stripe insisted that an Indian attack on Pakistani soil (including terrorist facilities) was tantamount to an act of war. Pakistan would retaliate and, in the process, would withdraw its troops from the North-West Frontier Province, where it was doing the bidding of the Bush administration by keeping an eye on the Taliban and al Qaeda. It appeared that for the first time two nuclear powers were about to go to war against one another. That prospect set off a flurry of diplomatic missions. India's foreign minister hurried off to Washington, and US envoys (including the secretary of state and the chairman of the Joint Chiefs of Staff) flew to New Delhi and Islamabad to defuse the issue.

* * *

George W. Bush had believed that regime change in Iraq would be the foundation of a democratic Middle East. The scenario, however, played out differently than he expected. It was not that Arabs did not try to warn Bush. The Egyptian dictator Hosni Mubarak predicted that the war would spawn "100 bin Ladens." The secretary-general of the Arab League warned that it would "open the gates of hell." As Mubarak had predicted, the war bred heightened resentment toward the United States and led to an increase in Muslim Brotherhood recruitment, with many of its radicalized recruits departing for Iraq. Mubarak, well aware of the threat he faced, responded with the most extensive crackdown in a decade against the Muslim Brotherhood.

Nearly eight years into the war on terror, the "world's sole superpower" was at a crossroads in Iraq and Afghanistan in 2009. Unwilling to pull out and unable to escalate the conflicts—because of fiscal constraints and lacking additional troops—the United States had reached a dead end, particularly in Afghanistan. (No one wanted to call it a *quagmire*, the term the journalist David Halberstam had popularized in his reports from Vietnam.)

Once more, historians began to write about the limits of US power, much to the frustration of the US body politic. It was a feeling reflected in the 2008

US presidential campaign, during which the major candidates promised to do a better job in securing "victory" without being able to define it. Bush's moral clarity—shored up by 725 US bases abroad and another 969 at home[46]— meant to rid the world of evil, was replaced by frustration and doubt. In the end, even Bush had to accept a limit on his ambitions in Iraq.

With no end in sight for the war in Iraq, nearly all of Bush's allies ended their involvement. Even UN secretary-general Kofi Annan, who tended to see things from Washington's point of view, had stated his opposition to the war— albeit a year and a half after it had begun. Absent an authorization from the UN Security Council, Annan argued, the US presence in Iraq was "illegal." Bush subsequently obtained UN Resolution 1790, a "mandate of the multinational force," which the UN extended "for the last time" until the end of 2008. The resolution gave Washington the temporary right to be in Iraq, but it also as-serted the "right" of Iraqis "to determine their own political future and control of their national resources."

In November 2008, the Iraqi parliament passed an "agreement" (not a treaty, which the US Senate would have to ratify) with the Bush administra-tion, one that emphasized Iraqi sovereignty and called for a "withdrawal" of US forces by 2011. In the meantime, the agreement placed considerable lim-its on the US military during the remainder of "their temporary presence in Iraq." It undermined the neocons' fond hope of a permanent US presence in Iraq. At the same time, it was a vague, compromise proclamation filled with numerous loopholes. It sought to lock in the US presence in Iraq for another three years, but without an ironclad guarantee that it would end in 2011. Not only did the agreement hold open the possibility of an extension of the US mil-itary presence; Pentagon officials openly expressed the view that they would abide by it only if nothing untoward happened.

Recommended Readings

Militant Islam

Armstrong, Karen. *The Battle for God.* New York: Ballantine Books, 2000.
    A discussion of the force of fundamentalism in Judaism, Christianity, and Islam
    since 1492.
Davis, Joyce M. *Innocence, Vengeance, and Despair in the Middle East.* New York:
    Palgrave Macmillan, 2003.
    A US journalist's explanation of the reasons for Middle Eastern violence.
Kepel, Gilles. *The War for Muslim Minds: Islam and the West.* New York: Belknap,
    2004.
Stern, Jessica. *Terror in the Name of God: Why Religious Militants Kill.* New York:
    Ecco Press, 2003.
    Based on interviews of zealots—Muslims, Jews, and Christians.

The War on Terror Under George W. Bush

Bacevich, Andrew J. *The Limits of Power: The End of American Exceptionalism*. New York: Metropolitan, 2008.
Blix, Hans. *Disarming Iraq*. New York: Pantheon, 2004.
By the head of the UN weapons inspection team.
Clancy, Tom, with Tony Zinni and Tony Koltz. *Battle Ready*. New York: G. P. Putnam's Sons, 2004.
A biography of the former commander of the US Marines.
Clarke, Richard A. *Against All Enemies: Inside America's War on Terror*. New York: Free Press, 2004.
The memoirs of the antiterrorist chief, who served both Bill Clinton and George W. Bush.
Coll, Steven. *Ghost Wars: The Secret History of the CIA, Afghanistan, and bin Laden, from the Soviet Invasion to September 10, 2001*. New York: Penguin, 2004.
The definitive account.
Hersh, Seymour M. *Chain of Command: The Road from 9/11 to Abu Ghraib*. New York: HarperCollins, 2004.
By an investigative journalist who was among the first to break the Abu Ghraib story.
Johnson, Chalmers. *The Sorrows of Empire: Militarism, Secrecy, and the End of the Republic*. New York: Metropolitan, 2004.
Mann, James. *The Rise of the Vulcans: The History of Bush's War Cabinet*. New York: Viking, 2004.
A former correspondent of the *Los Angeles Times* discusses the rise of the neocons.
The 9/11 Commission Report: Final Report of the National Commission on Terrorist Attacks upon the United States. New York: Norton, 2004.
Scheuer, Michael. *Imperial Hubris*. New York: Potomac Books, 2004.
By the operative in charge of the CIA's bin Laden unit, 1996–1999.
Woodward, Bob. *Bush at War*. New York: Simon and Schuster, 2002.
The first of four books by the *Washington Post* correspondent who had considerable access to Bush and his cabinet. It was followed by *Plan of Attack* (2004), *State of Denial* (2007), and *The War Within: A Secret White House History, 2006–2008* (2008).

Notes

1. Jacqueline Rose, "Deadly Embrace," *London Review of Books*, November 4, 2004, pp. 21–24; Raffi Khatchadourian, "Behind Enemy Lines," *The Nation*, May 15, 2006, p. 24.

2. Avishai Margalit, "The Suicide Bombers," *New York Review of Books*, January 16, 2003; Jessica Stern, *Terror in the Name of God: Why Religious Militants Kill* (New York: Ecco Press, 2003).

3. Christian Caryl, "Why They Do It," *New York Review of Books*, September 22, 2005; Scott McConnell, "The Logic of Suicide Terrorism: It's the Occupation, Not the Fundamentalism," *American Conservative*, July 18, 2005.

4. Jonathan Rabin, "My Holy War," *The New Yorker*, February 4, 2002; Steven Coll, *Ghost Wars: The Secret History of the CIA, Afghanistan, and bin Laden, from the Soviet Invasion to September 10, 2001* (New York: Penguin, 2004), pp. 470–474.

5. *The Battle of Algiers*, written and directed by Gillo Pontecorvo (Rialto Pictures Release and Janus Films, 1965).

6. Abdel Aziz al-Rantissi, cited in Rose, "Deadly Embrace," p. 24.

7. Cited in Coll, *Ghost Wars*, p. 380.

8. Lawrence Wright, "The Terror Web," *The New Yorker*, August 2, 2004, p. 47.

9. Ibid., pp. 40–53.

10. David B. Ottaway and Robert G. Kaiser, "Marriage of Convenience: The US-Saudi Alliance," *Washington Post*, February 12, 2002, p. A10; Max Rodenbeck, "Unloved in Arabia," *New York Review of Books*, October 21, 2004, pp. 22–25.

11. Cited in David Remnick, "Letter from Cairo: Going Nowhere," *The New Yorker*, July 12 and 19, 2004.

12. Lawrence Wright, "The Man Behind bin Laden," *The New Yorker*, September 16, 2002; Karen Armstrong, *The Battle for God* (New York: Ballantine Books, 2000), pp. 239–244; Rabin, "My Holy War."

13. Wright, "The Man Behind bin Laden."

14. Montasser al-Zayat, cited in ibid.

15. Coll, *Ghost Wars*, pp. 87, 155–157, 162–163, 185.

16. Clarke memo to Rice, "Presidential Policy Initiative/Review—The *Al-Qaeda* Network," January 25, 2001.

17. Lisa Meyers, NBC News, "Did Ashcroft Brush Off Terror Warnings?" June 22, 2004; Dan Eggen and Walter Pincus, "Ashcroft's Efforts on Terrorism Criticized," *Washington Post*, April 14, 2004.

18. *The 9/11 Commission Report: Final Report of the National Commission on Terrorist Attacks upon the United States* (New York: W. W. Norton, 2004), pp. 174–182, 254–277.

19. Bob Woodward, *Bush at War* (New York: Simon and Schuster, 2002), pp. 38, 141, 143.

20. Ibid., p. 314.

21. Barton Gellman and Thomas E. Ricks, "US Concludes Bin Laden Escaped at Tora Bora Fight," *Washington Post*, April 17, 2002.

22. Tommy Franks, *American Soldier* (New York: Regan, 2004), p. 309.

23. Eliza Griswold, "Where the Taliban Roam," *Harper's* (September 2003), pp. 57–65; Eliza Griswold, "In the Hiding Zone," *The New Yorker*, July 26, 2004, pp. 34–42.

24. Richard Clarke, *Against All Enemies: Inside America's War on Terror* (New York: Free Press, 2004), chapter 6, "Al Qaeda Revealed," pp. 133–154.

25. Peter Bergen, "Backdraft," *Mother Jones* (July–August 2004), pp. 40–45.

26. Bill Moyers and Michael Winship, "It Was Oil, All Along," *Bill Moyers' Journal*, June 27, 2008; "US Pushing for Privatized Iraq Oil Sector," *Petroleum Intelligence Weekly*, April 21, 2003; Greg Palast, "Secret US Plans for Iraq's Oil," *OfficialWire*, March 17, 2005; "Blood for Oil," *London Review of Books*, April 21, 2005, p. 13; James A. Baker III, Lee H. Hamilton et al., eds., *Iraq Study Group Report* (New York: Vintage, 2006), p. 2 and Recommendation #63, pp. 85–86; P. J. O'Rourke, "The Backside of War," *The Atlantic*, December 2003.

27. Cited in Paul Krugman, "Osama, Saddam, and the Ports," *New York Times*, February 24, 2006.

28. On the eve of Paul Bremer's departure for Iraq in May 2003, Bush told him, "it's important to have someone willing to stand up and thank the American people for their sacrifice in liberating Iraq"; L. Paul Bremer III, *My Year in Iraq: The Struggle to Build a Future of Hope* (New York: Simon and Schuster, 2006), p. 359. In his interview with Bob Woodward five years later, Bush returned to that sentiment.

29. For a scathing indictment of the press, see Michael Massing, "Iraq: Now They Tell Us," *New York Review of Books*, February 26, 2004.

30. Coll, *Ghost Wars*, p. 380.

31. During the first of five rehearsal sessions, Powell tossed the papers in the air, saying, "I'm not reading this. This is bullshit." Bruce B. Auster, Mark Mazetti, and Edward T. Pound, "Truth and Consequences: New Questions About US Intelligence Regarding Iraq's Weapons of Mass Terror," *US News and World Report*, June 9, 2003.

32. Cited by Danny Postel, "Look Who's Feuding," *American Prospect* (July 2004), p. 22.

33. Alexander Cockburn, "Because We Could," *The Nation*, November 8, 2004, p. 46.

34. Pamela Constable, "Paper Closed by US Is Back in Business," *Washington Post*, July 25, 2004, p. A15.

35. Naomi Klein, "Baghdad Year Zero: Pillaging Iraq in Pursuit of a Neocon Utopia," *Harper's* (September 2004), p. 51.

36. Cited in Mark Danner, "Abu Ghraib: The Hidden Story," *New York Review of Books*, October 7, 2004, p. 44.

37. Galbraith, "Iraq: The Bungled Transition," pp. 72–73; David Ignatius, "Kirkuk as Car Bomb," *Washington Post*, July 20, 2004, p. A17.

38. Figures are from www.iraqbodycount.com.

39. Peter Bergen, "Backdraft," pp. 40–45.

40. Steven Simon and Ray Takeyh, "Iran's Iraq Strategy," *Washington Post*, May 21, 2006, p. B2.

41. Lawrence Wright, "The Terrorist," *The New Yorker*, June 19, 2006, p. 31.

42. Sudarsan Raghavan, "In Fallujah, Peace Through Brute Strength," *Washington Post*, March 24, 2008.

43. Nir Rosen, "The Myth of the Surge," *Rolling Stone*, March 6, 2008; Steven Coll, "The General's Dilemma," *The New Yorker*, September 8, 2008, p. 37.

44. Jon Lee Anderson, "Inside the Surge," *The New Yorker*, November 19, 2007, p. 62.

45. Brookings Institution, *Afghanistan Index*, www.brookings.edu/afghanistanindex.

46. Tony Judt, "The New World Order," *New York Review of Books*, July 14, 2005, p. 16.

22 The Trajectory of the World Since 1945: A Summary

Historical processes are a combination of continuity and change. It was inevitable, therefore, that half a century after World War II, the world would be different from the one the Big Three had helped to create in their moment of triumph in 1945. The new order the victors established in 1945 had considerable staying power, but it was bound to end one day. Since the French Revolution of 1789, none of the international configurations of power survived much longer than a biblical generation of forty years.[1] Since 1945, the world has seen a number of major trends that, taken together, have put us at the beginning of a new, uncertain era. Among the major changes in the world since 1945 are the following.

1. The End of Colonialism

The first significant development after World War II was the demand for the rapid dissolution of European colonial control in much of the world. What Europe had accomplished between the time of the first Crusade in the late eleventh century and the turn of the twentieth century was largely undone in less than three decades. The colonial powers had been able to contain the anticolonial movements until the dam finally burst after World War II. At first blush, independence promised a happier future, free of foreign domination. In sub-Saharan Africa, in particular, the hope was that the continent now would develop its economic and human potential. Instead, the colonial powers left behind artificially drawn borders and governments that clung to power at all costs by canceling elections and murdering political opponents. Ethnic groups across the breadth of Africa repeatedly went to war against one another, leaving behind a devastated continent where the standard of living was lower in 1990 than it had been in 1960.

2. Superpower Competition in the Third World

In retrospect, it became clear that neither Cold War protagonist intended to begin a war in Europe. The contest moved to another venue, into the Third World, generally the former colonies. There, the superpowers competed for the hearts and minds of tyrants, their ideological beliefs (or generally the lack thereof) notwithstanding. The Soviet Union supported Nasser of Egypt, Sukarno of Indonesia, and Hussein of Iraq (none of whom had qualms about jailing local Communists). It also supported India against Communist China and the Sandinistas against the Nicaraguan Communist Party. The United States propped up a host of military dictators in Latin America, Africa, and Southeast Asia as well as in Southern Europe. It even supported Marxist insurgents and governments in Somalia, Yugoslavia, Angola, and China against Moscow, the ostensible center of international Marxism. In the process, the superpowers strengthened dictators around the globe, many of whom remained in power for decades. Gorbachev's "new thinking" led the Soviet Union to abandon its client states, such as Cuba, and the United States no longer had the need to prop up its own associates, such as El Salvador. The Cold War ended, but its legacy remained—devastated countries and military factions armed to the teeth. In many nations (Afghanistan, Somalia, Angola, Cambodia) the bloodletting continued. The sale of weapons also continued, this time for commercial reasons rather than those of state. Russia and the United States, as well as a host of smaller nations, continued to do what they had done efficiently, namely, produce weapons, and their economic woes dictated they sell them abroad. By the 1980s, they were joined in this by a new arms merchant—the People's Republic of China.

3. The Fall of Communism

The most surprising and sudden development since 1945 took place in Eastern Europe, where all the Communist parties gave up their once seemingly immutable hold on power in the short span of two years, from 1989 to 1991. Soviet socialism's most visible accomplishment had been the creation of a powerful security apparatus designed to deal with threats from without and within. East European Communist leaders, however, neglected what Communist ideology always had considered significant, the substructure upon which the socialist house rested, namely, the economic base. Gorbachev's perestroika eventually came to the conclusion that a new base was needed if the Soviet Union was to keep pace with the economies of the West. Once that position was reached, Communism as an ideology, as defined by Lenin and particularly Stalin, became a thing of the past.

4. The End of the Cold War

Equally astonishing was the end of the Cold War and its most dangerous feature, the military confrontation, when the Soviet army withdrew from Eastern Europe. The Warsaw Pact ceased to exist, making possible NATO's expansion into Eastern Europe. The nuclear arms reduction agreements, however, came at a late hour, as the genie of nuclear proliferation already had made its way out of the bottle. After the Soviet Union broke the US-British monopoly in 1949, France, the People's Republic of China, India, Pakistan, and Israel joined the ranks of nuclear powers, and a number of aspirants began to appear, among them North Korea and Iran.

5. The Reemergence of Germany

As the two superpowers declined, their old antagonists of World War II began to reassert themselves. Germany did so particularly after its reunification in 1990. The Gulf War witnessed the stationing of German troops abroad for the first time (in Turkey), and during the Yugoslav crisis German warships began to make their appearance in the Adriatic Sea and German airplanes over Kosovo. In the 1950s, the first West German chancellor, Konrad Adenauer, devoted himself to the integration of his nation into the West European community. In the early 1990s, Germany began to play once again its traditional role in Eastern Europe, taking the lead in the economic penetration of that region and in the recognition of breakaway republics of the Soviet Union and Yugoslavia.

6. The Reemergence of Japan

Japan's reassertion was more muted. After its disastrous defeat in World War II, it abandoned militarism in favor of pacifism and was content to remain under the US defensive and diplomatic umbrella as long as possible while pursuing economic growth. But shortly after the end of the Allied Occupation in the 1950s, the United States already began to urge Japan to take a more active role as an ally in the Cold War. Once the Cold War ended, it was the United States that encouraged Japan to play a greater part in international affairs, particularly since Japan had the financial means to assist in underwriting US and UN initiatives. Japan was cajoled into funding a portion of the Gulf War (after all, it was heavily dependent on oil from the region), and it played a leading role in the UN peacekeeping operation in Cambodia, where Japanese soldiers set foot on the Asian mainland for the first time since 1945.

At the turn of the century, however, Japan's role in East Asia was largely limited to economic activity due to resistance from nations it had controlled before and during World War II, notably Korea and a resurgent People's Republic of China. Moreover, Japanese (and German) military involvement abroad put to a severe test the clauses in their constitutions that permitted only acts of defense.

7. The Triumph of Capitalism

The demise of Communism and the ideological message of US president Ronald Reagan contributed to a return to a form of capitalism unchecked and deeply ideological in its content. Perestroika, designed to save Soviet socialism, opened instead the floodgate of criticism of Communism and produced a wild swing to a type of primitive capitalism the Western world had modified 100 years earlier because of its destructive and cruel nature. The primordial aspects of capitalism were making their way also into the arena of international trade, where the pretense of open and mutually beneficial trade at times began to give way to fierce competition, at times a zero-sum contest, the continuation of war by other means, in which there were invariably winners and losers. The unlimited "right" of one individual or nation to amass great wealth guaranteed the others' "right" to have little. By the early 1990s, the 1944 Bretton Woods ideals of free trade were severely tested by nationalist tendencies. This characteristic of international trade lay at the heart of the friction among the economic powers—the United States, the European Union, and Japan.

8. The Age of High Technology

Beginning with the 1970s, the world witnessed a new stage in the industrial revolution, a shift away from "smokestack" industries. The production of steel, once the yardstick by which industrial progress had been measured, lost its importance to knowledge-intensive industries such as computers and their offshoots—robots, digital communications, and the like. A fundamental flaw in the Soviet economy, for instance, had been the continued emphasis on the production of basic materials such as steel and oil in which it led the world. During the heyday of the smokestack industries, catching up with other industrialized nations was a difficult process, yet a relatively easy one compared to the hurdles underdeveloped countries faced at the end of the twentieth century. The gulf between the haves and the have-nots grew wider.

9. The Relative Decline of the Economic Power of the United States

The decades following 1945 witnessed a gradual yet steady erosion of US economic power relative to other parts of the world—East Asia (notably Japan) and Western Europe. The relative decline was the result of a number of factors. For one, the United States had spent vast sums of money on its national security without taking the necessary steps to shore up its economic base. It continued to lead the world in technological breakthroughs, particularly as they applied to weapons research and development, but gave up its dominant position in the production of consumer goods. With the demise of the Soviet Union, the United States stood as the sole remaining superpower, its economy and military still dominant, but facing yet another challenge: a revitalized China.

10. The Rise of East Asia

Beginning with Japan's "economic miracle" of the 1960s, East Asia emerged as an arena of dynamic economic growth and new prosperity. First, the Four Tigers (South Korea, Taiwan, Hong Kong, and Singapore) imitated Japan, registering in the early 1980s the world's highest economic growth rates. Then, by the early 1990s, this economic success was emulated by Southeast Asian countries (Thailand, Malaysia, and Indonesia) to attain honors as the world's fastest-growing economies. Then came the astonishing growth of the People's Republic of China after it converted to a market economy in the 1980s. The success stories in East Asia, like that of Japan, represented a blend of a Western-derived capitalist system and elements of traditional Asian culture, an amalgam featuring state-directed economic modernization and capital formation, high rates of personal savings and capital investment, abundant and cheap labor consisting of disciplined workers, emphasis on new high-tech industries, and export-driven industrial growth. The economic competitiveness of many Asian nations posed a challenge to a smug industrialized West and to a struggling Third World.

11. The Political Fragmentation of the World

The bipolar camps had been the result of the Cold War, and once that confrontation had come to an end, there was no further need to rally around one camp's flag or the other. Even at the height of the Cold War, a number of nations had refused to be drawn into it. De Gaulle of France, for example, feared too close an embrace on the part of the United States, and Nehru of India wanted no part of either bloc. Communist Yugoslavia's break with Stalin underscored the fact that "international Communist solidarity" existed primarily in theory only. Other Communist nations (China, Vietnam, Romania, Albania, and Cuba) tended to guard their independence against both Washington and Moscow. This fragmentation only increased after the end of the Cold War. The Soviet Union's East European bloc was no more, and the United States could no longer take its allies for granted.

12. Globalism Versus Nationalism

During the late 1980s, two conflicting currents came into collision. On the one hand, the "global village" was becoming smaller and many of its citizens began to see themselves as members of one large family facing common problems and a common future. This in turn gave rise to economic integration, to what some called the "borderless economy," to regional groupings and trade blocs such as the European Union and others formed in Asia and North America, and to regular summit meetings of the "Group of Eight," the heads of state of the leading market-economy nations.

Hitler and the horrors of World War II had discredited talk of blood that tied individuals to their collective tribe, but his defeat had only driven such talk underground, waiting for its recrudescence. In direct challenge to the concept of a "global village," the revival of nationalist tendencies produced an increasingly fragmented and parochial world.

Eventually, ethnic consciousness gradually began to make a resounding comeback. A case in point was the ethnic strife in the Soviet Union. After glasnost removed the restraints on its nationalities, the calls came for separatism and "ethnic cleansing." Russians demanded the expulsion of Jews, and Estonians demanded the expulsion of Russians. Elsewhere, the Irish wanted Britain out of Northern Ireland, and Quebec wanted out of Canada, the Biafrans wanted out of Nigeria, the Basques wanted out of Spain, the Uighurs and Tibetans wanted out of China, the Sikhs out of India, and the Kurds out of Turkey, Iran, and Iraq. Bulgaria expelled members of its Turkish minority; Arabs sought to drive Israelis into the sea, and Israelis demanded the expulsion of Palestinian Arabs; the nationalities of Yugoslavia decided they could not live in a Greater Serbia; and the misery in the Horn of Africa was in part the result of attempts to re-create a Greater Ethiopia and a Greater Somalia out of the same territory. Every East European nation had its "irredentists"[2] who claimed land at the expense of a neighbor. The Maastricht Treaty, the "deepening" of the European Union, came at a time when much of the world was threatening to break up into ethnic fragments.

13. The Emergence of Militant Islam

The late 1970s saw the appearance of a third global ideology challenging those of the superpowers—that of militant Islam as embodied in the sermons of Iran's Ayatollah Khomeini. It was the first significant ideological movement on a global scale since 1945. It was in part an appeal to the poverty-stricken masses of the Muslim world's more than 1 billion believers, most of whom lived in the Third World. It attacked the Western influence within Iranian society (as well as those of the Arab-speaking world, notably Lebanon, Kuwait, Iraq, Sudan, and Saudi Arabia). Militant Islam sought to restore the Muslim world to its former power and glory and to eliminate its dependency on outside forces that long had humiliated it.

The most dramatic manifestation of militant Islam was the emergence of al Qaeda under the leadership of Osama bin Laden. What had begun as a civil war within Arab Islamic societies—militants challenging corrupt Westernized dictators (notably in Egypt, Saudi Arabia, Iraq, Afghanistan, and Algeria)—morphed into direct attacks against the visible symbols of Western power and influence in (and outside) the Muslim world.

14. A Fragile Ecological Balance

By the early 1970s, the world became aware that the blessings of the industrial revolution had a darker side—a record growth in population and the ecological degradation of the globe. The world's population increased from approximately 2.4 billion in 1945 to 6.7 billion in 2008 and was accompanied by an even more explosive growth in polluting industry. US factories had polluted Lake Erie (but not irrevocably); Soviet irrigation had ruined Lake Aral (perhaps irreversibly); German, French, and Swiss industries had poisoned the Rhine River; and the air and water in large cities, especially in China (Shanghai, Beijing, and many others) and in the Third World (Mexico City, Cairo, Lagos, São Paulo, and others), had become scarcely suited for human habitation. Toxic wastes from nuclear weapons and power plants in many countries threatened serious ecological damage.

15. The Haves and the Have-Nots

The greatest challenges for the world's leaders in the twenty-first century were not of a technological nature. Neil Armstrong already had set foot on the moon, computers were able to conduct complex calculations in nanoseconds, and machines were able to perform what once had been backbreaking work. The potentially explosive problems were of a human nature. Many individuals faced a superfluous existence. They were the members of a dispensable underclass of great (and growing) numbers, primarily in the Third World. Mostly young and poverty-stricken, they witnessed a world capable of producing great wealth denied to them. This situation had the potential of producing great political turmoil. It was not something a magical "free market" or a "new world order" could resolve.

*   *   *

Year Zero came for Japan and Western Europe in 1945, when they began anew by putting the pieces back together again. For Eastern Europe, Year Zero came only in 1989; for the states of the former Soviet Union it came in 1991. China, with its billion people, started over after Mao's death in 1976. Year Zero came to the societies of sub-Saharan Africa in 1960; decades later they were still grasping for the takeoff point, another Year Zero that would take them to a happier future. The Shiite Muslims regard the Iranian revolution of 1979 as Year Zero. For the Arab world, Year Zero has yet to arrive.

Recommended Readings

Schell, Jonathan. *The Unfinished Twentieth Century.* New York: Verso, 2000.
  A survey of the twentieth century's slaughter, from World War I to Stalin's reign of terror, the Holocaust of World War II, and the use of atomic weapons. Schell focuses on three crucial Augusts—in 1914, when World War I began and launched an era of mass extermination made possible by the industrial revolution; 1945, when atomic weapons were first used; and 1991, when the Soviet Union's political and social experiment came to an end.

Notes

1. The French revolutionary system ended with Napoleon's defeat in 1815, and the "restored" conservative order lasted only until 1848. The wars for the unification of Germany and Italy rearranged the map of Europe by 1871, only to have that map be destroyed by World War I (1914–1918). The international system that came out of World War I lasted until the outset of World War II (1939–1945).

2. From the Latin *terra irredenta*, "land unredeemed," the land of our forefathers that must be returned; first used by Italian nationalists during the nineteenth century, as *Italia irredenta*.

Index

About the Book

Thoroughly updated, this new edition of *The World Since 1945* traces the major political, economic, and ideological patterns that have evolved in the global arena from the end of World War II to the present day.

The book provides not only the background that students need in order to understand contemporary international relations, but also new material about politics around the world. Among the issues covered in this edition are the impact of the ongoing global recession, China's growing role in the world economy, the unchecked nuclear arms race, NATO's eastward expansion, the wars in Afghanistan and Iraq, and the escalation of the Israeli-Palestinian conflict.

Beautifully written and student-friendly, *The World Since 1945* has made its place as the text of choice in scores of introductory international relations and world history courses.

Wayne C. McWilliams and **Harry Piotrowski** are emeritus professors in the Department of History at Towson University.